Fodor's Healthy Escapes

Bernard Burt

Fodor's Travel Publications, Inc.
New York • Toronto • London • Sydney • Auckland

Fourth Edition

ISBN 0-679-02723-8

Fodor's Healthy Escapes

Editor: Alison B. Stern
Contributors: Steven K. Amsterdam, Hannah Borgeson, David Low, Linda K. Schmidt
Creative Director: Fabrizio La Rocca
Cartographer: David Lindroth
Illustrator: Karl Tanner
Cover Design: Tigist Getachew
Cover Photograph: Ken Scott/TSW

Design: Vignelli Associates

About the Author

A resident of Washington, D.C., Bernard Burt has written two guidebooks to that city and contributed articles to *American Health, The Washington Flyer,* and *Maturity News Service.* The State of Maryland honored him as Travel Writer of the Year in 1985. I/SPA has named him to its board of directors and has honored him with its first award for service to the spa industry. He is also a founder of the International Spa & Fitness Association.

Special Sales

Fodor's Travel Publications are available at special discounts for bulk purchases for sales promotions or premiums. Special editions, including personalized covers, excerpts of existing guides, and corporate imprints, can be created in large quantities for special needs. For more information contact your local bookseller or write to Special Markets, Fodor's Travel Publications, 201 East 50th Street, New York, NY 10022. Inquiries from Canada should be directed to your local Canadian bookseller or sent to Random House of Canada, Ltd., Marketing Department, 1265 Aerowood Drive, Mississauga, Ontario L4W 1B9. Inquiries from the United Kingdom should be sent to Fodor's Travel Publications, 20 Vauxhall Bridge Road, London SW1 2SA, England.

MANUFACTURED IN THE UNITED STATES OF AMERICA
10 9 8 7 6 5 4 3 2

Contents

Foreword

The appeal of the fitness vacation—holiday time used for maintaining or achieving new levels of physical or mental well-being—continues to widen as new facilities, new programs, new technology, and new ideas attract health-conscious individuals.

Where yesterday's working men and women saw vacation time as an opportunity to escape and relax, today's traveler looks for opportunities to expend additional effort in pursuit of a stronger body, a better self-understanding, perhaps a new self-image. Those who invest vacation time to achieve health and fitness goals may groan about getting up before dawn to go on a hike, yet they tend to return home relishing the natural high it brings them.

Fodor's Healthy Escapes surveys the entire range of fitness holiday opportunities in North America. In the pages of this guide, the in-depth profiles of more than 240 resorts, facilities, and cruise ships provide the detailed information anyone needs to begin to plan a vacation with a purpose.

The fees and prices quoted in the resort and cruise ship profiles are based on tariffs that were current in 1994 and early 1995 and are subject to change as costs rise and the contents of program and package offerings are reformulated. Where applicable, taxes and gratuities are additional. Deposits must usually be received in advance of the guest's arrival, and a cancellation charge applies to most bookings. Each resort makes its own policy with respect to accepting payment by personal check, traveler's check, money order, or credit card. The following abbreviations are used in the resort profiles in noting credit card acceptance: AE, American Express; D, Discover; DC, Diners Club; MC, MasterCard; V, Visa.

Fees for medical services may be covered by health insurance and under some circumstances may be tax deductible; consult the resort's program director and/or your tax advisor for further information.

While every care has been taken to assure the accuracy of the information in this guide, the passage of time will always bring change, and consequently the publisher cannot accept responsibility for errors that may occur.

All prices and schedules quoted here are based on information available to us at press time. The availability of programs and facilities is subject to change, however, and the prudent fitness vacationer will confirm the details of resort or cruise line offerings before beginning to make serious plans.

Fodor's wants to hear about your travel experiences, both pleasant and unpleasant. When a resort or hotel fails to live up to its billing, let us know and we will investigate the complaint and revise our entries where the facts warrant it.

Send your letters to the editors of Fodor's Travel Publications, 201 East 50th Street, New York, NY 10022.

Acknowledgments

The author is grateful for the assistance of Naomi Wagman of Custom Spas Worldwide, Frank van Putten of Spa-Finders Travel Arrangements Ltd., J. J. Reynolds of the Association of Retail Travel Agents cruise ship committee, Judith Singer of Health Fitness Dynamics, Inc., Frank LaFleche of the Canadian embassy's tourism division, Augustin Ballina of the Mexican Government Tourist Office, and all the concerned professionals who worked out with him and contributed to the research and development of the original concept for this book.

The insights shared by T George Harris, founding editor of *American Health* and *Psychology Today* magazines, were a constant source of encouragement.

For personal support and advice, the author is indebted to Denise Austin, Jeffrey Burt, Nancy Love, and Duncan Farrell. Travel was facilitated by American Airlines, Continental Airlines, Mexicana Airlines, and USAir.

Additional information on programs and therapies is available from the International Spa and Fitness Association (6935 Wisconsin Ave., NW, Washington, D.C. 20815).

Directory 1: Alphabetical Listing of Resorts

Directory 2:
Listing of Resorts
by Program

Luxury Pampering

Nonprogram Resorts

Nutrition and Diet

Preventive Medicine

Stress Control

Taking the Waters

Vibrant Maturity

Weight Management

Introduction

By T. George
Harris

*Mr. Harris, the
founding editor of*
American Health
and Psychology
Today *magazines,
is executive editor
of* The Harvard
Business Review.

Americans are working harder than ever. In the past 15 years the leisure time of the average adult has shrunk by one-third to just 18 hours a week. The work week has grown longer by 20%, and for many working men and women it now approaches the 50-hour week once condemned in sweatshops.

This is not blue-collar sweat. The higher you rise in professional and executive ranks, the longer and harder you work. Then you labor still more hours learning new things, such as computer uses, that you need to do your job better. For many successful working men and women the stress of overload has become a badge of achievement: It comes with the territory. And those who in a previous generation might have been the idle rich often spend inherited wealth today on opportunities to try harder.

Stress has become the common cold of the busy classes. Fighting it, many strive to get into shape for peak performance. Fitness of body becomes the metaphor and means to fitness of mind. Gallup surveys for *American Health* magazine find that two out of three Americans now aim to do weekly exercise (though we don't always do as much as we intend). One in three of us considers health facilities in planning a vacation trip.

In fact the short, healthy trips become the turning point in many lives. When you go on vacation, it's foolish not to return in better shape than when you left. Travel is an investment in yourself, your productive capital. More and more people expect to get some good out of their trips. More people now take shorter and shorter vacations, and they vacation more often. Millions look for places where they will get the body back into motion, places where they will learn about fresh, tasty foods that are not larded down with fat, sugar, salt, and excessive calories.

That's the reason for this book. It fills the need for a detailed, easy-to-use guide to hundreds of places that now strive to provide meaningful recreation for the mind as well as the body. Moving far beyond the concept of the old European spa—those Marienbads where the elderly elite went to take the waters and be attended by doctors—some of the typically North American spots even offer specific programs to tone the brain and the spirit. The Golden Door in California invites a special few into "The Inner Door" to try the meditative lifestyle of serenity. Arizona's Canyon Ranch offers electronic feedback gear to help you tune in on your brain's alpha waves, long associated with meditation and creativity.

The Fodor's guides published by Random House have earned a reputation for practical, hard-to-get information. While other publishers bring out exotic volumes on "spas," this book provides the essential facts about healthy travel in a systematic way. *Fodor's Healthy Escapes* not only gives you prices and the details of programs, it provides such down-to-earth specifics as the kind of workout gear available in the exercise room.

The purpose is simple: to help you find the kind of place you want, nearest where you want to be. You will probably be astonished to discover that among the 243 resorts profiled in this book, several are an easy drive from your home or workplace. Then there is the chapter describing cruise ships that sail in Caribbean and Pacific waters.

The resorts described in this guide are grouped by region; if you want to find a facility in a specific area, the *Table of Contents* will tell you where to look. If you already have the name of a resort and want to learn what it has to offer, look for it in the alphabetical listing in *Directory 1*. If you want to find a resort that offers a particular kind of program or treatment, turn to *Directory 2*, which lists resorts under 13 categories of fitness program:

- Holistic health
- Kid Fitness
- Life enhancement
- Luxury pampering
- Nonprogram resort facilities
- Nutrition and diet
- Preventive medicine
- Spiritual awareness
- Sports conditioning
- Stress control
- Taking the waters
- Vibrant Maturity
- Weight management

n the search for an author, it was clear that this book did not want a health-food zealot, a weight lifter, a spa devotee, or an exotic travel writer who loves only funky or pricey places. We needed someone who could represent the needs of the hardworking woman or man with a limited time to spend on vacation.

The ideal choice turned out to be Bernard Burt, a marketing consultant out of the University of Pennsylvania's Wharton School, a prizewinning travel writer, and a practical-minded executive who had managed programs for Philadelphia's Civic Center. Like many a manager who strives for health, Burt had quite a few naive ideas about health behaviors and healthy food—and found himself totally unprepared, as most executives do, when his doctor told him his life would be shorter than normal if he did not get his weight down. At 58, Burt was ready to study the kinds of places that might help him change his lifestyle, and he signed on to research the new *Fodor's Healthy Escapes*.

Burt began with a test run for the April 1988 issue of *American Health*, an article on the most innovative places then rising in the U.S. spa world. Eager to discover the ancestry of such places, Burt investigated one of Europe's great spas, Brenner's Park Hotel in Baden-Baden, Germany. The historic Friedrichsbad, the emperor's bathhouse, had just been restored at great expense and was drawing Europe's and Japan's water-takers. Striding into the baths, Bernard paid little attention to the sign *Gemischt* (literally, "mixed"). Only when nude women and men appeared together did he realize the meaning of *Gemischt*. Being a gentleman of poise, he eased into the ancient European customs with hardly a blush.

Returned to the United States, Burt's poise underwent a more severe test at the Canyon Ranch in Arizona, one of the most innovative of American health centers. Mel Zuckerman, the founder and owner, has a missionary zeal about providing state-of-the-art programs, seminars, and nutrition. He and Dr. Bill Day, one of the fitness pioneers out of the national YMCA, have made Canyon Ranch the practical testing site for the fitness education.

Bernard Burt realized a clear break between the European spa tradition and American ideas. In different ways, the American industry strives to serve the individual's strong need for the enhancement of physical and mental resources. For most Americans, health means being the best each of us can be at the things we care about, from work to parenting to spiritual growth.

Burt found that other hardworking people seeking healthy turnarounds make wonderful companions. On his first dawn walks up a mountain, he learned that ordinary city clothes do not keep one warm in the desert. His feet seemed to be freezing until a companion executive dug out and passed on an extra pair of Brooks Brothers wool socks. In the supportive environment of the health resorts, guests as well as staff soon develop more than the customary concern for one another's welfare. The general feeling is, we're all in this together.

The most startling discovery Burt made concerned the cuisine. A gourmet who cares deeply about food, a wine lover and an honorary member of Washington's Sommelier Society, he expected to find tasteless brown things to eat, the bran-and-bean-sprout cuisine of the early health-food restaurants. Not so; in almost every resort he found the food so fresh "you don't need a lot of seasoning. And the beautiful presentation of the food always gets to me. Everything is low-fat. Part of the learning process is to find that you can enjoy these things without a lot of butter. All the intelligent and enthusiastic young people cooking in the resorts make it a pleasure to eat."

With help on his personal turnaround, Burt became even more faithful in his daily workouts at the Watergate Health Club in Washington, DC. The grinding work of the writer does not often lead to exercise, but Burt got his cholesterol and his triglycerides under control. He dropped 30 pounds before he finished this book, and his doctor no longer threatens him. His single purpose now as a writer is to guide you toward the place you'll choose for your own turnaround.

Glossary

A **Acupressure.** Finger massage intended to release muscle tension by applying pressure to the nerves.

Acupuncture. A Chinese system where fine needles are inserted at key points of the body that relate to different organs as a means of relieving muscular, neurological, and arthritic problems.

Aerobics. Exercise routines orchestrated to enhance cardiovascular and muscular strength.

Aerobics studio. A gymnasium used strictly for floor exercise; a cushioned or suspended floor aids in avoiding injury.

Aikido. Japanese martial art.

Air Dyne Bicycle. See *Schwinn Air Dyne Bicycle.*

Alexander Technique. A massage system created in the 1890s by the Australian actor F. M. Alexander to correct physical habits that cause stress and help improve posture.

Algotherapy. Seaweed bath. See *Thalassotherapy.*

Aquaerobics. Aerobics workouts in a swimming pool; stretch, strength, and stamina exercises that combine water resistance and body movements. Also *aquafit* and *aquacise.*

Aromabath. See *herbal wrap.*

Aromatherapy. Massage with oils from essences of plants and flowers intended to relax the skin's connective tissues and stimulate the natural flow of lymph.

Ayurvedic. 4,000-year-old Indian treatments, based on teachings from the Vedic scriptures, using oils, massage, and herbs.

B **Bach Cures.** Healing with floral essences and oils.

Balneology. Traditional study and practice of water-based treatments using geothermal hot springs, mineral water, or seawater.

Barre. Balance bar or rail used during exercise.

Behavior modification. Change in personal habits brought about through counseling and psychological conditioning.

Bindi. Bodywork combining exfoliation, herbal treatment, and light massage.

Bioenergetics. Exchange of energy between persons giving and receiving massage.

Biofeedback. Monitoring and control of physical functions such as blood pressure, pulse rate, digestion, and muscle tension with an electronic sensing device.

Body composition test. Evaluation of lean body mass and percentage of body fat, using standard weight charts; a computerized system compares personal data with standard percentages to determine whether an individual is overweight.

Body sugaring. Hair-removal process said to date from the time of Cleopatra.

C **Calipers.** Measuring device used in determining the percentage of fat in the body.

Cardiovascular endurance. Oxygen utilization by the body.

Cathartic. Laxative of natural or organic substances.

Chiropractic. Realignment of the spine and bone/body mechanics to relieve backache and postural problems.

Circuit training. The combination of aerobics and high-energy workout with weight-resistance equipment. Also see *Cross training.*

Circuit weight work. See *Circuit training.*

Cold plunge. Deep pool for the rapid contraction of the capillaries, stimulates circulation after sauna.

Colonic irrigation. Enema to cleanse high into the colon with water.

Contour. Calisthenics for deep toning of muscle groups.

Coordination. Connection and integration of parts of the body during movement.

Cross-country ski machine. A device that simulates the motions of cross-country skiing.

Cross-training. Alternating high-stress and low-stress exercise or sports to enhance physical and mental conditioning.

Crystal healing. Healing energy believed to be generated by quartz and other minerals.

Cures. Course of treatments. Also *kur.*

CYBEX. Patented equipment for isokinetic strength testing and training.

D **David System.** Pneumatic weight training units in which air is pumped. See *Circuit training.*

Drinking cure. Medically prescribed regimen of mineral water consumption.

E **Ergometer.** Exercise machine designed for muscular contraction.

F **Facial.** Deep-cleansing of the face and/or upper body with steam, light scrub.

Fango. A mud pack or body coating intended to promote the release of toxins and relieve muscular and arthritic pain.

Fast. Supervised diet of water, juice, nuts, seeds; intended to produce significant weight loss.

Feldenkrais Method. Developed by Israeli physicist Moshe Feldenkrais in the 1940s to reprogram the nervous system through movement augmented by physical pressure and manipulation.

Flex and stretch. Continuous movement exercises intended to increase endurance, flexibility, and muscular strength.

Flexibility. Muscular elasticity; the ability to stretch over joints.

Free weights. Hand-held dumbbells or barbells.

G **Gestalt.** Sensory awareness; the inner experience of being.

Guided imagery. Visualization to stimulate the body's immune system.

G5. Percussive hand massage to relax tense muscles.

H **Haysack wrap.** Kneipp treatment with steamed hay intended to detoxify the body.

Hellerwork. A system of deep tissue bodywork, stress reduction, and movement reeducation developed by Joseph Heller.

Herbal bath. See *herbal wrap*.

Herbal wrap. A treatment in which moisture, heat, and herbal essences penetrate the skin while the body is wrapped in hot linens, plastic sheets, and blankets; it is intended to promote muscle relaxation and the elimination of toxins. Also *aromabath*, *herbal bath*.

Herbology. The therapeutic use of herbs in treatments and diet.

Holistic health. A nonmedical approach to the healing and health of the whole person that seeks to integrate physical and mental well-being with lifestyle factors.

Homeopathy. Treating disease with tiny doses of natural substances.

Hot plunge. Deep pool for the rapid dilation of the capillaries.

Hot tub. A wooden soaking pool.

Hydromassage. See *hydrotub*.

Hydrotherapy. Underwater massage; alternating hot and cold showers; and other water-oriented treatments.

Hydrotub. Underwater massage in deep tubs equipped with high-pressure jets and hand-manipulated hose. Also *hydromassage*.

Hypnotherapy. Clinical use of hypnotism to stimulate positive habits.

I **Inhalations.** Hot vapors, or steam mixed with eucalyptus oil, inhaled to decongest the respiratory system; breathed through inhalation equipment or in a special steam room.

Interval training. A combination of high-energy exercise followed by a period of low-intensity activity.

Iridology. A theory that links markings in the iris of the eye to the condition of organs of the body.

Isokinetic exercise. Resistance balances effort applied against a device.

Isometrics. Pushing against a stable object to tone muscles.

Isotonics. Muscles are lengthened and shortened against a source offering constant resistance, such as barbells, known as free weights, or controlled weight-lifting stations.

Iyengar yoga. Exercise system developed in India by B.K.S. Iyengar.

J   Jacuzzi. A patented design of a whirlpool bath with underwater jets.

Jin Shin Jyutsu. Ancient Japanese form of body balancing.

K   Keiser Cam II. A patented system of pneumatic weight training units. Also, *Keiser Cam III*.

Kinesiology. The testing and strengthening of muscles through exercise and diet, intended to achieve better balance in the body.

Kneipp cures. Treatments combining hydrotherapy, herbology, and a diet of natural foods, developed in Germany in the mid-1800s by Pastor Sebastian Kneipp.

L   Lap pool. A shallow swimming pool with exercise lanes; the standard lap length is 50 feet.

Lifecycle. A computer-programmed exercise bike, made by Bally.

Liferower. A computer-programmed exercise machine that simulates rowing, made by Bally.

Lomi-Lomi. Hawaiian rhythmical rocking massage.

Loofah body scrub. Cleansing of the body with a mixture of sea salt, warm almond or avocado oil, and a loofah sponge.

Low-impact aerobics. A dancelike exercise in which one foot is always on the floor; intended to avoid muscle fatigue and to enhance cardiovascular fitness.

M   Macrobiotics. A vegetarian diet low in fat and high in antioxidant vitamins.

Manicure. Nail care.

Massage. Soothing, energizing deep-muscle manipulation, usually by hand, intended to reduce stress and fatigue while improving circulation. Various methods.

Maximal heart rate. An individual's highest attainable heart rate (the number of heartbeats per minute). It is best determined by means of a graded maximal exercise test, but an estimate can be made by subtracting one's age from 220. See *target heart rate*.

Mineral bath. A soaking in hot or cool water from thermal springs that contains mineral salts, natural elements, and gases.

N   Naturopathy. Natural healing prescriptions that use plants and flowers.

Nautilus. Patented strength training equipment designed to isolate one muscle group for each exercise movement that contracts and lengthens against gravity.

NordicTrack. A patented design of cross-country ski machine.

Nutrition counseling. The analysis of an individual's eating habits and dietary needs.

O **One-on-one training.** Personal instruction on exercise equipment from a professional exercise therapist.

Orthion. Stretching device for neck, spine.

Ovo-lacto diet. A regimen that includes eggs and dairy products.

P **Parafango.** Combination of mud and paraffin wax. See *fango*.

Parcourse. A trail, usually outdoors, equipped with exercise stations. Also *parcours, vitacourse*.

Pedicure. Nail care and treatment of the feet to remove dead skin with a pumice stone or razor; involves soaking feet, scraping, and massage.

Pilates Method. Strength training movements developed in Germany by Dr. Joseph Pilates during the 1920s.

Plyometrics. Jumps and push steps to strengthen leg muscles. See *Step aerobics*.

Polarity therapy. Balancing the energy within the body through a combination of massage, meditation, exercise, and diet; created by Dr. Randolph Stone.

Power. Anaerobic force exerted by a muscle.

Pressotherapy. Pressure cuffs used to improve circulation on feet.

R **Radiance technique.** See *Reiki*.

Rebirthing. A yoga breathing technique combined with guided meditation to relax and clear the mind. Also, reliving the experience of birth.

Rebounder. A miniature trampoline.

Reflexology. Massage of the pressure points on the feet, hands, and ears; intended to relax the parts of the body.

Reiki. An ancient healing method that teaches universal life energy through the laying on of hands and mental and spiritual balancing. Intended to relieve acute emotional and physical conditions. Also *Radiance technique*.

Rolfing. A bodywork system developed by Ida Rolf that improves balance and flexibility through manipulation of rigid muscles, bones, and joints. It is intended to improve energy flow and relieve stress (often related to emotional trauma).

Roman pool. A step-down whirlpool bath, for one or two persons.

Rowing machine. An exercise machine that simulates rowing; it can include computer graphics.

Rubenfeld Synergy. A method of integrating body and mind through verbal expression and gentle touch, developed by Ilana Rubenfeld.

Russian bath. Steam bath to flush toxins from the body.

S **Salt glow.** A cleansing treatment, using coarse salt to remove dead skin, similar to the loofah body scrub. Also *salt rub*.

Salt rub. See *salt glow*.

Sauna. A wood-lined room with dry-heat generated at temperatures of 160–210 degrees, intended to induce sweating to cleanse the body of impurities. In the Finnish tradition, which seeks even higher temperatures, heat is generated by a stove containing a heap of stones (*kiuas*) over which water is thrown to produce vapor (*löyly*).

Schwinn Air Dyne Bicycle. A stationary exercise bike that works the upper and lower body simultaneously.

Scotch douche. A treatment with high-pressure hoses that alternate hot and cold water, intended to improve circulation through rapid contraction and dilation of the capillaries.

Shamanism. Spiritual and natural healing performed by medicine men and women.

Shiatsu. A massage technique developed by Tokujiro Namikoshi that uses finger (*shi*) pressure (*atsu*) to stimulate the body's inner powers of balance and healing.

Sitz bath. Immersion of the hips and lower body in herbal hot water, followed by cold water, to stimulate the immune system. Also a Kneipp treatment for constipation, hemorrhoids, prostate problems, menstrual problems, and digestive upsets.

Spa cuisine. Fresh, natural foods low in saturated fats and cholesterol, with an emphasis on whole grains, low-fat dairy products, lean protein, fresh fruit, fish, and vegetables and an avoidance of added salt and products containing sodium and artificial colorings, flavorings, and preservatives.

StairMaster. A patented exercise machine that simulates climbing stairs.

Steam room. A ceramic-tiled room with wet heat generated at temperatures of 110–130 degrees, intended to soften the skin, cleanse the pores, and calm the nervous system.

Step aerobics. Rhythmic stepping on and off a small platform.

Stress management. A program of meditation and deep relaxation intended to reduce the ill effects of stress on the system.

Sweat lodge. Native American body-purification ceremony.

Swedish massage. A treatment that duplicates gymnastics movements with stroking, kneading, friction, vibration, and tapping to relax muscles gently; devised at the University of Stockholm early in the 19th century by Henri Peter Ling.

Swiss shower. A multijet bath that alternates hot and cold water.

T **Tai chi chuan.** Movements intended to unite body and mind; an ancient Oriental discipline for exercise and meditation.

Target heart rate. The number of heartbeats per minute an individual tries to attain during exercise; the figure is 60% to 90% of one's maximal heart rate. The American College of Sports Medicine recommends maintaining this rate for 20–30 minutes during exercise three to five days a week. See *maximal heart rate*.

Thalassotherapy. Water-based treatments that use seawater, seaweed, algae, and sea air; an ancient Greek therapy.

Trager massage. A technique developed by Milton Trager that employs a gentle, rhythmic shaking of the body to release tension from the joints. Intended for sensory repatterning.

Treadmill. An exercise machine that simulates walking.

U **Universal Gym.** A patented weight-training system.

V **Vegetarian diet.** A regime of raw or cooked vegetables and fruit, grains, sprouts, and seeds; natural foods with no additives.

VersaClimber. A patented exercise machine that simulates the climbing of a ladder.

Vodder Massage. Manual lymph drainage technique developed by Danish-born Emile Vodder in the 1950s.

W **Water volleyball.** The net game played in a pool.

Watsu. Underwater shiatsu massage.

Whirlpool. A hot pool with water rushing from jets on the sides at temperatures of 105–115 degrees, used to stimulate the system and relax sore muscles.

Y **Yoga.** A discipline of stretching and toning the body through movements or asana postures, controlled deep breathing, relaxation techniques, and diet. A school of Hindu philosophy that advocates physical and mental discipline for the unity of mind, body, and spirit.

Z **Zen shiatsu.** A Japanese acupressure art intended to relieve tension and balance the body.

1 Health & Fitness Programs

Planning a fitness vacation is a two-part process that involves determining your personal fitness goals and finding the right program or resort. You can begin by setting very specific goals for yourself and then look for the program that best suits your needs. Or you can start by surveying what a number of resorts offer and then decide what you want to achieve from your visit. This chapter will help with both kinds of planning process: It identifies and describes 12 different fitness programs plus the nonprogram category and explains what each attempts to do and what participants can hope to accomplish.

Never before have there been so many varied and challenging opportunities for exercising the mind, the spirit, and the body in a vacation with a purpose. The range of programs and facilities is wide, both for healthy men and women who want to stay in shape and for those who are determined to address a problem or improve a condition.

Since the first edition of this book was published in 1989, significant changes have evolved in spa programs. Several trends are expected to accelerate during the '90s: emphasis on preventive medicine and holistic health; less emphasis on weight loss but more education in nutrition and weight management through healthy eating and good exercise habits; and wider use of European hydrotherapy. Hopefully we will see more practical approaches to a total fitness vacation and more vacation spots that can be enjoyed year-round.

Some pleasure seekers may choose to relax amid the luxurious furnishings of a posh resort; others will find gratification in a week-long hiking adventure or the rugged atmosphere of a ranch, with a rigorous schedule that resembles boot camp. New Age retreats and yoga ashrams, naturopaths and natural healing ranches offer health and healing based on combinations of ancient therapies and the latest concepts in behavior modification. Some establishments preach preventive medicine, taking a holistic approach toward strengthening the body against illness through improved nutrition and an understanding of the relationship between mind and body. Others address such problems as the need to lose weight, to stop smoking, and to deal with stress. These programs educate participants, reinforce motivation, and provide a regimen not for quick results but for effective long-term improvement and well-being.

Increasingly sophisticated and often specialized resorts offer programs to help guests change their lifestyles at home. The establishment of new eating and exercise habits is now considered preferable to crash courses and 700-calorie daily diets. Techniques such as biofeedback have advanced to patterning weeks, where people learn how to achieve health goals over the long term. Hydrotherapy equipment from Europe appears alongside mud, seaweed, or algae for body cleansing and accompanies the latest in toning, shaping, and weight-loss techniques.

Crossover programs using European and Asian therapies have resulted in the implementation of new versions of the classic cure—a course of treatments available at spas in the United States. Among the notable programs are those at Marriott's Desert Springs Resort in California, where you'll find hydrotherapy tubs with underwater jets. Similar techniques are used at Christina Newburgh's SpaDeus in the Tuscan resort of

Chianciano Terme, Italy; and the Trianon Palace Givenchy Spa in Versailles, France. Thalassotherapy with fresh seawater and seaweed is added to the tub treatments at the Bobet Institute in the Miramar Hotel on the Brittany seacoast in France, as well as the new Hawaiian Ihilani resort and Canada's Sea Spa Nova Scotia. Bathers at California's Sonoma Mission Inn and the historic Baden-Baden in the Black Forest of Germany, relax in thermal water swimming pools and hydrotherapy tubs. At Osmosis Spa in California's wine country you can experience an exhilarating Japanese enzyme bath. Thermal mud baths are featured at Dr. Wilkinson's resort in Calistoga, California, and in ancient Abano near Venice, Italy. In Bangkok's Oriental Hotel Spa, the latest sensation is French thalassotherapy, using the same freeze-dried marine algae as Georgia's Sea Island Spa and the new Broadmoor spa in Colorado. Ayurvedic therapies from India are prescribed at the Raj in Iowa.

Similarly, American-style spa programs, traditionally focused on fitness or weight management, have reached Le Mirador Resort on Lake Geneva, Switzerland; Selma Lagerlof Hotel and Spa in Sunne, Sweden; the stately Hanbury Manor, 25 miles from London, England, which has a golf/spa program that includes a computerized fitness evaluation; and at the full-service clubs at London's Meridien Hotel, and Chewton Glen near Southampton, where seaside hikes are followed by aromatherapy massage.

No matter which spa you choose, computer technology is now applied at nearly all levels of fitness training. Interactive exercise machines analyze calories expended, adjust themselves to increase your effort, and calculate at what rate your body best functions. These machines are a valuable aid to staff members in designing health regimens to suit individual goals and physiology, but they don't take the sweat out of conditioning. The results of a fitness vacation remain yours to achieve, with personal training from spa professionals.

Basically, your choices fall into two categories: self-contained spas that focus on wellness, and resorts that feature a spa or health club along with sports and other diversions. In the wellness programs, you'll find group support and camaraderie from like-minded participants who are adhering, as you are, to a structured daily schedule. At the resorts, you may be more self-indulgent, as there are many options and temptations geared toward those who are on non-spa vacations.

The costs of a wellness week or spa holiday vary widely. Where luxury and personal attention are the formula and the staff outnumbers the guests, expect to pay premium prices. At the same time, the budget-conscious traveler will find options at $35 a day (including meals) and opportunities to use various resort facilities (without participating in a program) for a small daily fee. Many resorts will offer services (a facial or massage, for instance) at an additional cost, to complement the principal program you have chosen. In some areas the off-season brings markedly reduced rates and bargain packages.

Because rate policies differ widely among resorts, the wise traveler will want to have a clear understanding of precisely what features are included in a program rate and what taxes and tipping will be added to the rate quoted. The prices given in the resort profiles in this book were accurate at the time of writing, but they should be used only as a preliminary guide; they will vary throughout 1995 and 1996 as increases go into effect, new combinations of services are offered, and new programs and packages are formulated.

As this edition was being updated, new trends were becoming apparent. Regions experiencing the greatest growth were Canada, California, and the Southwest. In fact, we've added four Canadian resorts with all-inclusive programs; the new California center for mind/body studies, developed by Dr. Deepak Chopra; and a preventive medicine retreat, directed by Dr. Dean Ornish head of the Preventive Medicine Research Institute in Oakland, California.

Other new entries to look for in this edition are: the grandest spa at sea, aboard the *Queen Elizabeth 2*, which sails to the top of our chapter on cruises; the new spas at the historic Broadmoor Resort in Colorado Springs and at the Banff Springs Hotel in the Canadian Rockies; Ruth Stricker's visionary programs at the Marsh, near Minneapolis; the Wellness Program at Dr. Kenneth Cooper's Aerobics Center in Dallas; and Dr. John McDougall's diet and nutrition program in California's Napa Valley at St. Helena Health Center. The growing interest in Complementary Medicine—alternative therapies based on natural health—is reflected in our expanded coverage of hospital health centers that offer structured residential programs, such as the Claremont Resort, in Oakland, California.

Among those travel agents that are specialists in arranging spa packages are Custom Spa Vacations (tel. 800/443–7727 or 617/566–5144, fax 617/931–0599), Spa-Finders Travel Arrangements Ltd. (tel. 800/255–7727 or 212/924–6800, fax 212/924–7240), Spa Trek (tel. 212/779–3480 or 800/272–3480, fax 212/779–3471), and the Spa Connection (tel. 303/756–9939, fax 303/758–8862).

In the following pages, the descriptions of the 13 categories of fitness programs explain in general terms what you can expect to find in different kinds of programs. Each description concludes with Fodor's Choice of resorts that offer that program. Look up the resorts in the alphabetized *Directory 1* and turn to the profiles in the next chapter of this guide for details of the program offerings at each of the resorts. If you want to read about all the resorts offering a particular program, look at the lists in *Directory 2*. It gives the complete list of resorts for every program category and indicates the page on which each of the facilities is profiled. A glossary of terms for "spa speak" follows the introduction to the book.

Holistic Health

The premise of holistic health programs is that, in order to be truly fit and healthy, you must develop your emotional, intellectual, and spiritual self as well as your body. Nontraditional therapies are used to achieve a sense of wholeness with the world and oneself that will help the body to fend off illness.

Holistic-health training can be vigorous or mellow; it is usually a combination of exercise, nutrition, stress control, and relaxation. Activities include walking, hiking, biking, cross-country skiing, tennis, swimming, and aerobics classes. A wide range of alternative healing therapies stretches from massage to yoga, and the body can be cleansed with herbs, enemas, or psychic diagnoses.

The credo of holistic health retreats is that illness results from a lack of balance within the body, whether caused by stress or physical conditions, and that the balance can be restored without the use of medicine. When secluded in places of great natural beauty, the healing process may draw on spiritual sources as well as natural energy to help participants find inner strength.

Holistic Health: The Center for Mind/Body Medicine, California
Fodor's Choice Hawaiian Wellness Holiday, Hawaii
Hollyhock Farm, Vancouver Island, British Columbia, Canada
La Casa de Vida Natural, Puerto Rico
New Age Health Spa, New York
Northern Pines Health Resort, Maine
Omega Institute, New York
Pocket Ranch Institute, California
Preventive Medicine Research Institute Retreats at the Claremont, California
Royal Atlantic Health Spa, Florida

Kid Fitness

Programs to motivate children and teenagers to enjoy fitness through fun and exercise are designed to involve youngsters and their parents in a series of health-oriented experiences, complete with nutritious meals, sports, and excursions.

Kid Fitness: Green Valley Fitness Resort and Spa, Utah
Fodor's Choice The Marsh, Minnesota
The Peaks at Telluride, Colorado
Sea Island Beach Club Spa at The Cloister, Georgia
Sivananda Ashram, Quebec, Canada

Life Enhancement

The life enhancement program aims for long-term physical and psychological benefits. It involves a total assessment of one's condition, with medical tests and personal consultations on nutrition and fitness. Some programs have a spiritual element, others emphasize an educational approach through exercise, diet, and behavior modification.

Developed in many cases at specialized centers, life enhancement programs usually require complete commitment from participants. The size of the group is generally limited to about two dozen men and women, each working one-on-one with a team of health and behavioral specialists in an intensive experience that little resembles a resort-style program.

Life Enhancement: Cal-a-Vie Health Resort, California
Fodor's Choice Canyon Ranch, Arizona
The Cooper Aerobics Center, Texas
Duke University Diet and Fitness Center, North Carolina
Esalen Institute, California
The Greenhouse, Texas
The Heartland Spa, Illinois
La Costa Resort & Spa, California
Lake Austin Spa Resort, Texas

The Phoenician Centre for Well-Being, Arizona
Rancho La Puerta, Mexico
St. Helena Hospital Health Center, California
Skylonda Fitness Retreat, California

Luxury Pampering

Usually found at resorts where staff outnumber guests, luxury pampering is intended for those who long to be herbal wrapped, massaged, and soaked in bubbling pools fragrant with chamomile. The height of survival chic is lounging in an elegant robe and discussing a delicious spa meal; exercise classes and a weight loss diet can be part of the program, but no activity will put much strain on the body, if you don't choose to be so challenged.

An abundance of options makes luxury pampering a highly personalized regimen, designed for men as well as women. The services include exotic body and skin care treatments and the latest image-enhancers at the beauty salon, among them glycolic acid complexion peels, loofah body scrubs with sea salts and almond oil, aromatherapy massage, and paraffin facial masks for dehydrated skin. Recent advances have joined European spa treatments with American fitness concepts, such as an underwater massage, hydrotherapy with thermal water crystals, and thalassotherapy with seaweed products and seawater.

Deluxe accommodations and lots of amenities are basic to luxury pampering. Some resorts have Sunday-to-Sunday schedules, most offer pampering à la carte. To those who say, "No pain, no gain," the pampered reply, "No frills, no thrills."

Luxury Pampering: Avandaro Golf & Spa Resort, Mexico
Fodor's Choice Charlie's Spa at the Sans Souci Lido, Jamaica
The Doral Golf Resort and Spa, Florida
The Fontana Spa at the Abbey, Wisconsin
The Golden Door, California
Grand Wailea Resort and Spa Grande, Maui, Hawaii
The Greenbrier, West Virginia
The Greenhouse, Texas
Marriott's Spa at Camelback Inn, Arizona
Meadowood Resort, California
The Peaks at Telluride, Colorado
Sea Spa Nova Scotia, Nova Scotia, Canada

Nonprogram Resort Facilities

Nonprogram resort facilities—often a vacation resort that adds a fitness element with a health club—can be just the place for weekend getaways or family vacations. Some fill a gap in areas where fitness resorts are not available; others are close to cultural and historical attractions. Most offer outstanding facilities and special services geared to the fitness-oriented traveler.

Nonprogram Banff Springs Hotel, Alberta, Canada
Resort Facilities: The Broadmoor, Colorado
Fodor's Choice Cambridge Beaches, Bermuda
The Claremont Resort, California
Le Meridien Hotel & Villas, Bahamas
Ocean Pointe Resort, British Columbia, Canada

Privilege Resort, St. Martin, Caribbean
Scottsdale Princess, Arizona
Spa LXVI at Pier 66 Crown Plaza Resort, Florida
Spa Internazionale, Florida
Woodstock Inn & Resort, Vermont

Nutrition and Diet

Nutrition and diet programs maintain that well-being begins in the kitchen, that understanding the relationship between nutrition and diet can enhance one's lifestyle and promote sound, healthy habits. Here you may learn to evaluate product labels ("high in fiber," "low in cholesterol") and to cope with the variety of advertising claims.

Participants gain a new perspective on nutrition through lectures and first-hand experience in food preparation. How foods affect your health, how to shop, how to choose from restaurant menus, and how to plan and prepare meals are among the subjects covered. Classes are designed to generate menus and recipes for nutritious dining that participants will then take home with them.

Designed as an educational experience, with no attempt to provide a crash diet plan, the nutrition and diet program provides the fundamentals for following a regimen of eating healthy natural foods. And participants get to enjoy the meals prepared in class.

Nutrition and Diet:
Fodor's Choice
Canyon Ranch, Arizona
Canyon Ranch in the Berkshires, Massachusetts
Doral Golf Resort and Spa, Florida
Duke University Diet and Fitness Center, North Carolina
The Kushi Institute, Massachusetts
New Life, Vermont
Pritikin Longevity Center, California
Pritikin Longevity Center, Florida
Royal Atlantic Health Spa, Florida
Structure House, North Carolina
Tennessee Fitness Spa, Tennessee

Preventive Medicine

Preventive medicine centers take a scientific approach to health and fitness by combining traditional medical services with advanced concepts for the prevention of illness. Designed for healthy people who want to stay that way, the programs involve medical and fitness testing, counseling on nutrition and stress control, and a range of sports and exercise activities along with massage and bodywork.

Conceived as a regenerative experience for healing and relaxation, the programs can also treat problems associated with obesity, aging, and cardiovascular disease. These programs, usually developed in consultation with your personal physician at home, are carefully structured, supervised at all times, and require full participation.

Participants work with a team of physiotherapists and doctors in learning new techniques for survival; they discover how to eliminate negative habits and modify a lifestyle. The one-on-

one training with fitness instructors, nutritionists, and psychologists can reveal ways of accomplishing personal goals.

Along with hospital-related programs, specialized centers for preventive medicine can now be found at leading fitness resorts and at retreats under the auspices of medical services organizations. They bring together specialists in all fields of health and nutrition to provide a comprehensive prescription for healthy living.

Preventive Medicine: Fodor's Choice
Canyon Ranch, Arizona
The Cooper Aerobics Center, Texas
The Greenbrier, West Virginia
Maharishi Ayur-Veda Health Center, Massachusetts
Omega Institute, New York
Poland Spring Health Institute, Maine
Preventive Medicine Research Institute, California
St. Helena Hospital Health Center, California
Weimar Institute, California
Wildwood Lifestyle Center, Georgia

Spiritual Awareness

In celebrating human potential, spiritual awareness programs strive to stretch the individual's limits both mentally and physically. They try to foster a process of personal growth and transformation through workouts that synchronize mind and body and make one aware of one's inner resources. Specializing in alternative education, vegetarian diets, and natural therapies, they offer psychic tools for living.

The experience may draw on any number of Eastern and Western philosophies, and it might focus on yogic training or sensory awareness. Body therapies, visualization, and shamanism are among the healing processes that can be explored. Private counseling and group sessions are usually available for both beginners and advanced meditators.

Retreats rather than resorts, these centers for spiritual training are situated in places where nature's beauty can be enjoyed without distraction or tension.

Spiritual Awareness: Fodor's Choice
Breitenbush Hot Springs and Retreat, Oregon
Feathered Pipe Ranch, Montana
Harbin Hot Springs, California
Hollyhock Farm, British Columbia, Canada
Kripalu Center for Yoga and Health, Massachusetts
Omega Institute, New York
Pocket Ranch Institute, California
The Raj, Iowa
Sivananda Ashram, Quebec, Canada
Sivananda Ashram Yoga Retreat, the Bahamas

Sports Conditioning

For the active vacationer or the athlete seeking new challenges, sports conditioning programs offer advanced training in a variety of sports, workouts with experts, and high-tech training with the latest in exercise equipment.

The current buzzword is *cross-training*, which denotes a varied program that teaches the benefits of alternating sports such as tennis or swimming with exercises such as walking or weight lifting. Mountain hikes, beach runs, and cross-country skiing are programmed to stretch your endurance limits.

Mental training techniques can also be incorporated in sports conditioning programs. Following the lead of Olympic athletes and professional golfers, trainers are offering courses in guided relaxation, affirmations (positive statements), and visualization to improve the competitive edge. These practices are more than morale boosters; the visualization of successful performance may create neural patterns that the brain will use in telling the muscles what to do.

Therapy for sports-related injuries is a feature of some resorts. Others specialize in the mind-body relationship, with disciplines to promote both physical and spiritual development. Martial arts, yoga, and croquet are newly popular vehicles for integrating exercise and mental concentration.

Sports Conditioning: Fodor's Choice
The Aspen Club International, Colorado
Global Fitness Adventures, Colorado
The Hills Health Ranch, British Columbia, Canada
Le Sport, St. Lucia
Loews Santa Monica Beach Hotel, California
The Maui Challenge, Hawaii
The Peaks at Telluride, Colorado
PGA National Resort & Spa, Florida
Swept Away, Jamaica
Topnotch at Stowe, Vermont

Stress Control

Gaining control of the causes of stress is a basic element in the programs of most health and fitness resorts. The approaches to stress control, however, are varied; they include relaxation techniques, behavior modification, biofeedback, and meditation.

As a total experience, with a physical setting and food to lift one's spirits, stress-control programs can create a strong feeling of well-being. Some are offered as an executive retreat within a resort, as an antidote for job burnout, or as a recipe for self-renewal. The opportunity to work one-on-one with advisors, away from the causes of stress, can enhance a person's ability to cope with the stress factors of daily life.

Stress Control: Fodor's Choice
The Ashram Health Retreat, California
The Claremont Resort, California
Hilton Head Health Institute, South Carolina
The Himalayan Institute, Pennsylvania
The Integral Health Center, Virginia
Lake Austin Spa Resort, Texas
The Option Institute, Massachusetts
The Raj, Iowa

Taking the Waters

The practice of bathing in hot springs gave rise to the fashionable spas of Europe and America, where people congregated as much for social as for therapeutic purposes. Today taking the waters—which may involve drinking six to eight glasses of mineral water daily—is a practice enjoyed for health and relaxation.

The popularity of water-based therapies and mud baths at American fitness resorts is a recent phenomenon. The cross-fertilization of European and American approaches to maintaining a healthy body and a glowing complexion has revived interest in bathing at grand old resorts where natural waters are available free for the asking. Related but different treatments that involve seaweed, algae, and seawater are offered at spas that specialize in thalassotherapy.

For the purist, a secluded hot spring promises the best kind of stress-reduction therapy. Others need the added stimulation of body scrubs with sea salts by a masseur armed with a loofah sponge—or a whirlpool bath bubbling with herbal essences.

Taking the Waters: Alamo Plaza Spa at the Menger Hotel, Texas
Fodor's Choice Aqua-Mer Center, Quebec, Canada
Berkeley Springs State Park, West Virginia
Calistoga Mud Baths, California
Glen Ivy Hot Springs, California
Glenwood Hot Springs Lodge & Pool, Colorado
The Greenbrier, West Virginia
Harrison Hot Springs Hotel, British Columbia, Canada
The Homestead, Virginia
Hotel Ixtapan, Mexico
Hot Springs National Park, Arkansas
Ihilani, Hawaii
Murrieta Hot Springs Resort, California
Safety Harbor Spa and Fitness Center, Florida
Saratoga Spa State Park, New York
Two Bunch Palms, California

Vibrant Maturity

The aging of America has resulted in health and fitness programs designed for specific needs of men and women over age 50. Combining elements of spa vacations with medical services and lifestyle education, these programs can help achieve a healthier way of working, exercising, and eating. The emphasis is on prevention of illness by staying fit.

Vibrant Maturity: Canyon Ranch, Arizona
Fodor's Choice Camp Rediscovery, Virginia
The Cooper Aerobics Center, Texas
Duke University Diet and Fitness Center, North Carolina
Green Valley Fitness Resort and Spa, Utah
The Marsh, Minnesota
St. Helena Hospital Health Center, California
Structure House, North Carolina
The Oaks at Ojai, California
Weimar Institute, California

Weight Management

Learning how to lose weight properly and how to maintain a healthy balance in body mass is the basis of a weight management program. This is not a course for a dramatic loss of weight; rather, it teaches proper eating habits, beginning with what to buy in the supermarket and how to prepare meals.

The weight management resort integrates motivational sessions with exercise, diet, and pampering, re-education with recreation. Some programs involve fasting on juices and water.

Some resorts are residential retreats for the seriously obese; some offer a full range of sports and outdoor activities.

Carefully controlled and supervised, the typical regimen is tailored to the individual's fitness level and health needs. A team of specialists—therapists and nutritionists—coaches you on the basics of beginning and maintaining a personal program. Additional motivation and support arise in the camaraderie of being with a group of like-minded dieters.

Weight Management: Fodor's Choice

Canyon Ranch, Arizona
Duke University Diet and Fitness Center, North Carolina
Green Mountain at Fox Run, Vermont
Hilton Head Health Institute, South Carolina
National Institute of Fitness, Utah
New Age Health Spa, New York
Sans Souci Health Resort, Ohio
Structure House, North Carolina
Tennessee Fitness Spa, Tennessee

2 Health & Fitness Resorts

California

A trendsetter in food, fashion, and fitness, Southern California has been luring health-conscious visitors since the Spanish explorers first landed in San Diego. The 150 miles of coastline between Los Angeles and Mexico boasts more varieties of health spa than will be found in any other part of the nation: mud treatments, mineral waters, vegetarian diets, luxury pampering, and spiritual retreats are widespread.

Northern Californians consider themselves residents of a different state, with San Francisco at its center. For them the wine country north of San Francisco is a principal attraction, and taking mud baths at Calistoga ranks with visiting the vineyards of Napa and Sonoma counties. Inland, you have the natural grandeur of Yosemite National Park.

The Ashram Health Retreat

Life enhancement
Stress control
Weight management

California
Calabasas

Barbra Streisand called the Ashram "a boot camp without food." Others have found it a rite of passage to a new self-image. Shirley MacLaine described it in *Out on a Limb* as "a spiritually involved health camp."

The Ashram displaces old stresses with new ones. Most of the fairly affluent achievers who come here have high-pressure jobs, and by challenging themselves to a week of enormous physical exertion and minimal meals, they can experience what some speak of as a transcendent, positive change in attitude.

Guests live together in close quarters with a group of about 10, all of them following a routine of mountain hikes, exercise, and yoga. A daily massage and a few hours of relaxation are the only respite. Everyone joins in; participation in every activity is required.

Turning the concept of a retreat (the original meaning of ashram) into the ultimate challenge was an idea tested in a Guatemalan jungle by the Ashram's owner, Anne-Marie Bennstrom. A cross-country skiing champion in her native Sweden, she tested her personal limits by spending five months alone in the jungle. The mystical clarity of life's essentials, as opposed to the nonessentials, is what she shares with her guests in this retreat high above the Pacific Ocean.

The Ashram has operated at this site since 1975, accepting men and women, ages 20–70. The unpaved entrance road winds uphill to a plain, two-story stucco house. Surrounded by towering eucalyptus trees, the garden contains a small heated swimming pool, a solarium for sunbathing, and a geodesic dome where yoga and meditation sessions take place.

Each day begins at 6:30 AM with yoga, stretching, and breathing exercises that help take the kinks out of sore muscles and

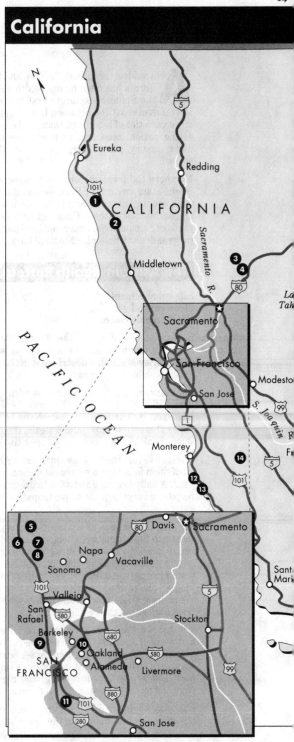

California

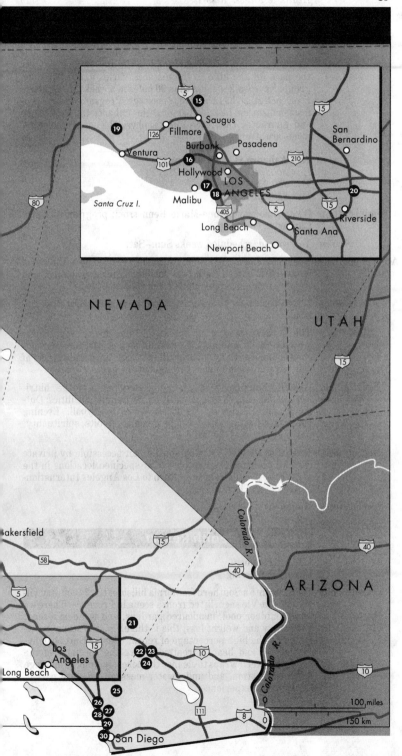

build energy for a strenuous hike into the hills. Breakfast is a glass of orange juice. The morning schedule usually includes an hour of weight lifting followed by an hour of exercise in the pool and winds down with a game of water volleyball. Calisthenics and at least a two-hour walk complete the day. Bennstrom sets the pace for the hike so the distance varies daily, but some groups have walked more than 90 miles in a week. In the afternoon each guest has a one-hour massage. Program leaders' professionalism and likeable personalities enhance the experience and guarantee that each guest's physical and psychological needs are attended to.

The Ashram Health Retreat
Box 8009, Calabasas, CA 91372
Tel. 310/222–6900
Fax 310/455–2572

Administration	Owner-manager, Anne-Marie Bennstrom; program director, Catharina Hedberg.
Season	Year-round, scheduled weeks Sun.–Sat.
Accommodations	Guests double up in 5 simply furnished bedrooms in the ranch house with shared bathroom facilities, library, lounge, and weights room. Exercise clothes and robe provided.
Rates	$2,200 per week, all-inclusive. Credit cards: V. Gratuities optional.
Meal Plans	The 3 lacto-vegetarian meals include fruit, vegetables, sprouts, seeds, and nuts. Lunch can be a yogurt-and-cottage-cheese blend with fruit slices, dinner a green salad. Snacks of raw vegetables and juices throughout the day.
Services and Facilities	**Exercise Equipment:** Free weights. **Services:** Massage, nutritional counseling, yoga, meditation. **Swimming Facilities:** Outdoor pool. **Recreation Facilities:** Water volleyball. **Evening Programs:** Lectures on developing healthy habits, spirituality, energy centers of the body.
Getting Here	*From Los Angeles.* 1 hr by shuttle; not accessible by private car. All guests picked up by van at specified locations in the area. Free pickup from and return to Los Angeles International Airport and local hotels.
Special Notes	No smoking.

Cal-a-Vie Health Resort

Life enhancement
Luxury pampering

California Vista — Terraced into a Southern California hillside, the 24 country villas of Cal-a-Vie seem lifted from a scene in Provence. There's a lovely outdoor pool, manicured gardens, and wonderful food. For luxury and weight loss, this is the ultimate escape, as attested by the high percentage of repeat clients. European hydrotherapy and beauty treatments are the specialty of the house. Seaweed wraps to cleanse the pores, lymphatic massage for detoxification, and underwater-massage tubs are part of the sybaritic experience.

You'll hear the words "detoxify" and "cleanse" on a daily basis here, since the program is designed to heal the body by restoring the balance of mind, body, and spirit. No intrusion from the outside world is allowed to disturb the peace and tranquillity of your week of hikes, aerobics classes, and calorie-controlled meals. Designed as a total environment for health and fitness with personalized attention, the 125-acre resort accepts only 24 guests a week for the Sunday-to-Sunday program.

Guests soon learn to relax as they receive total care. A toothbrush and personal things are all you need to bring; sweat suits, robes, shorts, and T-shirts are provided. As you go on to another activity, a fresh set of clothes is supplied. The staff has raised mothering to a fine art, and its members seem to care about clients. With a ratio of four staff members to each guest, little is left to chance.

The first step is your personal fitness evaluation. Your vital statistics and the results of a battery of tests to determine flexibility, cardiovascular capability, and upper and lower body strength are fed into a computer; your personal diet and exercise regimen will be based on the printout. Meals total between 1,200 and 1,400 calories per day on the maintenance diet, though you may opt for the cleansing or reduction programs.

The day begins with a prebreakfast hike into the hills—long or short depending on your preference—followed by cooling down exercises, and group workouts in the swimming pool, or in the gym with a personal trainer. Yoga, tai chi chuan, and aerobics are scheduled. Sparring in the "Boxercise" class helps build finesse and stamina.

During thalassotherapy, you are cocooned in a mixture of algae and seawater, coated with clay, and gently scrubbed and massaged. Another popular treatment, the aromatherapy massage, is intended to fight tension and its consequences, and is also geared to rid the body of cellulite. Essential oils from flowers and herbs are blended and applied to points of the body in varying combinations. As many as 25 oils can be combined for particular trouble spots. A dry-brush body scrub sloughs off old skin.

Cal-a-Vie Health Resort
2249 Somerset Rd., Vista, CA 92084
Tel. 619/945–2055
Fax 619/630–0074

Administration Founders-owners, William F. and Marlene Power; manager Deborah Zie.

Season Year-round, except mid-Dec.–Jan. 2.

Accommodations 24 private villas with heat, air-conditioning, French provincial furnishings, beam ceilings, stone fireplaces, flowered chintzes, carved wooden armoires. Each bedroom has TV, telephone, full bathroom with robes and amenities, and garden entrance. Meals served in main house.

Rates $3,950 per person per week, all-inclusive with meals, which covers service charges but not room tax (66.15); $3,650 for summer weeks. $500 non-refundable deposit required in advance. Credit cards: AE, MC, V.

Meal Plans 3 meals served to order daily, based on suggested calorie intake. Lunch can include a seafood salad, whole wheat pizza with *chèvre* cheese, sautéed tofu, and lentils. Dinner entrées can include sautéed free-range chicken with rosemary and roasted garlic, a pilaf of lentils and brown rice, and grilled swordfish. Special diets accommodated.

Services and Facilities **Exercise Equipment:** 2 Startrac treadmills, 2 StairMaster 4000, 2 Windracer bikes, 5 Bodymaster units, step aerobics, free weights. **Services:** Massage (Swedish, shiatsu, aromatherapy), thalassotherapy, hydrotherapy, water exercise class, Boxercise, dry brush body scrub, reflexology, pedicure, manicure; facial, hair, and skin care. **Swimming Facilities:** Heated outdoor pool. **Spa Facilities:** Indoor sauna and steam room; recessed Roman whirlpool. **Recreation Facilities:** Tennis court, volleyball; golf, horseback riding nearby. **Evening Programs:** Lectures on current topics, fitness, and nutrition; cooking demonstrations; movies.

In the Area San Diego museums, theaters, and waterfront; Sea World; San Diego Zoo and Wild Animal Park; herb farm; Mount Palomar Observatory.

Getting Here *From San Diego.* By car, Rte. 163 to I–15 to Vista (1 hr). Free pickup on Sun. and return to San Diego International Airport. Limousine, taxi, rental car available.

Special Notes No smoking on the property except in designated areas.

Calistoga Mud Baths

Luxury pampering
Taking the waters

California
Napa Valley Calistoga, a tiny town tucked into the vineyards of the Napa Valley, has been blessed with puffing fumerholes and steaming geysers, sources of thermal spring mineral waters and mud that has been tapped by a dozen spas, many of them within walking distance of the town's center, along Lincoln Avenue.

Calistoga is not a secret, however. Day-trippers from San Francisco have been coming here to combat stress; the springs attract families looking for a way to spend some meaningful time together; couples share romantic baths and massages; and people seeking relief from arthritis and rheumatism return regulary for the soothing effects of the mud baths.

The geysers, which were considered sacred to the Wappo tribe of Northern California, also attracted the 17th-century Spanish explorers who named them *agua caliente*, or hot springs. Later, in 1859, San Franciscan developer Sam Brannan coined the name Calistoga, a contraction of California and Saratoga Springs (the then-fashionable New York spa). Today the town has a mellow, laid-back look that's part Victorian restoration (no building over two stories) and part low-cost housing for Latino workers in the nearby wineries. Adding some spice to Calistoga is the newly opened western branch of the Culinary Institute of America, helping the area to become a rapidly growing mecca for gourmets.

Each of the dozen spas in town offers its own special variation on bathing bliss. Traditionalists head for Dr. Wilkinson's Hot Springs or the Indian Springs resort, where soaking in the volcanic mud is like floating gravity-free. Others prefer the privacy of whirlpool baths mixed with fango mud from Italy, or herbal essences that are not recycled and don't contain sulferous mineral water. Couples get special treatment at several places designed for duo bathing and massage.

The following is a selection of spas found in Calistoga. Come for a day or a week and try a few; each one has its own distinct personality.

Calistoga Spa Hot Springs. What's unique about this spa hotel is that it has the only exercise facility in town, in addition to four outdoor pools with naturally heated mineral water of varying temperatures. Aerobics classes and use of exercise equipment are complimentary for guests. The pools, mud bath, and massage are available to the public and can be booked on a daily basis if you are not staying on the premises. Admission to the pool is $5 with treatment, $9 without, $7 after 7 PM; towels are not provided. The pool is especially busy on weekends when families come to visit. Modern and well maintained, the two-story hotel has 52 simply furnished rooms with two twin beds, private bath, cable TV, telephone, air-conditioning; the kichenettes are equipped with hot plate (no oven), refrigerator, dishes, and utensils. *1006 Washington St., 94515, tel. 707/942–6269.* **Facilities:** *4 pools, whirlpools, aerobics classes, rowing machines, exercise bikes, Universal Gym, free weights.* **Services:** *Mudbath, massage, steambath, blanket wrap. Reservations for treaments: 8:30–4:30. MC, V.* **Rates:** *$64–$83 for standard double; $81–$105 for family unit.*

Dr. Wilkinson's Hot Springs. Dr. John Wilkinson, still active at age 80, came here as a chiropractor in the mid-1940s. Now run by his children, Mark and Carolyne, the resort encompasses 17 hideaway cottages, a five-bedroom Victorian house, and the 42-unit motel opened in 1952 and featuring the original mudbaths. A variety of treatments and packages are offered, including the "Stress Stopper," with spa and salon packages for $106 per person, $169 for two. Another option, "The Works" ($65), begins with a 10- to 15-minute soak in a 105°F mix of volcanic ash, peat, and mineral water. (Between bathers, mud vats are flushed with 212°F water, said to sterilize any residue.) Solicitous attendants swab your face with cool cloths, and offer cups of water. Next, after showering comes a bathtub soak in bubbling Calistoga water, and a blanket wrap to sweat out any remaining toxins. The finishing touch is a half-hour massage in a private room or alcove. Appointments are available to the public on a day-use basis. Additional salon services, including facials, mud mask, and acupressure facelift, are in a pretty pink cottage adjoining the motel. Guest rooms are well maintained, and the cottages are decorated with antiques. All rooms have a king-size bed or two twins and are equipped with air-conditioning, TV, phone, and coffee maker. *1507 Lincoln Ave., 94515, tel. 707/942–4102. 42 motel rooms.* **Facilities:** *Mudbaths, men's and women's bathhouse, mineral steamroom, indoor and outdoor pools.* **Services:** *Facials, cerofango and paraffin treatments for hands and feet, full-body massage. Bath appointments 8:30–3:30; massage appointments 9–4:30.* **Rates:** *$44–$76 single, $49–$84 double; bungalows with kitchen, queen-size bed: $59–$79 single, $69–$89 double; Hideaway cottages with queen-size bed: $47–$150 for double; Victorian* *house bedroom with queen bed: $69–$89 single, $79–$99 double. AE, MC, V.*

Harbin Hot Springs. Lying 16 miles from Calistoga, this secluded New Age retreat is a bit of a trek, but the holistic health community in the hills offers lodging and good treatments at a modest cost. There is a spiritual quality to bathing in the clothing-optional mineral pools, where the water-supported watsu massage can be experienced. A vegetarian restaurant and community kitchen (meals not included) are available to guests. Accommodations are in frame buildings with rooms (not air-conditioned) that open to a narrow veranda; both private facilities and dormitory space can be reserved. Private rooms are attractively decorated with wicker furniture and country-style bedding. *18424 Harbin Springs Rd., Box 82, Middletown, CA 95461, tel. 707/987–2477 or 800/622–2477 in CA; fax 707/987–9638.* **Facilities:** Mineral pools, restaurant, kitchen, hiking trails, evening lectures, concerts, movies. **Services:** *Massage, watsu, shiatsu, deep tissue, rebalancing, reflexology, rebirthing, hypnotherapy, chiropractic. Workshops (fee), daily meditation, and full moon ceremony open to guests and members ($5 fee). Day visitor pass $12–$17 per adult, children $10–$12.* **Rates:** *$40–$60 per room for single, $60–$90 double, without bath; $50–$80 single, $70–$110 double with half-bath; $80–$125 per couple with full bath; dormitory accommodations in rooms with 4–6 beds $23–$35; campsite $14–$23 per adult, $10–$14 per child. MC, V.*

Indian Springs Resort. The attraction here is the spring's all-volcanic ash mudbath, located on the site of the town's original spa. For just $65 the seaweed-based Repechage facial is a bargain: Not only is it heavenly, but it's given in the Mission-style bathhouse. With any spa service, guests can swim free in the naturally heated outdoor Olympic-size mineral water pool and get a discount on glider flights at the adjacent Gliderport. The 16-acre garden complex includes one-bedroom and studio cottages; a small one-bedroom house with full kitchen; and a three-bedroom house. All units have private bath, gas fireplace, TV, air-conditioning. *1712 Lincoln Ave., 94515, tel. 707/942–94515.* **Facilities:** *mudbaths, mineral-water outdoor swimming pool, bicycles, pedi-bikes, and barbecue equipment free to guests.* **Services:** *facials, mud bath, massage.* **Rates:** *cottages: $95–$150 double. $15 each additional guest; house: $140–$350, double. MC, V.*

Mount View Hotel. The newest and glitziest spa in town caters to couples looking for attention, luxury, and privacy. In 1993 the hotel was tastefully renovated, but still retains its history, as reflected in period furnishings and suites named for literary figures, Hollywood divas, and First Ladies who once signed the guest register. Six treatment rooms each contain a whirlpool tub and a separate shower with built-in steam bath that can be programmed for a number of soothing effects. Attendants draw the baths using non-thermal water, adding dehydrated Italian fango mud, salicyl, and an aromatherapy pine oil. The effect is relaxing and analgesic, and the mud does not cling to skin. Additional treatment rooms face the outdoor swimming pool (not heated) and a whirlpool with hot mineral water. An outdoor cafe serves refreshments in warm weather. You must make reservations for all services, including body and facial treatments, at the reception desk in the hotel lobby.

All facilities are clean. All hotel rooms with private bath with clawfoot tub, air-conditioning, TV, phone. Suites are decorated with Art Deco and Victorian antiques; (Ask for a room in the back: Front-facing rooms on the second floor can be noisy). Each cottage has a hot tub and sun deck. The hotel's new Catahoula Restaurant (tel. 707/942–2275 for reservations) and saloon are situated in what is now a National Historic landmark, and serve spa and regular cuisine for lunch and dinner. *1457 Lincoln Ave., 94515, tel. 707/942–6877; fax 707/942–6904.* **Facilities:** *Fango mudbath, whirlpools, steam baths, outdoor pool.* **Services:** *Aromatherapy, seaweed toning bath, Swedish-Esalen massage, reflexology, shiatsu, herbal wrap, mini-facial, customized baths with choice of fango, herbal crystals, oils, seaweed, or powdered milk whey. Spa appointments (tel. 707/942–5789) 9–7.* **Rates:** *2-night spa package (no meals) $359 single, $499 double. 33 standard rooms $90–$125; 6 suites $150–$165. 3 private cottages $189, double AE, MC, V.*

In the Area Sharpsteen Museum and Brannan cottage (Calistoga history), Old Faithful Geyser and geothermal museum, Culinary Institute of America, winery tours, Petrified Forest, state parks, public golf course, tennis, racquetball courts.

Getting Here *From San Francisco.* By bus, Greyhound (3 hr). By car, Rte. 101 to Novato, Rtes. 37, 121 to Napa, Rte. 29/128 to Calistoga (1½ hr). Taxi, rental car, bike rental available.

The Center for Mind/Body Medicine

Life enhancement
Preventive medicine

California
Del Mar
This week-long program at the Center for Mind/Body Medicine puts 12–15 residents through an intensive and highly regimented course designed to rejuvenate body and soul, supervised by a team of physicians, psychologists, and physiologists. The center, affiliated with the Sharp Institute, plans a permanent, self-contained facility to be open by 1996, but for now, sessions are being held in a private wing of a resort hotel in Del Mar (*see* L'Auberge Del Mar, *below*). The program, which links Eastern and Western concepts of natural healing and wellness with current anti-ageing research, has been inspired by the writings of Deepak Chopra, M.D., notably his best-sellers *Quantum Healing* and *Ageless Body, Timeless Mind*. In addition to lectures by Dr. Chopra and his colleagues, participants recieve medical evaluation, nutrition counseling, and rejuvenation therapies, including a daily Ayurvedic massage and yoga. Using biofeedback and meditation, the workshops teach both cognitive and non-cognitive techniques. Physical activity plays a role in rehabilitation after injury and to correct poor form and dysfunction in body movement.

This is a medically supervised, concentrated course in preventing illness. Healthy people learning to take control of their own ageing process will discover inner strengths, as well. Sessions are scheduled from Saturday to Saturday.

The Center for Mind/Body Medicine
8010 Frost St., Suite 300, San Diego, CA 92123
Reservations tel. 619/541–6730; program office tel.
619/793–6443
Fax 619/541–6706.

Administration	Executive director, Deepak Chopra, M.D.; medical director, David Simon, M.D.; program directors, Sarah McLean, Brent BecVar.
Season	Year-round.
Accommodations	Private rooms at L'Auberge have marble-walled baths with makeup lights, TVs, and air-conditioning. The hotel is built on several levels facing the sea, and has direct access to the beach as well as a small health club.
Rates	$3,200 for the all-inclusive week. Shorter programs are offered during holiday periods. Tax and gratuity not included. Credit cards: MC, V.
Meal Plan	Vegetarian meals served 3 times daily in private dining room.
Facilities	*See* L'Auberge Del Mar, *below.*
Special Notes	Shuttle transfers provided for Sat. pick up to and from resort and specified areas in San Diego area.

The Claremont Resort

Luxury pampering
Nonprogram resort facilities

California
Oakland

The San Francisco Bay area's premier urban getaway traces its origins to a romantic 1915 Victorian castle. The white-turreted hotel presides over 22 acres of landscaped grounds in the hills of Oakland and Berkeley. A fitness center with scheduled aerobics classes, spa, full-service salon, and bay-view cafe offering a low-calorie menu are some of the most noteable features of this resort.

The spa offers a wide range of services, including deep-tissue sports massage, shiatsu, and aromatherapy. There's also a personal trainer on staff to help you restyle your workout routine and improve your tennis technique. An aerobics studio, fully equipped weights room, outdoor heated pools for exercise and swimming laps, and 10 day/night tennis courts are open to all guests.

In the hydrotherapy area, there are rooms with specialized equipment for underwater massage, herbal wraps, and loofah body scrubs. Herbal and floral essences are used in baths, and aromatherapy massage helps detoxify the body. Separate locker rooms for men and women are each equipped with steam room, sauna, and whirlpool; workout clothing is provided daily. One-on-one attention is the focus of this spa: Among relaxation therapies offered is a one-hour restorative yoga session in which a trainer positions you so that gravity will work to help rejuvenate your whole body.

You can get half- to five-day spa packages, or you can use the facility on an à la carte basis.

The Claremont also hosts week-long retreats of the Preventive Medicine Research Institute. *See* Preventive Medicine Research Institute Retreat, *below.*

The Claremont Resort

Ashby and Domingo Aves., Box 23363, Oakland, CA 94623
Tel. 510/843–3000 or 800/551–7266
Fax 510/843–6239

Administration Managing director, Henry Feldman; spa director, Cindy Rudin.

Season Year-round.

Accommodations 239 spacious rooms with oversize beds (some are 4-posters) and sitting areas; bay-view rooms and suites command a premium. Fine contemporary art is displayed in the public rooms and halls. Facilities are available for social and business functions.

Rates Daily room rate $155–$194 single, $175–$215 double; suites $295–$720. Spa Retreat and overnight accommodations: $305 single, $223 double; 2 nights: $540 single, $383 double; 3 nights: $741 single, $527 double; 4 nights: $930 single, $666 double. Prices do not include tax and gratuities. Day packages, including service charge and facility fee, $79–$399. 1 night payable in advance or by credit card guarantee. Credit cards: AE, D, DC, MC, V.

Meal Plans Daily meal plan $60 per person for breakfast and dinner. Crossover cuisine—traditional seafood or meat dishes in heart-healthy portions—is served in the hotel's Pavilion Room and is calorie-controlled and low in cholesterol and sodium. Among the daily-changing specialties are mesquite-grilled swordfish with papaya chutney; grilled and steamed vegetables; grilled marinated prawns on linguini; roasted rack of Sonoma lamb, steamed sea bass; buckwheat ravioli with mushrooms, garlic, and tofu ginger in shallot broth.

Services and Facilities **Exercise Equipment:** 3 computerized Lifecycles, 2 Schwinn Air Dyne bikes, Turbobike, 2 Concept 2 rowers, 4 Startrac treadmills, 2 StairMasters, 4 Climb Max stairclimbers, Stairstepper, recumbent Lifecycle, 13-unit Cybex weight training circuit, dumbbells (3–50 lb); **Services:** Swedish, sports, and underwater massage, shiatsu, acupressure, aromatherapy, thalassotherapy, herbal wrap, loofah body scrub, facials; classes in aerobics, yoga, tai chi chuan, aquacise, body sculpting, stretching; biofeedback; salon for hair, nail, skin care; nutrition counseling; tennis and swimming lessons. **Swimming Facilities:** Olympic-size outdoor pool, lap pool. **Recreation Facilities:** Water volleyball, 10 tennis courts; golf, horseback riding nearby; hiking, parcourse.

In the Area Oakland's Jack London Square (entertainment, shopping, arts), The Oakland Museum, Berkeley and the University of California campus are a short hike from the hotel, including such attractions as a hillside botanical garden, concerts, sports activities, and dining at Chez Panisse. San Francisco, with its museums, beaches, and water sports, is just across the bay; downtown is only a 20-minute ride on the BART train. Free shuttle service to the BART station is provided from the hotel. Wine country tours also available.

Getting Here *From San Francisco*. By Bay Area Rapid Transit (BART), Rockridge Station (20 min). By car, Bay Bridge to Hwy. 24, Claremont Ave. exit to Ashley Ave. (30 min.). Limousine, taxi, rental car available. Airport transfers by scheduled van service.

Special Notes Specially equipped rooms, ramps, and elevators provide complete access to the spa for people with disabilities. Tennis and swimming clinics for children. No smoking in the spa or hotel. Spa open Mon.–Sat. 8:30–8:30, Sun. 8:30–6:30.

Esalen Institute

Life enhancement

California
Big Sur
The "human potential" movement nurtured in these cliff-top gardens and hot springs is alive and well after more than 25 years. Once considered a hippie haven, the Esalen Institute became an American utopia for seekers of ancient wisdom and new truths. Those goals gave birth to the Esalen style of sensuous massage and turned encounter therapy into an art form. If you're searching for self-awareness, there may be no more beautiful place to experience it than at Esalen Institute. Founded in 1962 by Michael Murphy and the late Richard Price, Esalen remains focused on personal and social transformation. If you enroll in this program, you must be comfortable with nudity, as clothing is optional during soaks at the hot springs.

Seminars and workshops on holistic health, esoteric religions, and emerging studies such as Gestalt therapy, psychosynthesis, shamanic healing, and neurolinguistics are offered throughout the year. Always popular are Esalen Massage bodywork workshops.

Many who come here simply want to unwind, and accommodations are available on a daily basis for $75 (includes lunch) with advance reservation (space permitting). Overnight guests can book a massage, hike in the Ventana Wilderness, and soak in natural rock pools filled by hot mineral springs. The institute also offers a hiking trip to Tassajara Zen Monastery (*see below*).

Esalen Institute
Hwy. 1, Big Sur, CA 93920
Tel. 408/667–3000; reservations 408/667–3005
Fax 408/667–2724

Administration Chairman, Michael Murphy; operations managers, Mary Mooney and Eric Erickson.

Season Year-round.

Accommodations 107 beds in rustic lodges; most rooms for 2, some with bunk beds. Comfortably casual furnishings with ocean views and the sound of the surf. No TV, radio, telephone, air-conditioning. Guests share rooms and baths, make their own bed.

Rates Tuition fee plus standard accommodations: weekend $380, 5-day $740, 7-day $1,110. Daily rate with meals $75–$125; bunk beds $75–$80. $100 deposit for weekends, $200–$300 for longer programs. Credit cards: AE, MC, V.

Meal Plans 3 meals daily, served buffet style. Meat, fish, and poultry, salads and fresh vegetables grown organically on the property served at lunch and dinner, with a vegetarian entrée such as spinach lasagna.

Services and Facilities **Services:** Massage (Esalen, Heller, Feldenkrais, deep-tissue), Rolfing, cranial-sacrial work; special studies. **Swimming Facilities:** Heated outdoor pool. **Recreation Facilities:** Hiking, tai chi chuan, morning exercise class, hot mineral baths. **Evening Programs:** Lectures, concerts.

In the Area Wilderness experiences (5 days or more); Hearst Castle at San Simeon, Mission of San Antonio de Padua (1771), Tassajara Zen Monastery in Los Padres National Forest (May 1–Labor Day), Big Sur State Park.

Getting Here *From San Francisco.* By bus, Greyhound via Monterey connecting in Big Sur with Esalen van (5 hr) for $30. By car, Hwy. 101 south to Monterey, west to Coastal marker 156, Hwy. 1, south to Esalen road marker (3½ hr). Esalen van service (for reservations, tel. 408/667–3000) Fri. and Sun. from Monterey airport or bus station ($30).

Special Notes Limited access for people with disabilities. Special activities and dining plan for children; limited child-care facilities. Nonsmoking cabins, nonsmoking areas in dining room.

Glen Ivy Hot Springs

Taking the waters

California
Corona
Nestled in the foothills of the Santa Ana coastal range, halfway between the desert and the ocean, is Glen Ivy Hot Springs, a day spa with mud baths, 15 rejuvenating mineral pools, concerts under the stars, and à la carte spa facilities that include massages, facials, and other salon services. The waters here have been known for their healing power, since the Luiseno tribe first built mud saunas around the springs during the pre-Hispanic era. (There are no traces of buildings.) The natives used an Aztec word imported by Franciscan missionaries, "temescal," meaning "sweat-house" to name the valley. In 1890, a 10-room adobe house opened as the first hotel to serve the orange ranchers from nearby towns. Artifacts and photos of these early days are on display in the Hot Springs Cafe. In 1912 the springs became popular with city dwellers who flocked from Los Angeles to the waters until 1969, when a flood wiped out the bathhouse and mudbath. With the rebirth of interest in natural therapies came new facilities and gardens. The homey country inn survived as a private residence, and the pools, sundecks, and landscaping were re-created in 1977 when the current management company was formed.

The white stucco buildings and clay-tile roofs counterpoint palm trees and bougainvillea. Warm desert sun, cool mountain breezes, and gardens provide the ambience for a relaxing, indulgent escape. Bathers float in the pools on rented rafts, dozing, reading, meditating. This is about as close to a tropical paradise as you can get for under $20 a day. The mud baths are free, and so is membership into the famous "Club Mud," for those who take a dip in the the vat of soft red clay that's been mined nearby. After you coat your body and hair, sit poolside and let the clay bake until it dries. Then rinse in the mineral water shower; your skin will feel satiny and healthy. The pools are drained and filled with fresh, chlorinated water every day.

Water temperatures vary between 90°F and 110°F at the two wells that supply a constant flow of mineral water to the pools. You'll be cautioned not to stay in the hot water too long, particularly if you're dieting or in poor health. The only organized activity is a 2 PM aquaerobics class held in the big swimming pool. Sign up for massage or salon services when you arrive, or call ahead for appointments. There are 16 massage rooms and well-equipped dressing areas for men and women.

Although sun protection is provided at a covered hot pool, you'll need to bring sunscreen. An old swimsuit and towel are recommended for the mud bath. Food and drink are available at the Spa Cafe, or you can pack a picnic and use shaded tables in a designated area. Perhaps a jog down the road to shop at the farm market will feel invigorating after lazing in the primal ooze.

Glen Ivy Hot Springs
25000 Glen Ivy Rd., Corona, CA 91719
Tel. 909/277–3529
Fax 909/277–1202

Administration Directors, John and Pamela Gray.

Season Year-round. Open daily, except Thanksgiving and Christmas.

Accommodations **The Mission Inn** (3649 7th St., Riverside, CA 92501, tel. 909/784–0300 or 800/843–7755), located in Riverside, provides admission to Glen Ivy Hot Springs and Continental breakfast with overnight accommodations: $101 single, $136 double. Credit cards: AE, MC, V.

Rates Daily admission to the pools, sauna, and mud bath: $14.50 weekdays for adults and children, $13.50 for senior citizens. All admissions Sat., Sun., and holidays $16.75. Children under 3 free. Credit cards: MC, V.

Services and Facilities **Services:** Aromatherapy massage, body polish, facials, anticellulite treatment, and nail and hand care. **Swimming Facilities:** Outdoor pool, 14 soaking pools. **Evening Programs:** Concerts (ticketed separately).

In the Area Temecula wineries, Old Town Temecula with its 1890s architecture.

Getting Here *From Los Angeles.* By car, I–10, I–60, or Hwy. 91 eastbound to I–15 south, exit right onto Temescal Canyon Rd., right on Glen Ivy Rd. (1 hr).

Special Notes All facilities accessible for people with disabilities.

The Golden Door

Life enhancement
Luxury pampering
Nutrition and diet
Spiritual awareness

California
Escondido The doyen of spas in Southern California, the Golden Door opened in 1959 a mile from its present location, which now encompasses 177 acres of canyon and orchard. Beyond the ornate

brass door lies an enchanted realm of Oriental gardens and inns. Guests in standard-issue sweat suits step peacefully to aerobics classes; *yukata* robes are supplied for lounging. The setting and the incredibly thoughtful staff create an air of calm order. The experience is restorative and regenerative.

The process of transforming yourself from sluggardly to energetic begins on your arrival Sunday afternoon with an interview about your fitness level, diet, and preferences. Do you prefer tennis, instruction in lap-swimming techniques, or a cooking class? A massage with a therapist, who gets to know every muscle in your body, is scheduled every day at the same time.

On the orientation tour for first-time guests, one can't help but be impressed by the attention to detail and devotion to comfort that have been incorporated into the spa's impressive design, a cross between a first-class resort and a Japanese country inn. The four spacious gyms have sliding glass walls that open to fresh air and the beauty of the lush gardens. A graceful bathhouse, tiled and topped with gray Oriental carving, contains a modern sauna, steam room, Swiss shower, whirlpool, and body-wrap facility.

Each day begins at 6 AM with a brisk mountain hike led by staff members who, Sherpa-like, supply flasks of cool water and fruit to sustain you until you are served breakfast. During your meal you're presented with a paper fan and schedule for the day. All decisions have been made for you, so all you can do is go with the flow. If you miss an appointment, a kimono-clad staffer will come searching for you.

The 50-minute exercise periods fill most of the morning; afternoons are for pampering and personal pursuits. You can have lunch by the pool, in the dining room, or in the privacy of your room. Massages can be alfresco or in your room, with a choice of shiatsu, traditional Swedish, deep-tissue, or aromatherapy. Daily beauty treatments are included in the program cost.

For fit guests who return whenever they need to recharge, there is an Inner Door program. It is an advanced course for a small group in problem solving, meditation, and body movement. For four days there are two-hour sessions for exploration of spiritual and inner forces, even tai chi chuan, designed for inner serenity.

The Golden Door

Deer Springs Rd.,
Box 463077, Escondido, CA 92046
Tel. 619/744–6677
Fax 619/471–2393

Administration President, Alex Szekely; manager, Rachel Caldwell; program director, Judy Bird.

Season Year-round, except Christmas week.

Accommodations Single rooms for 36 guests in buildings patterned after old Japanese honjin inns. 1-story ocher stucco buildings have bedrooms with sitting areas opening onto private gardens and decorated with muted colors and Japanese wood-block prints, parquet floors with carpets, sliding shoji screens, and jalousie windows. Private baths stocked with Golden Door skin-care products. Guest units cluster on courtyards, a short walk from the main building. 1 private cottage. All rooms have telephone and air-conditioning, but no TV.

Rates $4,250 weekly; $3,750 during July, Aug., and Thanksgiving week; $4,032 for Spa Trek package. $1,000 deposit with reservation, balance due before arrival. Credit cards: AE, MC, V. Gratuities included; for tax add $87.98 and $77.63, respectively.

Meal Plans 3 meals plus snacks served daily. 1,000 calories per day calculated for maximum energy with weight loss, 1,200 for maintenance. Low-cholesterol meals, rich in fiber and whole grains, low in salt, sugar, and fat, served with oriental flair. Lunch can include miso soup, stir-fry vegetables with tofu, or fresh Pacific shrimp sautéed with orange and ginger. Dinner entrées include boneless breast of chicken with wild mushrooms; whole wheat crepes filled with a mixture of spinach, mushrooms, and ricotta cheese; or cabbage rolls stuffed with bulgur pilaf and vegetables. Special needs accommodated.

Services and Facilities **Exercise Equipment:** 12 Hoggan CamStar weight training units, 6 Trotter treadmills, 3 Cardioaerobikes, 2 StairMasters, PTS Turbo bike, rowing machine, free weights. **Services:** Massage (Swedish, Trager, shiatsu, and others), aromatherapy, herbal wrap, body scrub, daily skin care, facials, manicure, pedicure, hair styling. Instruction in tai chi chuan, yoga, swimming, circuit training; fitness evaluations and submaximal stress test. **Swimming Facilities:** 2 outdoor pools. **Recreation Facilities:** 2 tennis courts, hiking, classes in flower arranging, crafts, gardening. **Evening Programs:** Lectures on nutrition, stress management, sports medicine, other health-related topics; movies.

In the Area Sea World.

Getting Here *From San Diego.* By car, Hwy. 163 to I–15, north to Deer Springs Rd. exit (40 min). Free pickup from and return to San Diego Airport.

Special Notes Ramps and 1-story structures make the entire complex accessible to people with disabilities. No smoking in public areas. Remember to bring appropriate shoes for hiking, walking, sports.

Green Gulch Farm Zen Center

Spiritual awareness

California
Sausalito
Standing amid pines and open fields that stretch to the Pacific, the wooden guest house at Green Gulch Farm seems far removed from the rest of the world, but it is only 25 minutes from San Francisco. A peaceful retreat for study and work, the center is suffused with the spirit of Zen.

Buddhist tradition is experienced here in many ways. You can join classes to study Zen texts on basic teachings and the bodhisattva spirit, practice playing the *shakuhachi* (Japanese bamboo flute), or partake of an ancient meditative tea ceremony. Workshops offer instruction in raku tea-bowl making (using clay dug on the farm), flower arranging, and organic gardening.

Guests are welcome to come and go as they please, joining in communal life and work on the organic farm or quietly meditat-

ing on long walks through the nearby woods and on Muir beach.
Miles of hiking trails surround the 200-acre Green Gulch, leading to Mount Tamalpais and Mill Valley.

As you enter the Lindisfarne Guest House, you'll gain an imme-
diate sense of ageless serenity. Constructed in the Japanese
temple style of handmade woodcraft, it has 12 rooms surrounding a high atrium.

A combination of vacation and partial participation in community work and practice is available from Sunday through Thursday nights. The morning schedule includes meditation, work,
classes, and group discussions; afternoons and evenings are
free. Called a "Practice Retreat," this program involves a minimum stay of three nights and earns you a modest reduction on
the daily rate, plus meals.

Green Gulch Farm Zen Center
Star Rte., Sausalito, CA 94965
Tel. 415/383-3134
Fax 415/383-3128

Administration	Spiritual leader, Abbot Tenshin Anderson; director, Nancy Schrader.
Season	Year-round.
Accommodations	12 rooms with shared baths, 1 suite. Simple wooden furniture, 2 beds in each room. Central heat, but no air-conditioning. Each room has outside patio or balcony.
Rates	$55–$70 per person in small single room, $90–$105 for 2 persons; weekends, $70–$85 daily, single in large room, $105–$120 for 2 persons. Meals $5 each. Practice Retreat, including meals, $30 per day single, $50 double occupancy (3-night minimum). Beginner's "sitting" $15, includes lunch; no lodging. Weekend workshop: $100 tuition includes all meals and $170 for shared accommodations, $200 for single room; add tax. Deposit: 1 night, plus $10 per person for each additional night. No credit cards.
Meal Plans	3 vegetarian meals daily, served buffet style, include eggs and dairy products. Organically grown vegetables from the farm are steamed, served with brown rice, miso soup.
Services and Facilities	**Services:** Instruction in Japanese arts, Zen, gardening, herbs. **Swimming Facilities:** Ocean beach, outdoor pool. **Evening Programs:** Lectures on Japanese arts in conjunction with scheduled workshops.
In the Area	Muir Woods, Napa Valley, Marin County Civic Center (Frank Lloyd Wright architecture, art galleries, theater), Sausalito waterfront (restaurants, boutiques).
Getting Here	*From San Francisco.* By car, Hwy. 101 to turnoff for Mill Valley, Hwy. 1 (Shoreline Hwy.) toward Muir Beach (25 min). By ferry, frequent bay crossings from the Embarcadero to Sausalito; then take a taxi.
Special Notes	Scheduled program for workshops/retreats varies weekly.

Heartwood Institute

Life enhancement
Spiritual awareness

California
Garberville

Set on 240 acres in the mountains on California's north coast, this rustic complex serves as a vocational school for practitioners in the healing arts, and also welcomes weekend visitors and participants in wellness retreats. The customized retreat programs are dedesigned for healthy people seeking to become even healthier. A full schedule of classes, exercise, and bodywork is offered during retreats by experts in Hatha Iyengar yoga, transcendental meditation, and nutrition.

The wilderness setting is perfect for walks in the woods, mountain biking, or participating in a group meditation under the wooden dome set in the forest. In the community center, a picturesque log lodge, are eight private treatment rooms, an outdoor hot tub, wood-fired sauna, and bedrooms. Meals are taken in the cozy dining room or on a spacious deck in nice weather. Typically there are 20 participants in a retreat program.

Heartwood Institute
220 Harmony La., Garberville, CA 95440
Tel. 707/923-2021
Fax 707/923-4906

Administration
Owners-managers, Robert Fasic and Roy Grieshaber; retreat coordinator, Susie Yong.

Season
Year-round.

Accommodations
15 rooms in 3-story dormitory, 36 campsites. Simple amenities include sheets, towels, comforters on beds, and shared bathrooms. No air-conditioning or maid service.

Rates
$110 per night for single room and meals, $90 per person for double room and meals; $55 for campsite. $126 tuition for weekend retreat, with $50 advance payment. Credit cards: MC, V.

Meal Plans
3 meals daily, served buffet style. All meals are primarily vegetarian: organic vegetables, grains, fruits, and nuts are supplemented with dairy products and eggs. Fish is served once a week. There is a snack kitchen for personal use in the community center. Special diets are accommodated.

Services and Facilities
Services: Yoga classes daily, Swedish/Esalen massage, polarity therapy, hypnotherapy, deep-tissue massage, shiatsu, acupressure, breathwork, Jin Shin Jytsu, transformational therapy, nutritional counseling. **Swimming Facilities:** Outdoor heated swimming pool. **Evening Programs:** Lectures, dances.

In the Area
Sinkyone Wilderness State Preserve, redwoods forest, Eureka and Arcata (Victorian architecture, museums, galleries).

Getting Here
From San Francisco. By car, Hwy. 101 north to first Garberville exit (3 hr). By bus, Greyhound to Garberville (6 hr). By plane, American and United Airlines to Eureka/Arcata Airport. Pickup arranged at airport or bus station (fee). Car rental, taxi available.

La Costa Resort & Spa

Life enhancement
Luxury pampering
Nutrition and diet
Weight management

California
Carlsbad

A mega-resort for the fun and fitness crowd, La Costa Resort & Spa is also known for its serious program for change of life-style. Nevertheless, the country club ambience is more suited to pampering than to preventive medicine. When the 1,000-acre complex was renovated several years ago, the idea was to offer something for every taste. The unfortunate result is over-crowding and lack of privacy in the spa building. The beauty salon, on the other hand, is state of the art.

The Healthy Lifestyles program is a one-week package designed to educate and motivate guests to adopt healthy habits. Each day begins with a brisk walk around the golf course. Power walking has now become the preferred exercise, for the fit and the not so fit, because it has none of the stress associated with running and jogging. Mornings are devoted to exercise at the gym, or therapy and massage, followed by workshops and lectures. Optional periods allow unlimited golf, tennis, or personal counseling.

Teamed with a personal trainer, nutritionist, and psychologist, you get a full wellness prescription. A computerized exerciser tests your strength, flexibility, and pulmonary function. Nutritional analysis and body composition determine your diet and measure the percentages of fat and muscle in your body. A take-home program is provided.

The Healthy Lifestyles program can begin any day of the week, and includes all meals, personal training, and seven hours of spa and salon services. It's wise to schedule early appointments at the spa, especially when a large group is meeting at the convention center across the way.

La Costa can be enjoyed simply as a luxury getaway as well as a structured spa program. Packages are available for two to seven nights, with a choice of eating in any of the dining rooms, all of which serve spa cuisine.

The true luxury of La Costa consists of the personal attention guests receive, even though the place is crowded. Locker-room attendants remember your name and slipper size and hand out fresh towels and robes without being asked; they deserve handsome tips. The separate facilities for men and women add to the clublike atmosphere. Included are a eucalyptus-scented inhalation room, steam room, sauna, Swiss multihead showers, hot and cold plunge pools, and an outdoor Jacuzzi. The gym and salon are coed.

La Costa Resort & Spa
Costa del Mar Rd., Carlsbad, CA 92009
Tel. 619/438–9111 or 800/854–5000; spa appointments
800/729–4772
Fax 619/931–7559

Administration
Managing director, Darryll Shaeffer; spa director, Judie Nixon.

Season Year-round.

Accommodations 478 deluxe rooms and suites in Spanish-style buildings and a campus-style spa complex. Newer rooms overlook the golf course. Fine furnishings. Fitness- and spa-program guests stay in large, poolside bedrooms with sitting areas, unless they request otherwise. 6 private residences.

Rates $590 weekdays for 2-night spa package for single or double, $700 weekends; $430 per night single for Healthy Lifestyles program, $639 per night for two people; $680 2-night Ultimate sport/spa package weekdays per couple, $780 weekends per couple. $215–$400 daily room rate, $375–$2,000 suite for single or double. Add 10% tax, 1 night payable on booking. Credit cards: AE, D, DC, MC, V.

Meal Plans You select from daily menus in 4 restaurants offering spa cuisine. Breakfast options include fruit, muffins, an egg-white omelet with salsa, and an energy mix of grains, apple butter, and raisins. For lunch, try cheese blintzes, papaya stuffed with crab, and beef Stroganoff. Chicken stuffed with foie gras, fettucine primavera, salmon fillet with horseradish sauce, and veal with artichoke sauce are dinner entrées, with fresh fruit, sherbet, or custard for dessert.

Services and Facilities **Exercise Equipment:** Eagle, Nautilus, and Universal weights units, Lifecycles, computerized treadmills, aerobic trainer, rowing machines, free weights, Rebounders. **Services:** Massage (Swedish, shiatsu, reike, aromatherapy, reflexology), Orthion, Myopulse, herbal wraps, loofah body scrub, spot toning, facials. Salon for hair, nail, and skin care. Coed exercise classes $10 (aerobics, Rebounder, yoga). Nutrition counseling, medical and fitness evaluations. Personal trainer for exercise, swimming, golf, and tennis. **Swimming Facilities:** 5 outdoor pools. **Recreation Facilities:** 21 championship tennis courts (8 lighted), 2 18-hole golf courses, driving range, horseback riding. Bike rental. **Evening Programs:** Lectures on health and fitness, stress management; movies and resort cabaret. Cooking demonstration.

In the Area Bus or limousine trips to Sea World, San Diego Zoo, Disneyland; Coronado beaches, San Diego museums, and Horton Plaza shops, Laguna Nigel (the Ritz Carlton); Del Mar Racetrack.

Getting Here *From San Diego.* By car, I–5 to Carlsbad, La Costa Ave. exit (40 min). By train, Amtrak to Oceanside (30 min). Limousine, taxi, rental car available.

Special Notes Access available for people with disabilities. Tennis and golf clinics and summer day-camp programs for children. No smoking in the spa building or the dining rooms. Spa open daily 7 AM–8 PM; minimum age 18.

Loews Santa Monica Beach Hotel

Nonprogram resort
Sports conditioning

California If you want a customized fitness program, Hollywood sports
Santa Monica trainer Jackson Sousa will give you primo one-on-one training in his own 3,200-square-foot facility, located in the Loews Santa Monica Beach Hotel. If he's not motivation enough for you to get into shape, nearby Venice Beach (a.k.a. Surfer's SoHo),

with lots of buffed bodies, should give you some impetus to pull in the waistline. This resort, opened in 1989 and refurbished in 1993, is located on the beach and is under an hour's drive from downtown Los Angeles.

Pamper yourself in the airy resort's health club and skin-care salon, and use the glass-dome indoor/outdoor swimming pool and Jacuzzi adjoining the fitness center. Training sessions and massages can be arranged, as well as a weekend hiking excursion. An optional package of salon services can be booked for $150, or you can combine fitness and massage services with a $120 day package. Special weekend packages are offered, including high-energy breakfast, personal training, nutritional counseling, and biometric evaluation.

Sousa's fitness center has a full line of state-of-the-art cardio-vascular and weight-training machines, plus a studio for aerobics and yoga classes. In addition to scheduled classes in step aerobics, stretch and tone, and water aerobics, physical therapy and orthopedic sports rehabilitation are offered. There are a sauna and a steam room in both the men's and women's locker rooms. Emphasis here is on strengthening, cross training, and prevention of further injury.

Loews Santa Monica Beach Hotel
1700 Ocean Ave., Santa Monica, CA 90401
Tel. 310/458–6700 or 800/235–6397
Fax 310/458–6761

Administration Managing director, Richard Casale; fitness center operator, Jackson Sousa.

Season Year-round.

Accommodations 350 rooms and 31 suites with ocean view. All have desk, 2 dual-line phones with data ports, phone in bathroom, robes, hair dryer, scale, TV, radio/clock, and air-conditioning. Rooms are refreshed twice daily, and are furnished with pale wood, rattan, and original art. On-site valet and self-parking, concierge service. Suites have marble-wall Jacuzzi, small balcony.

Rates $175–$225 single or double, suites to $2,500. $495 per person for Health-and-Fitness weekend package. Add 12% tax, gratuities. Credit cards: AE, DC, MC, V.

Meal Plans Healthy Options served à la carte or included in weekend package.

Services and Facilities **Exercise Equipment:** Cybex and Keiser weight-training equipment, StairMaster, Lifecycles, Gravitron, bikes, treadmills, free weights. **Swimming Facilities:** 65′ x 23′ indoor/outdoor pool, ocean beach. **Recreation Facilities:** Bike and skate path, inline skate rental, public tennis courts nearby. **Services:** Massage, facial, fitness evaluation, 1-on-1 training, salon. **Evening Programs:** Lobby lounge, nearby Center for the Performing Arts.

In the Area Santa Monica Pier (carousel, games, entertainment), Hollywood, J. Paul Getty Museum (art), Pacific Coast Bicentennial Bike Route, Malibu, Venice Beach, Santa Monica Mountains National Recreation Area, Universal Studios, Third Street Promenade (shopping and dining); Huntington Library (art collections and botanical gardens) 1 hr east in San Marino.

Getting Here *From Los Angeles International Airport.* SuperShuttle van (30 min). By car, Santa Monica Fwy. (I–10) to 4th St. exit, Pico Blvd. to Ocean Ave. (30 min). Taxi, limousine, rental car available.

Special Notes $8 daily facility fee for Fitness Center. Kid Fitness program on request.

Marriott's Desert Springs Resort

Luxury pampering

California
Palm Desert
The Desert Springs Resort, the elaborate flagship resort created in the desert by the Marriott Corporation, boasts an impressive design: To reach the health spa from the main lobby, guests step on a boat that glides gracefully to the oasis complex surrounded by lagoons and a golf course.

Guests at this airy 325-acre retreat find its elegance and desert views relaxing. Escape the midday sun at the juice bar or have your hair styled at the José Eber salon. Try the dry flotation unit, a space-age capsule appropriately named Superspace Relaxer that has its own audio, video, and sensory stimulation unit. When you're working out, enjoy the natural light that floods the newly expanded weight training gym and aerobics studios, where yoga, step aerobics, and body sculpting are among six classes scheduled daily.

Water is involved in the treatments and services offered, from hydrotherapy pools to hot and cold plunges, a Turkish steam room, and a vigorous Aquacise workout. Underwater massage in private tubs is enhanced with crystals from Hungarian mineral springs, developed for the spa's exclusive Kerstin Florian salon. Stimulating or relaxing aromatherapy oils—depending on your mood—and freeze-dried seaweed can be added to the bath. Moisturizing creams leave your skin glowing.

The new European Thermal Kur Program combines a series of baths and bodywork in a specially-priced package. The Spa Experience package is designed for flexibility, giving you a choice of services (one hour), unlimited aerobics classes, breakfast or lunch in the spa cafe, and a body composition test, plus hotel accommodations on a nightly basis. Or you can pay the daily admission of $20, which includes workout clothing and robe, unlimited fitness classes, and use of exercise equipment. The fee is waived when you book any one-day package that includes lunch, treatments, and exercise classes.

Skin-care products are formulated with natural ingredients that include lavender, chamomile, vitamins, collagen, seaweed, thermal mineral water, and glycolic acid. Applied by shiatsu acupressure technique, the ointments, gels, and sprays are intended to help prevent sun damage and aging. Treatments can be booked as part of a half-day pampering package or on a separate basis.

Marriott's Desert Springs Resort
74855 Country Club Dr., Palm Desert, CA 92260
Tel. 619/341–1856; spa appointments 800/255–0848; room reservations 800/228–9290
Fax 619/341–1872

Administration   Manager, Dave Rolston; executive spa director, John DeFontes; spa manager Patricia Sack.

Season   Year-round.

Accommodations   892 rooms and executive suites, with oversize beds, private bath, balcony. All rooms have refrigerator, mini-bar, 2 phones, TV, air-conditioning, contemporary Southwestern furnishings. Golf villas available.

Rates   1-night Spa Experience package priced by season, $150–$310 single, $220–$390 for 2, double occupancy. Day packages (no lodging) $85–$260. Daily room rates $120–$340 single or double occupancy; suites $350–$2,100. Add 9% tax, gratuities. Credit cards: AE, DC, MC, V.

Meal Plans   Spa cuisine is served in 3 of the resort's 10 restaurants, and at the spa cafe for breakfast and lunch. Meals are à la carte, or part of the Spa Experience package. Lunch can be a salad or cold poached salmon. Main dining room dinner entrées include grilled loin of veal, broiled chicken, pasta primavera. Coffee, herbal tea, dairy products. Special diets on request.

Services and Facilities   **Exercise Equipment:** 24-station Bodymaster weight training gym, 4 StairMasters, 6 Lifecycles, 4 Precor treadmills, free weights, including barbells, dumbbells, bench press. **Services:** Massage (Swedish, shiatsu, sports, aromatherapy), full-body masks (aloe, algae, mud), facials, herbal wraps, loofah body scrub, Bindi, reflexology. Nutrition counseling, computerized fitness and body-composition analysis. Beauty salon. **Swimming Facilities:** Outdoor pool. **Recreation Facilities:** 2 18-hole golf courses, 18-hole putting course, 20 tennis courts, croquet, water volleyball. Bike rental, horseback riding, skiing nearby. **Evening Programs:** Resort entertainment.

In the Area   Indian Canyons National Historic Park, sightseeing tours, aerial tramway to Mt. San Jacinto, ballooning, Desert Fashion Plaza (shopping), casinos, Bob Hope Cultural Center, Palm Springs Desert Museum (art, film series, concerts), Living Desert Reserve (nature studies), Polo Club, hot springs, Joshua Tree National Monument (hiking trails).

Getting Here   *From Los Angeles.* By bus, scheduled shuttle service from LAX and hotels or Greyhound (4 hr). By car, I-10 to Hwy. 111 (2½ hr). By train, Amtrak to Indio (2 hr). By plane, American Airlines and United commuter flights (30 min). Limousine, taxi, rental car available. Shuttle service by van to airport.

Special Notes   Limited access for people with disabilities. Supervised games, movies, tennis lessons for children. No smoking in the spa; nonsmoking areas in restaurants. Spa open 6:30 AM–7:30 PM daily. Exercise facilities available on daily basis ($20). Minimum age in spa, 16.

Meadowood Resort

Nonprogram resort

California Napa Valley   Meadowood, nestled in the heart of the wine country 60 miles north of San Francisco, recalls the grand old resorts of the early 1900s with its gabled lodges overlooking the manicured croquet lawn and golf course. Remarkably, most of the buildings are of recent vintage. The health spa was added in 1993 and epitomizes the Napa Valley lifestyle: easy informality and superb taste.

Wine plays an important role in spa treatments as well as on the dinner menu. Chardonnay cream is used in a body wrap and facial, exclusively formulated with aromatic essential oils from grape seeds, said to encourage natural revitalization. An extensive selection of massage therapies, body and facial treatments, and fitness classes is available at à la carte prices or as part of a personalized renewal program. (Lodging is not included in spa packages.).

The spa building is airy and sunlit, with an aerobics studio and weight-training room on the upper floor, and a suite of private rooms for massage and facials adjoining the men's and women's locker rooms. A robe is issued when you check in for your appointments, and full amenities are provided. Scheduled classes are open to all guests but rarely crowded: an early morning stretch session is followed by the 90-minute total body workout. One of the more creative classes offered here includes line-dance steps for country music fans; and aquaerobics, yoga, and step classes are listed on the daily schedule.

Vineyard tours begin right outside the resort. Mountain bikes with helmet and water bottle can be rented at the spa. For groups of four or more, the resident wine tutor, John Thoreen, sets up guided tours and tastings. Guided walks within Meadowood's grounds are another way to enjoy the rich, natural history of Napa Valley.

Meadowood Resort
900 Meadowood La., St. Helena, CA 94574
Tel. 707/963–3646 or 800/458–8080
Fax 707/963–3532

Administration General manager, Jorg Lippuner; spa directors, Eric and Catherine Chesky

Season Year-round.

Accommodations 99 guest rooms in lodges on hillside and in sports complex. French provincial furniture, with king- or queen-size beds trimmed in chintz, covered with down comforter. Most have fieldstone fireplace, high ceilings with fan, and gabled windows. All are air-conditioned, have TV, 2 phones, radiant heating, large tile bathroom. Amenities: coffee maker, toaster, wet bar, terry-cloth robes, basket of apples.

Rates $275–$385 per night for 2 persons. $295 per person for 3-day Renewal Program with 5 spa services. Add 15% service charge, plus taxes. Credit cards: AE, DC, MC, V.

Meal Plans Meals at Meadowood include a wide range of vegetarian and heart-healthy specialties. Chef Roy Breiman blends cooking techniques from the Provence region of France with the seasonal bounty from local farms and California's seacoast. Prix-fixe vegetarian dinner menu ($35) includes salad of couscous with layered zucchini, strudel with wild mushrooms and caramelized artichokes. Spa menu has crispy salmon with marinated tomatoes, vegetable spaghettini, fruit sorbet. Lunch selections at the Grill include grilled artichoke with crab salad, fettucine with mushrooms, tomatoes, basil, and garlic. Naturally an extensive wine list accompanies meals.

Services and Facilities	**Exercise Equipment:** Cybex 12-unit weight training circuit, Lifecycle 9500 recumbent bike, 2 Startrac treadmills, 3 Climb Max units, Monark bike, free weights (3–50 lbs), benches. **Swimming Facilities:** Outdoor heated 25-yd. lap pool. **Recreation Facilities:** 7 tennis courts ($8 per person), 2 croquet courts, 9-hole golf course, bike rental. **Services:** Massage (Swedish, deep tissue, aromatherapy), reflexology, facial, salt glow body scrub; Exercise consultation, personal training, body composition test, nutrition analysis.
In the Area	Calistoga mud baths (*see above*), Culinary Institute of America, St. Helena (shops, restaurants), ballooning, horseback riding, wineries.
Getting Here	*From San Francisco.* By car, Hwy. 101 via the Golden Gate Bridge to Hwy. 80, Hwy. 29 via Napa to St. Helena, Silverado Trail to Hopewell Mtn. Rd. (90 min). Limousine, taxi, car rental available.
Special Notes	Daily charge for spa use $15. Hours: 7AM– 8 PM daily. Minimum age in spa, 16.

Murrieta Hot Springs Resort

Taking the waters

California
Murrieta

A spa in the Old World style, the Murrieta Hot Springs Resort is a place to soak your body in warm mineral water, get a great massage, and enjoy vegetarian meals. The current ownership has given the rooms a facelift and added a second dining room that features chicken, fish, and wines from local vineyards (only vegetarian meals served in the original dining room). The atmosphere remains pleasantly laid-back. Rigid programs have been dropped in favor of letting guests do their own thing.

This tranquil resort stretches across 47 acres of landscaped grounds, land once roamed by the Temecula tribe, but more recently, in the 1940s, by Teamster Union executives who had the mission-style lodges built for their retreats. Hot springs from the Elsinor fault provide the mineral water of varying temperatures that fills the Olympic-size swimming pool and two smaller soaking pools.

Body work and skin care using natural products can be ordered à la carte, even if you aren't staying at the resort. A $10 day pass gets you a locker and admission to the mineral water pools. The bathhouse, a 1920s-style Spanish villa with mosaics and tiled tubs, has private rooms for soaking with essential oils and Bach flower mixes, Finnish saunas for men and women, and a full range of massage.

This is not a luxury facility, as the prices reflect. A 50-minute massage comes with a full-body mud wrap in the "Stress Release" package and costs $95. But the mineral water is the main attraction, said to be loaded with minerals as well as electromagnetic energy. It's a soothing way to treat sore muscles and stiff joints, and combined with mud treatments, the water helps relax the body and soften your skin. Murietta mud is a blend of tule root, sea kelp, betonite clay, and peat moss, plus tender care from a dedicated staff.

Murrieta Hot Springs Resort
39405 Murrieta Hot Springs Rd., Murrieta, CA 92362
Tel. 909/677–7451 or 800/458–4393
Fax 909/677–7451

Administration	General manager, Jeffrey Krulek; spa manager, Lynne Vertrees.
Season	Year-round.
Accommodations	242 guest rooms in private cottages and terraced stone lodges furnished with old oak dressers and new oversize beds. New suites with white wicker furniture, brass fixtures, and 2 queen-size beds. All with private bath, TV, and telephone. Air-conditioning by request.
Rates	$50–$75 a day single, $55–$80 double. 3-day/2-night midweek spa sampler $269 single, $225 double occupancy. 2-night weekend package $349 single, $279 double. Add gratuities, taxes. Credit cards: AE, MC, V.
Meal Plans	Vegetarian buffet, fish, or chicken dishes. Entrées include tofu-cauliflower curry, pasta, vegetarian enchiladas, bean burritos, Mexican-style salad. Mesquite-grilled fish and barbecue chicken served in a separate dining room. Coffee, tea, wine; fresh dairy products and cereals at breakfast.
Services and Facilities	**Exercise Equipment:** 11-unit Fisher weight training gym, 3 AeroSteps, 2 Schwinn Air Dyne bikes, 3 Windracer bikes, Bodyguard bike, Startrac treadmill, rowing machine, dumbbells and barbells (5–85 lbs.) with 6 benches, squat machine. **Services:** Massage (Swedish, polarity, lymph drainage, acupressure, shiatsu), herbal wrap, mud wrap, loofah body scrub, back scrub, foot care, facial. Beauty salon. **Swimming Facilities:** Outdoor pool. **Spa Facilities:** Outdoor pools, indoor Roman-style pools, and private baths. **Recreation Facilities:** 14 tennis courts (4 lighted), badminton, shuffleboard. Hiking, jogging trails. Golf at the nearby Rancho California Country Club's par-72 course. Horseback riding, lake fishing.
In the Area	Temecula's old-town district, antiques shops, wine tours, ballooning.
Getting Here	*From San Diego.* By bus, Greyhound to Temecula (90 min). By car, Hwy. 163 to I–15 past Temecula, Hot Springs Rd. exit (70 min).
Special Notes	Limited access for people with disabilities. Children are welcome to bathe with parents. No smoking in public areas. Spa bathhouse open weekdays 9–7, Sat. 9–8, Sun. 9–5.

The Oaks at Ojai

Nutrition and diet
Vibrant maturity
Weight management

California *Ojai*	Built as a country inn in 1918, the dignified wood-and-stone structure gained a new lease on life in the 1970s when Sheila Cluff and her husband became its owners. A former professional ice skater and physical fitness instructor, Sheila Cluff drew together a team of exercise physiologists. A sister spa in Palm Springs, the Palms, offers a similar no-frills program.

Ojai is an art center and a favorite of the practitioners of several healing faiths. The Oaks is located on the main square of the town, and appointments can be made with psychics, astrologers, pyramid enthusiasts, members of the Theosophy movement, or the Krishnamurti Foundation. All are attracted by the natural beauty of a fertile valley near the Los Padres National Forest, little more than an hour's drive north of Los Angeles.

At the Oaks at Ojai, fitness and weight-control programs are the main attractions for men and women who want to unwind or work out without fancy lodging or physical therapy. When you stick to the basics—up to 17 exercise classes and activities daily and a diet of fresh, natural foods that total only 1,000 calories—the Oaks helps you lose up to a pound a day safely.

The day begins with a challenging aerobic workout at 6 AM. Fruits, muffins, and vitamins are set out at the Winners Circle, a juice bar in the lodge. Lunch can be eaten by the pool or in the dining room. There is a midmorning broth break, and vegetable snacks are served in the afternoon. The program is aimed at burning calories, conditioning the heart and lungs, and toning the body. Guests here are diverse, ranging from young professionals to grandmothers; film industry folk, TV actresses, and housewives drop in to shape up or relax.

Most activities are held in the main lodge and garden. The complex includes saunas, an aerobics studio, a large swimming pool, and a cluster of guest bungalows. Classes, rated according to the guests' fitness level, last from 45 minutes to an hour. A nurse is on staff to help plan each person's schedule. Or you can work out on weight machines; facilities are open 24 hours.

The program operates on an all-inclusive American plan, and guests are welcome to stay a few days or weeks and take part in as many of the activities as they please. A number of special packages are available, including a spa-cooking week, and mother-daughter days.

The Oaks at Ojai
122 E. Ojai Ave., Ojai, CA 93023
Tel. 805/646-5573 or 800/753-6257
Fax 805/640-1504

Administration Owners, Don and Sheila Cluff; fitness director, Sally Dewar.

Season Year-round.

Accommodations 46 guest rooms in the main lodge and cottages, from small singles to a cottage for 3. Simply furnished with modern beds, all have private bath, color TV, telephone, air-conditioning.

Rates $135–$169 weekend rate, daily per person sharing small double lodge room with shower only; $179–$220 weekdays for single, $125–$159 per person double. $179–$220 for private rooms; 5-day program (Sun.–Fri. with 1 service) $895–$945 single, $625–$795 double; 7-day program with 2 services $1,253–$1,323 single, $875–$1,113 double. Spa Day (no lodging) $80. 1 night payable in advance. Add 14% service charge, 15.25% taxes. Credit cards: AE, D, MC, V.

Meal Plans 3 meals daily. Natural foods, no additives, salt, white flour, or sugar. Lunch can be soup, tuna salad with egg, mushrooms, and cheese, or vegetable crêpes. Dinner entrées: vegetarian lasagna, baked chicken, broiled fish, or pasta salad.

Services and Facilities **Exercise Equipment:** 16-station Paramount weight training system, 2 Trotter treadmills, 2 StairMasters, 2 Lifecycles, hand and ankle weights, stretch bands. **Swimming Facilities:** Outdoor pool. **Recreation Facilities:** Hiking; tennis, golf, and bike rental nearby. **Services:** Massage, facials; salon for hair, skin, and nail care; computerized body analysis. **Evening Programs:** Talks on health and fitness.

In the Area Lake Casitas, annual music and dance festivals; crafts boutiques; Bart's Corners book and sheet-music shop.

Getting Here *From Los Angeles.* By bus, Greyhound to Ventura (2 hr). By car, Hwy. 101 (Ventura Fwy.) to Ventura, Hwy. 33 to Ojai, Hwy. 150 to center of town (80 min). Taxi, rental car available.

Special Notes No smoking in rooms or inside hotel. Gym open 24 hr. Mother-daughter spa days in Jan.

The Palms

Nutrition and diet
Vibrant maturity
Weight management

California
Palm Springs
Finding an informal place in which to exercise and diet in the center of Palm Springs resort life is quite a feat. The Palms is a "come as you are" place, one with few frills, plenty of options, and no attendance requirements.

Activity centers on a large swimming pool, and additional classes are held indoors in a small aerobics studio and outdoors under the palms. With up to 16 activities offered daily, guests are encouraged to take part in as many or as few as they please. Special weeks feature high-powered speakers on health, nutrition, and fitness; a seminar on women in management; a 21-day course on quitting smoking; and, in January and May, a mother-daughter week.

The program operates on an all-inclusive American Plan, regardless of how long you stay (2-day minimum stay required), and guests may arrive on any day (unless a workshop is scheduled). The flexibility allows you to enjoy the attractions of the Palm Springs area, some within walking distance. Spa services also are available without lodging.

The converted manor house and cluster of private bungalows exude a Spanish-colonial ambience and sit handsomely beneath the dramatic starkness of mountains. Although there is no hydrotherapy, a sauna and whirlpool are tucked into the complex.

The Palms
572 N. Indian Canyon Dr., Palm Springs, CA 92262
Tel. 619/325–1111 or 800/753–7256
Fax 619/327–0867

Administration Manager, Bruce Taylor; fitness director, Marilu Rogers Horst.

Season Year-round.

Accommodations 37 rooms in the manor and bungalows, most on the ground floor with private patio. Motel-style furniture, double beds, generous closets. All rooms with private or shared bath, air-conditioning, TV, telephone.

Rates $155 per person, double occupancy, private bath, on a daily program basis; $125 with shared bath. Single rooms $195–$220. Spa Trek 7-night package with 2 treatments, $1,301 double, $1,645 single; 5-night midweek package $930 double, $1,173 single (1 treatment included). Add 9% tax; 14% service charge additional. 1 night's lodging payable in advance. Credit cards: AE, MC, V.

Meal Plans 3 meals totaling 1,000 calories served daily in the dining room. Breakfast is fresh fruit, diet muffin, and a vitamin supplement. Lunch includes soup, choice of chicken tostada seasoned with chili and cumin, or vegetable crepes. Veal loaf, broiled red snapper in tomato sauce, turkey divan, or vegetarian lasagna for dinner. No salt, sugar, or chemical additives. Coffee and hot or iced herbal tea all day. Midmorning broth break, afternoon vegetables.

Services and Facilities **Exercise Equipment:** 2 Paramount weight training gym units, 3 Bodyguard treadmills, StairMaster, 2 Lifecycles, hand and ankle weights, stretch bands. **Services:** Massage, body scrub, aromatherapy; salon for hair, nail, and skin care. Consultation on fitness, body composition analysis. **Swimming Facilities:** Outdoor pool. **Recreation Facilities:** Hiking. Bike rental, horseback riding, tennis, and golf nearby. Downhill and cross-country skiing in the mountains. **Evening Programs:** Talks on dressing for success, the history of Palm Springs, other subjects.

In the Area Local sightseeing tours; aerial tram ride, ballooning, baths at nearby hot springs; Desert Museum, living Desert Reserve.

Getting Here *From Los Angeles.* By bus, Greyhound (4 hr). By car, I–10 to Hwy. 111 (2½ hr). By train, Amtrak to Indio (2 hr). By air, scheduled service on Continental, American Airlines, and United commuter flights (30 min). Taxi service and rental car available. Desert City Shuttle bus ($65).

Special Notes Limited access for people with disabilities. No smoking in designated areas. Mother-daughter weeks in Jan. and May. Third week free July–Sept.

Pocket Ranch Institute

Life enhancement
Spiritual awareness

California
Geyserville

Here is a retreat for people who want to become more self-aware, in a peaceful, wooded setting. Founded in 1986 by Barbara Findeisen, a marriage counselor and specialist working with children and families, the Institute has serious educational programs for caregivers, as well as structured group workshops and personal retreats.

The ranch's spirituality is conveyed in a meditation cottage set on a hilltop, where you may encounter coyotes, horses, and cows roaming the canyons (also snakes in season) during the starry nights. Native American traditions are celebrated the week after Christmas, including a sweat lodge and intention-stick ceremony. Accommodations are available for just 50 participants (including children), which enables the Ranch to maintain an intimate, family-like atmosphere so guests can comfortably "reconnect heads with hearts, and set free the spirit within."

Bodywork is a key element in all programs; for short visits, book a massage to renew your energies. Beyond massage, therapists can work with you on breathing techniques and hypnosis to manage stress, and art as a means of self expression. Exercise, however, is not emphasized, although you are free to enjoy the large swimming pool or hike on trails into the surrounding hills. The bodywork building has two private rooms, sauna, and showers. For groups, a ropes course teaches team-building exercises.

Other exercises and programs include the 17-day "STAR" program, which confronts deep-rooted childhood trauma. Although you'll work in a group, you'll be assigned to a therapist for personal consultation, and you can set your own pace. Writing exercises as well as body work are included in the program fee. A popular three-day workshop is titled "Women & Spirituality." Participants are about 50:50 men and women.

Pocket Ranch Institute
Box 516, Geyserville, CA 95441
Tel. 707/857–3359
Fax 707/857–3764

Administration Business manager, Marsha Taylor; workshop coordinator, David Gaskin.

Season Year-round.

Accommodations 25 comfortably furnished bedrooms in 4-unit cabins. Specially designed rustic pine furniture, including desk, hand-crafted bedstead, country fabrics, and built-in lighting. Private bath, air-conditioning; no TV or telephone.

Rates $95 daily for self-directed retreat including single room and meals, $80 per person double occupancy. 17-day STAR program $4,200. Tuition for 3-day workshop $250, includes lodging and meals. Tax and gratuities not included. Credit cards: MC, V.

Meal Plans 3 meals daily, plus snacks, included in fee. Vegetarian and non-vegetarian selections. Special diets accommodated.

Services and Facilities **Exercise Equipment**: none. **Services:** Massage (Swedish, Esalen, shiatsu, deep tissue), hypnotherapy, breathing therapy, personal counseling. **Swimming Facilities**: Outdoor heated pool. **Recreation Facilities**: Hiking trails. **Evening Programs**: Lectures.

In the Area Harbin Hot Springs, Konocti Lake Resort and Spa.

Getting Here *From San Francisco*. By car, Golden Gate Bridge, north on Hwy. 101, Hwy. 128, ranch road (unpaved) for 7 mi. The total trip takes about 3 hr.

Post Ranch Inn

Nonprogram resort

California **Big Sur** Sensuous and environmentally sensitive, the new 98-acre Post Ranch Inn takes the posh to a higher level than most resorts. The first major resort to be developed in the area in almost 20 years blends into the redwoods of Big Sur, with only 30 guest rooms so the grounds still seem pristine. Each guest unit comes with a massage table, whirlpool tub, wood-burning fireplace, and stereo system. Also offered in your room is an herbal facial or body polish, and yoga instruction. The ultimate luxury is an hour-long massage in the privacy of your suite.

The ranch's spa is housed in a small cottage and takes advantage of the Ventana Range surrounding the resort. The sea air and refreshing scent of pines will invigorate you during your scheduled sessions of aerobic speed walking and guided nature and wilderness hikes. A personalized program can be arranged by contacting the spa director prior to your arrival. Appointments are scheduled until midnight. A larger spa building is scheduled to open by 1995. Presently, facilities include an aerobics studio, weight training equipment, and private treatment rooms. There's no tennis or golf; just smashing views of the Pacific Ocean and Ventana Peak. The meals at Sierrra Mar are as inspiring as the scenery.

Post Ranch Inn
Hwy. 1, Box 219, Big Sur, CA 93920
Tel. 408/667-2200 or 800/527-2200

Administration General manager, Lawrence Callahan; spa director, Roy Malcom.

Season Year-round.

Accommodations 30 suites in secluded wooden houses, accented by glass, marble, slate, and granite interiors. All have king-size bed, over-size bathroom with Jacuzzi tub, modern furniture, fireplace, air-conditioning, TV, phone. Amenities include terry-cloth robes. View varies in 7 Tree Houses, 12 Post Houses, 5 houses with ocean views, and the 6-suite Butterfly Houses.

Rates $255-$525 daily per suite. Add gratuities, taxes. Credit cards: AE, MC, V.

Meal Plan Continental breakfast buffet included in room cost. Dining room has prix fixe or à la carte menu for lunch (only on weekends) and dinner that includes Atlantic salmon with clams and mussels in dill-shallot broth with corn, peas, and potatoes and for dessert apricot steamed pudding with ginger ice cream, or coconut crème caramel with orange slices.

Services and Facilities **Exercise Equipment:** Weight training circuit, treadmills, bikes. **Services:** Massage (Esalen or sports), aromatherapy, herbal wrap, facial. 1-on-1 training, guided hikes. **Spa Facilities:** Outdoor hot tub for 20 persons; sauna, private treatment rooms. **Swimming Facilities:** Outdoor heated lap pool.

In the Area Esalen Institute, Tassajara Zen Monastery and hot springs, tour of Point Sur Lighthouse (ca. 1850).

Getting Here *From Carmel.* By car, Hwy. 1 south to ranch road (40 min).

Preventive Medicine Research Institute

Lifestyle enhancement
Preventive medicine

California
Oakland/Berkeley

Learning the power of lifestyle changes to reverse the progression of cardiovascular disease is the motivation for week-long retreats held at the Claremont Resort (*see above*) under auspices of the Preventive Medicine Research Institute. Directed by Dean Ornish, M.D., and led by health professionals from the institute, this highly structured program includes lectures and experiential sessions, as well as cooking instruction by celebrity chefs.

Stress management techniques, exercise in the resort's well-equipped fitness center, and group support help you discover how understanding your physical and emotional states can improve your mental health. The finishing touch is a visit to the spa and its salon, but those services are not included in the program cost.

Participation in the retreat is limited to 100, and includes all meals, accommodations, professional staff time, classes, and take-home material. Part of the fee contributes to ongoing programs at the Preventive Medicine Research Institute, a non-profit public institute associated with the University of California, San Francisco.

Preventive Medicine Research Institute
900 Bridgeway, Suite 2, Sausalito, CA 94965
Tel. 415/331-2323
Fax 415/332-5730

Administration President and director, Dean Ornish, M.D.; administrator, David Liff.

Season 7 week-long programs scheduled throughout the year.

Rates $3,450 for primary participant; additional $1,500 for spouse or companion sharing room.

Meal Plan 3 meals served daily in private dining room. Mainly vegetarian, the meals are low-fat, low-cholesterol.

Facilities *See* Claremont Resort, *above*.

Pritikin Longevity Center

Nutrition and diet
Vibrant maturity
Weight management

California
Santa Monica

The Pritikin Longevity Center, which occupies an entire beachfront hotel, is dedicated to the diet and exercise regimen espoused in the 1970s by the late Nathan Pritikin. It is the development center for programs offered elsewhere around the country, and since 1978 it has offered a vacation that presents the elements essential to preventing degenerative disease and improving the quality of one's life.

The medically supervised programs last for or 26 days, with a core curriculum that includes daily exercise, nutrition and health education, stress-management counseling, and medical services. The two-week program is recommended for weight loss, reducing cholesterol levels, and managing blood pressure. The four-week program is designed for persons afflicted with physical problems such as heart disease and insulin-dependent diabetes. The full course offers increased individual attention, counseling, and supervision. Optional exercise classes are scheduled daily.

Healthy people, too, come here to maintain their health, learn to control their diet, cook and eat Pritikin-style, and exercise. A free hot line is included for those who need continuing support after they leave the program.

The daily schedule includes cooking classes, lectures, and three supervised exercise sessions. A full physical examination is a major part of the program; it includes a treadmill stress test and a complete blood-chemistry analysis. Depending on your personal history and fitness level, you will be assigned to a specialist in either cardiology or internal medicine who will monitor your progress on the prescribed diet and exercise program. Restrictions are noted on your identification badge.

Ocean views from the dining room are a pleasure at mealtimes. The chefs cook without added fat, salt, or sugar, and no coffee or tea is served. Meals are largely vegetarian, although fish and chicken are served several times a week; there are many fresh fruits and whole grains. (The Pritikin diet is 5% to 10% fat, 10% to 15% protein, and 80% high complex carbohydrates.) Breakfast and lunch are self-service; dinners are served in the dining room.

Pritikin Longevity Center
1910 Ocean Front Walk, Santa Monica, CA 90405
Tel. 310/450–5433 or 800/421–9911
Fax 310/450–3602

Administration Director, Robert Pritikin; program director, David Pole.

Season Year-round.

Accommodations 128 rooms, from singles to suites, with desk, reading chair, tiled bath and glass-enclosed shower. Better rooms include a Jacuzzi bathtub ($250–$750 supplement for a 13-day program, $1,500 for 26-day program) and ocean views. Air-conditioning, TV, phone in all rooms, and just enough quiet comfort to make it feel like a resort.

Rates 13-day program for first-time visitors $5,373 single, $3,440 per person double, plus $1,933 medical fees (which may be covered by health insurance); repeaters $1,589 single, $3,029 per couple; 26-day program $11,181 single, $5,588 for partner. $500 in advance, 13-day program; $1,000 in advance, 26-day program. Add gratuities. Credit cards: AE, MC, V for deposit only.

Meal Plans 3 meals plus 3 snacks daily. Lunches may be vegetarian lasagna, chili relleno, and salad bar. Dinners are mostly vegetarian, but some entrées include fish, such as seafood crêpe or salmon teriyaki.

Services and Facilities **Exercise Equipment:** 51 Trotter treadmills, 9 combi bikes, 7 Schwinn Air Dyne bikes, 3 recumbent bikes, Concept 2 rower, 2 Precor rowers, Climb Max, 3 AeroStep, Schwinn Bow-Flex, 15-station weights system, dumbbells (5–50 lbs.), hand weights. **Services:** Medical, fitness, and nutrition counseling; massage, acupressure in four private rooms; beauty salon appointments. **Swimming Facilities:** Nearby outdoor pool, ocean beach. **Recreation Facilities:** Tennis, golf, fishing nearby. Optional weekend excursions to area attractions. **Evening Programs:** Lectures and films on health-related topics, music, and dancing. Concierge service for show and concert tickets.

In the Area Shopping centers, museums, guided food shopping, and restaurant dining; J. Paul Getty Museum, Norton Simon Museum, Venice Beach, Hollywood Park Race Track.

Getting Here *From Los Angeles.* By Bus, Santa Monica Blue Bus from downtown (tel. 213/451–5444) takes about 45 min. By car, Santa Monica Fwy. I–10) to 4th St. exit, Pico Blvd. (20 min). Taxi, limousine, rental car available. Parking on site. SuperShuttle from LAX airport.

Special Notes Elevator connects all floors. No smoking indoors.

St. Helena Hospital Health Center

Life enhancement
Preventive medicine
Spiritual awareness
Vibrant maturity
Weight management

California Vineyards spread for miles below the hillside perch of the St.
Napa Valley Helena Health Center. This is part of a hospital complex run by the Seventh-Day Adventists, but the center's structured residential programs are nondenominational and nonsectarian. The medically oriented programs are designed to teach self-management. Disease prevention is emphasized here. Following a physical examination and an analysis of your diet, doctors and health professionals prescribe a course of action intended to help you achieve a healthier lifestyle. Their specific recommendations for diet take into account your physical condition, nutritional requirements, and weight-loss goals. Together you devise an exercise schedule and discuss hydrotherapy treatments, massage, and medical tests that are available at an additional charge.

The health center's association with St. Helena Hospital enables it to draw on sophisticated medical facilities, biofeedback, and medical consultants appropriate to your special problems. The center offers programs in smoking cessation, lifestyle change through nutrition, alcohol and chemical recovery, pulmonary rehabilitation, pain rehabilitation, personalized health, and prime-of-life fitness.

The 12-day McDougall Program, dealing with diet and nutrition, includes group therapy and relaxation techniques, vegetarian cooking classes in a teaching kitchen, and bodywork—massage plus use of the steam baths, sauna, and whirlpool. Consultation with Dr. John McDougall, author of three books on the prevention and treatment of disease, focuses on lifestyle changes to lower cholesterol and improve personal health and well-being. The program is scheduled once a month.

Program participants have full use of a gymnasium, running track, indoor and outdoor swimming pool. A rest and relaxation program, designed for stress management, and a personalized health program (weekdays), including massages, are available.

St. Helena Hospital Health Center
Deer Park, CA 94576
Tel. 707/963–6200, 800/358–9195, or 800/862–7575 in CA

Administration Program director, Carol Williams, R.N., M.S.; coordinators DorAnne Donesky Neergaard, R.N., M.S., and Linda Schulz.

Season Year-round.

Accommodations 54 rooms with private bath, air-conditioning, many with balconies with views of Napa Valley; 2 beds and reading chair, TV, telephone. Furnished in motel-modern style.

Rates 4 day/3 night Personalized Health Program $1,551; 7-day smoking cessation program $2,470 single, $2,295 double; 12-day McDougall program $4,095 single, $3,887 double. Meals included. (Medical insurance may cover part of the cost.) Deposit required for some programs. Credit cards: MC, V.

Meal Plans 3 vegetarian meals daily, buffet style. No tea, coffee, or condiments. Cooking without butter and oil; vegetables sautéed in water. Specialties include vegetarian lasagna with mock cheese topping, baked tofu loaf, and eggplant "Parmesan" without cheese. Whole-grain breads baked without dairy products or eggs served in the McDougall program. Fresh fruit at all meals.

Services and Facilities **Exercise Equipment:** Weights room with treadmill, stationary bikes, rowing machines. **Services:** Massage, exercise instruction, private medical counseling, group discussions, group relaxation. **Swimming Facilities:** Outdoor pool (covered in winter). **Recreation Facilities:** Hiking, cycling, tennis, golf, aerobic dancing; horseback riding and glider rides nearby. **Evening Programs:** Informal lectures on health-related topics.

In the Area St. Helena (boutiques, restaurants), mineral baths in Calistoga, winery tours, Glen Ellen State Historic Park.

Getting Here *From San Francisco.* By car, I–80 north past Vallejo to Hwy. 37 going west, Hwy. 29 through St. Helena to Deer Park Rd., cross the Silverado Trail, turn left on Sanitarium Rd. (90 min). By bus, shuttle service at fixed prices to and from area airports.

Special Notes No smoking in guest rooms or health center facilities.

Sivananda Ashram Yoga Farm

Spiritual awareness

California
Grass Valley The Sivananda Ashram Yoga Farm follows the yogic disciplines of Swami Vishnu Devananda. Located in a peaceful valley north of Sacramento, the simple farmhouse provides lodging and space for two daily sessions of traditional postures (asanas), breathing techniques, and meditation. The intensive regimen of self-discipline is designed to foster a better understanding of the body-mind connection.

Meditation at 6 AM begins the morning session, brunch is served at 10, and then your schedule is open until 4 PM. Attendance at classes and meditations is mandatory.

The teachings of Swami Devananda have been widely documented as promoting both physical and spiritual development. His followers and new students join in practicing the 12 asana positions, from a headstand to a spinal twist, each believed to have specific benefits for the body. Participants learn that the proper breathing (*pranayama*) in each position is essential for energy control.

The 80-acre farm attracts a diverse group, families as well as senior citizens. Guests are asked to share bedrooms and to contribute time to communal activities. You may arrive on any day and stay as long as you wish.

Sivananda Ashram Yoga Farm
14651 Ballantree La., Grass Valley, CA 95949
Tel. 916/272-9322

Administration Manager, Avoram.

Season Year-round.

Accommodations 35 dormitory rooms have 5 beds each, 5 double rooms, minimal furnishings. Showers and toilets shared. Tent space on the grounds. Private rooms on request.

Rates $35 per person per day includes dormitory lodging, program, meals; $40 per person double, $50 single; campers pay $25. Supplemental charges for special programs. $25 in advance. No credit cards.

Meal Plans 2 lacto-vegetarian meals daily, buffet style. Morning meal of hot grain cereal, granola, yogurt, fruit. Stir-fry and steamed vegetables, rice, and scrambled tofu for dinner. Homemade soups, whole-wheat breads, green salads.

Services and Facilities **Services:** Massage. **Swimming Facilities:** None. **Recreation Facilities:** Meditation; skiing at nearby resorts. **Evening Programs:** Lectures on Hindu philosophy, concerts.

In the Area Lake Tahoe, historic gold-mining towns of Nevada City and Grass Valley, old-town Sacramento.

Getting Here *From Sacramento.* By bus, Greyhound to Auburn (2 hr). By car, I-80 to Auburn, Hwy. 49 (1½ hr). Pickup in the farm van $10 at Auburn, $25 at Sacramento Airport.

Special Notes Limited access for people with disabilities. Children are welcome to participate with parents. No smoking.

Skylonda Fitness Retreat

Life enhancement
Luxury pampering
Nutrition and diet

California Skylonda Retreat opened late in 1992 on 16 forested acres of
Woodside coastal hills south of San Francisco. During the seven-day retreats and weekend getaways guests recharge themselves physically, spiritually, and mentally while losing weight. The daily schedule incorporates hikes, yoga, meditation, strength

training, aerobics, aquatic exercises, and massage. All meals and services are included in the cost of the program.

Hiking the extensive network of trails surrounding Skylonda is basic to the rigorous program. The forested ridge separating San Francisco and the Silicon Valley from the sea is comprised of a series of microclimates, with tall redwoods, pine, oak, and the reddish madrone tree native to California. On any given day, the trail leader plans two hikes totalling 8–10 miles, with options for those who can't handle some of the more challenging terrain. Although you're expected to traverse vast meadows, sudden ravines, and intensely silent hollows, it's comforting to know that a van awaits at the end of the trail.

In this highly regimented program all 20–30 participants are expected to follow the posted schedule, and watchful staffers are on hand at all times for assistance. From the 6 AM wakeup call to the 9 PM close of evening programs, there is dynamic interaction with other members of the group. Sessions of yoga and circuit training recharge your energy for the hikes. An hour of silence is included "to reflect on things that are important." Evenings are devoted to discussion of stress management, songs in front of a great fireplace, and talks by wellness experts from Stanford University Medical Center.

The spacious log-and-stone lodge with a view of the forest has a multipurpose room for aerobics and yoga/stretching classes. Housed on the log-timbered upper floors are a library, dining room, and the main gathering room, which features stained glass windows, Oriental rugs, comfortable sofas, and VCR/music system. A glass-enclosed swimming pool and outdoor Jacuzzi adjoin the sauna and massage and facial rooms, on the ground floor of the lodge. Exercise clothing is laundered daily, and you pick up outfits as needed. The standard-issue gym suits are worn throughout meals, but warm gear comes in handy some evenings.

Three program options are available: Sunday–Saturday, with six nights lodging; Saturday–Sunday, with one night lodging, and a single day. As the program progresses you may experience unexpected physical and emotional reactions to the drastic changes in diet and exercise. Your body will metabolize food faster, as chef Sue Chapman aims for a diet that is 65–75% carbohydrates, 20–25% protein, and less than 10% fat. Most guests average about 1,400 calories per day, but the fixed menu does not list caloric content.

Skylonda Fitness Retreat
16350 Skyline Blvd., Woodside, CA 94062
Tel. 415/851–4500 or 800/851–2222
Fax 415/851–5504

Administration Founder-director, D. Dixon Collins.

Season Year-round.

Accommodations 15 rooms with private bath in 3-story log lodge. Each room contains 2 queen-size beds with down comforters, 2 wooden clothing cabinets. Small bathroom with shower. Rooms have open-beam ceiling, spectacular view of the redwoods, no air-conditioning.

Rates   7-day all-inclusive program $2,400 plus $15 tax and $120 gratuities. Weekend package $300 single, $250 per person double. Deposit 10%. Credit cards: AE, MC, V.

Meal Plans   3 meals daily included in program. Breakfast can be fresh fruit, whole grain muffin, or cereal. Lunch is a self-service salad or soup with whole-grain bread. Dinner includes cioppino, vegetarian lasagna or halibut baked in parchment, stuffed potato, or grain-stuffed artichoke. Specialties can be roast chicken breast on ragout of corn and blackeye peas, steamed prawns with Chinese long beans, tart of duck, morels, and roasted shallot. Deserts are seasonal berries with sorbet, peach shortcake, tart of buckwheat, poppyseed, and peaches. Coffee, herbal tea, and decaffeinated coffee available at all times. Energy breaks include a midmorning drink (orange juice, yeast, nonfat milk) and an afternoon snack of broth, fruit, vegetables, popcorn, or a cookie. Special diets and alternate menu selections are available on request.

Services and Facilities   **Exercise Equipment:** 20-unit HydraFitness system, 4 stationary bikes, rower, step units. **Services:** Swedish massage, facial, bodywrap, manicure, skincare. **Spa Facilities:** coed sauna, steamroom, outdoor whirlpool. **Swimming Facilities:** indoor 30-ft pool. **Evening Programs:** folksinger, movies, talks.

In the Area   Jasper Ridge Biological Reserve, Portola Valley, Palo Alto.

Getting Here   *From San Francisco.* By car, I–380 west to I–280 south, Hwy. 92W to Scenic Highway 35 (Skyline Blvd). Complimentary pickup at San Francisco International Airport. Pickup also scheduled at Stanford Shopping Center, Palo Alto, and other points.

Special Notes   No smoking in the lodge. Raingear provided.

Sonoma Mission Inn and Spa

Luxury pampering

California
Boyes Hot Springs   San Franciscans have been "taking the cure" at the Sonoma Mission Inn since the turn of the century, but fitness training and pampering are more recent attractions. The high-tech spa is a favorite escape for young couples from the city as well as a popular stopover on wine-country tours. Its first consideration is health maintenance rather than weight loss, and a few days here can do wonders for your spirits.

Several wings of deluxe rooms and mini-suites have been added to the big pink stucco palace since its new owners restored this grand old hotel in 1980. The resort accepts bookings for corporate conferences and sales meetings and, as a result, can be packed one day, quiet the next. Usually, however, weekends are busy so you'll want to avoid them if you yearn for peace and seclusion.

Midweek spa packages are the best buy; weekend rates are strictly à la carte. All adult guests are charged $10 daily ($20 weekends) for access to the spa (book a service and the fee is waived), which includes twin exercise rooms (one with cardiovascular equipment, one for weight training), sauna, steam room, and outdoor and indoor whirlpools beside a flower-bordered outdoor exercise pool. Scheduled daily are coed aerobics classes, aquacize groups, and yoga sessions. Robe and slippers are issued daily, and there are newly expanded locker rooms with full amenities. Despite its compact size, the spa has 10 massage rooms, four facial rooms, and a six-seat beauty salon. All facilities, except locker rooms, are coed and non-smoking. A heated outdoor swimming pool, which is open to all guests free of charge, adjoins the fitness pavilion.

Driving up to the main lobby is like arriving for a party at Jay Gatsby's. The baronial reception hall, awash in pastel pinks and peach against bleached wood, sets the mood of casual elegance. The inn and its fashionable dining room and wine bar seem far removed from the rigors of calorie counting. But the Grille and the Market Cafe have a spa menu; reservations should be made when you check in.

Down a path through gardens abloom with camellia and jasmine is the fitness pavilion, sandwiched between a conference center and tennis courts. After you check in with the spa director and schedule massage and beauty treatments, you are left pretty much on your own.

An airy, two-story atrium that belies the building's origins as a Quonset hut is the setting for most of the activities. The glass-walled exercise rooms, staffed with trainers, face a sunlit marble fountain. Report for treatments upstairs in a quiet lounge, where you can sip herbal tea and watch TV while you wait to be summoned. Classes are scheduled in the aerobics studio throughout the day, beginning at 7 AM with tai chi chuan and yoga, which attract a regular group of 10 or so local members. Hikers can sign up for 90-minute morning excursions ($10) which depart from the inn by van at 7 AM, and a wine-country picnic ($25) on Saturday.

Soaking in the natural, hot artesian mineral water is one of the most popular activities at the spa. In 1991 a new well was tapped, bringing to the surface another 135°F mineral-rich spring known for its restorative powers. Examples of the cure are documented in a brochure about the inn's history. The spring feeds into the exercise and swimming pools, and temperatures are regulated and adjusted to achieve maximum benefits from the therapy. Herbal, mud, and seaweed wraps are used to relax muscles, soften the skin, and draw out toxins. Treatments take place in two specially equipped "wet" rooms.

Sonoma Mission Inn and Spa

18140 Sonoma Hwy. 12, Boyes Hot Springs, CA 95416
(Reservations) Box 1447, Sonoma, CA 95476
Tel. 707/938-9000, 800/358-9022, or 800/862-4945 in CA

Administration Manager, Peter Henry; spa director, Jill Taylor.

Season Year-round.

Accommodations 170 rooms in the main building and garden units, all of them renovated in 1994 and 1995. Plantation shutters, canopied beds, and ceiling fans; king, queen, and twin beds. Each of 20 wine country–theme rooms in 3-story unit close to spa features wood-burning fireplace, spacious bathroom with bidet. Amenities include air-conditioning, TV, telephone, robes.

Rates Spa Sampler package per day (1–5 nights) $245–$305 single, $190–$210 per person double, including 3 meals; room and spa package $185–$245 single, $130–$160 double per night. Package available Sun.–Thurs. only, includes 3 meals, spa service, classes, gratuities, tax. Hotel tariff $110–$375 per room. 1 night in advance, $500 for package. Credit cards: AE, DC, MC, V.

Meal Plans Spa menu with calorie counts in the Grille. Choices at 1,000–1,200 calories per day include salmon poached in chardonnay with artichokes, breast of free-range chicken and steamed vegetables, grilled veal loin with leeks, saffron capellini with ratatouille, steamed shellfish. The Cafe offers vegetarian pizza, spa omelette, grilled prawns and scallops with wild rice pilaf. Wine, coffee (regular or decaffeinated), herbal tea, nonfat milk.

Services and Facilities **Exercise Equipment:** Cybex 6-station modular weight training gym, 2 Monark bikes, 2 Cycleplus, 2 Schwinn Air Dyne bikes, Concept 2 rowing machine, 3 Climb Max, 3 Startrac treadmills, Smith press and free weights (5–40 lb). Fitness Pavilion at inn has Trotter and Startrac treadmills, 2 StairMaster 4000, Lifestep, Lifecycle, Biocycle, Windracer, NordicTrack. **Services:** Massage (Swedish, Esalen), fango clay body pack, herbal and seaweed body wraps, loofah scrub, facials, manicure, pedicure/reflexology combination, shiatsu, aromatherapy; image consultation, personalized meditation, tarot card reading. **Swimming Facilities:** 2 outdoor pools. **Recreation Facilities:** 2 tennis courts, hiking. Horseback riding, golf nearby.

In the Area Sonoma Mission historic area, antiques shops, specialty food shops; Calistoga mud baths, Bodega Bay, winery tours.

Getting Here *From San Francisco.* By bus, Greyhound to Sonoma (90 min). By car, Golden Gate Bridge, Hwy. 101, Hwy. 37 to Sonoma, Hwy. 12 (45 min). Public bus at door; Sonoma Airporter scheduled van service to San Francisco airport; limousine, taxi, rental car.

Special Notes Limited access for people with disabilities. Spa open Mon.–Thurs. and Sun. 6 AM–9 PM, Fri.–Sat. until 10 PM. Non-registered guest fee: $35 or $20 plus treatment.

Spa at L'Auberge Del Mar

Nonprogram resort

California Del Mar The spa at the beautiful L'Auberge del Mar, which overlooks the Pacific, is a convenient getaway from San Diego. Although facilities are limited, you can exercise, get a massage, or be pampered at the beauty salon. Spa cuisine is served in the resort's Bistro Garden, open to the sunny beach breezes most of the year. The menu changes daily, with the calorie count posted beside each item. Emphasis is on fresh local ingredients, with low amounts of saturated fat, sodium, and cholesterol.

The original Del Mar Hotel was a legendary gathering place for the rich and famous, especially during the summer season of nearby Del Mar Race Track. The new inn on the same site combines the cozy comfort of a small European auberge with California-casual ambience. Built on several levels, the hotel can provide each guest room with a balcony and ocean view. On the first floor, close to the spa, rooms open onto a terrace surrounding the swimming pool.

While upscale La Jolla is only minutes away, the lifestyle in Del Mar is slow-paced and casual; the beach here is broad, uncrowded, and ideal for long morning walks. Guests can get here by Amtrak; the station is just below the hotel grounds.

Spa at L'Auberge Del Mar

1540 Camino Del Mar, Box 2889, Del Mar, CA 92014
Tel. 619/259–1515 or 800/553–1336
Fax 619/755–4940

Administration General manager, Terry Alder; spa manager, April Weinsoff.

Season Year-round.

Accommodations 123 deluxe rooms with balcony, marble bath and vanity, wooden armoire, minibar, TV. Some have gas fireplaces that ignite at the touch of a button; all are air-conditioned. Amenities include makeup lights in the bathrooms.

Rates $165–$250 for single or double room per night, $325–$750 suites. Spa Refresher packages to be announced. Add 8% state tax and gratuities. 1 night's payment required in advance. Credit cards: AE, MC, V.

Meal Plans Breakfast includes juice, Meuslix cereal, or egg-white omelet. Lunch may be a fruit salad or plate of grilled vegetables (Japanese eggplant, red peppers, zucchini, tomatoes, assorted squash), lightly brushed with extra-virgin olive oil. Dinner entrées include grilled fish or chicken and veal medallions in wine sauce.

Services and Facilities **Exercise Equipment:** Spectrum I weight training units, Sprint bike, Challenger rowing machine. **Services:** Swedish massage, shiatsu, acupressure, aromatherapy, fango, facials; beauty salon for hair, nail, and skin care. **Spa Facilities:** Underwater massage, coed sauna and steam room, 6 massage rooms. **Swimming Facilities:** Outdoor pool (45 ft), ocean beach. **Recreation Facilities:** 2 lighted tennis courts (concrete surface); golf nearby.

In the Area La Jolla (art museum, theater, shopping), Sea World, San Diego (zoo, Balboa Park museums and theaters, Old Town), Del Mar Race Track (July 25–Sept. 15).

Getting Here *From San Diego.* By car, I–5 (San Diego Fwy.) north to Del Mar Hts. Rd., Camino Del Mar to 15th St. (30 min). By train, Amtrak to Del Mar (25 min). By bus, Greyhound. Free transfers on arrival, departure.

Special Notes No smoking in spa. Minimum age 16. Spa open daily 9–8. Nonsmoking rooms available, some with access for people with disabilities.

Spa Hotel and Mineral Springs

Taking the waters

California
Palm Springs The Spa Hotel and Mineral Springs, boasting lush gardens and spacious rooms, is built on the site of hot mineral springs used by Native Americans for centuries. The Agua Caliente Band of the Cahuillia tribe owns the land and recently acquired the hotel, which was completely renovated in 1993. Although the spa is somewhat dated, it's well maintained and mostly serves as a day retreat (daily fee is charged). The hotel's location, in the

center of Palm Springs, is close to shops, restaurants, and recreational attractions.

The fitness program is based on European hydrotherapy methods. Decked out in white slippers and oversize terry-cloth towels, guests attend sessions of eucalyptus inhalation and use the sauna or the steam room. After a shower, they are escorted to sunken marble tubs. The "magical water" of the springs soon disposes of tension and promotes relaxation.

Herbal tea or ice water is served in the cooling rooms while guests, wrapped in sheets, wait for the masseur or masseuse. After the one-hour treatment guests are free to go for a swim in the Olympic-size outdoor mineral-water pool or a sunbathe in the rooftop solarium (clothes optional).

Spa Hotel and Mineral Springs
100 N. Indian Canyon Dr., Palm Springs, CA 92262
Tel. 619/325-1461 or 800/854-1279 (800/472-4371 in CA)
Fax 619/-325-3344

Administration	Manager, James R. Batt; spa director, Casey Olson.
Season	Year-round.
Accommodations	230 rooms (20 suites) in a completely renovated 5-story hotel. Contemporary Southwestern furnishings, with choice of king-size or double queen-size beds. All have balcony, bathroom, TV, air-conditioning.
Rates	Daily European plan per room, single or double: $55–$95 summer, $145–$185 winter. Spa Break 2-night package $295 per person double, $355 single (Mon.–Thur. only). 1 night payable in advance. Credit cards: AE, DC, MC, V.
Meal Plans	2 meals daily included in Spa Break: fresh fruit and yogurt at breakfast, cold salmon, choice of lamb medallions, whole-wheat pasta, or grilled shrimp and vegetables. Coffee, tea, and regular menu are available.
Services and Facilities	**Exercise Equipment:** 12-station Paramount weight training gym, 3 Lifecycles, Liferower, treadmill, free weights. **Services:** Massage (Swedish, sports, shiatsu), aromatherapy, herbal wrap, body scrub, facial; salon for hair, nail, and skin care. **Bathing Facilities:** 34 private Jacuzzis with mineral water, 2 soaking pools. **Swimming Facilities:** Outdoor pool. **Recreation Facilities:** Tennis, golf, and horseback riding nearby. Desert hiking, cross-country skiing nearby. **Evening Entertainment:** Village Fest street fair Thurs.
In the Area	Aerial Tramway, Desert Museum (nature and art exhibits, concerts, live theater), Living Desert Reserve (botanical gardens), Indian Canyons (jeep tour, hikes), Polo Club.
Getting Here	*From Los Angeles.* By VIP Shuttle (tel. 619/328-0222) or Desert City (tel. 619/320-0044) shuttle services from LAX airport, hotels (2–3 hrs); Greyhound (3 hr). By car, I–10 to Hwy. 111 in Palm Canyon or to Tahquitz way, turn left one block to hotel. By train, Amtrak to Indio (2 hr). By plane, American Airlines and United commuter service (30 min). Limousine, taxi, airport van service, rental car available.

Special Notes No smoking in the spa and in designated areas of the dining room. Native American–owned gaming casino planned to open in 1995.

Tassajara Zen Monastery

Nutrition and diet
Spiritual awareness
Taking the waters

California In 1966 Tassajara was acquired by the San Francisco Zen Cen-
Jamesburg ter, and it still maintains the tradition of welcoming overnight visitors as well as practitioners of Zen Buddhism. Guests are invited to join in meditation, receive basic instruction, and attend lectures, but no activity is required. Those who wish to participate in a Practice Retreat are required to perform about a half-day of work on the buildings and farm. Workshops in yoga, poetry, and sensory awareness are also offered.

This site, surrounded by formidable mountains and overlooking the Pacific Ocean, has been a place of healing and purification for centuries. Native Americans used the hot springs, and Spanish hunters gathered here. Now, among other activities, Tassajara guests bathe in the slightly sulfurous water until parboiled, then stretch out on the rocks to contemplate nature. A clothing-optional policy prevails.

Your day begins at 5:40 AM when a bell ringer awakens you for meditation in the Japanese-style hall, or Zendo, which is the center of the Zen monastery at Tassajara. Students in black garb and with shaved heads join visitors seeking to become familiar with Buddhist practices.

Among the retreat's most popular traditions is its Zen cuisine. Those who know Tassajara primarily through its cookbooks on vegetarian meals and bread baking can begin to experience Zen cooking in a one-week workshop dubbed "Cooking as Meditation," led by Ed Brown, former head chef here and author of *The Tassajara Bread Book*. In addition to actually preparing food, guests learn that cooking embodies many of the elements of spiritual practice: "working sincerely with the ingredients available, giving more than you ever thought possible, being patient with the fact that everything has a mind of its own, [and] trusting your own sensibilities."

Tassajara Zen Monastery
Jamesburg, CA
Reservations: Zen Center, 300 Page St., San Francisco, CA 94102
Tel. 415/431-3771

Administration Guest manager, Cassandra Bramucci.

Season May–Sept.

Accommodations 36 guest rooms in a 1-level structure of stone and pine. Some have 2 beds, others a foam cushion on the floor. Dormitory room has 4 beds. 1 large corner unit, Stone Suite, for 4–6 persons. All rooms open to sundeck, with access to spring-fed pools and stream. No electricity; kerosene lamp provided. Communal bathhouse or shared bathroom. No housekeeping services.

Rates $115–$200 single, $95–$110 per person double occupancy, with 3 meals. Practice Retreat (3-night min.) $40–$45 per day. Dormitory $67 per night; 2-room suite with private bath $130 per person (4–6 beds); add 7.1% tax. Workshop $580–$740. Deposit $35–$65. No credit cards.

Meal Plans 3 vegetarian meals served daily, buffet style. Breakfast includes oatmeal, tamari-roasted cashew nuts, French toast, yogurt with blackberries. Different breads baked daily. Organically grown vegetables are steamed, served with tofu and brown rice, and baked. Japanese udon and pasta are among entrées.

Services and **Services:** Meditation retreats, workshops in yoga, cooking,
Facilities Japanese arts. **Swimming Facilities**: Jr.-Olympic-size outdoor pool. **Recreation Facilities:** Natural rock pools with circulating thermal water (clothing optional); steam room, outdoor swimming pool. **Evening Programs:** Lectures, meditation.

In the Area Big Sur State Park (hiking, beaches), Carmel (art galleries, boutiques), San Simeon State Historic Park (Hearst Castle), Monterey (Spanish colonial historic site, aquarium), Esalen Institute.

Getting Here *From San Francisco.* By car, I–280 south to Hwy. 17, via Monterey to Carmel, Rte. G16 (Carmel Valley Rd.) for 23.2 mi, right on Tassajara Rd. to Jamesburg (3 hr).

Special Notes Park at Jamesburg for the Tassajara stage ($26 per person round-trip for shuttle from parking to lodge) to avoid steep mountain road. No smoking in compound. Bring bath towel, flashlight, blanket. Day visitors $10–$15.

Two Bunch Palms

Luxury pampering
Taking the waters

California Al Capone, so the story goes, had the rock-walled fortress-like
Desert Hot house built at the desert oasis called Two Bunch Palms in the
Springs late 1920s. His casino became the resort's dining room, but the massage parlor below is still in use. Complete with stained-glass windows and Art Deco furnishings, Two Bunch Palms is like stepping into the past.

Popular as a hideaway for Hollywood stars and writers, the spa offers privacy (only registered guests get past the guardhouse), intimacy (44 villas and suites), and total relaxation. No spa packages are offered (26 services are à la carte), no gym or golf course exists, and no children are allowed. For those who crave exercise, however, there are stationary bikes, yoga classes, and a jogging trail.

The dry heat of the desert induces a certain lethargy. To avoid the sun, guests indulge inside in the spa's extraordinary repertoire of bodywork and beauty treatments. One innovation is the esoteric massage, "designed to balance and harmonize the physical, emotional, and spiritual bodies." Another specialty is watsu (reflexology) massage in the pool: You float in the hot pool on six inner tubes while undergoing hand and foot massage.

Geothermal springs on the north slope of the Coachella Valley supply hot mineral water (148°F) for the spa's swimming pool. Cooled a bit for comfort, the water splashes over a rock waterfall into a turquoise grotto framed by tropical shrubbery, and under a canopy of fan palms and tamarisk trees.

Total immersion is offered at the Clay Cabana, a palm-shaded mud bath. While you soak in warm, green clay dug from mineral water wells on the property, your muscles relax as toxins are drawn out. For total bliss follow this with a shower, soak in the mineral pool, and massage.

Two Bunch Palms

67425 Two Bunch Pkwy., Palms trail, Desert Hot
Springs, CA 92240
Tel. 619/329–8791 or 800/472–4334 in CA
Fax 619/329–1317

Administration General manager, Jerry Greenbach; spa director, Dana Bass-Smith.

Season Year-round.

Accommodations 44 guest rooms in villas or motel-like buildings situated near pool. The 2-bedroom suite No. 14 is popular, at $395 a night, complete with the initials A.C. inscribed in a desktop, plus a bullet hole in a mirror and lookout tower (with wet bar) that doubles as a tanning deck. Casa Blanca minisuite with Jacuzzi, $315. Villas are spacious, have private garden with whirlpool, kitchen, living room with TV, bedroom with king-size bed. All rooms air-conditioned, with TV, telephone.

Rates $105–$412 for 2 persons, includes Continental breakfast. Advance payment for 1 night. 2-night minimum. Add 10% tax, gratuity. Credit cards: AE, DC, MC, V.

Meal Plans 3 meals daily served in the resort dining room. No spa diet, but selections of salads, grilled fish or chicken, and seasonal fresh fruit.

Services and Facilities **Services:** Massage (Swedish, Trager, shiatsu, jin shin do, reflexology, deep-tissue), aromatherapy, 90-min salt-glow body scrub and herbal steam, facials, herbal wraps, mud baths. **Swimming Facilities:** Outdoor mineral-water pool. **Recreation Facilities:** 2 lighted tennis courts, bicycles. **Evening Programs:** Informal entertainment.

In the Area Joshua Tree National Monument (desert habitat), Palm Springs (shopping, museums, mountain cable ride).

Getting Here *From Los Angeles.* By car, I–10 to Hwy. 111 (2 hr). By bus, Greyhound (4 hr). By train, Amtrak to Indio (2 hr). Private planes and scheduled air service to Palm Springs (30 min).

Special Notes Limited access for people with disabilities. No smoking in spa. No children (minimum age 18).

Weimar Institute

Life enhancement
Preventive medicine
Vibrant maturity
Weight management

California
Weimar

A diabetic housewife, a stressed-out doctor, and an overweight retiree are representative of the older generation of fitness converts who come to the Weimar Institute, nestled in the Sierra Nevada foothills between Sacramento and Reno, to learn healthy habits. Medically oriented yet devoted to education and exercise, the 19-day Newstart program teaches guests to help themselves through a combination of physical, mental, and spiritual healing.

Although Weimar is a nondenominational and nonsectarian place, all the doctors and staff are Seventh-Day Adventists, who see prevention as the best medicine. They will accept anyone willing to adhere to a strictly vegetarian diet and exercise regimen at home. The physicians and educators here encourage patients to get off medication as soon as is safely possible. They believe modern technology has overshadowed simple cures for common ailments. Their programs help participants to quit smoking, control weight, and cope with such degenerative diseases as arthritis, diabetes, cancer, and cardiovascular problems. With the help of computers, the staff makes specific recommendations for diet based on assessments of your physical condition, nutritional requirements, and weight-loss goals. After you undergo a complete physical, a physician will create a personal schedule, and will continue to monitor your progress throughout the three-week program.

The first activity of the day is calisthenics, and everyone is encouraged to walk and enjoy the miles of woodland trail on the 457-acre campus. "Stretchercise" classes that won't strain bodies unaccustomed to exercise are scheduled between cooking classes and private counseling or therapy sessions. Hydrotherapy and massage are also part of the program. Included are a 16-head enclosure of contrasting hot and cold showers, Russian-style steam baths, and whirlpools. Those afflicted with neuromuscular problems learn to relieve themselves of pain.

Newstart shares resources with Weimar College, a training institution for health-related ministries that offers an intensive, outpatient type of program with live-in accommodations. Weekend seminars are often scheduled for those who want a refresher course in health cooking or controlling stress. Others come simply to relax at the Weimar Inn, which also has a weights room.

Weimar Institute
Box 486, 20601 W. Paoli La., Weimar, CA 95736
Tel. 916/637–4111 or 800/525–9192

Administration President, Paul Roberson; medical director, Thomas Mullen, M.D., F.A.C.S.

Season Newstart program June–mid-Dec.; weekend seminars year-round.

Accommodations 29-room no-frills country lodge. Large rooms with sitting area and private bath, single or king-size beds. Informal gatherings around the fireplace in the lobby; self-service laundry. Also 23 rooms with cherry furnishings, quilted bedspreads, mirrored closet doors, and flowered wallpaper at the Weimar Inn.

Rates 19-day live-in Newstart program, including medical fees (some insurance policies will cover fees), $4,475; $3,975 for participating spouse or partners, $2,500 for accommodations only at lodge. $43 per night for 2, $38 single, without meals, at the Weimar Inn. Newstart program $500 per person in advance; inn accommodations 50% in advance. Credit cards: AE, D, MC, V. Rates include tax, gratuity.

Meal Plans 3 vegetarian meals daily in the Weimar Country Cafeteria. Specialties include a "haystack" of chili, rice, sprouts, lettuce, and tomato on corn chips, vegetarian lasagna, steamed vegetables on rice with Oriental sauce. Breads baked daily. Whole and sprouted grains. No eggs, cheese, or dairy products.

Services and Facilities **Exercise Equipment:** 3 Exercycles, Schwinn Air Dyne bike, 2 rowing machines, 2 treadmills, cross-country ski machine, tiltboard, free weights, 10-unit hydraulic weight-training system. **Services:** Newstart program includes complete physical and medical history evaluation, blood tests, treadmill stress tests, consultation with physician; hydrotherapy and massage; cooking classes; 24-hr nursing staff. **Swimming Facilities:** River bathing and wading. **Recreation Facilities:** Volleyball; golf course nearby. **Evening Programs:** Music, video presentations, and talks on inspirational and health-related topics.

In the Area Weekend outings to the Empire Mine State Historic Park, the California State Capitol, and the Railroad Museum in Sacramento; sightseeing and shopping in the Lake Tahoe area; Yosemite National Park, the Nevada casinos, Old Sacramento.

Getting Here *From Sacramento.* By car, I–80 north to Weimar, exit on W. Paoli La. (60 min). By bus, Greyhound to Weimar (60 min). By train, Amtrak to Colfax (45 min). Transportation from bus or train station to Weimar Institute provided (fee) on request. Taxi, rental car available.

Special Notes 1 room at the lodge and the inn has access for people with disabilities. No smoking.

The Southwest

Health resorts are the new bonanza in the Old West. Ranches and lodges in the desert offer the latest in diet, nutrition, and exercise programs, and fitness routines can include skiing, mountain biking, and hiking.

The pioneer among fitness resorts in the Southwest is the Canyon Ranch near Tuscon, Arizona, with innovative lifestyle programs. In the Rocky Mountain states, Colorado has the newly renamed Peaks at Telluride (formerly the Doral) for sports conditioning accented by Southwest traditions and the newest spa, a spectacular addition to The Broadmoor in Colorado Springs. Summer music festivals in Aspen and Vail add another dimension to holidays for healthy bodies and minds. Scottsdale, Arizona, now offers the widest range of spas, from the upscale Marriott's Spa at Camelback Inn to The Phoenicians Centre for Well-Being. With a dry, warm climate to match superb fitness and beauty facilities, these are world-class destination resorts. The area is also optimal for outdoor adventure, family-oriented hot springs, and ranch vacations.

Stress-control and weight-management courses are the attraction in modern, palm-studded oases near St. George, two hours north of Las Vegas casinos in an area of intense development commonly referred to as "Utah's Banana Belt" or the "Other Palm Springs."

Buckhorn Mineral Wells Spa

Taking the waters

Arizona
Mesa
Locals and sufferers from arthritis and skin problems know Buckhorn Mineral Wells Spa, a small resort in the desert near Phoenix that offers treatments on an à la carte basis to overnight guests and day visitors. Bathers enjoy private rooms with tile tubs into which hot mineral water flows continuously; a whirlpool unit enhances the effect, and a licensed masseur or masseuse is on hand from Tuesday to Saturday 9 to 5.

Surrounded by cactus and palm trees, the motel-style lodge looks like a combination of hacienda and gymnasium. Separate men's and women's entrances lead to the cement bathing cubicles. The mineral water, unchlorinated and naturally heated at 106°F, flows at the rate of 7,000 gallons per hour. Cooler water can be added, but the nurse in attendance recommends the high temperature to relieve sore muscles and aching bones. Tubs are drained, cleaned, and refilled after each use.

Built in the 1940s, the Buckhorn Spa was expanded in 1993 by the current owner and operator, and now guests can stay in adobe cottages equipped for housekeeping. Restaurants and a shopping center adjoin the resort, and there is a small museum on the grounds displaying native birds and animals.

Buckhorn Mineral Wells Spa
5900 E. Main St., Mesa, AZ 85205
Tel. 602/832–1111

Administration	Manager, Alice A. Sliger
Season	Year-round.
Accommodations	15 cottages with twin beds, private bath, kitchenette. Dishes and linens provided. Units have Spanish-colonial furnishings, air-conditioning.
Rates	$35 a day for 2, Jan.–Mar.; $225 weekly. Lower rates in summer. 1 night payable in advance. No credit cards.
Services and Facilities	**Exercise Equipment:** None available. **Services:** Whirlpool mineral baths ($12), Swedish-type massage with vibrator ($20). Series rates and combination treatments. **Swimming Facilities:** Nearby lake. **Spa Facilities:** Hot mineral well water in 27 private rooms. **Recreation Facilities:** Golf courses, horseback riding nearby; fishing, picnic areas, parks, water sports.
In the Area	Scottsdale resorts and restaurants; Phoenix; the Heard Museum (Indian art); Paolo Soleri's Arcosanti village.
Getting Here	*From Phoenix.* By car, Hwys. 60, 80, 89, Recker Rd. (30 min). Rental car available.
Special Notes	No smoking in the bathhouse.

Canyon Ranch

Holistic heath
Life enhancement
Luxury pampering
Preventive medicine
Vibrant maturity
Weight management

Arizona
Tucson

This 70-acre spread in the foothills of the Santa Catalina Mountains is a high-tech emporium of good health that positively radiates energy. From the moment you are welcomed in the big clubhouse and shown to your casita, you'll encounter good attitudes and a nonstop pursuit of health and well-being. Even the most stressed-out Type A personalities tend to find the extensive schedule of special programs, exercise classes, hiking, bike trips, and bodywork to their liking.

The prebreakfast required walk begins at dawn. Typically, about 50 men and women dressed for the predawn chill warm up on the tennis courts. The fitness instructor sets a brisk pace on paths through the desert landscape of cacti, mesquite, acacia, and palo verde trees. Conversations come naturally with fellow ranchers, and newcomers quickly learn the lay of the land. Later, over a breakfast of Spanish omelet (made of egg whites), orange juice, and freshly brewed decaf coffee, intense debates on the merits of shiatsu and Swedish massage can develop.

The scope and scale of the sprawling ranch will probably be slightly daunting at first, but you'll soon become familiar with the various centers and residential clusters. Unlike more rigidly programmed resorts, the ranch allows you to select your activities. Many outdoor activities, however, require signing up in advance to reserve a spot, and you may find that your appointments clash with other outings or classes.

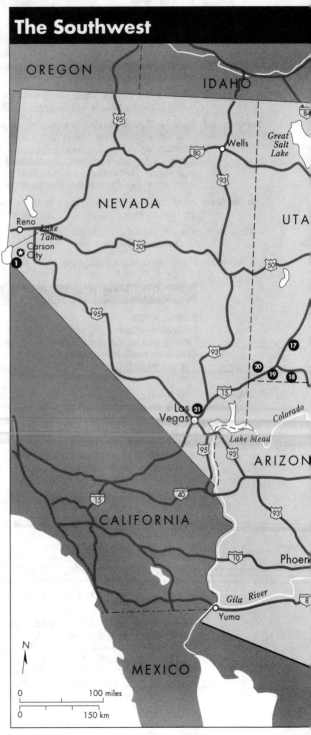

The Southwest

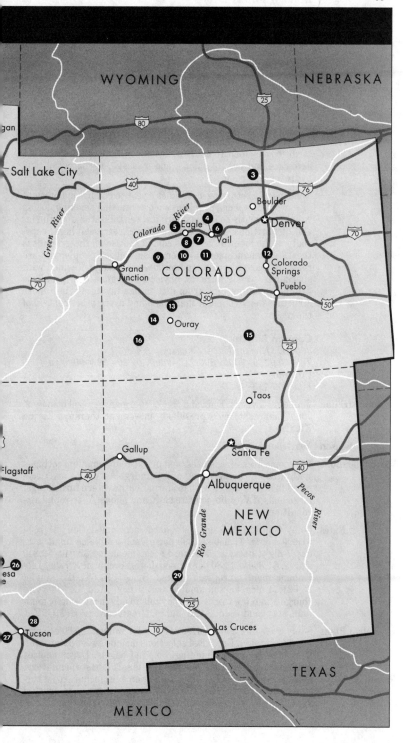

Since its opening in 1979, Canyon Ranch has developed many lifestyle programs that emphasize fitness of mind, body, and spirit. Age extension and food management are among the current entries. Group psychodynamics—a shared experience that builds synergy among the participants—is an important aspect of the ranch's philosophy.

The fully air-conditioned spa complex has seven gyms, aerobics studios, strength and cardio machines, one squash and three racquetball courts; other casitas house and men's and women's locker rooms with separate sauna, steam, and inhalation rooms, whirlpool baths, and private sunbathing areas. The spa facilities are open 16 hours a day. Also in the spa building are skin-care and beauty salons, and massage, herbal wrap, and hydrotherapy rooms.

Some people return several times a year to combat job burnout or to work on special problems such as quitting smoking, losing weight, arthritis relief, and physical rehabilitation for injuries and disfunctions. Preventive medicine is stressed here, especially in the medical/wellness complex. Also on the grounds is the Life Enhancement Center, designed for people who are ready to make a serious commitment to change. Teamed with specialists, you'll work on physical and emotional problems dealing with anything from diet to healthy aging, in a more structured environment than you'll find in the other centers of the resort.

Canyon Ranch
8600 E. Rockcliff Rd., Tucson, AZ 85715
Tel. 602/749–9000, 800/742–9000, or 800/327–9090 in Canada
Fax 602/749–1646

Administration	Founders-owners, Enid and Mel Zuckerman; general manager, Jona Liebrecht; vice president, movement therapy, Karma Kientzler
Season	Year-round.
Accommodations	140 rooms in casitas, suites, and private condominium cottages with kitchen, living room, and laundry. All rooms are decorated in desert colors with modern, Southwestern furnishings, large beds, TV/radio, private bath, and phone. Year-round air-conditioning.
Rates	5-day/4-night package, standard accommodation $1,160–$1,690 single, $1,050–$1,390 per person double occupancy. 8-day/7-night package, standard accommodation $2,040–$2,840 single, $1,860–$2,380 per person double occupancy. 7-day Life Enhancement program (Sun.–Sun.) $4,084.91 single, $3,021.74 per person double occupancy. Add 18% service charge and 6.5% tax. 2 days payable in advance. 4-night minimum stay (mid–Sept.–mid–June). Credit cards: AE, MC, V.
Meal Plans	8-day cycle of 1,200 calories per day for women, 1,800 calories per day for men. Breakfast selections include sweet potato waffles, sunshine bread pudding, lox, and bagels. Lunch choices may be chicken fajitas, Oriental noodle salad, pasta primavera, hearty vegetarian bean chili. Dinner entrées include roast turkey with garlic mashed potatoes, cioppino, mustard crusted rack of lamb, and fresh fish. Vegetarian items on menu.

Services and Facilities **Exercise Equipment:** Full line of BodyMaster weight training machines, 11 stationary bikes, 2 recumbent bikes, 15 treadmills, 8 stair machines, Gravitron, 3 rowing machines, 2 NordicTrack cross-country ski machines, 3-station Versa-Climber, free weights. **Services:** 9 types of massage, aromatherapy, herbal wraps, body scrub with crushed pearls; hair salon, nail and skin care. Consultation on nutrition and diet, holistic health, body composition, and fitness level. Biofeedback program, smoking cessation. Cooking class. **Swimming Facilities:** Indoor pool, 3 outdoor pools. **Recreation Facilities:** 8 tennis courts, 3 racquetball courts, squash court, outdoor running track, basketball, volleyball, 21-speed mountain bikes; golf and horseback riding nearby. **Evening Programs:** Talks by psychologists, authors, naturalists, and other specialists.

In the Area Daily hiking, biking trips in Sabino Canyon; Biosphere 2; Arizona-Sonora Desert Museum, crafts market in Nogales, Mt. Lemmon (pine forest); Tucson's old-town arts district, Mission San Xavier del Bac in Santa Cruz Valley.

Getting Here *From Tucson.* By car, Speedway Blvd. east to Kolb Rd., Tanque Verde to Sabino Canyon Rd., Snyder Rd. to Rockcliff (30 min). Free transfer from Tucson airport on arrival and departure. Rental car, taxi service available.

Special Notes Limited access for people with disabilities. Minimum age of guests is 14. Smoking not permitted indoors or in public areas. Alcoholic beverages permitted only in private guest rooms. Remember to bring completed medical questionnaire, hiking shoes, walking shoes, clothing for warmth, and sun protection. Spa open daily 6 AM–10 PM.

Global Fitness Adventures in Sedona

Holistic health
Spiritual awareness
Sports conditioning

Arizona
Sedona
The week-long Global Fitness Adventure in Sedona is a journey of self-awareness where guests absorb energy from the canyons, towering rock monoliths, and fire-red buttes of the area; visit four primary vortexes—said to emit positive and negative charges that affect human physiology—and take 8- to 15-mile hikes to the remains of ancient settlements.

Guests begin most mornings with yoga and tai chi chuan on a rock vortex surrounded by incredible views. A purification ceremony in a traditional Native American sweat lodge is optional. The daily schedule also includes a sunset horseback ride, natural healing bodywork, and fitness classes. The group is housed in wooden houses in Oak Creek Canyon, and a private chef cooks organic meals in the main lodge, where evening programs are held.

Global Fitness Adventures in Sedona
Box 1390, Aspen, CO 81612
Tel. 303/927–9593
Fax 303/927–4793

Administration Founder-director, Kristina Hurrell

Season Mar.–May and Sept.–Nov.

Accommodations 10 wooden houses, each with 2 bedrooms, 2 fireplaces, large living room, kitchen, wood decks. The air-conditioned houses
have Southwestern decor, TV, phone, and large modern bathroom for each bedroom.

Rates $1,950 per week includes 3 massages, all meals. $500 check deposit, balance due 30 days prior to arrival. Gratuities suggested ($50–$100). No credit cards.

Meal Plan Organic vegetarian meals served family style. Breakfast can be
a power drink made from fruit, soy protein powder, and wheat
germ or granola. Lunch is a mixed salad or curry tempeh
sprout sandwiches. Dinner is Tex-Mex vegetarian chili with
jalapeño corn muffins, mixed greens, or vegetable soup with
salad.

Services and Facilities **Services:** Massage, natural healing bodywork, fitness classes.
Recreation Facilities: Horseback riding. **Evening Programs:**
Motivational talks, sweat lodge.

In the Area Jerome (Victorian mining town), Tuzigoot and Montezuma's
Castle (prehistoric ruins), the Grand Canyon, Sedona arts and
crafts shopping.

Getting Here *From Phoenix.* By car, I–17N (90 min). By plane, commuter
flights to Sedona airport (20 min). By bus, shuttle service from
Skyharbor International Airport (reservations, tel. 602/282–
2066).

Special Notes Programs also in Aspen, CO; Santa Barbara, CA; Dominica in
the Caribbean.

Marriott's Spa at Camelback Inn

Life enhancement
Luxury pampering
Non-program resort

Arizona Within a spectacular hacienda-style structure in the foothills of
Scottsdale Mummy Mountain, the Spa at Camelback Inn is a retreat for
fitness buffs as well as leisure and business guests. Programs
include the latest bodyworks technologies and old-world therapies combined with heart-healthy cuisine. The spa has the most
complete facilities in the Phoenix-Scottsdale area with special
packages for men and women. In 1994 it was renovated and expanded, adding state-of-the-art exercise equipment, five massage rooms, and more tables in the restaurant. Ask for
accommodations in casitas near the spa; both the desert ambience and spacious rooms are conducive to total relaxation.

Start your day with a 4-mile power walk up the mountainside
for grand views of the Phoenix valley and surrounding desert,
then through lushly landscaped residential areas. The daily
walk at 6:30 AM is open to all resort guests without charge, and
if you book at least an hour of services, the daily spa admission
charge ($18) is waived. If you're not staying at the complex,
plan a full day at the spa, so you can sample different physical
activities and then indulge in a bodywork session and salon services. Workout clothes, robes, and slippers are provided; just
bring exercise shoes.

Advancing the art of fitness evaluations, Camelback has linked
up with the Institute of Aerobic Research in Texas, where test-

ing procedures are based on those of aerobics pioneer Dr. Kenneth R. Cooper. FITCHECK is a one-hour assessment of body composition, flexibility, cardiovascular endurance, and body strength. For an additional $85, you can enroll in the comprehensive Personalized Aerobics Lifestyle System (PALS), and work one-on-one with an instructor who will prepare a binder with all your customized information, as well as a specific routine that will help you achieve your fitness goals.

There is no question that staffers take their work seriously; many have University of Arizona degrees in physiology and some are trained in esoteric massage techniques at workshops in nearby Sedona or California. New treatments applied here include a European Kur using Hungarian crystals and creams, the Parisian Body Polish with a cream made from crushed pearls, and Jin Shin Jytso stress-reduction massage from Japan.

Southwestern art and ceramics brighten the locker rooms and lounges, where bottles of water are always at hand to ward off dehydration in the dry Arizona climate. Having a massage outdoors under a crystal-blue sky can be followed by a body scrub with a mixture of sea salts and oils or an herbal wrap. Specially equipped treatment rooms and the sauna and steam room are in an atrium, which has a cold plunge pool and hot whirlpool.

Marriott's Spa at Camelback Inn
5402 E. Lincoln Dr., Scottsdale, AZ 85253
Tel. 602/948–1700 or 800/242–2635
Fax 602/596–7018

Administration General manager, Wynn Tyner; spa director, John Town

Season Year-round.

Accommodations 423 guest casitas on 125 acres. Rooms have king-size bed or large twins, decorated in conservative pastels and earth tones. Some have fireplace, upper bedroom and balcony with extra bathroom. All are air-conditioned, have TV, bath amenities, and phones; parking lot adjoins casita clusters.

Rates $275–$340 Jan.–May 21, $110–$170 May 22–Sept. 10, $210–$265 Sept. 11–Dec. 31; suites $180–$1,450. Add 9.05% room tax. Deposit: one night. Spa Day (lodging not included) packages for men and women, $60–$185; Focus on Fitness day with FITCHECK evaluation $140. All spa services available à la carte, plus 18% service charge and 6.7% sales tax. Credit cards: AE, DC, MC, V.

Meal Plans Choice of spa cuisine in Sprouts Restaurant at the spa building or Chaparral Room. Breakfast menu offers egg-white omelet, French toast, cereal, freshly squeezed juices, freshly baked muffins, coffee. Lunch at Sprouts can be a salad, grilled pompano stuffed with crabmeat, or cold skinless breast of chicken. Dinner only in the Chaparral Room offers à la carte choices of pasta bow ties with poppy seeds in tomato-basil sauce, poached loin of lamb, grilled aki tuna with papaya relish, and roasted breast of capon stuffed with ricotta cheese.

Services and Facilities **Exercise Equipment:** Universal multistation weight training gym, 4 Precor treadmills, StairMaster 4000, Gauntlet, 2 Windracer rowers, 2 Windracer bikes, 2 Schwinn Air Dyne bikes, Lifecycle, 2 recumbent PTS-Turbo 400 bikes, free weights. **Services:** Swedish, shiatsu, and sports massage, un-

derwater massage (women only), thalassotherapy, aromatherapy, herbal wrap, loofah body scrub, facial; fitness/well-
ness evaluations, body-composition analysis, nutritional counseling, one-on-one training, beauty salon for hair, nail, and skin
care. **Swimming Facilities:** Outdoor lap pool; 3 resort pools.
Recreation Facilities: 2 golf courses (36 holes), 9-hole pitch-
and-putt course, 10 tennis courts (5 lighted); horseback riding,
hiking nearby. **Evening Programs:** resort entertainment.

In the Area The Heard Museum (Native American art and history),
Taliesin West (Frank Lloyd Wright home), Cosanti Foundation
sculpture garden, Paolo Soleri's Arcosanti, Sedona spiritual
energy tour, Buckhorn hot mineral-water baths, Mexican
crafts market in Nogales, Biltmore Fashion Park. Big Surf water theme park, Desert Botanical Gardens, equestrian center,
Camelback Mountain hiking.

Getting Here *From Phoenix.* By car, north on 44th St., Tatum Blvd. to Lincoln Dr. (30 min). Shuttle bus service from Skyharbor International Airport. Taxi, rental car available.

Special Notes Reciprocal guest privileges at Marriott's Mountain Shadows
(tel. 602/948–7111), which has golf, tennis, and a health club.
Organized activities for children 5 and older include games,
dinner, movies, tennis clinic, tennis day camp. No smoking in
the spa. Spa open weekdays 6:15 AM–7:30 PM, weekends 6:15
AM–7 PM.

The Phoenician Centre for Well-Being

Life enhancement
Luxury pampering
Nutrition and diet

Arizona Nestled on 235 acres of manicured lawn and desert terrain at
Scottsdale the base of Camelback Mountain is The Phoenician, a Sheraton
resort that combines elgant accommodations, sports, and a
wide range of spa services. Though the hotel caters to conferences and family vacationers, the private-club atmosphere is
still maintained. Exceptional service matches the grandeur of
the public areas; oversize guest rooms are quiet retreats, with
all the amenities of a world-class resort. In fact, a second golf
course is planned for 1995, and will adjoin The Phoenician with
the property that was Elizabeth Arden's Maine Chance.

Inspired by the therapeutic climate of the Southwest, the center offers treatments using desert plants and minerals. Jojoba,
clay, and aloe-vera preparations appear on the menu along with
Pevonia European skin-care products. Special "signature" programs are customized to fit the skin-care needs of guests. Herbal wraps with sage, juniper, and rosemary are offered as
calming treatments.

The resort provides a multitude of options for sports and recreation. The two-level Centre for Well-Being is an escape from
the desert sun, where you can meditate in a secluded atrium,
work out on state-of-the-art equipment, or join an aerobics
class in studios equipped with sprung-wood floors. The exercise facilities, along with beauty salon and barber shop, are on
the upper level, enhanced by views of the resort.

The Phoenician Centre for Well-Being
6000 E. Camelback Rd., Scottsdale, AZ 85251
Tel. 602/941-8200 or 800/888-8234
Fax 602/947-4311

Administration General manager, Alan Furstman; director, Josie Feria

Season Year-round.

Accommodations 442 guest rooms in the main hotel, 107 rooms in casitas including 12 parlor suites. Oversize bathrooms in Italian marble, hair dryer, terry-cloth robes, 3 telephones. Desert tones accent wood furniture; suites have hand-carved travertine fireplace. Air-conditioning, TV, daily paper delivery.

Rates Summer: $160–$265, suites $525–$700; winter: $310–$465, suites $950–$1,550. 4-day/3-night Turnaround $1,315 single, $1,820 per couple. 8-day/7-night Luxury of Choice package $2,760 single, $3,560 per couple. Twice-as-Nice 4-day/3-night golf/spa package $1,000 per couple. 1-day Retreat (no lodging or meals) $170. Daily spa admission ($16; $6 after 5 PM) waived in conjunction with treatments or program. Packages include tax; gratuity extra. Credit cards: AE, DC, MC, V.

Meal Plans Breakfast included in some programs. All four of the resort restaurants and room service offer "Choices" cuisine, low in fat, cholesterol, and sodium. Mary Elaine's serves contemporary cuisine, others offer Italian and Southwestern specialties.

Services and Facilities **Exercise Equipment:** Eagle Cybex circuit training, 4 StairMaster 4000 PT, Concept 2 rower, Liferower, 3 Lifecycle 9500, 2 Schwinn Air Dynes, PTS Turbo recumbent bike, StairMaster crossaerobics, 6 Precor treadmills, Olympic free weights, punching bags. **Services:** Massage therapy includes Swedish, shiatsu, sports, reflexology, aromatherapy, jin shin jyutsu, seaweed body wrap, MoorMud wrap, body scrub; desert clay, herbal, or aloe-vera body wrap; OJA Shirodhara therapy; facial, eye-lifting, back facial; fitness consultation, body composition analysis, cholesterol testing; astrology, herbology, tarot card reading; scheduled classes for self defense, aerobics, tai chi chuan, yoga; salon and barbershop for hair, nail care. **Swimming Facilities:** 7 outdoor pools. **Recreation Facilities:** 18-hole golf course, 11 tennis courts, croquet, lawn bowling, volleyball, badminton, archery, walking, jogging, water basketball and volleyball, bike rental.

In the Area Camelback Mountain hiking, Borgata Mall (shopping), Desert Botanical Garden, Taliesin West (Frank Lloyd Wright Foundation), Heard Museum (Native American art), Sedona arts and spiritual community, Maine Chance.

Getting Here *From Phoenix.* By car, north on 44th St. to Camelback Rd., right to Jokake, left into resort (20 min). Shuttle bus from Skyharbour International Airport. Taxi, rental car.

Special Notes Funicians Club for children has daily supervised program. Teenage programs available at certain times of the year. Spa open 6 AM–8 PM. Minimum age in spa: 16.

Scottsdale Princess

Nonprogram resort

Arizona The towers of the Scottsdale Princess rise from the Sonoran
Scottsdale Desert like a mirage surrounded by a velvet green golf course.
The 450-acre resort, member of a hotel chain noted for its upscale facilities in Mexico and Bermuda, was renovated in 1993.
It has a king-size spa and fitness center and offers packages as
well as daily use ($12) of the exercise equipment and participa-
tion in the five daily aerobics classes.

A fitness staff member sets the pace on a 45-minute morning
walk in the crisp desert air along the grounds and golf course.
The rest of the day is your own to schedule with bodywork and a
bit of luxury pampering. Participating in a wide range of outdoor sports is the major attraction for most guests: walleyball,
Ping-Pong, a fun run, and desert biking are scheduled daily, in
addition to tennis, golf, and water aerobics.

Escape the desert sun in the mirrored aerobics studio, with
suspended hardwood floors ideal for step, low-impact, stretch,
and body-sculpture classes. Encompassing 10,000 square feet
of workout space, the Fitness Center has an array of exercise
equipment, and separate men's and women's locker rooms with
steam, sauna, and whirlpools. Other options include nearby
hiking trails in the McDowell Mountains and a 400-acre equestrian park.

Scottsdale Princess
7575 E. Princess Dr., Scottsdale, AZ 85255
Tel. 602/585–4848 or 800/344–4758
Fax 602/585–0086

Administration Manager, Stephen Ast; health club manager, Jill Eisenhut

Season Year-round.

Accommodations 600 guest rooms and suites range in style from Mexican colonial
to contemporary high-rise. All with living and work areas, terraces, wet bars, and large baths. 75 villas, 125 casitas with
wood-burning fireplaces near the tennis courts. All are air-conditioned, have TV, 3 phones with data jacks, bathrooms with
double sinks, and separate bath and shower stalls.

Rates $216–$312 single or double occupancy, Jan.–May 21; $120–
$140 May 22—Sept. 17; $205–$275 Sept. 18–Dec. 31. Suites
$500–$1,700. 2-night spa package $389–$456 per person, includes Continental breakfast, services. Credit cards: AE, DC,
MC, V.

Meal Plans The Grill (golf clubhouse) and Las Ventanas (garden atrium
and golf-course view) feature grilled seafood and chicken and
salads. La Hacienda serves Mexican specialties, and the Mar-
quesa features Catalan cuisine. Vegetarian meals are available.

Services and **Exercise Equipment:** 15-station Universal weight training
Facilities gym, 3 Quinton treadmills, 4 Lifecycles, Schwinn Air Dyne and
Monark bikes, Concept 2 rower, 2 treadmills, free weight
dumbbells to 65 lb, 4 StairMaster 4000. **Services:** Herbal wrap,
loofah body scrub, mud wrap, aloe or algae body mask, massage (Swedish, aromatherapy, therapeutic, reflexology); salt-
glow treatment; beauty salon for facials, hair and nail care.

Swimming Facilities: 3 outdoor pools, 1 (75 ft) for swimming laps and aquatic exercise. **Recreation Facilities:** 9 tennis courts, 2 18-hole golf courses, racquetball and squash courts, indoor/outdoor basketball, croquet, bike rental, wallyball, volleyball, fishing; nearby equestrian center offers riding, shows, and polo. **Evening Programs:** Resort entertainment.

In the Area Desert tours by jeep; Sedona arts and spiritual center; hiking trails in the McDowell Mountains.

Getting Here *From Phoenix.* By car, north on 44th St. to Camelback Rd., turn right to Scottsdale Rd., then left to Bell Rd. (45 min). By bus and van service from Skyharbor International Airport.

Special Notes Some rooms equipped for persons with disabilities; ramps and elevators to all areas. No smoking in health club. Spa open weekdays 6 AM–8 PM, weekends 7–7. Kids Klub ($20 per session). Minimum age in spa 16.

3HO Ranch

Holistic health

Arizona
Tucson
In 1973 the 3HO Ranch opened as a treatment center for addictive behavior (therefore some fees may be covered by insurance companies); today there are focus weeks devoted to health and revitalization, as taught in the one-week SuperHealth programs. Situated among wooded acres in the Santa Catalina Mountains above Tucson, the ranch makes the most of its optimal setting by using the tranquil, profoundly spiritual environment, clean desert air, and year-round sunshine, in combination with Eastern and Western therapies. The weekly enrollment runs between 10 and 15 guests, to ensure an unregimented, customized program that suits individual needs.

The all-inclusive program begins with Friday dinner and orientation. Guests receive a medical assessment of their fitness level and a daily schedule listing sessions of yoga and meditation, body-language work, and massage and acupuncture. "Breathwalks" combine meditation and breathing exercises during walks for an hour each morning. Another important component of the program is the diet of healing and cleansing foods, based on ayurvedic principles and Chinese herbalism. The goal is to teach techniques for improving everyday life.

The Ranch is owned and operated by members of the Sikh community, but is open to everyone interested in a no-frills introduction to alternative and complementary medicine.

3HO Ranch

2545 N. Woodland Rd., Tucson, AZ 85749
Tel. 602/749–0404
Fax 602/749–0407

Administration Director, Sat Kirpal Khalsa; medical advisor, Dharma Singh Khalsa, M.D.

Season Year-round, 1 week per month.

Accommodations 8 bedrooms in rustic, 1-story bunkhouse. Each room has 2 beds, bath and shower, air-conditioning. Simply furnished, with no amenities.

Rates $1,995 per person, double occupancy per week. Nonrefundable deposit: $200. Credit cards: AE, MC, V.

Meal Plans 3 vegetarian meals daily included in the program. Vegetarian lasagna, enchiladas, pasta and vegetables, mung beans, and rice are among items served family style.

Services and Facilities **Exercise Equipment:** none. **Services:** massage, acupuncture; medical assessment, Life Pattern counseling, Kundalini yoga. **Swimming Facilities:** outdoor pool. **Recreation Facilities:** Tennis court, Jacuzzi; horseback riding nearby.

In the Area Mission San Xavier del Bac, Nogales crafts market, Biosphere 2, Old Town Tucson, Mt. Lemmon (pine forest).

Getting Here *From Tucson.* By car, Tucson Blvd. north, Valencia Blvd., Kolb St., rt. on Tanque Verde Ave. to Woodland Rd. (25 min). From airport, complimentary transfers.

The Aspen Club International

Life enhancement
Sports conditioning
Stress control
Weight management

Colorado
Aspen

The program here is designed to help you improve your general health and fitness level by integrating exercise, healthy eating, and modern medicine. The schedule on a typical Monday in February includes cross-country and downhill skiing, tennis, and snowshoeing, but it's the personal training at the Aspen Fitness and Sports Medicine Institute, the club's high-tech health facility, that sets this property apart from the others.

The center for therapy and training employs a comprehensive approach to well-being that considers the individual's personal needs and goals in prescribing short-term lifestyle modifications aimed at making significant health improvements. Rehabilitation after injuries is a specialty here.

The fitness program, which is open to nonmembers, is concerned chiefly with weight loss, stress reduction, and the rehabilitation of sports-related injuries. Visitors stay a few days or a few weeks, scheduling exercise classes and diagnostic appointments among the activities of a world-class resort.

A complete physical evaluation by a team of physicians, physical therapists, and trainers is the first order of business; you undergo a stress test with EKG readings, pulmonary-function tests, and body-fat, strength, and flexibility measurements. A nutritionist evaluates your eating habits and body chemistry (and schedules blood tests when appropriate) prior to recommending a diet that meets your nutritional needs.

Athletes make up a large percentage of the institute's members, as the special equipment attracts pro football players and amateur skiers, alike.

The Aspen Club International

Fitness and Sports Medicine Institute
1450 Crystal Lake Rd., Aspen, CO 81611
Tel. 303/925–8900; lodging 303/925–6760, 800/882–2582,
or 800/443–2582 in CO
Fax 303/925–9543

Administration   General manager, Mark Overstreet; program director, Julie Anthony

Season   Year-round.

Accommodations   Studios, 4- and 5-bedroom condominiums, private home rentals—all with Jacuzzi, fireplace, sun deck—by arrangement with the Aspen Club Management Company. 91 rooms and suites at the Aspen Club Lodge have oak furnishings, queen-size and twin beds, bath, and kitchen. Maid service, newspaper delivery. Continental breakfast and health-club facilities included.

Rates   The Fitness and Sports Medicine Institute 5-day training program includes lodging, gratuity, tax. $1,875–$6,375 single, $1,675–$6,175 per person double occupancy. Deposit: 50%. Some costs may be covered by medical insurance. Credit cards: AE, MC, V.

Meal Plans   Meals are not included in the program. Heart-healthy cuisine is available for breakfast and lunch at the Club dining facility. Recommended restaurants in Aspen include Gordon's, Syzygy, Piñons, Cache Cache, and range from moderate to expensive.

Services and Facilities   **Exercise Equipment:** 12-unit David circuit, 4 Keiser Cam III, 3 Nautilus units, Eagle leg press, 2 Polaris units, 7 StairMasters, 5 Quinton, 1 Precor treadmill, 6 Lifecycles, 2 Liferowers, Precor rower, 6 Tunturi bikes, 5 Monark bikes, 2 Schwinn bikes, Turbo and Nautilus recumbent bikes, NordicTrack, free weights, dumbbells and barbells (3–100 lbs). **Services:** Swedish massage, nutritional and food-allergy evaluation, strength and flexibility tests, blood-profile analysis, maximal stress test, body-composition analysis, private exercise training; post-injury therapy. **Swimming Facilities:** Indoor lap pool. **Recreation Facilities:** Skiing, 2 indoor and 7 outdoor tennis courts, 3 racquetball courts, 3 squash courts, basketball, volleyball, walleyball, fencing, cycling, aikido. Golf and horseback riding nearby. **Evening Programs:** Athletics, tournaments, fitness and nutrition seminar.

In the Area   Mountain hiking and dogsledding offered by local tour operators. Aspen Music Festival and Ballet/Dance Festival (July–Aug.), ballooning, rafting. Crafts shows and classes at the Anderson Ranch at Snowmass. Nature walks at Hallam Lake Wildlife Sanctuary. Mineral-water baths at Glenwood Springs.

Getting Here   *From Denver.* By train, Amtrak to Glenwood Springs (2 hr). By bus, Greyhound to Glenwood Springs (3 hr). By car, I–70 to Dillon, Rte. 91 to Hwy. 24, Rte. 82 via Independence Pass (closed in winter) is scenic route (3½ hr). By plane, flights on United or Continental Express (40 min). Free pickup from and return to Aspen airport. Rental car, taxi, limousine available.

Special Notes   Full facilities for people with disabilites. Children's athletic programs in swimming, tennis, squash, racquetball, and dance; nursery and toddler swim class by reservation. No smoking in public areas. Some nonsmoking apartments and rooms. Spa open 6:45 AM–10 PM daily.

The Broadmoor

Luxury pampering

Colorado
Colorado Springs

Celebrating a 76-year legacy as the premier health and sports resort in the Rocky Mountain region, in 1994 the Broadmoor introduced an exclusive line of body treatments utilizing native Colorado ingredients. The newly constructed spa facilities include hydrotherapy, balneology, and inhalation rooms. Combined with your choice of sports-specific training, bodywork, or fitness activities, the spa offers personalized programs rather than a structured schedule.

The new sports-and-fitness complex includes 17 tennis courts and the Dennis Ralston training program, three championship golf courses, three heated swimming pools, bike rentals, and boating on a private lake. Set in the heart of 3,000 well-groomed acres, the Broadmoor has its own pharmacy, movie theater, ice skating arena, and stables for horseback riding. Within a few miles are the mineral waters of Manitou Springs, which once served as the house water for the Waldorf Astoria Hotel in New York.

The two-level lakefront spa has an aerobics studio for scheduled classes in step, slide, body sculpting, and box aerobics. There is an indoor swimming pool where aquatics classes are held and a dedicated, three-lane adult lap pool. The weight training and cardio rooms are available to all resort guests for a daily fee ($5–$10), or as part of spa packages. Separate locker rooms for men and women have steamroom and sauna.

The Broadmoor
Box 1439, Colorado Springs, CO 80901
Tel. 719/577–5777 or 800/634–7711, ext. 5770
Fax 719/577–5700

Administration
President, Stephen Bartolin, Jr.; spa director, Marguerite Rivell

Season
Year-round.

Accommodations
700 rooms including 67 suites, with full bathroom, porcelain bathtub, sink with brass fixtures. Traditional furniture, air-conditioning, TV, telephones. Choice of king-size or 2 double beds, view of mountains or city. Amenities include clock radio, toiletries; evening turn-down service.

Rates
Daily rates per room $225–$295 peak season, $155–$195 off season, suites $250–$1,800, depending on season and room. Spa packages including accommodation and meals are introduced seasonally. Credit cards: AE, D, MC, V.

Services and Facilities
Exercise Equipment: 15 Cybex stations, free weights and dumbbells (5–50 lb) in weight resistance room; 3 Cybex bikes, 4 Schwinn Pro bikes, 2 Trotter 685 treadmills, 2 Concept II rowers, 2 Cross-Conditioning Systems XL180, 4 StairMaster PT4000 in cardiovascular room. **Services:** Swedish and aromatherapy massage, shiatsu, Floraspa body wraps and aromabaths, salt glow body scrub, mud baths, milk-whey baths, underwater massage tubs, facial room. **Swimming Facil-**

ities: 2 outdoor pools, indoor pool and lap pool. **Recreation Facilities**: 17 tennis courts, 3 golf courses, horseback riding, ice skating, paddleboats, jogging trail, shuffleboard; bike rental, rifle club with skeet, trap, and sporting clays. Downhill skiing nearby.

In the Area   Garden of the Gods (hiking), Pikes Peak (cog railway, hiking), Manitou Springs (historic spa, Indian cliff dwellings), US Olympic Training Center, Air Force Academy, Royal Gorge (whitewater rafting), Van Briggle Pottery.

Getting Here   *From Denver.* By car, I-25 to Lake Ave. (90 min). By air, Colorado Springs Airport has scheduled service to major cities. Taxi, limousine, rental car available at airport and hotel.

Special Notes   Spa hours: 6:30 AM-8:30 PM daily. Minimum age: 16. Daily facilities fee: $10. Facilities are accessible for people with disabilities.

Eden Valley Lifestyle Center

Preventive medicine
Spiritual awareness
Vibrant maturity
Weight management

Colorado   This homelike retreat set amid woods, lakes, and streams on
Loveland   550 acres in the foothills of the Rocky Mountains teaches physical conditioning and nutrition in comprehensive programs lasting 7 to 24 days. The Eden Valley Lifestyle Center's approach emphasizes the pursuit, under medical supervision, of traditional Seventh-Day Adventist philosophies of diet and mental and spiritual health.

Following thorough individual physical evaluations by the medical director, small groups of guests are counseled on health and disease prevention. Cooking demonstrations show how the vegetarian diet can be adapted to one's own kitchen routines.

The doctor monitors each guest's progress and may suggest additional activities. Drinking lots of pure water, walking in the clean mountain air and sunshine, and taking hydrotherapy and whirlpool baths are all part of the program.

Personalized strategies for attaining a healthy lifestyle are prepared for those with heart disease, diabetes, degenerative disease, and digestive problems. Chronic fatigue, obesity, arthritis, and high blood pressure are also treated, and there is therapy for those who want to stop smoking.

The Lifestyle program began in 1987 as an extension of services at a nearby home for senior citizens. People of all ages come here to gain new vitality and stamina and to relax in the company of a small supportive group.

Eden Valley Lifestyle Center
6263 N. County Rd. 29, Loveland, CO 80538
Tel. 303/669-7730 or 800/637-9355

Administration   Administrator, Daniel McKibben; medical directors, Joseph Shidler, M.D. and Kilson Koh, M.D.

Season   Year-round, with schedules 3 weeks per month.

Accommodations 5 guest rooms with twin beds in a new ranch-style facility, 3 with private bath; 5 rooms in private homes. Draperies and flowered bedspreads. Private sun deck.

Rates 7-day program $745–$795, 14 days $1,395, 21 days $1,995, all per person, double occupancy. Medical costs may be covered by health insurance. $300 in advance for the 14- and 21-day programs, $100 for the 7-day program, nonrefundable. Credit cards: MC, V. Companion rates available.

Meal Plans 3 vegetarian meals daily, buffet style. Adventist diet of fruit, raw vegetables, legumes, and grains. No butter, oils, or dairy products. Some olives, nuts, and avocado. Entrees for lunch and dinner include vegetarian lasagna with mock-cheese topping, bean haystack with rice on corn chips, topped with cashew-nut mixture, green salads, steamed vegetables, and baked tofu.

Services and Facilities **Exercise Equipment:** Stationary bike, treadmill, trampoline. **Services:** Physical examination, blood-chemistry analysis, computerized lifestyle inventory, daily hydrotherapy treatments with massage, Jacuzzi, sauna. **Swimming Facilities:** Community pool and lakes. **Recreation Facilities:** Mountain trail hiking, fishing, boating; downhill and cross-country skiing. Golf course, tennis courts, horseshoe pitch and picnic facilities nearby.

In the Area Estes Park (mountain resort), greyhound racetrack, county fair and rodeo, trail rides, ghost towns, antiques shops. Performing-arts and museum exhibitions.

Getting Here *From Denver.* By car, I–25 north to Loveland, County Rd. 27 to County Rd. 29 (90 min).

Special Notes No smoking.

Filhoa Meadows

Holistic health
Preventive medicine
Stress control
Taking the waters
Vibrant maturity

Colorado
White River
National Forest

This family-oriented health retreat close to Aspen is designed to help balance your mental, physical, spiritual, and social selves. Created for the person who is at high risk for lifestyle diseases (cancer, heart problems, arthritis), this is therapy to help change old behavioral habits that are self-defeating and debilitating. For couples with marital problems, founder-owner Robert Durham provides conflict-resolution counseling, with an emphasis on personal communications, family relationships, and Christian values. Sessions can involve children as well as adults.

Coordinated by medical consultants and specialists in physical education and cardiac rehabilitation, the programs are planned on an individual basis to meet the needs and fitness level of participants. Activities center around a big wooden lodge close to the historic Indian Springs, which provide a constant source of hot mineral water for the indoor and outdoor hydrotherapy pools. Guest rooms are divided between the lodge, a private house, and two cabins with duplex apartments, outdoor decks, and hot tubs. In addition to the soothing mineral-water baths, downhill skiing in winter and biking in summer, and the natural scenic beauty at 7,000-feet in the Rockies, you can enjoy a full range of entertainment and sports.

The health education concentrates on understanding diet, exercise, and how our minds work. No meals are served, so come prepared to do your own cooking as well as participate in discussions on nutrition and a healthy lifestyle. Supervised workouts are scheduled in an indoor pool that is equipped with hydrojets and in a small exercise area that has panoramic views of the Rockies.

Filhoa Meadows

14628 Hwy. 133, Redstone, CO 81623
Tel. 303/963–1989 or 800/227–8906

Administration Director, Robert Durham; seminar coordinator, Melody L. Durham, R.N.; medical consultants, Bernarr Johnson, M.D., F.A.C.S. Claudia and Alan Nelson, M.D. F.A.C.S.

Season Year-round.

Accommodations 4 private bedrooms in the main lodge share 3 bathrooms, kitchen; 2-bedroom River House sleeps 8, has full bathroom, kitchen, family room with additional sofa beds. Choice of single beds, queen- or king-size. 2 rustic cabins with duplex apartments each have queen-size bed, sofabed, kitchenette, bathroom, deck, and hot tub. No air-conditioning, TV, or phone.

Rates $60 per night in the lodge, $50 per night in the River House, single or double occupancy, $65–$70 per couple in cabin. Add taxes. Counseling $40 per hour. Advance payment of 1 night, nonrefundable, by check. No credit cards.

Meal Plans None. Guests do their own cooking.

Services and Facilities **Exercise Equipment:** Total Gym exercise unit, 2 Schwinn bikes, 2 rowing machines, Sears treadmill, free weights. **Services:** Massage, counseling, cooking demonstration. **Swimming Facilities:** Indoor static lap pool. **Recreation Facilities:** 3 outdoor Jacuzzis, parcourse, running track; nearby downhill and cross-country skiing, trout fishing, hiking, biking, rafting, horseback riding.

In the Area Aspen (summer music and ballet festivals), Glenwood Springs (swimming, golf), jeep tours to the Snowmass Wilderness (ghost towns, nature photography), Colorado River (white-water rafting), Redstone (Victorian mining town).

Getting Here *From Denver.* By car, I-70 to Glenwood Springs, Hwy. 82 to Hwy. 133 (3 hr). By bus, Trailways to Glenwood Springs (3 hr). By train, Amtrak to Glenwood Springs (1 hr). By plane, scheduled flights to Aspen (30 min). Transportation by prior request to and from Glenwood Springs and Aspen.

Special Notes Limited access for people with disabilities. No smoking indoors.

Glenwood Hot Springs Lodge & Pool

Taking the waters

Colorado
Glenwood Springs

This facility has one of the largest natural mineral-water pools in the Rockies, and is popular year-round, even in subfreezing temperatures.

In summer and winter the 130°F water is cooled for comfort in the 405-foot-long outdoor swimming pool, fed with naturally hot water. In a smaller therapy pool equipped with underwater jets for massage, the water temperature is 104°F. Together the pools contain 1.1 million gallons of mineral water, changed three times daily. The entire complex, with a 3-story lodge and athletic club is two blocks long.

Lodge guests use the Hot Springs Athletic Club and can participate in aerobic workouts, use championship racquetball, handball, and walleyball courts, and relax in coed saunas and whirlpools. The club's scheduled fitness classes include water and low-impact aerobics, and Jazzercise.

Nearby are vapor caves (coed), where the hot springs create temperatures that reach 115°F and provide a great sweat. Cold-water hoses are available, but there is no soaking pool. Day visitors are welcome here and at the pools; lodge guest admission to the caves is $4 adults, $2.75 children.

Glenwood Hot Springs Lodge & Pool
Box 308, Glenwood Springs, CO 81601
Tel. 303/945–6571

Administration Manager, Kjell Mitchell

Season Year-round.

Accommodations 107 modern rooms furnished with 2 queen-size beds (some are king-size), private bath and double vanity. Deluxe rooms with balcony or patio overlooking the pools, coffee maker, safe, air-conditioning, geothermal heating.

Rates $57–$73 per day single, $62–$78 double; deluxe rooms with 2 queen-size beds $78 for 2 persons. Add 7.75% tax. Daily pool admission $6 adults, $3.75 children. Discount on admission to pools and athletic club for lodge guests. 1 night payable in advance. Credit cards: AE, DC, MC, V.

Meal Plans No meal plan. Meals served at the lodge cafe.

Services and Facilities **Exercise Equipment:** 10-station Nautilus units, 4 Lifecycles, 2 StairMasters. **Services:** Massage, facials, chiropractic adjustment. **Swimming Facilities:** 4 outdoor pools. **Recreation Facilities:** Hiking, water slide, trout fishing, 4 indoor racquetball courts, 2 handball and walleyball courts.

In the Area Ski resorts, Aspen Music Festival, Wheeler Opera House, Anderson Ranch arts center at Snowmass.

Getting Here *From Denver.* By train, Amtrak twice daily (3 hr). By bus, Greyhound (4 hr). By car, I–70 (3 hr). Rental car available.

Special Notes No smoking in athletic club or caves.

Global Fitness Adventures

Holistic health
Life enhancement
Spiritual awareness
Stress control
Weight management

Colorado Inspired by the majesty and splendor of the Rockies, former
Aspen fashion model Kristina Hurrell and her husband, Dr. Rob
Krakovitz—author and holistic health authority—designed a
life-energizing program filled with fun activities for guests of
all ages. This Rocky Mountain health retreat accommodates up
to 10 participants for its one-week programs.

The picturesque 52-acre ranch is located 45 miles from Aspen
and is surrounded by 2 million acres of the White River National Forest. Welcomed at the main lodge, you are assigned to a
room or private cabin. A variety of natural healing techniques
and bodywork are included in the program. Days begin with an
hour of yoga and end with dinner by candlelight.

Outdoor recreation is the focus here. Hiking and touring the
backcountry fill most days. Horseback riding continues to be a
major attraction at this former dude ranch. The seasonal excursions include cross-country skiing, snowshoe hiking, sleigh
rides, and downhill skiing (at an additional $45 fee). An option-
al vision quest, involving a 24-hour ceremony, sweat lodge, and
drumming, is often available. A daily massage (1-hour) is included in the program rate.

The combination of healthy eating and extensive daily exercise
forms a basis for weight loss. Spa-cuisine meals total 800 calories per day. Vegetarian meals and supervised juice or water
regimens are also offered. By adhering to a course of exercise
and attending classes on topics ranging from improving communication skills and personal relations to enhancing mental,
emotional, and physical energies, you'll achieve a sense of well-
being in this magical place that will put you on the road to peak
vitality.

Global Fitness Adventures
Box 1390, Aspen, CO 81612
Tel. 303/927-9593 or 800/488-8747
Fax 303/927-4793

Administration Founder-director, Kristina Hurrell; holistic medicine director,
Rob Krakovitz, M.D.

Season Year-round.

Accommodations 18 rooms in main lodge and guest cabins. Rustic charm, ranch-
style furnishings, private modern baths. Lodge with high
beam ceiling and open fireplace. Jacuzzi on sun deck.

Rates $1,900–$2,300 per person, double occupancy for 1 week. $300
per person per day; includes all meals, massages. Deposit $500,
balance due 30 days prior to arrival. $50–$100 per week gratuity suggested. No credit cards.

Meal Plans 3 meals daily, family style, plus snacks. Breakfast is either
pineapple or papaya (high in enzymes that aid digestion), granola, or a power drink made from fruit, soy protein powder, and
wheat germ. Lunch is either a salad with tofu, nuts, seeds, and

sprouts, or a lemon, garlic, tempeh, and sprout sandwich. Dinner is steamed squash, steamed brown rice with vegetables, grilled trout, or vegetarian lasagna.

Services and Facilities **Services:** Massage, natural healing bodywork, yoga and meditation training, detoxification techniques, diet plan with nutritional supplement. Personal consultation on medical and health problems, with holistic therapies (fee). Horseback-riding instruction (fee). **Swimming Facilities:** Nearby lake. **Recreation Facilities:** Horseback riding, trout fishing rowing, canoeing, snowshoeing, mountain biking; golf and tennis nearby. **Evening Programs:** Informal workshops on health and nutrition.

In the Area Cross-country and downhill skiing, trail rides; shopping, summer arts festival in Aspen; mineral baths at Glenwood Springs; Olympic training center at Colorado Springs.

Getting Here *From Denver.* By car, I–70 to Glenwood Springs, Rte. 82 to Basalt (3 hr). By air, American, Continental, and United commuter flights to Aspen (40 min). Free pickup in Aspen on Sun.

Special Notes Laundry service provided. No smoking indoors, smoking discouraged elsewhere. Program also in Sedona, AZ; Kauai, HI; Santa Barbara, CA; and island of Dominica.

Great Sand Dunes Country Club and Inn

Nonprogram resort
Spiritual awareness

Colorado Even though it opened in 1990, the Great Sand Dunes Country
San Luis Valley Club and Inn resembles a frontier settlement, with rough-hewn log cabins and 800 head of buffalo roaming the grounds. Don't imagine that you'll have to rough it, however. The native crafts and Western antiques scattered about make the accommodations feel authentic, but all the modern conveniences are present as well. Amenities include a sauna, Jacuzzi, ozone-filtered heated swimming pool, glassed-in gym, and 18-hole golf course.

And you can't beat the scenery: The unique sand dunes, waves of ever-shifting sand lapping at the base of snow-capped mountains, cut a 57-square-mile swath through the valley that is clearly visible from every vantage point on the ranch. The atmosphere is conducive to meditation and contemplation, as well as to fun: Children love climbing the sandy slopes, and Nordic skiers often don Arab robes for an outing on a sea of sand.

Great Sand Dunes Country Club and Inn
5303 Hwy. 150, Mosca, CO 81146
Tel. 719/378–2356

Administration Owner-director, Hisayoshi Ota; general manager, George Kellof

Season June–Sept.

Accommodations 15 guest rooms in 3 vintage log buildings. Handmade wooden furniture, some king-size beds. Private bathrooms, no air-conditioning, TV, or telephone. Terry-cloth robes provided.

Rates $130–$180 per room for 2 people, includes Continental breakfast. 2-night golf package $245 per person. Add 7.75% gratuity.
Credit cards: AE, D, MC, V.

Meal Plans The restaurant's à la carte menu features local mountain trout
and buffalo steaks and burgers (lower in cholesterol and higher
in protein than beef). Specialties include Middle Eastern and
Italian dishes. Continental breakfast is included daily.

Services and **Exercise Equipment:** 8-station Universal gym, StairMaster,
Facilities Lifecycle, Schwinn Air Dyne bike. **Recreation Facilities:** 18-
hole golf course, stables for guided 2-hour trail rides. **Services:**
Swedish massage, shiatsu. **Swimming Facilities:** outdoor pool
(heated).

In the Area Rio Grande National Forest, Great Sand Dunes National Monument, Valley View Hot Springs (warm mineral springs), Creed
(boom town),the Zen Center, Haidakhandi Universal Ashram,
Tibetan Buddhist Center, and Carmelite Hermitage.

Getting Here *From Denver.* By car, I–25 south to Hwy. 160, west to Colorado Hwy. 150 to County Rd. 6 east (5 hr). By air, Continental
Express to Alimosa; complimentary pickup at airport with advance request.

Indian Springs Resort

Taking the waters

Colorado At the historic Indian Springs Resort you can swim in mineral
Idaho Springs water surrounded by tropical foliage beneath a translucent
arched roof. Built in 1869, the lodge is a Victorian relic down to
its ornate dining room; in 1992 the 20-room inn opened.

The soaking pools cater to guests' who are interested in nude
bathing; in fact, no bathing suits are allowed. Separate caves
for men and women have walk-in pools hewn into rock. Water
flows from three springs at temperatures ranging from 104°F
to 112°F. Couples and families may soak together by reserving
private tubs (booked by the hour).

Sacred to Native Americans, the hot springs were first developed for prospectors during the local gold rush, and devotees
have traveled from around the world to bathe in them ever
since.

Chemical analysis of the water has found that it contains trace
minerals essential to good health. While no conclusive scientific
claims have been made for the waters, experts cite the benefits
of bathing for those who suffer from arthritis and rheumatism.
Unlike most hot springs, the waters here do not smell of sulfur.

Both day visitors and overnight guests are welcome. Located
on Soda Creek, with a national forest to the west, this bargain
getaway is easily reached from Denver.

Indian Springs Resort
Box 1990, Idaho Springs, CO 80452
Tel. 303/567–2191

Administration Manager, Jim Maxwell

Season Year-round.

Accommodations 32 lodge rooms, single and double, furnished with Victorian antiques and brass beds; few modern conveniences. 20 deluxe rooms in the inn with king-size or double beds, color TV, coffee maker, full modern bath.

Rates Lodge rooms $44–$50 for 1 or 2 persons; deluxe inn rooms $55–$59; campsite $14. Bathhouse admission $10. 1 night payable in advance by credit card. Credit cards: MC, V.

Meal Plans No meal plan, but the dining room serves 3 meals daily.

Services and Facilities **Services:** Massage. **Swimming Facilities:** Indoor pool. **Recreation Facilities:** Hiking, horseback riding, fishing, coed Jacuzzi.

In the Area St. Mary's Glacier.

Getting Here *From Denver.* By car, I–70 east to Idaho Springs exit, Hwy. 385.

Special Notes No smoking in pool area or baths. Pool open daily 9 AM–10 PM. Caves open daily 7:30 AM–10:30 PM.

The Lodge at Cordillera

Life enhancement
Luxury pampering

Colorado
Vail Valley

With its small state-of-the-art spa and expansive views of the Rocky Mountains, the Lodge at Cordillera is an ideal hideaway for those seeking luxury accommodations along with a workout. Built on 2,000 acres overlooking the ultradeveloped ski resort of Vail, the lodge is secluded and intimate. There are just 28 guest rooms in the three-story lodge, and most are large enough to rate as suites. The architecture is interesting: Walls are made of stone and stucco and the roof is Chinese slate; downstairs within the spa, facilities for fitness and body treatments are the very latest.

The guests (never more than 60 at one time) are an interesting mix of seasoned spa goers, sophisticated travelers, and exacting corporate executives. The staff caters to this upscale clientele, usually successfully, but still some guests criticize service in the restaurant. The spa lacks camaraderie, but has a light-filled ambience to relax even the most demanding visitor.

Outdoors are 15 miles of groomed, private trails for hiking, biking, or cross-country skiing, as well as skating and sledding areas, a swimming pool, and tennis courts. Activities at the spa include fitness classes, aerobics, and morning hikes. The coed exercise room, with an array of hightech equipment, adjoins a cushion-floored aerobics studio, and atrium. The lap pool and Jacuzzi offer mountain views. Body treatments feature Decleor products, and there is a complete salon for men and women. Programs are available for two to five days, or you can drop in for an afternoon or full-day escape. Plan ahead, reservations are required.

Adventure-minded guests explore the backcountry on a five-day hiking program led by staff members several times during the summer. Complete with gourmet picnic lunches and soothing spa treatments, the itinerary includes parts of the White River National Forest and the spectacular El Mirador peak. In winter, ski tours of the area are offered.

After a day on the slopes or in the spa, you're ready for an epi-curean performance in the Picasso restaurant. First, there are preliminary samplings in front of a carved limestone fireplace in the cavernous lobby. The maple-coffered ceilings and plush sofas might be in the home of an oil-industry executive, which is precisely what managing partner William Clinkenbeard planned when he retired from Exxon. This is getting away in style.

The Lodge at Cordillera
Box 1110, Edwards, CO 81632
Tel. 303/926–2200 or 800/548–2721
Fax 303/926–2486

Administration	General manager, Bruce Kendall; spa manager, Kail Christensen
Season	Year-round.
Accommodations	28 rooms and suites, many with fireplace, balcony, or sun deck. 2 queen- or king-size beds, covered with European-style duvets. Handcrafted pine furniture, gemstone-color accents. Spacious bathroom with terry-cloth robes. TV with VCR, air-conditioning, phones.
Rates	$145–$260 per night, single or double occupancy for standard room; with fireplace, $170–$230. Suites $225–$385. 2-night Getaway with spa services and meals, $512 plus lodging. 5-day Adventure, $1,160 plus lodging. Add gratuities and tax. Advance payment $100 per person. Credit cards: AE, DC, MC, V.
Meal Plans	Continental breakfast included in room rate. Nutritionally balanced menus for guests on a fitness program offer such entrées as salmon fillet wrapped in grape leaves, roasted, veal loin Provençale, salad of chicken breast marinated in sherry vinaigrette, and fish of the day steamed with vegetable julienne. Restaurant Picasso has prix-fixe and à la carte menus emphasizing new French *cuisine de qualité*.
Services and Facilities	**Exercise Equipment:** 8-unit Keiser Cam II pneumatic weights machines, 3 Trotter treadmills, 3 Lifecycles, StairMaster 4000, PTS Turbo recumbent bike, Precor rowing machine. **Services:** Swedish massage, hydrotherapy, aromatherapy or sea-algae body wrap, body polish, facial, leg-circulation treatment, bust care, waxing, manicure, pedicure; fitness assessment, personal training, endurance testing. **Swimming Facilities:** Indoor 3-lane Olympic (25 m) lap pool, outdoor heated pool. **Spa Facilities:** Separate saunas and steam rooms for men and women, 2 hydrotherapy tubs, lap pool, weights room, aerobics studio, massage rooms. **Recreation Facilities:** 2 outdoor tennis courts, cross-country skiing, ice skating, snowmobiling, dog-sled rides, mountain hiking and biking, bowls, croquet, volleyball, badminton; nearby downhill skiing, golf, trout fishing.
In the Area	Vail (cultural center, shopping), Beaver Creek (white-water rafting, skiing), Arrowhead (downhill skiing).
Getting Here	*From Denver.* By car, I–70 to Exit 163 at Edwards, Rte. 6 to Squaw Creek Rd., Cordillera Way (2½ hr). By plane, scheduled flights to Avon Airport (25 min); private planes land at Eagle County Airport; helicopter landing pad at Cordillera.

The Peaks at Telluride

Kid fitness
Life enhancement
Luxury pampering
Sports conditioning
Weight management

Colorado
Telluride

The $75 million Peaks at Telluride (formerly the Doral Resort) opened in 1992 as a luxury retreat catering to both spa lovers and outdoors enthusiasts. Set amid the ski slopes in Southwest Colorado, the 10-story hotel is surrounded by majestic views of the Rocky Mountains and presents a spa program that capitalizes on Southwestern traditions and Native American lore. Options include hiking and trail rides, mountain biking and rock climbing, and skiing. Guests can enjoy morning walks in the crisp mountain air, sunrise yoga in a glass-walled studio, and guided vision quests.

In a hushed enclave atop the hotel's 42,000-square-foot spa and fitness center guests experience the widest range of skin-care treatments and bodywork in the Rockies. The 40-room facility is open to both day visitors and hotel guests. Creams and thermal-mud packs are moisturizing and soothing, especially if you've been on the slopes all day.

The Peaks' Sports Performance package focuses on your sport of choice by working with an exercise physiologist, nutritionist, and the sports psychologist. After an assessment of your current performance level, the team designs an "exercise prescription" to enhance performance, off-season training, and injury prevention. A sport-specific diet is set up for you by the nutritionist. And workouts with a sports performance specialist help you learn to visualize and mentally prepare yourself for performance on the "next level."

The weatherproof facilities include both indoor and outdoor swimming pools, cardiovascular deck with inspiring views, and a weight room packed with the latest Cybex equipment. Rock climbing can be practiced indoors, as well as racquetball, squash, and badminton. For family fun there is KidSpa, a high-tech concept in day camps, and a water slide into the indoor/outdoor swimming pool. Workout clothing is provided in locker rooms.

The Peaks at Telluride
624 Mountain Village Blvd., Box 2702, Telluride, CO 81435
Tel. 303/728–6800 or 800/789–2220; 800/SPA–KIVA for spa appointments
Fax 303/728–6175

Administration

General manager, Richard M. Houston; spa director, Gayle Moeller

Season

Year-round.

Accommodations

177 rooms surrounding a 4-story atrium. Included are 35 suites with living-dining area. Luxury rooms open to terrace. All have extra-large bathroom with stall shower, Southwestern decor, TV, minibar, air conditioning, 2 phones, hair dryer, magnifying mirror, and full amenities.

Rates 3-day/3-night Alpine Spa Retreat without meals $460–$617 single, $275–$359 per person double occupancy. 5-day/5-night Next Level package with spa breakfast or lunch daily, $1,037–$1,317 single, $727–$867 double. 5-day/5-night Sports Performance package, or weight loss program, with 2 spa meals daily, not including hotel room $1,200. Daily hotel room tariff for 2 persons $120–$395 deluxe, $125–$435 luxury, $245–$700 suite. Other spa packages priced seasonally. 1-day spa packages (no lodging) $95–$295; facility fee $35 for nonhotel guest booking a spa service. Vision Quest excursion $110–$180. Add 12% tax, 18% gratuity. Deposit for 1 night by credit card. Credit cards: AE, DC, MC, V.

Meal Plans Spa breakfast and lunch included in some packages. Prepared under specific nutritional guidelines for minimal sodium, fat, and caloric content, the menu might include pizza made with tomatoes, fresh mozarella, and basil, or a grilled chicken breast sandwich on a whole-wheat pita for lunch. Dinner may be fresh Atlantic salmon, pasta, and mixed salad.

Services and Facilities **Exercise Equipment:** 42-unit Cybex weight training system, 2 Concept 2 rowers, 2 StairMaster Gauntlets, 3 StairMasters 4000PT, VersaClimber, 6 Precor 9.5 treadmills, 2 Nordic-Tracks, 2 Lifecycles 9500R, 4 Lifecycles 9500, 2 Precor bikes, Pilates, dumbbells (3–100 lbs), free weights. **Services:** Massage (Swedish, shiatsu, aromatherapy, sports), OJA Shirodara therapy, body facial, fango wrap, or cellulite treatment, hydrotherapy bath with seaweed, fango; salon for hair, nail, and skin care; personalized training, fitness evaluation, nutrition plan; stress management using biofeedback, respiration, hemi-sync goggles, InnerSea dry float system; kiva with purification bath, sauna, steam room; Ultratone body shaping. **Swimming Facilities:** 25-yard indoor lap pool, heated outdoor/indoor pool. **Recreation Facilities:** 1 indoor racquetball court, 1 squash court, 5 outdoor tennis courts, mountain bike rental, flyfishing, cross-country and downhill skiing equipment rentals, 18-hole golf course; Preferred Peaks room with climbing wall.

In the Area Crested Butte, Black Canyon National Monument, Million Dollar Hwy. (scenic drive), Mesa Verde National Park (Anasazi cliff dwellings), Durango (historic district, narrow-gauge railroad), Ouray and Pagosa hot springs.

Getting Here *From Denver:* By car, I–70 west to Grand Junction, Hwy. 62 south via Ridgeway, Hwy. 145 (6½ hr). By plane, Continental Express and United Express (60 min). Complimentary shuttle service from Telluride Airport to hotel. Car rental, taxi available.

Special Notes KidSpa activities and day care available for half- or full-day fee. High altitude at hotel (9,490 ft. elevation) will require an initial adjustment. Smoking is permitted in all public areas; some guest rooms and designated tables in dining rooms are nonsmoking; no smoking in the spa. All areas are accessible for people with disabilities.

The Vail Athletic Club

Nonprogram resort

Colorado
Vail

When skiers and hikers come to bustling Vail Village, a replica of an Alpine town, they get a choice of athletic clubs. All offer spa services and exercise classes, but the best equipped is the Vail Athletic Club, the 3-story modern lodge with indoor swimming pool, squash court, and climbing wall.

The aerobics studio doubles as a basketball court, and from 7:15 AM to noon guests can take step, body sculpting, yoga, and water aerobics. There's more of the same after 5 during the winter season. You can also sign up for an hour of cross-training in the fitness room, or a consultation with the resident exercise physiologist to help you shape up. To de-stress, there are facials, body scrubs, and a mud treatments. Salon services (manicure, pedicure, hair care) and skin treatments with the Dr. Hauschka herbal creams, and massage (sports, reflexology, shiatsu) are on an à la carte basis. The facility fee for nonresidents is $20; club residents and members fees are complimentary.

Vail Athletic Club
352 E. Meadow Dr., Vail, CO 81657
Tel. 303/476-0700 or 800/822-4754
Fax 303/476-7960.

Administration
General manager, Bob Moroney; spa director, Lisa de Koster

Accommodations
38 rooms renovated in 1994, including studios with kitchens, and multi-bedroom penthouses. Some have a fireplace; all are air-conditioned, with TV, phone, full bathroom, down-filled comforters, contemporary furnishings.

Rates
Daily tariff per room, single or double occupancy: $175–$1,300 winter season, $100–$700 spring–fall. Add tax, gratuity. Credit cards: AE, MC, V.

Meal Plans
Continental breakfast buffet is complimentary. Terra Bistro specialties include marinated chicken breast with corn salsa and greens, coriander rubbed tuna with tamari vinaigrette, sesame encrusted salmon, roasted lamb coated with Indian spices, and chickpea tamales. No special spa menu.

Services and Facilities
Exercise Equipment: Hoggan CamStar weight training equipment, treadmill, 2 StairMasters, 2 Biocycles, 2 Lifecycles, 2 VersaClimbers, rowing machine, NordicTrack ski unit, boxing bags, free weights. **Services**: Sports massage (8–8), bodywork, facial; beauty salon. **Spa Facilities**: indoor and outdoor Jacuzzis, steam baths, saunas, Swiss showers, lockers. **Swimming Facilities**: Indoor lap pool (20 m), outdoor pool (25 m; summer only). **Recreation Facilities**: 8 outdoor tennis courts, 20-ft indoor climbing wall, racquetball/squash court, skiing.

In the Area
Vail Nature Center, Colorado Ski Museum, Dobson Ice Arena (indoor skating), Eagle River (white-water rafting).

Getting Here
From Denver: By car, I-70 (2 hr). By plane, commuter flights on Continental, United, and American airlines to Avon Airport (45 min). Taxi, rental car, limousine available.

Waunita Hot Springs Ranch

Taking the waters

Colorado
Gunnison
National
Forest

This family-oriented dude ranch with a thermal-water swimming pool, offers a taste of the Old West but with modern comforts. The 200-acre ranch, family owned and operated since 1962, was among the first settlements in western Colorado. Today horseback riding and outdoor recreation are the main attractions.

Nature lovers and families with children make up most of the 45-person guest list. You can bird-watch, collect rocks, or hike in the national forest. Bring casual clothes, jeans, and boots and discover real Western hospitality.

A log barn houses the riding instruction program, with classes for children and adults. There are corral games and an all-day ride to snow-capped peaks near the Continental Divide. Other activities, scheduled daily, include hayrides and an overnight mountain camp out. Local outfitters offer stream and lake fishing, river floats, and hikes.

Hot mineral water flowing through the swimming pool is cooled to a temperature of 95°, is soothing and relaxing after riding or hiking. There are heated dressing rooms, and the area is lit at night.

The weekly program begins on Sunday afternoon, and includes riding instruction, trail rides, fishing, and cookouts. As the week progresses, rides become more advanced for those who enjoy this activity, but sightseeing vehicles are available for the others. Anglers need not acquire a fishing license since the private lakes are stocked by the ranch; gear is available from the office.

Meals at the ranch house consist of hearty buffets. A bowl of fresh fruit is always on hand, and you can help yourself to coffee, tea, hot chocolate, or punch. Alcoholic beverages are not permitted, and nondenominational religious services are held on Sunday.

Waunita Hot Springs Ranch
8007 County Rd. 887, Gunnison, CO 81230
Tel. 303/641-1266

Administration Manager, Junelle Pringle

Season June–Sept.

Accommodations 22 rooms in the ranch house and a log lodge, all with private bath, wood paneling, leather chair. TV in the library. Thermal-water heating system. Queen-size beds. Laundry facility.

Rates $900 a week per person, double occupancy, $1,000 single; children's rates on request. $150 deposit per person. No credit cards.

Meal Plans 3 meals daily, buffet style. Cookouts and steak-fry dinners. Home-cooked food to suit any diet. Barbecued chicken and grilled trout specialties.

Services and Facilities **Swimming Facilities:** 90-ft outdoor pool. **Recreation Facilities:** Hiking, horseshoes, Ping-Pong, corral games, fishing, softball, volleyball. **Evening Programs:** Country-Western Music Hall, movies.

In the Area Cookout rides, overnight camp out; river float trip, mountain rides, Jeep trips offered by local outfitters; Continental Divide, ghost towns, mining relics.

Getting Here *From Denver.* By car, Hwy. 285 to Salida, Hwy. 50 to Doyleville, County Rd. 887 (3 hr). By air, Continental Express and United Express (40 min). Complimentary pickup at Gunnison Airport.

Special Notes No smoking indoors.

The Westin Resort

Nonprogram resort

Colorado
Cascade Village/
Vail
Upvalley and upscale, the 17-acre Westin Resort includes the two-level, 67,000-square-foot Cascade Athletic Club. With indoor and outdoor tennis, squash, and racquetball, an indoor running track, workout equipment, bodywork, and a range of professional health and fitness programs, this is truly a full-service spa at a la carte prices. While the club charges a daily admission fee to resort guests ($10), the facilities are open to the public ($16–$25, depending on season).

Beyond skiing, you can focus on fly fishing, hiking, biking, riding, and sport shooting. Superbly located on Gore Creek, the resort is close to private sports preserves where activities are scheduled both for individuals and groups. At the Four Eagle Ranch, a 50-acre spread roamed by prize cattle, you can join a trail ride and participate in a cattle roundup, like in the movie "City Slickers." A few miles down the road, Vail Rod & Gun Club offers instruction for marksmen with sporting clays and fly fishing on miles of private streams.

You can rent mountain bikes and take off on the path into Vail Village, just over a mile away. Walking is probably your best option, and you can always get a ride back on the hotel's complimentary shuttle bus. Clearly, roughing it is not the style at this Westin. Opened in 1982, the four-story wings resemble European chateaux, and have been decorated in jewel tones as a result of refurbishment in 1994. For skiers, the Cascade Village chairlift provides easy access from the Westin's back door to all of Vail Mountain (3,150-feet incline).

The Westin Resort
1300 Westhaven Dr., Cascade Village, Vail, CO 81657
Tel. 303/476–7111 or 800/420–2424, 800/228–3000
Fax 303/479–7025

Administration General manager, Christopher M. Hanen; Cascade Club manager, Gay Speinke

Accommodations 300 rooms and suites in 4-story chateau-style lodges. Interiors feature luxurious furniture, wood armoire with TV, air conditioning, phones, minibar. Some suites add kitchen, fireplace, Jacuzzi, and/or sauna. Most rooms have a balcony, with either mountain or garden view.

Rates Daily tariff per room: $89–$350 for double, suites from $375. Admission to Cascade Club $10. Add tax, gratuity. Confirmation by credit card. Credit cards: AE, DC, MC, V.

Meal Plans No meal plan. The Cafe provides casual fare, Alfredo's serves Northern Italian and New American cuisine.

Services and Facilities **Exercise Equipment**: 17-unit Nautilus circuit, StairMaster, 8 Lifecycles, 4 Lifesteps, 2 StarTrac treadmills, Trotter treadmill, Trackmaster, 2 Schwinn Air Dyne bikes, UBE, NordicTrack ski unit, Concept II rower, Liferower, free weights. **Services**: Swedish and sports massage, fitness and nutritional evaluation. **Swimming Facilities**: heated indoor/outdoor pool. **Recreation Facilities**: 7 tennis courts, 3 squash courts, 2 racquetball courts, bike rental, golf, indoor driving range. Nearby white-water rafting, hikes in White River National Forest.

Getting Here *From Denver*: By car, I–70 to Vail (2 hr). By plane, commuter flights to Avon Airport on Continental and United Express (25 min).

Wiesbaden Hot Springs Spa & Lodgings

Taking the waters

Colorado **Ouray** Begun as a mountainside motel with mineral-water baths, the family-owned-and-operated Wiesbaden Hot Springs Lodge has become a full-fledged health resort in recent years. Its facilities include an exercise room with video monitors but no instructors, a weights room, a sauna, and an indoor soaking pool with rock-walled vapor cave.

At an altitude of 7,700 feet, the picturesque old mountain town of Ouray is sheltered from winds by the surrounding forest. Few roads traverse these mountains that are the source of the Rio Grande and several hot springs. The geothermal water that heats the motel and swimming pool flows from two springs at temperatures of 111°F–134°F. The mineral water is also circulated through soaking pools, avoiding the need for chemical purification.

Scenic canyons in the national forest are a major attraction for hikers. The makings for a picnic can be found in town, a few blocks away (the lodge has no dining room). Dinner at the Bon Ton Restaurant in the nearby St. Elmo Hotel is recommended for a taste of the town's Victorian gold-rush days.

Wiesbaden Hot Springs Spa & Lodgings
625 5th St., Box 349, Ouray, CO 81427
Tel. 303/325–4347 or 303/325–4845
Fax 303/3325–4845

Administration Manager, Linda Wright-Minter

Season Year-round.

Accommodations 18 modern rooms, each with private bath, king-size or twin beds. Private apartments. Glass-walled lounge overlooks the swimming pool and sun deck. Rooms decorated with antiques, some have wood stove. Complimentary morning coffee and tea.

Rates	Daily rate per room for 2 persons $80–$140. Add 8.2% tax. 1 night payable in advance. Credit cards: MC, V.
Services and Facilities	**Exercise Equipment:** Universal weight training gym, stationary bike, NordicTrack. **Services:** Swedish massage, reflexology, acupressure, aromatherapy, facials. **Swimming Facilities:** Outdoor pool. **Recreation Facilities:** Hiking; bike rental.
In the Area	Antiques shops, Box Canyon falls, Telluride (historical mining town) film festival, Ute Indian reservation, Durango.
Getting Here	*From Denver.* By car, I–70 to Grand Junction, Hwy. 550 (4 hr). By air, Continental or United Express to Montrose (1 hr). Car rental and taxis available.
Special Notes	No smoking on premises. No pets. Thermal pools open daily 8 AM–midnight.

Sheraton Desert Inn Hotel & Casino

Luxury pampering

Nevada
Las Vegas

The combination of a health and fitness club within a country club and casino resort has made the Desert Inn popular. Devoted to exercise and pampering, this well-equipped facility can be enjoyed without entering the casino. Guests pay a daily facilities charge ($18) or sign up for a package plan. However, since the resort and spa facilities were acquired in 1994 by ITT Sheraton Corporation, they have been undergoing a tremendous expansion and will be closed for construction until the end of 1995. During renovation, spa services will be offered temporarily elsewhere in the hotel.

By 1996 the new 30,000-square-foot spa building will be completed, and will feature a stunning floor-to-ceiling glass wall in the central rotundas of the men's and women's pavilions. Separate facilities include private therapy pools, hot or cold water plunges, and a big central Jacuzzi. The steam rooms, saunas, and hydrotherapy room are a few steps away.

Part of the expansion will include a lap pool for swimming and water volleyball, and an indoor coed facility with two gyms: one for weight training and cardiovascular workouts.

The water-focused treatments include loofah body scrub with sea salts and herbal wraps. Thalassotherapy consists of varied baths and wraps with seaweed-based products to soothe and cleanse the body.

Sheraton Desert Inn Hotel & Casino
3145 Las Vegas Blvd. S, Las Vegas, NV 89109
Tel. 702/733–4444, 800/634–6906, or 800/634–6906 for room reservations
Fax 702/733–4795

Administration	V.P. general manager, John Koster; spa director, Jeffrey Bliss
Season	Year-round.
Accommodations	821 rooms with a desert theme in original tower. New 1,800-room tower planned, plus 3,000 room Sheraton Desert Kingdom hotel scheduled to open in 1997. Recently refurbished minisuites in the Wimbeldon and Pebble Beach buildings have balconies and are closest to the spa and tennis complex.

Rates $90–$105 a day, single or double; minisuites $150–$175. Spa packages $165 a day, $110 for half-day, plus lodging. Daily facility charge $18 (refunded when services are booked); add 17% gratuity, 7% tax. 1 night payable in advance. Credit cards: AE, DC, MC, V.

Services and Facilities **Exercise Equipment:** 2 Lifecycles, free-weight dumbbells (2–60 lbs.), 2 StairMaster 4000, Concept 2 rowing ergometer, 2 StarTrac treadmills. **Services:** Massage, paraffin treatment, salt-glow and loofah body scrub, facials, herbal wrap; nail and skin care. **Swimming Facilities:** Lap pool, Olympic-size recreational pool. **Recreation Facilities:** 10 tennis courts, water volleyball, golf. **Evening Programs:** Celebrity shows in casino.

In the Area Waterworld theme park, Lake Mead recreational area and Hoover Dam, the Grand Canyon. Fashion Show shopping mall.

Getting Here *From Los Angeles.* By bus, Greyhound (5 hr). By car, I–15 (4½ hr). By plane, scheduled flights (1½ hr). Limousine on request; rental car, taxi.

Special Notes Ramps and elevators provide access for people with disabilities; all facilities are on 1 level. During construction of new spa building, scheduled to open late in 1995, spa services and limited exercise equipment are in a temporary facility.

Walley's Hot Springs Resort

Taking the waters

Nevada
Genoa A health club and hot mineral baths are the attractions at the charming cluster of Victorian cottages called Walley's Hot Springs Resort. Located in the foothills of the Sierra Nevada, 12 miles from Lake Tahoe's south shore and 50 miles from Reno, the secluded resort offers a pay-as-you-go treatment plan and free exercise classes.

The main building, a two-story health club, has separate men's and women's sections, each of which contains a sauna, steam bath, and massage rooms. A coed weight-training room is modestly equipped, but there are plans for expansion.

Thermal water is piped from an artesian well into the bathhouse, where it continuously flows through the baths. For an outdoor soak, the 104°F water is collected in six cement pools, where it is cooled for the swimming pool.

Walley's Hot Springs Resort
2001 Foothill La., Box 26, Genoa, NV 89411
Tel. 702/782–8155

Administration Owner, Connie Atwood; director, Katherine Vanderbrake

Season Year-round.

Accommodations 5 private cottages, 1 with queen-size bed, others with 2 double beds. Private baths, country antiques, turn-of-the-century ambience. All units have TV, telephone, and air-conditioning.

Rates $85–$120 per day for 2, plus tax; 1 night payable in advance. Credit cards: AE, MC, V.

Services and Facilities **Exercise Equipment:** 7-station Universal weight training gym, free weights, stationary bikes. **Services:** Massage. **Swimming Facilities:** Outdoor pool. **Spa Facilities:** Indoor and outdoor mineral-water pools. **Recreation Facilities:** 2 tennis courts, downhill and cross-country skiing nearby. **Evening Programs:** 2 exercise classes weekly.

In the Area Lake Tahoe resorts and casinos, Reno casinos, historic Carson City.

Getting Here *From Reno.* By car, Hwy. 395 south to Genoa, Genoa La. to Foothill La. (60 min). By bus, Greyhound to Gardnerville (45 min). Rental car, taxi available.

Special Notes Limited access for people with disabilities. Children under 12 not permitted in the health club. No smoking in the health club.

Truth or Consequences

Taking the waters

New Mexico
Truth or
Consequences

Many consider the town of Truth or Consequences (named for the popular 1950s radio show) the bargain basement of health spas. Spring water is channeled to bathhouses and guest lodges along Broadway, the main drag, and the adjoining streets. Some properties offer little more than a tub, and most do not accept credit cards, but you also pay blue-light special rates: A 20-minute soak in unchlorinated 110°F mineral water typically costs $3, a 60-minute massage with hand-held massager costs $25.

Naturopathic treatments are offered at some of the older establishments, but a massage is the principal therapy after bathing. Water sports in mile-long Elephant Butte Lake just outside town, hiking, and tubing on the Rio Grande are mentioned in Chamber of Commerce publications. What is not mentioned, however, is the run-down appearance of the town and its once famous baths. Yet local operators say the area is picking up, and there are newer motels on the main road.

At the **Artesia** (312 Marr St., tel. 505/894–2684; open daily, 8–8), sunken tubs in three private massage rooms are sanitized and filled with fresh, hot mineral water after each use. The **Indian Springs** (200 Pershing St., tel. 505/894–3823) rely on nature for water circulation, inviting a potential for algae buildup.

Bathers at **Ye Olde Hot Springs Bath Haus** (Pershing and Austin Sts., no phone) can exercise in two big pools equipped with metal support bars (for people with disabilities), or soak in three private pools at water temperatures varying from 107°F to 110°F. The **Charles Motel,** in town, has separate facilities for men and women, each with sauna, steam bath, and four individual tubs.

Truth or Consequences
Chamber of Commerce, Drawer 31, Truth or
Consequences, NM 87901
Tel. 505/894–3536

Season Year-round.

Accommodations Standard motels on the highway, without mineral baths, include Super 8 and the Best Western Motel. Rooms are available in town at the Charles Motel (tel. 505/894–7154).

Rates $40 per room for 2 at the Charles Motel. At Best Western Hot Springs Inn rooms cost $47–$49 for 2. Confirmation by credit card. Credit cards: AE, MC, V.

Services and Facilities **Swimming Facilities:** Nearby lake. **Recreation Facilities:** Hiking, tubing.

Getting Here *From Albuquerque.* By car, I–25 north (2½ hr).

Cliff Lodge at Snowbird

Luxury pampering
Sports conditioning

Utah
Snowbird

Alpine views from a penthouse spa, mountaineering courses, and 1,900 acres of groomed ski slopes are the attractions at the sports-oriented Cliff Lodge. Set in Utah's scenic Wasatch Mountains near Salt Lake City, the 11-story lodge hosts university and corporate groups for Life Enrichment workshops, which will be open to the public under a new program.

The Mountaineering Center complements the spa-and-ski program with rock-climbing classes, overnight backpacking trips, bike tours, and guided treks to the peaks of the national forest. Open from July through mid-October, the center attracts outdoors people and climbers of all achievement levels. For golfers, there is helicopter service to the courses in nearby Wasatch National Park and at Jeremy Ranch. Skiers can also be whisked up to powder snow conditions on upper slopes.

The active, youthful vacationers here get into shape at the two-story fitness center on the top floors of the hotel. Sport-specific training, as well as bodywork, are available in the spa on an à la carte basis. There are saunas and steam rooms for men and women and private treatment rooms for sophisticated therapies, such as the French Phytomer process of cleansing and toning the bust with marine products. A skin treatment for the back, popular with men, uses steam, a prep scrub, a Phytomer marine peel, and massage cream to deep-cleanse the pores and moisturize the skin.

There's plenty for children to do while their parents exercise or pamper themselves. Special skiing (children's lift tickets are free when accompanied by adults) and tennis training are offered for children 5 and older, and kids stay free in their parents' room.

Another spa option is the Canyon Raquet Club, a tennis and fitness complex 10 miles from the ski area. Squash, racquetball, and tennis, plus weight training, cardiovascular exercise, and an Olympic-size pool, are open to guests.

Cliff Lodge at Snowbird
Little Cottonwood Canyon Rd., Snowbird, UT 84092
Tel. 801/742-2222 or 800/453-3000
Fax 801/742-3204

Administration Manager, David M. Hale; spa director, Todd R. Randall

Season Year-round.

Accommodations 532 rooms and suites with mountain views and or balconies that open onto the 11-story atrium. Luxury furnishings and baths, king-size beds, cable TV, full service.

Rates Standard rooms $89–$178 for 2 persons per day, deluxe bed-room $285. Mountaineering Center activities charged separately. Deposit: 1 night's rate in summer, 2 nights' rate during winter season. Credit cards: AE, DC, MC, V.

Meal Plans The Aerie's low-fat, low-cholesterol offerings may include vegetarian lasagna or pizza, grilled salmon, broiled chicken, luncheon salads, chicken teriyaki, meatless chili. The Spa Cafe serves fruit smoothies, high-fiber breakfast, and lunch.

Services and Facilities **Exercise Equipment:** 12 Keiser Cam III pneumatic weight-resistance units, Lifecycles, Bodyguard 900 bikes, 2 Stair-Masters, rowing machine, 2 Trotter treadmills. Aerobics studio with suspended wood floor. **Services:** Massage, hydrotherapy, herbal wrap, parafango wrap, Phytomer deep-cleansing treatments, manicure, pedicure, facial, hairstyling. Daily classes in aerobics and stretching. Stress-management course (additional fee). **Swimming Facilities:** Outdoor lap pool, Olympic-size indoor pool. **Recreation Facilities:** 23 tennis courts (10 indoor), 2 squash courts, 2 basketball courts; hiking, skiing, rock climbing. Golf and horseback riding nearby. **Evening Programs:** Outdoor adventure films and talks.

In the Area Helicopter rides, Western barbecues, backpacking, mountain-bike tours, tram rides; Salt Lake City sports and entertainment centers, Mormon Tabernacle, mineral springs at Heber City, historic Alta (19th-century silver mine).

Getting Here *From Salt Lake City.* By bus, Utah Transit Authority scheduled service from city terminal and airport during winter season (45 min). By car, I–75, I–80, Rte. 210 to Little Cottonwood Canyon (40 min). Free pickup on arrival and departure at Salt Lake City airport with package plans. Also, Canyon Transportation (tel. 800/255–1841) provides van service for $32 round-trip. Limousine, taxi, rental car available. Resort parking; valet service and indoor parking at the lodge only.

Special Notes Ski-training course for people with disabilities. Ski and tennis instruction, day-care center for children. No smoking in the spa, the 9th-floor guest rooms, or designated areas of the dining room.

Green Valley Fitness Resort and Spa

Kid Fitness
Luxury pampering
Nutrition and diet
Vibrant maturity
Weight management

Utah
St. George Discovering a full-service spa along with a concentrated weight-loss and fitness program in the dry desert of southern Utah is reason for many to spend a week or two at the Green Valley resort. Guests can also enjoy full resort facilities plus sophisticated bodywork with locally formulated herbal, mud, and mineral products used exclusively in the spa center's color-coded relaxation center. Native American healing traditions are integrated into treatments and services.

The one-week Spa Aerobics program, with bodywork and pampering services, offers you a choice of two electives: hiking or tennis. Beginning with an introduction to how the body's weight-regulating mechanism works, your learning experiences include trips to restaurants and supermarkets, cooking workshops, and discussion groups. The nutritious high-energy meals are a revelation regarding the variety and quantity of food that one can enjoy while losing weight. Even exchanging tips with the Green Valley cook in a dining room–cum–demo kitchen is encouraged.

The fitness training emphasizes correct posture and body movements, shaping and contouring as weight is lost. With only 52 participants per week, the staff physiologists and nutritionists can maintain personal interaction with guests. Relax in a private Jacuzzi surrounded by lush greenery and brightly lit candles, and follow it up with a massage or facial.

Other programs include a Native American Awareness week, a Shaman's Journey, and Vic Braden's Tennis College.

Green Valley Fitness Resort and Spa

1515 W. Canyon View Dr., St. George, UT 84770
Tel. 801/628–8060 or 800/237–1068
Fax 801/673–4084

Administration Owner-director, Alan Coombs; spa director, Carole Coombs; Fitness director, Linda Davis

Season Year-round.

Accommodations Each guest or couple is housed in one of 50 furnished condominium apartments with spacious contemporary interiors with one or two bedrooms, living room, dining counter, kitchen, private bath, balcony. Some have a Jacuzzi on the deck; all have TV, phone, air-conditioning.

Rates 7-night Spa Aerobics week $2,350 per person, double occupancy. Tax and gratuity included. Single occupancy add $238. Daily rate is $350 per night (for lodging; 5-night minimum). $500 deposit. Credit cards: AE, D, MC, V.

Meal Plans 3 meals daily. Low-fat diet, no sugar or salt. Breakfast is scrambled eggs, buttermilk biscuits, turkey sausage, assorted fresh fruit. Lunches include soup, salad, steamed vegetables, a tuna-salad sandwich on whole-grain bread or turkey salad on pita. Typical dinner entrées are baked salmon or orange roughy, stuffed Cornish game hen, beef kebab, or chicken barbecue. Desserts include banana pudding and apple strudel.

Services and Facilities **Exercise Equipment:** 2 Lifecycles, 2 Lifesteppers, 1 Lifecycle bike, 13 CamStar weight training units. **Services:** Swedish massage, hand and foot reflexology, mud and herbal wraps, facials, powdered-pearl body rub; hair, nail, and skin care. Personal counseling on tension control, wardrobe, coloring and makeup, skin care, shopping. **Swimming Facilities:** Outdoor and enclosed pools, diving pool. **Spa Facilities:** Steam rooms, saunas, whirlpool. **Recreation Facilities:** 15 outdoor and 4 indoor tennis courts, volleyball, shuffleboard, basketball, lawn chess, 9-hole executive golf course, putting green, bowling alley, roller skating, 2 racquetball courts. Rental of bicycles. Horseback riding, downhill skiing, water sports nearby. **Evening Programs:** Talks on health and nutrition.

In the Area Zion National Park excursion with picnic lunch, Vic Braden Tennis College (on site), North Rim of Grand Canyon, Snow

Canyon sandstone cliffs, Bryce Canyon National Park, Nevada casinos, country and western entertainment, river rafting.

Getting Here *From Las Vegas.* By car, I–15 to St. George (2 hr). By plane, commuter flights on Skywest (40 min). Free pickup from and return to St. George airport. Van service from/to Las Vegas on St. George Shuttle (tel. 801/628–8320) costs $30 each way. Car rental, taxi available.

Special Notes Elevators, oversize bathroom facilities for people with disabilities. Summer fitness/health and tennis camp for children, with Vic Braden Tennis College. No smoking. Bring a medical release from your doctor, casual workout clothing, walking shoes.

The Last Resort

Nutrition and diet
Spiritual awareness

Utah
Sunset Cliffs

Yoga studies, meditation, and nature walks are the cornerstone programs for rejuvenating the body and the mind at the Last Resort, an informal mountain retreat. Located in southern Utah about 40 miles southwest of Bryce Canyon, the two-story log building 8,700 feet above sea level boasts spectacular mountain views and accommodates up to 10 guests.

Marked trails attract hikers and backpackers in summer and autumn. In winter the light powder snow makes ideal conditions for cross-country skiing.

Directors Pujari and Abhilasha offer a multidimensional experience, a seven-day retreat that includes Iyengar yoga workouts twice a day, hiking, and a soak at nearby hot springs. During year-end retreats, total silence is observed for 10 days. A five-day natural-foods cooking course in August teaches meal planning and preparation of tofu, tempeh, whole grains, beans, fresh vegetables, and other healthy ingredients. Spring is celebrated with a 10-day detoxification and spring cleaning of the body.

The Last Resort
Box 6226, Cedar City, UT 84720
Tel. 801/682–2289 or 619/283–8663

Administration Program directors, Pujari and Abhilasha (Ed and Barbara Keays)

Season Year-round, with retreats scheduled in June, July–Aug., Dec., and Jan.

Accommodations Dormitory beds and private rooms for couples. Simple furnishings, communal bath.

Rates 7-day yoga retreat $695 per person, 5-day cooking course $495, 10-day spring retreat $795; year-end Vipassana meditation, 5 days $295, 10 days $495.

Meal Plans Vegetarian meals prepared by a nutritionist, tea, and juice come with retreats. Menus include steamed fresh vegetables, whole grains, rice, casseroles.

Services and Facilities Swimming Facilities: Nearby lakes. **Spa Facilities:** Mineral baths at Pah Tempe Hot Springs. **Recreation Facilities:** Hiking, cross-country skiing. **Programs:** Meditation instruction, re-birthing, Iyengar yoga classes, lectures on lifestyle.

In the Area Bryce Canyon National Park, North Rim of the Grand Canyon, Zion National Park, Cedar Peaks, Shakespeare Festival in Cedar City (mid-July–Aug.).

Getting Here *From Las Vegas.* By car, I–15 to Cedar City, Rte. 14 (3 hr).

Special Notes No smoking.

National Institute of Fitness

Nutrition and diet
Weight management

Utah
Ivins
Designed by an exercise physiologist, the National Institute of Fitness's no-frills fitness and weight-loss program is based on nutrition, movement, and recreation in some of the most glorious canyon country in the West. Often called the "Walking Spa," the program includes training with certified coaches on hikes as well as in aerobics classes. The 100–150 participants are divided into groups classified C (most fit), B (average) A (moderate) and Special A (limited fitness).

Vigorous exercise, rather than pampering or bodywork, is central here. On arrival participants are given a fitness evaluation that includes a cardiovascular endurance test. The results-oriented program is designed to get you off diets and drugs and to restore normal cholesterol and sugar levels. Guests with serious weight problems stay a month or more, often shedding 50 pounds. Bodywork and personal services are optional extras.

The program moves along at a fast pace, and instructors concentrate on teaching techniques that guests can practice on their own at home. The indoor facilities include an aerobics studio, weights room, racquetball court, and covered swimming pool for laps and aquaerobics. The Megahealth building, added in 1992, has a 200-seat dining room, aerobics studio, lecture hall, and 12 treatment rooms.

National Institute of Fitness
202 N. Snow Canyon Rd., Box 938, Ivins, UT 84738
Tel. 801/673–4905
Fax 801/673–1363

Administration Founder-director, Dr. Marc Sorenson; program director, Vicki Sorenson; nutrition director, Ralph Ofcarik, Ph.D.

Season Year-round; programs begin on Mon.

Accommodations 127 air-conditioned rooms with 1–4 beds each. Modern furnishings, private bath. Semiprivate rooms have partitions, single beds. Daily maid service weekdays. No TV or phone.

Rates 1-week program $814 per person double occupancy, $1,175–$1,754 single. $100 (nonrefundable) payable in advance. Gratuities and tax included. Credit cards: MC, V.

Meal Plans 3 meals served daily (included in Program fee). Low-fat weight-loss diet, nutritionally balanced, controlled portions. Low in salt, fat, sugar; high in complex carbohydrates. Pritikin-style entrées for lunch are turkey loaf, tuna sandwich on wheat bread; dinner includes vegetarian lasagna, pizza with turkey. Salad bar daily.

Services and Facilities **Exercise Equipment:** 11-station weight training gym, 2 PT 6000 and 6 PG 4000 StairMasters, 6 Cateye Exercycles, 14 Challenger treadmills, NordicTrak Quinton cross-country unit, 3 Enduricisers, free weights, Rebounders. **Services:** Massage, aromatherapy, facials, loofah body scrub; hair, nail, and skin care; fitness evaluation; complimentary makeup session and exercise instruction. **Swimming Facilities:** Heated indoor pool. **Recreation Facilities:** Tennis court, indoor racquetball court; horseback riding nearby. **Evening Programs:** Workshops on nutrition and health; line dancing, yoga, cooking class.

In the Area Snow Canyon State Park, Las Vegas, Salt Lake City, Zion National Park.

Getting Here *From Las Vegas.* By car, I–15 to St. George, Bluff St. north to Santa Clara, Sunset Blvd. to Ivins (2 hr). By plane, commuter flights on Skywest Airlines to St. George (45 min). Free pickup from and return to St. George Airport. Van service from/to Vegas available on St. George Shuttle (tel. 801/628–8320) for $30 each way. Taxi, rental car available.

Special Notes No smoking. Remember to bring exercise clothing, aerobic and hiking shoes. Spa open daily 6 AM–9:30 PM.

Pah Tempe Hot Springs Resort

Nonprogram resort
Taking the waters

Utah Deep in a canyon near Zion National Park, hot springs gush
Hurricane from the muddy bottom of the Virgin River to fill a series of pools cut into the rocks surrounding the Pah Tempe resort. Here, bathing is a sybaritic experience for body, mind, and spirit, and conversation comes easily among guests soaking in the warm, sulfur-rich waters or sinking into the mud for a natural body scrub. Swimsuits are required.

Pah Tempe operates as a bed-and-breakfast lodge; meals are served on a terrace overlooking the river, and the primarily vegetarian menu changes seasonally. The resort and the ambience are completely informal, and the inexpensive lodging and camping sites draw many European campers.

Bodywork is available by pre-arrangement, and yoga, water aerobics, and health-related workshops are scheduled from time to time; inquiries and advance planning are necessary for those who want to participate. Travelers who are not staying at the lodge may use the pools, showers, and restaurant for a daily fee ($10). Guides for nature walks, bird-watching, and local archaeology are available to introduce guests to the colorful desert and mountain terrain.

Pah Tempe Hot Springs Resort
825 N. 800 East; Box 35–4,
Hurricane, UT 84737
Tel. 801/635–2879 or 801/635–2353

Administration Managing partner, Ken Anderson

Season Year-round.

Accommodations Cabins and 7 rooms in the lodge accommodate 24 guests; all are furnished simply (no TV or air-conditioning), all have double bed, some have private bath. Private lodge (capacity 20–30) for groups. RV and campsites. No maid service.

Rates $45 per day single, $55–$75 per day for 2, including breakfast; additional person $15, children (age 5 or under) $10. Senior-citizen (63 and older) rates available. RV and camping, $25 single, $35 for 2, $10 additional adult. Rates include use of pools, facilities. Credit cards: MC, V.

Meal Plans Vegetarian menus for breakfast, lunch, dinner. Entrées include lasagna and a spinach and pinenut spanakopita.

Services and Facilities **Services:** Massage, facials, scalp and hair treatments by appointment. **Swimming Facilities:** Outdoor concrete pool with 95° thermal water. **Spa Facilities:** Natural rock pools with circulating thermal water (103°F–106°F), 2 indoor Jacuzzis.

In the Area Zion National Park, Dixie College Amphitheater, Bit 'n Spur Café for country music, Chums factory outlet for sportswear, St. George Mormon Temple (c. 1877).

Getting Here *From St. George.* By car, I–15 to Rte. 9 via Hurricane; entry road at Virgin River Bridge (25 min).

Special Notes No smoking in pool areas or restaurant. Bring old swimwear, beach towel, flashlight.

The Northwest

Native Americans believed long ago that the Great Spirit lived at the earth's center and that steaming hot springs produced "big medicine" waters. Rediscovered by a new generation, the hot springs of the Northwest can be enjoyed in settings of great natural beauty or at large new resort developments. One such sacred spot in Oregon is now the popular resort Kah-Nee-Ta, owned and operated by the Confederated Tribes of the Warm Springs. Wyoming has developed Hot Springs State Park on land near Yellowstone National Park purchased from the Shoshone and Arapahoe Indians. The Sol Duc Hot Springs Resort in Olympic National Park, Washington, is another warm watering spot.

Montana's "big sky" country offers the family-oriented Fairmont Hot Springs Resort and the rustic Chico Hot Springs Lodge, along with 39 ski runs and posh dude ranches. In a verdant valley rich with gold-rush lore outside Fairbanks, Alaska, the sulfur sprites of Chena Hot Springs have welcomed homesteaders and "cheechako" travelers since 1905.

The region's newest destination resort and conference center, Skamania Lodge, has a fitness center overlooking the Columbia River Gorge in Oregon. Welcome to wilderness adventures with workouts and luxury pampering.

Chena Hot Springs Resort

Taking the waters

Alaska
Fairbanks
A soak at the historic Chena Hot Springs Resort near Fairbanks comes accompanied by reminders of pioneer days. There are cabins and pools here that were built in the early 1900s, when most visitors were gold miners who had traveled by dogsled and on horseback in search of relief from rheumatism and arthritis in the hot springs. Images of the miners still smile from the photographs of the Victorian era that decorate the dining room and lounge.

The old-time character of the resort has not changed, despite recent renovations. The bathhouse was rebuilt recently, with tile floors and showers in the locker rooms, and expansive use of glass walls in the pool area. The hot mineral water that bubbles to the surface at 156°F is cooled to a tolerable 110°F in the soaking pools, 90°F for swimming. Thermal water also heats the lodge rooms and three whirlpools.

The cluster of cabins around the main lodge has the general appearance of a mining camp. In the gardens between the steaming ponds, where the spring waters run into a creek, the machinery, carts, and tools that the miners once used have taken on the role of memorabilia. Moose have been spotted wandering on the grounds, and antlers adorn some of the buildings.

A lively crowd from the university in Fairbanks 60 miles down the road comes to ski the nearby slopes and well-marked trails.

Don't expect calorie-counted food or any fancy dietetic dishes.
Wild blueberry daiquiris are the specialty at the bar.

Chena Hot Springs Resort

Chena Hot Springs Rd., Fairbanks, AK 99707
Reservations: Box 73440, Fairbanks, AK 99707
Tel. 907/452-7867
Fax 907/456-3122

Administration	Manager, Frank Rose
Season	Year-round.
Accommodations	54 plainly furnished lodge rooms. Baths private or shared, geothermal hot water, maid service. 7 Trapper Cabins with double and single beds, wood-burning fireplace for heat, propane lights, washbasin, chemical toilet. RV hookup, campsites. Single rooms on request.
Rates	$50-$110 per day for 1-4 persons. $25 per night in advance. Credit cards: AE, DC, MC, V.
Meal Plans	Pancakes with berries, hot cereal for breakfast; generous servings of roast beef, ham, roast turkey for lunch and dinner. Fresh produce in season.
Services and Facilities	**Spa Facilities:** 2 indoor whirlpools, swimming pool, outdoor whirlpool. **Recreation Facilities:** Volleyball court, croquet, horseshoe pitch; fishing, hiking, mountain climbing; downhill and cross-country skiing, ice skating, snowmobiling, sledding.
In the Area	Chena River cruise, University of Alaska at Fairbanks Museum (Native cultures, Gold-rush history).
Getting Here	*From Fairbanks.* By car, Rte. 2 (Steese Hwy.) to Chena Springs Rd. (80 min). Rental car available.
Special Notes	Limited access for people with disabilities. Pool open 8 AM–10 PM ($8 for nonguests).

McKinley Chalet Resort

Nonprogram resort

Alaska
Denali National Park

Overlooking majestic mountains at a scenic turn in the Nenana River, is the McKinley Chalet Resort, consisting of a cluster of chalets, rustic cabins, and a modern mountain lodge in an accessible area of the wilderness of Denali National Park. Guests enjoy free use of the only indoor health club and swimming pool this side of Mt. McKinley. Fitness facilities at the resort's Chalet Club include an exercise room with weights, whirlpool, and sauna, and an aerobics studio is used for classes.

Dominated by Mt. McKinley, the Denali experience is a mixture of rugged outdoor treks and guided bus tours. Naturalists and park rangers accompany trips along park roads that are closed to private cars in the summer. River rafting and a scenic float are other possibilities here.

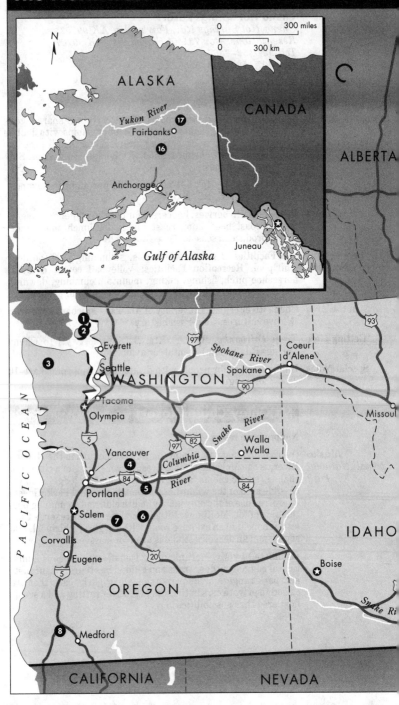

The Northwest

0   300 miles
0   300 km

N

ALASKA

CANADA

ALBERTA

Yukon River   17
Fairbanks

16

Anchorage

Gulf of Alaska

Juneau

1
2
Everett

97   *Spokane River*   Coeur d'Alene

3

Seattle   WASHINGTON   Spokane

90

PACIFIC OCEAN

Tacoma

Olympia

5

Snake River

97   82

Walla Walla

Missoul

Vancouver

4

Columbia   84

5   *River*   84

Portland

Salem   7   6

Corvallis

Eugene

20

IDAHO

Boise

5

OREGON

Snake Ri

8   Medford

CALIFORNIA   NEVADA

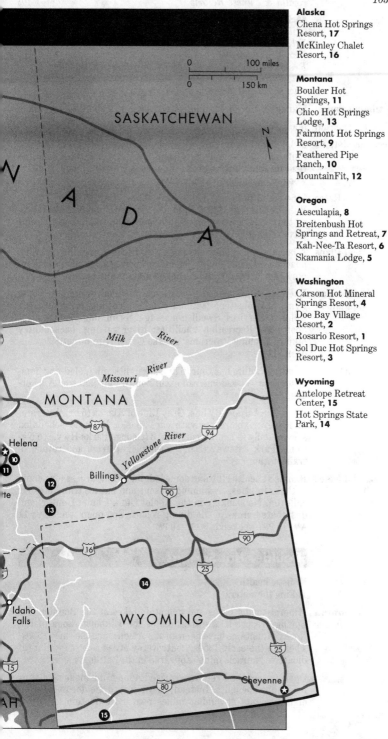

Alaska
Chena Hot Springs
Resort, **17**
McKinley Chalet
Resort, **16**

Montana
Boulder Hot
Springs, **11**
Chico Hot Springs
Lodge, **13**
Fairmont Hot Springs
Resort, **9**
Feathered Pipe
Ranch, **10**
MountainFit, **12**

Oregon
Aesculapia, **8**
Breitenbush Hot
Springs and Retreat, **7**
Kah-Nee-Ta Resort, **6**
Skamania Lodge, **5**

Washington
Carson Hot Mineral
Springs Resort, **4**
Doe Bay Village
Resort, **2**
Rosario Resort, **1**
Sol Duc Hot Springs
Resort, **3**

Wyoming
Antelope Retreat
Center, **15**
Hot Springs State
Park, **14**

McKinley Chalet Resort

Milepost 239 Parks Hwy. Denali Park, AK 99755
Tel. 907/683–2215
Fax 907/683–2398
Reservations: Box 202516, Anchorage, AK 99520
Tel. 907/683–2215
Fax 907/258-3668

Administration Manager, Margaret Kelly; club manager, Deborah Kingston

Season May–Sept.

Accommodations 288 deluxe 2-room suites in alpine chalets, with hotel service. Suites include simply furnished sitting rooms with sofa and reading chair, 2 twin beds (or double with twin), modern bath, wooden balconies and walkways.

Rates $154 for 2 persons, double occupancy. Daily 7-hour Tundra Wildlife bus tour, $49 per person; 3-hour Denali Natural History tour, $27 per person. 1-night's lodging in advance. Credit cards: AE, MC, V.

Meal Plans À la carte menu offers fresh salmon baked and grilled, salads, poached halibut, roast leg of lamb, pasta, steaks, chicken, pork. For breakfast, home-baked muffins and breads.

Services and Equipment **Exercise Equipment:** 10-station Universal weight training gym, StairMaster, stationary bikes, rowing machine, free weights. **Services:** Swedish massage. **Swimming Facilities:** Indoor pool. **Recreation Facilities:** River rafting, backcountry hiking. **Evening Programs:** Alaska Cabin Nite buffet $29, children $17.

In the Area Tundra Wildlife bus tour (6 hr), air sightseeing, sled-dog demonstration, Vistadome rail excursion to Fairbanks or Anchorage.

Getting Here *From Anchorage.* By bus, Gray Line of Alaska (5 hr). By train, McKinley Explorer private car, Alaska Railroad scheduled service daily (6 hr). By car, Rte. 3 (George Parks Hwy.) to National Park gateway (5 hr). Free pickup from and return to train station.

Special Notes Ramps at health club and some lodgings allow access for people with disabilities. Swimming lessons and nature trail hikes for children. No smoking in the Chalet Club, Chalet Center, and designated areas of the dining rooms. Spa open weekdays 11 AM–10 PM, weekends 9 AM–10 PM.

Boulder Hot Springs

Holistic health
Taking the waters

Montana
Boulder
Mineral-spring baths and mountain hikes at the Boulder Hot Springs resort in the foothills of the Elkhorn range of the Rocky Mountains have been an attraction since the early 1800s. Then, in the early 1950s, controversy arose as stories of a radioactive "miracle mine" appeared in the national media.

Operators of the Free Enterprise Radon Mine make no claims for medical benefits. Instead, they point to the documentation of treatments at similar mines near Bad Gastein, Austria, where more than 7,000 patients a year breathe radon under medical supervision.

Those who come to the Free Enterprise mine seeking relief from asthma, arthritis, bursitis, and other forms of chronic, crippling pain bundle up in sweaters and coats and stretch out in deck chairs to breathe the radon gas and drink the radioactive water. Some visitors have claimed to experience improved freedom of movement and relief from pain after a week.

As for the degree of radioactivity involved, the Montana Health Department says that guests are exposed to less than 10% of the maximum legal allowance of radiation to which miners may be exposed. No authoritative medical evaluation of the theraputic value of the mines has been established.

Located 3 miles from the hotel and 85 feet below ground, the mine is surprisingly dry and comfortable. A large elevator, capable of handling wheelchairs, descends to well-lighted, timbered tunnels equipped with warming lamps. Visits last a maximum of 80 minutes, and a series of up to 32 treatments is suggested. The temperature of the mineral water is 175°F when it reaches ground level. It's pure enough to drink, but it does have the effect of a laxative and diuretic. Call the mine office (tel. 406/225-3383) for more information.

Boulder Hot Springs
Box 1020, Boulder, MT 59632
Tel. 406/225-4339

Administration	Manager, Barbara Reiter
Season	Year-round.
Accommodations	7 bedrooms in turn-of-the-century mansion. Furnishings have a well-worn look: heavy wooden pieces, oversize beds, old-fashioned baths. Hostel beds, camp sites, RV connections available.
Rates	$40–$60 single, $60–85 for 2 persons. RV $10. Credit cards: MC, V.
Meal Plans	Breakfast included in lodging rate. Hotel restaurant only serves groups.
Services and Facilities	**Services:** Massage (acupressure, deep-muscle), biofeedback therapy, consultation on nutrition and health. **Swimming Facilities:** Naturally heated outdoor mineral-water pool. **Spa Facilities:** Separate men's and women's bathhouses have hot and cold plunge pools. **Recreation Facilities:** Hiking, fishing; cross-country skiing.
In the Area	Glacier National Park, Lewis and Clark Caverns, Montana State Capitol in Helena, Yellowstone National Park.
Getting Here	*From Helena.* By car, I–15 to Boulder, Hwy. 69 to Boulder Springs (40 min). Free pickup from and return to Helena or Butte. Service to the radon mine. Rental car available.
Special Notes	Limited access for people with disabilities. No smoking in dining room.

Chico Hot Springs Lodge

Taking the waters

Montana
Pray

After a day in the saddle, the prospect of a hot soak makes sore muscles bearable. There's nothing glamorous about the Chico Hot Springs Lodge, but the two hot-springs pools on its 157-acre grounds encourage many visitors to Yellowstone Park to detour. Located about 30 miles from the park's northern gateway, the resort offers horseback riding and pack trips into the Gallatin National Forest and the Absaroka range of the Rockies.

Surrounded by spectacular mountain scenery, the open-air pools are fed by 110°F untreated mineral water from several springs. Four private areas in the bathhouse have redwood hot tubs large enough for a family of four. Rustic facilities are available for changing; bring a towel if you're not staying at the ranch. The pools are open to the public as well as to registered guests, and as you soak you might even spot deer on the slopes.

Chico Hot Springs Lodge
Pray, MT 59065
Tel. 406/333-4933

Administration	Managers, Michael and Eve Art
Season	Year-round.
Accommodations	52 rooms in the main lodge, 12 motel units, several family-size condominium apartments in A-frame cabins. Lodge rooms have Western furnishings, twin beds, private or shared bath.
Rates	Lodge rooms $39–$69, motel room $59 for 2 persons per day. 2-bedroom cabin $69–$74 per day. $179–$275 in condominium. Confirmation by credit card. Credit cards: MC, V.
Meal Plans	À la carte lunch menu includes grilled fish, salad, fruit plate; dinner entrées can be roast venison, saddle of lamb, grilled or sautéed trout.
Services and Facilities	**Swimming Facilities:** Mineral-water outdoor pool. **Spa Facilities:** 4 private tubs, 2 outdoor pools, Jacuzzi. **Recreation Facilities:** Boating, trout fishing (private lake), horseback riding; cross-country skiing, snowmobiling, mountain bike rental.
In the Area	Trail rides; Yellowstone National Park; Crow Indian Reservation, river float trips.
Getting Here	*From Bozeman.* By car, I–90 to Hwy. 89 (2 hr).

Fairmont Hot Springs Resort

Taking the waters

Montana
Anaconda

Big Sky country and big springs come together here. Nestled near the Pintlar Wilderness in an area of boundless views and numerous springs, the Fairmont Hot Springs Resort combines striking modern architecture and Western hospitality. The range of amenities and activities makes it ideal for a family vacation in summer or a skiing holiday in winter.

Native Americans worshiped the "medicine water" of the natural hot springs. The mineral water, 160°F when it surfaces, is treated and cooled for the two Olympic-size swimming pools and the indoor and outdoor soaking pools. Resort facilities include men's and women's steambaths but no bodywork. There are many organized activities to keep children busy.

Fairmont Hot Springs Resort

1500 Fairmont Rd., Anaconda, MT 59711
Tel. 406/797–3241, 800/443–2381, or 800/332–3272 in MT

Administration Manager, Edward Henrich

Season Year-round.

Accommodations 135 guest rooms in the lodge; time-share condominium apartment rentals. Double beds, quality furnishings, private bath. RV hookup, campsites.

Rates Rooms $72–$87, depending on season; suites $175–$295; condominium $105–$195 for 1 or 2 persons. 1 night payable in advance. Credit cards: AE, D, MC, V.

Meal Plans Standard American breakfast and dinner in the restaurant.

Services and Facilities **Swimming Facilities:** Outdoor and indoor Olympic-size pools. **Spa Facilities:** Large soaking pools, indoor and outdoor. **Recreation Facilities:** 2 tennis courts, 18-hole golf course, horseback riding, hayrides; trout fishing, cross-country skiing, sleigh rides.

In the Area Yellowstone National Park, Glacier National Park, Discovery Basin (downhill skiing).

Getting Here *From Butte.* By car, I–90 (15 min). Complimentary transportation by lodge van. Rental car available.

Special Notes Limited access for people with disabilities. Hayrides, sleigh rides for children. Pools open 24 hours.

Feathered Pipe Ranch

Holistic health
Spiritual awareness

Montana
Helena

Feathered Pipe Ranch is a magical place that sets spirits soaring, and attracts world-renowned teachers and practitioners. Almost every week from spring to autumn sees an intensive program here on subjects as diverse as astrology, women's studies, shamanism, massage training, and Iyengar yoga. Since 1975 people from many backgrounds, professionals in the healing arts, and novice students have been coming here to gain new ideas and experiences and to attend workshops in yoga and holistic health. The number of participants ranges from 35 to 50, and some families attend with young children.

Located in the Montana Rockies close to the Continental Divide, the retreat sits on land that was once inhabited by a Native American tribe. Climbing to "sacred rocks" for meditation, you gain a panoramic view of the 110-acre ranch. Miles of hiking trails, a sparkling lake and stream, and the dry, clear air make a heady combination that can generate a tremendous feeling of release.

Log and stone buildings give the impression of a frontier outpost. Beyond the main lodge are Native American tepees, Mongolian yurts, cabins (some with bath), and basic tents. A cedar bathhouse holds huge hot tubs, a sauna, and a massage room staffed by professional therapists.

The search for insight is the ranch's principal attraction. Serious concentration is the norm here, with little of the fun-and-fitness holiday atmosphere.

Feathered Pipe Ranch
2409 Colorado Gulch, Helena, MT 59601
Tel. 406/443-0430
Foundation programs: Box 1682, Helena, MT 59624
Tel. 406/442-8196
Fax 406/442-8110

Administration	Executive director, India Supera; seminars director, Katherine Smith
Season	Late Apr.–Sept.
Accommodations	4 dormitory rooms with bunk beds for 2–6 people in the main lodge. Linens, blankets, towels provided. Tents, yurts, campsites; 6 cabins (3 with bath); tepees sleep 2 persons each.
Rates	1-week program $1,025 in dormitory, $1,325–$1,525 per person in cabin. Lodging, meals, instruction included. $300 payable in advance. Credit cards (4% surcharge): MC, V.
Meal Plans	3 gourmet vegetarian meals daily, cafeteria style. Organically grown produce. Breakfast includes yogurt, home-baked bread or muffins, fresh fruit; lunch may be tuna-fish salad with pita bread, green salad, or pasta with vegetables; typical dinner selections are baked trout, eggplant and cheese casserole, zucchini baked with tomatoes. Special diets accommodated.
Services and Facilities	**Services:** Massage, bodywork. **Swimming Facilities:** Mountain lake. **Recreation Facilities:** Volleyball, hiking. **Evening Programs:** Talks related to study programs; entertainment.
In the Area	Helena historical area and shopping; Gates of the Mountains boat tour, hot springs.
Getting Here	*From Helena.* By car I–15 (15 min). Rental car and limo available. Van service ($30 round-trip) is provided by the resort upon request.
Special Notes	No smoking indoors. Remember to bring flashlight, sun protection. Lodging only for program participants.

MountainFit

Sports conditioning

Montana
Bozeman

The week-long MountainFit programs in Montana combine strenuous exercise and scenic beauty. Hard-core hikers can enjoy challenging treks in Yellowstone National Park, the Absaroka-Beartooth Wilderness, and along the Bridger Range, where the peaks rise above 9,000 feet.

Each day's route, selected from among 25 charted hikes, is geared to the average capability of group members (usually guests choose between two destinations), who range in age from 30 to 70 and may include both beginners and experienced hikers. Outfitted with lunch, snacks, and fannypack, their water bottles refilled and frozen nightly, a group of 6–10 hikers sets off daily with a leader and a guide at the rear. South-central Montana offers forests of tall lodgepole pines, alpine meadows carpeted with rare ferns and bear grass, limestone cliffs with the fossil remains of marine animals, and living deer, moose, mountain goats, elk, bison, golden eagles, and cutthroat trout. Staffers recount local lore and identify plants and wildlife en route.

Safety is a priority: Hikes are registered with park rangers, while the staff carries two-way radio equipment and checks individuals regularly for foot blisters or signs of stress.

Based at the Gallatin Gateway Inn, a historic railroad hotel, the six-day program includes spa cuisine with regional produce and perhaps game. Yoga instruction and hiking are major parts of the program. (Transportation to the trailheads is provided.)

MountainFit

Gallatin Gateway Inn, Bozeman, MT 59715
Reservations: 633 Battery St., San Francisco, CA 94111
Tel. 415/397-6216 or 800/926-5700

Administration	Owner and director, Diane Wechsler
Season	June–Sept.; scheduled every week.
Accommodations	6-room lodge (2 doubles, 4 singles), with brass beds, flowered comforters, and matching curtains; each bedroom has a large, modern bathroom. No air-conditioning, TV, or phone.
Rates	$1,750 for shared room; Sun.–Sat. program includes meals, outings. Single supplement $445. $300 nonrefundable deposit on reservation; balance due 30 days before start of program. Credit cards: AE.
Meal Plans	Daily menu of 1,200–1,500 calories. Breakfast choices are freshly baked muffins, cereals, fruit, pancakes. Trail lunch consists of cold gazpacho soup, couscous salad, peanut butter and jelly sandwiches, fruit. A typical dinner, served family style, includes green salad, homemade pasta, salmon poached or baked in phyllo crust, asparagus tips, 4-grain pilaf, sorbet dessert.
Services and Facilities	**Services:** Massage. **Swimming Facilities:** Outdoor pool. **Recreation Facilities:** 2 tennis courts, Jacuzzi. **Evening Programs:** Lecture-demonstrations, films.
In the Area	Lewis & Clark Caverns, Chico Hot Springs Resort, Yellowstone River; Yellowstone and Grand Teton national parks; Museum of the Rockies.
Getting Here	*From Bozeman.* Participants' transportation provided on arrival and departure (30 min). By car, I-90, Hwys. 10/191 (30 mins).
Special Notes	No smoking in lodge. Hiking boots required; bathrobe provided. Daily maid service.

Aesculapia

Holistic health
Spiritual awareness

Oregon
Wilderville

Named after the Greek god of healing and ancient dream temples, Aesculapia is a retreat that teaches self-healing. Visitors take part in shamanistic ritual, hike in the woods, or meditate in a sanctuary cabin.

Located on 80 acres of mountain wilderness in the Siskiyou Mountains of southwest Oregon, Aesculapia fosters the visionary experience of founder-director Graywolf (Fred) Swinney. Dream-healing sessions help participants examine visionary experiences. Among special events scheduled are spring and fall weeks devoted to healing communion, weekend retreats, and a two-week combination of spiritual and outdoor adventure that climaxes with a journey on the Rogue River.

Guided by Graywolf, the wilderness quest begins with 3–4 days of mental and physical training, including a sweat lodge ceremony, drumming, meditation, and discussions of dreams. After a few days on the river, you are challenged by whitewater rapids. There are evening campfires and mornings devoted to sharing dreams before you return to Aesculapia and prepare for the outer world.

Aesculapia
Box 301, Wilderville, OR 97543
Tel. 503/476–0492

Administration Founder-director, Graywolf (Fred) Swinney

Season Year-round.

Accommodations Rustic, 4-bedroom house and 4 cabins. Guests bring their own towels, blankets. Campsites and tents available.

Rates 1-week retreat $550, 2-week retreat with Whitewater Wilderness Quest $1,100, 2-day sanctuary $100. 1 night payable in advance. No credit cards. Work-scholarship aid available.

Meal Plans All meals included in retreat price. Vegetarian meals, fresh fruit and produce in season.

Services and Facilities **Services:** Massage; counseling on nutrition and health. **Swimming Facilities:** Lake. **Recreation Facilities:** Hiking. **Evening Programs:** Informal workshops, rituals.

In the Area Ocean beaches, vineyard tours, hot springs; Shakespeare Festival (July–Aug.); Rogue River (white-water rafting); Kalmiopsis Wilderness (hiking).

Getting Here *From Eugene.* By bus, Greyhound to Medford (2 hr). By car, I–5 south to Grants Pass (90 min), Hwy. 199. Rental car available.

Breitenbush Hot Springs and Retreat

Holistic health
Spiritual awareness
Taking the waters

Oregon
Detroit

The Esalen of the Northwest, the Breitenbush Hot Springs and Retreat is a holistic community for groups and individuals; its rustic cabins cluster on the banks of the Breitenbush River, surrounded by the Willamette National Forest. The daily schedule begins at 7 AM with meditation, then stretching classes. Participation is optional, no charge. Bodywork services at the bathhouse are moderately priced.

The hot mineral waters are a major attraction: Natural springs and artesian wells supply 180°F water for the steam bath and outdoor pools. At an idyllic spot in the woods, the water flows through four hydrojet pools for alfresco baths with adjustable temperatures. In the meadow you can dip into footbaths where the hot mineral water flows naturally.

Beyond sybaritic pleasures, the community is dedicated to fostering personal health and spiritual growth. Visitors can join daily well-being workshops and ceremonies, even experience a meditation pyramid and a Native American sweat lodge. A sanctuary building provides space for a private retreat.

Cabins are simply furnished, with only a sheet on the bed. Bring your own blankets, sheets, and towels. Nights can get cold during summer, so no air-conditioning is needed.

Breitenbush Hot Springs and Retreat
Box 578, Detroit, OR 97342
Tel. 503/854–3314
Fax 503/854–3819

Administration Manager, Ross McKeen

Season Year-round.

Accommodations 40 cabins for 2–4 people, bath with toilet, no air-conditioning, TV, or telephone. Sheets and towels can be rented. 20 tents with mattresses, some bare campsites.

Rates $45–$55 a day in shared room includes meals. Private cabin with bathroom $75. Tent $35–$40, campsite $30–$35 with meals. 1 night payable in advance. Credit cards: MC, V.

Meal Plans Ovo-lacto vegetarian diet. Breakfast is granola, hot cereal of mixed grains, yogurt, fruit, and home-baked wheat breads. Lunch can be a salad with sprouts or tuna fish, vegetarian pizza. Dinner entrées may include lasagna, Mexican casserole, or vegetarian pizza. Special diets accommodated.

Services and Facilities **Services:** Massage, hydrotherapy, aromatherapy, herbal wrap; counseling on health and healing. **Swimming Facilities:** Outdoor pool to be renovated; glacial river. **Spa Facilities:** 4 outdoor tiled pools, indoor hot tubs. **Recreation Facilities:** Hiking; cross-country skiing. **Evening Programs:** Workshops on health and nutrition.

In the Area Native American cultural center at Warm Springs Indian Reservation; Mt. Hood National Forest, Mt. Jefferson Wilderness.

Getting Here *From Portland.* By car, I–5 south to Salem, Hwy. 22 to Detroit, Hwy. 46 to Breitenbush (2 hr). By bus, Greyhound (3 hr).

Special Notes Smoking only in designated outdoor areas. Remember to bring a flashlight.

Kah-Nee-Ta Resort

Taking the waters

Oregon
Warm Springs
The Kah-Nee-Ta Resort, owned and managed by a confederation of tribes whose ancestors once worshiped at the springs on their reservation, strikes a delicate balance between tradition and modernity. Guests are invited to tribal ceremonies and festivals and to a salmon-bake feast. Huge swimming pools attract families, and bathhouses offer private soaks and a massage.

The imposing guest lodge and conference center, opened in 1968, sit atop a rocky ridge overlooking the Warm Springs River and a recreation complex. Open to the public, the Indian village of tepees and vacation villas offers mineral baths and pools, a golf course, tennis courts, and stables. Trails for biking, hiking, and riding fan out toward the distant Cascade Mountains on the 60,000-acre reservation.

All activities are priced à la carte, and the fees are modest: $20 ($15 for teenagers) for an hour on horseback, $5 for a 25-minute mineral bath. Arrangements can be made on short notice on any day of the week. In the separate men's and women's bathhouses, the five tiled sunken tubs are refilled after each use. The odorless mineral water is piped in at 140°F and cooled to suit the bathers.

Kah-Nee-Ta Resort
Box K, Warm Springs, OR 97761
Tel. 503/553–1112 or 800/554–4786
Fax 503/553–1071

Administration Manager, Ron A. Malfara

Season Year-round.

Accommodations 139 luxury rooms in the cedar lodge, 25 cottages in the village, and furnished tepees accommodate 325. Lodge rooms have balconies with views, oversize beds, full bath, air-conditioning, TV, telephone; 2-bedroom suites have fireplace in living room. Campsites, RV and trailer hookup available. Tepees each accommodate 10 campers.

Rates Lodge rooms $89.95–$99.95 per day, single or double; suites (2 bedrooms) $159.95–$179.95; cottages $123.95 for up to 4 persons. Tepee $49.95 for 1–3 persons, $12 for additional persons. RV hookup $28–$32. Prices include tax. 1 night payable in advance. Credit cards: AE, DC, MC, V.

Meal Plans No meal plan offered, but guests can dine on a variety of dishes in the lodge dining room.

Services and Facilities Services: Massage. **Swimming Facilities:** Olympic-size outdoor pool (village), outdoor pool (lodge). **Spa Facilities:** 5 tiled Roman tubs in men's and women's bathhouses. **Recreation Facilities:** 2 tennis courts, 18-hole golf course, horseback riding, trout fishing, mountain-bike rental. **Evening Programs:** Drumming, ceremonies, rituals; salmon bake.

In the Area Nature walks with resident naturalist; Mt. Hood National Forest, the Dalles recreation area, white-water rafting on the Deschutes River; American Indian Museum.

Getting Here *From Portland.* By car, Hwy. 26 east to Warm Springs (2½ hr). By air, scheduled commercial service to Redmond (30 min); private and charter flights land at Madras Airport 25 mi away. Rental car available.

Special Notes Limited access for people with disabilities. No smoking in pool area and designated dining areas.

Skamania Lodge

Nonprogram resort

Oregon
Columbia Gorge

The panoramic sweep of the Cascade Mountains and the mighty Columbia River welcomes visitors to the new Skamania Lodge, built on a ridge in the Gorge National Scenic Area, 45 minutes from Portland. This is a dramatic area, well known for the blustery winds that blow through the Gorge and make it a thriving center for sailboarding. But the history of this region long predates the construction of the first windsurfer: This is Chinook tribe territory, and Skamania Lodge's architecture helps convey the past. Creating the casual, calming interior are Native American–style rugs, Pendleton fabrics, and mission-style wood furnishings. A stone fireplace dominates the three-story Great Room, close to the library and dining room.

A midweek spa package includes dinner and two treatments, as well as use of the sports facilities, but there are no aerobics classes. Guests can use a coed Jacuzzi and two tennis courts outside; and indoors is a 60-foot lap pool with its own waterfall. Adjoining the men's and women's locker rooms are saunas and whirlpools, and two massage rooms. The spa is open 6 AM to 11 PM, and the fitness center has a trainer on staff. You may use the fitness center for $6 a day.

Also on the grounds is a 18-hole golf course that winds through the forest. Guided trail rides on horseback ($20 per hour) are reserved through the lodge's guest services desk. In winter trails are groomed for cross-country skiing. For some great scenery, head out to the lush botanical areas and waterfalls.

Skamania Lodge
Box 189, Stevenson, WA 98648
Tel. 509/427–7700 or 800/221–7117
Fax 509/427–2547

Administration General manager, Ian Muirdon; spa manager Shelly Arrowood

Season Year-round.

Accommodations 195 rooms, 39 with fireplace. All have contemporary and mission-style wooden furniture, full modern bathroom, air-conditioning, TV, phone. Amenities include terry-cloth robes, coffee maker.

Rates 1-night spa package for 2, $129; daily $85–$155 for singles or doubles. Add tax, gratuity. Credit cards: AE, DC, MC, V.

Meal Plans   No spa menu. The dining room serves fine Pacific Northwest cuisine, such as coulibiac of salmon and halibut, sea bass with corn and clam sauce, Dungeness crab legs, roast leg of venison with wild berry relish, buffalo fillet.

Services and Facilities   **Exercise Equipment**: Apollo multipurpose gym, 3 Lifestride treadmills, 2 Bodyguard stairsteppers, 2 Arrow rowers, 6 Tunturi bikes, Fonday step unit. **Services**: Massage. **Swimming Facilities**: Indoor 60-ft lap pool. **Recreation Facilities**: 2 tennis courts outdoor, unlit; 18-hole golf course with driving range, mountain bike rental, volleyball court, horseback riding, trail hikes.

In the Area   Mt. St. Helens Volcanic Monument, Mt. Hood Railroad, sternwheeler river cruise, Bonneville Dam, the Dalles recreation area, Maryhill Museum (European art and fashion).

Getting Here   *From Portland*: By car, I-84 east to Bridge of the Gods, or Hwy. 14 (45 min).

Special Notes   Minimum age in spa: 16.

Carson Hot Mineral Springs Resort

Taking the waters

Washington
Carson   The claw-foot enamel tubs are characteristic of the old-fashioned friendliness bathers enjoy at the Carson Hot Mineral Springs Resort. Proud of using "the same bath methods for over 100 years," the management strives to remain unpretentious and comfortable. The rustic cabins, a landmark hotel, and bathhouses located on the banks of the Wind River near its junction with the mighty Columbia date from 1876. The oldest remaining structure, a two-story wood hotel, was built in 1897 to accommodate bathers who traveled by steamboat from Portland, Oregon. The cabins were built in the early 1920s.

Taking the waters is a simple, two-step procedure: A tub soak is followed by the traditional sweat wrap, in which an attendant wraps bathers in sheets and heavy blankets to induce a good sweat. Separate bathhouses for men and women offer some privacy.

The 126°F mineral water is piped directly into the tubs (eight for men, six for women), which are drained and refilled after each use. The water is not treated with chemicals; analysis shows it to be high in sodium and calcium, like springs at principal European spas. The crowning touch is the hour-long massage ($26–$32).

Carson Hot Mineral Springs Resort
Box 370, Carson, WA 98610
Tel. 509/427–8292

Administration   Manager, Rudy Beilkowsky

Season   Year-round.

Accommodations   9 large hotel rooms, 23 cabins, all simply furnished with double beds. No private bath, TV, or telephone. Cabin rooms have toilet and sink, kitchenette.

Rates   Rooms $29–$34 and cabins $31–$36 for 2 persons, $5 each additional person. 1 night payable in advance. Credit cards: MC, V.

Meal Plans No meal plan available. The hotel restaurant serves 3 hearty meals daily, à la carte. Lunch menu includes pasta salad, beef lasagna, vegetarian sandwiches. Dinner entrées are a vegetarian "gardenburger," fruit platter, grilled salmon, steak, ham.

Services and Facilities **Services:** Massage. **Spa Facilities:** Individual tubs in men's and women's bathhouses ($6). **Recreation Facilities:** Hiking, fishing, golf.

In the Area River trips, the Dalles recreation area, Bonneville Dam, Shakespeare Festival (summer), Portland museums and cultural centers, 18-hole golf course.

Getting Here *From Portland.* By car, I–84 east to Bridge of the Gods, Rte. 14 to Carson (70 min).

Special Notes Limited access for people with disabilities. No smoking in the bathhouses.

Doe Bay Village Resort

Taking the waters

Washington The hot tubs at the rustic Doe Bay Village Resort afford spec-
Orcas Island tacular views of the San Juan Islands, and the constant, 106°F temperature of the mineral water from nearby springs protects bathers from the chilly mist. Waterfalls, the ocean, hidden beaches, and a sauna with stained-glass windows help to create a special feeling of seclusion and communion.

Native Americans were the first to make a sanctuary here. Loggers and trappers came to enjoy the springs and a tavern in the town, where a general store and post office have operated since the early 1900s. In time the area became an artists' colony and a human-potential center; today the resort is a laid-back haven for people who love bathing in hot springs, hiking, kayaking, and participating in other outdoor activities. A large number of day visitors come here by ferry from the mainland for a soak at the springs.

The open-air hot tubs at the resort are equipped with Jacuzzi jets; two have hot water, one is naturally cold. A wood deck surrounds the bathing complex, which is attached to a big sauna hut in which 20 people can enjoy the wood-fired heat comfortably. The price for eight hours is $6 (including parking if you drove over from the ferry). Bring your own towels.

The paint is peeling and the plumbing doesn't always work, but the prices are reasonable. There are campsites (with communal baths and showers) for those who go for seclusion in the woods. Some sites have a dome of plastic sheeting for protection from the rain. Hostel-style dormitory beds at $10, and a Retreat House for $50, accommodate groups and individuals.

Doe Bay Village Resort
Star Rte. 86, Olga, WA 98279
Tel. 206/376–2291 or 206/376–4755
Fax 206/376–3637

Administration Management committee

Season Year-round.

Accommodations	Rustic cabins for up to 100 guests range from duplexes to large cottages with private shower, heat, and bedding. No maid service, TV, telephone. Campsites, tents, RV hookups ($16) and dormitory lodging ($10.50) available.
Rates	Cottages $40.50–$91 a day for singles or doubles; $10.50 per additional person. 1 night payable in advance. Credit cards: AE, MC, V.
Meal Plans	Vegetarian cuisine, chicken, seafood à la carte.
Services and Facilities	**Services:** Massage, kayaking instruction. **Swimming Facilities:** Ocean beach, mountain lake. **Spa Facilities:** 3 outdoor tubs, steam room, Jacuzzi. **Recreation Facilities:** Guided kayak tours, fishing, hiking, golf, tennis nearby.
In the Area	Ferry trips to nearby islands; whale-watching boat trips; Seattle museums and cultural life; Olympic National Park.
Getting Here	*From Seattle.* By car, I–5 to Mt. Vernon, ferry from Anacortes. Drive through Olga to east end of the island (3 hr).

Rosario Resort

Nonprogram resort

Washington
Orcas Island

Sea-inspired treatments for the body and the seaside setting are the lure of the Rosario Resort, built around the former mansion of the shipbuilder Robert Moran. Many of the guest lodges and public rooms have a nautical look; portholes and other parts salvaged from old ships pop up in the indoor swimming pool and other unexpected places. An organ room with a spectacular cathedral ceiling and stained-glass windows is the setting for concerts and lectures.

The resort has a small indoor spa with whirlpool, coed sauna, aerobics studio, and weights room. The daily schedule includes low-impact and aquatic aerobics, dance exercise, stretching and toning (flexercise) calisthenics, and yoga. Spa services are reserved on an à la carte basis; use of the spa is free.

Simple pleasures, such as hunting for driftwood on the 2-mile-long beach, wandering in the pine woods, and relaxing in the sauna, attract most visitors. Families with children, senior citizens, and fitness buffs come for a few days or weeks. Canada, the Rockies, and sophisticated Vancouver are a few hours' drive north; charming Victoria is just 7 miles away by water. Orcas Island is protected by hills on one side, warmed by the Japanese current of the Pacific Ocean on the other. The winters are mild and see no snow accumulation.

Rosario Resort
Eastsound, Orcas Island, WA 98245
Tel. 206/376–2222 or 800/562–8820

Administration	Owner-manager, Sarah Geiser; spa director, Pamela Edwards
Season	Year-round.
Accommodations	179 rooms, condominium apartments, villas, all with country antique furnishings, modern beds, private bath, color TV, air-conditioning, patio; studios have a fireplace. No room service.

Rates Double rooms $63–$210 per couple. Add 7.5% tax. 1 night payable in advance. Credit cards: AE, DC, MC, V.

Meal Plans Menu à la carte in the Orcas Room. Lunch can be a green salad dressed with fresh fruit juice and cayenne pepper or chicken baked in romaine lettuce. Dinner entrées may include grilled salmon with peppercorn, basil, and red-pepper sauce; veal topped with crab and asparagus. Special diets on request.

Services and Facilities **Exercise Equipment:** 4-station Marcy weights unit, 4-station Apollo II gym, Precor rower, stepmachine, 2 Lifecycles, NordicTrack, Rebounders, dumbbells (3–50 lbs.). **Services:** Massage (Swedish, shiatsu, reflexology), facials, salt-glow body scrub, pedicure, manicure; full-service beauty salon. **Swimming Facilities:** 2 outdoor pools, indoor pool, ocean beach, mountain lake. **Recreation Facilities:** 2 tennis courts, hiking; 9-hole golf course nearby; marina; kayaking center.

In the Area Whale-watching boat trips, kayaking excursions, ferry trips; island crafts and antiques shops in Eastsound; Orcas Island Historical Museum. Seattle; Vancouver; Olympic National Park, Doe Bay Hot Springs.

Getting Here *From Seattle.* By car, I–5 to Mt. Vernon, ferry from Anacortes to Eastsound (2½ hr). By plane, scheduled flights to Rosario Resort in Eastsound by Kenmore Air (tel. 800/543–9595); by seaplane (60 min). Van service to the ferry landing provided by Rosano Resort, to and from Eastsound.

Special Notes Limited access for people with disabilities; some ground-floor rooms wheelchair accessible. No smoking in the spa or in designated dining areas.

Sol Duc Hot Springs Resort

Taking the waters

Washington
Olympic National Park

Here's the place to bring the family for a soak and a swim after a drive or a hike in Olympic National Park. Located within the park, the Sol Duc Hot Springs Resort maintains public and private pools, including four indoor whirlpools, filled with mineral water that flows from springs on federal land.

Piped into a heat exchanger at a temperature of 123°F, the mineral water is cooled for use in the three large outdoor soaking pools. The water's continuous flow into the pools makes chlorination unnecessary. Creek water is heated and treated for the large outdoor swimming pool.

Operating as a concession of the Department of the Interior, the resort has been updated and expanded in recent years.

Sol Duc Hot Springs Resort
Soleduc River Rd., Olympic National Park, WA
Reservations: Box 2169, Port Angeles, WA 98362
Tel. 206/327–3583

Administration Manager, Connie Langley

Season May–Oct.

Accommodations 32 cabins with double bed (or twin beds and sofa bed), 6 with kitchen, all with modern bath. RV sites. No TV, telephone, dresser, or air-conditioning.

Rates Cabin with kitchen $89.08 day, without kitchen $80.46, including tax, for 2 persons. 1 night payable in advance. Credit cards: AE, MC, V.

Meal Plans Vegetarian, fish, and chicken dishes. Granola, yogurt, smoked salmon omelet, buckwheat pancakes with fresh berries for breakfast; burgers and deli selections for lunch; charbroiled chicken, baked cod with mushrooms, steaks, steamed vegetable platter, or zucchini-cheese casserole for dinner.

Services and Facilities **Swimming Facilities:** Large public pool. **Spa Facilities:** 4 indoor whirlpools, outdoor soaking pools. **Recreation Facilities:** Fishing, hiking. **Evening Programs:** Talks by park rangers.

In the Area Nature hikes with park rangers. Seattle museums, cultural centers, Pioneer Square (Klondike Gold Rush museum).

Getting Here *From Seattle.* By car, Hwy. 101 to Fairholm, Soleduc Rd. 11 mi to resort (4 hr). By car ferry, scheduled service to Winslow, Hwy. 101 to Soleduc Rd. (2 hr).

Special Notes Ramps at geothermal pools allow access for people with disabilities; rooms are wheelchair accessible. Nature walks for children with park ranger. No smoking in the bathhouse.

Antelope Retreat Center

Holistic health
Spiritual awareness

Wyoming
Savery
An isolated ranch in the foothills of the Continental Divide, the Antelope Retreat Center puts you to work preparing meals, joining in ranch chores, and gardening. Among the special weekly programs are vision quests based on the Native American rite of passage, which include a three-day wilderness fast, and a nature-awareness week devoted to learning survival skills while camping in the Red Desert and Medicine Bow National Forest. Focus programs include gender weeks, with a personal sojourn in the desert; and Sacred Hoop week, which involves exploring Dakota traditions.

John Boyer grew up on the ranch, founding the retreat center in 1986 to share his love of nature and the inner quiet learned from neighboring Native Americans. Guests are initiated at a sweat-lodge ceremony and taught personal awareness exercises. Some even get to help with lambing the small herd of sheep.

Antelope Retreat Center
Box 166, Savery, WY 82332
Tel. 307/383–2625

Administration General manager, John Boyer; program directors, Gina Lyman and Tom Barnes

Season Year-round.

Accommodations 16 guests in the ranch house in 4 bedrooms, plus 2 4-bed native yurts. Shared bathroom; no air-conditioning. Bedrooms have wooden furniture, single or double beds.

Rates $500–$600 weekly (Sat.–Sat.) with all meals. Deposit: 50% of program fee. No credit cards.

Meal Plans 3 meals served daily, family style. Breakfast can be homemade grain cereal with honey, buckwheat pancakes with fruit, or an omelet. Lunch is soup and salad, sandwiches on homemade bread. Dinner main courses are barbecued chicken, baked or grilled fish, spaghetti, tofu casserole, and vegetable stir-fry. Special diets are accommodated. Vision Quest includes 3-day fast.

Services and Facilities **Swimming Facilities:** Stream. **Recreation Facilities:** Hiking, skiing, outings to rodeos and nearby attractions; gardening, ranching. **Evening Programs:** Sweat lodge.

In the Area Steamboat Springs (downhill skiing, hot springs), Medicine Bow National Forest, Red Desert.

Getting Here *From Denver, Co.* By car, I–70 via Idaho Springs, exit at Dillon, Rte. 9 to Kremmling, Rte. 40 west via Steamboat Springs to Craig, Hwy. 13/789 to Biggs, right on Rte. 70 via Dixon to Savery, left on Creek Rd. (5½ hr). By air, scheduled flights to Steamboat Springs (40 min.); van transportation Saturday ($50 round-trip) provided on requested by Antelope Retreat.

Special Notes Children accompanying program participants charged $75 up to age 4, $200–$362 ages 5–15.

Hot Springs State Park

Taking the waters

Wyoming
Thermopolis Long before explorers discovered the Big Spring, it was a bathing place for the Shoshone and Arapahoe tribes. When the land was purchased by the federal government in 1896, the deed stipulated that the springs remain open and free to all. Thus there is no charge to bathe in the indoor and outdoor pools maintained by the State of Wyoming. A Holiday Inn, resort apartments, and a rehabilitation center are located within the 1-square-mile Hot Springs State Park.

The water wells from the earth at a temperature of 135°F and spills down a series of mineral-glazed terraces on its way to the Big Horn River. Some of the flow is diverted to privately operated bathhouses and swimming pools and into the state-run baths. The sparkling clean and airy facilities are patronized by families en route to Yellowstone and by senior citizens from a nearby retirement home. Park and pools are open daily, 9 AM–10 PM.

The Holiday Inn on the bank of the Horn River offers the most complete facilities. There are separate men's and women's bathhouses for private soaks (coed on request), and an outdoor hydrojet pool is filled with warm mineral water. The outdoor swimming pool contains chlorinated tap water. The Athletic Club facilities are free to inn guests.

Located in central Wyoming, the town of Thermopolis is surrounded by high buttes and range land where herds of bison still roam free; it's a pleasant stop on the way to Yellowstone from Denver and Cheyenne.

Hot Springs State Park
Thermopolis Chamber of Commerce
220 Park St., Thermopolis, WY 82443
Tel. 307/864-2636

Holiday Inn of the Waters
100 Park St., Box 1323, Thermopolis, WY 82443
Tel. 307/864-3131 or 800/465-4329

Administration Manager, James Mills

Season Year-round.

Accommodations 80 rooms with modern furniture, bath, queen-size or twin beds or waterbed. Separate exercise rooms for men and women in the Athletic Club.

Rates $65 a day for 2 in twin-bed room, $59 single. Meals à la carte. 1 night payable in advance. Add tax (6%) and gratuities. Credit cards: AE, MC, V.

Meal Plans No meal plan available. The hotel restaurant serves 3 meals daily; special diets accommodated. Western steaks, grilled fish, baked mountain trout, salads in season.

Services and Facilities **Exercise Equipment:** 9-station Universal weight training gym in men's and women's areas; punching bag, stationary bikes, 2 racquetball courts. **Services:** Massage, beauty shop. **Swimming Facilities:** Outdoor heated pool. **Spa Facilities:** 4 private mineral water tubs, outdoor Jacuzzi; sauna, steam bath, men's and women's bathhouses. **Recreation Facilities:** Bicycle rental (tandem, single); golf, fishing, skiing, snowmobiling nearby.

In the Area Outfitters offer hunting and fishing trips, scenic tours, river floats. Yellowstone National Park, Wind River Canyon, County Historical Museum (Hole in the Wall Bar), Jackson wintersports area, Wind River Indian Reservation.

Getting Here *From Cheyenne.* By car, I-25 to Casper, Hwy. 20 via Moneta (3 hr). By bus, Powder River Line (4 hr).

Special Notes No smoking in the Athletic Club and designated areas of the dining room; nonsmoking rooms available. Club open weekdays noon-8:30, weekends 10-8:30.

The Central States

Dallas has been in the forefront of recent fitness developments in the Central States. Dr. Kenneth Cooper, who did pioneering research in exercise and nutrition in the U.S. Air Force and at the Cooper Clinic, is the guiding spirit for the Aerobics Center's residential program. In the suburbs, the Greenhouse offers luxury pampering and body conditioning for women only. Executives-on-the-go can work out or relax at Loews Anatole Hotel; the Crescent Court Hotel's full-service spa; and the health club at the Four Seasons Resort.

Texans have taken to European hydrotherapy with the Kneipp herbal baths and Kur Program at the Alamo Plaza Spa in San Antonio and at the Lake Austin Spa Resort near Austin. Close to the heart of Houston, the Houstonian Hotel has a well-equipped health club but no longer operates the Phoenix Spa program.

Akia

Stress Control　　　　　　　　　　　　　　　*Women only*
Weight management

Oklahoma
Chickasaw
National
Recreation Area

A rigid weight-loss diet, and getting lots of exercise are the main ingredients of the no-frills program at Akia, a fitness retreat for a dozen women. Guests participate in full days of hiking, stretching, and body toning in a rigorous dawn-to-dusk schedule that takes advantage of the scenic Arbuckle Mountains and nearby lakes and forests.

The day begins with exercise on the redwood deck that surrounds the main building. The 2-mile hike before breakfast is followed by more stretching and toning in a lakeside pavilion. Aerobics classes, contouring, and relaxation exercises begin the afternoon. Then participants have the option of soaking in the hot tub, getting a massage, walking, bicycling, or swimming in a nearby lake. Private consultation on nutrition with a registered dietitian and one-on-one training with the exercise instructor help you plan a personal fitness program.

Akia
Sulphur, OK
Office: 2316 N.W. 45th Pl., Oklahoma City, OK 73112
Tel. 405/842-6269

Administration　Founder-director, Wilhelmina Maguire

Season　10-week spring and fall seasons.

Accommodations　Stone cottages and wood duplex for 11 guests. Cottages have 3 single beds, shared bathroom, carpeting, wooden deck.

Rates　$415 for 5-day session, $350 for 4-day weekend, $260 for 3-day, $175 for 2-day. $150 advance payment. No credit cards.

Meal Plans　3 simple meals daily total 950–1,000 calories, with options at breakfast and lunch; 3-course dinner. Breakfast can be cereal with fruit and juice, lunch a high-fiber protein shake. Typical dinner entrées are spinach lasagna, baked fish, eggplant Par-

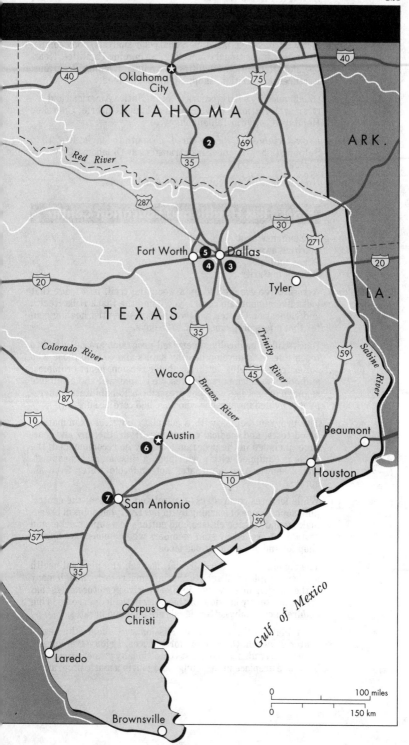

mesan, peppers stuffed with lentils and brown rice; ricotta cheesecake is a favorite dessert.

Services and Facilities **Services:** Massage, facial, personal color analysis, body composition test, nutritional counseling. **Swimming Facilities:** Nearby lake. **Recreation Facilities:** Bicycling. **Evening Programs:** Lectures on nutrition, shopping for health food.

In the Area Oklahoma City's Kirkpatrick Center (Native American and African art), National Cowboy Hall of Fame, Guthrie, Cherokee Heritage Center in Tahlequah.

Getting Here *From Oklahoma City.* By car, I-35 south to Davis, Rte. 12 to Sulphur (2 hr). By bus, free transfers at Oklahoma City Airport, and from Davis.

Special Notes No smoking. Bring your own linens and towels.

Black Hills Health and Education Center

Life enhancement
Spiritual awareness
Stress control
Vibrant maturity

South Dakota Across three creeks and up a woodland trail, in a lodge that
Hermosa looks like a mountain resort, you'll find the Black Hills Health and Education Center, a Seventh-Day Adventist healing center that offers programs of 12 to 25 days.

Black Hills's medically supervised programs are designed to teach guests to develop healthy habits and to help those who suffer from diabetes, arthritis, hypertension, heart problems, and obesity. Each person's lifestyle is analyzed and a suitable regimen of exercise and diet prescribed. Rehabilitation therapy is provided for persons who have had cardiac surgery.

The program begins with a complete physical examination, blood tests, and medical counseling. Hydrotherapy and massage (included in the program fee) may be recommended; the lodge is equipped with a whirlpool, a Russian steam cabinet, and a shower that alternates hot and cold water from six sprays.

While lectures cover stress control and nutrition, the central philosophy is one of learning by doing. Everyone joins in breadmaking and cooking classes, and outings to a supermarket and restaurant are led by staff members who demonstrate how to shop for and order nutritious foods.

The combined focus on spiritual, mental, and physical health attracts people of all ages to this informal resort, though many of the participants are over 50. They arrive in motor homes that can be hooked up outside, or they stay in the lodge; some bring children and a baby-sitter. Meals are included in rates.

An affiliate of the Black Hills Missionary College, the health center draws on the campus for services. Friday evening is a time when students and guests traditionally gather around the big stone fireplace in the lounge and join in a music program.

Black Hills Health and Education Center
Box 19, Hermosa, SD 57744
Tel. 605/255-4101
Fax 605/255-4622

Administration President, Robert Willard; medical director, Melvyn Beltz, M.D.

Season Year-round.

Accommodations 12 rooms in a 2-story lodge, modern furnishings, mostly double beds, private and shared baths. Motor-home services.

Rates 12-day program $1,550 single, $2,395 couple; 25-day program $2,395 single, $3,495 couple. $100–$200 reduction for motorhome use. Daily rate $30–$35 per room. $100 per person advance payment. Credit cards: MC, V.

Meal Plans 3 vegetarian meals daily, buffet style. Fruits, vegetables, legumes, and such natural fat sources as nuts and avocadoes. Lunch and dinner include salad bar, water-steamed vegetables, such entrées as vegetarian lasagna with mock-cheese topping, baked tofu, cashew chow mein. Whole-grain bread baked daily. No dairy products, eggs, coffee, tea, condiments.

Services and Facilities **Exercise Equipment:** Schwinn Air Dyne bikes, Trotter treadmill, rowing machine, trampoline, multipurpose gym. **Services:** Massage, hydrotherapy, medical consultation. **Swimming Facilities:** At nearby fitness center. **Spa Facilities:** Mineral hot springs nearby. **Recreation Facilities:** Gold panning, rock collecting; downhill skiing nearby. **Evening Programs:** Informal talks and films on health-related topics. Music program Fri.

In the Area Evans Plunge hot springs, a naturally heated indoor mineral-water pool; Custer State Park wildlife preserve; Rapid City's Aka Lakota Museum (Native American art and history); Mt. Rushmore; the Black Hills Passion Play (summer); the Homestead, a working gold mine at Lead; antique train ride from Hill City; Badlands National Park; Wind Cave National Park (caverns); prehistoric excavations. Deadwood casinos.

Getting Here *From Rapid City.* By car, Hwy. 79 south to Hermosa, Hwy. 40 west to entrance road (40 min). Free pickup from and return to Rapid City airport and bus station.

Special Notes Specially equipped rooms, ramps for people with disabilities. No smoking indoors.

Alamo Plaza Spa at the Menger Hotel

Luxury pampering
Taking the waters

Texas
San Antonio Kneipp herbal baths are the latest addition to the historic Menger Hotel, which has a European hydrotherapy program at its Alamo Plaza Spa. Trained at the Kneipp center in Bad Wörishofen, Dr. Jonathan Paul de Vierville adapted these popular European traditions to American lifestyles, opening the Alamo Plaza Spa in 1993 while continuing his state-certified school for bodyworkers.

Located directly across from the Alamo, the shrine of Texas independence, and built on the site of a pioneer beer brewery and Russian-Turkish bathhouse, the hotel taps its own Edwards

Aquifer for spring water to fill the big claw-foot Victorian bath-tubs in its original 1859 building and the new spa located beneath the fitness center. This is an urban retreat for body and mind.

Personalized regimens are set up for guests by advance reservation. The spa has five treatments rooms, a steam room, and whirlpool. An esthetician is available for facials and treatments on hands and feet. Using Kneipp herbal essences and aromatic oils made in Germany, your program can include water applications, exercise, diet, and combinations of dry heat, wet massage, wet heat, dry massage.

Alamo Plaza Spa at the Menger Hotel
204 Alamo Plaza, San Antonio, TX 78205
Tel. 210/223-5772; reservations: 800/345-9285
Fax 210/228-0022

Administration	Director, J. Paul de Vierville, M.S.W., Ph.D; hotel general manager, J. W. McMillin
Season	Year-round.
Accommodations	320 rooms (23 suites) including the restored 1859 wing with Victorian furnishings. All with private bathroom, air-conditioning, TV, telephone. Many feature ornate balconies overlooking an interior garden that has tropical foliage and a swimming pool. Choice of king-size or twin beds, nonsmoking rooms.
Rates	Daily rate $102 single, $82–$122 per person double occupancy; suites from $546. 3-day/2-night Victorian Kur Spa Holiday $395 per person, double occupancy, $463 single; American Kur Spa Classic including evening program $494 double, $559 single. Kur Spa Day (no lodging) $195. Deposit: $50. Add tax, gratuities. Credit cards: AE, D, MC, V.
Meal Plans	Breakfast, lunch, and beverage breaks included in spa packages; one dinner only in American Kur Spa Classic. Menu choices in hotel dining room include low-fat healthy selections.
Services and Facilities	**Exercise Equipment**: 2 Tectrix stairclimbers, 2 bikes, Trotter treadmill, stretch board, free weights. **Services:**Swedish massage, hydrotherapy, herbal body scrub, wrap, facial, inhalation, hand and foot treatment. **Swimming Facilities**: 25-meter outdoor swimming pool with spring water. **Recreation Facilities**: River Walk.
In the Area	The Alamo, Sea World, Fiesta Texas, Rivercenter Mall, IMAX theater.
Getting Here	*From San Antonio.* By bus, Star Shuttle ($5 for the 45-min. ride) leaves the San Antonio Airport every 30 mins. By car, I–35 south, Commerce Street exit, right on Bowie St., to Crockett, left to fountain (20 min.).
Special Notes	Spa open 9–9 daily. Minimum age 18, or accompanied minor. No smoking in spa. Facilities accessible for people with disabilities.

The Cooper Aerobics Center

Nutrition and diet
Preventive medicine
Vibrant maturity
Weight management

Texas
Dallas

A recognized leader in the study of the medical value of exercise, the Aerobics Center has a residential Cooper Wellness Program designed to help participants achieve permanent changes in lifestyle. Programs of 7 days and a 4-day wellness weekend teach the adoption and cultivation of healthy habits. You can also schedule an intensive one-day workout, with optional workshop.

Your stay can begin with an optional physical examination. The first day's schedule sees a chest X-ray, a test for pulmonary function, and vision, hearing, and dental exams. A standard skinfold test and weigh-in on an underwater scale determine your ideal body weight. Blood pressure is measured during and after exercise, and an ECG treadmill test measures stress. Before and after the program, 24 blood tests, including HDL and LDL for cholesterol, are administered. (Your health insurance may cover this.) The comprehensive medical report determines the exercise program that will be recommended for you.

Four exercise sessions are part of each day's program. You can work out on a treadmill or walk and jog on paved and lighted trails that wind through the 30-acre wooded estate. A gymnasium has basketball and racquetball courts and a three-lane running track. Two heated outdoor lap pools are six lanes wide and 75 feet long. The four outdoor Laykold lighted tennis courts are equipped with automatic ball machines.

Classes include lectures on nutrition and health, and you participate in cooking and bread-making demonstrations. Volleyball, aerobics in the swimming pool, and other forms of group exercise are scheduled. The whirlpool, sauna, and steam room are open every night; massage appointments cost extra.

Programs are limited to groups of no more than 20, and appeal to high-powered executives who have lost control of their health. Here they work with a team of nine full-time physicians, a dentist, nutritionists, and exercise technologists. Guided by Dr. Kenneth H. Cooper, whose pioneering research on aerobics inspired the founding of the center in 1970, these professionals make wellness meaningful to everyday life. Lodging and a medical evaluation are not included in the program prices.

The Cooper Aerobics Center
12230 Preston Rd., Dallas, TX 75230
Tel. 214/386–4777 or 800/444–5192
Telex 791578/AEROBICCTR DAL
Fax 214/386–0039

Administration Founder-president, program director, Kenneth H. Cooper, M.D.

Season Sessions scheduled Sept.–July.

Accommodations 60 rooms, 12 suites, with heavy mahogany king- or queen-size beds, wing chairs, private bath. A grand staircase dominates the marble lobby.

Rates 13-day program $3,310–$4,110; 7-day $2,210–$3,010; 4-day $1,510–$2,310; 1-day $265 (optional workshop fee $195 additional). Rooms at Guest Lodge $88, single or double occupancy, suites on request. Add 13¼% lodging tax, 8¼% meal tax. Credit cards: AE, MC, V (5% charge).

Meal Plans 3 calorie-controlled meals daily from planned menu, plus snacks. Breakfast can be whole-grain pancakes with hot blueberry topping, seasonal fresh fruit, low-fat milk, decaf tea or coffee. Lunch is tossed salad with Lite dressing, Hawaiian chicken with potatoes and baked tomato, fresh fruit tray, mineral water, diet drinks, or decaf coffee/tea. Dinner is beef Burgundy on a bed of pasta, snap peas, spinach salad, skim milk, beverage.

Services and Facilities **Exercise Equipment:** Cybex strength equipment, cardiovascular equipment. **Services:** Personal counseling on fitness, diet, and exercise; medical testing and evaluation. Swedish massage. **Swimming Facilities:** 2 heated outdoor pools. **Recreation Facilities:** 4 25-yard racquetball courts, 4 tennis courts, volleyball, basketball, handball. Golf course nearby. **Evening Programs:** Talks on nutrition and health; cooking school; dinner at local restaurant.

In the Area Dallas Baseball Stadium; White Rock Lake; the Omnimax film theater in Fort Worth; Dallas Museum of Art, Kennedy Memorial, Fort Worth Science Center, Dallas Arboretum and Botanical Garden.

Getting Here *From Dallas.* By car, Hwy. 635 (LBJ Freeway), Preston Rd. (20 min). Limousine, rental car, taxi available.

Special Notes For people with disabilities, ramps and elevator provide access to all areas. No smoking indoors. Remember to bring recent medical records, a watch with second hand, calculator, exercise clothing.

Four Seasons Resort and Club

Life enhancement
Luxury pampering
Sports conditioning

Texas Space-age design and Old World architecture meet at Las
Dallas/Irving Colinas, an urban center where since 1963 the Four Seasons Resort and Club has combined sports and spa programs.

Programs can be tailored to suit your needs: You can work out on the advanced Nautilus equipment, do aerobics and body-building exercises, and play a round of golf or team up for tennis. Personal trainers, nutritional counseling, and fitness evaluations are available at an hourly rate that can be combined with any of the resort's special packages. In addition to overnight packages, one-day packages are offered to nonresidents.

More than 25 spa treatments and beauty salon services can be booked on an à la carte basis. Services range from massage to aromatherapy, herbal wraps, and baths. There are two sets of

Jacuzzis, saunas, steam rooms and hot/cold pools. The spa program assures personal attention from the staff.

Local families, executives, and serious golfers enjoy the Four Seasons, with its two golf courses, indoor and outdoor tennis courts, and jogging tracks, among the sports facilities. Squash and racquetball courts, indoor and outdoor swimming pools, clinics, and private instruction are also available to spa guests in the newly expanded four-level Sports Club, which is the centerpiece to the 400-acre resort.

In 1994 there were 50 villa rooms added and all guest accommodations in the hotel were upgraded. The "alternatives" menu served in the main dining room keeps dieters on course. Regular selections are available as well.

Four Seasons Resort and Club
4150 N. MacArthur Blvd., Irving, TX 75038
Tel. 214/717-0700 or 800/332-3442, Telex 735319
Fax 214/717-2477

Administration	General manager, Jim FitzGibbon; spa director, Kathryn Waldman; Sports Club manager, Mark Herron; health/fitness director, Tracy York
Season	Year-round.
Accommodations	315 rooms in the 9-story tower, 50 rooms in new 2-story golf villas. Tastefully styled with executive amenities: toiletries, hair dryer, terry robes; comfortable living area, 3 telephones, cable TV, marble bath with separate tub and shower. Private balcony with most rooms; ask for golf course view.
Rates	Weekday $215, weekend $135–$145, suites to $1,000. Fresh Start spa package 2 night/3 days $1,220–$1,280 per couple, $730–$800 single. Add 11% tax, and gratuities. Credit cards: AE, DC, MC, V.
Meal Plans	3 meals daily in 2–6 night spa packages. Four Seasons Alternative Cuisine is low in cholesterol, fat, calories, sodium. Menu selections are broiled chicken, Mexican chicken enchilada, grilled salmon, roast quail with fresh berry sauce. Daily caloric intake under 1,000; vegetarian meals available.
Services and Facilities	**Exercise Equipment:** 12-station Nautilus circuit, NordicTrack, recumbent cycle, 3 Bodyguard cycles, 2 Windracer cycles, free weights room, 5 Lifecycles, 8 StairMasters, 6 treadmills, 2 rowing machines, 5 Schwinn Air Dyne bikes, water rowing machine. **Services:** Swedish, shiatsu, reflexology, sports, and aromatherapy massage, herbal and sea-kelp wraps and baths, loofah body scrub, facial, heated mud pack. Personal training, fitness evaluation, Tae Kwon Do. **Swimming Facilities:** 25-yd indoor lap pool, 25-m outdoor lap pool, 2 recreational pools. **Recreation Facilities:** 8 outdoor, 4 indoor tennis courts, 6 indoor racquetball courts, 3 squash courts, 1 softball, 2 handball courts, 1/2 court basketball gymnasium, 2 18-hole golf courses.
In the Area	Dallas Arts District, West End Historic District, Baseball Stadium, Texas Stadium, Market Center, State Fair Music Hall.
Getting Here	*From Dallas.* By car, Hwy. 35 to Hwy. 183 (Airport Freeway), MacArthur Blvd. exit. (20 min). Limousine service. Taxi, rental car available.

Special Notes Limited access for people with disabilities. Professionally managed child-care center (6 months to 8 years of age). No smoking in the spa or designated dining areas. Nonsmoking rooms available. Spa open weekdays 6 AM–10 PM, weekends 7 AM–9 PM.

The Greenhouse

Life enhancement   *Women only*
Luxury pampering
Stress control

Texas   Privacy and freedom from stress are precious commodities to
Arlington   the harried young career women and female celebrities who
              check into the Greenhouse for a week of physical and emotional
              rejuvenation. Completely self-contained, with a staff of more
              than 125 serving just 39 guests, the retreat specializes in the
              classic spa tradition of total pampering.

From the airport you'll be whisked in a chauffeured limousine
to the Greenhouse, set amid gardens and fitness trails. A special destination for the knowledgeable spa set since 1965, it was
built by the fashion trendsetters of Neiman Marcus. While the
elegant enclave has maintained its high standard of service and
accommodations, it has expanded its program to appeal to the
special needs of its guests. Repeaters make up 75% of the clientele.

Each guest is assigned a personal esthetician, hairdresser,
manicurist, and masseuse for the week. A resident exercise
physiologist, nurse, and other staff members plan a schedule to
the individual's needs.

Breakfast in bed begins the day at 7 AM. Your daily schedule
comes on the tray, and a fresh leotard and robe await you. A
brisk guided walk through the garden is followed by exercise
classes to energize and tone the body. Choices include aerobics
(high and low impact), step classes, yoga, tai chihuan, strength
training, aquatics (Hydrotone, Splashdance, and step), relaxation and breathing, and boxing. Your personal trainer studies
your fitness profile (prepared on your arrival) and works with
you at your pace. Lunch is served poolside, followed by a daily
massage and serious pampering. Daily schedules are adhered
to unless guests request otherwise. Evenings can be dressy or
informal, depending on the guests, yet the setting reflects
everything you've ever seen on TV about Texan elegance and
style.

The Greenhouse
107th St., Box 1144, Arlington, TX 76004
Tel. 817/640–4000
Fax 817/649–0422

Administration President, Lee Katzoff; co-director, Shirley Ogle; program director, Cynthia Lefferts

Season Year-round except early July and Dec. Programs begin and end on Sun.; 3-day miniweeks sometimes available.

Accommodations 37 single rooms, 2 suites with queen-size half-canopied beds, matching drapes. Hand-embroidered linens, large dressing area, marble bathroom, sunken tub, air-conditioning, TV, telephone.

Rates $3,795 per week single; suite shared by 2, $3,895; Mini-week $2,500. $1,000 deposit. No credit cards.

Meal Plans Choice of weight loss or maintenance: 1,000–1,200 or 1,500 calories a day. 3 meals plus midmorning snack and afternoon fruit frappe. Homemade bran muffin, fresh melon and raspberries, coffee or tea for breakfast; vegetarian pizza with baby greens salad, lobster-and-crab salad, cheese soufflé with fruit at lunch; Cornish hens stuffed with shallots and breast meat, broiled lamb chops, grilled salmon at dinner.

Services and Facilities **Exercise Equipment**: Gravitron, Step & Slide, Strongput, 6-station Universal weight training gym, Nautilus units, 4 Trotter treadmills, 8 stationary bikes, cross-country NordicTrack, 2 StairMaster, body-ball weights, hand weights, poles, elastic Thoro-bands. **Services:** Massage (Swedish, shiatsu, reflexology, sports, acupressure, watsu), facials; hair, skin, and nail care; one-on-one workouts. Personal fitness, nutrition, health, beauty, and relaxation programs. Cooking classes. **Swimming Facilities:** Indoor and outdoor pools. **Recreation Facilities:** tennis court, parcourse, jogging track. **Evening Programs:** Discussion topics are stress, wellness, makeup, cosmetic surgery; entertainment, feature films, fashion shows.

In the Area Kimbell Art Museum, Dallas Museum of Art, Amon Carter Museum, Dallas Baseball Stadium, State Fair Music Hall, Texas Stadium, shopping malls.

Getting Here *From Dallas.* By car, I–30 to Arlington, Hwy. 360 to Avenue II, left to 107th St. (20 min). Free transportation from and return to airport; taxi, rental car available.

Special Notes No smoking in public areas.

Lake Austin Spa Resort

Life enhancement
Luxury pampering
Weight management

Texas Hill-country walks, water aerobics, and a range of body-
Austin strengthening exercise classes make up the program at the Lake Austin Spa Resort. The coed retreat provides a great escape in a part of Texas noted for scenic rolling hills and placid lakes.

You pay a basic daily rate, which includes fitness classes, meals, and programs on lifestyle enhancement. Also available, for an additional fee, are European facials with Repechage skin-care products, and other personal services in the salon.

The day begins at 7 AM with group walks ranging from 2 to 4 miles. The facilities include a lap pool with resistant jets, a coed Jacuzzi, sauna, and steam room, and indoor and outdoor swimming pools. The glass-walled gym and aerobics studio, with suspended wood floor, overlooks beautiful Lake Austin. Hiking and jogging trails plus parcourse are nicely laid out, and extend into the woods.

The meals are designed to help you maintain a balanced diet of fresh fruit, vegtables, and herbs from an organic garden on the property. Snacks and energy drinks are available throughout the day.

One of the nice touches here is a roommate-matching service. If you want to share accommodations for extra savings, ask about a compatible person who is registered for the program. Up to four roomates can share one of the pretty lakeside cottages. Arrival is any day of the week; minimum stay is two nights.

Lake Austin Spa Resort
1705 Quinlan Park Rd., Austin, TX 78732
Tel. 512/266–2444 or 800/847–5637
Fax 512/266–1572

Administration Executive director, Deborah Evans; program director, Gayle Moffett

Season Year-round.

Accommodations 40 recently renovated cottages provide country B&B amenities, TV, phone, air-conditioning, private bath. Bedrooms have 2 full-size beds. Nightly turndown service is provided.

Rates Daily rate $110–$172 single, $102–$152 per person double. Add service charge and 6% tax, $200 per person deposit. Credit cards: AE, MC, V.

Meal Plans 3 meals daily, high in complex carbohydrates and fiber, low in fat, sugar, and salt. Breakfast buffet has muffins, fresh fruit, coffee, tea, juices, choice of tacos, whole-wheat pancakes, blintzes, French toast, cereals. Lunch and dinner entrées may be enchiladas, lasagna, fajitas, pizza, barbecued chicken.

Services and Facilities **Exercise Equipment:** Flexmaster weight training equipment in 3 gyms, recumbent bike, 2 StairMasters, 2 Schwinn Air Dyne bikes, treadmill, rowing machine, free weights. **Services:** Swedish, aromatherapy, shiatsu massage; reflexology; body brushing; polish; Bindi; herbal wrap; clay body masque; seaweed body masque; facials. Salon for hair, nail, care, makeup consultation. Personal consultation on fitness, nutrition, skin analysis, special dietary needs. **Swimming Facilities:** Indoor and outdoor pools. **Recreation Facilities:** Volleyball, badminton, paddleboats, Jacuzzi, tennis; golf and horseback riding nearby. **Evening Programs:** Talks on health and fitness.

In the Area University of Texas, state capitol, L. B. Johnson Library and museum.

Getting Here *From Austin.* By car, Ranch Rd. 2222, FM, 620 to Quinlan Park Rd. (45 min). Free transfers to and from Austin Airport. Taxi, rental car available.

Special Notes Smoking and nonsmoking rooms available. Laundry rooms available. Hiking weeks spring and fall.

The Middle West

Fitness resorts are a relatively recent phenomenon in the Middle West; their programs are informal and outdoors oriented, they capitalize on scenic locations, and their focus tends to be on weight loss and general well-being.

Wisconsin offers the widest variety of choices, from the sports-oriented American Club to the sophisticated pampering of the Fontana Spa at the Abbey Resort on Lake Geneva, and the Aveda Spa Osceola, a riverside retreat near the twin cities, Minneapolis and St. Paul. In Ohio you can work out in a registered historic landmark at the Kerr House, or at Mario's International Spa near Cleveland, with its Americana decor and Victorian antiques. For another kind of spa experience take the thermal waters at French Lick Springs in Indiana and the Elms in Missouri: Both have been popular since the turn of the century.

Destination spas such as Birdwing in Minnesota, and the Heartland near Chicago, offer personal attention and the support of group camaraderie. Perhaps the most unusual new example is the Raj in Fairfield, Iowa, devoted to the ancient system of preventive natural medicine known as ayurvedic therapy. The Marsh near Minneapolis is another new example of state-of-the-art facilities and programs. At these country retreats you learn to handle stress, manage your diet, and balance mind, body, and spirit.

The Heartland Spa

Life enhancement
Nutrition and diet
Stress control

Illinois
Gilman

Guests are made to feel at home in the Heartland Spa's lakefront mansion, which is rather like being at an adult camp in the country. The 30-acre estate boasts a guest list limited to 28, and your day can be as structured or unstructured as you please. You don't need to sign up for scheduled exercise classes, but do make appointments for massage and facials. Since bodywork and beauty treatments are included in the package, most guests take advantage of them—and add further pampering services at their own expense.

High-tech workouts with weight machines are held in the barn, an impressive three-level fitness center reached through an underground passage from the house. This barn is unlike anything on the neighboring farms; it has a full complement of cardiovascular workout equipment, pneumatic resistance muscle movers, an indoor swimming pool, whirlpool, sauna, steam room, and private massage rooms.

Personal consultation with staff is included in the five- and seven-day programs. They advise you to concentrate on activities you enjoy and to continue them when you return home. (Try yoga and race walking!) Scheduled classes include

The Middle West

aerobics, aquacise, step aerobics, martial arts, and self-aware-ness. Options include a ropes course and Pilates exercises.

The weekend is the busiest time of the week, when van loads of Chicagoans arrive on Friday evening via complimentary trans-portation from the Loop. Yet the best deal is a five-day stay, from Sunday to Friday noon. Longer, discounted stays can be arranged to concentrate on weight loss or recuperation from ill-ness.

The Heartland Spa
Rte. 1, Box 181, Gilman, IL 60938
Tel. 312/6465 in Chicago; 815/683–2182 at spa, or
800/545–4853
Fax 312/427–7746

Administration Founder, Jerry Kaufman; director, Mary Quinn

Season Year-round.

Accommodations 14 pine-furnished rooms, refurbished 1992, have country an-tiques, down-filled comforters, twin beds, private bath with hair dryer, toiletries, large fluffy towels.

Rates 2-day weekend $500 per person double occupancy, $700 single; 5 days $1,375 double, $1,875 single; 7 days $1,650 double, $2,300 single. Roommate matching on request. Taxes and gra-tuities included. 50% deposit. Credit cards: AE, MC, V.

Meal Plans 3 meals daily (table service). Snacks and fruit all day. Break-fast includes freshly baked muffins, hot and cold cereal, coffee on request. Vegetarian menu; dairy products, fish served occa-sionally. No salt, sugar, or added fats. 1,200 calories a day for women, 1,500 for men. Lunch can include hearty soup, vegeta-ble pâté, or Japanese mushroom salad; typical dinner entrées are grilled swordfish with rosemary, Peruvian fish stew, corn crepes with spinach soufflé, fish and vegetable brochettes.

Services and Facilities **Exercise Equipment:** 8 Keiser Cam II pneumatic resistance units, 3 Cybex exercycles, Pilates, 2 Schwinn Air Dyne bikes, 2 rowers, 3 treadmills, 3 Tunturi exercycles, free weights, hand weights, StairMaster, soft joggers, NordicTrack, trampolines. **Services:** Massage therapy (sports, relaxation, foot), facial, manicure, pedicure, hair and skin care; personal fitness assess-ment, nutrition evaluation, underwater body composition test. **Swimming Facilities:** 15-m indoor pool, 3-acre lake. **Recreation Facilities:** 2 lighted outdoor tennis courts, parcourse, hiking, cross-country skiing (equipment provided), 2-person bike, ¼-mi running track. **Evening Programs:** Informal discussions on health-related topics. Guest speakers on stress management, life enhancement, dependency, financial planning.

In the Area Architecture of Frank Lloyd Wright in Oak Park, Abraham Lincoln's home and tomb in Springfield.

Getting Here *From Chicago.* By car, the Dan Ryan Expwy. south, I–57 to Kankakee Exit 308, Hwy. 52/45 (becomes Hwy. 49) to Rte. 24, R.R. 122 (90 min). Free van service from and return to down-town Chicago Fri. and Sun. By train, Amtrak to Gilman (1 hr). By bus, Greyhound (2 hr).

Special Notes No smoking indoors.

French Lick Springs Resort

Nonprogram resort
Taking the waters

Indiana
French Lick

Modeled on the great spas of Europe, the French Lick Springs Resort was built in the early 1840s and attracted a wealthy elite who came from all over the country to "take the waters" in as many ways as they could. The sulfurous spring water was bottled and marketed as Pluto Water, and today it is still used in the Pluto Bath in the hotel health club.

Recently restored to its original Victorian elegance in a costly renovation, the hotel has high-ceilinged rooms with ceiling fans, French doors, carved woodwork, and verandas that overlook formal gardens. Its 2,600 acres of lawns and rolling woodland add to the charm and attract families and conventions.

The spa can be enjoyed on a daily-rate basis or with baths and beauty services included in two-night and five-night packages. No formal program of activities is offered; you set your own schedule. The spa director will consult with you on a meal plan, exercise classes, and bodywork. There is an exercise room, sauna, and whirlpools.

French Lick Springs today is a place to have fun and enjoy a bit of pampering. With two championship golf courses, tennis courts, and other recreation facilities at hand, the springs are no longer the sole attraction. Yet you can still have a sip from a well beneath a gazebo or take a bath in spring water piped into a claw-foot tub.

French Lick Springs Resort
French Lick, IN 47432
Tel. 812/936–9300 or 800/457–4042

Administration   General manager, Greg James; spa director, Doris Todd

Season   Year-round.

Accommodations   502 deluxe suites and large double rooms with king- or queen-size bed, antique furniture, modern private bath, color TV.

Rates $149 spa day package with lunch. 5-night spa program, $662 per person double occupancy, $860 single; 2-night midweek package $299 per person double, $384 single. Winter rates lower. Gratuities and tax extra. Credit card confirmation or $100 per person deposit for spa packages. Credit cards: AE, DC, MC, V.

Meal Plans   3 meals daily with spa packages. Low-calorie selections include poached salmon for dinner, shrimp shish kebab and teriyaki chicken for lunch. Vegetarian meals on request.

Services and Facilities   **Exercise Equipment:** 10-unit Universal weight training gym, 2 Air Dyne bikes, rowing machines, Tredex, Stairobic, Aerobi-Cycle. **Services:** Swedish massage, aromatherapy, reflexology, salt rub, facials, pedicure, manicure, loofah body scrub; makeup lessons, beauty salon for hair and skin care; personal consultation on exercise. **Swimming Facilities:** Indoor and outdoor pools. **Recreation Facilities:** 2 18-hole golf courses, 18 tennis courts (8 indoors and lighted), horseback riding, bicycling, bowling, billiards; fishing, sailing, skiing. **Evening Programs:** Resort entertainment.

In the Area Surrey rides. Evansville historic district (19th-century homes), Old Vanderburgh County Courthouse, New Harmony colony near Vincennes, Amish farms.

Getting Here *From Louisville.* By bus, Greyhound (2 hr). By car, I-64 west, Hwy. 150 to Paoli, Rte. 56 west (60 min). Hotel limousine, rental car available.

Special Notes Elevators and ramps connect hotel rooms and spa facilities for people with disabilities. Supervised day camp for children during summer; playground, miniature train ride, wading pool. No smoking in the spa.

Indian Oak Resort

Luxury pampering

Indiana This nonstructured resort offers a variety of spa services in ad-
Chesterton dition to 100 acres of lush, well-maintained grounds, around which many activities—including hiking and watersports—take place. In 1990 the resort was expanded and now offers spa packages that include an extensive selection of personal services such as massages and facials, as well as meal coupons.

There are five rooms for massage, facials, and reflexology, and a newly designed room for wet treatments with mud and seaweed. All guests can use the facilities and participate in exercise classes without charge. Scheduled are aquacize, StepReebok, and Stretch & Tone. While exercising you can enjoy a view of the lake. There is also an indoor lap pool and whirlpool.

Indian Oak Resort
558 Indian Boundry, Chesterton, IN 46304
Tel. 219/926-2200 or 800/552-4232

Administration General manager, Cathy Chubb; spa manager, Wendy Krantz

Season Year-round.

Accommodations 100 rooms, some with king-size beds; modern furniture, private bath, cable TV, phone, air-conditioning. Lakeside rooms have terraces.

Rates $70–$125 for 2 persons double occupancy, $65–$99 single; suites $160–$190. 2-night spa package $225–$247 per person double, $286–$341 single; 3-night spa package $418–$461 per person double, $506.50–$589 single. Taxes included; add gratuities. Deposit for first night by credit card. Credit cards: AE, DC, MC, V.

Meal Plans Continental breakfast included in all room rates. Spa package includes 2 meals daily, low in fat, salt, and calories.

Services and **Exercise Equipment:** Universal gym, 2 StairMasters, 2 tread-
Facilities mills, Schwinn Air Dyne bike, rowing machine, free weights. **Services:** Swedish massage, herbal wrap, facial, shiatsu, body buff; salon for hair, nail, and skin care. **Swimming Facilities:** 50-ft indoor lap pool, private lake. **Recreation Facilities:** Boating, fishing, hiking trails.

In the Area Lake Michigan, Dunes National Lakeshore, Indiana Dunes State Park.

Getting Here *From Chicago.* By car, I–80/90 to I–94 (1 hr). By train, South Shore 9 to Chesterton (80 min). Free shuttle service from train.

Special Notes Spa open Tues.–Fri. 8–8, Sat. and Mon. 8–5, Sun. 8–1. Minimum age 16.

The Raj

Life enhancement
Preventive medicine
Spiritual awareness

Iowa The secluded Raj health center, opened in 1992 in the heart of
Fairfield rolling meadows and woodlands, introduces a new level of luxury to the country's array of destination spas devoted to the ancient system of preventive natural medicine known as ayurvedic therapy. Here, the soothing and refreshing treatments first introduced in America at Massachusetts's Maharishi Ayur-Veda center can be combined with programs incorporating fitness and exercise.

Treatment begins with an assessment of your physiological makeup by a physician concerned with both physical and spiritual health. Maharishi therapies, designed to restore balance in your body, are deeply relaxing. Traditionally known as *panchakarma*, treatments include warm herbal-oil massages, herbal steam baths, and internal cleansing. Aromatic ayurvedic oils are used to enliven engery points (*marmas*) to create a feeling of well-being. For stress reduction and to expand inner awareness, you are introduced to Transcendental Meditation (TM) and given a mantra.

The Raj
24th St. NW, Fairfield, IA 52556
Tel. 515/472–9580 or 800/248–9050
Fax 515/472–2496

Administration Owners/directors, Candace and Rodgers Badgett, Jr.; medical director, Christopher Clark, M.D.; fitness director, Barbara McLaughlin

Season Year-round.

Accommodations 46 deluxe rooms and suites in 2-story villas and in the Raj Court Hotel. The Spa Wing of the hotel has 19 standard rooms, while the Hotel Wing has 18 larger deluxe rooms. Each private villa has 3 guest suites. All rooms have queen-size beds, carpeting, air-conditioning, and telephone and are decorated with flowered wallpaper, carved-wood furniture, and silk and cotton draperies. Baths are marble-walled with twin vanities, shower and bath (separate in deluxe rooms and suites), and amenities including hair dryer, robes, and slippers.

Rates 3-day program $1,095; 5-day program $1,685; 7-day program $2,255. TM training not included in program fee. Lodging $85 single per night, $120 for doubles; villa apartment $125–$185. Add gratuity and 5% tax. Deposit 50%. Credit cards: AE, MC, V.

Meal Plans 3 gourmet vegetarian meals daily that follow the ayurvedic principles are included in program. Breakfast includes home-baked bread, jam, cereal. Lunch can be fresh organic vegetable soup, eggplant pilaf with basmati rice and cilantro sauce, lemon broccoli or dilled green beans, and dessert. Dinner menus include jade soup, fresh green peas in coconut milk, summer squash sauté, couscous pilaf, asparagus phylo rolls, and dessert.

Services and Facilities **Exercise Equipment:** 2 treadmills, 2 stairsteppers, 2 stationary bikes, free weights. **Services:** Ayurvedic massage, transcendental meditation, stress management, self-pulse diagnosis, nutrition and diet counseling, internal cleansing. **Recreation Facilities:** Nearby golf, horseback riding, tennis. **Programs:** Videotapes and lectures on health-related topics.

In the Area Maharishi International University, Pella (Dutch historic settlement), Des Moines.

Getting Here *From Cedar Rapids.* By car, I–380 south, Rte. 1 south to Fairfield airport, right turn on Rural Road 8 (1¼ hrs). Private planes land at Fairfield Airport, where pickup by a Raj car can be arranged upon request (fee). Limousine or hotel car picks up at Cedar Rapids Airport (fee).

Special Notes No smoking. Special accommodations available for people with disabilities. Hotel accommodations and dining open to the public.

Birdwing Spa

Life enhancement
Luxury pampering
Nutrition and diet

Minnesota The first full-service spa in the upper Midwest, Birdwing Spa
Litchfield blends European therapy and Minnesota traditions. The Tudor mansion set on a lakeside estate accommodates up to 25 guests; an exercise studio occupies the former barn, and an outdoor swimming pool and 12 miles of groomed walking and cross-country ski trails are on the grounds.

Oriented to outdoor activity, the spa provides equipment for skiing, canoeing, and biking, in addition to circuit weight training. In two daily "image sessions," guests have a choice of facial, massage, or manicure. Aerobic exercise or an hour of yoga completes the daily schedule in the 3,500-square-foot fitness building.

Birdwing ranks high as a relaxing experience on a 300-acre country estate. The chalet has a sauna and Jacuzzi and is adjacent to the beauty-treatment facilities. The owners have developed a fitness program to complement a diet regimen of 1,000–1,200 calories daily for women, 1,300–1,500 calories for men.

Birdwing Spa
21398 575th Ave., Litchfield, MN 55355
Tel. 612/693–6064

Administration Owner-directors, Richard and Elisabeth Carlson

Season Year-round.

Accommodations 9 bedrooms (singles and doubles) with Ethan Allen furnishings, draperies, shared baths. The master suite has fireplace, private bath, Jacuzzi, and steam bath.

Rates 7-day program $1,650 single occupancy of the master suite, $1,550 per person double; $1,275 single, $1,195 double in other rooms. 5-day program $1,350 single in the master suite, $1,250 per person double; $1,075 single, $995 double in other rooms. 2-day retreat $475–$550 per person in the master suite; $350–$395 other rooms. 1-day overnight package $225–$295. Add 15% service charge and tax. $150 in advance for weekends, $300 for other programs. Credit cards: MC, V.

Meal Plans 3 weight-loss meals daily: cinnamon raisin French toast with 3-berry sauce for breakfast, fruit kebabs followed by chicken tacos with salsa or turkey pizza for lunch, chicken asparagus rolls and butterscotch brownies for dinner.

Services and Facilities **Exercise Equipment:** 2 treadmills, 2 Schwinn Air Dyne bikes, StairMaster, free weights. **Services:** Swedish and Esalen massage, facials, hair and nail care, aromatherapy, paraffin therapy, back treatment. Nutritional counseling, fitness evaluation, exercise instruction. **Swimming Facilities:** Outdoor pool. **Spa Facilities:** Men's and women's saunas, coed whirlpool, massage room. **Recreation Facilities:** Bicycling, canoeing, cross-country skiing, bird-watching. Tennis and golf nearby. Special weeks for art and nature studies. **Evening Programs:** Guest speakers on stress control, nutrition, cardiac health, and problems of career women. Cooking classes and feature films.

In the Area Minneapolis–St. Paul museums, Mall of America.

Getting Here *From Minneapolis.* By car, I-394, Hwy. 12 west to Litchfield, Rte. 1 and 23 (90 min). Birdwing makes arrangements for local transportation on request ($50).

Special Notes No smoking in public areas indoors. Minimum age 16.

The Marsh

Kid fitness
Life enhancement
Vibrant maturity
Weight management

Minnesota Designed as a center for balance and fitness, the Marsh inte-
Minnetonka grates architecture and aerobics, nutrition and nurturing, to help you balance the mind and body. Begun in 1985 on the edge of marshland near Minneapolis, the dramatic wooden structure seems to grow from the earth: The inside opens to the sky. The spa addition opened in 1993 as part of an expansion that more than doubled the Marsh, and for the first time there are overnight accommodations for 12 guests.

Ruth Stricker practices what she preaches as the founder-director of the Marsh. Despite the onset of crippling lupus, Stricker discovered how meditation and body movements work together to restore health. As the Marsh membership grew, an Over-50 Club was formed to push the envelope in exercise programs for mature bodies. And a KidFitness center serves the community as well as visitors, inspiring teenagers to incorporate fitness regimens with an active lifestyle.

The new, 27,000-square-foot structure includes a climbing wall, a flotation tank, and a silo-shape meditation tower equipped with a computer-controlled "mind gym," with sounds that help guests to meditate. During the day you can sign up for tai chichuan, yoga, somatics (movements to help manage chronic back pain), centering (exercises for alignment and stretching), flo-motion in the pool, and back therapy with physio-gymnastic balls, among other workouts.

This is the most comprehensive spa in the Midwest, with everything under one roof, including cardiovascular and weight-training equipment, a 75-foot lap pool, sauna, and nine treatment rooms. Educational programs, classes, and special services can be part of a retreat program, but there is no package or group activity.

The Marsh
15000 Minnetonka Blvd., Minnetonka, MN 55345
Tel. 612/935-2202
Fax 612/935-9685

Administration Founder-director, Ruth Stricker; spa director, Linda Yard

Season Year-round.

Accommodations 6 bedrooms, each with 2 single beds, private bathroom, chair, bureau. Cozy rather than elegant, the rooms have views of the marsh, are air conditioned, with TV, phone. Robes are provided.

Rates 6-night spa package $1,800–$2,200 single, $1,700–$2,100 per person double occupancy. Gratuities and tax included. Credit cards: AE, MC, V.

Meal Plans Breakfast included with room; lunch and dinner served in restaurant, and can be ordered à la carte. Menu choices include fresh grilled salmon, chicken breast with wild mushrooms, pork medallions with salsa, and choice of wine, beer, or herbal tea. Coffee and bottled waters available.

Services and Facilities **Exercise Equipment**: Versa Climber, CYBEX, Concept II Rowers, Combi Ergopower Bicycle, StairMasters, Stretchmate, Equinox 2000, Quinton treadmills, NordicTrack Pro X-C ski machines, Keiser equipment, Nautilus. **Services**: Swedish massage, Feldenkrais Method, Alexander Technique, Somatics; herbal wrap. **Swimming Facilities**: 75-ft indoor pool. **Recreation Facilities**: Nature trail, racquet ball, squash court, golf, rock-climbing wall.

In the Area Minneapolis/St. Paul museums and theaters, Mall of America.

Getting Here *From Minneapolis.* By car, I–394 west to Carlson Pkwy., Hwy. 494 south to Minnetonka Blvd., right for ¼ mile (30 min).

Special Notes All facilities accessible for people with disabilities. No smoking indoors. Classes scheduled 7–7 daily. Childcare and developmental activities for children 6 wks–6 yrs.

The Elms Resort

Nonprogram resort
Taking the waters

Missouri
Excelsior Springs

In the 1800s high-living health seekers descended on this sleepy little Missouri town each season to take the mineral waters. The Elms, built to accommodate them in the grand manner, became a tradition that survived two devastating fires; the present limestone and concrete structure was built in 1912 and incorporates the New Leaf Spa.

Ten "environmental rooms" are programmed for jungle rain, wet steam, or dry sauna and equipped with a hot tub for two. The European swim track, which can be mildly claustrophobic, is a one-lane lap pool filled with tap water.

There's a lot of nostalgic charm about the Elms. Croquet and badminton are played on the lawn, and the tennis court is free to guests. A quaint village of boutiques completes the resort. Popular for conventions and sales meetings, the 23-acre wooded resort is less than an hour from Kansas City.

The Elms Resort
Regent St. and Elms Blvd., Excelsior Springs, MO 64204
Tel. 816/637–2141, spa reservations: 816/637–0752 or 800/843–3567
Fax 816/637–1222

Administration Manager, Douglas Morrison; spa manager, Sandra Kennedy

Season Year-round.

Accommodations 136 rooms furnished with traditional wood dresser and table, desk, ceiling fan, cable TV, old-fashioned tiled bath.

Rates $49–$79 per night for doubles Sun.–Thurs., $149.88 summer weekend package for doubles. Suites $95–$130. Condos $150. Add tax (6.975%) and gratuities. Credit cards: AE, DC, MC, V.

Meal Plans American and European cuisine. Salads, fresh fish, meat, or chicken for lunch and dinner. Buffet dinners and brunch included in weekend package.

Services and Facilities **Exercise Equipment:** Nautilus circuit gym, Liferower, Lifecycle, treadmill, stationary bike. Indoor running track circles the lap pool (23 circuits = 1 mi). **Services:** Swedish massage, facial, cosmetology, beauty salon. **Spa Facilities:** Private mineral baths by appointment ($12.50). Hot and cold whirlpools, 3-level spa complex with separate saunas and steam rooms for men and women. **Swimming Facilities:** Outdoor pool; municipal indoor pool. **Recreation Facilities:** Golf, tennis, croquet, badminton, volleyball, horseshoes, shuffleboard; racquetball court nearby; bicycle rental. **Evening Programs:** Resort entertainment.

In the Area Watkins Woolen Mill (19th-century textile factory) in state park; fishing, swimming, hiking, picnicking, camping. Kansas City Zoo, Country Club Plaza (shopping), Crown Center (Hallmark museum), Nelson Atkins Museum of Art.

Getting Here *From Kansas City.* By car, I–35 north to Excelsior Springs, Hwy. 69 to Rte. 10 (30 min). Limo, rental car, taxi available.

Special Notes   No smoking in the spa. Spa open Fri.–Sat. 8 AM–11 PM, Sun.–Thur. 8AM–9 PM.

Marriott's Tan-Tar-A Resort & Spa

Nonprogram resort

Missouri   Outdoor recreation is the principal attraction of Marriott's
Osage Beach   Tan-Tar-A Resort, surrounded by 400 acres in the Lake of the Ozarks region. The lake, created by a dam in 1931, has countless coves for water sports, boating, and fishing. The hotel caters to conventioneers as well as family vacationers. New in 1992 was the Windjammer Spa, a privately operated facility connected to the resort's indoor swimming pool and fitness center.

Guests enjoy use of an indoor/outdoor fitness center. Aerobics classes are offered three mornings a week, aquatics two mornings. The weights room, staffed by fitness specialists, is open daily. Massage and aromatherapy are available à la carte in the spa building, which features the Aveda Concept products and services, and has a private steam room and whirlpool.

Marriott's Tan-Tar-A Resort & Spa
State Road KK, Osage Beach, MO 65065
Tel. 314/348–3131, 800/826–8272, or 800/268–8181 in Canada; Windjammer Spa: 314/348–3535

Administration   Manager, Bill Bennett; spa manager, Michelle Bennett

Season   Year-round.

Accommodations   1,000 rooms in the hotel and cottages have fireplace, kitchenette, bar (in some rooms and suites), coffee maker, TV, private bath.

Rates   Double rooms $105–$159, 1-bedroom suites $180–$249, 2-bedroom suites $240–$335. 2-night golf package for doubles, $328–$432, includes breakfast and unlimited golf. Deposit of 1 night's lodging applied to last night reserved (and forfeited on early departure). Credit cards: AE, DC, MC, V. Rates include tax.

Meal Plans   The Cliff Room has Continental cuisine and light fare as well as fried catfish. Windrose on the Water serves fish cooked to order (broiled, baked, sautéed, blackened).

Services and   **Exercise Equipment:** 3 Trotter treadmills, 2 Liferowers, 3 Nau-
Facilities   tilus stationary bikes, 9-station Universal weight training gym, abdominal-muscle exerciser. **Services:** Swedish massage, reflexology, acupressure, facial, body wrap, salt glow scrub, sea salt bath, aromatherapy; hair, nail, and skin care for men and women. **Swimming Facilities:** 4 outdoor pools, private beach on lake. **Recreation Facilities:** 6 outdoor and 2 indoor tennis courts, 4 indoor racquetball courts, 2 golf courses, 8 bowling lanes, billiards, moped rental, boat rental with fishing guide, trapshooting range, miniature golf, ice skating. **Evening Programs:** Resort entertainment.

In the Area   Trail rides, fishing; Bridal Cave, HaHa Tonka Castle monument and state park, antiques shops; Abraham Lincoln home and tomb in Springfield, IL; Harry Truman home and library in Independence, MO.

Getting Here *From St. Louis.* By car, I–44 to Rte. 65 (70 min). Limousine
service to and from the airport; rental car available.

Special Notes Supervised morning play camp for youngsters, teenage games
and indoor activity in summer. No smoking in the weights
room. Spa open 9–5 daily; $10 facility fee refunded with ser-
vices.

The Kerr House

Life enhancement
Luxury pampering

Ohio The Kerr House is an antiques-filled Victorian mansion that
Grand Rapids functions as a hideaway for men and women who seek privacy
and a complete overhaul. With just five to seven guests in residence at a time, the facility takes on the atmosphere of a private club. Some weeks are reserved for men only, women only,
or corporate groups.

Yoga, the specialty of the house, is taught in a carpeted exercise
room on the top floor. Laurie Hostetler encourages guests by
providing her own book of *asanas*, the exercise positions of
Hatha yoga. But don't come here looking for weight machines
or a luxurious swimming pool: You won't find them. Exercise is
limited to low-impact aerobics, walking, and three hours of
yoga daily.

Personal counseling makes this spa experience attractive for
those who want to learn healthy habits. A good deal of time is
spent discussing ways to build self-esteem and to deal with
everyday stress. Addictions to smoking, caffeine, and sugar
can be addressed. Avoiding temptation, changing one's daily
routine, and being in a supportive group often inspire success.
During the initial chemical withdrawal, positive support and
breathing exercises to cleanse the lungs and flush impurities
from the body are prescribed. Drinking lots of water, eating
natural foods, and cleansing the colon are also advised. Whirlpool, sauna, and massage sessions are part of the pampering.

The Kerr House
17777 Beaver St., Grand Rapids, OH 43551
Tel. 419/832–1733

Administration Director, Laurie Hostetler

Season Year-round.

Accommodations 5 guest rooms with high ceilings, antiques, lace curtains. The
house has massive wood doors, stained-glass windows, a hand-
carved staircase.

Rates 5-day program (Sun.–Fri.) $2,150 per person double occupan-
cy, $2,550 single. Tax and services included. Weekends $575
double, $675 single. Gratuities optional. 50% payable in ad-
vance. Credit cards: AE, MC, V.

Meal Plans Diet of 750–1,000 calories per day, mainly vegetarian, with fish
and chicken. Low in fat and cholesterol; no salt, sugar, refined
flour, additives. Lunch can include a Senegalese carrot soup,
lettuce salad, pita bread with couscous stuffing, and herbal tea.
Typical dinner entrées are eggplant Parmesan with tomato

sauce; baked chicken breast on wild rice; shrimp and baked potato.

Services and   **Exercise Equipment:** Rebounders, NordicTrack, backswings.
Facilities   **Services:** Massage, pedicure, facial, hair and skin care, reflexology, polarity, herbal body wraps, mineral baths. **Swimming Facilities:** Community pool nearby. **Recreation Facilities:** Hiking along the Maumee River and the Miami & Erie Canal towpath; paddleboat rides. **Evening Programs:** Speakers.

In the Area   Visit to a glass craftsman's studio, the Ludwig Mill (water-powered saw and grist mill), the restored Fort Meigs, farms and country fairs, hydroplane races (Sept.).

Getting Here   *From Toledo.* By car, Ohio Turnpike (I–75) to Rte. 6, Rte. 65 to Rte. 24 (30 min). Complimentary pickup and return at Toledo Express Airport.

Special Notes   No smoking indoors.

Mario's International Spa

Luxury pampering

Ohio   Clevelanders enjoy formal dinners by candlelight, business ex-
Aurora   ecutives shift from meetings to massage appointments, and a dozen or so spa guests in terry-cloth robes take tea in a Victorian parlor, all at Mario's International Spa. Located a few miles from the Ohio Turnpike, this country inn cum spa gives you a sense of having journeyed back to another century; one of the buildings was a stagecoach inn more than 130 years ago.

In addition to the spa building and a conference center, the complex is headquarters for Mario's International, owned and operated by Mario and Joanne Liuzzo, who have combined their experience in the beauty salon business with a love of Victoriana. Their salon outgrew two Victorian houses in eight years. Planned are an Olympic-size pool in the manner of ancient Roman baths, an enclosed jogging track, and 10 new guest rooms.

Fitness is the focus of the programs for corporate members and health-conscious men and women who come here. Aquaerobics, a Dynastic stretch-and-tone class, weight-loss diets, and thalassotherapy are new features. Recreation includes hiking, biking, and other outdoor sports. The spa has widened its selection of exercise equipment and worked on nutrition with Cleveland Clinic. Specialists from the clinic consult on preparation for and recovery from plastic surgery.

Esthetics is what the spa does best: eight facial and throat treatments for men and women, massages, pedicures, manicures, makeup application, and a top-quality salon for hairstyling and dressing. Repechage, a house specialty facial, involves a layered thermal mask with applications of concentrated aloe vera juice, powdered seaweed, and clay. When the hardened clay mask is removed, your complexion feels softer and firmer. The price is $70. Also new is an oxygen treatment to enhance the effect of facials.

Mario's International Spa
35 E. Garfield Rd., Aurora, OH 44202
Tel. 216/562–9171, Fax 216/562–2386

Administration	Director, Joanne Liuzzo
Season	Year-round.
Accommodations	14 rooms in the hotel wing and the original mansion, furnished with period pieces and modern comforts: Jacuzzi, large modern bath, hair dryer, terry-cloth robe. Executive suite has fireplace.
Rates	Day at the Spa package with treatments, lunch, and aerobics $209 per person; 3-day/2-night Retreat package $1,779 per couple, $1,069 single. Tax included, add gratuities. One-third of total payable on booking. Credit cards: AE, MC, V.
Meal Plans	3 meals daily with packages. Oatmeal buttermilk pancake topped with fruit sauce (breakfast), shrimp and vegetable kebab (lunch), ricotta-stuffed zucchini rounds with tomato puree, grilled veal medallions with shiitake mushrooms, and grape mousse made with skim milk (dinner).
Services and Facilities	**Exercise Equipment:** Nautilus and Universal weight machines, stationary bikes, StairMasters, and treadmills planned in fitness center scheduled to open 1995. **Services:** Massage, facials, body scrub with dulce (a nutrient-packed seaweed) and almond oil, manicure, pedicure, parafango muscle treatment with mud/paraffin mix, hydrotherapy tub, Vichy shower, aromatherapy, hairstyling, makeup consultation, personalized exercise instruction, Habitat environmental sauna; health and diet analysis, pre- and post-plastic surgery esthetics treatments. **Recreation Facilities:** Bicycling; golf, tennis, horseback riding nearby; downhill and cross-country skiing. **Evening Programs:** Lectures on health topics.
In the Area	Antiques shops, flea markets, shopping areas, Sea World. Blossom Music Center (Cleveland Orchestra) June–Aug.
Getting Here	*From Cleveland.* By bus, Greyhound (50 min). By car, I–480 to Rte. 91, Rte. 82 and 306; or the Ohio Turnpike (I–80) to Exit 13 (40 min). Limousine service from Cleveland Hopkins Airport; rental car available.
Special Notes	Limited access for people with disabilities. Nonsmoking areas designated.

Sans Souci Health Resort

Luxury pampering
Stress control
Vibrant maturity
Weight management

Ohio *Bellbrook*	On a beautiful, secluded 80-acre estate, a small band of health seekers follows the owner and director of the Sans Souci Health Resort, Susanne Kircher, on a parcourse fitness trail across the immaculate lawn of the country retreat. Birdsong and gentle breezes enhance the outdoor sessions of stretching, breathing, and wakeup exercises. Miles of hiking trails crisscross the woods and meadows of the estate, which borders a 600-acre wildlife preserve.

Kircher, a registered nurse and a former consultant to Olympic athletes, mixes European spa philosophy with no-frills fitness training. The daily agenda is full of aerobics, from dance steps to slimnastics, and water workouts in the swimming pool during warm months. Meals are mainly vegetarian.

The programs in the spacious country home where the Romanian-born Kircher began her fitness resort in 1978 are devoted to stress management and stopping smoking. Kircher's philosophy spells LSD: long, slow, distance achievements. Rather than fast fixes, the program helps you plan practical goals. A stern taskmaster, she summons you to join a meditation walk to the pine forest, or race-walking practice. "You will join us for exercise this morning?" is more statement than question. Your answer will be yes.

Sans Souci Health Resort
3745 Rte. 725, Bellbrook, OH 45305
Tel. 5/848–4851

Administration Director, Susanne Kircher, R.N.

Season May–Oct.

Accommodations Spacious, airy rooms furnished English country style, with private bath, dressing area.

Rates 5-night program Sun.–Fri. $1,280 per person double occupancy, $1,480 single; weekend retreats $550 per person double, $650 single. Daily rate $152 (no room). 30% payable in advance. Tax and gratuity included. Credit cards: MC, V.

Meal Plans 800–1,000 calorie daily diet includes breakfast (sprouted wheat berries in soy milk or homemade granola), snacks, mineral water, lunch (whole-grain crepe, green salad, and steamed vegetables), and dinner (seafood divan, fruit-garnished chicken) served by candlelight. Juice fast recommended on day of arrival.

Services and Facilities **Exercise Equipment:** Stationary bike, Rebounder, 18-station parcourse. **Services:** Massage, aromatherapy, acupressure, loofah scrub, facials, herbal wraps, manicures, pedicures, hair and skin care; cooking demonstrations, personal consultation on nutrition and diet. **Swimming Facilities:** Outdoor pool, lake. **Recreation Facilities:** Horseback riding, badminton, volleyball, croquet; golf, tennis, and fishing nearby. **Evening Programs:** Workshops on behavior modification, stress management, nutrition; assertiveness training; therapeutic massage and Jacuzzi relaxation. Guest lecturers and films.

In the Area Picnic lunches, tour of Bellbrook, 600-acre Sugarcreek Reserve.

Getting Here *From Dayton.* By car, I–75 to Rte. 725 East (30 min). Free service to Dayton International Airport; $20 for pickup on arrival.

Special Notes No smoking indoors.

The American Club

Nonprogram resort

Wisconsin In a town dominated by the nation's leading manufacturer of
Kohler plumbing fixtures and bathtubs, it can be no surprise that luxury and bathing are synonymous at the American Club's 237-room hotel owned and operated by the Kohler Company. Part of the club's charm lies in being in a place that looks like a Hollywood vision of middle America yet functions with the precision of a posh resort. The original Tudor-style dormitory, reminiscent of a country inn, has been duplicated across a garden courtyard where a Victorian greenhouse serves as an ice cream parlor.

With a 36-hole golf course designed by Pete Dye, a Sports Core with indoor and outdoor tennis courts and a spa salon, and a 500-acre nature preserve where country gourmet meals are served in a secluded log lodge, the American Club has become an oasis of fitness in the Midwest.

Whirlpools for two are set on glass-covered terraces and in mirrored baths. For the ultimate in hedonism, ask for a suite equipped with the Kohler Shower Tower (similar to Swiss shower) or the Habitat, a master bath with an hour's serenity programmed into it: The sounds of a rain forest, soft breezes, a gentle mist, a steam bath, even desert tanning are simulated.

Checking in at the Sports Core, you get a locker and towel and the opportunity to schedule herbal wraps, massage, and court times. In addition to racquetball courts (used for handball and wallyball, too), six indoor tennis courts are available for an hourly fee, while the outdoor courts are free. The Peter Burwash International staff offers professional instruction. Exercise rooms, aerobics studio, and health services are downstairs. A glass-walled 60-foot swimming pool and the Lean Bean restaurant (a happy discovery for dieters) are off the lobby.

River Wildlife is a place apart, one where the outdoors and good food are celebrated. Marksmen practice, hikers explore more than 30 miles of woodland trails, and canoeists and fishermen enjoy the winding Sheboygan River. Horseback rides can be solo or escorted. In winter the trails are groomed for cross-country skiing. Lunch is served daily in a rustic lodge, dinner on weekends in front of the huge fireplace. American Club guests need only a $7 pass to use the facilities; the trails are open to all.

The American Club
Highland Dr., Kohler, WI 53044
Tel. 414/457–8000 or 800/344–2838
Fax 414/457–0299

Administration General Manager, Alice Hubbard

Season Year-round.

Accommodations 237 rooms with a range of whirlpool baths, 4-poster brass beds with feather comforters and pillows, wood paneling, carved oak doors, sitting areas, glassed-in terrace with hot tub, wet bar, and mirrored bath in some rooms. Rooms in the renovated Carriage House are reached by crossing the parking lot or using an underground walkway. Free transportation between facilities.

Rates $114–$550 for 2 in double room, $89–$550 single. 2-day escape packages for 2 persons, including a bubble massage at the Sports Core and some meals, $308 and up. For golfers, 2 rounds at Blackwolf Run, plus amenities, $694 for 2 persons double occupancy. 1-day Gold Program with spa services $264. 1 night payable in advance. Tax and gratuity not included. Credit cards: AE, DC, MC, V.

Meal Plans   Breakfast buffet in the Wisconsin Room, expanded menu at Sunday brunch. Dinner at the Immigrant is a dress-up affair in small rooms dedicated to the club's original European occupants; specialties are Wisconsin whitefish caviar roe, scallops, shrimp, seafood sausage on spinach pasta, mesquite-roasted loin of Iowa pork, Kohler Purelean beef. The River Wildlife menu, changed every weekend, can feature pheasant pâté, grilled rabbit, broiled fresh brook trout stuffed with vegetables, veal scallops with pesto and 5-cheese sauce. Salad of sprouts and seasonal greens or hamburgers at the Lean Bean or the Horse & Plow pub restaurant for lunch.

Services and Facilities   **Exercise Equipment:** 14-station Nautilus circuit, 8 Lifecycles, 3 StairMasters, Liferower; 16-station Universal gym, 6 Schwinn Air Dyne bikes, 2 rowers, Olympic free weights, NordicTrack, 3 step machines. **Services:** Massage, herbal wrap, body wrap, facial, manicure, pedicure; fitness consultation; hydrotherapy. Aerobics classes throughout the day ($6.50 each). Clay marksmanship course, crazy-quail shooting, archery instruction. **Swimming Facilities:** Indoor lap pool, lake with sandy beach. **Recreation Facilities:** 6 indoor and 6 outdoor tennis courts, 2 handball/racquetball courts, fishing, canoeing and boating, bicycle rentals, hiking, cross-country skiing, 2 golf courses.

In the Area   Half-day canoe trip, nature walks, charter-boat fishing on Lake Michigan; Kettle Moraine State Forest (Ice Age formations), dunes on Lake Michigan beaches, nature trail at Sheboygan Indian Mound Park, Kohler Arts Center, Kohler Design Center, cheese plant tour, Kohler Company tour, Manitowac Maritime Museum, shops at Woodlake Kohler.

Getting Here   *From Milwaukee.* By car, I–43 to Exit 126, Rte. 23 west to Kohler (about 60 min). By bus, Greyhound to Sheboygan (70 min). Limousine Service (tel. 800/236–5452) to and from Milwaukee's Mitchell Airport, Amtrak, and bus stations.

Special Notes   Elevators link all floors. The Sports Core has supervised activities for children 1½–6. Older children can join week-long summer-camp programs or sign up for tennis and swimming lessons. No smoking in Sports Core athletic and therapy areas.

Aveda Spa Osceola

Life enhancement
Luxury pampering
Weight management

Wisconsin   On the banks of the St. Croix river, about an hour's drive from
Osceola   Minneapolis/St. Paul, is the Aveda Spa Osceola, opened in 1990. A former estate on 80 acres, the prairie-style three-story house dating from 1908 has been rejuvenated with hydrothera-

py rooms, European shampoo bed, a few pieces of exercise equipment, and a beauty salon.

The resort, owned and managed by the Aveda Corporation, a Minneapolis-based producer of natural products for the hair and skin, serves as both a day spa and a country getaway. In summer, you can enjoy walking, running, or biking on scenic trails surrounding the spa, or spend hours canoeing on the placid St. Croix River. In winter, cross-country skiing, snowshoeing, and ice-skating outings are organized. You may also choose to visit their Native American sweat lodge.

Spa treatments, enhanced with flower and plant essences and the pure water of St. Croix Springs, are designed to refresh and relax your body. Advanced cellular skin-care technology has been incorporated into the spa's skin-care treatments, which include aromatherapy.

Much of the decor is retained from the 1920s, along with antiques from the 17th century. A mammoth fireplace fills one end of a living room stripped of furniture for the daily session of yoga. Up the wide oak stairway are six bedrooms with polished wood floors; bright Pakistani, Indian, and Turkish carpets; and antique wooden beds laden with down pillows and duvets.

In the lower level of the house, past the sauna and exercise salon, are areas for treatments plus grottolike single bedrooms. Private rooms for massage, facials, and a hydrotherapy tub are reserved for guest use. Additional treatment and guest rooms are in the carriage house.

Programs are individually tailored to each guest's needs. Organized activity is minimal, as are the meals, but if you want the ultimate in skin care while shedding a few pounds, this is the place.

Aveda Spa Osceola
1015 Cascade St., Rte. 3, Box 72, Osceola, WI 54020
Tel. 715/294–4465 or 800/283–3202
Fax 715/294–2196

Administration General manager-owner, Horst Rechelbacher

Season Year-round.

Accommodations 10 guest rooms, including suites. Furniture ranges from Indian to antiques to Art Deco, with wicker chairs, brass beds. Most rooms have private bath, air-conditioning; no TV or telephones.

Rates A weekend stay with spa services and meals is $550 single, $525 per person double occupancy. 5-day stays are $1,300 single, $1,010 double. Gratuities for meals and taxes included. A 1-day package with lunch is $210 without lodging, $295–$329 overnight. Deposit 50% payable in advance. Credit cards: AE, MC, V.

Meal Plans Organic menu includes lunch choices of tomato aspic with guacamole, endive, and nasturtium salad. Dinner entrées include organically raised trout or grilled salmon with jalapeño and roasted tomato sauce, stuffed baby artichokes, Peruvian potatoes, and steamed green beans. Macrobiotic meals are available.

Services and Facilities **Exercise Equipment:** StairMaster, NordicTrack, Windbike, incline bed. **Services:** Swedish massage, shiatsu, reflexology, aromatherapy, underwater massage; beauty salon for hair, nail, and skin care. **Swimming Facilities:** Community outdoor pool. **Evening Programs:** Speakers on self-management, organic cooking, stress management, personal success, and the science of flower and plant essences.

In the Area Antiques shops in the village of Osceola, canoeing, antique airplane flying (Aug.).

Getting Here *From Minneapolis.* Transportation from the Minneapolis/St. Paul International Airport, $50. By car, I–35 north to Hwy. 97 east, Rte. 95 north to Hwy. 243, east to Rte. 35 north (1 hr). Rental car available.

Special Notes Minimum age in spa is 18. Limited access for people with disabilities. No smoking in the mansion. Mosquitoes can be annoying between June and Sept.

The Fontana Spa at the Abbey

Luxury pampering
Nutrition and diet
Vibrant maturity
Weight management

Wisconsin Surrounded by panoramic views of Lake Geneva and the
Lake Geneva woods, the glass-walled swimming pool and aerobics studio at the Fontana Spa have an indoor-outdoor feeling that is enhanced by the changing seasons. The spa's opening in 1989 marked a radical innovation for the landmark resort. The ambience here, unlike that of the traditional country inn, is modern with accents in furniture and leaded-glass inspired by Frank Lloyd Wright's prairie designs.

Unexpected amenities add to the feeling of well-being: pitchers of fresh fruit juices along with muffins and fruit are laid out in the morning; the spa salon exudes the aroma of herbs and oils used in the imported French body and skin-care products by Phytomer.

The wide range of services in the spa packages (or on an à la carte basis for resort guests) distinguishes the Fontana as a destination that will appeal to sophisticated spa goers. Treatments range from loofah scrubs, thalassotherapy, and herbal wraps to European hand and foot treatments, from mud masks and aromatherapy facials to massages. In all, 33 different services are offered in combination with aerobic and aquatic exercise classes, and one-on-one training with the latest in exercise equipment.

Popular with women who are trying to shed a few pounds, the spa also has programs geared to the special needs of older guests. The staff includes a registered nurse who conducts an initial fitness and health evaluation. Programs are individually tailored to the needs of guests, and maximum enrollment is 30 participants at one time.

The Fontana Spa at the Abbey
Hwy. 67/Fontana Blvd., Fontana, WI 53125
Tel. 414/275-5910 or 800/772-1000
Fax 414/275-5910

Administration General manager, Steve Kostechka; spa director, Karen Saia

Season Year-round.

Accommodations 358 rooms in modern lodge (24 new spa wing rooms in 1991). Twin double beds, TV, telephone, air-conditioning. Some locations noisy; lodge has direct entrance to spa building.

Rates 2-night spa sampler midweek $501.86-$579.21 single, $430.04-$468.71 per person double, weekends $523.96-$634.46 single, $441.09-$496.34 per person double; 5-night package $1,439-$1,604 single, $1,260-$1,343 per person double. Spa packages include gratuities and taxes. 50% advance payment. Credit cards: AE, DC, MC, V.

Meal Plans Menu selections in the spa's dining room are low in calories, saturated fat, and cholesterol. Breakfast can be cinnamon French toast, apple compote, or miniblueberry muffins. 3-course lunch and dinner include barbecued chicken, sea bass wrapped in spinach and served on a bed of saffron couscous.

Services and Facilities **Exercise Equipment:** 10-unit Eagle weight training gym, 2 Lifecycles, 2 Turbo bikes, 2 Precor treadmills, StairMaster, 2 rowing machines, free weights, Sierra cross-country ski machine. **Services:** Swedish massage, shiatsu, acupressure, aromatherapy, fango, herbal wrap, loofah body scrub, facials, body polish, mineral baths, Scotch hose/Swiss shower, 3 underwater massage tubs; aerobics and aquacise classes, fitness evaluation; full-service beauty salon. **Swimming Facilities:** Indoor lap pool (18½ yds), outdoor pool, lake. **Spa Facilities:** Separate men's and women's sauna, steam room, whirlpool; coed Jacuzzis, aerobics studio, pool. **Recreation Facilities:** 6 outdoor tennis courts (lighted), horseback riding, parcourse; golf, boating, racquetball, bike trips nearby; hiking. **Evening Programs:** cooking demonstration, resort entertainment.

In the Area Live theater and concerts, shopping, antiques shops.

Getting Here *From Chicago.* Limousine service (fee) from O'Hare International Airport. By car, I-94, Routes 50 and 67 (2 hr). By bus, Wisconsin Limo (tel. 312/427-3100) runs twice daily, takes 2 hrs, and costs $20 each way. By air, Delavan Airport handles private aircraft. Rental car available.

Special Notes No smoking in spa or spa dining room. Ground-floor accommodations for people with disabilities. Minimum age in spa 18; daily charge ($33) for guests not on package plan.

Olympia Village Resort

Nonprogram resort

Wisconsin
Oconomowoc
Olympia Village, a first-class vacation resort for relaxation and rejuvenation, is a good place to escape for a few days or a week. The spa's aerobics studio with a cushioned floor, offers a full schedule of classes that includes a workout in the pool.

A three-day spa package includes two lunches and personal services. You're free to exercise in the weights room or work on your appearance. A personalized fitness program and daily diet will be tailored to your needs and physical abilities by the staff director. (Salon services are available in the main lodge, on an à la carte basis.)

Coed whirlpools and sunken Roman baths allow socializing or a private soak. Separate saunas and steam rooms for men and women and private massage rooms are among the extensive facilities for guests and residents of nearby condominiums. Luxuriously tiled and carpeted, the spa combines glamorous atmosphere and gentle discipline.

Olympia Village Resort
1350 Royale Mile Rd., Oconomowoc, WI 53066
Tel. 414/567–0311 or 800/558–9573

Administration General manager, Ron Droegmyer; spa manager, Lois Stallman

Season Year-round.

Accommodations 380 modern rooms facing a lake and ski lifts. Fully carpeted and air-conditioned, all rooms have private bath and color TV.

Rates 2-night spa package $294 per person double occupancy. Suites $75 additional per day. Gratuities and tax included. Advance guarantee by credit card. Credit cards: AE, MC, V.

Meal Plans Dinner choices include broiled herbed chicken, broiled pike in lemon dill sauce, steamed lobster. Luncheon menu changes daily, features spinach quiche, chef's salad.

Services and Facilities **Exercise Equipment:** 2 Lifecycles, Biocycle, 2 StairMasters, 12-station Universal weight training gym, rowing machine, dumbbells, 30 free weights, wrist weights. **Services:** Exercise classes, massage, herbal wrap, facial, pedicure, manicure, loofah body scrub, hair and skin care. **Swimming Facilities:** Indoor and outdoor pools, private beach on lake. **Recreation Facilities:** Indoor and outdoor tennis, racquetball courts, golf, horseback riding, bicycle rental, water sports; downhill and cross-country skiing. **Evening Programs:** Resort entertainment, movie theaters.

In the Area Old World Wisconsin (living history village), Octagon House (historic home), fishing, Milwaukee Brewers baseball.

Getting Here *From Milwaukee.* By car, I–94 to Rte. 67 (40 min).

Special Notes Elevators and ramps connecting all floors provide access for people with disabilities. No smoking in the spa or spa dining room. Spa open daily 6:30 AM–10 PM in summer; winter schedule varies.

The South

From hot-springs spas to holistic mountain retreats, the range of health facilities in the South includes some of the oldest and some of the newest resorts in the nation. Virginia's Warm Springs baths, Hot Springs National Park in Arkansas, and the ultramodern Sea Island Beach Club Spa at The Cloister in Georgia, make dramatic contrasts that show how far the pursuit of fitness has come over the last century.

The Diet and Fitness Center, sponsored by Duke University Medical Center in North Carolina, advances programs for health maintenance, as do the Wildwood Lifestyle Center, a Seventh-Day Adventist medical center in Georgia, and the private Hilton Head Health Institute set amid sea pines in South Carolina. The only Pritikin Longevity Center on the East Coast combines its weight management program with a Miami Beach vacation.

For the combination of fitness facilities and sports opportunities, few resorts can match the programs of the PGA National Resort & Spa, Fisher Island Spa Internazionale, and the Safety Harbor Spa and Fitness Center, all in Florida. Georgia's Chateau Elan, the world's only spa at a winery, has its own bottled waters and wines, as well as three golf courses plus equestrian and tennis centers, less than an hour's drive from Atlanta.

Budget-conscious vacationers get a bonus in weight management programs at the Tennessee Fitness Spa and Miami's Lido Spa Hotel, both of which cater to mature guests. The holistic approach at the new Royal Atlantic Health Spa, in Florida, may be the best value on the beach.

Uchee Pines Institute Health Center

Preventive medicine
Vibrant maturity
Weight management

Alabama
Seale

This homelike retreat offers health conditioning and special diets in comprehensive 18-day sessions that appeal mostly to persons over 50. The medically directed programs at the Uchee Pines Institute treat most degenerative diseases.

The Health Conditioning Center expounds traditional Seventh-Day Adventist (but is nondenominational and nonsectarian) philosophies on nutrition and mental and spiritual health. Led by three physicians, the staff combines medical and natural healing. A nutritional analysis, aided by computers, gives each patient specific diet recommendations and takes into account each individual's physical condition, nutritional needs, and weight loss goals. Following each guest's complete physical examination (some of which may be covered by medical insurance), a physician prescribes a personal schedule and continues to monitor the patient's progress throughout the program. Treatments to stop smoking, drinking, or other lifestyle problems are also offered.

The South

Alabama
Uchee Pines Institute
Health Center, **2**

Arkansas
Hot Springs National
Park, **1**

Florida
Bonaventure Resort &
Spa, **29**
The Don CeSar Beach
Resort, **21**
Doral Golf Resort and
Spa , **35**
Fisher Island Spa
Internazionale, **30**

Fontainebleau Hilton
Resort and Spa, **33**
Hippocrates Health
Institute, **25**
Lido Spa Hotel, **31**
Palm-Aire Spa Resort
& Country Club, **27**
PGA National Resort
& Spa, **24**
The Pier House
Caribbean Spa, **23**
Pritikin Longevity
Center, **34**
Royal Atlantic Health
Spa, **26**
Saddlebrook Sports
Science, **19**

Safety Harbor Spa and
Fitness Center, **20**
Sanibel Harbour
Resort & Spa, **22**
Spa LXVI at Pier 66
Crown Plaza
Resort, **28**
Turnberry Isle Resort
and Club, **32**

Georgia
Chateau Elan, **5**
Sea Island Beach Club
Spa at The Cloister, **18**
Wildwood Lifestyle
Center, **4**

North Carolina
Duke University Diet
and Fitness Center, **15**
Structure House, **14**
Westglow Spa, **6**

South Carolina
Hilton Head Health
Institute, **16**
Hilton Head Westin
Resort, **17**

Tennessee
Tennessee Fitness
Spa, **3**

OHIO

WEST VIRGINIA

★ Washington, D.C.

I-95

⑧

⑨

I-64

Richmond ★

⑦

nkfort

Lexington

I-64

I-80

⑩ ⑪

I-12 I-13

Norfolk

Roanoke

I-85

I-13

KENTUCKY

I-75

I-81

VIRGINIA

Knoxville

⑥

I-77

Greensboro ⑭ ⑮

Winston-Salem

Rocky Mount

Raleigh ★

NORTH CAROLINA

attanooga

I-75

I-85

I-26

Charlotte

Greenville

⑤

I-20

Columbia ★

SOUTH CAROLINA

★ Atlanta

Augusta

I-85

Macon

I-16

Savannah R.

I-95

Charleston

I-17

GEORGIA

⑯

⑰

Chattahoochee River

Flint River

Valdosta

Savannah

⑱

Tallahassee ✪

I-10

Jacksonville

I-75

I-95

Daytona Beach

FLORIDA

Orlando

I-4

0   200 miles
0   300 miles

⑲

⑳

㉑ Tampa

㉔ ㉕

㉖

Fort Myers

㉗ ㉘ Fort

㉒

I-41

㉙ Lauderdale

Miami

㉚

㉛—㉟

Key West ㉓

ATLANTIC OCEAN

N

Virginia

Camp
Rediscovery, **8**

Hartland Wellness
Center, **9**

The Homestead, **7**

The Integral Health
Center, **10**

The Kingsmill
Resort, **12**

The Tazewell Club, **13**

Yogaville, **11**

Secluded in a 200-acre woodland preserve near the Chattahoochee River, the center's live-in accommodations for 14 guests provide privacy and comfort. Walks, gardening, exercise, and hydrotherapy balance out daily lectures on preventive medicine, nutrition, and lifestyle change.

The health center is equipped with a heated, full-body whirlpool, steam bath, massage tables, and ultrasound therapy units. Special treatments include fomentation—application of moist heat to the body for relief from congestion or pain—and the use of ice packs to slow down circulation or arrest a physical reaction. Only a few pieces of exercise equipment are available to those who want an active program.

Uchee Pines Institute Health Center
Rte. 1, Box 273, Seale, AL 36875
Tel. 205/855-4764

Administration	Manager, Joseph Anaman; medical director, David Miller, M.D.
Season	Year-round.
Accommodations	7 twin-bed rooms with modern furniture, flowered bedspreads, ceiling fans, reading lamps. Private bath.
Rates	$2,595 for an 18-day live-in session, all-inclusive; $2,395 for a spouse as a patient, $1,495 as a nonpatient (includes physical exam and medical consultation). $500 per person advance payment; 5% discount for full payment. Credit cards (4% surcharge): MC, V.
Meal Plans	3 vegetarian meals daily, family style. Adventist diet of fruits, vegetables, legumes, and grains. No fats, butter, or oils. Olives, nuts, and avocado in moderate amounts. Entrées include vegetarian lasagna, whole-wheat pizza, baked tofu.
Services and Facilities	**Exercise Equipment:** Stationary bike, jogger trampoline. **Services:** Massage, showers. **Spa Facilities:** Whirlpool, steam bath. **Recreation Facilities:** Nature hiking, bicycling, gardening, orchard work. **Evening Programs:** Informal discussions of health-related topics.
In the Area	Group outings to Callaway Gardens; Providence Canyon, Tuskegee Institute Museum (history and agriculture).
Getting Here	*From Atlanta.* By bus, Greyhound to Columbus, GA (5 hr). By plane, Delta Airlines to Columbus, GA (30 min). By car, I-185 via Columbus, Rte. 80 to Rte. 431, south to Rtes. 24 and 39 (about 5 hr). Free pickup to and from airport and bus station.
Special Notes	No smoking indoors.

Hot Springs National Park

Taking the waters

Arkansas
Hot Springs

Hot Springs National Park was once called the Valley of the Vapors. Native Americans and Spanish conquistadores were attracted by clouds of steam from the 47 springs that bring hot mineral water to the surface in what is now a national park within a resort city. Local lore has it that Hernando de Soto and his explorers relaxed here in 1541. The park rangers tell visitors about the spring water's 4,000-year journey from deep within the earth, where it is heated to 143°F, and its mineral content from which its therapeutic properties derive.

In 1832, the federal government set aside four sections of the springs as a health reservation, the first in the country's history. A partnership evolved with private bathhouse and hotel operators, so the National Park Service now regulates operations and maintains the reservoirs, where the spring water cools down to 100°F for bathing.

Six bathing facilities are open to the public, and plans are underway for renovation and adaptive reuse of several Art Deco buildings on Bathhouse Row. The most splendid of the eight buildings surviving here, The Fordyce, was built in 1915 by a Colonel Fordyce, who credited the spring waters with saving his life. The interior has stained-glass windows and a skylight with scenes of water nymphs, appropriate for the Museum of Bathing, created as part of the building's restoration in 1989.

In the Buckstaff Bathhouse, a stately three-story brick-and-marble edifice, bathers step into a private porcelain tub filled with mineral water heated to 103°F. Plan on about 1½ hours for a soak in the thermal waters, the whirlpools, and a massage. The entire treatment at Buckstaff Baths, including hot packs on sore muscles and a multineedled shower, costs about $35. Reservations are essential.

Vacationing here is like taking a step back in time. Grand old hotels as well as mansions offer bed and breakfast. Hot Springs is also a modern medical center for advanced therapy of degenerative diseases and rehabilitation treatments for postcardiac or surgery patients. The town has the flavor of a 19th-century European spa—all the charm without the exaggerated claims.

Hot Springs National Park
Box 1860, Hot Springs, AR 71902
Tel. 501/623–2308

Hot Springs Convention & Visitors Bureau
Box K, Hot Springs National Park, AR 71902
Tel. 501/321–2835 or 800/543–2284

Administration	Superintendent, Roger Giddings
Season	Year-round.
Accommodations	Bathing facilities and 53 rooms with spring water piped into the bathroom at the 488-room Arlington Hotel (tel. 800/643–1502). Other public pools at the Hilton, Downtowner, and Majestic hotels. Guest houses and camping facilities nearby. Rehabilitation therapy and baths at Hot Springs Health Spa, open daily 9–9.
Services and Facilities	**Swimming Facilities:** Indoor and outdoor pools at hotels; lakes nearby. **Spa Facilities:** 6 bathhouses operate under the auspices of U.S. Department of the Interior. All open Mon.–Sat. 7 AM–11:30 PM, 1:30 PM–4 PM; hotel hours vary. Arlington open Sun. morning. **Services:** massage, hot packs, baths. **Recreation Facilities:** Hiking trails in Ouachita Mountains, boating, fishing, biking, horseback riding; cross-country skiing. Hotels offer tennis, golf. **Programs:** 12-min. slide program scheduled in park headquarters auditorium.
In the Area	Ouachita Lake recreational area, Oaklawn Park (Thoroughbred racing, late Jan.–mid-Apr.), Hot Springs Mountain Tow-

er, Ozark Folk Center at Mountain View (concerts, exhibits), Cowie Wine Cellars in Eureka Springs, Alligator Farm, Toltec Mounds State Park (Indian earthworks).

Getting Here *From Little Rock.* By bus, Greyhound (60 min). By car, I–30 to Hot Springs Exit, Rte. 70 West (60 min).

Special Notes Ramps and specially equipped rooms in most hotels and Buckstaff Baths. No smoking in bathhouses.

Bonaventure Resort & Spa

Luxury pampering
Nonprogram resort
Weight management

Florida If you want to go first class on a tight budget, consider a holiday
Fort Lauderdale at the Bonaventure Resort & Spa, where you can arrange first-rate services à la carte or as a package. The difference between the two is in quantity of services, not quality. You can stay a weekend, four days, or a full week; take unlimited exercise classes and enjoy expert bodywork and beauty treatments; or orient your visit around sports—tennis, golf, and horseback riding. But beware adding too many extras to your spa schedule, as your bill will quickly run up.

Sybaritic pleasures aside, management takes a serious approach to fitness here. A staff nurse interviews you on arrival and may suggest consultation on a diet plan. Guests can opt for calorie-controlled meals or dine in the gourmet dining room.

A typical day begins with a walk or jog around the golf course before breakfast, then an hour-long aerobics class. Three levels of conditioning are offered in a dozen different classes that range from easy stretches and yoga to deep toning calisthenics and energizing routines. Workouts in the water are popular, especially for people with orthopedic problems; there's support for joints and the back while doing aquatics in the pool. There are cardiovascular exercises for men only, as well as a thermal mineral water body scrub and massage to condition the male physique.

What sets this spa apart from others is the wide range of body and skin-care treatments. Always on the cutting edge, Bonaventure recently introduced the European Kur program developed by Kerstin Florian with thermal-water crystals from Hungary. Adding to its repertoire of hydrotherapy, the kur includes bodywork with an imported line of essential oils used in the aromatherapy massage.

Families with children have the extra advantage with the sports program for teenagers and day camp for youngsters. Ocean beaches are just 30 minutes away by car, making outings a reasonable alternative to staying on resort grounds throughout your vacation.

Bonaventure Resort & Spa
250 Racquet Club Rd., Fort Lauderdale, FL 33326
Tel. 305/389–3300 or 800/327–8090
Fax 305/384–6157

Administration Managing director, Don DeFeo; spa director, Tanya Lee

Season Year-round.

Accommodations 493 luxury guest rooms and suites in 9 4-story buildings; Spacious rooms with balconies overlook lake or golf course with 2 beds (queen-size or twin) or 1 extra-large king-size. Rattan seating and tropical colors. Oversize bath with dressing area.

Rates $150–$250 daily for 1 or 2 persons; Perfect Day package at spa $195 per person (lodging not included), plus tax and gratuity. Bonaventure spa package without services (2-night minimum stay) $172–$277 single, $129–$179 double. Add tax, service charges. Additional bodywork and beauty treatments, golf and tennis packages available. 1 night's advance payment 7 days after booking or credit card confirmation. Credit cards: AE, D, MC, V.

Meal Plans 3 meals with calorie-counted selections served daily in private Spa Dining Room included in packages. 1,200 calories suggested for those not on weight-loss diet. Lunch specialties include pasta primavera, curried chicken soup, baked vegetables marinara with tofu, and fresh fruit. Dinner entrées include Maine lobster with asparagus spears, stir-fried chicken and vegetables on cellophane noodles, dessert crepe with blueberry and cheese filling.

Services and Facilities **Exercise Equipment:** 10-station Keiser gym, 3 Lifecycles, 5 Quinton treadmills, 3 stationary bikes, 2 StairMasters, Gravitron, 2 Lifesteps, Liferower, free weights (5–50 lb). **Services:** Massage (Swedish, shiatsu, aromatherapy, reflexology), aromatherapy bath, loofah body scrub, herbal wrap, sea-kelp body wrap, thermal back treatment, baths, and facials. Men's and women's salons for skin and nail care, hairstyling. Private exercise, golf, tennis, and horseback-riding instruction. Individualized fitness profile, nutrition profile, and body composition analysis. **Swimming Facilities:** Outdoor pools; ocean beach nearby. **Spa Facilities:** 3½-foot exercise pool, outdoor Jacuzzi, Finnish sauna, Turkish steambath, hot and cold plunge baths. **Recreation Facilities:** 24 tennis courts, 2 18-hole golf courses, 6 racquetball and squash courts, horseback riding, bicycle rental. **Evening Programs:** None.

In the Area Shopping trip to Sawgrass Mill Mall, beach shuttle; local sightseeing on request. Everglades tour by airboat, jai-alai fronton, Bahamas cruises, dog- and horse-racing tracks, Seminole Indian village, Fort Lauderdale museums and performing arts center.

Getting Here *From Miami.* By car, I–75 to Fort Lauderdale, Arvida Parkway Exit, State Rd. 84 (40 min). By plane, scheduled service (15 min). Taxi, rental car available.

Special Notes Ramps, elevators, and specially equipped rooms for the disabled. No smoking in spa building or in designated areas of the dining room. Spa open daily 7–7 winter season, summer hours vary.

The Don CeSar Beach Resort

Nonprogram resort
Taking the waters

Florida
St. Petersburg
Beach

Thalassotherapy is featured at the new spa facilities of The Don CeSar Beach Resort. This historic hotel's location on the Gulf of Mexico makes it easy to provide a course of treatments using seaweed, marine plant extracts, and spirulina to rejuvenate the body after the ravages of time and sun exposure. Rather than offering a fixed program, the spa, which is the first on Florida's Coast to use such treatments, offers services à la carte and is open to nonguests as well as hotel residents. While facilities are limited (there is no indoor seawater exercise pool), the spa offers a fitness assessment and take-home program.

Redolent of the Roaring Twenties, this pink palace is affectionately called "The Don" by visitors who relish its stately public rooms trimmed with crystal chandeliers and marble fountains. Recently it underwent a $14 million facelift to restore its Moorish/Mediterranean ambience. Below the lobby a grand staircase leads to the sleek, cool confines of the spa. Offering daily beachside exercise classes, and the latest in exercise equipment, this can be a welcome retreat from the sun.

Selecting from a menu of eight sea-oriented body treatments, you can set a course to rejuvenate, relax, or restore. Scrubs and polishes are recommended to prepare your skin for the full benefits of body wraps and massage therapies. Seaweed body wraps, using Floraspa products imported from France, are said to revitalize.

Most of these treatments are priced at $60–$70, with the ultimate combinations up to $149. Issued a robe, slippers, and locker at check-in, you're free to use the Beach Club facilities for the rest of the day, including sauna and whirlpool. The $10 facility fee shows up on your bill, along with 7% sales tax.

The Don CeSar Beach Resort

3400 Gulf Blvd., St. Petersburg Beach, FL 33706
Tel. 813/360–1881, 800/282–1116, or 800/637–7200
Fax 813/367–3609

Administration General manager, Lawrence Trainor; spa manager, Thor Holm

Season Year-round.

Accommodations 277 rooms including 50 suites and 2 penthouses. All have bathroom with marble walls, traditional bedroom furniture, TV, phone, air-conditioning.

Rates $175–$215 per room for 2 during summer. Credit cards: AE, D, MC, V.

Meal Plans No meal plan. Healthy selections appear on the menus of 4 restaurants and room service.

Services and Facilities **Exercise Equipment:** 2 modular CYBEX weight training units, 2 CYBEX treadmills, 2 StairMaster 4000PT, 2 Lifecycles, 2 Schwinn Air Dyne Cycles. **Services:** Massage, aromatherapy, body wraps, sea scrub, spirulina body masque, reflexology; personal training, fitness assessment. **Swimming Facilities:** Olympic-size outdoor pool, ocean beach. **Recreation Facilities:**

2 tennis courts with lighted hard surface; beachfront water sports. Nearby 18-hole golf course, deep sea fishing, sailing.

In the Area Busch Gardens, Disney World, Dali Museum, St. Petersburg Historical Museum, Florida International Museum, Ybor City (historic Tampa), Sarasota Ringling Museum, Asolo State Theater (opera and plays), Ruth Eckerd Hall (concerts), seabird sanctuary, marine mammal center, Florida Suncoast Dome (sports), baseball spring training, Tampa Bay Buccaneers football.

Getting Here *From Tampa.* By car, I–275 (25 min). By van, scheduled service from Tampa International Airport. Rental car, taxi, and limousine available.

Special Notes Facilities accessible for people with disabilities. Kids Ltd. day care program for ages 5–12. Spa hours Mon.–Sat., 7 AM–9 PM, Sun. and holidays 9–5.

The Doral Golf Resort and Spa

Life enhancement
Luxury pampering
Sports conditioning
Stress control

Florida Like a vision of Tuscany, the villa's red-tile roof rises above for-
Miami mal gardens, statuary, and cascading fountains at the Doral Country Club. The mood inside is modern, without a trace of sweaty workouts to disturb the calm. The spa is self-contained, with a wing of suites and a dining atrium just for those participating in one of the deluxe fitness and beauty packages.

Around the upper levels of the central atrium are the men's and women's locker rooms, equipped with whirlpool, saunas (dry and steam), sun deck, and lounge; 26 private massage rooms with a selection of treatments; a coed beauty salon and skin-care treatment rooms; and a running track.

The spa at the Doral blends European and American health concepts, but keeps daily regimens flexible. The classes tend to be jazzy, low-impact workouts that appeal to men as well as women. There are one-on-one workouts with state-of-the-art CYBEX equipment and cardiovascular machines.

Appointments for personal services begin in the locker room–lounge, where fresh workout clothing is issued. A therapist then escorts you by elevator to private rooms around the lofty rotunda. Serious regimens are planned after consultation with staff specialists who compare your health profile with a computerized model. All this personalized attention—a three-to-one ratio of staff to guests—comes at a price: about $350 per day, including three meals. Treatments are priced individually.

Stress management is taught in a seven-day program scheduled at various times throughout the year. Dr. Eric Goldstein, a psychologist at the University of Miami who has worked with Olympic athletes, developed the program with spa trainers and nutritionists. Biofeedback and respiratory training routines and a "Stress Relief" workout teach participants how to control stress in every aspect of their lives.

Beyond beauty, the spa provides tools for taking control of your life. Counselors meet with newcomers to develop a program which can include treatments drawn from several natural sources: marine seaweed body wraps, tropical fruit enzyme facials, herbal ayurvedic hydrotherapy, and the new Kerstin Florian Kur program using thermal water crystals and mud from springs in Hungary.

Evenings are devoted to new experiences with fellow spa goers: talks by health specialists, an astrologer, and cooking demonstrations. But many guests simply enjoy the luxurious accommodations, perhaps a feature film from the library for their VCR, and prepare for an early morning walk around the golf course. The spa villa is air-conditioned, which is essential during the high-humidity summer months. Weather permitting, breakfast is served alfresco, with your choice of newspapers.

Doral Golf Resort and Spa

8755 N.W. 36th St., Miami, FL 33178
Tel. 305/593–6030 or 800/331–7768 (800/247–8901 in FL)
Fax 305/593–6030, ext. 5101

Administration General manager, Hans Turnovszky; spa director, Cathy Blum

Season Year-round.

Accommodations 48 suites in spa villa, all with twin baths, Jacuzzi, wet bar and refrigerator, VCR, 2 dressing areas, hair dryer, queen- or king-size bed. Suites with private terrace or balcony overlook golf courses or garden.

Rates Spa plan includes suite accommodations, 3 meals daily, and choice of services. 2-nights $968–$2,390 single, $746–$1,543 per person double occupancy; 4 nights $2,063 (includes extra services and limo)–$4,307 single, $1,594–$2,889 per person double occupancy; 7-night package $2,764–$4,795 per person double, $3,369–$7,337 single. Tax and gratuities included. Flexi-Plan 1-night suite package $423–$612.86 single, $423–$613 double. $500 advance payment within 7 days after booking 7-night plan, balance 14 days before arrival. Full payment within 7 days after booking short stays. Refundable (less $50) up to 14 days prior to arrival date. Credit cards: AE, DC, MC, V.

Meal Plans Specialties include buckwheat waffles with fruit topping or 1-egg omelet with spinach (breakfast), small pizza topped with turkey sausage (lunch), steamed lobster with mussel sauce or grilled honey basil chicken with rice and fresh vegetables (dinner), polenta lasagna with layers of smoked chicken, spinach, sliced tomato, or pork loin sautéed with mushroom and marsala sauce. Seafood is offered nightly; special diets accommodated.

Services and Facilities **Exercise Equipment:** complete CYBEX system, free weights (3–65 lb), Versaclimber, 2 StairMasters, 2 Lifecycles, 2 Liferowers, 2 StairMaster cross aerobics units, 3 Schwinn Air Dyne bikes, 5 Trotter treadmills, barbells (10–50 lb), Hydrofit. **Services:** Fango mud facial and body treatments; facials, herbal wraps, underwater massage, Body cream cleansing, hand and foot therapy, Swedish, aromatherapy, acupressure massage; beauty salon; cooking class; tai chi chuan. **Swimming Facilities:** Large outdoor pool with cascades, separate Olympic-length lap pool, indoor pool for aquatics. **Recreation Facilities:** 5 golf courses, 15 tennis courts, horseback riding, hiking trail. **Evening Programs:** Lecture and discussion group daily.

In the Area Complimentary use of beach club at Doral Hotel On-the-Ocean; shopping at Bal Harbour, Coral Gables; performing-arts seasons and festivals in Miami and Miami Beach; museums and Vizcaya mansion; Orange Bowl games and concerts; jai alai and racetracks; sailing and deep-sea fishing. Major-league baseball and basketball.

Getting Here *From Miami International Airport.* 15 min. away, served by major airlines. Amtrak station in Miami. Airport transfers by Doral limousine service included in the spa villa plan (4-day minimum). Taxi, rental car, limo arranged by concierge. Free scheduled shuttle bus to Miami Beach. Free parking, restricted to spa guests.

Special Notes Barrier-free facilities and dining rooms for people with disabilities; elevators throughout the spa center and villa. No smoking indoors. Spa open daily 8–6.

Fisher Island Spa Internazionale

Luxury pampering

Florida Secluded on Fisher Island off the southern tip of Miami, the Spa
Biscayne Bay Internazionale welcomes a limited number of guests to experience a very private world of luxury amid gardens ablaze with tropical flowers. The concierge can explain the island's development from 1925 hideaway built by William K. Vanderbilt to 1990s condominium community complete with beach club and marina.

In what was once Vanderbilt's seaplane hanger, the spa is a sybaritic temple to the body. Beyond swimming pool with underwater jets, you discover a patio pool and open-air massage rooms, where a waterfall cascades refreshingly cool water into a heated Jacuzzi. Nero never had it so good.

The spa also has 12 treatment rooms, one private room, a salon, two aerobics studios, and a cardio/weight-training room. Separate men's and women's saunas, steam rooms, and lounges stocked with fruit and juices add to the club-like atmosphere.

With a maximum of 20 guests padding about, the spa staff lavishes attention on you. For beginners, this eliminates problems during yoga and aerobics. The daily schedule lists six classes, from Reebok Bodywalk to step, waterworks, and body-toning. Interval training is organized with a full line of Keiser equipment.

Fisher Island Spa Internazionale
1 Fisher Island Dr., Fisher Island, FL 33109
Tel. 305/535–6020 or 800/537–3708
Fax 305/535–6003

Administration Fisher Island Club managing director, Michael Thomas; Spa Internazionale director, Deborah A. Smith

Season Year-round.

Accommodations 60 suites, guest rooms in cottages, 2-story villas, and condominium apartments. Vanderbilt cottages (3) and seaside contemporary suites have kitchen and living room, full bathroom, 1–3 bedrooms, each with bathroom. All accommodations are air-conditioned, with TV, telephone. Terraced for ocean views, some suites have whirlpool outdoors; cottages have private patio and whirlpool.

Rates 3-night spa package $2,076–$2,530 single, $1,547–$1,771 per person double occupancy; 7-night spa package $4,432–$5,297 single, $3,185–$3,709 double. Guest rooms $302–$357 daily for 2 persons, villa suites $385–$825 for 2, private cottage for 2–6 persons, $440–$1,182. Add 9.5% tax, $25 daily club membership fee. Perfect Spa Day package for island residents $195. Credit cards:AE, DC, MC, V.

Meal Plans Spa packages include 3 gourmet spa cuisine meals daily. Breakfast can be oat bran pancakes with banana and yogurt, or fresh fruit plate. Lunch choices include grilled mahimahi pita sandwich, Southwestern shrimp grilled with red pepper relish. Dinner entrées include grilled fillet of salmon on spinach with sorrel sauce, whole wheat pasta with fresh vegetables.

Services and Facilities **Exercise Equipment**: Cardio-weight room with 17 Keiser units, 3 StairMasters PT4000, 4 Startrac treadmills, 2 Schwinn Air Dyne bikes, Gravitron, Liferower, Cybex UBE, 2 Lifecycles, 12 free weight stations with overhead and underhand cable, Smith machine, dumbbells (3–50 lb), barbells (15–65 lb). **Services**: Massage, shiatsu, aromatherapy, body polish, reflexology, hydrotub, herbal wrap, algae body masque, reflexology, facials. Salon for manicure, pedicure, hair treatment, parafin hand/foot treatment. **Swimming Facilities**: Indoor lap pool, outdoor recreation pools, ocean beach. **Recreation Facilities**: 18 tennis courts (grass, clay, hard surface; lit for night play), 18-hole golf course, bike rental, marina for deep-sea fishing and yacht charter.

In the Area Miami Beach and South Beach, Theatre of the Performing Arts, Bayside Mall (free ferry at scheduled times from and to island), Vizcaya museum.

Getting Here *From Miami.* MacArthur Causeway to Fisher Island ferry terminal. Complimentary airport transfers for spa package guests. Rental car, taxi, limousine available. Helicopter and seaplane base nearby.

Special Notes Facilities accessible for people with disabilities. Spa open Sat.–Sun. 8–7, Mon. and Wed. 7–9, other days 7–8. Minimum age in spa is 16.

Fontainebleau Hilton Resort and Spa

Luxury pampering
Sports conditioning

Florida Behind the monumental lobby, the half-acre lagoon with rock
Miami Beach grotto and cascades, and the deli bar is the spa. Located in the Fontainebleau's old South building, where convention guests stay, it is developing into a self-contained fitness and health retreat. The ambience is more that of a city club than a fitness resort. The clientele includes local members and visiting businesspeople. Access to a health food restaurant and salons for skin care expand the range of this glamorous beach resort.

A computer program measures cardiovascular strength and evaluates diet. It might help beforehand for you to compare notes with your personal physician at home and start working under the supervision of experts on the link between diet, exercise, and health.

The exercise facilities here are perhaps the most extensive to be found in the area. With 105 aerobics classes scheduled weekly, the sprung-wood floors workout rooms are constantly in action. The array of weight training equipment includes a full line of Nautilus, and the staff includes 30 massage therapists on duty in seven private rooms. For a real treat, reserve time to be massaged al fresco, then slip into the sauna, steam bath, or jacuzzi.

Fontainebleau Hilton Resort and Spa

4441 Collins Ave., Miami Beach, FL 33140
Tel. 305/538-2000, 800/445-8667, or 800/548-8886
Spa reservations, tel. 305/538-7600
Fax 305/534-7590

Administration General manager, Leo Salom; Spa director, Norman Siegel

Season Year-round.

Accommodations 1,224 rooms, all with private bath, and 61 suites. Deluxe bedrooms with king-size or large double beds, TV, and balcony.

Rates Spa Daybreak package $175. Room-only for 2 persons $104–$215 per day in summer, $250–$270 in winter; suites from $375. Add 9.5% tax and gratuity. Daily spa pass $12.78. 1 night's lodging advance payment. Credit cards: AE, DC, MC, V.

Meal Plans Paradise Health Bistro (open 8–7) serves sandwiches, pizza, salads, low-cal drinks, juice, and fruit. Heart-healthy items at the hotel's 6 restaurants are the snapper, pasta primavera, and broiled chicken. All meals à la carte.

Services and Facilities **Exercise Equipment:** 20-unit Nautilus circuit, 8 Lifecycles, rowing machines, StairMasters, treadmills, free weights. **Services:** Massage, aromatherapy, loofah body scrub, herbal wrap; personal instruction on exercise, fitness profile, private whirlpool mineral baths, skin-care treatments, manicure, pedicure, nutrition consultation, skin consultation. **Swimming Facilities:** Exercise pool, free-form recreational pool, and ocean beach. **Recreation Facilities:** 7 lighted tennis courts, Hobie and Catyak catamaran sailboats, windsurfing, beach volleyball. Nearby golf course and horseback riding. **Evening Programs:** Resort entertainment, cabaret.

In the Area Local sightseeing tours and cruises, Caribbean cruises, 1-day Bahamas flights and cruises, Thoroughbred horse races, harness track, dog races, jai alai fronton, Miami Dolphins stadium. Metropolitan Museum (major art shows), Gusman Performing Arts Center (concerts), opera season (winter), chamber music series, theater, baseball, basketball seasons.

Getting Here *From Miami International Airport.* Shuttle van service operates at all times (20 min). Taxi, rental car, limousine, public bus available. Free indoor parking included in spa package.

Special Notes Elevator to all floors and some specially equipped rooms for the disabled. Free children's accommodation with parents. No smoking in spa or designated dining areas. Spa open weekdays 6:30 AM–10 PM, weekends 8–7.

Hippocrates Health Institute

Holistic health
Weight management

Florida
West Palm Beach

A vegetarian diet, medical consultation, chiropractic therapy, and psychological consultation are central to the health-renewal program at the Hippocrates Health Institute. Sessions three weeks or longer are planned on an individual basis for 15 to 20 participants. Highly structured, the program includes nutritional education, regular exercise, massage, reflexology, detoxification, and relaxation.

Guests stay in a spacious hacienda or at private cottages on the 20-acre wooded estate. A peaceful, healing serenity pervades the grounds, where walkways wind through tropical surroundings to a dry sauna and ozonated swimming pool.

The Hippocrates lifestyle involves learning to be self-sufficient in matters of food and medicine. A typical day begins at 8 AM with light exercise before breakfast, then a blood-pressure check, and discussion session on health and diet. Guests learn and practice how to sprout and grow greens for home use.

Personal counseling comes with the program. A psychologist and an M.D. work closely with the medical director to monitor your progress and advise you on personal problems. Deep-relaxation techniques are taught to enhance healing, creativity, and inspiration.

Hippocrates Health Institute
1443 Palmdale Ct., West Palm Beach, FL 33411
Tel. 407/471–8876 or 800/842–2125
Fax 407/471–9464

Administration   Co-directors, Brian R. Clement and Anna Maria Gahns

Season   Year-round; scheduled 3-week programs.

Accommodations   20 guest rooms, from 3 luxury suites in Spanish-style hacienda to garden apartments and 2 cottages, some with marble-walled bath and whirlpools. New England-style furnishings in most rooms.

Rates   3-week Health Encounter $5,900–$7,800 with private room, $2,600–$4,500 in shared accommodations with up to 5 persons. Shorter and longer stays on space-available basis. 50% of room rate required as a nonrefundable deposit by certified check or major credit card. Credit cards: AE, MC, V.

Meal Plans   3 meals daily, buffet style, with days designated for juice fasting. Live Food diet of unprocessed organic raw vegetables, fruits, nuts, seeds, sprouts, sea plants and algae, and herbs. Raw juices and legumes in enzyme-rich menu, including combination of red pepper stuffed with mix of nuts and seeds or sauerkraut and seed loaf.

Services and Facilities   **Exercise Equipment:** Universal multistation gym, Lifecycle, LifeClimber, treadmill. **Services:** Health consultations, chiropractic treatment, full body massage, facials, supervised exercise program, wheatgrass detoxification schedule. **Swimming Facilities:** Outdoor pool, ocean beach nearby. **Recreation Facilities:** 2 tennis courts, golf and boating nearby. **Evening Programs:** Lectures and discussions nightly.

In the Area   Trips to the beach, local museums, shopping excursions.

Getting Here   *From Miami.* By bus, Greyhound to West Palm Beach (90 min). By car, Florida Turnpike (I–75) to Palm Beach Exit 40, Okeechobee Blvd. to Skees Rd. (1 hr). Free service to and from West Palm Beach airport and bus station. Taxi, rental car available.

Special Notes   Ramps provided for people with disabilities; 1 specially equipped guest room. No smoking.

Lido Spa Hotel

Vibrant maturity
Weight management

Florida   An all-inclusive daily rate that covers massage, exercise
Miami Beach   classes, and nutritional guidance makes the Lido Spa Hotel a good alternative to luxury spas. It's really more a residential hotel than a resort. Occupying choice frontage on Biscayne Bay, it is linked to Miami Beach by the scenic Venetian Causeway, a toll road for Miami commuters.

Family-owned and operated, the Lido has a comfortable, lived-in look, but shows its age. The main building opened in 1962 and is flanked by two-level wings of motel-like accommodations. Garden-level rooms are popular with older guests, who make up the majority of the Lido's regular clientele; they are a friendly community of mature adults, and many return year after year. The managers of the men's and women's spas provide a limited amount of guidance but, at the same time, are responsive to guests' personal needs and interests. If you are self-motivated and can set your own schedule, this could be a pleasant, relaxed vacation.

The daily schedule includes two low-impact exercise classes in the air-conditioned gym and occasional workouts in the swimming pool. Otherwise you're on your own to schedule massage appointments, swim in the two outdoor pools (one is filtered saltwater), or sunbathe in private cabanas.

Lido Spa Hotel
40 Island Ave., Miami Beach, FL 33139
Tel. 305/538–4621 or 800/327–8363.

Administration   Director, Aaron "Chuck" Edelstein

Season   Nov.–May.

Accommodations   106 rooms, mostly in 1- or 2-story garden wings. Fully equipped apartments (15) nearby. Furniture has plastic, 1960s look, well maintained and serviced daily. TV, telephone, air-conditioning; extra charge for refrigerator.

Rates   Varies with season, $65–$125 single, $56–$95 per person, double occupancy. Daily rate includes massage (30 min), 3 meals, exercise classes, outings. Add 9.5% tax, gratuities. Deposit $100 per room. Credit cards: AE, MC, V.

Meal Plans   Selections from menu include grilled snapper, pasta salad, baked chicken. Eggs, dairy products; coffee and tea available. Kosher food on request.

Services and   **Exercise Equipment:** 3 Precor treadmills, 10 stationary bikes
Facilities   (Tuntori, Monark), StairMaster, 3 Lifecycle, Universal multi-

station gym, free weights, pulleys, barbells, tiltboard, Rebounder. **Swimming Facilities:** Outdoor lap pool, recreational pool. **Spa Facilities:** Steam room, private whirlpools, Swedish massage; loofah body scrub, facial for women only. Beauty salon. **Evening Programs:** musicals or movies.

In the Area Bass Museum of Art, Lincoln Road (arts district), Theater of the Performing Arts (concerts, opera, ballet, musicals), Dade County Cultural Center, Art Deco hotels and cafés, Bayside shops.

Getting Here *From Miami.* By car, Biscayne Blvd. to Venetian Causeway. Free transfer to airport or Amtrak station on departure.

Special Notes No smoking in spa or special areas of dining room.

Palm-Aire Spa Resort & Country Club

Life enhancement
Luxury pampering
Weight management

Florida Surrounded by five 18-hole championship golf courses, 37 clay
Pompano Beach and hard-surface tennis courts, and condominium apartment buildings, the Palm-Aire Spa Resort has built a clientele of local residents and "snowbird" winter visitors for 25 years.

The spa is beginning to show its age, but it doesn't skimp on service. Separate men's and women's pavilions have private sunken Roman baths, Swiss showers (17 nozzles that alternate warm and cool water), and some of the most experienced hands in the massage business. Each side has sauna, cold plunge, steam room, and outdoor exercise pool (try aquaerobics in the buff). There's a well-equipped coed gym, racquetball courts, and junior-Olympic-size outdoor swimming pool. Ocean swimming, however, is about a 20-minute ride away.

A typical day begins with 10 minutes of warm-up stretches after breakfast, then a brisk walk on a half-mile parcourse. An instructor monitors your pulse rate on every lap. Fresh workout clothing is handed out in the locker room, and you can relax in the lounge while waiting for your next appointment or aerobics class. There's a clublike atmosphere as resident members and regular guests swap gossip and watch the stock market reports. Staff members are attentive and accustomed to gratuities.

Calories count in the private spa dining room; the food is portion controlled, high in carbohydrates, and low in fat. The 1,000-calorie-per-day plan is sufficient, but second helpings are available. A regular, "fattening" menu is served in the adjoining dining room.

Salon services for men and women, in a newly decorated facility adjoining the spa, are charged à la carte. If you plan to stay two nights or longer, ask about package plans, such as the mother-daughter week available June–September. A discount is available for repeat visitors.

Palm-Aire Spa Resort & Country Club
2501 Palm-Aire Dr. N, Pompano Beach, FL 33069
Tel. 305/972-3300 or 800/272-5624
Fax 305/968-2744

Administration Hotel director, Bruce W. Dunbar; spa director, Kathy Eggleston

Season Year-round.

Accommodations 166 spacious rooms and 18 golf villas. All with separate dressing rooms and some with 2 baths. Private terraces, about half overlooking golf course. King-size beds and sofas, remote-control TV, built-in wet bar.

Rates 3-night/4-day spa package includes meals and spa services: seasonal prices $334.17–$423.09 single, $303.69–$357.04 per person double. Taxes, gratuities included. 2-night minimum. Ultimate Day (no room) $200–$210 includes tax and gratuity. Golf and tennis packages available. Deposit: 1 night's advance payment by credit card. Credit cards: AE, DC, MC, V.

Meal Plans 3 meals daily in Spa Dining Room. Breakfast can include poached egg on wheat bread or cottage cheese and a bran muffin. Lunch choices include spinach-mushroom salad followed by baked potato stuffed with cottage and Jarlsberg cheeses or Spanish omelet made with egg whites. Broiled or poached snapper, chicken cacciatore, and vegetable lasagna for dinner.

Services and Facilities **Exercise Equipment:** 2 Trotter treadmills, 4 Precor treadmills, 2 StepMasters, 2 Liferowers, 4 Lifecycles, 2 StairMasters, Heartmate bike, 2 Bodyguard ergometer bikes, 3 Schwinn Air Dyne bikes, 2 recumbent bikes; 16-unit Bodymaster strength conditioning system; complete Olympic free-weight gym, barbells (1–100 lbs.). **Services:** Body massage (Swedish, Trager, deep muscle), thalassotherapy, Sarvar mineral bath, full-body fango mudpack, facial treatments, loofah body scrub, herbal wrap, body composition analysis. Separate men's and women's salons for hair, nail, and skin care. Golf and tennis clinics, personal conditioning. **Swimming Facilities:** 2 outdoor pools; separate men's and women's fitness pools. **Recreation Facilities:** 37 tennis courts, 3 18-hole golf courses, 2 racquetball courts, indoor squash court. **Evening Programs:** Lectures on behavior modification, stress management, nutrition, other health-related topics.

In the Area The Everglades, Fort Lauderdale Museum of the Arts, performing arts center, Parker Playhouse; 1-day Bahamas cruise; Pompano Harness Track, Dania Fronton (jai alai), dog and Thoroughbred racing; deep-sea fishing charters, canal cruises; Yankee spring training games.

Getting Here *From Miami.* By car, I-95 north to Exit 34, Atlantic Blvd., 27th Ave. to second entrance road (45 min). Limousine service (fixed fee) available to and from Fort Lauderdale International Airport and Miami. Rental car, taxi available. Valet service at hotel.

Special Notes Spa facilities on ground level and elevators make this hotel accessible for people with disabilities. No smoking in the spa, the spa dining room, or the lounge.

The Pier House Caribbean Spa

Nonprogram resort

Florida
Key West

The Caribbean Spa is a special enclave within the popular Pier House resort. Working out here is both liberating and seductive, mirroring the laissez-faire attitude of Old Town Key West itself. While for most guests the big event of the day is watching the spectacular sunset with beer in hand, you can also indulge in a sybaritic escape.

Decorated in tropical color schemes, the spa building has 22 guest rooms and a boutique spa on the ground floor, where a professional trainer or esthetician will develop your personalized program. Facilities include men's and women's locker rooms with steam room and sauna, outdoor whirlpool, complete exercise circuit, and salon for hair styling, facials, manicures and pedicures.

The salon's specialty is Prescription Plus creams and lotions formulated for your skin type by the esthetician doing your facial. Try the "Coma," a 90-minute combination of massage, reflexology, and paraffin treatment on your hands and feet. Services are available à la carte or as part of packages with hotel accommodations.

Workouts with a harbor view are a bonus when you join one of the daily aerobics classes held in the resort's waterside disco. Options include step and low-impact. All hotel guests can join the water aerobics session held in the swimming pool.

The convenient, fun location in the heart of a sometimes boisterous town, gives you plenty of opportunity to stroll to shops and tourist attractions—all the while knowing you can retreat to the spa's hushed quarters. The resort's beach is not up to the quality of the accommodations. Really a small, rocky cove, it does offer some attraction, if you enjoy nude bathing; local rules are tolerant. With all the temptations in Key West, the Caribbean Spa offers a healthy alternative.

The Pier House Caribbean Spa
1 Duval St., Key West, FL 33040
Tel. 305/296–4600 or 800/327–8340
Fax 305/296–4600

Administration General manager, Joyce Matt; spa director, Dennis Delaney

Season Year-round.

Accommodations 22 spa rooms; corner minisuite with fireplace, some have Habitat baths with steam/sauna, some have bathrooms with marble-topped double vanity, whirlpool tub. White wicker furnishings, sitting area, king-size bed, ceiling fans, French doors opening into a private patio or balcony. Amenities include color TV with VCR, CD players, AM/FM radio, air-conditioning, telephones. The main buildings have 123 guest rooms, including 13 suites.

Rates 4-day/3-night Island Escape package $1,450 for 2 double occupancy, $1,030 single; 3-day/2-night Island Unwinder $580–$890 per couple; 4-day/3-night Stress Breaker Plus $580–$950 per couple. Full-day package with lunch (no lodging) $149, half-day $100. Other rooms from $165–$225 single or double, suites $295–$675. Add tax and service charge. Daily facility charge for resort guests ($10) is waived when services are booked. Advance payment for 1 night (longer during holidays). Credit cards: AE, DC, MC, V.

Meal Plans 3 spa cuisine meals daily included in residential package. Breakfast can be tropical fruit with yogurt or egg-white omelet with spinach, onions, and cottage cheese, cereal with skim milk. Lunch choices are grilled seafood; chicken salad; flank steak. Dinner can begin with conch bisque or conch eggroll, salad of field greens in vinaigrette; entrées include Key West shrimp with pasilla chili barbecue sauce, sautéed yellowtail with Key lime sauce, papaya, and avocado.

Services and Facilities **Exercise Equipment:** 9-unit Keiser weight training gym, 2 StairMasters, 2 Precor treadmills, 2 Lifecycles, "Wave Webb" gloves, dumbbells (5–45 lbs.), bench press. **Services:** Massage (sports, therapeutic, aromatherapy, combination), deep pore cleansing, loofah scrub, facial with Key West aloe; salon for hair styling, waxing, manicure, pedicure. 1-on-1 training. **Swimming Facilities:** 2 outdoor pools, salt-water beach.

In the Area Audubon House and studio, Sloppy Joe's, Hemingway's house, Conch Train tour of historic district, Sunken Treasure Museum, Harry Truman Little White House Museum.

Getting Here *From Miami.* By bus, Greyhound (3 hr). By car, Hwy. 1 (Overseas Highway) via Seven-Mile Bridge (3 hr). By air, scheduled service on USAir, American Eagle commuter. Rental car, taxi available; bike and moped rental.

Special Notes Spa open weekdays 7 AM–9 PM, weekends 8–8. No smoking in spa.

Pritikin Longevity Center

Nutrition and diet
Weight management

Florida
Miami Beach

Dieting at the Pritikin Longevity Center may be the healthiest part of a holiday on Miami Beach. Everyone, from the doctors on staff to the exercise instructors, eats Pritikin-style.

The revolutionary diet introduced by the late Nathan Pritikin in 1974 is the foundation of 13- and 26-day programs designed to treat and control medical problems. The medically supervised live-in program here provides the support many people need in changing their lifestyles.

The regimen demands discipline, so don't expect a fun-in-the-sun holiday. Along with 50 other participants, you work out in the gym or pool and walk on the beach. If you enjoy ocean swimming, it can be part of your exercise plan. The staff doctor decides what's best.

Exercise, nutrition, stress management, health education, and medical services are the core curriculum. The 13-day program is recommended for sufferers of heart disease, insulin-dependent diabetes, obesity, or uncontrolled high blood pressure. The full course offers individual attention, counseling, and close supervision.

Healthy people come to learn how to safeguard their health, and to gain knowledge and self-assurance in the face of temptation. The daily schedule includes cooking demonstrations, lectures, and three exercise sessions. A full physical examination is a major feature of the program and includes a treadmill stress test and complete blood chemistry analysis. Depending on your personal history and fitness level, you are assigned to a specialist in cardiology or internal medicine who monitors your progress on the prescribed diet and exercise program.

Pritikin Longevity Center

5875 Collins Ave., Miami Beach, FL 33140
Tel. 305/866-2237 or 800/327-4914 (Flamingo Hotel, 305/865-8645)
Fax 305/866-1872

Administration Executive director, Joan Mikus

Season Year-round, scheduled dates.

Accommodations 100 rooms in beachfront hotel, some facing traffic on Collins Ave., others with an ocean view on penthouse floor, and suites. Smaller rooms included in program with single or double beds, private baths, and comfortable furniture. All with air-conditioning, color TV, telephone, maid service.

Rates 13-day program $5,973 single, $2,587 spouse or companion; 26-day program $9,991 single, $4,711 spouse or companion. More for larger rooms. $500 advance payment for 13-day program, $1,000 for 26-day. Credit cards: AE, MC, V (for deposit only). Discount for repeat visitors.

Meal Plans 3 meals plus 3 snacks daily. Buffet-style breakfast and lunch, table service and menu choices at dinner. Lunch and dinner salad bar. Lunch includes Pritikin vegetarian pizza, eggplant patties with marinara sauce, and rice-tofu moo goo gai pan; chicken teriyaki or poached salmon in dill sauce for dinner.

Services and Facilities **Exercise Equipment:** 23 Trotter treadmills, Trotter multi-station gym, 8 Schwinn Air Dyne bikes, 2 rowing machines, StairMaster, bench press, hand weights. **Services:** Private counseling on nutrition and health, complete medical and physical examination, including blood tests. Massage, acupressure appointments by request. **Swimming Facilities:** Olympic-size outdoor pool for aerobics; direct access to beach. **Recreation Facilities:** Nearby tennis courts and golf course, boardwalk. **Evening Programs:** Nightly entertainment by local talent; exercises.

In the Area Group trips to shows and jai alai games; Miami museums and sightseeing, deep-sea fishing.

Getting Here *From Miami.* By car, I-95 to Rte. 195 exit, Arthur Godrey Causeway to 41st St., left on Collins Ave. (15 min). Public bus, airport shuttle service, taxi, rental car available. Private parking on site.

Special Notes Ramps and elevators provide access for people with disabilities. No smoking on the premises. Spa open daily 6:30 AM–10:30 PM.

PGA National Resort & Spa

Luxury pampering
Sports conditioning
Vibrant maturity
Weight management

Florida
Palm Beach
Gardens

Golf and tennis champions exercise here during tournaments, but the spa at the PGA National Resort can be enjoyed as a sybaritic getaway combined with sports conditioning year-round. With five golf courses, five croquet courts, a 26-acre sailing lake, biking and jogging trails, and the Health & Racquet Club, the resort provides a comprehensive health and fitness regimen.

The instructors recommend a varied workout program to develop specific muscle groups and cardiovascular strength. Skiers might train on a cross-country exercise machine, a stair-climbing machine, and alternate 20-minute sessions on Nautilus equipment. For the tennis player, there's the treadmill, selected Cybex units, and tennis aerobics, taught by a tennis pro.

The European philosophy of cleansing the body of impurities and toxins is carried through at the spa building. Hydrotherapy treatments, thalassotherapy, and body masks with natural plants and sea extracts are offered à la carte or in spa packages. The spa is connected to the main resort building and has a private outdoor pool complex, called "Waters of the World," where imported salts and mineral crystals are added to two of the pools. You can experience a soak in the Dead Sea and the French Pyrenees, a hot tub, cold plunge, or just swim.

Golf, however, is the principal recreation here. The home of the Professional Golfers' Association of America, the five courses challenge any style player, professional or Sunday duffer. Getting in shape for the ultimate golfing experience, a round on the General (a course designed by Arnold Palmer), could be the goal of a fitness regime devised by a team of golf pros and fitness instructors.

There is a specific circuit of Cybex equipment to help golfers loosen up muscles and gain strength and flexibility. To work on golfing technique, try the daily clinics, private lessons, or three-day Nicklaus/Flick Golf School. Another option is the advanced PGA National Golf Academy, included as part of a four-day resort package.

The nutritional needs of a sports regimen are the specialty of resident Registered Dietician Cheryl Hartsough. Personal consultation on diet, meals, and fitness training are included in the four-night Healthy Weight program. To learn the secrets of counteracting the aging process, guests are now offered a four-night Ageless Beauty Retreat. The full-service spa salon is open to the public.

PGA National Resort & Spa
400 Ave. of the Champions, Palm Beach Gardens, FL 33418
Tel. 407/627–2000 or 800/633–9150
Fax 407/622–0261

Administration Managing director, David Bagwell; spa director, Karen Antenucci; fitness director, Randy Myers; Health & Racquet Club director, Ruth Barnett

Season Year-round.

Accommodations 335 spacious guest rooms, including 59 suites with tile floors and Mediterranean Revival fabrics and furniture, and 85 cottage units along golf courses, each with 2 bedrooms, 2 baths, and kitchen. Renovated 1992, all rooms have balcony or terrace, private bath, coffee maker, and walk-in closet.

Rates Daily: $99–$300 for singles or doubles, suites $175–$950, cottage suites $230–$365. Spa plan, per day with deluxe accommodations and meals, $509 single, $395 per person double occupancy; 4-night Rejuvenation Program $2,387 single, $1,929 per person double; 4-night Ageless Beauty Retreat $2,381 single, $1,923 double; 4-night Healthy Weight Program $2,373 single, $1,915 double; 2-night golf/spa package $588 per person double (no meals). Full-day spa package with spa cuisine lunch (no lodging) $239. Tax, service charges, and gratuity included in spa packages. 1 night advance payment. Credit cards: AE, DC, MC, V.

Meal Plans 3 low-fat spa cuisine meals daily in 4-day packages. At the Citrus Tree restaurant, menu selections include Florida red snapper grilled over mesquite wood, Cajun blackened beef, grilled chicken. Lunch options are pizza with chicken sausage and fresh tomato marinara, steamed yellowtail snapper in an eggplant boat, chilled fruit soup served in coconut shell, or mixed seafood with Asian noodles and stir-fry vegetables. New World cuisine dinners include brie and grape quesadilla, chicken potstickers with sun-dried cherry, pan-seared shrimp and scallops. Sports cuisine with high carbohydrate counts may be Thai cucumber role with crab, tuna taco shimi, Chimayo red chicken, or Maverick beef tenderloin.

Services and Facilities **Exercise Equipment:** 2 18-station Nautilus circuits, 12-unit Cybex room, 5 Trotter treadmills, 4 Lifecycles, 4 StairMasters, 4 Monark stationary bikes, NordicTrack cross-country ski machine, free weights (5–50 lbs.) **Services:** Massage (Swedish, sports, shiatsu, aromatherapy, reflexology, acupressure, lymphatic, cellulite), salt glo marine algae body wrap, seaweed body polish, aromatherapy wraps, hydrotherapy tubs with sea salts, essential oils, Vichy shower, facials. 1-on-1 training, wellness lifestyle, stress management, fitness and nutritional assessment, tennis, golf, and croquet instruction. **Swimming Facilities:** Family pool at hotel, 5-lane lap pool at health club; outdoor pool and Jacuzzi at the spa. **Recreation Facilities:** 5 golf courses, 19 outdoor tennis courts (12 lighted), 5 indoor racquetball courts, croquet lawn, sailboats, aquacycles, bicycles; walking and jogging trails, horseback riding nearby; fishing in private lake. **Evening Programs:** Disco, resort entertainment; lectures during scheduled weight management, golf and tennis programs.

In the Area Palm Beach Worth Avenue shops, Flagler Museum (Whitehall), Golf Hall of Fame, the Gardens (shopping), Burt Reynolds Dinner Theater, Palm Beach Symphony Orchestra, opera and pops concerts at Kravis Center, Polo Club, Morikami Museum and gardens (Japanese arts).

Getting Here *From West Palm Beach.* By car, I–95 to Exit 57, PGA Blvd. west to resort entrance; Florida Turnpike to Exit 44, PGA Blvd. (20 min). Limousine and van service (fixed fee) to and from airport. Taxi, car rental available.

Special Notes Ramps, elevators, and specially equipped rooms provide access for people with disabilities. Daily baby-sitting, summer day-camp; golf and tennis clinics or private instruction for children. Spa hours daily 8:30–6. Daily facility fee $25 included in spa packages.

Royal Atlantic Health Spa

Holistic health
Weight management

Florida After a dozen years down the beach in Hallandale (at the Re-
Pompano Beach gency), the owners opened this self-contained retreat in 1993. Friendly, with no frills, this is an affordable place to practice prevention of illness.

When you want to veg out or fling off flab, the Royal Atlantic Health Spa has structured programs to support your goals. The holistic spa program addresses your emotional and physical well-being. The daily schedule of lectures and workshops covers stress management, nutrition, and the dynamics of fitness. Exercise classes are held in a large gym that adjoins the poolside dining room. Cooking classes in gourmet vegetarian cuisine are held most afternoons, teaching how fruits, vegetables, and starches can eliminate cravings and reduce the fats and proteins that contribute to weight problems, heart disease, diabetes, cancer, and aging.

Each day begins with an aerobic walk along the beach, followed by low-impact, step, and aquatics classes. To improve body awareness and flexibility you can join a session of yoga, held under the palm trees. The spa treatment rooms and a beauty salon are in the U-shape hotel complex surrounding a private garden with open-air swimming pool and Jacuzzi.

Royal Atlantic Health Spa
1460 S. Ocean Blvd., Pompano Beach, FL 33062
Tel. 305/941–6688 or 800/583–3500

Administration Owner-directors, Hyland Gross and Ruth and Morton Pine; medical director, Michael Klaper, M.D.

Season Year-round.

Accommodations 50 guest rooms in 3-story court with swimming pool. Renovated in 1993, rooms are furnished motel-style, with 2 queen-size beds, private bathroom, air-conditioning, TV, telephone. Garden level rooms have private patio open to pool and beach; ocean-view rooms have balcony.

Rates 1-week program with meals and accommodations $995–$1,345 single, $895–$1,245 per person double. Add tax and gratuities. $100 advance payment. Credit cards: AE, MC, V.

Meal Plans 3 low-cal vegetarian meals daily. Breakfast is all fresh fruit. Lunch buffet of salads, baked potato, and fruit. Dinner served by candlelight may include vegetarian lasagna or stuffed pepper with salad. Juice and water diets optional.

| Services and Facilities | **Exercise Equipment**: Universal weight training gym, treadmill, stationary bikes, step machine, free weights. **Services:** Facial, herbal body wrap, massage, mud or seaweed, and anti-cellulite wraps, aromatherapy, reflexology; salon for hair and nail care. **Swimming Facilities:** Outdoor pool; ocean beach. **Recreation Facilities:** Tennis, and golf nearby. Bicycles, snorkeling, and fishing gear can be rented. **Evening Programs:** Informal discussion groups. |

In the Area Disney World, Morikami Museum, Fort Lauderdale Performing Arts Center, art museums.

Getting Here *From Fort Lauderdale International Airport.* By car, I–95 to Commercial Blvd., east to Hwy. A1A (35 min). Rental car, taxi, limousine available.

Special Notes No smoking in rooms or on premises. All facilities accessible for people with disabilties. Minimum age 18.

Saddlebrook Sports Science

Sports conditioning

Florida
Wesley Chapel
(Tampa Bay)

An active, sports-oriented vacation comes in a variety of packages at Saddlebrook. In 1993 Saddlebrook Sports Science, a new training facility, was opened by sports trainer Dr. Jack Groppel and psychologist Dr. James Loehr. Clinics are designed for business executives interested in improving productivity, and athletes seeking peak performance. Both groups learn to handle stress more efficiently while maintaining high levels of energy.

Six services are available, including a psychological profile of how you handle stress in the office or in competitive sports. Based on these assessments, along with your interests and goals, a personal exercise program is designed for you.

Rolling greens and tree-lined fairways surround a traffic-free "walking village" where everything is conveniently located. The centerpiece is a 270-foot Superpool, big enough for racing, water aerobics, or volleyball. The Jockey Club fitness center nearby has ultramodern saunas, whirlpools, and steam rooms in separate facilities for men and women, massage rooms, and a fully equipped exercise room. Families feel comfortable in this community, too, where there are sports activities for young people as well as competitive-minded parents.

Saddlebrook Sports Science
5700 Saddlebrook Way, Wesley Chapel, FL 33543
Tel. 8/973–1111 or 800/729–8383; Sports Science Center
8/973–8022

Administration Co-directors, Dr. Jack Groppel, Ed.D., and Dr. James Loehr, Ph.D.; General manager, Richard Boehning

Season Year-round.

Accommodations 700 guest rooms in 10 resort clusters, from spacious rooms with large baths to 1- and 2-bedroom suites with fully equipped kitchens. All units have cable TV, modern furniture, queen- and king-size beds, balcony or patio.

Rates Deluxe room, single or double, $190–$325 Jan. 15–Apr. 30; $90 in summer. Golf Escape package (2-night minimum) $261–$291

single, \$186–\$201 per person each night. Tennis packages available. 1 night's advance payment for short visits, 25% for longer. Sports Science private consultation \$150–\$200 per hr. Credit cards: AE, DC, MC, V.

Meal Plans Meals not included in packages. The Cypress Room open for Fri. night seafood buffet and Sun. brunch. The Little Club (open daily) features American cuisine.

Services and Facilities **Exercise Equipment:** 12-station Nautilus circuit, computerized Biocycle, Monark stationary bike, StairMaster, free weights (2–50 lbs.) and curl bar. **Services:** Swedish massage, facial, manicure. Computerized fitness analysis, health-risk appraisal, nutrition profile, stress management index, competitive sports profile. Tennis and golf clinics, including videotaped swing analysis. **Swimming Facilities:** 3 outdoor pools. **Recreation Facilities:** 37 tennis courts (hard and clay, some with lights), 2 18-hole golf courses designed by Arnold Palmer. Also fishing (equipment provided), 2-mile jogging trail.

In the Area Busch Gardens (family-oriented theme park and wildlife preserve), Sea World (performing whales and dolphins), Disney World, Cypress Gardens, Ybor City (Tampa's Cuban quarter).

Getting Here *From Tampa.* By car, Rte. 275 to I–75, Hwy. 54 (40 min). Limousine, rental car, taxi available.

Special Notes Ground-floor accommodations for people with disabilities, ramps to fitness center. Programs for children 6–12: tennis and golf instruction, special camps, supervised activities during holidays. No smoking in fitness center and designated dining areas.

Safety Harbor Spa and Fitness Center

Life enhancement
Luxury pampering
Taking the waters
Weight management

Florida
Safety Harbor
(Tampa Bay)

Walking along Bayshore Drive in the morning, swimming laps under swaying palms, and soaking in mineral spring water are among the pleasures of a vacation at Safety Harbor. After a major face-lift in 1992, the Spa & Fitness Center emerged with new owners, new dining room, conference theater, and a Clarins salon for skin care. For its 50th anniversary in 1995, the resort finished renovating all guest rooms.

Modern chemical analysis shows that each spring has a different proportion of calcium, magnesium, sodium, potassium, and other minerals. This water is used for filling two coed Jacuzzis and a chlorinated indoor pool.

Aquatics is a strong feature of the health-oriented program. Private hydrotherapy tubs in the men's and women's bathhouses are enhanced with blends of herbs and marine algae for stress reduction, relief of muscular tension, and toning treatments. Exercising in the specially designed shallow indoor and outdoor pools burns calories efficiently without straining the body. Even out of the water, though, exercise instructors promote low-impact routines, and the shock-absorbing floors are specially constructed to help avoid tendonitis and shin splints.

The instructors here specialize in a variety of routines, from gentle to active, to keep you from getting bored.

A member of the fitness staff will check your overall physical condition, monitor your aerobic heart rate, and analyze your body-fat to muscle ratio. Based on a computer analysis, a specific combination of exercise and diet will be recommended.

Bodywork appointments are made through a guest coordinator, and charged on an à la carte basis. Both men's and women's locker rooms have sauna, steam room, and direct access to the exercise pool, but it's a good idea to bring footwear, even aquatic socks for water aerobics.

Safety Harbor Spa and Fitness Center
105 N. Bayshore Dr., Safety Harbor, FL 34695
Tel. 8/726–1161 or 800/237–0155
Fax 8/726–4268

Administration	Owner-director, Roger Kumar; spa director, Bina Kumar; medical director, Richard Gubner, M.D.
Season	Year-round.
Accommodations	210 bedrooms and suites; 30 full-service apartments in annex across the street. Newer large deluxe units in the towers with balcony or terrace, 2 queen-size beds, dressing room, oversize bath. All air-conditioned, with TV, telephone, robes.
Rates	1-day package, full American plan with lodging, $190–$400 per person. 5–day/4–night package $1,142–$2,045 single, $1,113–$1,687 per person double occupancy. 8–day/7–night package $2,142–$3,449 single, $1,885–$2,830 double. Gratuities and tax included. Deposit: 1 night advance payment. Credit cards: AE, DC, MC, V.
Meal Plans	3 meals daily in formal dining room. Fitness plan breakfast includes fresh-baked pumpkin muffins, whole-wheat pancakes with raspberry puree, and egg-white omelet with farmer cheese. Lunch includes vegetable chili with white or brown rice, vegetable lasagna, pizza with whole-wheat crust, and breast of chicken with herbed ricotta cheese. Special dinner salads, such as romaine lettuce with Parmesan dressing, then broiled lobster, crab Mornay, shrimp with linguini. Coffee and herbal tea. Suggested daily 900–1,100 calorie menu provides 50% complex carbohydrates, 25% protein, 20% fat.
Services and Facilities	**Exercise Equipment:** Paramount sports trainer system with adductor, abductor, abdominal pullover, pull-down, butterfly back press, lateral raise, leg-kick pulley, bicep/tricep machine. Nautilus hip/back, leg curl, lower back, and abdominal machines. 12 Precor treadmills, 3 StairMasters, LifeStep, Lifecycle, 2 Windracers, 2 Heartmate TV bikes, 2 Schwinn Air Dyne bikes, Versaclimber, 2 Concept II rowing machines, upper body ergometer, 4 trampolines, Hydra Fitness Total Power machine, Roman Chair abdominal unit. Free weights (1¼–45 lbs.) and dumbbells (3–40 lbs.) with bench press, incline bench, Uniflex unit. 2 speed bags for boxers. **Services:** Fitness evaluation, massage, herbal wraps, salt-glow loofah body scrub, facials, haircuts and styling, makeup consultation, manicure, pedicure. Tennis instruction. **Swimming Facilities:** outdoor and indoor pools. Mineral spring water in all swimming pools and Jacuzzis. **Recreation Facilities:** 7 Har Tru tennis courts, 2 hard

courts, putting green, free use of bikes, basketball, water volleyball. Golf and horseback riding nearby (fee). **Evening Programs:** Lectures on stress management and health-related topics, cooking demonstrations, cultural programs, lounge dancing on weekends.

In the Area Organized outings for beach, biking, fishing (fee). Evening trips to performing arts centers in Tampa and Clearwater, shopping centers, movies; Ybor City (Tampa's colorful Cuban quarter), 1-day Bahamas cruise, Busch Gardens (family theme park and wildlife preserve), history museums, Tarpon Springs sponge harvest and sales center, Disney World.

Getting Here *From Tampa.* By bus, scheduled van service every 20 mins. ($12) by Airport Limo Connection (tel. 800/282–6817) from Tampa International Airport. By car, I–275 south to Exit 20, Rte. 60 toward Clearwater, exit on Bayshore Blvd. (20 min). Hotel van to the airport. Taxi, rental car available.

Special Notes Elevators but no specially equipped rooms for people with disabilities. No smoking in the spa and in designated dining areas. Arrival can be any day; no group program.

Sanibel Harbour Resort & Spa

Luxury pampering
Sports conditioning

Florida Located on 80 wooded acres overlooking island-studded San
Fort Myers Carlos Bay, the resort is memorable for its easy access to Sanibel and Captiva islands and its top-quality tennis courts and fitness facilities. A private beach, marina, and bayfront swimming pool add to recreation options.

More than 40 aerobics classes a week are taught at variable impact levels in a plush studio with carpeted floor. The spa's indoor lap pool is used for an energizing aquafit class. For more active pursuits, four air-conditioned racquetball courts can be booked by the hour. The Racquet Club offers day-long tennis workouts.

A surprising range of body treatments comes with your spa day package: Swiss showers, aromatherapy, salt glow body scrub, herbal and seaweed wraps, and a salon for hair, nail, and skin care. Both men's and women's sections have sauna, steam room, 5 whirlpools, and hot and cold plunge pools. For a sonic massage, relax on the BETAR bed, a combination of stress-releasing musical energy impulses. A "Sensation" afternoon has sauna, Swiss shower, body buff, mud masque, and reflexology massage. Individually tailored fitness packages can begin any day, as there is no group program. You can also pay the daily facility fee ($10) and use services à la carte.

Sanibel Harbour Resort & Spa
17260 Harbour Pointe Dr., Ft. Meyers, FL 33908
Tel. 8/466–2166 or 800/767–7777
Fax 8/466–2150

Administration Managing director, Robert Moceri; spa director, Susan Brewer

Season Year-round.

Accommodations 240-room hotel in resort complex with 100 2-bedroom luxury condominium apartments facing San Carlos Bay. Hotel rooms offer private balcony, king- or queen-size beds, cable TV, Florida furniture, bath with robes, hair dryer; air-conditioning, telephone, nightly turn-down service. Condominiums in 2 12-story towers have bath with each bedroom, full kitchen, washer/dryer, dining room. Suites available in hotel.

Rates $105–$300 daily per room for 2 persons, suites $150–$840; condominium for 4 persons $145–$495. 5-day/4-night Health & Beauty package without meals $1,162–$1,662 single in hotel, $944–$1,202 per person double in hotel. 3-day/2-night Spa Sampler $494–$744 single in hotel, $389–$514 per person double in hotel. Spa gratuities included in packages, room tax added. Meal plan $61 per person daily (breakfast, lunch, dinner) includes taxes and gratuities. Deposit: 1 night advance payment by credit card. Credit cards: AE, DC, MC, V. Day package (without lodging) $165–$235 includes gratuity.

Meal Plans Breakfast can be buckwheat pancakes or yogurt with fresh fruit, coffee or herbal tea. Light gourmet specials at lunch include chicken terrine appetizer or marinated tuna and grouper carpaccio with baby mixed greens. Entrées are chilled Floridian grouper with lightly spiced papaya coulis, wholewheat pizza with goat cheese, grilled lamb chop, steamed chicken breast stuffed with mushrooms. "Cuisine of the Sun" nightly special menu uses all natural ingredients.

Services and Facilities **Exercise Equipment:** 18-unit Keiser circuit, 7-station Paramount weights gym, dip station, Icarian 7 station, Smith machine, tricep bar, Preacher curl, 4 Schwinn Air Dyne bikes, 4 Trackmaster treadmills, 3 Heart Mate computerized bikes, 2 PTS Turbo recumbent bikes, 3 Lifecycles, Liferower, 2 StairMasters. **Services:** Massage (Swedish, reflexology, sports, aromatherapy), loofah salt glow body scrub, herbal or seaweed wrap, facial with paraffin, mud masque, apricot scrub, salon for hair, nail, skin care. Fitness evaluation, nutritional counseling, personal training, tennis instruction. **Swimming Facilities:** Indoor lap pool, outdoor resort pool, bay beach. **Recreation Facilities:** 12 lighted tennis courts (8 clay, 4 Spin-flex), center court stadium, fitness trail, 4 racquetball courts at spa, marina for sailing and fishing charters; golf, horseback riding nearby. Fishing pier. Water sports, canoe rental.

In the Area Everglades National Park (sightseeing boat, overnight canoe trip from Everglades City), Corkscrew Swamp Sanctuary (Audubon Society boardwalk tour) J. N. Ding Darling Wildlife Refuge (naturalist tour), baseball spring training camps, Thomas Alva Edison winter home and laboratory, Henry Ford estate, Burroughs Home (19th-century Georgian Revival mansion), Bonita Springs Dog Track, Seminole Gulf Railway, Sanibel Island, Captiva Island (shelling), Florida International Museum.

Getting Here *From Fort Meyers or Southwest Florida Regional Airport.* By car, I–75 to Daniels Rd, left at Six Mile Cypress, which becomes Gladiolus Rd., left on Summerlin Rd. to Sanibel Island causeway entrance, right on Harbour Pointe Dr. (20 min). Airport shuttle service on request ($13 per person). Taxi, limousine, and rental car available.

Special Notes Supervised children's program (ages 5–12) daily. No smoking in spa. Spa open Mon.–Sat. 7 AM–9 PM, Sun. and holidays 9–5.

Daily spa admission fee ($12.75) included in packages, waived with services. Minimum age 16.

Spa LXVI at Pier 66 Crown Plaza Resort

Florida
Ft. Lauderdale

The landmark Pier 66 Tower Hotel underwent changes in 1994. Rahn Properties took it over, gave it a complete renovation, and renamed it The Pier 66 Crown Plaza Resort. Located directly on the Intracoastal Waterway, the resort's 22-acre tropical gardens and 142-slip marina contrast with the busy beach scene just down the road. When you want to swim in the ocean, hail the water taxi at the resort's dock for a three-minute trip to the beach.

Spa LXVI is refreshingly tucked away in gardens and has a full-service salon for body, skin, and hair treatments. Owned and managed by MCM Hospitality, Inc., this sybaritic hideaway has indoor and outdoor heated whirlpools, private massage rooms, and a room full of exercise equipment. Aerobics classes are offered poolside, and all guests can join an exercise session in the swimming pool.

Spa LXVI at Pier 66 Crown Plaza Resort
2301 S.E. 17th St. Causeway, Ft. Lauderdale, FL 33316
Tel. 305/525–6666, 800/327–3796, or 800/432–1956 in FL
Fax 305/728–3541

Administration
Executive spa director, Toni Miller Parkyn; hotel general manager, James R. Allmand

Season
Year-round.

Rates
Daily room rate single or double occupancy from $199 (from $139 May–Dec. 15). 1-night spa package with hotel accommodations, from $175. Credit cards: AE, DC, MC, V.

Accommodations
380 deluxe rooms with ocean, Intracoastal, or pool view located in 17-story tower and garden lanais. All have private bathroom, air-conditioning, TV, and telephone.

Services and Facilities
Exercise Equipment: 6 Nautilus units of "Next Generation" weight training equipment, 3 StairMasters, 2 Precor treadmills, 5 Lifecycles, rower, free weights. **Services:** Swedish and sports massage, aromatherapy, seaweed wrap, facial, pineapple or salt glo body scrub; salon for hair, nail, and skin care; fitness evaluation, personal training, aerobics and aquatics classes. **Swimming Facilities:** 2 outdoor pools. **Recreation Facilities:** 2 Har-Tru clay tennis courts (lighted), snorkeling, scuba, parasailing, deep-sea fishing; marina with pleasure craft charter. Golf privileges at nearby course. **Evening Programs:** None.

In the Area
Everglades National Park, jai alai fronton, horse racing tracks, Fort Lauderdale museums and performing arts center, convention center.

Getting Here
From Ft. Lauderdale International Airport. By car, east on 17th St. Causeway to bridge (15 min). Rental car, taxi, limousine available.

Special Notes
Specially equipped rooms for people with disabilities. Minimum age in spa is 16. No smoking in spa.

Turnberry Isle Resort and Club

Luxury pampering

Florida
Aventura
(North Miami)

Here's a luxury hideaway for the executive who wants to shape up in privacy. Turnberry Isle Resort & Club accepts guests to share the members' spa and sports privileges, including spacious accommodations on the Intracoastal Waterway, and two Robert Trent Jones championship golf courses. A well-guarded secret, the 300 tropical acres and waterfront resort is overseen by the Rafael Group, international hoteliers who know how to maintain a very private club atmosphere.

Rarely crowded, the club has two air-conditioned racquetball courts, indoor and outdoor whirlpools, and lounges with sundecks. Scheduled aerobics classes in the sprung-wood–floor studio are attended by club members, and attract some of the area's best instructors. Yoga also is popular as an afternoon unwinder.

For a break in the sports routine, try the beach. There are cabanas, a swimming pool, and light fare for lunch at the members-only Ocean Club. Relax in a Turkish steam bath and Swedish sauna, or get one-on-one cardiovascular training in the weights room, complete with large-screen TV. The entire array of equipment is top-of-the-line.

Turnberry Isle Resort and Club
19999 W. Country Club Dr., Aventura, North Miami,
FL 33180
Tel. 305/932–6200, 800/223–1588, 800/327–7028, or
800/447–7462 in Canada
Fax 305/933–3811

Administration General manager, Jens Grafe; spa director, Frederick Benke

Season Year-round.

Rates 2-night mini-spa plan $419–$869 single, $289–$519 per person double occupancy, including taxes and service charges but no meals. 4-night Spa Indulgence plan $1,269–$2,199 single, $1029–$1,499 double; 7-night Fitness Plan, $1,989–$3,619 single, $1,569–$2,389 double. 1 night's advance payment with credit card. Credit cards: AE, DC, MC, V.

Accommodations 271 deluxe rooms in Mediterranean-style country club and hotel complex, all air-conditioned, with king-size beds, marble bath with hair dryer, whirlpool tub, 3 phones (2 lines), cable TV with VCR. Also 60 spacious rooms in 5-story Yacht Club hotel adjoining spa; 27 1- and 2-bedroom villas.

Meal Plans Personalized diet/nutrition consultation included in spa plans, but no meals. All meals served à la carte. High-carbohydrate luncheon includes grilled swordfish, pasta primavera, and cold shrimp plate. Typical dinner entrées are steamed lobster tail, tenderloin brochette, eggplant Parmesan, mesquite-grilled redfish with scallions.

Services and
Facilities
Exercise Equipment: 20-unit Nautilus circuit, Plus II Cybex units, 2 Liferowers, 5 StairMasters, VersaClimber, 5 Lifecycles, 9 Precor treadmills, Precor 3-D bike, Biocycle, recumbent bike, 2 Cybex ergometers, 2 Bally Lifesteps, hand weights. Dumbbells (3–80 lbs). **Services:** Therapeutic massage, Swedish massage, shiatsu, aromatherapy, reflexology; back cleansing

and heat treatment, Phytomer marine mask, herbal wrap, loofah body scrub, Swiss shower, hydrotherapy tub, skin care. Computerized body-composition analysis, nutrition consultation, blood cholesterol test, medical consultation. Spa salon for hair, nail, and skin care. **Swimming Facilities:** 2 pools at spa, Ocean Club, Country Club. **Recreation Facilities:** 2 championship golf courses, 24 tennis courts (18 lighted), 2 indoor racquetball courts, walleyball, basketball, yacht charter.

In the Area Aventura Mall, Thoroughbred races at Gulfstream Park, Disney World, Miami and Fort Lauderdale museums. Joe Robbie Stadium (Miami Dolphins), Dania Fronton (Jai Alai), Biscayne Dog Race Track, baseball.

Getting Here *From Miami.* By car, I-95 to Exit 20, Ives Dairy Rd., U.S. Rte. 1, Biscayne Blvd. (25 min). By boat, Intracoastal Waterway to Turnberry Isle Marina. Taxi, limousine, rental car available.

Special Notes No smoking in the spa and in designated areas. Spa open daily 7 AM–9 PM. Shuttle bus to beach, mall, country club, and spa.

Chateau Elan

Life enhancement
Luxury pampering
Stress control

Georgia
Braselton

A new and unique addition to the Atlanta area in 1992, the spa at Chateau Elan is a restful retreat within a 3,400-acre gated resort community. The chateau is, in fact, a working winery, complete with vineyards and a reproduction of a 16th-century French manor house. Follow the woodland trails to a private lake and discover the elegant spa building where a full-service health and exercise facility complements beautiful accommodations in 14 guest rooms.

The professional staff at the spa is supplemented by Atlanta area medical consultants, and specialists in nutrition and smoking-cessation programs. Behavior-modification services also are an option. On arrival you will be offered a menu of services, and the concierge will make dining reservations in the winery's Le Clos if you're not counting calories. The spa also has its own dining room where breakfast and lunch are served as part of packages for 2–8 days.

A quiet, warm, and friendly atmosphere prevails, encouraging you to discover the best of yourself. Mornings begin with easy stretches, and a short hike is scheduled after breakfast. Nature trails, horseback riding, and golf can be scheduled on your daily program along with one-on-one training and beauty services. Personalized rather than organized group activity is what guests seem to prefer.

Within the Chateau complex are the South's largest equestrian center, with three all-weather arenas, riding trails, and Grand Prix show facility, a 10-court tennis center by Stan Smith, a beauty salon with private treatment rooms, 150-room inn and conference center managed by Marriott, and vineyards where summer concerts and picnic dinners are an added attraction.

Also offered are art and sculpture classes, and spa cooking demonstrations, and special therapy is available for recuperation from illness or surgery and post-holiday recovery.

Chateau Elan
Haven Harbour Dr., Braselton, GA 30517
Tel. 404/867–8200 or 800/233–9463
Fax. 404/867–8714

Administration	President, Nancy C. Panoz; spa director, Judie Rustin; fitness manager, Cathy Carroll
Season	Year-round.
Accommodations	The spa building has 14 rooms, individually decorated in themes ranging from Oriental to Greek, Western, Art Deco, and Victorian. Antiques and high-tech amenities, queen-size or twin beds, lavish bathroom fixtures. 2 Loft suites feature upper level bedroom with 4-poster bed, 2 bathrooms. All air-conditioned, with VCR, phone, concierge service.
Rates	Daily rate $129–$284 single, $144–$289 per person, double occupancy. Spa Getaway (2-night/3-day) $1,000 per couple, $750 single; golf package with spa services, 2 meals daily (3-night/4-day) $1,424 single, $1,128.50 per person double; luxury week (7-night/8-day) $3,207.90 single, $2,271 per person double. Day package, including lunch, spa services, no lodging, $125–$175. Add 6% tax, optional gratuities. Deposit $1,000 for a week's stay, $500 for other packages. Credit cards: AE, MC, V.
Meal Plans	Basic plan includes 3 spa meals daily, afternoon tea, evening snack. Breakfast specials are blue corn pancakes with fresh homemade quark, yolkless omelet with steamed spinach and mushroom or cheese, gravlax, and cereals, muffins, croissants. Lunch begins with salad or Belgian endive, choice of 2 soups, entrée choice such as duckling breast, salmon supreme on black noodles, vegetarian goulash. Dinner main course can be petit fillet of beef or grilled chicken. Desserts include yogurt fruit ice, fresh fruit, and berry cocktail.
Services and Facilities	**Exercise Equipment:** Landice treadmill, 2 Alpine stairclimbers, Preference stationary bike, Bodyguard ergometer, hand weights (complete cardiovascular circuit at the Inn). **Services:** Massage (Swedish, shiatsu, therapeutic, sports, aromatherapy), reflexology, body wrap, loofah, body gommage, collagen masque, facials, glycolic acid series, thalassotherapy, paraffin hand and foot moisturizing, mineral bath; salon for hair, nail, and makeup; tanning bed; fitness evaluation, skin analysis, makeup instruction. **Spa Facilities:** Coed sauna, steam bath, whirlpool. **Swimming Facilities:** Outdoor heated pool with resistance jets; nearby health club's indoor/outdoor pool. **Recreation Facilities:** Bicycles, horseback riding (extra charge), 3 18-hole golf courses (greens fee), tennis center. **Evening Programs:** concerts.
In the Area	Atlanta museums, Buckhead Mall, Atlanta Underground.
Getting Here	*From Atlanta.* By car, I–85 north, Exit 48, turn left on Old Winder Hwy. 211 (45 min). Airport transfer by limousine through Chateau Elan transportation service, taxi, rental car.
Special Notes	Minimum age 16.

Sea Island Beach Club Spa at The Cloister

Life enhancement
Luxury pampering

Georgia
Sea Island

After 75 years as the grande dame of southern seashore resorts, The Cloister opened its Sea Island Spa at the Beach Club in 1989. Group activity is minimal, because programs are tailored to each guest's fitness level and personal goals, but all guests join a morning beach walk and stretch class. Thalassotherapy by the sea is a major attraction here.

The power of the sea inspires services and products such as seaweed masks and salt scrubs offered at the Beach Club Spa. In the licensed hands of an esthetician, the facial masque treatment becomes a succession of cleansing and soothing experiences as four layers of aloe, seaweed, and Repechage creams are applied. While your complexion is being detoxified and moisturized to combat the ravages of time and sun, your feet are softened with a paraffin waxing. The final touch may be a reflexology massage, one of 18 different techniques offered by staff therapists.

The aerobics studio and exercise rooms attached to the spa are open to all resort guests for modest daily fees. In addition, other sports add a special dimension to this seaside escape. The Cloister offers 54 holes of golf at two clubs, plus an acclaimed golf academy with indoor and outdoor training by professionals. Water sports, a tennis club with 18 courts, three skeet ranges, and a cycling center with 300 bikes for rent, stables with 60 horses, a gun club, and docks for boat rental on the Intracoastal Waterway are also available to guests.

The Sea Island Spa at the Cloister
Sea Island, GA 31561
Tel. 916/638–3611 or 800/732–4752
Fax 912/638–5814

Administration
Managing director, Ted Wright; Beach Club director, Jane Segerberg

Season
Year-round.

Accommodations
264 guest rooms in spacious, modern lodges overlooking the beach and waterway, plus private cottage rental. Choice of twin or king-size bed, patio or balcony. Air-conditioned, with TV, sitting area, walk-in closet, full bathroom, telephone and desk. Original Spanish Mediterranean architecture by Addison Mizner, 1928.

Rates
Spa package priced per day (minimum stay 3 nights), $347–$641 single, $282–$429 per person double occupancy. For cottage renters: 2-day spa retreat without lodging $330, 5-day package $825. Add 6% tax, 15% service charge, spa gratuities. Deposit $250. No credit cards.

Meal Plans
Full American Plan, 3 meals daily, included in spa package with lodging. Limited selection of spa cuisine on menu in main dining room; lunch and breakfast buffet at the Beach Club. Seafood buffet, fresh fish featured daily at beachside restaurant. Formal dinner menu and dancing nightly in main building.

Services and Facilities   **Exercise Equipment:** 12-unit Eagle Cybex weight training circuit, 2 StairMasters, LifeRower, Cycleplus bike, 2 MasterMill treadmills, dynabands. **Services:** Massage including acupressure, deep-muscle therapy, aromatherapy; facial, paraffin hand and foot treatment, herbal or seaweed wrap, body scrub. Fitness evaluation, nutrition consultation, exercise program, personal training and exercise video. **Swimming Facilities:** 2 freshwater pools, ocean beach. **Recreation Facilities:** Horseback trail rides with lunch or evening cookout, 18 tennis courts, 2 golf clubs, skeet range, bike and boat rental, sea kayak tour of marshes, windsurfer rental.

In the Area   Ft. Frederica (British colonial village, ca. 1740); St. Simons Island (historic church); Jacksonville; FL, Savannah, GA.

Getting Here   *From Jacksonville.* By car, I–95 north, Exit 6, east on Hwy. 17 (45 min). Van service scheduled by The Cloister transportation desk from Jacksonville Airport ($30). By plane, Delta Express to Brunswick, GA; hotel van on request ($12). Limousine, car rental, taxi available.

Special Notes   Teenage skin care and makeup classes during holidays. Teenage golf clinic. Supervised program for children 3–11 daily and evenings, Family Festival June 12–Sept. 4.

Wildwood Lifestyle Center

Life enhancement
Preventive medicine
Vibrant maturity

Georgia
Wildwood

Converts to fitness come here to learn a healthier way of life. Up to 26 middle-aged professionals and housewives participate in each session of the Wildwood Lifestyle Program. Medically oriented and devoted to education and exercise, the 22-day program provides a basis for self-help.

Wildwood, a hospital as well as a lifestyle center, has been devoted to preventive medicine for more than 40 years. The doctors, nurses, and staff, all Seventh-Day Adventists (although programs are nondenominational and nonsectarian), see diet as a means of disease prevention. Their nutritional computer analysis makes specific recommendations for diet and takes into account present physical condition, nutritional requirements, and weight-loss goals. After a complete medical examination a physician—who monitors your progress throughout the three-week program—prescribes a program for you. One-week programs to stop smoking are scheduled at various times during the year. Personal counseling tailored to the health needs of the individual and 10- to 17-day programs are available. The philosophy is to treat the causes of disease rather than the symptoms. High blood pressure, coronary heart disease, angina, arteriosclerosis, diabetes, stress, constipation, arthritis, and obesity are addressed.

Wildwood Lifestyle Center
Box 129, Wildwood, GA 30757
Tel. 706/820–1490 or 800/634–9355
Fax 706/820–1474

Administration   Director, Wilbur Atwood; Lifestyle Program director, Mary Fisher; medical director, Scott Grivas, M.D.

Season   Year-round.

Accommodations   26 mountain lodge bedrooms with twin beds, private patio; some share large bath. Woodland views. Lounge for informal lectures around fireplace, laundry facility.

Rates   22-day program $3,145, 14-day program $2,295 sharing accommodation. Private rooms when available. 20% discount for spouses participating in nonmedical parts of program. Transportation included certain times of year. 7-day stop-smoking program $1,495. $100 per person advance payment, refundable up to 2 weeks before program begins. Credit cards (4% surcharge): MC, V.

Meal Plans   Fruits, vegetables, legumes, and grains. No butter or oil, but nuts, olives and avocados available. 3 daily buffets without dairy products, fish, or meat. Specialties include vegetarian lasagna with melted "cheese" topping of tahini, pimiento, and tomato; oat-burger roll; steamed vegetables with rice; 7-grain bread.

Services and Facilities   **Exercise Equipment:** 2 Lifecycles, 2 trampolines, rowing machines. **Services:** Swedish massage, hydrotherapy showers, medical treatment. **Swimming Facilities:** Lake on property. **Spa Facilities:** Sauna and steam room. **Recreation Facilities:** Hiking, boating. **Evening Programs:** Lectures on health-related and spiritual topics.

In the Area   Picnics, outings to historical sites and Civil War memorials; Atlanta museums, shopping; Chattanooga museums.

Getting Here   *From Atlanta.* By bus, Trailways to Chattanooga (2 hr). By plane, scheduled flights to Chattanooga metropolitan airport. By car, I–24 past Chattanooga, Exit 169 (about 2 hr). Free service to and from Chattanooga airport and bus station. Rental car available.

Special Notes   All rooms on ground level; wheelchair patients accepted when accompanied by companion. No smoking indoors. Remember to bring an alarm clock, laundry detergent, umbrella, rain gear.

Duke University Diet and Fitness Center

Life enhancement
Nutrition and diet
Vibrant maturity
Weight management

North Carolina **Durham**   Durham has been known as a hub of the diet and fitness industry for more than 40 years. During 25 of those years, the Duke Diet and Fitness Center (DFC) has provided an on-campus program for weight and health management that resembles a college course in healthy living. Four-week stays are typical, although two-week and longer programs are offered.

Starting with a physical examination Monday morning (including testing, treadmill exercise, and body-composition evaluation) and personal assessments, the specialized faculty of physicians, dieticians, and psychologists set up a schedule based on your fitness level and personal interests. Choices range from workshops on stress management to cooking classes, fitness training to psychological counseling. The daily schedule keeps you busy from around 8 AM through dinner.

There is some free time on weekends and evenings to explore the area, taking in sports events and entertainment. Throughout the week you work out on fitness equipment, take stretch and aerobics classes, and exercise in the pool and gym.

Learning strategies for lifestyle change and long-term success keeps you busy in classrooms, on local supermarket tours, and on dining out at local restaurants. The DFC encourages family members or close friends to accompany program participants, to make it easier when you bring home new, healthy habits. (After receiving medical clearance, support persons can participate in most of the daily activities offered at the DFC.) For smokers, there is a special program to help kick the habit. Program graduates are encouraged to return periodically for continuing education and reinforcing healthy goals.

Duke University Diet and Fitness Center
804 W. Trinity Ave., Durham, NC 27701
Tel. 919/684-6331 or 800/362-8446
Fax 919/684-6176

Administration Director, Michael A. Hamilton, M.D.; administrative director, Dawn Schiffhauer, R.D.

Season Year-round.

Accommodations Local inns cater to dieters. Duke Tower, across the street from the center, has furnished apartments with bedroom, living room, kitchen for $315 per week. Rooms in private homes $75–$110 per week.

Rates 4-week program $4,795, 2-week program $3,895. $500 refundable deposit required. Credit cards: AE, MC, V.

Meal Plans 3 low-calorie, portion-controlled meals daily at center are also low in sodium, fat, and cholesterol. Vegetarian and kosher diets accommodated. Lunch entrées include seafood gumbo with rice, lamb stew, and eggplant Parmesan. Italian baked fish, barbecued chicken, sirloin steak, and black bean tortillas for dinner. Menu published weekly, with calorie counts.

Services and Facilities **Exercise Equipment:** Treadmills, stationary bicycles, stair climbers, NordicTrack ski machine, rowing machines, weight machines, steps for gym and pool aerobics, recumbent bicycles, free weights. **Services:** Massage, personal fitness training, swimming instruction, body composition testing, individual psychotherapy, career counseling; on-site medical clinic. **Swimming Facilities:** 25-m indoor pool. **Recreation Facilities:** University campus and city parks provide full range of sports, including tennis, golf, fishing. Basketball and volleyball in DFC gymnasium. **Evening Programs:** Lectures on health-related topics scheduled nightly weekdays: Image consultant, dance instructor, Overeaters Anonymous speakers. Duke University performing arts and cultural programs open to participants.

In the Area Atlantic Ocean beaches, Blue Ridge Mountains, outlet shopping, furniture shopping in High Point and Charlotte, Brevard Music Center concerts late June–mid-Aug., Asheville folk arts, Biltmore Estate near Asheville.

Getting Here *From Raleigh-Durham Airport.* By car, I–40 to Durham Fwy. (Rte. 147), exit at Duke St., right on Trinity Ave. (20 min). Taxi, rental car available.

Special Notes Ramps in most buildings provide access for people with disabilities; All facilities at DFC on 1 floor. Theater, arts, recreational outings for children through community organizations. No smoking indoors and in patio area. Remember to bring appropriate seasonal clothing, exercise and swimming outfits, jogging or walking shoes; notebooks and pens, wristwatch, alarm clock, padlock for gym lockers.

Structure House

Vibrant maturity
Weight management

North Carolina
Durham
Founded in 1977, Structure House specializes in serious weight problems for first-time visitors and alumni who return for a week or more of reinforcement; many bring their spouse or a companion. Most people stay a month or more to learn the program that is designed to teach long-term weight control. The new environment helps, particularly if you have failed to lose weight at home or in other programs. Over 40 qualified professionals help you to understand the reasons behind unhealthy lifestyles and to practice problem solving.

Settling into your apartment in "the village" will be like getting a new lease on life. The cluster of residential units around the new Life Extension Center and the large Georgian-style Structure House, where one goes for meals, classes, and professional services, convey a college campus atmosphere. A healthy lifestyle, in fact, is what you learn here.

The medically managed program involves mental and physical conditioning. A full physical examination and diagnosis precedes the planning of an individual diet and exercise regimen. For the elderly, the handicapped, and those with health problems, the medical staff consults with patients' private physicians in order to monitor and continue health services.

The integration of medical and psychological aspects of weight loss, alongside dietary and exercise programs, makes this program work for people who need a structured environment. The exercise facilities and classes at the Life Extension Center are the equal of many leading spa resorts. Classes are varied: step aerobics, aquacise and dynabane.

Structure House
3017 Pickett Rd., Durham, NC 27705
Tel. 919/493–4205 or 800/553–0052
Fax 919/490–0191

Administration Program director, Gerard J. Musante; medical director, Steven Hirsch, M.D.; fitness director, Ann Archer

Season Year-round; sessions begin 8 AM Mon., new arrivals on Sun.

Accommodations 76 1- and 2-bedroom apartments in 9 2-story houses on campus. New modern units, sliding glass door opens onto porch. Washer/dryer, linens, telephone, color TV with HBO, weekly maid service.

Rates $1,400 per week single, $1,277.50 per person double occupancy, for all-inclusive program and apartment. (Health insurance may cover some services.) $500 per person advance deposit. Credit cards: MC, V. No tax. Gratuities optional.

Meal Plans Selections from weekly menus that individuals plan for themselves. Suggested 700-calorie menu includes 3-cheese quiche, chef's salad, bean chowder, and French toast. Fri. lunch is a potato bar with toppings. Dinner entrées include sea scallops in wine, baked chicken, and filet mignon. Vegetarian and special diets accommodated.

Services and Facilities **Exercise Equipment:** 5 Nautilus machines, 3 treadmills, 6 Schwinn Air Dyne bikes, step machine, rowing machine, bench press and free weights, trampoline. **Services:** Massage (Swedish, Trager, deep-muscle, polarity), medical consultation and testing, consultation with clinical psychologist, dietary reeducation workshops. **Swimming Facilities:** Indoor and outdoor pool, lakes nearby. **Recreation Facilities:** Nature trails, basketball, badminton, Ping-Pong, tennis; golf, horseback riding nearby. **Evening Programs:** Occasional parties.

In the Area Eastern Piedmont mountains and lakes, plus numerous historic sites; minor-league baseball at *Bull Durham* park.

Getting Here *From Raleigh-Durham Airport.* By car, I–40 west (20 min. to Structure House). Shuttle service prearranged by Structure House, $20. Taxi, rental car available.

Special Notes Ramps for wheelchairs; some apartments equipped for people with disabilities. No smoking indoors and in designated dining areas. Remember to bring recent medical records, exercise clothing, wristwatch with second hand, walking or jogging shoes.

Westglow Spa

Life enhancement
Weight management

North Carolina
Blowing Rock

This historic 20-acre mountain retreat overlooking Grandfather Mountain in the Blue Ridge, was converted in 1991 into North Carolina's first European-style spa resort. The graceful Colonial-style mansion built in 1916 now houses six guest rooms and the spa's main dining facility. Additional accommodations are found in two new guest cottages equipped with kitchen, fireplace, TV, and phone.

The Life Enhancement Center has an indoor swimming pool, men's and women's whirlpools, dry sauna, six body treatment rooms, beauty salon, weights room, aerobics studio, and poolside café. Health and beauty services range from fitness and nutrition training to massage and body therapy; a daily schedule of classes is posted, though the staff will also do training and aquatics on request.

The miles of forest surrounding the resort provide vacationers with the opportunity to hike, take rafting trips in nearby white-water rapids, or go canoeing. From May to October the spa organizes week-long Hiking and Adventure Programs. There is a tennis court on the estate, and arrangements can be made nearby for horseback riding, golf, and in winter, downhill skiing.

Westglow Spa
Hwy. 221 S, Box 1083, Blowing Rock, NC 28605
Tel. 704/295-4463 or 800/562-0807
Fax 704/295-5115

Administration Founder-director, Glynda McPheters; spa manager, Jean Teague

Season Year-round.

Accommodations 6 guest rooms in main house, 2 cottages with 1-2 bedrooms. Vintage furnishings, Oriental rugs, large library retain mansion's original elegance. Modern bathrooms and amenities added in 1989. Cottages have fireplace, air-conditioning, phone, TV, and kitchenette.

Rates 2-night package $539-$618 single, $439-$483 per person double occupancy; 5-night package $1,329-$1,462 single, $1,109-$1,219 double; 7-night package $1,769-$1,949 single, $1,439-$1,584 double; day guest (no lodging) $199-$219; 8-day/7-night Hiking and Adventure Program, $1,869-$2,059 single, $1,539-$1,699 double. Add 6% tax, 10% gratuities. Deposit: 50% in advance. Credit cards: AE, MC, V.

Meal Plans 3 meals daily included in program. Breakfast can be cereal, blueberry pancakes, with herbal tea, decaffeinated or regular coffee, low-fat milk, yogurt. Lunch choices include Oriental pasta, vegetarian sandwich, or sliced pork tenderloin on wheat bread, garden salad, soup. Dinner entrées are mountain trout, mixed grill, vegetarian platter, and baked chicken.

Services and Facilities **Exercise Equipment:** 15-unit Cybex weight training circuit, 12 Cybex Fitron bikes, 4 Lifecycles, 2 Challenger treadmills, 2 Cybex Lifesteps, dumbbells. **Services:** Swedish or deep-muscle massage, aromatherapy, herbal wrap, reflexology, body scrub, facial, cellulite/lymphatic drainage; fitness assessment, exercise, nutrition and diet consultation, personal trainer; salon for hair and nail care. **Swimming Facilities:** indoor lap pool. **Recreation Facilities:** Outdoor tennis court (composition surface), croquet court, walking trails; horseback riding, 18-hole golf course nearby.

In the Area Tweetsie Railroad and theme park (vintage trains, country music), Blue Ridge Parkway, Great Smoky Mountains National Park.

Getting Here *From Charlotte.* By car, I-77 north, I-40 west to exit 123, Hwy. 321 north to Blowing Rock Bypass exit for Sunset Blvd., Main St. to Hwy. 221 south (2½ hr). By air, USAir Express to Hickory (45 min). Pickup charge $75. Rental car, taxi available.

Special Notes No smoking indoors.

Hilton Head Health Institute

Life enhancement
Nutrition and diet
Stress control
Vibrant maturity

South Carolina The concentrated courses held here since 1976 are concerned
Hilton Head with modifying behavior in order to achieve practical results:
Island changes in your daily life and work habits, nutritional education for weight maintenance, smoking cessation, and managing
stress. The highly structured program has a maximum of 40
participants.

Health education begins with an understanding of your body.
Lectures, workshops, exercise classes, and meals designed to
advance that understanding are scheduled in the institute's
main building, a short walk from your living quarters. The effect of nutrition and exercise on the body's metabolism and the
effect of stress on productivity and health are taught by a team
of psychologists, nutritionists, and physical fitness specialists.

The subtropical climate, 12 miles of white, sandy beach, and
ample walking and biking trails through local nature preserves
go far to enhance and renew the spirit. Other activities center
in a campuslike cluster of Low Country cottages. Participants
share well-decorated apartments, fully equipped for laundry
or cooking. The medically supervised programs are suited for
individuals and couples who have reached a point in their
lives where change is necessary and they need a boost to get
started.

Hilton Head Health Institute
Box 7138, Hilton Head Island, SC 29938
Tel. 803/785–7292 or 800/292–2440; 800/348–2039 in
Canada
Fax 803/686–5659

Administration Executive director, Peter M. Miller, Ph.D.; medical consultant, Jack M. Catlett, M.D.; fitness director, Robert Wright

Season Scheduled programs year-round; closed during Christmas.

Accommodations Cottages in Shipyard Plantation have traditional furniture,
fine fabrics, color TV. Each participant has a private bedroom
and bath, sharing the living room and fully equipped apartment and laundry facilities with another person in the program. Private porch, parking space, pedestrian walkways.

Rates 5-day program $2,450, 12-day program $3,675, 26-day program $5,725. Deposit: 5-day $500, 12-day $800, 26-day $1,200.
All rates are per person; 10% discount for couples. Credit
cards: MC, V.

Meal Plans 3 meals and "Metabo" fruit snack daily. Weekday diet totals approximately 800 calories daily, more on weekends, when out-
door activity increases. Food high in complex carbohydrates,
moderate protein, low fat, no sugar or salt. Lunch can feature
pasta primavera with raw vegetables, dinner entrées include
chicken enchilada with salsa and brown rice.

Services and **Exercise Equipment:** 8-station Paramount weight system, 5
Facilities Schwinn Air Dyne stationary bikes, 2 rowing machines, 3
treadmills. **Services:** private massage therapist on request;

beauty salon nearby. **Swimming Facilities:** Outdoor pool, ocean beach. **Recreation Facilities:** 24 tennis courts and 3 golf courses within walking distance, for a fee. Nature preserve of subtropical marshes for hiking. Horseback riding, bicycling, windsurfing, sailing, deep-sea fishing available through resort.

In the Area Community theater, cinema, shopping mall. Nature tours by boat; Historic Savannah, GA (1 hr), Beaufort, Charleston (antebellum homes and gardens, 2 hr north).

Getting Here *From Savannah.* By car, I–95 to Rte. 278 (50 min). By plane, Hilton Head Island airport has scheduled service on USAir (via Charlotte) and American Eagle (via Raleigh/Durham). Limousine service hourly from Savannah airport. Taxi, rental car available.

Special Notes Programs for children at community centers. No smoking indoors. Bring an alarm clock, flashlight, medical records. Group size limited to 40.

Hilton Head Westin Resort

Nonprogram resort

South Carolina
Hilton Head Island
On an island noted for golf, tennis, and fishing, Port Royal Plantation's health facilities at the posh Westin Resort are a happy addition. Equipment, classes, and outdoor recreation on 24 acres of landscaped, subtropical beach are available for a fee; guests in the hotel get complimentary health-club privileges.

Mornings may begin with a beach walk, led by a trainer at the Spectrum Health Club. Invigorated by sun, sea, and air, you can join an exercise class or have a personal program planned for you. The club's full-time fitness pro is available for consultation and cardiovascular testing.

The sprawling, five-story hotel has big-city airs and a breezy, Southern Low Country ambience. Enjoy the view of the grand courtyard and three swimming pools from the mirrored weights room. One of the pools is glass-enclosed for year-round swimming and water aerobics classes. Scheduled daily are three or four aerobics classes ($5 charge each), including step and low-impact, held in a studio with suspended wooden floor that has room for 10–12. Other facilities include a steam room with Swiss shower, a sauna misted with eucalyptus oils, three outdoor whirlpools, and private rooms for massage appointments.

Hilton Head Westin Resort
2 Grasslawn Ave., Hilton Head Island, SC 29928
Tel. 803/681–4000 or 800/228–3000
Telex 62893418
Fax 803/681–1087

Administration General manager, Anthony Cherone; health club manager, Spencer Kurtz

Season Year-round.

Accommodations 410 luxury rooms (including 38 suites), with separate dressing areas, hair dryers, large baths. Furnishings and architecture are reminiscent of grand southern homes. All have balcony.

Rates $215–$315 for 2 people in summer. Suites $365–$780. Add 7% tax and $5.50 daily service charge. Golf and tennis packages available. Deposit: 1 night by credit card. Credit cards: AE, DC, MC, V.

Meal Plans Carolina Cafe buffet serves breakfast, lunch, dinner. Barony Restaurant's low-cholesterol and sodium menu includes free-range chicken with black-pepper pasta and chanterelle mushroom sauce, sautéed shrimp Provençale over angel-hair pasta, and broiled fish of the day. All meals à la carte; dinner in the Barony about $50 per person, including tip, tax, and wine.

Services and Facilities **Exercise Equipment:** Weights room with 14 Universal units, free-weight dumbbells (3–50 lbs.), Lifecycle, rowing machine, 2 StairMasters, treadmill, NordicTrack, Schwinn Air Dyne bike, bilateral board equipment, Nautilus abdominal machine. **Services:** Fitness testing, personal instruction on exercise equipment, classes and beach activity; massage by appointment (fee); golf and tennis clinics. **Swimming Facilities:** Indoor pool, 2 outdoor pools (1 with lap lanes); ocean beach. **Recreation Facilities:** Beach runs and walks, volleyball, water polo; 3 golf courses, 16 tennis courts (clay, hard, and grass, 6 lighted), croquet lawn; horseback riding, windsurfing, sailing, and fishing nearby. **Evening Programs:** Resort entertainment.

In the Area Historic Savannah (1 hr), Beaufort, and Charleston (antebellum homes and gardens, 2 hr north).

Getting Here *From Savannah.* By car, I–95 to Hardeeville, Rte. 278 (50 min). By plane, Hilton Head Island airport has scheduled service on Piedmont-Henson (via Charlotte). Also, private aircraft facilities. Hourly limousine service from Savannah airport. Taxi, rental car available.

Special Notes Ramps, specially equipped rooms, elevators to all floors provide access for people with disabilities; beach wheelchair with dunebuggy wheels available. The Kids Korner for children has arts and crafts, games, pool and water activities morning and evening May–Sept., Nov.–Apr. Health club open Mon.–Sat. 7 AM–8 PM, Sun. 9:30–6. No smoking in the health club.

Tennessee Fitness Spa

Nutrition and diet
Weight management

Tennessee
Natural Bridge At this mountain camp for healthy living, guests get back to nature, and back in shape at the same time. The Tennessee Fitness Spa organizes hikes, swimnastics, canoeing, bike rides, and walks through the area's scenic surroundings for fitness and to aid in weight management.

Regularly scheduled classes on nutrition are held in the natural stone dining hall, where the spa chef demonstrates how to cook meals that are low in fat, sodium, and sugar. Most guests are concerned with weight management, and some come for several months to develop a workable weight-loss regimen that they can continue at home.

Guests, who range in age from 20 to 70, join a group leader for a 7 AM hill walk, a 2½-mile warmup followed by stretch class and aerobics. The daily schedule rotates among step aerobics, line dancing, aquacise, floor work, and lectures. Cross-training can be followed by a volleyball game or a soak in the big hot tub. Personal services, such as massages and facials, are optional extras.

Tennessee Fitness Spa

Rte. 3, Box 411, Waynesboro, TN 38485
Tel. 615/722–5589 or 800/235–8365
Fax 615/722–7441

Administration	General manager, John Alexander; program director, Valerie Shaw
Season	Mid-Feb.–mid-Dec.
Accommodations	36 double rooms, 2 with 4 beds, in 6 2-story wooden chalets. Simply furnished, with private bathrooms, shower for every 2 guests, heat. No air-conditioning, TV, or telephone. New deluxe rooms have bathtub, phone connection.
Rates	$799 per week for private room including meals and program, $529 per person double; $1,499 for 2 weeks in private room, $999 double. Deposit is $100, gratuities optional. Local tax added. Credit cards: MC, V (4% surcharge).
Meal Plans	3 meals daily included in program, low in fat, sodium, and sugar. Breakfast can be pancakes, apple spice cake, French toast, or cereal with skim milk. Herbal tea, fruit juices available all day; no coffee. Lunch choices are pizza or black beans and rice, salad bar. Dinner entrées include chicken enchiladas, turkey burgers, Friday night seafood, salad bar.
Services and Facilities	**Exercise Equipment:** 4 Nautilus units, 3 StairMasters, 3 Precor treadmills, 2 Windracer bikes, free weights. **Services:** Massage, facial, hair styling, manicure/pedicure. **Swimming Facilities:** Covered, heated pool. **Recreation Facilities:** Bicycles, canoes (charge), racquetball court, fishing. **Evening Programs:** Cooking class, cross training, volleyball, pool games, movies, entertainment.
In the Area	Natural Bridge (world's only double-span natural rock bridge formation), Natchez Race (scenic highway), Nashville (country music).
Getting Here	*From Nashville.* By car, I–65 south, Exit 46 (Columbia), Hwy. 412 via Hohewald, Rd. 20 to Hwy. 99 southwest (2 hr). By bus chartered by the spa: Sunday pickup at 1 PM in Nashville ($25 round-trip). Rental car available.
Special Notes	Roommate matching service and 4-person rooms with 2 bathrooms available.

Camp Rediscovery

Life enhancement
Vibrant maturity

Virginia *Front Royal*	Designed for adults (the average age of participants is 68), Camp Rediscovery blends popular traditional camp activities with personalized health and fitness programs. Challenging participants to expand physical boundaries, the week-long program provides a chance to rediscover the simple pleasures of staying fit. Based on personal consultations, camping experiences are geared to the fitness level of participants. At the end

of camp, each person is tested again to measure improvement in heart and lung efficiency, flexibility, balance, and strength.

Staffed by members of the Adult Health and Development Program at the University of Maryland, Camp Rediscovery offers one-on-one support in achieving your goals. Warm and enduring friendships develop between campers and staff, all of whom have degrees in health-related subjects.

Taking a multidisciplinary approach, the program imposes no mandatory activities; you can join a supervised canoe trip, play tennis, or practice archery and yoga. Discussions on osteoporosis, loneliness, dental care, stress management, and coping with loss and grief are part of the daily agenda.

Accommodations are in two-story lodges which have 40 rooms, some air-conditioned. The grounds include a lake for sailing, boating, and fishing. Campers who require more assistance or are in wheelchairs get special attention (some are chauffeured from one activity to another).

Camp Rediscovery
Administrative Office: 2007 Pelden Rd., Adelphi, MD 20783
Tel. 301/431–3733 or 301/405-2528

Administration	Director, Dr. Daniel Leviton, Ph.D.
Season	Aug.–Sept.
Accommodations	Shared double room in lodge, for 2 to 3 occupants. All rooms have private bath, screened windows; some are air-conditioned. Beds supplied with linens; no maid service.
Rates	$500 for 7-day session, shared room; no extra charge for private room if available. Discount for participating group members and camp alumni. No credit cards.
Meal Plans	Buffet-style meals served 3 times a day, plus snacks. Prepared with low sugar, salt, and fats, the selections include whole grains and salad, fish, chicken.
Services and Facilities	**Exercise Equipment:** Screened gymnasium with exercise mats. **Services:** Group or individual classes in tennis, archery, riflery, yoga, aerobics. **Swimming Facilities:** Lake. **Recreation Facilities:** Volleyball, canoeing, paddleboats; horseback riding nearby (additional fee). **Evening Programs:** Nightly health seminars, folk dancing, or campfire talk.
In the Area	Monticello (Thomas Jefferson's Palladian home), Montpelier (home of President James Madison), Ash Lawn-Highland (home of President James Monroe), University of Virginia campus designed by Jefferson, vineyard tours, Ruckersville (antiques shops), Skyline Drive.
Getting Here	*From Washington, DC.* By car, I-66 (90 min). Rental car available.

Hartland Wellness Center

Preventive medicine
Vibrant maturity
Weight management

Virginia The 10- to 18-day program incorporating health, education,
Rapidan and exercise at Hartland Wellness teaches you how to help
yourself. The core program consists of cooking school experience, private and group counseling, and physical therapy
guided by a team of physicians, dietitians, educators, chap-
lains, and therapists.

The doctors and staff, all Seventh-Day Adventists (although
the program is nondenominational and nonsectarian), focus on
disease prevention. Their computer-aided nutritional analysis
makes specific recommendations for diet and takes into account
physical condition, nutritional requirements, and weight-loss
goals. Heart disease, arthritis, cancer, diabetes, and obesity
are among the diseases dealt with here, on this 575-acre estate
in the foothills of the Blue Ridge Mountains. Spouses are encouraged to participate at a reduced fee.

Your personalized schedule begins with breakfast at 6:45 on
weekdays. Hydrotherapy, including contrasting hot and cold
showers, hot packs, or sitz baths may be recommended.

The program is associated with Hartland College, a small,
four-year training program for health professionals. The intensive, outpatient-style program has motel-like facilities adjacent to physicians' offices and treatment areas in the mansion.
The dedicated physicians and educators believe medical
technology often overshadows simple ailments that can be pre-
vented with good living habits.

Hartland Wellness Center
Box 1, Rapidan, VA 22733
Tel. 703/672–3100

Administration Director, William Evert

Season Sessions monthly except Dec.

Accommodations 15 rooms in a 2-story residential-treatment building. Furnished with antiques, cherrywood dresser and bed; 5 rooms
have 2 queen-size beds, 10 have 2 beds. All have private bath.

Rates 10-day program $1,500, spouse $1,350; 18-day program $2,500,
spouse $2,250; Deposit 50% of program fee. Credit cards: MC,
V (5% surcharge).

Meal Plans 3 vegetarian meals daily. Lunch may include baked tofu loaf,
water-steamed vegetables, green salad, baked potato, and
homemade bread. Fruit served only at breakfast and dinner,
along with grains, cereals, and legumes. No butter or oils. The
vegan diet is high in complex carbohydrates. No dairy products, cheese, eggs, meat, fish.

Services and **Exercise Equipment:** 2 stationary bikes, 2 treadmills, rowing
Facilities machine, NordicTrack cross-country ski simulator, free
weights. **Services:** Hydrotherapy, massage, stress-management classes, exercise counseling, smoking-cessation program, cardiac and cancer rehabilitation; medical tests, body-
composition evaluation, physician's visits; cooking school,

weight-control counseling; spiritual guidance. **Swimming Facilities:** Indoor pool. **Recreation Facilities:** Hiking, jogging trails; cross-country skiing (no equipment provided). **Evening Programs:** Medical lectures.

In the Area   Scheduled weekend tours to Monticello (estate of Thomas Jefferson), Montpelier (home of James Madison), museums in Washington, DC; Shenandoah National Park and the Skyline Drive, Colonial Williamsburg, historic Fredericksburg, factory outlets.

Getting Here   *From Washington, DC.* By train, Amtrak to Culpeper (80 min). By bus, Trailways to Culpeper (90 min). By car, I–66 to Lee Highway (Rte. 29) into Culpeper, Rte. 15 toward Orange, to Rte. 614 (about 2 hr). By plane, Dulles International and National Airports, commuter service to Charlottesville. Pickup arranged at airports, bus and train stations for fixed fee. Rental car available.

Special Notes   No smoking indoors. All facilities accessible for people with disabilities.

The Homestead

Nonprogram resort
Taking the waters

Virginia
Hot Springs
Style accounts for the enduring popularity of this historic spa. The mineral springs that made the Homestead famous as long ago as 1766 still gush in front of the Bath House (renovated in 1994 in celebration of its centenary), furnished with 1920s-style wicker furniture and flowered chintz draperies, and there are huge marble tubs for mineral-water soaks.

The Olympic-size indoor swimming pool, built in 1903, is great for laps and crowded only on weekends. Daily aerobic and aquacise classes are scheduled. Admission is free of charge for resort guests. Nonresidents can book services and use the facilities.

Relaxation therapy begins with a private soak in one of the marble tubs. The naturally heated thermal water, high in sulfur, magnesium, and 16 other minerals, reaches your tub at 104°F and overflows to keep the temperature constant. After a few minutes in the sauna or steam room (the men's side has a Turkish bath), you're led to a marble slab for a rubdown with coarse salt, then hosed off in the Scotch spray (hot and cold shower). After cooling down, you're treated to a massage by a real pro.

Three golf courses and 19 tennis courts, playable most of the year, are big outdoor attractions. For the family, there's horseback riding, mountain trout fishing, archery, and trap shooting. Surrounded by a 15,000-acre mountain preserve, the Homestead has miles of hiking trails. Snowmaking equipment on the slopes and groomed trails for cross-country skiing are winter attractions. Despite its rambling size, the Homestead makes you feel at home, even as it caters to conventions. The East wing and tower rooms, renovated in 1994, have dramatic views of the surrounding mountains. Each season, from blossoming spring dogwood to blazing fall foliage, has special appeal.

The Homestead
Hot Springs, VA 24445
Tel. 703/839-5500 or 800/336-5771
Fax 703/839-7656

Administration	President, Gary Rosenberg; spa managers, Donna Keyser and Hugh Hite
Season	Year-round.
Accommodations	600 guest rooms including 75 suites in main section and tower, built 1902–1929, and South Wing, added with conference center in 1973. Choice rooms and best views in the tower. Mahogany bedsteads, writing tables, lounge chairs, lacy white curtains, damask draperies. Some rooms with French doors that open on to private balconies or screened porches have fireplace, walk-in closet. All are air-conditioned, with TV, telephone, large tiled bathroom.
Rates	MAP (2 meals daily) per person double occupancy, $149–$259; single $99–$154. Suites $333–$408 double, $284–$359 single. Children with adults free through age 12, packages for golf and tennis. $200 advance payment. Add 5% tax, 16% service charge. Credit cards: AE, MC, V.
Meal Plans	The Modified American Plan includes breakfast and dinner. Country breakfasts include grits, omelets, steak, mountain trout. Dinner features Virginia ham stuffed with greens, roast beef, broiled chicken, farm produce, sautéed whole trout or smoked fish appetizer.
Services and Facilities	**Exercise Equipment:** Universal weights gym, with leg extension, chest press, shoulder press, hip and arm units; StairMaster, 2 treadmills, stationary bikes, abdominal board, rowing machine, free weights. Exercise room open daily 6 AM–10 PM. **Services:** Salt-glow body scrub, mineral tub, therapeutic whirlpool, fitness evaluation, personal trainer, aromatherapy, Swedish massage; salon for facials, manicure, pedicure, and hair styling. **Swimming Facilities:** Large indoor pool with mix of mineral and well water, 2 outdoor pools. Indoor pool open daily 6 AM–10 PM. **Recreation Facilities:** 3 golf courses, 19 tennis courts (Har-Tru and Gras-Tex), horseback riding, hiking, skeet and trap shooting, archery, fishing, lawn bowling, carriage rides, bowling alley; downhill skiing, ice-skating, cross-country skiing (equipment rental). **Evening Programs:** Movies, dancing.
In the Area	Carriage rides, country boutiques, the baths at Warm Springs (Jeffersonian structure), chamber music concerts at Garth Newel, historic Lexington (Washington and Lee University), Virginia Military Institute (George Marshall Library).
Getting Here	*From Washington, DC.* By train, Amtrak from Union Station or Alexandria, VA, to Clifton Forge (4 hr). By car, I-66 west to I-81, at Mt. Crawford Exit, Rtes. 257 and 42 to Goshen, Rte. 39 to Warm Springs, Rte. 220 south to Hot Springs (about 6 hr). By plane, USAir to Roanoke, VA (1 hr). Private aircraft land at the Homestead Ingalls Field. Limousine meets train or plane by arrangement (fixed fee). Rental car available.
Special Notes	Ramps and elevators in all buildings and some specially equipped rooms provide access for people with disabilities. Swimming, tennis, and skiing lessons for children; supervised playroom (summer only) and outdoor activity at the spa build-

ing (fee). No smoking in the spa and designated areas of the dining room. Spa services available Mon.–Thurs. 9–6, Fri. and Sat. until 7 PM, Sun. until 5PM.

The Integral Health Center

Holistic health
Spiritual awareness
Stress control

Virginia
Buckingham

Healthy living is taught at the Integral Health Center in a residential setting where small groups focus on programs to achieve and sustain maximum health. Formerly a private home, the center was remodeled to resemble a bed-and-breakfast inn, with accommodations for up to 12 guests.

The four-day Heart Retreat programs concentrate on coping with specific physical conditions, including immune deficiency, heart disease, and cancer. Weekend programs address diet and nutrition, weight loss, herbal healing, smoking, and general health and well-being. Chiropractic treatments are available.

Meditation helps guests find quiet and understanding, and breathing techniques build energy. The scenic location, overlooking the James river valley, contributes to a sense of peace. Spiritual teacher Sri Swami Satchidananda teaches that our whole being can be healed even when it's not possible to entirely heal the body.

Staff members are certified in holistic health sciences. Guest speakers and program leaders add expertise. Yogaville, a residential community for yoga students and monastics on the adjoining Satchidananda Ashram enhances the spiritual atmosphere.

The Integral Health Center
Rte. 1, Box 1681, Buckingham, VA 23921
Tel. 804/969–1451
Fax 804/964–1303

Administration Program administrators, Michael Sullivan and Sandra McLanahan, M.D.

Season Year-round.

Accommodations 7 modern bedrooms, private or shared baths. Dormitory rooms have 3–4 beds.

Rates 2-night weekend $225 in dormitory room, $325 private. 4-night Heart Retreat $295 dormitory, $395 private. Service charges and gratuities included. Deposit 25% advance payment. Credit cards: MC, V.

Meal Plans 3 vegetarian meals served family style in dining room. Rice, dahl, steamed vegetables with brown rice, green salad, tofu dishes, fruit, homemade soups, breads.

Services and Facilities **Services:** Guided relaxation, medically supervised fasting, instruction in yoga, meditation, cooking, visualization; Swedish massage, shiatsu, herbal wraps, oil baths, chiropractic treatments. **Swimming Facilities:** Outdoor pool, beach on nearby lake. **Recreation Facilities:** Country roads, hiking trails. **Evening Programs:** Meditation.

In the Area Yogaville and the Universal Light and Truth Shrine; Charlottesville (University of Virginia), Monticello (Palladian villa designed by Thomas Jefferson), Civil War sites (Appomattox Courthouse), Ash Lawn (estate of President James Monroe).

Getting Here *From Washington, DC.* By train, Amtrak to Charlottesville (3 hr). By bus, Greyhound to Charlottesville (4 hr). By car, I–66 south to Rte. 29, at Lovingston Rte. 56 to Rte. 604 (3½ hr). By plane, commuter flights on USAir to Charlottesville. Service to and from Charlottesville train and bus stations or airport by prior arrangement (fixed fee). Rental car available.

Special Notes Ashram classes in yoga, meditation, and cooking for children. No smoking. Remember to bring slippers and walking shoes.

The Kingsmill Resort

Nonprogram resort

Virginia For a family vacation combining sports and entertainment, the
Williamsburg Kingsmill Resort villas provide an ideal base from which to explore Busch Gardens, Colonial Williamsburg, the scenic Tidewater area, and Atlantic beaches. Built and managed by Anheuser-Busch, the 2,900-acre resort borders the historic James River, where there's a private marina. Golfers play the River Course, designed by Pete Dye, the Plantation Course, designed by Arnold Palmer, or a 9-hole course. The Sports Club, a 23,000-square-foot structure with indoor and outdoor exercise facilities, restaurant, and adjacent conference center, complements a tennis complex.

In southeastern Virginia's rolling hills and forests, Kingsmill Resort possesses both cosmopolitan sophistication and Colonial gentility. It's big enough so corporate conferences and vacationers needn't mix. The atmosphere is more residential than resort, and if you enjoy planning your own program, the elements are all here.

The Kingsmill Resort
1010 Kingsmill Rd., Williamsburg, VA 23185
Tel. 804/253–8201 or 800/832–5665

Administration General manager, Terry Haack; Sports Club manager, Beverly Cutchins

Season Year-round.

Accommodations Private villas overlooking river or golf course. 1–3 bedrooms, some complete kitchens, living rooms with fireplace. Residential furnishings, daily maid service. Air-conditioning, king- or queen-size beds, color cable TV.

Rates Seasonal pricing. $101–$165 for guest room, $424–$555 for up to 6 adults in 3-bedroom suite in Riverview Rooms. 3-day golf school $590 per person, double. Add 8.5% tax, optional gratuities. Credit cards: AE, MC, V.

Meal Plans Sports Club bistro-style restaurant serves light fare, including grilled chicken breast on brioche, pasta salad, and individual pizzas 11 AM–10 PM. Fruit dishes, nut breads, and whipped drinks of yogurt, honey, and fruit prepared daily. Peyton spa specials at dinner (4–9:30) are sautéed chicken breast over pasta and grilled pork tenderloin with a spicy mango sauce.

Services and Facilities **Exercise Equipment:** 15-station Nautilus exercise machines, 2 treadmills, 2 stationary bikes, 2 Schwinn Air Dyne bikes, 2 rowing machines, 2 StairMasters, NordicTrack, power rack incline bench, bench press, free weights. **Services:** Aerobic classes and water aerobics ($5 per class), instruction on exercise equipment. **Swimming Facilities:** Indoor 56-ft lap pool, outdoor recreational pool. **Recreation Facilities:** 3 golf courses, 15 tennis courts (Vel-Play, Deco-Turf, lighted), 2 racquetball courts, game lounge with billiards, table-top shuffleboard; coed whirlpool, separate saunas and steam rooms for men and women. **Evening Programs:** Summer season of pop and rock concerts.

In the Area Colonial Williamsburg (88 restored 18th-century buildings, shops, and residences), James River plantation tour, Jamestown Festival Park (replicas of 3 historic ships), Yorktown (Revolutionary War battlefield), Williamsburg Pottery (outlet shops and boutiques), Virginia Beach, Mariner's Museum, Nature Museum and park.

Getting Here *From Washington, DC.* By train, Amtrak from Union Station or Alexandria, VA, to Williamsburg (all seats reserved, 3 hr). By bus, Greyhound (3 hr). By car, I–95 south to I–64 east, Exit 57A to Rte. 199W. By air, commuter service to Norfolk and Newport News on USAir and American Eagle.

Special Notes Interpretive tours for children at historic sites. No smoking in sports club.

The Tazewell Club

Nonprogram resort

Virginia The first health club in the old Colonial capital opened in 1988. *Colonial* A part of the Williamsburg Lodge and Conference Center com- *Williamsburg* plex, facing a golf course, the Tazewell Club is minutes from the 173-acre historic area. It's an escape to the latest in pampering and exercise after immersing in 18th-century life.

Designed for newcomers to fitness, the club also challenges fitness buffs. Low-impact aerobics classes are taught on weekdays; aqauaerobics on weekends. The swimming pool is popular with families, but certain hours are reserved for lap swimmers.

The workout area has views of the surrounding valley, once part of the Tazewell estate. The swimming pool opens onto a sun deck. The spa, with separate saunas, steam rooms, whirlpools for men and women, and private massage areas, is on the same floor. Try a loofah body scrub or massage.

The club is open to guests staying in any of the five hotels operated by the Colonial Williamsburg Foundation. Two Robert Trent Jones golf courses, eight tennis courts, croquet court, bowling green, and two outdoor swimming pools are nearby. Personal services, court time, and greens fees are extra.

The Tazewell Club
Williamsburg Lodge
Box C, Williamsburg, VA 23187
Tel. 804/220–7690 or 800/447–8679
Fax 804/221–8797

Administration	Club manager, Robert Sweel
Season	Year-round.
Accommodations	25 Tazewell Club guest rooms in the Williamsburg Lodge, color TV, spacious baths. Also 5 hotels and group of Colonial houses, plus 2 deluxe suites with Jacuzzi, fireplace, wet bar, and private balcony on penthouse level of club. 235 guest rooms in the Williamsburg Inn, a short walk from the health club and 85 rooms in restored homes with Colonial atmosphere. All air-conditioned, with TV, telephone, private bath.
Rates	Double or single occupancy in Tazewell wing $129–$199; regular lodge rooms $119–$165; suites $425 for 1–4 persons. Williamsburg Inn room $275–$315 suites $425–$650. Colonial House rooms $119–$250. Variable deposits, about $90–$100 per room. Add 8½% tax, optional gratuities. Credit cards: AE, MC, V.
Meal Plans	No meals at the Tazewell Club, but guests can charge meals at historic area restaurants to their room. In Regency Dining Room (jacket and tie required) at the Williamsburg Inn, specialties include Chesapeake crabmeat sautéed in wine, picatta of shrimp and veal, and scaloppine of lamb with garlic. Traditional Virginia recipes in the town's taverns—King's Arms, Christiana Campbell's, Josiah Chowning's—run the gamut from peanut soup to stuffed trout. Chesapeake Bay specialties are available at the Friday seafood buffet at the Williamsburg Lodge.
Services and Facilities	**Exercise Equipment:** 11 Keiser Cam II stations, Nautilus gym, 2 Lifecycles, 2 Liferowers. **Services:** Massage, loofah scrub, herbal wrap, facial, manicure, pedicure, nonsurgical face-lift, hair/skin care; individual instruction on exercise equipment. **Swimming Facilities:** 60-ft 4-lane lap pool, large outdoor pool. **Recreation Facilities:** 18- and 9-hole golf courses, 8 tennis courts, lawn bowling and croquet, jogging trail, bicycle rentals; badminton, volleyball, and water aerobics on request. Miniature golf. **Evening Programs:** 18th-century concerts, tavern entertainment. Shakespeare productions.
In the Area	Busch Gardens (family-oriented theme park), James River plantation tour, Jamestown Festival Park (replicas of 3 historic ships), Yorktown (Revolutionary War battlefield), Virginia Beach, Mariner's Museum, Nature Museum and park.
Getting Here	*From Washington, DC.* By train, Amtrak from Union Station or Alexandria, VA, to Williamsburg (all seats reserved, 3 hr). By bus, Gold Line (tel. 301/386–8300) or Trailways (3 hr). By car, I–95 south to I–64 east (3 hr). By plane, scheduled flights to Norfolk or Richmond, VA (30 min.). Taxi, car rental available; limousine on request. Scheduled van service to airports from Williamsburg hotels.
Special Notes	Elevator to all floors, some specially equipped rooms provide access for people with disabilities. Tours of historic sites and golf lessons for children. No smoking in club. Remember to bring fitness shoes (white-soled aerobics), workout clothing, leotards.

Yogaville

Holistic health
Spiritual awareness
Vibrant maturity

Virginia
Buckingham

The body-mind connection is strengthened at Yogaville through in-depth workshops in three essential yoga practices: asana (physical postures), meditation, and pranayama (breathing techniques). A permanent community in the beautiful James River valley near Charlottesville, the ashram welcomes people of all faiths and backgrounds to study and practice the teachings of Integral Yoga under the guidance of the Rev. Sri Swami Satchidananda. Guests are free to participate or observe, and special training in Hatha Yoga is available for beginners. Classes begin at 6:30 AM, alternating with meals and meditation until 6 PM. Meditation techniques and an understanding of karma also are taught, and guided nature walks provide an introduction to the valley's ecology.

Guest accommodations range from a two-story wooden lodge, the Lotus Inn, which has a health food cafe and offers private rooms, to dormitory or tent space. Motor homes can be parked on the grounds of the 750-acre retreat. The main meal is lunch, served in a communal hall. Those who volunteer for work in the organic garden, kitchen, or other areas of the community may earn free meals.

The ashram offers a variety of 2- to 5-day workshops, retreats, and yoga-training programs.

Yogaville
Rte. 604, Buckingham, VA 23921
Tel. 804/969–3121 or 800/858–9642
Fax 804/969–1303

Administration
Founder, Rev. Swami Satchidananda; program director, Ram Wiener

Season
Year-round.

Accommodations
The Lotus Inn has 6 private rooms with kitchenette, full bath, 1 double bed and a sofa bed, individually controlled heat and air-conditioning. 15 dormitory rooms (4–6 beds) have air-conditioning, communal bath, in a 2-story building that includes classrooms. 8 campsites are in a wooded area, some with platforms, near the dormitory with shower and laundry facilities.

Rates
$80 for 2 in private room, $35–$42 per person in dormitory, $55 single room including meals, program. 4-day Hatha yoga program $145 dormitory, $245 in private room; 5-day silent retreat $250. Campers $22 single, $37 couples per day. Motor home $50 per couple daily, $300 per week. Special rates for children. Advance deposit for visits of 2 weeks or more, $100. Add tax. Credit cards: MC, V.

Meal Plans
3 meals daily included in guest rate. The lactovegetarian diet includes whole grains, protein sources such as tofu and legumes, fresh fruit, and vegetables. Lunch is the main meal of the day; breakfast and supper are light buffets with cereals, herbal tea, yogurt, low-fat milk. Dinner favorites are brown rice pasta or baked tofu. The Lotus Cafe offers coffee and snacks throughout the day, plus yogurt drinks.

Services and Facilities **Services:** Instruction in meditation, Hatha Yoga, daily schedule of classes. **Swimming Facilities:** Private beach on 16-acre lake, river. **Recreation Facilities:** Nature walk, gardening, sauna, hot tub. **Evening Programs:** Classes or spiritual concert.

In the Area Charlottesville (University of Virginia), Monticello (Jefferson's Palladian villa and orchards), Richmond (Confederacy museum, historic mansions), Shenandoah National Park, Skyline Drive (scenic highway).

Getting Here *From Washington, DC*. By train, Amtrak to Charlottesville (3 hr). By bus, Greyhound to Charlottesville (4 hr). By car, I–66 west to Rte. 29, I–64 west (toward Lynchburg), 29 Bypass to I–64 east (toward Richmond), Rte. 20 south, Rte. 655 into Rte. 601, left on Rte. 604 (5 hr). By plane, USAir, United Express, or Delta, (45 min). Pickup from airport, train, or bus, $15. Rental car available.

Special Notes Elderhostel for senior citizens, October. Cleaning and linen service provided twice weekly for guests staying 1 week or more at Lotus Inn. Specially equipped facilities for people with disabilities. No smoking, alcohol, illegal drugs, or pets allowed. Bring blanket or towel for yoga, alarm clock, slip-on shoes.

The Middle Atlantic States

George Washington made taking the waters in West Virginia fashionable at about the same time that Europeans discovered a place called Spa in Belgium. Health resorts flourished over the years in the Poconos, the Alleghenies, and the southern Appalachians. These resorts tend to be small-scale and conservative, emphasizing service and personal attention, and oriented to golf and tennis rather than to high-energy workouts. While the renowned Greenbrier Resort in White Sulphur Springs, West Virginia, made the great leap from traditional to contemporary in its health spa, Berkeley Springs—where George Washington bathed—remains a sleepy country town with modest accommodations for spa-goers in a West Virginia state park. The Coolfont Resort, secluded in a valley near Berkeley Springs, brings together the past and present with its own blend of holistic health programs and luxury pampering. The introduction of snow-making equipment has added a new dimension to resorts throughout the area, with downhill and cross-country skiing now complementing indoor exercise.

In building the nation's first boardwalk, Atlantic City touched off a development boom along the New Jersey shore. The introduction of casino gambling in 1978 brought the town out of a long decline, and when the manufacturer of Lifecycles and other exercise equipment became a Bally company, the shore gained its first full-scale fitness center at Bally's Park Place Hotel. Like most spas in the area, it is an amenity rather than a comprehensive health vacation program, but Bally's exclusive combination of nutritious meals, bodywork, and workouts by the sea adds up to a healthy escape.

Diversity makes the Middle Atlantic states a rewarding destination for the fitness-oriented traveler. Your choices range from charming Deerfield Manor in the Poconos to the most sophisticated facilities this side of the Alleghenies at Nemacolin Woodlands in the Laurel Highlands of Pennsylvania. Affordability also distinguishes spa programs in the Mid-Atlantic region. Mid-week packages offer full services at substantial savings. Weekend packages near New York City are featured at two New Jersey Hiltons, in Short Hills and Long Branch.

The Hilton at Short Hills

Luxury pampering

New Jersey
Short Hills

The combination of a luxurious hotel and deluxe European health spa has made the Hilton at Short Hills a popular hideaway for Manhattanites as well as corporate executives visiting the Newark area. With full-service spa facilities—from Roman-style pool to hydrotherapy and fango treatments—and a fitness center and calorie-conscious cuisine, this Hilton offers all the amenities of many fitness resorts. Even complimentary workout attire is provided.

The salon at the spa provides a wide range of face and body programs. Under the direction of Pierre Pellaton, the therapists use European techniques and products for facials, skin rejuvenation treatments, and mud baths. Along with gentle underwater hydromassage, they offer an herbal wrap or an exfoliation combined with seaweed wrap. Completing your new look are hair and nail services, and waxing.

Appointments for all salon services are à la carte, and it's wise to call ahead for a schedule on busy weekends. The hotel offers a Spa Sampler package with a Friday or Saturday night stay that includes health consultation, half-hour massage, aquacise and exercise classes, use of equipment and brunch. A shuttle carries guests to the elegant Short Hills Shopping Mall.

The Hilton at Short Hills
41 JFK Pkwy., Short Hills, NJ 07078
Tel. 201/379-0100 or 800/455-8667
Fax 201/376-0481

Administration	General manager, Eric O. Long; spa directors, Christine De Maio, Dan Klauser
Season	Year-round.
Accommodations	300 rooms in a 10-story glass-walled office complex. The Towers has additional amenities in 70 rooms and 37 suites with French doors dividing bedroom and living room. All have TV, 2 phones, marble bathroom with hair dryer, scale, and an array of toiletries. Concierge and private lounge for complimentary breakfast, cocktails, and dessert buffet.
Rates	Spa Sampler weekend package $135 per person. Rooms $125–$175 single, $125–$195 per night for 2, double occupancy in standard room; Towers rooms $145–$205 single, $145–$225 for 2 double, suites $235 single, $255 for 2 double. Add 6% tax plus gratuities. Deposit: 1 night. Credit cards: AE, DC, MC, V.
Meal Plans	No meal plan. Spa cuisine served in the casual Terrace Restaurant. Breakfast choices include eggbeater omelet with salsa, Mueslix cereal, steamed Irish oatmeal; lunch entrées include vegetable frittata, chilled poached salmon with cucumber/onion compote, lobster/angel-hair pasta with mushrooms; dinner menu has shellfish consommé, crispy red snapper with lime-salsa glaze, seared tuna with ratatouille and crisp leeks, grilled chicken breast with pink lentils. Dinner selections also available in the Dining Room prix fixe.
Services and Facilities	**Exercise Equipment:** 8 Keiser pneumatic weights units, 2 Concept 2 rowing machines, 3 Bodyguard treadmills, 2 StairMasters, 4 stationary bikes, free weights (3–50 lbs). **Services:** Massage (Swedish, shiatsu), herbal wrap, facial, body polish, fango, salon for hair, nail, and skin care. Fitness assessment, computerized nutritional analysis, 1-on-1 training. **Swimming Facilities:** Indoor 50-ft lap pool, outdoor pool. **Recreation Facilities:** Access to racquetball and squash courts (fee); golf, tennis nearby.
In the Area	Short Hills Mall (150 shops and boutiques), the Meadowlands (baseball and entertainment complex).
Getting Here	*From New York City.* By car, New Jersey Turnpike to Rte. 78N, or Garden State Parkway to Exit 142, Rte. 78 west in local traffic lane to JFK Pkwy (20 min). By bus, NJ Transit from Port Authority Terminal (45 min). By air, complimentary shuttle service to Newark International Airport (15 min)

The Middle Atlantic States

New Jersey
The Hilton at Short Hills, **3**
Ocean Place Hilton Resort & Spa, **4**
The Spa at Bally's Park Place Casino Hotel, **5**

Pennsylvania
Deerfield Manor, **2**
The Himalayan Institute, **1**
Nemacolin Woodlands, **6**

West Virginia
Berkeley Springs State Park, **7**
Coolfont Resort, **8**
The Greenbrier, **10**
Lakeview Resort, **9**

Lake Erie

Allegheny River

West

OHIO

Ohio River

Pittsburgh

Wheeling

Morgantown

Parkersburg

Clarksburg

Potomac River

WEST VIRGINIA

Charleston

0   50 mi

0   75 km

210

Special Notes Nonsmoking rooms available. Spa open weekdays 6 AM–10 PM, weekends 8–8. No smoking in spa; poolside lunch service. Business Center weekdays.

Ocean Place Hilton Resort & Spa

Luxury pampering

New Jersey
Long Branch Located within commuting distance of Manhattan, the Ocean Place Hilton's seafront spa is a popular weekend escape for young executives. Skin care to repair damage wrought by the climate and sun is a specialty here. The French moor therapy mud, a black organic natural product by Remy Laure, is used in facials and underwater massage. This is preceded by a vigorous scrubbing with mineral salts and body oils to stimulate circulation, remove dead skin cells, and unclog pores. For those who prefer a more soothing experience, aromatherapy wraps, facials, or massages are suggested. All treatments can be booked à la carte or as part of one- to three-day packages, with or without hotel accommodations.

Fitness classes in the new aerobics studio and the indoor pool can be charged to your bill individually or a program package with spa meals. Over 25 hours of classes are scheduled weekly on the studio's cushioned floor. The spa guests enjoy an ocean front promenade and a nearby state park beach.

Ocean Place Hilton Resort & Spa
1 Ocean Blvd., Long Branch, NJ 07740
Tel. 908/571–4000 or 800/445–8667
Fax 908/571–3314

Administration General manager, Frank Gaynor; spa manager, Cindy Luebbert

Season Year-round.

Accommodations 254 rooms, all air-conditioned with balcony, TV, phone, modern bath. Contemporary furniture includes desk in oceanfront rooms. Direct access to spa and beach promenade.

Rates $130–$205 single, $150–$225 double for 2 persons. 2-day Spa Getaway $149–$189 single, $229–$275 for 2, double occupancy. 3-day Getaway $770–$876 single, $1,352–$1,458 for 2, double occupancy. Full-day Revitalizer with lunch, no lodging $239. Packages include tax, gratuities. Daily spa fee $15, class $15. Credit cards: AE, DC, MC, V.

Meal Plans Hilton Food For Life lunch (choice of salads, fruit platters, seafood) included in spa packages. Spa cuisine dinner includes choice of grilled catch of the day, broiled chicken with local vegetables in season, salad bar, fresh fruit.

Services and Facilities **Exercise Equipment:** 11-unit Maxicam circuit, 2 Lifecycles, 2 Stairobic machines, 3 Startrac 2000 treadmills, dumbbells (3–55 lbs), 2 benches. **Services:** Massage, MoorMud hydromassage or wrap, aromatherapy, herbal wrap, French body polish with Vichy shower, salt glow loofah scrub, facials, reflexology, seaweed body masque or facial. Personal goal training, body fat analysis, fitness assessment, circuit training, swimming and tennis lessons. **Swimming Facilities:** Indoor lap pool, outdoor resort pool on sun deck, ocean beach. **Evening Programs:** dancing.

In the Area Monmouth Park Race Track, Garden State Arts Center, Presidents' Park (beach dunes).

Getting Here *From New York City.* By car, I–95 (New Jersey Turnpike) south to Garden State Pkwy., Exit 105 to Rte. 36 (1 hr). By train, NJ Transit commuter services from Penn Station via Newark (2 hr). Taxi, rental car available.

Special Notes Children's day camp Memorial Day–Labor Day. Bike rental available. Specially equipped rooms for physically handicapped guests available. Spa open weekdays 7 AM–9 PM, Sat. 8 AM–10 PM, Sun. 8–6. Beach conditions posted at Presidents' Park.

The Spa at Bally's Park Place Casino Hotel

Luxury pampering

New Jersey
Atlantic City
Amid the glitz and glamour of the beachfront casinos, the Spa at Bally's Park Place Hotel & Tower is a health and fitness oasis. The spacious facilities and top-of-the-line equipment would be the pride of any fitness resort, though here they serve as a complement to gambling and entertainment. It's possible not to set foot in the casino, but most of the people working out in the weights room also exercise the one-armed bandits.

The pool, saunas, whirlpools, and treatment rooms are open to hotel guests and members; others must pay a daily fee, which is waived if you book services such as massage or herbal body wrap. Check-in at the sixth-floor reception desk to confirm appointments and to join the action in one of the three racquetball courts.

Terraced gardens dotted with whirlpools, showers, and a coed glass-walled sauna flank the swimming pool. Upstairs are men's and women's locker rooms with Turkish bath, treatment rooms, and exercise equipment. The ultimate relaxer here is a private session in the MVP Suite, which boasts a marble whirlpool and steam shower. Also try aromatherapy, Swedish, or shiatsu massage.

The mid-week spa package includes a meal plan that allows you to dine in the hotel's restaurants on a fixed menu. Among the services included in the package are salon treatments that feature Sothys products, and daily exercise classes, such as slimnastics, low-impact aerobics, stretch and tone, and aquafit, scheduled from 11 to 3 in the aerobics studio.

The spa's exotic gardens and waterfalls and dramatic terrace overlooking the Atlantic give visitors a sense that they have found a luxurious escape from the routine.

The Spa at Bally's Park Place Casino Hotel

Bally's Park Place Casino Hotel & Tower
Boardwalk and Park Pl., Atlantic City, NJ 08401
Tel. 609/340–4600, 800/772–7777, or 800/225–5977

Administration General manager, Ronald Mann

Season Year-round.

Accommodations 1,260 rooms with private bath; 110 suites; 9 restaurants. Art Deco touches in the original building; luxury rooms with sitting area in the new tower have marble-walled bathroom, hair dryer,lighted makeup mirror, robes.

Rates Rooms $115–$205 per day. Spa admission $20 for hotel guests, $30 others. Treatments priced individually. 1-day spa package $99, 6-day/5-night program with calorie-controlled meals $795 double occupancy, $995 single. 3-day/2-night package $395 double, $475 single. Add tax, gratuities. (Saturday night is not included in any package plan.) Credit cards: AE, DC, MC, V.

Meal Plans Spa packages include 3 meals daily. Breakfast can be an egg-substitute omelet or French toast, fresh fruit with yogurt. Buffet lunch in the Spa Cafe includes salads, soup, fruit. Spa cuisine in the hotel dining rooms features fresh fish, lean meats. Dinner choices include pan-seared scallops with saffron rice, steamed salmon with onions in balsamic vinegar sauce, lobster and shrimp casserole, and scallops Newburgh with lemon-dill rice. Daily diet has 55% carbohydrates, 15% protein, 30% fat.

Services and Facilities **Exercise Equipment:** 10 computerized Lifecycle bikes, Pyramid weight training equipment room, 3 Quinton treadmills, 10-unit Cybex weight training circuit, 5 Trotter treadmills, 2 Lifesteps, 5 StairMasters with video, cross-country ski machine, 2 Nautilus recumbent bikes. **Services:** Massage, herbal wrap, aromatherapy massage, algae body masque, loofah body scrub, facial; salon for hair, nail, skin care. **Swimming Facilities:** Indoor pool, ocean beach. **Recreation Facilities:** 4 indoor racquetball courts; bike rental on the Boardwalk; golf and tennis nearby. **Evening Programs:** Cabaret and celebrity shows.

In the Area Brigantine National Wildlife Refuge, Farley State Marina, the Noyes Museum (contemporary art), Historic Town of Smithville, Atlantic City Race Track.

Getting Here *From Philadelphia and New York.* Atlantic City is served by daily casino bus from points throughout the region. By plane, USAir commuter flights. By train, Amtrak or commuter service via Philadelphia offers daily service. By car, the Garden State Pkwy. from points north and south, the Atlantic City Expressway from Philadelphia (60 min). Taxi, rental car, minibus available locally.

Special Notes Facilities for treatments and hotel accommodations available for people with disabilities. Spa open Mon.–Satur. 7:30 AM–9 PM, Sun. 8–7. No smoking.

Deerfield Manor

Life enhancement
Vibrant maturity
Weight management

Pennsylvania
East Stroudsburg The program at Deerfield Manor takes an individualized approach to diet and nutrition and encourages you to achieve a healthy lifestyle. Participation is limited to 33 men and women who want to unwind and shape up. The daily activities include guided walks, exercise classes, aerobics, yoga, and calisthenics in the heated outdoor pool. Surrounded by mountains, the 12-acre spa retreat encourages moderate exercise and diet amid

lots of country charm. Weekend as well as Sunday to Sunday packages are offered.

The attractive white clapboard farmhouse, dating from the 1930s, has a warm, supportive environment nurtured by a 16-member staff, with occasional visits from lecturers and health professionals. A family-like feeling tends to develop among guests, many of whom are repeat visitors in the over-50 age bracket.

Guests make informed nutritional choices when following the "Total Fitness" program: Each guest selects a menu plan according to personal need and based on the consumption of 750–800 calories per day. In some cases guests opt for the 350-calorie-a-day diet limited to freshly squeezed fruit and vegetable juices. Meals are served in a bright, spacious dining room. Exercise equipment is minimal and no activity required.

Deerfield Manor

R.D. 1, Rte. 402N, East Stroudsburg, PA 18301
Tel. 717/223–0160 or 800/852–4494
Fax 717/223–8270

Administration	Owner-manager, Frieda Eisenkraft; fitness director, Susan Lipkin
Season	Apr.–mid-Nov.
Accommodations	22 single and double rooms in main country house and deluxe annex rooms with private bath. Furnished with wicker furniture, antiques. Informal lounge with VCR, records. Sauna.
Rates	Weekend $250–$301 per person double occupancy, $324–$363 single. Weekly (Sun.–Sun.) $699–$899 per person double occupancy, $899–$1,099 single. Add gratuities (15%), taxes (6%). $200 payable in advance. Credit cards: MC, V.
Meal Plans	3 meals daily; fish and chicken, locally grown produce, fresh fruit. Vegetarian meals optional.
Services and Facilities	**Exercise Equipment:** StairMaster, treadmill. **Services:** Massage (Swedish, shiatsu, reflexology), facial, wrap. **Swimming Facilities:** Heated outdoor pool. **Recreation Facilities** (nearby): 2 tennis courts, golf, roller skating, ice skating, horseback riding. **Evening Programs:** Guest lecturers on health-related topics, handwriting analysis; concerts.
In the Area	Shopping tours, summer theater, antiques markets.
Getting Here	*From Philadelphia and New York.* By car, I–80 from New York, I–84 from New England, I–83 from the Baltimore–Washington area connect with Rte. 402. By plane, major airlines serve Allentown, PA. By bus, Martz Lines to Stroudsburg. Taxi, rental car, and limousine service available locally.
Special Notes	No smoking indoors. Ramps and accommodations for people with disabilities.

The Himalayan Institute

Spiritual awareness
Stress control
Weight management

Pennsylvania
Honesdale

Physicians and psychologists at the 422-acre international headquarters of the Himalayan Institute of Yoga Science and Philosophy use biofeedback, aerobic exercise, breathing, meditation, diet, and fasting to train people to live with stress. Their leader is Swami Rama, the Indian yogi who stopped his heart from pumping blood for 17 seconds in a Menninger Foundation clinic experiment in 1970, thereby reinforcing theories about the relationship between the body and the mind.

Biofeedback, a technique that uses machines to teach regulation of the nervous system, is linked with the practice of Eastern philosophy and yoga exercises to form the institute's holistic approach to living. Meditation and relaxation can enable one to gain control of the body and the mind, according to Swami Rama, and the serene atmosphere at this mountaintop retreat provides the appropriate setting for exploring the mind and exercising the body.

Research into ancient healing and self-development techniques by the resident faculty is used as the basis for much of the program. Meditation is employed as a systematic method for developing every level of individual consciousness. Sessions of yoga (an hour and 45 minutes) and "silent time" are scheduled throughout the day. Guests are asked to maintain quiet from 10 PM until 8 AM, and to abstain from emotional relationships and other distractions while at the institute. For residencies of a month or more, work-study programs are available.

The Himalayan Institute
R.R. 1, Box 400, Honesdale, PA 18431
Tel. 717/253-5551 or 800/822-4547

Administration President, Rudolph Ballentine, M.D.

Season Year-round.

Accommodations 100 guests are housed in the main building, a 3-story redbrick structure with austerely furnished rooms with communal toilet and showers. Each room has 1 or 2 beds, a sink, sheets, and towels; no lock on the door.

Rates Weekend seminar tuition $75-$85; shared room $100-$110 per person double. 2-week Health Transformation program (Western medical sciences combined with Eastern concepts) $1,750-$2,100 single, $2,550-$3,825 for 2 people. Twenty-eight-day Health Transformation or weight-loss and self-awareness program $2,500-$3,000. Personal retreat with meals on request. Deposit for seminars. Credit cards: MC, V.

Meal Plans 3 vegetarian meals daily, cafeteria style, and herbal tea included in program rate. Breakfast is oatmeal with apples, fresh banana, whole-grain bread with butter. Lunch can be minestrone soup, hummus, and green salad, or steamed rice with raisins. Dinner includes soup (butternut squash or potato), homemade bread, graham crackers, apples, or tofu-and-lentil casserole. Dairy products, no eggs. Vegetables from organic garden. Nondairy options available.

Services and Facilities **Exercise Equipment:** Stationary bikes. **Services:** Biofeedback training (5 sessions $125), aerobics classes, cooking classes, medical and psychological consultations, tennis lessons, breath tests. Massage and body therapies not available. **Swimming Facilities:** Pond on property, with sandy beach and bathhouse. **Recreation Facilities:** Tennis and basketball courts, handball court, hiking trails; cross-country skiing, ice skating. **Evening Programs:** Lectures.

In the Area Pocono Mountains sightseeing.

Getting Here *From New York City.* By bus, Short Line from Port Authority Terminal (3 hr) or weekend charters (tel. 212/243–5994 from 78 5th Ave. (13th St.) by reservation. By car, via Lincoln Tunnel to I–80 W, Hwy. 6 through Milford and Honesdale to Rte. 670 (3 hr).

By air, scheduled flights to Scranton. Taxi, rental car available.

Special Notes Preschool, kindergarten, and elementary school programs combine Eastern and Western educational concepts, Montessori methods, and yoga philosophies. No smoking indoors.

Nemacolin Woodlands

Luxury pampering
Stress control
Weight management

Pennsylvania Atop a scenic bluff in the Laurel Highlands of southwestern
Farmington Pennsylvania stands the Woodlands Spa, a $6 million centerpiece of the Nemacolin Woodlands resort and conference center. Despite its name, this is no rustic retreat. The four-level building of native stone, buff brick, and glass is the best-equipped spa this side of the Allegheny Mountains.

The range of bodywork available is exceptional—scrubs and wraps using sea salts, oils, mud, and herbal mixtures; aromatherapy or Swedish massage; foot reflexology—and facilities in separate wings for men and women provide everything from toothbrushes to workout clothing and robes. After a session in the steam room or the sauna, you can relax in a glass-walled whirlpool and enjoy the view of woods and distant mountains.

Downstairs is devoted to exercise: an array of Keiser pneumatic weight training machines, plus bikes, treadmills, and a StairMaster with video monitors to help you meet your goals; a four-lane indoor lap pool 65 feet long that's also used for water aerobics; and a mirrored aerobics studio with sprung-wood floor that can hold groups of 40 or more.

Upstairs is the beauty salon and a suite of treatment rooms; both are spacious and airy and warmed in winter by a fireplace. Dermalogica skin-care system treatments are offered to retard aging, control blemishes, and rejuvenate your complexion.

At the Woodlands Spa you set your own pace, but the basic program includes a prebreakfast walk in the woods led by staffers, scheduled exercise classes, and energy breaks for vegetable broth or fruit smoothies. Treatments are included in spa packages of one to six days, or booked à la carte. Nonprogram guests pay a daily fee for classes and services.

The 550-acre resort features a full range of sports, with equipment supplied at the Activities Center adjoining the spa. The indoor Equestrian Center offers dressage training as well as trail rides. Outdoor tennis courts, championship croquet, horseshoes, biking, and trout fishing in a stocked lake are among the options. In winter, trails are groomed for cross-country skiing and snowmobiles, and the lake is filled with ice skaters. The Golf Academy offers instruction on the 6,600-yard par-70 course from March until November.

Nemacolin Woodlands
Box 188, Farmington, PA 15437
Tel. 412/329-8555 or 800/422-2736
Fax 412/329-6198

Administration President, Maggie Hardy Magerko; director and general manager, Charles Ingalsbee; spa director, Tammy Pahel

Season Year-round.

Accommodations 96-room lodge is closest to spa building; new wing with spacious bedrooms and terrace suites furnished in traditional English or Art Deco style. 2 queen-size beds are standard, some have 4-posters. Separate bathroom and commode, some with whirlpool bathtub, balcony; TV, 3 telephones, air-conditioning. Also, furnished condominiums and cottages with kitchens.

Rates 1-night Mini-Spa package $162–$230 per person double or single, without meals. 2-day/2-night Woodlands Discovery package $256–$321 per person, single or double, with meals, gratuities. Daily room rates include use of spa facilities, $139–$215 single or double, suites $179–$395, condominium $129–$175 for 1 or 2 persons, plus tax and gratuity. Golf and tennis packages available. Deposit $150. Credit cards: AE, MC, V.

Meal Plans Spa dining room in lodge has breakfast buffet with muffins, hot and cold cereals, juices, yogurt, fruit. Lunch, served at spa or in café, can be salad with chef's award-winning New England clam chowder. Dinner selections include brook trout stuffed with scallops, shrimp, grilled chicken breast, veal scallops. Menu on 14-day cycle, special diets accommodated.

Services and Facilities **Exercise Equipment:** 10 Keiser pneumatic weight training machines, Biocycle, StairMaster, Trotter and Trakmaster treadmills, VersaClimber, Monark and Rosso bikes, free weight dumbbells (5–50 lbs.). **Services:** Massage (Swedish, sports, aromatherapy, reflexology), facials, back cleansing; body wrap, loofah body polish; hair, nail, and skin treatments. Personalized fitness-assessment, stress-management program, diet and nutrition lectures, body-composition evaluation, 1-on-1 training. Scheduled walks and group exercise. **Swimming Facilities:** Indoor lap pool, outdoor recreational pool. **Spa Facilities:** Coed weights room, aerobics studio with Reo-Flex floor, treatment rooms, beauty salon, 4-ft.-deep lap pool. Separate men's and women's saunas, whirlpools; workout clothing and robes provided in locker room; juice bar, boutique. **Recreation Facilities:** 4 tennis courts (Omni surface, lighted), bicycle rental, Equestrian Center, 2 18-hole golf courses, miniature golf, Golf Academy, croquet, boating, trout fishing, badminton, shuffleboard; winter skating, cross-country skiing, snow-mobiles. Racquetball nearby. Greenhouse, table tennis. **Evening Programs:** Music weekends, chess, sports bar.

In the Area White-water rafting at Ohiopyle State Park, Fallingwater (Frank Lloyd Wright architecture), Laurel Caverns, Fort Necessity (French & Indian War), Antietam Battlefield (Civil War), Western Maryland Scenic Railroad (June–Oct.).

Getting Here *From Washington, DC.* By car, Capital Beltway (I–495), I–270 north to Frederick, MD., I–70 west to Cumberland, Rte. 48 to Keyser's Ridge, Rte. 40 (Old National Road) to Farmington, PA. (4 hr). By air, USAir to Pittsburgh (45 min). Transfers on request; private airstrip. Rental car.

Special Notes No smoking in spa or spa dining room. Children's playground, petting zoo, and Family Activities Center open year-round. Plants sold in greenhouse. Pony ride, canoe rental, golf instruction available.

Berkeley Springs State Park

Taking the waters

West Virginia
Berkeley Springs
Berkeley Springs State Park has been called the K-Mart of spas: An hour-long "tub and rub" treatment costs $30, and in the summer you can swim in the big outdoor pool. All the mineral water you care to drink or take home is free. Although no larger than a town square, the tiny park wins high marks for cleanliness and no-frills treatments: Bring your jeans and a sense of humor.

Spartan and a bit old-fashioned by today's standards, the state-run facilities offer a down-home Blue Ridge brand of healing. In the original 1815 Roman bath building, step-down tubs rent for $10 an hour per person. Filled with 750 gallons of spring water heated to 102°F, the recently renovated pools hold several people—coed company is fine—in privacy. The eight pools can be rented by the hour and can hold up to four people at a time. No reservations are taken; the policy is first come, first served.

Both the main bathhouse and the Country Inn hotel across the street date from the 1920s. In the women's bath, heated mineral water spurts from enormous pipes into two 3-foot-deep tiled plunge pools where patrons soak in privacy. The men's masseurs operate in open cubicles, steam cabinets line yellow brick walls, and bathtubs provide a relaxing soak. Adjoining the park is the Country Inn (tel. 800/822–6630) and its Renaissance Spa, which provides limited beauty salon treatments and private mineral water whirlpools open to the public.

Berkeley Springs State Park
Washington St., Berkeley Springs, WV 25411
Tel. 304/258–2711 or 800/225–5982

Administration Superintendent, Robert Ebert

Season Year-round.

Accommodations The adjacent Country Inn (tel. 800/822–6630) has rooms with shared bath for $35 for 2, $65–$80 with private bathroom, choice of king-size or twin beds. The inn's 2-night Ultimate Spa package is $449–$525 for 2. There are several bed-and-breakfasts in town or nearby. The Highlawn Inn (tel. 304/258–5700), a hilltop Victorian mansion, has antiques-filled rooms, each with modern bath or shower, and full breakfast for $70–$105 for 2. Add 9% taxes. Also, Coolfont Resort (*see below*) has tent sites, RV hookups, and a wide range of accommodations, with or without spa packages. Cacapon State Park (tel. 304/258–1022 or 800/225–5982), 10 mi south of town, offers cabins, lodge rooms, restaurant, and golf course. Credit cards: AE, MC, V.

Rates   Bath and massage $30 (60 min); thermal water bath $10 (60 min).

Services and Facilities   **Services:** Massage (30 min), private bath, Roman plunge pool, steam cabinet. **Swimming Facilities:** Outdoor pool open May 30–Sept. 1 ($2 adults, $1.25 children).

In the Area   Cacapon State Park, Berkeley Castle mansion (1887), Harpers Ferry National Historical Park, Charles Town racetrack, Antietam Battlefield (Civil War), Blue Ridge Outlet Center (shopping), C&O Canal, Berkeley Springs State Parkland, Berkeley Springs Museum, Prospect Peak Overlook (3-state view), Winchester (apple orchards, festivals), Whitetail Resort (downhill skiing).

Getting Here   *From Washington, DC.* By car, I–270 to Frederick, Md., I–70 west to Hancock, MD, cross Potomac River on Rte. 522 (90 min). By train, Amtrak to Martinsburg, WV.

Special Notes   Facilities accessible for people with disabilities. Discount on bathhouse admission and services for senior citizens. No smoking in bathhouses. Spa open Apr.–Oct., Sat.–Thurs. 10–6, Fri. 10–9; Nov.–Mar., daily 10–6. Old Roman Bathhouse open weekends only Columbus Day–Memorial Day. Summer concerts at bandstand, Sat. 5 PM.

Coolfont Resort

Holistic health
Life enhancement

West Virginia
Berkeley Springs   A relaxed, informal, budget-priced mountain retreat occupying 1,300 acres in the foothills of the Appalachian Mountains, Coolfont has the laid-back look of a summer camp for adults. With the opening of the Spectrum Spa in 1992, the resident owners culminated 20 years devoted to creating an environment for healthy vacations. In addition to a fitness center with indoor spring-water swimming pool, the spa has 16 private rooms for a wide range of bodywork, a full-service salon, demonstration kitchen, and aerobics studio with sprung-wood floor. In the Swim and Fitness Club are a coed whirlpool and sauna, weights training room with exercise bikes, and Paramount equipment. The daily schedule of classes is open to all resort guests, and runs from morning stretch to aquatics, body sculpting, and yoga.

Members of the resident staff combine expertise in physical fitness, nutrition, massage, and holistic health. In addition to regularly scheduled programs, guest instructors lead workshops on natural nutrition, creative problem solving, and stress reduction. Also offered regularly is a weekend of massage instruction for couples, and a week-long Breathe-Free program for smoking cessation.

The emphasis here is on health awareness, yet there is a cultural dimension to the Coolfont community. Folk singers, string quartets, and artists in residence perform on weekends. A woodsy lounge bar comes alive Saturday nights with country music and sing-alongs.

Coolfont Resort

Cold Run Valley Rd., Rte. 1, Box 710, Berkeley Springs, WV 25411
Tel. 304/258-4500 or 800/888-8768
Fax 304/258-5499

Administration	Owner-managers, Martha and Sam Ashelman; program director, Diane Mickelson
Season	Year-round.
Accommodations	240 rooms, some with fireplace and whirlpool bath, in the modern 3-story Woodland Lodge and 20 mountain chalets. The deluxe chalets have 2 bedrooms, double beds, 2 baths, and can be shared or as 2 private units. All are air-conditioned, with telephone, TV, coffeemaker, wet bar, daily maid service. Lodge rooms offer choice of queen-size or twin beds, patio or balcony; all have modern bathroom with shower/tub, TV, telephone, air-conditioning. Also guest rooms in the historic Manor House (no smoking); tent sites, RV hookups, and log cabins available.
Rates	Daily Modified American Plan $72-$112 per person double occupancy, $102-$142 single, includes admission to Swim & Fitness Center; 2-night Spa & Fitness package $320-$360 per person double occupancy, $360-$420 single; 2-night Massage Workshop $640-$750 per couple; 6-night Health Retreat $900-$1,020 per person double occupancy, $1,020-$1,170 single; Breathe-Free program $1,395 single. Spa for a Day (no lodging) $104.94. Add 9% room tax, optional gratuities. Deposit: 50% payable in advance (refund when canceled at least 48 hr before start of program). Credit cards: AE, DC, MC, V.
Meal Plans	3 meals daily included in spa packages, 2 meals daily in MAP rate. Breakfast in spa dining room can be omelet, hot cereal, fruits. Lunch menu has lentil stew, pita sandwich with turkey, vegetarian pizza, tempeh burger. Dinner may be salmon baked in parchment, chicken dijon, cajun beans and rice. Salad bar, fruit bowl, herbal teas, decaffeinated coffee available. Juice and fruit snacks. Vegetarian meals available; special diets accommodated.
Services and Facilities	**Exercise Equipment:** 15-unit Paramount weight training system, Trotter treadmill, StairMaster, Tunturi ergometer, Precor rowing machine, 2 Monark bikes, Schwinn Air Dyne bike, free weights (3-20 lbs.), hand weights. **Services:** Massage (neuromuscular, cranial/sacral, sports, deep-tissue therapy, Swedish), sugaring or clay body masque, herbal wrap, loofah body scrub, facials; salon for hair, nail, and skin care. Fitness evaluation, nutrition consultation. **Swimming Facilities:** Indoor pool; beach on private lake. **Recreation Facilities:** 8 tennis courts; boating, hiking, horseback riding; team sports; cross-country skiing, ice skating; 18-hole golf course nearby. **Evening Programs:** Concerts, health lectures.
In the Area	*See* Berkeley Springs State Park, *above*.
Getting Here	*From Washington, DC.* By car, I-270/70 to Hancock, MD, Rte. 522 (2 hr); or the Pennsylvania Turnpike (I-76) at the

Breezewood exit. By air, USAir has scheduled service to Hagerstown, MD; private planes use Potomac Airport. By bus, Greyhound to Hagerstown, MD. By train, Amtrak or MARC to Martinsburg, WV. Rental car, taxi available.

Special Notes Special accommodations for people with disabilities. Supervised camp for children, summer only. No smoking in the dining room or designated accommodations. Swim and Fitness Center open weekdays 10–8, weekends 8 AM–9 PM. Elderhostel in December.

The Greenbrier

Luxury pampering
Preventive medicine
Taking the waters
Weight management

West Virginia
White Sulphur
Springs

The legendary Greenbrier resort blends old-fashioned comfort with high-tech spa treatments. The spa wing was opened in 1987 and has separate soaking pools and therapy rooms for men and women, a mirrored aerobics studio, and interactive exercise equipment. Hydrotherapy comes with mineral water—your choice of sulfur soak or bubbly herbal foam. Sports, riding, and hiking in the foothills of the Allegheny Mountains are significant attractions within the 6,500-acre resort, which includes three golf courses and a rifle club.

While the hotel is a busy scene of conferences and afternoon teas in vast halls filled with "oriental" decor, the spa is serene and small, awash in pinks and greens, with sprigs of rhododendron painted on tiles. The staff includes both old hands and university-trained physiology specialists; they make newcomers feel comfortable about trying some of the exotic-sounding treatments. Seaweed body wraps, aromatherapy, and facials with European floral products are among the à la carte offerings.

The Greenbrier Clinic, established in 1948, occupies a separate building that is completely equipped for diagnostic and preventive medicine. Health examinations can now be combined with spa therapy. Checking in with the resident medical staff, the participant undergoes a two-day diagnostic assessment plus advanced fitness evaluation. A doctor will confer with the spa nutritionist and physiologist to plan a personalized diet and exercise regimen.

Spa cuisine is available to guests in a five-day package that includes breakfast, lunch, and dinner, unlimited exercise classes, luxury pampering, and individual nutrition consultation. The meals contain 30% fat or less, are moderate in cholesterol and sodium, and include high-fiber selections. Presented with classic Greenbrier flair, the menu capitalizes on fresh, natural foods from nearby farms.

Constantly refurbished, guest suites are huge, with parlor and walk-in closet, traditional furniture, and Greenbrier green carpet. There is a Greenbrier look and style, an aspect of artistic rightness and service that starts at the white brick gateway. The great white neoclassical hotel rises from beds of flowers. Its lobbies have flooring of black and white marble squares,

Dorothy Draper decor, flowers massed on tables, and full-length Gilbert Stuart portrait of George Washington.

The Greenbrier
White Sulphur Springs, WV 24986
Tel. 304/536–1110 or 800/624–6070
Fax 304/536–7854

Administration	General manager, Ted J. Kleisner; spa director, Judy Stell
Season	Year-round.
Accommodations	650 rooms in main building, deluxe cottages, and guest houses.
Rates	$149–$326 daily per person double occupancy, $176–$441 single, including breakfast and dinner. Suites from $215 per person. Daily service charge $14.25 plus 6% tax per person. 5-night/6-day spa package $2,300 per person double or single, 2-day spa package $1,050 per person double or single, including 3 meals daily. 5-day Spa and Clinic program $2,300 per person double or single. Deposit: $300 per room payable in advance. Tax and gratuities included in spa packages. Credit cards: AE, DC, MC, V.
Meal Plans	American fare plus low-calorie alternatives at breakfast and dinner in the main dining room. Dinner can begin with smoked duck salad, mushroom consommé, an entrée of grilled swordfish or mountain trout with lentil ragout, braised spinach leaves, followed by a salad of red-oak leaf lettuce with tomatoes in yogurt dressing. Dessert is pear strudel in fresh berry sauce. Cafe service for lunch. Tea daily.
Services and Facilities	**Exercise Equipment:** 7-unit Nautilus weight training circuit, 3 Trotter treadmills, 3 Schwinn Dynavit bikes, UBE ergometer, 2 StairMasters, dumbbells (4–40 lb); $10 facility fee includes use of sauna/steam room. **Services:** Full-body massage, back facial, pressure-point facial, herbal wrap, scalp massage, mineral or herbal bath, paraffin hand treatment, aromatherapy; hair, nail, and skin care in salon; 1-on-1 training, fitness evaluation, personal exercise program. Aerobics class $6. **Swimming Facilities:** Indoor Olympic-size pool, outdoor pool. **Recreation Facilities:** 15 outdoor and 5 indoor tennis courts, platform tennis, 3 golf courses, fishing, skeet- and trapshooting, bowling, croquet, horseback riding, carriage rides, jogging and hiking trails, parcourse, bicycle rental. **Evening Programs:** Feature films, food and wine weekends, dancing.
In the Area	Presidents' Cottage Museum (displays memorabilia of famous visitors), crafts studios, mineral water springhouse.
Getting Here	*From Washington DC.* By car, I–95 or Skyline Drive, I–64 (6 hrs) to Richmond. By plane, Lewisburg Airport has scheduled flights by American Airlines via Raleigh/Durham and by USAir via Pittsburgh and Charlotte. By train, Amtrak's Cardinal between New York City, Washington, and Cincinnati stops at the Greenbrier Fri., Sun., and Tues. Private limousine connects with flights at Lewisburg. Rental car, taxi available.
Special Notes	Special accommodations provided for people with disabilities. Sports school for children June–Labor Day. No smoking in the spa and areas of the dining room. Spa open daily 7–7.

Lakeview Resort

Nonprogram resort

West Virginia The fitness and sports center of the Lakeview Resort comple-
Morgantown ments an executive conference center and two championship
golf courses. Surrounded by woodland and a scenic lake, it's a
place for both rigorous workouts and simple relaxation.

The action is continuous in the fitness center (a separate facility), and registered guests enjoy unlimited access to facilities at
no extra cost. Inside is a 40-foot lap pool, jogging track (22 laps
equals a mile), and aerobics studio with 20 classes scheduled
during the week. Indoor and outdoor tennis facilities are available, too.

A personal fitness evaluation is offered when you arrive, and
the only extra fees are for massage, use of the racquet-sport
courts, and aerobics classes. A nursery will take care of the
kids while parents work out. Lunch and snacks are available at
the spa juice bar.

Lakeview Resort
Rte. 6, Box 88A, Morgantown, WV 26505
Tel. 304/594–1111 or 800/624–8300

Administration Manager, W. G. Menihan; fitness director, Greg Orner

Season Year-round.

Accommodations 2-story inn with 187 well-appointed rooms and 55 2-bedroom
condominium units with maid service.

Rates Daily rate per room $80–$139, single or double occupancy.
Condominium apartments (up to 6 persons) $280 per day. Cred-
it card guarantee for 1 night. Credit cards: AE, DC, MC, V.

Meal Plans Light fare in the lakeview restaurant; juice bar and snacks in
the fitness center.

Services and **Exercise Equipment:** 10-station Nautilus circuit, Marcy
Facilities weight-resistance gym and recumbent bike, StairMaster, Lifecycle, Liferower, free weights. **Swimming Facilities:** Indoor lap
pool and outdoor pool, lake. **Spa Facilities:** Coed whirlpool, separate saunas. **Recreation Facilities:** Racquetball and walleyball
courts, 2 indoor, 4 outdoor tennis courts; fishing, boat rentals,
horseback riding, waterskiing, 2 golf courses. **Evening Programs:** Dancing, cabaret.

In the Area Lakeview Theater (summer stock), Cheat River Gorge (white-
water rafting), Star City (glassmaking), Cooper's Park State
Forest (hiking trails).

Getting Here *From Pittsburgh.* Located 75 mi south of Pittsburgh, the resort is accessible by interstate routes and commuter airlines.
By car, Rtes. 48 and 79 (90 min). By plane, Morgantown's Hart
Field is served by USAir. Courtesy car pickup to and from airport.

Special Notes No smoking in the fitness center, some guest rooms, designated areas of the dining room. Fitness & Sports Center open
weekdays 6:30 AM–10 PM, weekends 7–5. Minimum age in center is 16.

New England and New York

A return to elegance marked a decade of intensive development throughout the northeastern states. Grand old estates have been rejuvenated, hotels have updated their fitness facilities and introduced European therapies. The result has been a broader range of vacation options for both luxury-minded and budget-conscious travelers.

Tradition blends with the latest concepts in nutrition and bodywork at the Norwich Inn & Spa, a Connecticut landmark. In the Berkshires, Arizona's famed Canyon Ranch offers innovative health programs only minutes away from the Boston Symphony Orchestra's popular summer home at Tanglewood. The facilities at this first destination spa and fitness resort in the Northeast are among the most comprehensive in America. Nearby, the modestly priced Kripalu Center for Yoga and Health exercises your body and mind in a sanctuary unlike traditional ashrams in its size and scope of programs.

Advancing the concept of preventive medicine, spas are teaming up with doctors, nutritionists, and psychologists in new programs that address stress control, aging, and lifestyle. In Vermont, Green Mountain at Fox Run has a Liquid Diet Recovery program. At the New Age Health Spa in New York, you can participate in a challenge course designed by experts from Outward Bound, or luxuriate in the newly expanded spa building. In the Hudson Valley, Omega Institute has been at the forefront of personal and professional development in holistic health since 1977.

Norwich Inn & Spa

Luxury pampering

Connecticut
Norwich
Combine a 1920s country inn with a contemporary spa, and you have a perfect escape for city dwellers. Located two hours north of New York City, the imposing Georgian-style Norwich establishment took on a new life in 1987 with the addition of the spa. Today the inn blends sophisticated cuisine and beauty treatments with New England tradition.

The spa philosophy of the owner, Edward J. Safdie, is one of nurturing and unadulterated pampering, and this is evident throughout the inn's operation. From flowered chintz and hand-rubbed pine in the old-fashioned bedrooms to high-tech workouts in the gym, the regimen and comfort complement each other.

The 35-foot swimming pool under a soaring cathedral ceiling is the spa's centerpiece. An aerobics studio and an exercise room equipped with Keiser Cam II pneumatic resistance units flank the pool. You can sign up for massages, deep-cleansing facials, body scrubs, hydrotherapy, and a full range of skin and beauty treatments. Classes, scheduled throughout the day, are open to other guests at the inn as well as to program participants.

New England and New York

Connecticut
Norwich Inn & Spa, **23**

Maine
Northern Pines Health Resort, **1**
Poland Spring Health Institute, **2**

Massachusetts
Canyon Ranch in the Berkshires, **17**

Kripalu Center for Yoga and Health, **18**
The Kushi Institute of the Berkshires, **19**
Maharishi Ayur-Veda Health Center, **16**
The Option Institute, **20**
Rowe Conference Center, **14**
Smith College Adult Camp, **15**

New Hampshire
Waterville Valley Resort, **3**

New York
Aegis, **13**
Gurney's Inn, **30**
Living Springs Lifestyle Center, **29**
Mohonk Mountain House, **26**
Mountain Valley Health Resort, **23**

New Age Health Spa, **25**
Omega Institute, **27**
Omni Sagamore Resort & Spa, **10**
Saratoga Spa State Park, **12**
Sivananda Ashram Yoga Ranch, **27**
Tai Chi Farm, **28**
Zen Mountain Monastery, **24**

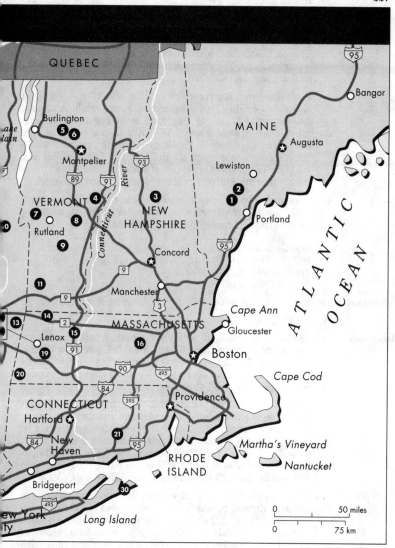

QUEBEC

Bangor

MAINE

Burlington **5** **6**

Augusta

★ Montpelier

Lewiston

VERMONT **4** **3**

Portland

NEW HAMPSHIRE

7 **8**

Rutland

9

Concord

Connecticut River

ATLANTIC OCEAN

11

Manchester

13 **14**

MASSACHUSETTS

Cape Ann

Lenox **15**

Gloucester

19 **16**

Boston

20

Cape Cod

CONNECTICUT

Providence

Hartford ✿

Martha's Vineyard

84

New Haven

21

Nantucket

RHODE ISLAND

Bridgeport

30

New York City

Long Island

0   50 miles

0   75 km

Vermont
The Equinox, **11**
Four Seasons
Healing, **4**
Golden Eagle, **6**
Green Mountain at
Fox Run, **9**
New Life, **7**
Topnotch at Stowe, **5**
Woodstock Inn &
Resort, **8**

The range of treatments makes this spa special. Choices include polarity therapy, acupressure, thalassotherapy, body wraps with Canadian glacial clay or algae imported from France, facials, and hydrotherapy in a deep tub with a 60-jet water massage. The Personal Escape Plan lets you tailor a spa package to your daily needs.

Introduced into the recent renovation here was an excess of charm and comfort, but standard rooms are small. Antiques, four-poster beds, ceiling fans, handwoven rugs, and lace curtains enhance the bedrooms. A 6-foot birdhouse in the lobby is home to a pair of finches. Public areas include a taproom with a large stone fireplace and a quiet sunroom full of palms and wicker. Spa guests have a choice of accommodations in a villa or the historic inn, and must walk through a garden to the spa.

Surrounded by 37 acres of woodland and situated near a state park, the inn offers rural diversions after workouts, including casino gaming in nearby Foxwoods and Shantok.

Norwich Inn & Spa
607 W. Thames (Rte. 32), Norwich, CT 06360
Tel. 203/886–2401 or 800/275–4772
Fax 203/886–9483

Administration President, Raymond Mellette; spa director, Mark Vinchesi

Season Year-round.

Accommodations 65 rooms, 16 suites, all with private bath, furnished with antiques and reproductions. The 16 villa suites come with fireplace, deck, Ralph Lauren prints, and kitchen serviced by the inn and have access to a private clubhouse, gym, and swimming pool. All rooms have TV, phones, air-conditioning.

Rates Personal Escape Plan per day $325–$425 single, $280–$340 per person double, includes accommodations, spa services, meals, tax (2-night minimum midweek, 3-night minimum weekends; deposit $250). Getaway Country Retreat with 2 meals daily, $170–$260 single, $115–$165 double. Spa facility fee $10 per day. Inn room $115–$185, single or double occupany; villa $200–$230. Add 12% tax. Credit cards: AE, DC, MC, V.

Meal Plans Three meals daily in Escape plan; breakfast and dinner in Country Retreat package. Breakfast choices include spa omelette or buffet with fruit, scrambled egg substitute, pancakes, cereals. Lunch includes butternut squash chowder, choice of grilled chicken salad or crab cakes, white bean and tuna salad or chicken fajita, spinach salad or spa pizza. Dinner entrées can be sole Florentine, roulade of veal, scallops on pasta, vegetable plate, Polynesian shrimp. Desserts include pear-cranberry parfait, baked apple, brown-rice pudding.

Services and Facilities **Exercise Equipment:** 5 Keiser Cam II pneumatic resistance units, 4-station Universal gym, Liferower, 5 Lifecycles, 4 Challenger treadmills, 2 StairMasters. **Services:** Facials, body massage, loofah scrub, hydrotherapy, herbal or clay wrap, fango bath, cellulite massage, thalassotherapy, aromatherapy massage; skin-care salon. **Swimming Facilities:** Indoor exercise pool, outdoor recreational pool. **Spa Facilities:** Men's and women's sauna and steam room, whirlpool; aerobics classes, private workouts. **Recreation Facilities:** Tennis courts. Norwich Golf Course and Fort Shantok State Park adjoin the inn's

37 acres. Rental bicycles. **Evening Programs:** Cooking demonstrations, fitness lectures, color analysis.

In the Area Mystic Seaport Maritime Museum, General Dynamics submarine base in Groton, Old Lyme art center and historic homes. Cathedral of St. Patrick in Old Norwich, Essex summer beach colony, Eugene O'Neill Theater Center, Goodspeed Opera House in Haddam, Foxwoods Casino, Gilette Castle.

Getting Here *From New York City*. By train, Amtrak from Grand Central Station to New London (90 min). By air, scheduled flights to New London by American Airlines and USAir. By car, I–95 to I–395, Rte. 32 to Norwich (3 hr). Hotel limousine service to the airport and Amtrak station in New London ($21 each way). Taxi and rental car available in Norwich and New London. Ample free parking.

Special Notes No smoking in the spa and dining room. Spa open Sun–Thurs. 8–8, Fri.–Sat. 8 AM–9 PM. Minimum age in spa, 18.

Northern Pines Health Resort

Holistic health
Preventive medicine
Stress control
Weight management

Maine
Raymond

Getting back to nature can be a healthy experience on the 68-acre lakefront Northern Pines Health Resort. The diet and fitness programs, based on a holistic approach, are designed to help participants develop a positive attitude toward weight loss and stress control; the transition is a gradual process, not a quick fix. Lifestyle management, rather than exercise, is emphasized.

Essentially a year-round self-help camp with a limited number of optional services, Northern Pines offers a program designed for men and women who want to take control of their lives. Campers range widely in age, but many are over 40. The affordable rates make it popular with singles. About 50 guests are resident in summer, 30 during the ski season, allowing for a friendly mix with lots of personal attention from the staff.

Each day begins with stretching exercises and a brisk walk through the woods, followed by a choice of focus sessions or aerobics. Instruction is available in transcendental meditation, art, and music. Morning and afternoon yoga are optional. Evenings offer more learning activities, from cooking classes to massage demonstrations. Fasting regimens are offered, and about 20% of the guests opt to go on a week-long juice fast.

The camp's lakeside log cabins date from the 1920s and provide total seclusion for couples. New lodge rooms and cabins with two bedrooms are on the hillside amid towering pines, spruce, and hemlock. There are also two-person yurts (earth-covered cabins) that have carpeting and modern conveniences.

The informality and laid-back pace appeal to stressed-out professionals who come here to rejuvenate and relax.

Northern Pines Health Resort
Rte. 85, R.R. 1, Box 279, Raymond, ME 04071
Tel. 207/655-7624

Administration Owner-director, Marlee Turner; manager, Susan Lubner

Season Year-round, except Nov.–mid-Dec. and mid-March–May.

Accommodations Private cabins and lodge rooms for 50. Some share a bathroom, others a communal facility; most have private toilet and shower. Well-worn wood furniture and buildings. Self-service laundry.

Rates 1-week summer program (Sun.–Sun.) $675–$1,300; weekend (2 nights) $230–$440. Rooms $90–$220 per day. 50% deposit per person. Add gratuities, 7% tax. Credit cards: AE, MC, V.

Meal Plans Modified vegetarian diet, 800 calories per day. 3 daily buffets include pasta, salads with home-grown sprouts, poached salmon. Supervised fasts begin with 2 days of raw fruit, vegetables, juices, and broth.

Services and Facilities **Exercise Equipment:** NordicTrack cross-country ski machine, 2 stationary bikes, Solaflex unit, slant board, Rebounders, free weights. **Services:** Massage, shiatsu, reflexology, aromatherapy, facials, hair treatment, herbal wrap, float tank sessions, Clearlight therapy. **Swimming Facilities:** Lake with sandy beach. **Recreation Facilities:** Hiking, canoeing, sailing; jogging trails. **Evening Programs:** Cooking demonstrations, massage techniques, sauna baths, salt rubs; videos, storytelling.

In the Area L. L. Bean store, ocean beaches, White Mountain Range; Acadia National Park; ferry trips to Nova Scotia; Portland's restored Old Port, summer theater, Portland Museum of Art; factory outlets in Freeport.

Getting Here *From Portland.* By car, I-95 to Exit 8, Rte. 302 northwest to Rte. 83 (45 min). Rental car, taxi available.

Special Notes Summer camp for children, 3½ or 7 weeks. No smoking in public areas. 2 rooms accessible for people with disabilities.

Poland Spring Health Institute

Preventive medicine
Vibrant maturity

Maine
Poland Spring An extended visit to Poland Spring Health Institute is more like taking a holiday in the country than being at a clinic. Poland Spring has been synonomous with healthy water for more than a century, largely due to a commercial bottling plant near the institute. Everything here that has to do with water—from drinking 8–10 glasses a day to soaking to steaming in a room where you receive body wraps preceding a massage—uses the Poland Spring. Additionally, following a vegetarian diet and participating in rigorous outdoor exercise are requirements of the program.

Just 10 guests are accommodated in old-fashioned comfort in the big New England farmhouse, where the average stay is two weeks. A special program for smoking cessation (14 days) is offered, as well as five-day nutrition and health seminar.

Guests work closely with specialists on diabetes and stress related ailments. A series of exercises and hydrotherapy treatments is prescribed that is appropriate for your physical condition. Testing by the medical office, when needed, is an additional charge; everything else is included in the weekly fee.

This nonprofit, private wellness center was founded in 1979 and emphasizes Christian prayer. The 260-acre property is bounded by a 2-mile-long lake, with hiking and biking trails and a parcourse, and in winter guests can cross-country ski and ice skate.

Poland Spring Health Institute

R.F.D. 1, Box 4300, Summit Spring Rd., Poland Spring, ME 04274
Tel. 207/998–2894; clinic 207/998–2795
Fax 207/998–2164

Administration	Medical director, Richard A. Hansen, M.D.; program director, Ulla Hansen
Season	Year-round.
Accommodations	5 large rooms, most sharing a bath.
Rates	Semiprivate room $745 a week with meals, private room $950, tax and service charge included. $200 nonrefundable reservation fee. No credit cards.
Meal Plans	Salads and steamed vegetables, fresh fruit, and homebaked bread make up the diet of complex carbohydrates. Lunch buffet may consist of gluten roast, baked potato, green beans, salad. Dinner is fruit, salad, toast. No eggs, dairy products, fish, or meat is served.
Services and Facilities	**Exercise Equipment:** Stationary and outdoor bikes. **Swimming Facilities:** lake, steambath, whirlpool. **Recreation Facilities:** Boating, canoeing, biking, horseback riding; nearby golf. **Evening Programs:** Lectures on health-related subjects.
In the Area	Shopping and sightseeing trips, Shaker village at Sabbathday Lake.
Getting Here	*From Boston:* By air, Portland International Airport (40 min). By car, I–95 to Rte. 302 (2 hr). Courtesy transfers.
Special Notes	No smoking indoors. Remember to bring sturdy walking shoes, rain gear, and personal medical records as requested. Special attention is paid to people with disabilities and heart patients.

Canyon Ranch in the Berkshires

Holistic health
Life enhancement
Luxury pampering
Preventive medicine
Vibrant maturity
Weight management

Massachusetts
Lenox

Canyon Ranch has a mind-and-body approach to fitness that focuses on improving your lifestyle. Skiers can get in shape before tackling cross-country trails, and executives can use the latest biofeedback systems to de-stress. A 100,000-square-foot fitness center includes racquetball, squash, and tennis courts; a running track; a 75-foot swimming pool; and separate spas for men and women with saunas, steam rooms, inhalation rooms, and Jacuzzis.

The Arizona Canyon Ranch's hiking and biking programs have been adapted to the Berkshire terrain, but don't expect to find Southwestern food and decor. The spartan accommodations opened for overnight guests when the fitness center was built in 1989, and in no way compare to the grandeur of the property's centerpiece, a mansion that dates from 1897 with formal gardens. Glass-walled walkways connect to the inn and fitness center.

In addition to daily yoga, meditation, and more than 30 fitness classes, you can schedule private consultations to reduce stress or stop smoking.

Canyon Ranch in the Berkshires
165 Kemble St. (Rte. 7A), Lenox, MA 01240
Tel. 413/637–4100 or 800/742–9000
Fax 413/637–0057

Administration	Manager, Mary Ellen St. John
Season	Year-round.
Accommodations	120 rooms and suites, with New England–style functional furnishings. Rooms are air-conditioned, have telephones, digital clock radio with alarm, no TV. Terry-cloth robe and thongs supplied; hair dryer and makeup mirror in bathrooms. Self-service laundry.
Rates	4-day/3-night package with deluxe accommodations $730–$1,210 per person double occupancy, $880–$1,410 single; 8-day/7-night package $1,750–$2,580 per person double, $2,040–$2,980 single. Minimum 3-night stay July 1–Aug. 31 and holiday weekends; 2-night minimum at other times. Nightly rates $225–$410 double, $275–$480 single. Service charge (18%) and tax added. 2 nights' deposit in advance. Credit cards: AE, MC, V.
Meal Plans	Menu for a là carte choices at 3 meals daily. Also salad bar. Selections include New England specialties cooked with a minimum of salt and fat. Recipes are 60% carbohydrate, 20% protein, and 15–20% fat. 1,200–1,800 calorie balanced menu available. Vegetarian meals and special diets available. Coffee, tea, milk served; no alcohol.
Services and Facilities	**Exercise Equipment:** State-of-the-art treadmills, stair climbers, stationary bikes, rowing machines, free weights, 2 Gravitrons, 2 NordicTracks, complete circuit of Keiser CAM 300 pneumatic units. **Services:** Herbal wraps, 7 types of massage, aromatherapy, hydrotherapy, acupuncture. Salon for hair, nail, skin care; holistic health counseling, biofeedback training; medical checkup and fitness evaluation. **Swimming Facilities:** Indoor and 50-foot heated outdoor pool. **Spa Facilities:** Separate wings for men and women with sauna, steam room, Jacuzzi; studios for aerobics, yoga. **Recreation Facilities:** Cross-country skiing, hiking; bicycles for daily group outings; 3 indoor tennis courts (hard surface), 3 outdoor courts (Har-Tru), 2 racquetball courts, squash court, indoor track; canoeing. **Evening Programs:** Visiting specialists speak on health and lifestyle topics.

In the Area Optional tours to local museums and festivals, Tanglewood Music Festival, Jacob's Pillow Dance Festival, the Sterling and Francine Clark Art Institute in Williamstown (25 mi), Williamstown summer theater, Appalachian Trail.

Getting Here *From Boston and New York City.* By car, Massachusetts Turnpike (I–90) (3 hr). By train, daily Amtrak service to Rensselaer, NY or Pittsfield, MA; complimentary transfer. By air, scheduled flights to Albany Airport or Bradley International at Hartford/Springfield. Taxi, rental car, limousine available. Complimentary transfers to/from airports.

Special Notes Minimum age of guests is 14. Smoking not permitted indoors or in public areas. Alcohol not permitted in public areas. Ramp entry to all buildings and facilities. Some bedrooms specially equipped for people with disabilities. Spa open daily 6:30 AM–10 PM.

Kripalu Center for Yoga and Health

Life enhancement
Preventive medicine
Spiritual awareness

Massachusetts Kripalu synthesizes the ancient science of yoga with modern
Lenox approaches to holistic health and personal growth in a series of programs designed to fight stress and increase well-being. The Kripalu Center occupies a former monastery (built in 1957) on a 300-acre wooded site adjacent to the Tanglewood Music Festival grounds. Although the four-story brick building lacks exercise equipment and has mostly dormitory accommodations, this is a suitably expansive setting to experience spiritual balance.

On a typical day you have a choice of lectures, workshops, bodywork, and several yoga sessions. Mornings begin at 5:45 in the main chapel, or with a yoga session from 6AM to 7:25, followed by breakfast eaten in silence. Most of the guests, who can number over 300, start their day walking about the grounds, and join evening sessions of chanting.

In addition to the daily schedule, there are week-long programs with such names as DansKinetics℠, Men and Yoga, Life After 50, Self-Esteem, and Meditation Retreat. Women's issues are addressed in week-long programs where practicing the gentle movements of Kripalu yoga becomes a metaphor for taking control of one's life. Options include all-juice fasting, an inner quest intensive, and a week of women-only outdoor treks.

Drawing on Sanskrit philosophy, anatomy, and psychology, these programs teach energy balancing techniques that can be used to develop a healthy lifestyle. An understanding of love is the basis for optional weekend programs, another is devoted to transforming stress by using meditation and yoga techniques. Experiential in concept, each day is structured to involve you in a new awakening to your personal needs and powers.

Family-oriented, Kripalu offers supervised programs for teenagers and children, encouraging noncompetitive and loving friendships. Teenagers can participate in the one-week "Coming of Age" camp which mixes yoga and sports. Creative exercise for children ages 4 to 13 is scheduled daily during summer, and weekends year-round. Parents can enroll children on a daily fee basis in the supervised sessions of yoga, dance, and sports.

Participants range in age from 18 to 80 and work together to rediscover themselves through a variety of inner-attunement techniques. Some come for a few days of rest and renewal; others seek compassion and healing through private consultation.

Kripalu Center for Yoga and Health
Box 793, Lenox, MA 01240
Tel. 413/448–3400 or 800/967–3577
Fax 413/448–3384

Administration Spiritual director, Yogi Amrit Desai; manager, Sudhir

Season Year-round.

Accommodations Dormitory rooms with 10–20 beds; sheets, blankets, and towels provided; standard rooms have 2 low beds, access to hall bath; deluxe rooms with double, queen, or twin beds, have either private bath or access to hall bathroom. Private rooms have access to a breakfast and tea lounge. No maid service. Lakeview rooms (2 beds) at extra cost.

Rates Weekend 3-night programs $160–$390 single, $180–$310 double; week-long (6 nights) workshop $495–$1,395 single, $570–$885 double. Nightly rate $64–$195 single, $72–$124 double. Daily rate (no lodging) $30–$40. Children's Program $45 per day; without lodging $30; child's day pass only, $10; Teen's 1-week program $495. Deposit: 25% in advance. No refunds, but deposit can be applied to future programs. Credit cards: MC, V.

Meal Plans 3 vegetarian meals daily, buffet style, includes whole grains and vegetables, dairy products. Full salad bar, several entrees, fresh-baked bread, variety of condiments. Hot or cold tea served at noon. Food is low in fat and sweeteners. Special diets accommodated by advance request. Silence is maintained during breakfast and lunch.

Services and Facilities **Services:** Massage therapies, including Kripalu bodywork, polarity, shiatsu; facial and foot care; medical tests. **Swimming Facilities:** Private lake. **Spa Facilities:** Saunas for men and women, whirlpool. **Recreation Facilities:** DansKinetic aerobic exercise class; skiing in winter. **Evening Programs:** Communal meditation and chanting; Indian dancing and concerts.

In the Area Tanglewood Music Festival (July–Aug.), summer theater and dance; the Sterling and Francine Clark Art Institute in Williamstown.

Getting Here *From Boston.* By car, Massachusetts Turnpike (I–90) to Exit B-3, Rte 22 south, Rte 102 east via West Stockbridge, Rte 183. (2 hr). By air, scheduled service to Albany or Bradley International Airport at Hartford/Springfield. By train, Amtrak has 1 train daily from Boston to Pittsfield, with connections to Lenox by Bonanza Bus (tel. 800/556–3815). Taxi, limousine service, and car rentals available in Lenox, Albany and Bradley airports. By bus, Peter Pan Lines (tel. 800/237–8747) to Lenox (3 hrs).

Special Notes Facilities and rooms specially equipped for people with disabilities. Day camp for children 4–13, July–Aug., $30–$45 per day. No smoking in or near the center. Remember to bring mat or cushion for meditation and yoga; bedding and towels for dormitory accommodations.

The Kushi Institute of the Berkshires

Nutrition and diet
Spiritual awareness

Massachusetts Since 1978, the Kushi Institute has been in the forefront of
Becket macrobiotic research and education. The center offers an intensive seminar in cooking, plus four or five days of instruction on preventing cancer and heart disease. For newcomers to macrobiotics, there is a week-long introductory course that includes exercise and massage.

Secluded on 600 acres of woodlands and meadows, the Berkshire center provides a peaceful, natural environment for study and relaxation. In a former Franciscan abbey, the bedrooms and working kitchen accommodate up to 15 participants in year-round programs. Many of these seminars are taught by founders Aveline and Michio Kushi.

The daily activities begin with a session of *do-in*, stretching exercises that are simple and easy to learn. Periods of meditation alternate with lectures and workshops in food preparation. Individuals, couples, and families often participate together.

The Kushi Institute of the Berkshires
308 Leland Rd., Box 7, Becket, MA 01223
Tel. 413/623-5742
Fax 413/623-8827

Administration Manager, Carolyn Heidenry; program director, Charles Millman

Season Year-round. Macrobiotic residential seminar is offered twice a month, beginning on a Sun. and running through lunch the following Sat. Cooking intensives and topical seminars run 4–5 days. Multipart spiritual training seminar scheduled at various times of the year.

Accommodations 10 guest rooms in main lodge, simply furnished with 1 or 2 beds; 3 rooms have private bath or shower facility. New building scheduled for completion in 1994 has 12 large rooms with private bath.

Rates 6-day Way to Health seminar (Sun.–Sat.) with meals and a shared bedroom, $985 for participant, $825 accompanying person. 1-month Dynamics of Macrobiotics program $3,250 per person double occupancy. Private bath $25 additional per day. $100 advance deposit per person. Credit cards: AE, MC, V.

Meal Plans 3 meals daily, family style. Brown rice, miso soup, beans, and cooked vegetables with salads, natural desserts. Specialties include tofu and seitan dishes, sushi, noodles and pasta, amasake pudding.

Services and Facilities **Services:** Shiatsu massage. Acupressure. **Swimming Facilities:** Nearby lake. **Evening Programs:** Workshops and discussions on diet and nutrition; informal entertainment.

In the Area Tanglewood Music Festival at Lenox (35 min), summer theater and the Sterling and Francine Clark Art Institute in

Williamstown (90 min), Jacob's Pillow Dance Festival in Becket.

Getting Here *From Boston.* By car, Massachusetts Turnpike (I–90), exit for Lee (2½ hr). By bus, Peter Pan Bus Lines (800/237–8747) or Bonanza Bus Lines (tel. 800/556–3815) to Lee (3 hr). By air, Bradley International Airport at Hartford/Springfield. Free pickup at bus station in Lee; taxi, car rental available.

Special Notes No smoking on premises except in smoking lounge.

Maharishi Ayur-Veda Health Center

Nutrition and diet
Preventive medicine
Spiritual awareness
Stress control

Massachusetts Ancient Indian healing techniques and modern biofeedback
Lancaster technology are the means to relaxation and good health in the elegant mansion of the Maharishi Ayur-Veda Health Center. Ayurvedic medical treatments are based on an analysis of one's *dosha*, or physical and emotional type. The therapy includes a special diet related to body type, massage with warm oil and herbal essences, and total relaxation.

The healing process of *panchakarma* begins with a physical examination, pulse measurement, and a thorough questionnaire to determine whether you are *vata* (quick, energetic, movement prone), *pitta* (enterprising and sharp), or *kapha* (tranquil and steady). Therapy and diet are prescribed accordingly.

The medically supervised program is based on ayurvedic principles, as practiced in Asia. The center's doctors and registered nurses are trained in both Eastern and Western medicine. Cancer and other disease sufferers frequently come for treatment.

A daily two-hour session to rid the body of impurities includes massage, heat application, and a gentle laxative. Neuromuscular training may be recommended through yoga exercises. Aromatherapy is also available, and a course in transcendental meditation is taught for an extra fee. Sound therapy is the focus of the stress-reduction program.

Furnished with large beds and heavy but comfortable chairs, the high-ceiling rooms retain a look of luxury from the 1920s, when this was the country cottage of a shipping magnate involved with the *Titanic*.

Maharishi Ayur-Veda Health Center
679 George Hill Rd.,
Box 344, Lancaster, MA 01523
Tel. 508/365–4549
Fax 508/368–0674

Administration Director, Jay Glaser

Season Year-round.

Accommodations 14 bedrooms and several suites. Some small single rooms share a bath. All rooms air-conditioned.

Rates 1-week program $2,850–$3,950 single or double occupancy. Week-long deluxe Royal Program with suite $3,950 single, $3,450 per person double occupancy. No credit cards.

Meal Plans 3 vegetarian meals daily in the formal dining room or guests' rooms. Indian rice and dal with cooked vegetables, herb seasoning, and cooked fruit. Specialties include vegetable pâté. Bland diet with few fats and no dairy products other than milk. Herbal teas and lassa as recommended by the doctor.

Services and Facilities **Services:** Transcendental meditation (TM) instruction in stress-management techniques, psychophysiological audio program, self-pulse diagnosis, aromatherapy. Most programs include massages, herbal steam bath, heat treatments, and internal cleansing. **Evening Programs:** Videotapes and lectures on health-related topics.

Getting Here *From Boston.* By car, Massachusetts Turnpike (I–90) west to Rte. 495 north, exit on Rte. 117 West to Rte. 70. Entrance is on George Hill Rd. (about 3 hr). Limousine, rental car for local use.

Special Notes No smoking.

The Option Institute

Holistic health
Life enhancement
Spiritual awareness
Stress control

Massachusetts Sheffield The goal at the Option Institute, a mountain retreat, is to nurture healthy attitudes toward life rather than emphasize physical fitness. Personal attitudes, beliefs, and feelings are examined to develop a fuller understanding of how to improve one's physical and mental health. Working in group sessions and private consultations, participants are taught to be more accepting of themselves, to learn to find alternatives, and to form more loving relationships.

Founded in 1983 by Barry Neil Kaufman and Suzi Lyte Kaufman, who have written and lectured on interpersonal relationships, the Option Institute sets out to provide a stimulating environment for people from all walks of life. Young professionals as well as families of children with special needs come for weekends and intensive programs of up to eight weeks. A participant is expected to gain a profound sense of energy and vigor from the release of tensions. The 85-acre campus set amid grassy meadows, forests, and streams provides the setting that can inspire a fresh attitude toward life.

The Option Institute
R.D. 1, Box 174A, Sheffield, MA 01257
Tel. 413/229–2100
Fax 413/229–8831

Administration Program directors, Susan Abrams and Richard Magan

Season Year-round.

Accommodations Lodges have 18 bedrooms, each with 2 beds, shared bath, and shower. The simply furnished, newly constructed buildings use natural wood and lots of windows for an open, rustic feeling.

Rates 3-day weekends (Thurs.–Sun.) $395 per person double occupancy, meals included. 1-week intensives exploring the impact of attitude on body and health $995–$1,125. Specially designed programs, about $150 per day. Some kitchen-equipped cottages for families with autistic or learning-impaired children. 50% deposit. Credit cards: MC, V.

Meal Plans Vegetarian meals 3 times daily, buffet style. Specialties include vegetarian lasagna, whole-grain casseroles, legumes, seasonal vegetables, Greek salad, pasta. Limited amounts of eggs, cheese, milk.

Services and Facilities **Services:** Swedish massage; private counseling. **Swimming Facilities:** Pond. **Recreation Facilities:** Hiking the Appalachian Trail; downhill skiing at Butternut and Catamount, cross-country skiing. **Evening Programs:** Workshops and group discussions on health, personal relationships, communication.

In the Area Tanglewood Music Festival at Lenox, summer theater, the Sterling and Francine Clark Art Institute in Williamstown, Jacob's Pillow Dance Festival in Lee.

Getting Here *From New York City.* By car, I–95 to the Massachusetts Turnpike, exit for Sheffield (3 hr). By bus, Bonanza Bus Line (tel. 800/556–3815) from Port Authority Terminal to Sheffield (3 hr). By air, Bradley International Airport at Hartford/Springfield. Free pickup at bus station in Sheffield; private limousine service from airport.

Special Notes Limited access for people with disabilities. Special training for children who have mental disabilities, autism, or learning problems. No smoking indoors.

Rowe Conference Center

Spiritual awareness

Massachusetts **Rowe** Weekend programs to stimulate the mind on spiritual and health topics are the specialty of the Rowe Conference Center, a mountain retreat affiliated with the Unitarian Universalist Association. The white clapboard farmhouse and a pair of three-story lodges host a small, nondenominational community that offers a warm, uncompetitive atmosphere for personal and spiritual growth.

Surrounded by 1,400 acres of forest in western Massachusetts, Rowe provides a quiet place to discuss current health issues. Topics include clinical and spiritual healing, mastering the mind-body connection, and shamanism. Special weeks are devoted to adult recovery from alcohol problems, gender issues, and issues concerning single parenting.

The center is operated like a camp, but offers no organized fitness program and lets visitors take advantage of natural attractions on their own schedule. Recently expanded guest accommodations provide basic comforts, including a coed sauna. Guests do their own housekeeping; in the dormitory, bring your own bedding (linens available at extra charge).

Rowe Conference Center
Kings Highway Rd., Rowe, MA 01367
Tel. 413/339–4216

Administration Administrative assistant, Barbara Rivard

Season Year-round.

Accommodations 12 private bedrooms, all with semiprivate bath and 2 beds, linens, and towels. Also dormitory rooms for 6–8 people.

Rates Weekend program $110–$170 (depending on guests' financial situation). Room and meals $120 per person double occupancy, $150 single, $90 dormitory. All require deposit. Credit cards: MC, V.

Meal Plans Meals from Fri. dinner to Sun. lunch. Vegetarian food served family style, including homemade bread, lentil loaf, squash casserole, and pasta primavera. Eggs and dairy products served, meat on request; special diets accommodated.

Services and Facilities **Services:** Swedish massage. **Swimming Facilities:** Lake. **Recreation Facilities:** Hiking, cross-country and downhill skiing. **Evening Programs:** Discussion groups, sweat lodge.

Getting Here *From Boston.* By car, Mass. Turnpike or Rte. 2 to Hwy. 91 in Greenfield, MA, then west on Rte. 2 (the Mohawk Trail) 19 mi to Rowe (3 hr). By bus, Peter Pan Line (tel. 413/781–2900) to Greenfield (2¾ hr). Pickup by Rowe on request.

Special Notes Guest house accessible for people with wheelchairs. Summer camp for children; weeks for 4th graders to high school seniors. No smoking indoors. Bring sheets and blanket for dormitory rooms.

Smith College Adult Camp

Sports conditioning
Vibrant maturity

Massachusetts
Northampton

Based on the campus of Smith College in the scenic Berkshire Mountains, this one-week program offers cross-training with professionals and faculty members in a variety of sports. In addition to tennis, squash, swimming, and track there is a fully equipped gym.

Scheduled activities include aerobics classes, yoga, tai chi chuan, and group hikes. Organized bike trips and outings to nearby attractions are available at no additional charge. Also offered is an introduction to stress control using biofeedback equipment.

Nutrition and dietary consultations with the staff nutritionist helps those concerned with weight loss. Meals are served cafeteria style in the college dining hall; vegetarian meals can be provided with advance request.

Limited to 35 participants, the program attracts a mix of men and women. Average age, 50; minimum age, 22.

Smith College Adult Camp
Northampton, MA 01063
Tel. 413/585–3975
Fax 413/585-2712

Administration Manager, James A. Johnson

Season June.

Accommodations Dormitory rooms with 2 beds, shared bathroom. Laundry room.

Rates $650 for the 6-day program, includes room, meals, activities, 50% advance payment. No credit cards.

Meal Plan 3 meals daily.

Services and Facilities **Services:** Massage. **Exercise Equipment:** Eagle weight training gym, indoor and outdoor running tracks. **Swimming Facilities:** 25-yd. indoor pool, lake. **Recreation Facilities:** 12 indoor tennis courts (lighted, Mondo surface), 4 outdoor tennis courts, 6 squash courts. **Evening Programs:** Orienteering, panel discussions, dances, cookouts.

Getting Here *From Boston.* By car, Mass. Turnpike (I–90) to Hwy. 91, Northampton exit (2½ hr). By bus, Peter Pan Lines (413/781–2900) to Northampton (3 hrs). Rental car available.

Waterville Valley Resort

Nonprogram resort

New Hampshire
Waterville Valley

Surrounded by mountain peaks and forests of green fir and silver birch, this 500-acre recreational complex became a four-season resort in 1987 with the opening of a $2-million sports center. The use of the facilities is a bonus for guests at the deluxe lodges and condominiums of the Waterville Valley Resort. In warm weather, you can play tennis on one of 18 clay courts, use mountain bikes, in-line skates, or play golf with a $20 recreation pass sold daily at your lodge. In winter, world-class downhill and cross-country skiing covers 225 acres. Services and classes at the center are offered on an à la carte basis.

At the foot of Mt. Tecumseh a full-service ski shop rents equipment and offers instruction. Thirty-five downhill trails are ranked for beginner, intermediate, and advanced skiers. Snowmaking equipment assures good snow conditions from mid-November through mid-April. The Cross Country Ski Center at one end of the valley is another attraction. Fourteen trails lead into the heart of the forest.

The Sports Center, open every day of the year, offers indoor and outdoor tennis and swimming, racquetball, squash, and a weights room. A coed sauna and Jacuzzi are available in addition to separate facilities and steam rooms for men and women.

The range of activities makes Waterville Valley a good choice for family vacations. A community bus service provides free transportation all day.

Waterville Valley Resort
Box 417, Waterville Valley, NH 03215
Tel. 603/236–8303; reservations 800/468–2553

Administration Sports center manager, Ralph Trinque.

Season Year-round.

Accommodations 4,000 beds in quarters that range in variety from deluxe chalet-style inns to modest condominium apartments. Leading choices are Snowy Owl Inn, Black Bear Lodge, and fully equipped 2-story houses. Bookings through the lodging bureau.

Rates 1-bedroom apartments at the Black Bear $119–$281 daily for 1 to 2 persons. Add 8% tax. 50% advance payment. Credit cards: AE, DC, MC, V.

Meal Plans No meals in ski or spa packages. Spa food at 2 restaurants: O'Keefe's has vegetarian burgers, fitness salads; Chili Peppers has light fare such as broiled fish, fruit plate with cottage cheese, roast chicken.

Services and Facilities **Exercise Equipment:** 4 Nautilus, 1 lats unit, Lifecycle, Alpine stairclimber, rowing machine, free weights. **Services:** Swedish massage, aerobics classes, aquacise. **Swimming Facilities:** Indoor and outdoor 25-m pools, pond. **Recreation Facilities:** 2 indoor tennis courts, 2 racquetball courts, squash court, indoor running track, golf, canoeing, horseback riding, skiing, ice skating, hiking, sailing, biking. **Evening Programs:** Seasonal entertainment.

In the Area Mt. Washington cog railway.

Getting Here *From Boston.* By car, Rte. 3 to I–93, exit for Waterville (28), then 11 mi on Rte. 49 (2½ hr). By bus, Greyhound to North Conway, NH (3 hr). By air, scheduled flights to Manchester, NH. Rental car, Valley shuttle bus available.

Special Notes Ramps and elevator in Sports Center will accommodate wheelchairs. Sports Center open 8 AM–9:30 PM daily. Ski camps, tennis camps, and outdoor wading pool for children. No smoking in Sports Center.

Aegis

Spiritual awareness

New York
New Lebanon A philosophy of the interrelatedness of all spiritual traditions is at the heart of the study programs offered by Aegis in historic Shaker buildings on the grounds of a 430-acre mountaintop compound. Life is celebrated here in all its diversity with topics ranging from Taoist healing to Zen dance. A visit is an experience in living together harmoniously and learning how to share life's bounty.

Founded in 1975 as an esoteric school for the Sufi Order in the West, the permanent community here is known as the "Abode of the Message." The teachings of their spiritual leaders, notably Pir Vilayat Inayat Khan, focus on the nature of healing. The Sufi path is explored at weekend retreats and in a summer series of workshops and retreats.

Aegis brings together people from diverse walks of life in a common quest for self-fulfillment and inner growth. You can pitch a tent or work in the kitchen at the Abode as part of a personal retreat. Each weekend program attracts up to 75 participants.

Aegis
R.D. 1, Box 1030D, New Lebanon, NY 12125
Tel. 518/794–8095 or 518/794–8090

Season Year-round.

Accommodations	Log cabins with 2–4 beds, shared bathroom. 1-person huts, and camping space in the woods; rooms and dormitory shared in the Abode community. Washhouses have hot showers and toilets for men and women. Bedding and towels not provided.
Rates	2-day weekend tuition $75 plus lodging. Rooms for 2, $45–$68, single $40 per night, including meals. Tent space $20 with meals. 50% advance payment. Credit cards: MC, V.
Meal Plans	3 vegetarian meals a day, with dairy and nondairy choices.
Services and Facilities	**Swimming Facilities:** Nearby lakes. **Recreation Facilities:** Hiking, cross-country skiing.
Getting Here	Located between Albany, NY, and Pittsfield, MA, the Abode provides pickup service at Bonanza Bus Lines (tel. 800/556-3815) station, and at Albany airport. *By train,* Amtrak to Albany (2 hrs). *From New York City.* By car, Taconic Pkwy. north to Rte. 295, Rte. 22 to Rte. 20 in New Lebanon.
Special Notes	No smoking in communal areas. Remember to bring sleeping bag or bedding, warm clothing, insect repellent. No children.

Gurney's Inn

Luxury pampering

New York
Montauk

At the International Health and Beauty Spa the specialty is seawater therapy by the water. Located on the tip of Long Island, with all the amenities of a big beach resort, the spa at Gurney's Inn draws on the ocean for inspiration. The sybarite can revel in seaweed baths, swim in a 60-foot indoor seawater pool, have a seaweed facial, and dine on seafood while enjoying a view of the sea. Modeled after European spas where ocean water is an integral part of advanced hydrotherapy, Gurney's adds aerobics, stress control, diet programs, and beauty-salon services.

Sea air and miles of white sandy beach come with your room at the inn. Brisk morning walks along the shore start the daily program. Add to that a 14-station parcourse, with instruction twice daily, for exercise at your own pace. Invigorated by the ocean, you can join an aquatics exercise class in the pool, relax in a sunken Roman bath, or swim in the surf.

The diversity of the seawater treatments makes Gurney's special among spas on this side of the Atlantic. Filtered and heated water from the ocean is pumped into whirlpools designed for underwater massage, mixed with volcanic mud from Italy, used in wraps with seaweed products from France, and added to body scrubs with salt from the Dead Sea. Treatments are scheduled 8 AM–10 PM. Spa-plan guests receive priority.

The spa building is a world apart from the convention and timeshare vacation crowds that keep Gurney's Inn busy much of the year. The pool and classes are open to all guests, however, and this puts a strain on the facilities during the peak summer season. For peace and quiet, schedule your visit when the beach crowd goes home or during the winter.

Gurney's Inn
Old Montauk Hwy., Montauk, NY 11954
Tel. 516/668-2345 or 800/445-8062 in NY, CT, and PA;
spa 516/668-2509

Administration Innkeepers, Lola and Nick Monte; spa director, Margaret McNeill-Byrnes

Season Year-round.

Accommodations 126 bedrooms in time-share rentals, including suites and cottages. None connect to the spa. All are air-conditioned, have full modern bathroom, TV, telephone; some with seaview from balcony.

Rates 5-day Marine Renewal plan, $490 plus accommodations; fall-winter-spring "Escape" 3-day package without room $523 per person; 5-day Health and Beauty Plan package $675 per person. Lodging $130–$155 per person double occupancy, $230–$290 single. Daily facility fee for nonpackage visit $16.50; 1-day package $280. Add 15% service charge, 8.5% tax. 25% payable in advance. Credit cards: AE, DC, MC, V.

Meal Plans 3 spa meals daily included in packages. Spa cuisine in a private room and the main dining room. Calorie-controlled meals (1,000–1,200 calories per day) low in salt and sugar. Lunch can begin with tortellini en brodo or egg-drop soup, 3-bean salad; entrée choice of manicotti, grilled salmon, steak stirfry, or whole-wheat pasta. Dinner entrées include seafood brochette, paella, vegetarian lasagna, chicken breast with asparagus. Herbal teas and espresso are available, as are vegetarian meals on request.

Services and Facilities **Exercise Equipment:** 15-station Universal gym, 4 Nautilus units, 2 Lifestep, 2 Lifecycle, Maxicam, 2 treadmills, dumbbells (3–75 lb), Olympic plates (2½–45 lb). **Services:** Massage, loofah scrub, herbal or seaweed wrap, facial, fango pack, aromatherapy, seawater private bath; health/fitness profile, biofeedback, private training. Full-service salon. **Swimming Facilities:** Indoor pool, ocean beach. **Recreation Facilities:** Hiking, jogging, disco dancing, yoga; tennis and horseback riding nearby; golf at Montauk Downs public course. **Evening Programs:** Lectures on health and nutrition; dancing and entertainment.

In the Area Historic homes, art galleries, whale-watching, museum, wineries, and boutiques in Montauk; summer theater; bird-watching.

Getting Here *From Connecticut and New England.* By ferry, at New London and Bridgeport. *From New York City.* By bus, Hampton Jitney and Montauk Express. By car, Long Island Expressway to Sunrise Highway (Rte. 27). By train, from Grand Central Station, the Long Island Railroad (tel. 212/526–0900) has daily round-trip schedules. By air, USAir has scheduled flights to MacArthur Airport at Islip, private planes land at Montauk and East Hampton airports. Courtesy car meets trains and private planes. Rental car, taxi available.

Special Notes Children's swimming at midday and after 6 PM; under 18 not permitted in spa treatment areas. No smoking in the spa.

Living Springs Lifestyle Center

Preventive medicine
Vibrant maturity

New York
Putnam Valley

A budget-priced alternative to health resorts, the Living Springs Lifestyle Center, run by the Seventh-Day Adventists, is a residential retreat where you can improve your life and tone your body with spa-quality treatments. It's nondenominational and open to persons of all faiths, particularly to people over 50 who want to recharge their lives holistically. The medically supervised educational and conditioning programs focus on disease prevention, stress control, nutrition, weight management, and quitting smoking.

Set on 68 acres at the edge of a clear lake in the Taconic Mountains, the retreat, which was founded in 1977 as a nonprofit corporation, offers a homelike atmosphere that can be conducive to establishing lasting new habits. Healthy cooking is taught, and methods for preventing heart and other diseases are discussed. Daily exercise is geared to your level of fitness and personal goals.

The holistic approach teaches you how to focus on weight management, smoking cessation, and lifestyle enhancement. The center has a resident physician, and offers a medical package with tests and consultations. Following a consultation, you can schedule hydrotherapy treatments to promote healing or focus on relaxation. Saunas, alternating hot and cold showers, and exercise are also prescribed.

Natural foods and lots of spring water are key nutritional features, and the retreat specializes in vegetarian meals that are high in complex carbohydrates and fiber and free of fats and oil. (Also note that the kitchen is kosher.)

Living Springs Lifestyle Center
136 Bryant Pond Rd., Putnam Valley, NY 10579
Tel. 914/526–2800 or 800/729–9355

Administration Manager, Charles Cleveland; medical director, David DeRose, M.D.

Season Year-round.

Accommodations 2-level modern lodge with 5 semiprivate rooms, 3 private rooms.

Rates 7-day program $895 in private room, $695 semiprivate. Medical plan $1,045 in private room, $845 sharing. $100 payable in advance. Credit cards: MC, V.

Meal Plans 3 meals a day, buffet style. Lunch can include steamed vegetables, cashew chow mein, salad, fruit. No coffee or spices.

Services and Facilities **Exercise Equipment:** Treadmill, rowing ergometer, 2 stationary bikes; outdoor parcourse. **Swimming Facilities:** Spring-fed lake. **Recreation Facilities:** Hiking and nature trails, boating; cross-country skiing; biking. **Evening Programs:** Lectures and films on health-related topics.

In the Area West Point, Bear Mountain.

Getting Here *From New York City.* By car, Taconic Pkwy. to Rte. 6 exit. By train, from Grand Central Station, Metro-North Commuter to

Peekskill (free transfers). Pickup at airports on request. Courtesy car available.

Special Notes No smoking.

Mohonk Mountain House

Life enhancement
Sports conditioning

New York
New Paltz

Nature walks have been a way of life at Mohonk Mountain House in the Hudson River Valley since 1875, and members of the founding family of Quakers are still active in organizing health and fitness weeks. Hikers, runners, and cross-country skiers choose from more than 100 miles of trails, paths, and carriage roads that link scenic sites within the 2,500 acres of private woodland. Others ride horseback or enjoy the crystal-clear lake.

In the hotel, a turreted and gabled Victorian structure that rambles an eighth of a mile and accommodates up to 500 guests, 19th-century manners and ambience are preserved. Choice rooms in the towers have original Victorian woodwork, working fireplace, balcony. There is no bar or smoking in public rooms, and a dress code is in effect for dinner.

Golfers are challenged by a nine-hole par-35 course designed along Scottish lines, complete with driving net, and there is a lighted 18-hole putting green. Equestrians can join guided trail rides, English or Western, at the resort's stables. In winter, the riding trails are groomed for cross-country skiing. Indoors, the fitness center has exercise equipment, an aerobics studio with ballet bar, and saunas and showers. Low-impact aerobics and stretch classes are scheduled regularly, as are classes in nutrition and back care. Physiologists, sports trainers, and fitness buffs get together at Mohonk for exercise workshops and lectures. Programs range from designing a personal fitness plan to nutrition and kinesiology. Weeks are devoted to quitting smoking, stress management, and the holistic way.

Mohonk Mountain House
Lake Mohonk, New Paltz, NY 12561
Tel. 914/255-1000, 914/255-4500, or 800/772-6646

Administration President, Bert Smiley; general manager, Gillian Murphy; fitness director, Geri Owens

Season Year-round.

Accommodations 300 rooms, many with balcony and working fireplace, some with washbasin only, some sharing an adjoining bath. Rooms and bed-sitting rooms with private bath, double or twin beds.

Rates Rooms and 3 meals daily $145–$277 single occupancy, $237–$359 for 2 persons; tower room with fireplace $420 for 2 persons. Add 15% service charge, taxes. Deposit: 1 night payable in advance. Credit cards: AE, DC, MC, V.

Meal Plans 3 meals and afternoon tea included with room. The menu follows the American resort tradition, with some light selections. Buffet-style lunch.

Services and Facilities	**Exercise Equipment:** 6-station Universal gym, 2 Schwinn Air Dyne bikes, 2 Monark bikes, StairMaster, Lifecycle, Nordic-Track cross-country unit, hand weights. **Services:** Massage. **Swimming Facilities:** Mohonk Lake, ½-mi-long 60-ft-deep freshwater lake with swimming and diving areas. **Spa Facilities:** Separate saunas for men and women. **Recreation Facilities:** 6 tennis courts (4 clay, 2 Har-Tru), platform tennis courts; 9-hole golf course; ice skating and downhill skiing; croquet. **Evening Programs:** Concerts, films, dancing; speakers on health and fitness.
In the Area	Carriage rides, trail rides, hayrides.
Getting Here	*From New York City.* By car, New York State Thruway (I–87) to New Paltz (Exit 18). By train, Amtrak to Poughkeepsie. By bus, (Port Authority Terminal) and other cities served by Adirondack Trailways. Hotel transfer service to bus or train station and New York City and airports.
Special Notes	Weekday outdoor adventures and walks for children. No smoking in public areas indoors.

Mountain Valley Health Resort

Luxury pampering
Nutrition and diet
Weight management

New York
Hunter Mountain
Shedding 7–10 pounds per week is the goal of most guests at the Mountain Valley Health Resort, which opened here in 1992. (It was formerly the Garden Spa, in Colt's Neck, New Jersey.) Set on 23 acres at the base of Hunter Mountain, the resort displays the backdrop and foreground of the majestic Catskill mountain range. Hiking trails lead into the Catskill State Park, and the Hunter Mountain Ski Center is only a mile away.

A brief medical background check and orientation is given for new arrivals. The spa director determines your level of fitness and your nutritional needs. A computerized body-composition analysis (additional fee) may be recommended. The program includes daily massage, full fitness program with low-impact aerobics, step aerobics, swimnastics, stretching, toning, yoga, and guided walks. There is no mandatory schedule or arrival day.

Mountain Valley Health Resort
Rte. 214, Box 395, Hunter, NY 12442
Tel. 518/263–4919 or 800/232–2772
Fax 518/263–4994

Administration	Director, Natalie Skolnik
Season	Year-round.
Accommodations	32 rooms, each with private bath, color TV (with cable and satellite), telephone. Some rooms are lofts with skylights, 2 have whirlpool bath.
Rates	Weekly (7 nights) package rates $595–$1,150. 4-night packages $450–$850 Weekend packages (3 nights) $350–$750. Add tax and 15% service charge. Deposit $200–$300. Credit cards: AE, D, MC, V.

Meal Plans 3 meals daily based on 650-, 900-, or 1,200-calorie diets; optional juice fast, vegetarian meals, and special dietary requests. Breakfasts feature egg-white omelet, hearty grain
cereals, and fresh fruit. Lunches offer tomato bisque, zucchini
lasagne, spinach frittata. Dining-room service, candlelight
dinners include Cornish game hen with apple glaze, chicken
Parmesan, flounder Florentine, haddock with Creole sauce,
chocolate mousse.

Services and **Exercise Equipment:** 3 treadmills, StairMaster, 2 recumbant
Facilities bicycles, rowing machine. **Services:** Theraputic massage,
reflexology, shiatsu, facial, seaweed and cellulite body wraps,
exfoliating body polish, body waxing, manicure, pedicure. Individual nutritional fitness and stress counseling available.
Body-composition analysis, cholesterol testing, Innerquest behavior-modification technology. **Swimming Facilities:** Indoor
pool and heated outdoor pool. **Recreation Facilities:** 2 tennis
courts, basketball and volleyball courts, hiking trails, cross-
country skiing.

Getting Here *From New York City.* New York Thruway to Exit 19 (Kingston), Rte. 28 west to Phoenicia, follow signs to Exit 214 north
(Pine Hill, 2 hrs away). Mountain Valley Health Resort will be
15 min farther on the left.

Special Notes Ramps and some ground-floor rooms offer access people with
disabilities. No smoking in public areas but smoking and no-
smoking rooms are available.

New Age Health Spa

Holistic health
Life enhancement
Nutrition and diet
Sports conditioning
Weight management

New York Committed to a holistic lifestyle, the New Age Health Spa is a
Neversink country retreat that offers a wide range of physical treatments
to enhance your new appearance. The tranquil, 160-acre farm
estate in the Catskill Mountains is an ideal setting in which to
balance body, soul, and mind.

The farm is a full-fledged spa whose owners live on the ground
and are active in all the decision-making. They have added
sophisticated bodywork as well as stress management and
preventive medicine therapies. An Outward Bound type of
challenge course features a 45-foot alpine tower, used for building corporate teamwork and teaching self-reliance.

No one goes hungry here, but diet options are offered at a dedicated table in the dining room. The daily menu is planned along
guidelines set by the American Heart Association (high carbohydrates; low protein, fats, and salt; no sugar). For determined
dieters, "juicing" is the recommended program for fast weight
loss, and supervised participants are advised to sign up for an
accompanying colonic cleansing, a water treatment that serves
to speed up "detoxification" of the body. Other food plans include Spartan (700- to 800-calorie vegetarian) and Rotation
(900- to 1,100-calorie plan consisting of vegetarian meals alternating with a fish, turkey, or chicken meal).

The programs allow you to set your own pace; opt for exercises in Zen meditation, a tai chi chuan class, or a 3- to 5-mile aerobic walk before breakfast. Move on to a weight-management lecture followed by a series of innovative low-impact aerobics and floor-work classes that enable you to match activities to your energy level.

With the expansion of the spa building in 1994, there are 14 massage rooms and two wet rooms, and separate saunas and steambaths for men and women. Options include herbal wraps, facials, treatments with paraffin or Dead Sea mud, and weight training.

New Age Health Spa
Rte. 55, Neversink, NY 12765
Tel. 914/985-7601 or 800/682-4348
Fax 914/985-2467

Administration Owner-directors, Stephanie Paradise and Werner Mendel; fitness director, Sandra Lachaga

Season Year-round.

Accommodations 39 rooms in 2-story cottages, each with "country charm" decor, air-conditioning, private bath. TV and phone in main house lounge.

Rates 1-week package, including diet and exercise program, $699–$969 per person double occupancy. Single and triple rooms available. Mini-week package (Sun.–Fri.) with 2 spa services $665–$885 per person double, $910 single. Add 15% service charge, 8% tax. 25% payable in advance. Credit cards: AE, MC, V.

Meal Plans 3 meals daily included in package rates. Salad bar and fresh vegetables grown in the spa's greenhouses featured with such dinner entrées as vegetarian lasagna, poached fish and baked chicken. Special dietary requests accommodated. Juice fast available with staff consultation.

Services and Facilities **Exercise Equipment:** 2 StairMasters, 3 treadmills, Cat's Eye rowing machine, NordicTrack, stationary bikes, free weights, weight training circuit. **Services:** Massage (Swedish, shiatsu, sports), herbal wrap, loofah scrub, colonic, Dea Sea mud body mask, paraffin body waxing, aromatherapy. Salon for hair, nail, skin care. **Swimming Facilities:** Indoor lap pool (30′ × 50′), outdoor pool. **Recreation Facilities:** Volleyball; cross-country skiing and snowshoeing. **Evening Programs:** Talks on healthy living and personal growth; workshops in astrology, psychology, awareness; movies, disco.

In the Area Grossinger resort (golf), Lake Minnewaska (nature preserve), Hudson Valley (historic homes).

Getting Here *From New York City.* By New Agevan, express service Fri. and Sun. morning and return ($40 each way) at 72nd St. & Madison Ave. By bus, Greyhound from Port Authority (2 hr). By car, New York State Thruway (I–87) to the Catskills, Rte. 17 to Liberty, Rte. 52 and 55E to Neversink (2 hr). Local taxi available.

Special Notes No children under 16; no alcohol, smoking, or drugs. Bring personal radio with earphones, clock, flashlight.

Omega Institute

Holistic health
Life enhancement
Preventive medicine
Spiritual awareness
Stress control

New York
Rhinebeck

Call it a New Age mecca or a quest for higher consciousness; it's chiefly an adult summer camp where you can strive to develop physical and mental balance alongside people on the leading edge of preventive medicine and holistic health.

Sometimes referred to as Esalen East, the Omega Institute brings together people of different backgrounds—doctors, lawyers, housewives, college students—who want to function more positively as individuals and as members of society. More than 250 educational workshops, from Native American studies to wellness and stress control, last two to five days. The classes, including diet workshops and "Shamanic Journey, Power and Healing," are led by faculty and guest lecturers comprising a veritable *Who's Who* of the human potential movement.

Located about 100 miles north of Manhattan, the rustic, 80-acre campus features a new Wellness Center complete with sauna, massage rooms, flotation tanks, nutrition- and stress-reduction counseling, and holistic medical consultations. On campus are a theater, gift and bookshops, and cafe. Yet there's not a Nautilus gym in sight.

A Wellness Week integrates study and practice of a healthy lifestyle. Omega's core faculty offers a sound medical understanding of the roles that diet, nutrition, exercise, and fitness play in the ongoing development of health. Through experiential sessions in massage, yoga, tai chi chuan, group support, and games, each participant forms a positive attitude toward wellness.

On a typical morning, when as many as 350 people are camping out or living in the dormitories and cottages, groups assemble before breakfast for optional yoga, meditation, and tai chi chuan sessions.

Omega Institute
260 Lake Dr., Rhinebeck, NY 12572
Tel. 914/266-4444 or 800/944-1001
Fax 914/266-4828

Administration
Program director, Thomas Valente; general manager, Skip Backus; president, Stephan Rechtschaffen, M.D.

Season
June–mid-Oct. Winter programs in the Caribbean, New Mexico, and New England.

Accommodations
Rooms in cottages, dormitory beds, camping facilities. Private rooms with shared bath. No rooms have TV, phone, or air-conditioning.

Rates
5-day Omega Wellness Program tuition $285 plus lodging. Accommodations in dormitory for 5-day program $200; cottage rooms for 5-day program $285–$350 per person, double occupancy (limited number of single rooms available). 2-day lodging $98 dormitory, $138–$170 rooms. Campsites $40 per person,

per day. Meals and tax included in lodging fee. 50% payment in advance. Credit cards: MC, V.

Meal Plans Cafeteria service of 3 meals daily included in lodging. Mainly vegetarian, with some fish and dairy products. Many locally grown fresh fruits and vegetables. Whole grains, beans, and bean products. No artificial sweeteners.

Services and Facilities **Swimming Facilities:** Private lake. **Services:** Massage, aromatherapy, counseling in nutrition, antistress, wellness. **Recreation Facilities:** Basketball, canoeing, jogging, tennis, volleyball. **Evening Programs:** Concerts, films, lectures.

In the Area The historic village of Rhinebeck, Old Rhinebeck Aerodrome.

Getting Here *From New York City.* By car, New York State Thruway (I–87) or the Saw Mill River Parkway north to the Taconic Parkway, Bull's Head Rd. west to Lake Dr. (2 hr); By train, Amtrak from Grand Central Station stops at Rhinecliff, where Omega vans pick up guests (for train schedules, tel. 800/872–7245). By bus, Bonanza Bus Line (tel. 800/556–3815) from Port Authority Terminal to Rhinebeck (2 hr). Omega vans pick up in Rhinebeck at Beekman Arms Hotel.

Special Notes Some cottages and facilities equipped for people with disabilities. Family Week in August includes nature studies and creative games for children. No smoking indoors.

Omni Sagamore Resort & Spa

Luxury pampering

New York
Bolton Landing
Surrounded by the Adirondack Mountains and set on a 70-acre private island, the huge white clapboard Omni Sagamore Resort & Spa suggests an escape to the quiet pleasures of a bygone era. Rejuvenated by new owners, the resort now includes a modern health club, indoor swimming pool, and indoor tennis and racquetball courts. Fitness classes are scheduled throughout the day, from walks and low-impact aerobics to water exercise, at no charge to hotel guests who book one or more spa treatments and services.

The health club has separate sauna, whirlpool, and steam-room facilities for men and women. There is a coed exercise area, with newly expanded space to accommodate the equipment, and a wet area specially equipped for body scrubs. Appointments are made for treatment on an à la carte basis, which includes the daily charge for club facilities and workout clothing. A flexible spa plan is available for two days or more.

In addition to massage, facials, and beauty makeovers, the specialty here is moormud therapy using natural healing mud from an Austrian moor, Neydharting, in body wraps, facial and scalp treatments, and packs for sports injuries. You can wind down your treatment with a full-body rubdown using a mixture of sea salt and massage oil that leaves your skin tingling. After the scrub with loofah sponges, the salt mixture is hosed off. Next, peppermint soap is applied, leaving you with a glowing feeling. The cost: $30–$70 for each treatment; or this could be included as part of a two-day spa package. (A 17% gratuity is added to the cost of services.)

The classic 1930 hotel is on the site of the original Sagamore, opened in 1893. Recent additions include seven lakeside lodges. At the fitness center you can work out and enjoy an unbroken vista of Adirondack State Park.

Omni Sagamore Resort & Spa
Box 450, Bolton Landing, NY 12814
Tel. 518/644–9400 or 800/358–3585
Fax 518/644–3033

Administration Manager, Robert MacIntosh; spa director, Damian Alessi

Season Year-round.

Accommodations 350 rooms, including 178 deluxe suites, and cottages. The main hotel's 100 rooms embody history and contemporary comfort. Condominium-style suites in new lodges.

Rates Weekend Spa Sampler $279 plus lodging. Spa Day $89–$195 (accommodations not included). Rooms $85–$390 per night in main hotel, lodges $79–$295 Deposit: 1 night payable in advance. Add $4 daily service charge, tax. Spa gratuity and tax included in package rate. Credit cards: AE, MC, V.

Meal Plans Meals not included in spa plan. Choices from Trillium restaurant's dinner menu include as appetizers seafood terrine or fresh berries, spinach consommé, green salad. Entrée choices include poached salmon, grilled chicken breast, linguine. Desserts are apple strudel or blueberry cake, Grand Marnier Bavarian. 5 restaurants provide low-calorie options, emphasizing fish and local produce.

Services and Facilities **Exercise Equipment:** 10-station Keiser training circuit, 3 StairMasters, 2 Lifecycles, 2 Trotter treadmills, 3 Concept 2 rowers, Windracer, free weights. **Services:** Massage (Swedish, shiatsu, sports), loofah salt glow, reflexology, facials, herbal wrap, seaweed and mud wrap, aromatherapy. 4 aerobics classes daily including aquacise, step aerobics, stretching; beauty salon. **Swimming Facilities:** Indoor pool; lakeside docks. **Recreation Facilities:** 18-hole golf course, 4 outdoor lighted and 2 indoor tennis courts, jogging trails, hiking, boating, water sports; snowsledding, ice skating, cross-country and downhill skiing, tobogganing; horseback riding and horse-drawn sleigh rides. **Evening Programs:** Dancing, jazz club, scheduled entertainment.

In the Area Cruises on Lake George aboard a classic 72-foot Morgan wooden yacht, the Adirondack Museum (history and art), Fort Ticonderoga (circa 1755 war memorabilia), the Hyde Collection (European and American art), Saratoga Springs' Victorian area, summer season of concerts, ballet, and horse races (Saratoga Springs), Colonial Fort William Henry (setting for *Last of the Mohicans*), Lake George Village.

Getting Here *From New York City.* By car, 4-hr drive on the New York State Thruway (I–87) to Exit 24 (Bolton Landing). By air, Albany is served by Eastern, USAir, and Continental airlines, among others. By train, Amtrak to Fort Edward, from Boston or New York City. A hotel car meets guests at Albany or the train station ($50 round-trip).

Special Notes No smoking in the spa. Facilities charge ($15) includes shorts, T-shirts, robe, slippers.

Saratoga Spa State Park

Taking the waters

New York
Saratoga Springs

Once a rival of Europe's glamorous spas, Saratoga is better known today for Thoroughbred racing and the arts. But the mineral springs at Saratoga Spa State Park remain a major attraction, and plans are underway to develop a complete health and fitness center in some of the original buildings. Meanwhile, the Roosevelt Bath operates year-round, and the Lincoln Baths are open during July and August.

The mineral-rich water bubbles up all around the town, but at the park you can drink for free; in town you pay for the bottled water. Pick up a map from the Old Drink Hall, downtown, or the spa visitor center operated by the State of New York. If you park at the Geyser Picnic Area lot and follow the path, you will encounter three of the best-known springs, all of the saline-alkaline variety. First is the Hayes Well, which has a breathing port at one side for inhaling carbon dioxide—said to be good for the lungs and sinuses. The gas also carbonates the water and powers geysers that spout up 10 feet or higher at this spot.

For a diuretic effect, try Hathorn Spring No. 1, a block east of Broadway on Spring Street. This water contains large amounts of sulfur, iron, lime, and other minerals. Dense, green-tinted, and faintly smelly, it has been prescribed for everything from sinus to complexion problems.

More palatable is the 90-minute relaxer offered spa visitors: a 15- to 25-minute mineral bath followed by a half-hour massage, then a 30-minute rest. Your float in the salty, effervescent warm mineral water induces relaxation by slowing breathing; studies have shown that some carbon dioxide is absorbed through the skin, where it dilates the blood vessels, improves circulation, and aids the flow of blood. Wrapped in warm sheets, you cool down before enjoying a relaxing massage. The cost of this treatment varies according to season; it is $36–$40 in July and August.

The Gideon Putnam Hotel, a sprawling, neo-Georgian lodging with old-fashioned country-club charm, was built during the New Deal era, refurbished 1992, and is the only hotel in the spa park. However, to get a full taste of the town and its Victorian landmarks, stay at the venerable Adelphi Hotel on Broadway, built in 1870 and lovingly restored by the current owners.

Saratoga Spa State Park
The Gideon Putnam
Box 476, Ave. of the Pines, Saratoga Springs, NY 12866
Tel. 518/584–3000
Fax 518/584–1354

Administration Manager, Kenneth Boyles

Season Year-round.

Accommodations 132 rooms, 12 suites, with traditional furnishings, modern bathroom. All have phone, flowered drapery, TV, air-conditioning.

Rates 2-night package $264 for 2, double occupancy (lower Nov.–Apr.). Program includes mineral baths, meals, raceway pass, gratuities, taxes. Daily rate $114–$236 single or double. Suites from $104. Add tax, optional gratuity. 1 night payable in advance. Credit cards: AE, DC, MC, V.

Meal Plans   Salads and light cuisine on the spa menu.

Services and Facilities   **Services:** Swedish massage, baths, hot pack. **Swimming Facilities:** Victoria Pool in the spa park ($5), Great Scandaga Lake in nearby Adirondack State Park. **Spa Facilities:** Mineral-water baths in private tubs at the spartan facilities of Roosevelt Bath No. 1 (518/584–2011); semiprivate at Lincoln Baths (518/584–2010). Days and times of operation vary with season; call for reservations. **Recreation Facilities:** 8 free public tennis courts and 2 golf courses in the spa park; hiking trails at Spruce Mountain near town; guided history walks; jogging in Congress Park. **Evening Programs:** the Saratoga Performing Arts Center (tel. 518/587–3330) in Spa State Park presents the New York City Ballet in July, the Philadelphia Orchestra in Aug., and popular and jazz artists. Dance companies perform at the Little Theater (tel. 518/587–3330).

In the Area   900 buildings on the National Register of Historic Places; tours include the rose garden at the Yaddo artists' colony and the 1864 gable-roof clubhouse at the track. Polo matches and a harness-racing track nearby. Saratoga Battlefield National Historical Park has a scenic 9.5-mi drive open to bicyclists. Museums in former spa buildings are devoted to dance, racing, and local history.

Getting Here   *From New York City.* By car, New York Thruway (I–87; 3½ hrs away). By train, Amtrak from Montreal (3 hrs), Boston, and New York City. By air, USAir flights to Albany. By bus, Adirondack Trailways (tel. 800/858–8555). Rental car at airport; taxi in town. Park admission: $3 per car, free for Gideon Putnam hotel guests.

Special Notes   Specially equipped baths and rooms for people with disabilities. Nonsmoking rooms available. Remember to bring drinking cups.

Sivananda Ashram Yoga Ranch

Spiritual awareness

New York
Woodbourne   When stressed-out urbanites join members of the farm community to exercise and meditate or to jog through 80 acres of woods and fields, the effect is spiritual as well as physical. Guests from diverse social and professional backgrounds around the world meet at Sivananda Ashram Yoga Ranch to share their interest in yoga.

Morning and evening, everyone participates in classes devoted to traditional yogic exercise and breathing techniques. The dozen asana positions range from a headstand to a spinal twist, and each has specific benefits for the body. You will be taught that proper breathing, *pranayama*, is essential for energy control.

The daily schedule includes meditation and chanting at 6 AM and 8 PM, yogic posture and breathing exercise classes at 8 AM and 4 PM, and vegetarian meals served at 10 AM and 6 PM. Participation in program activities is mandatory, including karma yoga classes and various talks on yogic practice and philosophy. The ideal is to become harmoniously balanced; the discipline can provide physical, psychological, and spiritual benefits.

Sivananda Ashram Yoga Ranch

Box 195, Woodbourne, NY 12788
Tel. 914/434-9242
Fax 914/434-1032

Administration Founder-director, Swami Vishnu Devananda; director, Swami Sankarananda

Season Year-round.

Accommodations 50 small rooms: singles, doubles, apartments in the farmhouse and cottages. Apartments have private bath. Tent space.

Rates Room $35–$40 daily per person, including meals; 1-month work-study program $100. $25 payable in advance. No credit cards.

Meal Plans 2 meals daily, buffet style. Lacto-vegetarian diet with fresh vegetables grown on the ranch and dairy products. No coffee, eggs, alcohol.

Services and Facilities **Swimming Facilities:** Pond. **Spa Facilities:** Communal sweat lodge and sauna. **Recreation Facilities:** Woodland trail hiking. **Evening Programs:** Meditation, chanting, lectures.

Getting Here *From New York City.* By bus, Short Line (Port Authority Terminal) to Woodbourne, then arrange for pickup; during the summer, van service operated by Sivananda provided every weekend (243 W. 24th St., $20 round-trip). By car, Rte. 17N to Exit 105B, Rte. 42 to Woodbourne (2 hr).

Special Notes No smoking. Remember to bring towels and meditation mat.

Tai Chi Farm

Spiritual awareness
Sports conditioning

New York Martial arts and inner discovery bring harmony to participants
Warwick in workshops at the Tai Chi Farm. Founded and led by Master Jou Tsung Hwa, the farm has a summer schedule devoted to understanding and perfecting the tai chi chuan postures and meditations. Specialists teach such exercises as Swimming Dragon Chi Kung, a complete muscle and organ toner that makes your body seem to flow like a swimming dragon. From the Creative Being Centre in England, a master teaches how to transform stress into self-discovery using Dragon Breath Energy.

The Chinese have been studying chi for 4,000 years. Here the concepts of leading, sticking, neutralizing, and attacking are discussed and practiced with experts in many specialized forms of tai chi chuan. Characterized by a spirited give-and-take, San Shou is an ingeniously choreographed set of 88 matched movements that refine your form and sensitivity. In the body mechanics of tai chi chuan, you discover how to root and balance the yin aspect of letting go with the yang aspect of connecting and projecting energy.

Tai Chi Farm
Box 828, Warwick, NY 10990
Tel. 914/986-9233

Administration Master, Jou Tsung Hwa; manager, David Pancarician

Season May–Oct.

Accommodations 10 wooden cabins with cots or mattresses for 2–10 persons. Bedding not supplied. No electricity or running water. Outhouse shared by campers. Campsites available.

Rates $30 per person for weekend lodging, $95 tuition; $50 per person for 5-day workshop lodging, $170 tuition. Campsites $10–$20.

Meal Plans No meal service. Participants prepare their own meals.

Services and Facilities Services: Individual and group instruction. **Exercise Facilities:** Indoor studio. **Swimming Facilities:** Pond.

Getting Here *From New York City.* By bus, NJ Transit from Port Authority Terminal to Warwick (2 hr). By car, Rte. 80W, 23N to I-94N, exit 1 mi past NJ-NY state line in New Milford.

Zen Mountain Monastery

Spiritual awareness

New York
Mt. Tremper

Joining a group of Buddhist monks as they work in silence, meditate, and celebrate Zen rituals and arts is the unique experience at the Zen Mountain Monastery. You can sip green tea at a Zen tea ceremony, hear the broken notes of a Shakuhachi bamboo flute, learn Sumi-e ink painting or traditional wood carving, and explore the subtleties of Ikenobo flower arranging. There are weekends devoted to Taoist martial arts, poetry, and Zen photography.

Founded in 1980 by Zen priest John Daido Loori, who is addressed as *sensei* (teacher), it is the only monastery in America that offers concerts and programs for visitors throughout the year. Scheduled monthly retreats attract 60–100 participants.

The day's activities move to a measured cadence, sometimes with chanting, often in silence. Everyone does caretaking, an hour of giving back to the buildings and land some of the benefits received from them. Periods of *zazen* (meditation) provide concentration during intensive *sesshin* silent retreat weeks.

Located in a state forest preserve, a 10-minute drive from Woodstock, the monastery seems to be of another time and world. It was, in fact, built at the turn of the century by Catholic monks and Norwegian craftsmen. There are endless mountain trails, ponds, and streams for hiking and recreation, and the atmosphere of peace and solitude is conducive to introspection.

Zen Mountain Monastery
Box 197PC, S. Plank Rd., Mt. Tremper, NY 12457
Tel. 914/688-2228

Administration Director, John Daido Loori; program director, Geoffrey Arnold; coordinator, Kathy Nolan; registrar, Jimon.

Season Year-round; weekend programs scheduled in summer, retreats in fall and winter.

Accommodations 4-story stone monastery with 175-bed dormitory. Main hall, classrooms, dining hall, library. All facilities shared on a communal basis. Rustic cabins available for couples.

Rates Weekend programs $125–$185, retreats of 3–7 days (Tues.–Sun.) $185–$325 per person, including 3 meals daily. Advance payment of $50. Credit cards: MC, V.

Meal Plans Vegetarian meals and some fish or meat, served buffet style 3 times a day. Weekends begin with Fri. dinner (steamed fish with rice and vegetables) and end with Sun. lunch. Dairy products served. Much of the food from the monastery garden.

Services and Facilities **Services:** Zen training, intensive meditation, artist retreats. **Swimming Facilities:** Nearby mountain lakes. **Recreation Facilities:** Hiking; tubing on creek; skiing at Hunter Mountain. **Evening Programs:** Occasional concerts of contemporary and Oriental music; an introduction to Zen.

In the Area Woodstock artists' colony, Catskill Mountain Forest Preserve, Beaverkill River scenic area.

Getting Here *From New York City.* By bus, Adirondack Trailways (tel. 800/858–8555) from Port Authority via Kingston to Mt. Tremper (about 3 hr). By car, New York State Thruway (I–87) to the Catskills, Rte. 28 and 212 to Mt. Tremper (2½ hr).

Special Notes No smoking.

The Equinox

Life enhancement
Luxury pampering

Vermont
Manchester
Village

The 2,300-acre historic Equinox resort has a newly renovated 18-hole par 71 golf course, three tennis courts, and spa facilities that include a coed Turkish steam bath, indoor and outdoor swimming pools, whirlpools, and a Swedish sauna. Guests have unlimited use of the spa facilities, but if skiing at Mt. Equinox or exploring the historic town is more desireable, such options are also available.

The comprehensive facilities are complimentary to all hotel guests, and specialized spa programs are available à la carte. A three-night spa package includes three spa meals daily and treatments or salon services. There is also a two-night Fun and Fitness package, with breakfast and dinner. Before you begin your regime, a staff member will give you a computerized body-composition analysis, which will be used to tailor your exercise schedule, and you'll participate in an informal discussion on exercise physiology, nutrition, and stress management. Advance planning with the spa director will help you focus on weight loss, stress management, or behavior modification.

Workout options include brisk walks and personalized training with weights, and programs are limited to 16 participants, so early reservations and travel plans are suggested.

In 1992 the hotel and golf course were refurbished, but the 1800s charm has been retained, especially in the dining room, which dates back to 1769 when it was a tavern. Guest rooms have a fresh but historic style, with Audubon prints and Vermont country charm. All bathrooms have been reconstructed with 18th-century tile, pedestal sinks, and natural finish beaded pine-paneled ceilings.

The Equinox

Rte. 7A, Manchester Village, VT 05254
Tel. 802/362–4700 or 800/362–4747
Fax 802/362–4861

Administration   General manager, S. Lee Bowden; fitness director, Susan Thorne-Thomsen

Season   Year-round.

Accommodations   163 bedrooms and 10 suites, furnished in classic New England style with pine beds and dressers, flowered chintz fabrics, modern conveniences. Beds turned down at night; *New York Times* delivered. All with large modern bathroom, TV, phone, air-conditioning. Also available, 9 town houses with 1–3 bedroom suites.

Rates $130–$270 single, $140–$280 for 2, double occupancy. 1-bedroom parlor suite $245–$295 daily. 3-night spa package $915 single, $720 per person person double, $675 triple. 2-night Fun & Fitness package $585 single. $410 double, $365 triple. Add 7% tax, gratuity. Deposit of 1 night. Credit cards: AE, DC, MC, V.

Meal Plans   Meals included in spa packages. Spa breakfast offers choice of fruit, buttermilk pancakes with blueberry coulis, hot oatmeal or bran cereal with skim milk; lunch can be ceviche of sole with cilantro, grilled medallion of beef with shallots, or chilled asparagus with seasoned wild rice; dinner choices include herbed pasta with mushrooms, poached salmon, or veal medallion.

Services and Facilities   **Exercise Equipment:** 8-station Nautilus circuit, free weights, 2 Lifecycles, 3 AMF semirecumbent bikes, NordicTrack, stairclimber, computerized rowing machine. **Services:** Massage, thalassotherapy, herbal wrap, loofah body scrub, pedicure, paraffin treatments, hair and skin care. **Swimming Facilities:** 47′ indoor and 75′ outdoor heated pools. **Recreation Facilities:** 3 HarTru tennis courts, golf course, hiking trails, bicycle rental, nearby downhill and cross-country skiing, horseback riding, canoeing, horse-drawn carriage rides. **Evening Programs:** Resort entertainment.

In the Area   Antiques shops, shopping at factory outlets, summer theater, jazz concerts, Marlboro Music Festival, Brattleboro Museum, Norman Rockwell Museum, Bennington crafts center, Hildene (Robert Todd Lincoln's estate).

Getting Here   *From New York City.* By car, New England Thruway (I–95) north to I–91, exit at second Brattleboro turnoff for Rte. 9 to Rte. 30 (4 hr). By bus, Greyhound from Port Authority Terminal (4½ hr). By air, scheduled flights to Albany, NY; bus service to Manchester by Vermont Transit (tel. 800/451–3292). Taxis and rental cars available.

Special Notes   No smoking in the spa. Spa open weekdays 7–7, weekends 8–7:30. No minimum age until 6 PM; 15 years after 6 PM.

Four Seasons Healing

Holistic health
Spiritual awareness

Vermont
Norwich
The mountain lodge is the base for wilderness programs and workshops that encourage personal health and exploration. Counseling comes from a team of doctors, psychologists, psychotherapists, and Vision Quest guides. Among the relaxing activities that weekend-program guests can participate in are lounging in front of a fire, hiking through the woods, and sitting by a stream with other visitors.

The Four Seasons Healing, a private retreat, was founded 15 years ago as a nonprofit organization in southern New England, and in 1994 it acquired the 20-acre site in the Upper Connecticut River Valley of Vermont. Action-oriented healing practices, drawn from psychodrama, shamanism, depth, existential, humanistic, and transpersonal psychologies are practiced. Groups are limited to eight people for the six-day Vision Quest; and 20 people at the Breakthrough Weekends devoted to gender reconciliation for individuals and couples.

Programs can be customized for individuals, couples, or a group that wants a private retreat. The scheduled events, held during summer and the fall leaf-changing season, include weekend gatherings for men or women, and a one-day introduction to shamanic journeying. Bring your own tent or use equipment supplied for overnight wilderness experiences. The philosophy of the nature-oriented activities is that spending time alone can enable you to face the cycles of life and death, where spiritual rebirth happens naturally.

The communal attitude at the lodge helps participants share problems and connect with their deeper selves. Meals are vegetarian, with lots of grains and steamed vegetables, served family-style. This is a very informal place, where guests share outhouse and communal shower facilities.

Four Seasons Healing
New Boston Rd., R.R. 1, Box 399, Norwich, VT 05055
Tel. 802/649–5104

Administration Directors, Israel Helfand, M.S., Ph.D, and Ari Kopolow, M.D.

Season July–Oct.

Accommodations Shared rooms in rustic lodge with communal shower and outhouse.

Rates Weekend program $85, Breakthrough Weekend $250, 6-day Vision Quest $485–$725.

Meal Plans 3 meals daily served family style, included in program. Vegetarian main dish for dinner can be tofu casserole or spinach lasagna. Breakfast is hot cereal, lunch a pita sandwich, salad, fruit. Herbal tea, decaf coffee available.

Services and Facilities **Services**: Counseling, guided hikes and backpacking treks; lifework planning, couples relationships.

In the Area Marlboro Music Festival, Brattleboro, Woodstock Dartmouth College Hopkins Center (performing arts), Saint-Gaudens Studio (sculpture), Manchester Village.

Getting Here *From New York City.* By car, I–95 north to I–91, exit at Norwich to New Boston Rd. (4 hr). By air, scheduled commuter flights to Lebanon, NH. (1 hr). Car pools arranged; taxi, rental car available.

Special Notes Additional weekend retreats planned in Virginia/Maryland.

Golden Eagle

Nonprogram resort

Vermont
Stowe

Toning and body shaping are what this budget spa does best, and it draws a mixed crowd of singles and families mostly between 30 and 60. The traditional mountain lodge has winter and summer activities, and a health spa open to guests.

Set on 80 acres near the center of Stowe, the resort has well-developed nature trails. A self-guided tour brochure includes descriptions of local flora and fauna. Staff members accompany guests on walks if requested in advance. For longer hikes and bike rides, try the Stowe Recreation Path, a 5½ mile scenic route through the valley, which runs past the entrance to Golden Eagle and out toward Mt. Mansfield ski area. Nonstructured, this is a good base for families.

Golden Eagle
*Box 1110B, Mountain Rd. (Rte. 108), Stowe, VT 05672
Tel. 802/253–4811 or 800/626–1010*

Administration Manager, Neil Van Dyke; spa director, Vicki Demeritt

Season Year-round.

Accommodations 80 rooms with private bath; suites, cottages, apartments with cooking facilities, color TV, air-conditioning, oversize beds. Some rooms with Jacuzzi and fireplace. Also a Bavarian-style chalet.

Rates $59–$200 daily per room for 2, single occupancy $5 additional. 1-night deposit on booking. Credit cards: AE, DC, MC, V.

Meal Plans Heart-healthy selections on breakfast and dinner menus. Dinner may include veal marsala, fish rolled with vegetables, or broiled scrod. Special diets are accommodated.

Services and Facilities **Exercise Equipment:** 8 Universal gym stations, 2 Trotter treadmills, 3 Schwinn Air Dyne bikes, Concept II rowing machines, free weights. **Services:** Massage, reflexology. **Swimming Facilities:** Indoor lap pool, 2 outdoor pools. **Recreation Facilities:** Tennis courts, bicycles, scenic path for jogging. **Evening Programs:** Resort activities.

In the Area Shelburne Museum, Cold Hollow Cider Mill, Trapp Family Lodge, Ben & Jerry's Ice Cream Factory.

Getting Here *From Boston and New York City.* By train, Amtrak to Waterbury, VT (10 mi from Stowe). By car, I–91, I–89 to Stowe exit (3 hr from Boston, 6½ hr from NYC). By air, scheduled flights to Burlington, VT. Hotel limousine arranged on request to meet trains and planes; taxi, rental car in area.

Special Notes Ground-floor rooms for people with disabilities. No smoking in the spa and sections of the dining rooms. Spa open daily 9–9.

Green Mountain at Fox Run

Life enhancement   *Women only*
Weight management

Vermont   Located on more than 20 acres of private land in the Green
Ludlow   Mountain National Forest, overlooking the Okemo Valley and
ski area, this is the country's oldest all-women program devoted to developing a self-directed plan for eating and exercise
that can be integrated into your life at home. Participants
range in age from 17 to over 80.

For women with a serious weight problem, coming to Green
Mountain at Fox Run is a commitment to change. The difference
is not just a new diet or vigorous exercise, but a new lifestyle
based on healthy habits. The program provides a practical approach to eating, exercise, and stress management that can ensure long-term success.

One of the first lessons you learn here is that diets don't work.
Instead of deprivation, moderation becomes the key. Eating
three balanced meals a day is required, and you are encouraged
to give in, ever so slightly, to an occasional yearning for sweets.
Guests learn to cope with food fads and are shown that being
more active can be as pleasant as taking a walk down a country
lane. For women who have unsuccessfully attempted to manage
their weight with liquid diets, there is a special program to
overcome negative effects and resume a livable and enjoyable
approach to eating. Professional workshops for nurses and social workers also are also offered.

Working with a team of registered dietitians, exercise physiologists, and behavioral therapists with specialties in weight,
health, and addiction, you develop a personalized weight and
health program that becomes part of your daily routine. A follow-up program helps you to maintain this routine at home. Tuition costs cover individual nutrition/dietary counseling,
exercise prescription and modification, and private behavioral
counseling sessions. The only extra expense, if desired, is for
massage therapy.

Owner-operated since 1973, management keep this a homey
place. There is some high-tech gym equipment and an outdoor,
heated pool, but it's otherwise quite simple. Pampering services are à la carte. Exercise classes, running, walking, hiking,
biking, and cross-country skiing in winter fill most of the day.
Aerobic dance and body-conditioning sessions teach that exercise can be fun, something that fits easily into everyday life.

Green Mountain at Fox Run
Fox La., Box 164, Ludlow, VT 05149
Tel. 802/228-8885 or 800/448-8106
Fax 802/228-8887

Administration   Program directors, Alan H. Wayler, Ph.D. and Marsha J.
Hudnell, M.S., R.D.; fitness director, Sandy DiNatale

Season   Year-round. Special seminars scheduled weekends.

Accommodations   26 rooms: singles, doubles, and duplexes (2–4 persons), all with
modern bath. Lounge with fireplace, TV; high-ceiling, raftered
dining room.

Rates 1-week session $1,150–$1,800; 2-week $2,150–$3,350; 4-week $3,750–$5,700. Rates based on type of accommodation, single or double occupancy (roommates matched on request). $500 deposit with application. Tax and gratuity included. Credit cards: MC, V.

Meal Plans 1,200-calorie (per day) diet low in fat and sodium, high in complex carbohydrates. Menus include a salad plate, pasta, eggplant Parmesan, tortilla dishes, liver and onions, baked potato with trimmings, even ice cream. Coffee and tea available throughout the day.

Services and Facilities **Exercise Equipment:** 2 Trotter treadmills, 2 Schwinn Air Dyne bikes, NordicTrack, Concept 2 rower, Ross stepper, Nautilus recumbent bike, free weights, mountain bikes. **Services:** Swedish massage, facial, manicure, pedicure; sports instruction. **Swimming Facilities:** Olympic-size heated outdoor pool; nearby indoor pool and Jacuzzi. **Spa Facilities:** Sauna. **Recreation Facilities:** 2 tennis courts, outdoor track, nearby golf course; downhill and cross-country skiing, snowshoeing. **Evening Programs:** Cooking classes, movies, group discussions, lectures.

In the Area Trips into town for shopping (including antiques shops), scenic mountain drives, summer stock theaters.

Getting Here *From New York City.* By car, I–95 north to I–91, Exit 6 in Vermont (Rte. 103 North) to Ludlow (4½ hr). By bus, Vermont Transit (tel. 800/451–3292) from Port Authority Terminal to Ludlow. By air, scheduled flights to Lebanon, NH, on Delta, Northwest Airlines. Complimentary pick-up from airports and bus station. Transfers upon departure included in tuition.

Special Notes Smoking only in specified areas. Remember to bring recent physical report, walking and aerobics shoes.

New Life

Holistic health
Life enhancement
Nutrition and diet

Vermont
Killington
Two vacations rolled into one is the concept of New Life fitness guru Jimmy LeSage: His program mostly attracts hikers who want to get in shape and enjoy the outdoors. The Inn of the Six Mountains, where New Life is housed, is set in a picturesque alpine valley, and operates from mid-May through autumn (dates depend on when the leaves stop turning).

A former professional cook and hotel manager, LeSage caters to his guests' needs while exhorting them to learn ways to improve their habits. His philosophy on food and eating is published in a book given to each guest and experienced first-hand in a cheery dining room. Fresh fruit, herbal teas, decaffeinated coffee, and spring water are always on hand in the hospitality lounge.

Exercise classes are held in a tent with specially designed floor, and are scheduled around outdoor activities. Sivananda-style yogic movements gently stretch muscles and prepare the body for vigorous outdoor activity; the afternoon program relaxes the body and works off fatigue. Other options are offered at the indoor complex with swimming, steam room, and heated whirlpool that guests can use at any time.

Hiking the lush valleys of the Green Mountain Range is a great way to strengthen your heart and muscles. Guided by New Life staff members, groups hike daily. The treks become more challenging as your stamina increases. The climax is an all-day hike that includes a picnic lunch.

New Life
The Inn of the Six Mountains, Killington Rd.,
Killington, VT 05751
Tel. 802/422-4302 or 800/228-4676
Fax 802/422-4321

Administration Founder-director, Jimmy LeSage

Season Mid-May through Oct.

Accommodations 100 rooms with double beds, private baths, color TV, and phone. Pine-paneled lobby, lounge with fireplaces and comfy chairs.

Rates Weekend sampler $400 single, $395 per person double; 6 day/5 night program (Sun.–Fri.) $1,099 single, $980 double. $200 advance payment per person. Add 15% service charge, 7% tax. Credit cards: MC, V.

Meal Plans 3 meals served daily. Modified Pritikin diet (1,000–1,200 calories per day) low in fats and high in complex carbohydrates. Chicken, fish, vegetables, and fruit among the choices. Specialties include lentil loaf, chicken curry salad, sandwich with spicy tofu filling. Special diets accommodated.

Services and Facilities **Exercise Equipment:** Cardiovascular power circuit with Lifecycle rowing ergometer, Rebounders, NordicTrack ski machine, StairMaster, Precor rower, Cybex multigym, Mohawk stationary bike. **Services:** Swedish massage, shiatsu, facials; classes in aerobics, yoga, tai chi chuan; aquacise. **Swimming Facilities:** Indoor lap pool, heated outdoor pool. **Recreation Facilities:** Outdoor tennis, racquetball courts; golf course and horseback riding nearby; mountain-bike rentals. **Evening Programs:** Discussions on healthy living, talks on beauty, lectures on nutrition and stress.

In the Area Antiques shops, summer theater, jazz concerts, Marlboro Music Festival.

Getting Here *From New York City.* By car, New England Thruway (I–95) north to Exit 24, Northway to Exit 120 (Fort Anne/Rutland), Hwy. 4 east via Rutland to Killington Rd., Rte. 100 (5 hr). By train, Amtrak to White River Jct. (4 hr). By bus, Vermont Transit to White River Jct. (5 hr). Complimentary pickup at bus station. By air, Delta Business Express or Northwest Link to Lebanon, NH (1 hr). Limousine, car rental available.

Special Notes No smoking in public areas. Remember to bring warm clothing, hats, walking shoes. Spa open daily 8 AM–10 PM.

Topnotch at Stowe

Luxury pampering
Nutrition and diet
Sports conditioning
Stress control

Vermont Perched in Vermont's Green Mountains, Topnotch is a classic
Stowe country inn that caters to sports enthusiasts and weary urbanites seeking escape from civilization. Complementing its four-
season outdoor activity, the resort opened a full-service spa in
1989.

Topnotch emphasizes health education by putting each guest
through a "Fitness Profile" analysis. Based on your body composition, strength and flexibility, cardiovascular and blood
tests, an exercise program is planned. Outfitted with a daily issue of shorts, T-shirt, robe and slippers, you have a choice of
classes, one-on-one workouts, and circuit weight training.
There are coed sauna, steam room, and Jacuzzi.

Sport-specific fitness and conditioning classes get you in shape
for tennis and skiing. The program for three to seven days includes instruction as well as time on the courts and slopes. The
resort has an indoor tennis center with four lighted courts
(Deco Turf II), and transports guests to nearby Mount Mansfield, Vermont's highest peak, top-rated for downhill skiing.
Also, there are 30 kilometers of groomed cross-country trails
winding through the 120-acre resort, which link with the Catamount Trail along the ridge of the Green Mountains. For the
riding enthusiast, the Topnotch Equestrian Center provides
horses, trail rides, riding rings, lessons, and a gallop across the
meadows and backwoods.

Golfers get guest privileges at the Stowe Country Club. A popular focal point for swimmers is the cascading waterfalls alongside the 60-foot heated indoor swimming pool. Tennis clinics
and an Orvis school for fishermen are scheduled throughout
summer.

While the spa is sophisticated, the inn is comfortable and homey. Its 92 guest rooms are spacious, many with views of the
mountains. A massive fireplace warms the main lounge, and
there is a cushy sofa for reading by the fire. If you're not too
sleepy after a day of sports and spa followed by evening-fitness
rap sessions, there's a well-stocked library in your room for
bedtime reading.

Topnotch at Stowe
Mountain Rd., Box 1458, Stowe, VT 05672
Tel. 802/253–8585 or 800/451–8686
Fax 802/253–9263

Administration General manager, Lewis Kiesler; spa director, Helen Priestly

Season Year-round.

Accommodations 92 rooms furnished with antiques, fine wooden beds, some with
canopy, and library. Modern bathroom with imported soaps
and bath gels, plush towels. All have air-conditioning, cable
TV. Also, suites, condominiums.

Rates Daily without meals $64–$89 per person double occupancy. Spa
packages with meals: $189–$214 per night for 5-night program;

$172-$197 per night for 3-night program. Add 17% service charge, 5% taxes. Credit cards: AE, DC, MC, V.

Meal Plans 3 meals daily included in spa packages. Menu choices for breakfast are tofu omelet, buckwheat pancakes with fruit topping, hot or cold whole-grain cereals. Lunch selections include mushroom-barley soup, salad of asparagus and roasted red peppers, whole-wheat pizza, chicken breast in cilantro-mint sauce. Dinner entrées can be seafood pasta in creamy 3-mustard sauce, or grilled chicken. Vegetarian meals, snacks available. Coffee, tea, milk served.

Services and Facilities **Exercise Equipment:** 9-station Cybex weight training unit, 2 Schwinn Air Dyne bikes, 4 Precor treadmills, pulley machine, ProTec PT5-1000 recumbent bike, Liferower, 3 StairMasters, 2 Lifecycles, Gravitron, free weights. **Services:** 2 aerobics studios with 13 scheduled classes, aquacise, yoga; massage (Swedish, shiatsu, reflexology), acupressure, aromatherapy, hydrotherapy, herbal wrap, loofah body scrub, facials; beauty salon for hair, nail, and skin care; instruction in tennis, skiing, riding. **Swimming Facilities:** Indoor 60-ft lap pool, outdoor pool. **Recreation Facilities:** 12 tennis courts (4 indoor), equestrian center, putting green, lawn croquet, bikes, table tennis, billiards, art studio; spa sauna, steam room, coed Jacuzzi. Nearby golf, downhill skiing, squash, and racquetball. **Evening Programs:** bike rides and walks, nutrition seminars, scheduled events 5 nights per week.

In the Area Stowe Village (antiques shops), Trapp Family Lodge (concerts), Shelburne Museum (Americana), Cold Hollow Cider Mill, Ben & Jerry's Ice Cream Factory, Smuggler's Notch, Bingham Falls (swimming, picnics).

Getting Here *From Boston.* By train, Amtrak to Waterbury, VT (4 hr). By bus, Greyhound and Vermont Transit (tel. 800/451–3292) (5 hr). By air, scheduled flights on USAir to Burlington, VT (1 hr), private-plane airport at Stowe. By car, I–93 to Concord, NH, I–89 north to Exit 10 (Stowe/Waterbury), Rte. 100N to Stowe, left on Rte. 108 (Mountain Rd.) 4 mi (4 hr). Taxi, car rental available; town trolley service, hotel limo.

Special Notes No smoking in spa or spa dining room. No-smoking guest rooms available. Limited access for people with disabilities. Spa open weekdays 8–6, weekends 8–7. Daily facility fee ($10–$20) included in spa packages.

Woodstock Inn & Resort

Nonprogram resort

Vermont *Woodstock* Picture the perfect New England town: the county courthouse and library facing an oval green, a covered bridge leading to immaculate farms, a cluster of fancy boutiques, and a Colonial inn. Add a $5-million sports center, 50 miles of cross-country ski trails, nearby mountains with more than 200 downhill trails, and you have the Woodstock Inn & Resort.

The current inn, the fourth on the site, spreads from the historic town center to the sports center. Included are a golf course and croquet lawn, outdoor and indoor swimming pools, tennis courts, and a 69-station parcourse. The weight equipment and aerobics studio are luxury-spa caliber, and they can be used for a nominal fee. Classes cost $5 each. A winter ski package includes lift tickets and equipment rental.

Traditions are alive at the inn from the dress code to the hearty New England menu. The nearby Billings Farm Museum has exhibits of early New England farm life, and offers visits to a prize-winning dairy barn. Phone and power lines were buried with a grant from a neighbor, Laurence Rockefeller, to preserve the view of the town green.

Woodstock Inn & Resort
14 The Green, Woodstock, VT 05091
Tel. 802/457–1100 or 800/448–7900

Administration	General manager, Chet Williamson; sports director, Douglas Keleher
Season	Year-round.
Accommodations	121 bedrooms with patchwork quilts, cable TV, air-conditioning, clock radio. Modern baths.
Rates	In summer, $139–$495 for 2 persons. Meals not included. Midweek sports package (3 days, 2 nights) $374 single, $450 per person double occupancy, includes racquetball or tennis, massage. Add 7% tax, and gratuities. Deposit: 2 nights. Credit cards: AE, DC, MC, V.
Meal Plans	Modified American plan (breakfast and dinner) $46 per person per day. Courtside Restaurant in Sports Center serves a chicken salad plate or assorted melon slices with cottage cheese, sherbet, or yogurt sauce for lunch. The main dining room offers poached chicken, roast young pheasant, and sea scallops for dinner.
Services and Facilities	**Exercise Equipment:** 11 Nautilus units, 2 Concept 2 rowing ergometers, 2 Monark bikes, Trotter treadmill, incline station, hyperextension station, free weights. **Services:** Swedish and deep-tissue massage, sports instruction, yoga and aerobics classes, aquatics for arthritics. **Swimming Facilities:** Indoor and outdoor pools. **Spa Facilities:** Coed steam room, separate men's and women's saunas, whirlpools in the Sports Center. **Recreation Facilities:** 10 outdoor and 2 indoor tennis courts, 2 indoor racquetball courts, 2 indoor squash courts; cross-country skiing, downhill skiing at Suicide Six, Killington, Ascutney Mountain, Okemo Mountain; horseback-riding center nearby, sleigh rides and nature walks. **Evening Programs:** Resort entertainment.
In the Area	Quechee Village (crafts), Dartmouth College Hopkins Center (performing arts), Saint-Gaudens Studio (sculpture), Marlboro Music Festival (chamber music), walking tours of historic Woodstock.
Getting Here	*From Boston.* By car, I–90 to I–91 (100 mi). By air, scheduled flights to Lebanon, NH. Taxi, rental car available.
Special Notes	Ramps and specially equipped rooms for people with disabilities. Tennis camp for children June–Aug. only. No smoking in the sports center.

Hawaii

Polynesian culture has given new dimensions to the pursuit of fitness. On the volcanic island of Hawaii, guests at Kalani Honua live in traditional lodges made of cedar logs or camp out among the palm trees. On Maui you can join a week-long fitness adventure called "The Maui Challenge," which allows participants to cross train in sports as they encounter the natural features of the island.

At the same time, developers of luxury resorts have competed for the distinction of having the most opulent health club on the island. On Maui, you can indulge in a combination of Japanese, Hawaiian, European, and American fitness fantasies at the Grand Wailea Resort, while at the Spa Grande, you can work out in a two-level cardiovascular-fitness and weight-training center. On Oahu, close to Pearl Harbor, the new Ihilani Resort has a spa with "Hawaiian Thalasso" seawater treatments.

While the water sports of Hawaii are famous, the islands are full of more unexpected fitness opportunities, such as bicycle rides down the slope of Maui's extinct volcano, Mt. Haleakala. Local outfitters will drive you to the top of the 10,023-foot slope to see the sunrise and provide bikes for the leisurely ride down. Or you can cruise the islands on one of the twin liners of American Hawaii Cruises and make use of the on-board spa.

Home of the strenuous Iron Man Triathalon, Hawaii offers a full range of sports ventures for every taste—from horseback riding on ranches to kayaking up the Huleia River on Kauai through a wildlife refuge. Polo matches abound on Oahu and the Big Island; the Hawaii Polo Club even offers five-day training programs. For fishermen the waters off the Kohala coast are legendary for deep-sea catches, and the Kona coast has spectacular sites for scuba diving—Napoopoo Beach Park and Keei Beach are favored spots. In the winter, you can go skiing on the Big Island. From December through May, the upper slopes of Mauna Kea, 13,796 feet above the sea, frequently have enough snow to make for sun-baked skiing.

Waikiki Beach hotels have some of the smallest fitness facilities and encourage guests to take part in water sports or use private clubs. Anyone can join the daily 8 AM aerobics class on the beach opposite the Pacific Hotel, where Gold's Gym sponsors sessions with TV fitness trainer Gilad Jancowicz. The military club at Ft. DeRussy offers beach aerobics at 9 AM Mon.–Sat. There's even a free clinic at the local YMCA to prepare runners for the Honolulu Marathon.

Island parks allow hikers the opportunity to enjoy the real Hawaiian paradise. For information on organized treks, contact clubs such as Hawaii Ike Travel Society (tel. 808/326-5775) and the Waikiki Community Center (tel. 808/923-1808). Leeward Community College (tel. 808/956-8946) publishes a statewide *Eco-Tourism Directory*. The comprehensive *Hawaii Health and Fitness Guide* is available from Aurora Productions (4400-4 Kalanianaole Hwy., Honolulu, HI 96821, tel. 808/988-7975).

One word of caution, however, when venturing into secluded areas on any of the islands, be sure you aren't wandering onto a farm or other private property, as there have been shooting incidents in the past. Check with local park-service officials before you start out on a hike or ride.

Grand Wailea Resort and Spa

Luxury pampering
Nutrition and diet
Preventive medicine
Stress control

Hawaii
Wailea (Maui)

Amid the splendor of the $600 million Grand Wailea Resort, the 50,000-square-foot Spa Grande offers the most extensive health and fitness facilities in Hawaii. In addition to 10 individual and private Jacuzzi areas, there are Roman-style whirlpools 20 feet in diameter located in the atriums of the men's and women's pavilions as well as 42 individual treatment rooms for everything from facials and loofah scrubs to mud treatments and massage.

Water sets the mood for the entire 40-acre resort. Located on Maui's south shore, 25 minutes from Kahului Airport, the eight-story hotel and two-level beachfront spa overlook formal gardens and placid surf.

Hydrotherapy comes with the spa's daily admission fee or as part of 4- to 7-night packages. The Terme Wailea circuit begins with a choice of two treatments designed to exfoliate and cleanse the skin: a loofah scrub or Japanese goshi-goshi scrub, sitting shower, and soak in a furo tub. Next you have a choice from five specialty baths in marble and gold mosaic tubs: aromatherapy for relaxation, Maui mud to remineralize, limu (Hawaiian seaweed) for detoxification, herbal for rejuvenation, and tropical enzyme bath for toning and softening the skin. To stimulate circulation there are saunas, steam rooms, and cold-water plunges. Upstairs are private, oceanfront treatment rooms where seven types of massage and five different facials are offered.

Aerobics classes are held several times daily. Also available is an air-conditioned racquetball court (convertible for squash) and weight-training rooms. Water sports on the hotel beach include catamaran cruises, canoe rentals, snorkeling, windsurfing, and scuba diving. The Wailea resort area contains two 18-hole golf courses in its limits, and a tennis club with 14 courts, three of which are grass. Guests at the neighboring Four Seasons resort also have access to Spa Grande.

Grand Wailea Resort and Spa

3850 Wailea Alanui Dr., Wailea, Maui, HI 96753
Tel. 808/875–1234 or 800/888–6100
Fax 808/874–2442

Administration Manager, Mark Hodgdon; spa director, Darryll Leiman

Season Year-round.

Accommodations 787 rooms in an 8-story tower, all with ocean view, private lanai, modern bath. Included are 53 suites and 100 rooms of

Hawaii

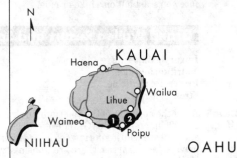

N

KAUAI

Haena

Wailua

Lihue

Waimea

Poipu

NIIHAU

OAHU

Ka

Honolulu

Wai

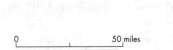

0   50 miles

0   75 km

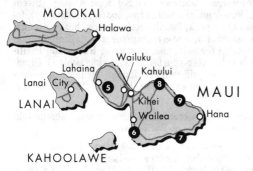

MOLOKAI
Halawa

Wailuku
Lahaina Kahului
Lanai City **5** **8** MAUI
LANAI Kihei **9**
Wailea Hana
6 **7**

KAHOOLAWE

PACIFIC OCEAN

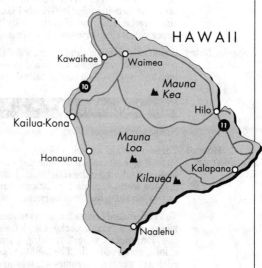

HAWAII

Kawaihae Waimea

Mauna
Kea ▲

10

Hilo
Kailua-Kona **11**

Mauna
Loa ▲

Honaunau Kalapana

Kilauea ▲

Naalehu

Napua Club floors. Air-conditioned, telephones, TV, and full amenities.

Rates Ocean front $400–$450 per night; Ocean view $375 per night; Terrace $325 per night; Suites $700–$8,000 per night for 2; Napua Club–Ocean Front $550 per night; 7-night Grande Plan spa package $5,140–$5,713 single, $3,562–$3,848 per person double occupancy; 4-night spa package $2,304–$3,084 single, $2,296–$2,460 per person double occupancy. Package rates include tax and service charge; tax added to room-only rate. Deposit: 50%. Credit cards: AE, DC, MC, V.

Meal Plans 2 spa cuisine meals per day included in 4-night or 7-night Grande Plan. Spa café lunch features organically grown island food with Italian and Provençal touches: Grilled breast of chicken with mango chili sauce, mahimahi with snap peas and roasted red peppers, black-bean salad with cilantro. Breakfast at café typically may be egg-white omelet or tropical fruit. Optional Italian, Japanese, and Polynesian restaurants.

Services and Facilities **Exercise Equipment:** 14-unit Keiser system, 3 StairMasters, 4 Lifesteps, 4 WindRacer bikes, 2 Cybex cycles, 2 Biocycles, 2 Accufit, 5 StarTrac treadmills, Gravitron, LifeRower, Concept 2 rower, free weights, and barbells. **Services:** Massage (Swedish, shiatsu, lomi-lomi, aromatherapy, sports, reflexology), facial, seaweed body pack, loofah scrub, wraps, healing baths. Consultation on health, stress management, nutrition, fitness. Full-service salon for hair, nail, skin care. **Recreation Facilities:** Ocean beach water sports, 2 swimming pools (1 Olympic size), 2 18-hole golf courses, indoor racquetball/squash courts, billiards, 14 tennis courts, 8,000 sq. ft. "Keiki"-land for kids.

In the Area Mt. Haleakala (volcano crater), Skyline Drive, Lahaina (old port), Hana Highway, Seven Sacred Pools.

Getting Here *From the U.S. mainland.* Direct flights by United, Delta, American, and Hawaiian Airlines to Maui's Kahului Airport. By car, Hwy. 380 to Hwy. 350 via Kihei Hwy. 31. Complimentary transfers included in Grande Plan. Taxi, rental car, limousine available. *From Honolulu.* By interisland airlines and American Hawaii cruises. Rental car available.

Special Notes Children's activities and lunch, $35 daily. Accommodations for people with disabilities available. Separate spa facilities for men and women. Spa hours: daily 6 AM–8 PM.

Halekulani Hotel

Nonprogram resort

Hawaii Three mornings a week, at 7:30, guests gather on the beach for
Honolulu (Oahu) stretching exercises and a morning jaunt with Max Telford, fitness consultant for the Halekulani Hotel. Telford, holder of numerous world records for distance running, offers fitness tips as you jog along his favorite route.

The Halekulani fitness facility is modest, but is like a hideaway where you can plan a workout with free weights, multiple-exercise Paramount weight-training gym, bicycles, rowing machines, and treadmills. The facility is available free of charge to all hotel guests. Aerobics classes are scheduled at 7:30 AM

Tuesday, Thursday, and Saturday, although there are rarely more than a handful of participants. For serious workouts, the hotel concierge arranges admission to the nearby Honolulu Club, where for a modest fee you can enjoy one of the best-equipped health clubs in the world.

The Halekulani is a small, private enclave, and the five-building complex and lush gardens meticulously maintain island traditions.

Halekulani Hotel
2199 Kalia Rd., Honolulu, HI 96815
Tel. 808/923–2311 or 800/367–2343
Fax 808/926–8004

Administration	Manager, Patricia Tam; fitness-program director, Max Telford
Season	Year-round.
Accommodations	456-room luxury hotel, 5 wings (1930s building and new additions). Rated best hotel in Hawaii. Rooms have sitting area, full bathroom with deep-soaking tub, glassed-in shower, marble vanity. Most have views of the beach and Diamond Head. 3 telephones, nightly turn-down service, cable TV (CNN), work desk.
Rates	Rooms for 1 or 2 persons $265–$430 daily, suites $580–$3,500 single or double. Confirmation by credit card. Credit cards: AE, DC, MC, V.
Meal Plans	Orchids Restaurant specializes in Pacific seafood and contemporary American cuisine. La Mer specialties include Lanai venison in a poivrade sauce, Norwegian salmon smoked over kiawe wood, onaga fish baked in herbed salt crust. Meals are à la carte.
Services and Facilities	**Exercise Equipment:** Paramount weight-training multigym, 2 Lifecycles, 2 Precor treadmills, Lifestep, Precor rower, dumbbells (3–35 lb), bench press. **Services:** Shiatsu massage; aerobics class. **Swimming Facilities:** Outdoor pool, ocean. **Recreation Facilities:** At Honolulu Club: racquetball, volleyball, golf driving range; nearby tennis and golf. Water sports equipment on beach. **Evening Programs:** Resort entertainment.
In the Area	Honolulu Museum of Art, Pearl Harbor, Ihilani Resort and Spa.
Getting Here	*From Honolulu International Airport.* Limousine, shuttle service, rental car, or taxi available (20 min).
Special Notes	For people with disabilities, elevators, ground-floor lanai suites, and 14 specially equipped rooms are barrier free. Supervised activities and excursions for children. No smoking in designated dining areas; some nonsmoking rooms. Fitness room open daily 7 AM–10 PM.

Hawaiian Wellness Holiday

Holistic health
Life enhancement

Hawaii *Koloa (Kauai)*	Combine a holistic approach to health and nutrition with a beach condominium resort, add therapeutic massage and chiropractic treatments, and you have Dr. Grady Deal's prescription

for a fitness holiday. Dr. Deal—a psychologist, licensed massage therapist, gourmet cook, and practicing chiropractor—and his wife, Roberleigh, have created a warm, homelike atmosphere for their guests. Using facilities at the Sheraton Beach Resort, the Hawaiian Wellness Holiday is tailored to individual needs and interests. By keeping the group small—an average of 10 per week—the Deals aim for a high level of success in meeting each person's goals.

Yoga, aerobics, and aquacise in the swimming pool are part of the daily program. Included in the program cost are three massages or chiropractic therapy. Detoxification, weight loss, and body toning are the primary objectives. Invigorating exercise and a cleansing diet are supplemented by natural therapies.

Spending most of the day outdoors, on scenic hikes and walks as well as at aerobics classes, guests quickly discover the natural healing effect of the island. Excursions included in the basic fee take the group to such scenic places as Waimea Canyon; the NaPali coast; Lumahai beach, where *South Pacific* was filmed; and the Seven Sacred Pools. Kauai is said to have a rare energy vortex, a metaphysical natural beauty that relaxes the mind and body. Exploring the island with a like-minded group of health seekers adds a special quality to the fitness holiday. Each person is encouraged to search for inner energy.

Rounding out the program are cooking demonstrations based on the macrobiotic and vegetarian meals that are served, workshops on nutrition and health, meditation, and deep-breathing exercises for relaxation. At the end of the day, you can unwind in the steam room, sauna, or Jacuzzi while awaiting yet another memorable sunset.

Hawaiian Wellness Holiday
Box 279, Koloa, HI 96756
Tel. 808/332-9244 or 800/338-6977

Administration	Program director, Roberleigh Deal; medical director, Grady A. Deal, Ph.D., D.C.
Season	Year-round.
Accommodations	Deluxe room or suite at Sheraton Kauai Beach Resort, with king- or queen-size beds, full bathroom, balcony, TV, telephone, air-conditioning, ceiling fans; choice of oceanfront or garden view.
Rates	All-inclusive week $2,095 single, $3,295 for 2 double occupancy in ocean-view room; $1,795 single, $2,895 for 2 in garden view room. Add 7% tax; gratuities optional. (5% discount for 2-week program.) Deposit: $500 on booking, balance due 30 days prior to arrival. Credit cards (5% surcharge): AE, MC, V.
Meal Plans	Vegetarian, cleansing, or macrobiotic meals with whole grains, raw and cooked vegetables, fruit, juices, legumes, and fish. Breakfast can be wheatless waffles with berries; lunch, a vegetable stew or baked macaroni with cashew-pimiento cheeseless topping. Dinner includes green salad with oil-free dressing, brown rice cooked with sesame seeds, and herb tea. Special dietary needs accommodated.
Services and Facilities	**Exercise Equipment:** Cybex circuit with 10 variable resistance units, 3 Stairsteps, 2 Aerobicycles, 2 Monark bikes, computerized rower, Olympic free weights, dumbbells. **Services:** Mas-

sage (Swedish, shiatsu, deep tissue), reflexology, G-5 vibrator massage, chiropractic, physical therapy; hair, nail, and skin care (added fee). Nutritional counseling, cooking classes. Detoxification/colonic program ($250 additional). **Swimming Facilities:** 2 outdoor pools, ocean beach. **Recreation Facilities:** 2 tennis courts, water sports, hiking. Golf, horseback riding, bicycle rental nearby. **Evening Programs:** Talks and slide shows on health-related topics; Hawaiian cultural performances.

In the Area Scheduled group hiking and sightseeing trips to various parts of the island; botanical garden, fern grotto, Spouting Horn blowhole, Kokee State Park, Waimea Canyon. Optional: helicopter tour, scuba dives, day cruises.

Getting Here *From Koloa.* By car, Poipu Rd. to Poipu Beach (15 min). Transfers on arrival/departure at airport (and for all excursions) included in program fee. Taxi, rental car available.

Special Notes Accommodations for people with disabilities. Full program for children over 12; resort activity available. No smoking in program areas. Remember to bring medical or chiropractic records.

Hilton Waikoloa Village

Luxury pampering
Nonprogram resort

Hawaii
Waikoloa (Hawaii) Created on a mammoth scale, the Hilton Waikoloa Village has the secluded Kohala Spa, which serves as an escape from the beach scene. Opened in 1988 by Hyatt and managed since 1993 by Hilton, the spa is part of a 62-acre resort that includes cavorting dolphins, horse-drawn carriages for rides into the countryside, and catamarans for surfing. Instead of walking to your room, you ride a canal boat or the "tubular tram." There is also a spiritual walk with guided meditation recalling the ancient kahunas.

The spa offers European thalassotherapy in baths, herbal wraps, body masks, and loofah scrubs. Seaweed-based cosmetics and natural oils nourish the body and prevent sun damage to winter-weary complexions. Participants are provided with workout clothing and robes. In one of the spa's posh, private massage rooms you can experience a traditional Hawaiian Lomi-Lomi massage, a form of lymphatic cleansing. With rhythmic rocking, the massage relaxes muscles while stimulating circulation. Services are billed to your room on an à la carte basis, plus $15 for daily use of spa facilities; $10 after 4 PM if you include a massage or treatment.

Extensive facilities are at your disposal. In separate sections for men and women are Turkish steam rooms, Finnish sauna, outdoor whirlpool, showers and locker room with full amenities. A beauty salon, a gym for aerobics classes, and a weights room are all part of the freestanding spa building.

The spa's combination of Eastern and Western health philosophies includes daily tai chi chuan and yoga classes as well as stress reduction, water aerobics, and meditation. The ancient Chinese tai chi chuan movements are demonstrated on the beach at 7:30 and 9:30 in the morning. All guests are invited to join a power walk around the property, called the Sunrise Pacer (3–5 mi). Classes are complimentary.

From the mile-long museum walkway filled with $3.5 million of Oriental and Pacific art to the acre-size swimming pool with its waterfalls, hidden grotto bar, and twisting water slide, nonstop fantasy rather than fitness is the reason for vacationing here.

Hilton Waikoloa Village
1 Waikoloa Beach Resort, Waikoloa, HI 96743
Tel. 808/885–1234 or 800/445–8667

Administration General manager, Dieter H. Seeger; spa manager, Donna Gordon

Season Year-round.

Accommodations 1,241 guest rooms in 3 low-rise towers. Contemporary furnishings include king-size or 2 queen-size beds, marble-floored bathroom, full amenities. 75% of rooms have ocean view. Regency Club with 80 exclusive rooms, complimentary breakfast and beverage service.

Rates From $225 a night, single or double occupancy. Spa sampler $99 (includes service charge and gratuity). Add 4.167% state sales tax. Deposit: Confirmation by credit card. Credit cards: AE, MC, V.

Meal Plans No meal plan available. Lunch at the spa can include chili chicken salad with confetti of marinated rice and vegetables in cilantro vinaigrette; poached salmon with cucumber and tomato on Bibb lettuce with dill couli; vegetable antipasto with tuna.

Services and Facilities **Exercise Equipment:** 10-unit Keiser weight-training gym, 2 StairMaster 4000 PT, Gravitron, 4 PTS Turbo recumbent bikes, 2 Biocycles, 2 Precor treadmills, Concept 2 rowing machine, dumbbells (2½-50 lb). **Services:** Massage (Lomi-Lomi, aromatherapy, shiatsu, sports, Swedish), reflexology, seaweed pack, body facial, body mask, loofah buff, herbal wrap, herbal or aroma bath, hydrating facial. Beauty salon with French Phytomer products for hair, nail, and skin care. **Swimming Facilities:** Outdoor freshwater pools, seawater lagoon, ocean beach. **Recreation Facilities:** 8 tennis courts (2 clay, 6 plexi), 2 championship 18-hole golf courses plus 2 courses nearby, horseback riding, windsurfing, snorkeling, scuba diving, sailing.

In the Area Hawaii Volcanoes National Park (2 active volcanoes, Kilauea and Mauna Loa), Kona coffee plantations, Captain Cook (fishing port), Hilo (shopping), Mookini Heiau (royal palace), Puukohola Heiau (temple), Lyman House Museum (missionary home), downhill skiing (Jan.–Mar.).

Getting Here *From Honolulu.* Interisland air services to Keahole Kona Airport (45 min), transfer by hotel van ($17.50 each way) or rental car (20 min).

Special Notes Specially equipped rooms for people with disabilities. Children's day camp with lunch ($35). No smoking in spa. Spa open daily 6 AM–8 PM.

Hyatt Regency Kauai

Nonprogram resort

Hawaii
Poipu Beach
(Kauai)

Secluded within the Hyatt Regency Kauai resort is the full-service Anara Spa. ANARA stands for "A New Age Restorative Approach," best experienced while relaxing with a Lomi-Lomi massage followed by a facial using coconut oil scented with gardenias. Attentive staff members blend ancient Hawaiian healing therapies with state-of-the-art technology: This effective combination leaves guests feeling like a million bucks. There is a courtyard, lap pool, and lava rock showers, as well as a complete health facility, including steam room, sauna, sprung-floor aerobics studio, small fitness room with weights, and Jacuzzi. Scheduled daily are aerobics classes, weight training clinics, and aqua-trim water exercise.

Services worth noting include the Ti Leaf Cool Wrap, designed to alleviate the discomfort of sunburn and elevated body temperature. Guests are spread on a bed of the cooling leaves, covered with a gel made from aloe vera and comfrey, then covered with more heat-absorbing leaves and wrapped in a sheet for 20 minutes to sweat out any toxins. Another treatment is the Sacred Bath of Hawaiian elders or kapunas: red colloidal clay from the base of Kauai's Mt. Waialeale is mixed with sea salts and spread on the body after a session in the steam room. This treatment is followed with a botanical bath with a limu or seaweed and salt mixture, which simulates thalassotherapy in helping to stimulate blood circulation.

This plantation-style resort, set on 18 acres of lush beachfront, comes complete with a private jungle lagoon and includes a museum of Asian and Pacific art, a collection of wildlife, and fine restaurants. Joggers can enjoy a 2-mile course on the beach. Family-oriented programs include an introduction to island archeology.

Hyatt Regency Kauai
1571 Poipu Rd., Koloa, Kauai, HI 96756
Tel. 808/742–1234 or 800/228–9000
Fax 808/742–1557

Administration General manager, Rick Riess; spa director, Shelly Widen-Hall

Season Year-round.

Accommodations Spread out on 3 floors, the 600-room resort includes concierge service floors in the Regency Club. Spacious, contemporary rooms, full bath, lanais, balconies; luxury amenities. Air-conditioning, TV, telephone.

Rates $230–$360 per day for 1 or 2 persons; Regency Club $410. Pamper Yourself 1-day spa package $175, plus room. Ultimate spa package for 2 (including breakfast or lunch) $445; if reserved with 4-night Hyatt Vacation, from $510 per person, double occupancy, including rental car, tax, and gratuity. 2 nights' advance payment or credit-card confirmation. Credit cards: AE, DC, MC, V.

Meal Plans No special meal plan. Selected low-calorie, low-fat items for heart-healthy dining available daily.

Services and Facilities **Exercise Equipment:** Nautilus weight-training units (6 stations), Lifecycle, treadmill, free weights. **Services:** Massage (shiatsu, Lomi-Lomi, Swedish, Esalen), beauty salon, tennis clinics, private lessons, scuba course. **Swimming Facilities:** Free-form ½-acre pool, ocean beach. **Recreation Facilities:** 5 tennis courts, hiking; bicycle rental. **Evening Programs:** Resort entertainment.

In the Area Hanalei National Wildlife Refuge (kayak tour), Kokee State Park (mountain lodge), Waimea Canyon (scenic drive), Waimea (Capt. Cook landed here in 1778), Na Pali Coast State Park (hiking trails), Fern Grotto.

Getting Here *From Lihue.* By car, Hwy. 50 to Poipu Beach Rd. (20 min). Rental car, taxi, airport shuttle van available.

Special Notes Crafts programs and Camp Hyatt ($34) day camp for children. Ground-floor rooms for people with disabilities. Daily spa admission $10. Open daily 6 AM–8 PM; salon services by appointment, 9–6.

Ihilani Resort and Spa

Luxury pampering
Taking the waters

Hawaii Inspired by the sea and ancient Hawaiian healing therapies,
Oahu the spa program at the new Ihilani Resort provides revitalization and relaxation. Located on Oahu's leeward western coast, 25 minutes from Honolulu International Airport, the 640-acre resort opened late in 1993. Designed for upscale travelers and members of the Ko Olina Golf Club, the luxury hotel is set amid thousands of coconut palm trees, banyans, monkeypods, and silver buttonwood trees, as well as flowering bougainvillea, firecracker plants, and fragrant plumeria. Surrounded by four tranquil lagoons and the Waianae mountains, this property may be the ultimate Hawaiian escape.

Aerobics classes are scheduled in a coed studio on the top floor of the three-level spa, where there is also a weights room. Jacuzzi and locker rooms are on the second floor, where you enter from the hotel. An ocean environment is created with French thalassotherapy technology and fresh saltwater piped directly from the Pacific. Specially-designed treatment rooms have a hydrotherapy tub by Doyer, a Vichy-style shower massage table, and a Needle Shower Pavilion with 12 shower heads for water massage. The treatments involve seaweed packs and wraps, salt scrubs, and facial masques with marine algae.

Four program packages are offered. The seven-day Revitalization package can begin on any day, but a Sunday welcome is suggested by the spa director who prepares a personal program for each guest. Postural and body alignment sessions may be included, as well as Swedish and shiatsu massage, or a more challenging fitness component. The four-day Energy Booster package allows you to sample therapies, Tuesday through Saturday. There is also a four-day Getaway package for weight loss or maintenance.

The spa's selection of treatments includes Hawaiian herbs and medicinal plants such as ti leaves. In addition, the Essensa and Nina Ricci skin care products are used. Managed by a subsidiary of Japan Air Lines, the resort's lovely accommodations are a perfect complement to the spa facilities.

Ihilani Resort and Spa
92-10001 Olani St., West Oahu, HI 96707
Tel. 808/679–0079 or 800/626–4446
Fax 808/679–0080

Administration General manager, Charles Park; spa director, Lisa Dobloug

Season Year-round.

Accommodations 387 guest rooms and 42 luxury suites in a first-class hotel dominated by a 15-story, glass-dome atrium. Oceanfront guest rooms include 7 with private garden terrace lanais and access to outdoor spa. All rooms have ceiling fan, air-conditioning, TV, 3 telephones, oversize marble bathroom with deep-soak tub, glass-enclosed shower stall, double vanities, lighted mirror, and private lanai with cushioned teak furnishings, a dining table, and reclining "Queen Mary" lounge chair. Amenities include robes, custom toiletries, hair dryer.

Rates 7-day Revitalization program $3,646 single, $2,834 per person, double occupancy. 7-day Vitality package $3,554 single, $2,749 double. 4-day Energy Booster package $2,021 single, $1,530 double. 4-day Getaway $2,093 single, $1,618 double. Prices include tax, gratuity, and airport transfers. Spa Day package (no lodging) $295. Daily room tariff $275–$425 for 1 or 2 persons, plus taxes; spa rooms $550, suites $700–$5,000. Deposit: 1 night. Credit cards: AE, DC, MC, V.

Meal Plans 3 spa cuisine meals daily included in program packages. Meals are served the main dining room: daily salad, fish entrée, fresh tropical fruit. Breakfast may be egg-white omelet or banana whole-wheat pancakes with yogurt. Lunch selections include vegetarian pizza or lasagna, seafood Mediterranean style.

Services and Facilities **Exercise Equipment**: Fitness Master cross country skier, 2 rowing machines, Vigor 10-station training equipment, including 3 Quinton treadmills, 2 Cateye bikes, and 3 StairMasters. **Services**: Swedish massage, shiatsu, hydrotherapy, thalassotherapy, body scrub, herbal wrap, marine masque, and facial; beauty salon. **Swimming Facilities**: outdoor lap and exercise pools, ocean beach. **Recreation Facilities**: 6 tennis courts (Kramer Sports Surface), 18-hole golf course, water sports, complimentary snorkling equipment, croquet, bocci balls.

In the Area Pearl Harbor Memorial, Waikiki Beach, Honolulu Museum of Art, Iolani Palace.

Getting Here *From Honolulu.* By car, Hwy. 1 west, past Honolulu International Airport, to Ko'Olina exit (30 min). Limousine, rental car, taxi available.

Special Notes Spa open daily 7–7. Minimum age is 16. Supervised child-care facility available.

Kalani Honua Conference Center

Holistic health
Life enhancement
Taking the waters
Weight management

Hawaii
Pahoa (Hawaii)

Suspended between fire and water, the Kalani Honua Conference Center sponsors a full range of health-oriented activities. An intercultural program, with yoga and hula, complements workshops scheduled throughout the year. Subjects covered by workshop retreats include men's health, organic gardening, and the body-mind-spirit connection. Visitors can participate or venture off to explore on their own.

Founded in 1982, the center attracts an interesting mix of robust, healthy men and women, families hiking the volcano trails, and professional bodyworkers attending seminars on holistic health and preventive medicine, but there is no fixed program. Of special interest are presentations on native Hawaiian cleansing rituals by islanders Leon Kalili and Delton Johnson.

In keeping with the spirit of old Hawaii, guests are housed in *hales*, wood lodges made of cedar logs. Each hexagonal lodge has its own kitchen and ocean-view studio space, with dormitory rooms, but mostly private accommodations. Campers can sleep under the stars at 25 sites among the palm trees.

Therapeutic services and exercise classes are the focus of a Japanese-style spa. The wooden bathhouse has a communal hot tub, sauna heated by wood-burning stove, and private massage rooms. Four pavilions with suspended wooden floors are used for yoga, aerobics, and dance performances. Nearby are an 85-foot swimming pool and a Jacuzzi, plus a fitness center.

Kalani Honua Conference Center
Box 4500, Pahoa, HI 96778
Tel. 808/965–7828 or 800/800–6886
Fax 808/965–9613

Administration Director, Richard Koob; program director, Michael Kraft

Season Year-round.

Accommodations 4 2-story lodges, 37 rooms double or multiple occupancy. Cedar walls and floors, minimal furniture, many windows; Hawaiian prints and fabrics, fresh flowers. Baths shared, except for 2 private suites in each lodge. No maid service; communal kitchen. Also available: private cottages with cooking facility, 25 tent sites. Amenities: coin-operated laundry, rental of water sports gear. No air-conditioning.

Rates Lodge room $65 per night single with private bath, shared bath $52; $75 for 2 persons double occupancy with private bath, shared bath $62. Suites on request. Cottages $85 for 2 in a duplex unit with private bath. Dormitory bed $28. Tent site $15. Deposit: 1 night. Credit cards: AE, DC, MC, V.

Meal Plans Primarily vegetarian, meals at Cafe Cashew are à la carte. Hawaiian-style breakfast includes papaya, passion fruit, banana smoothies, buffet of tropical fruits, brown rice, French toast. Lunch can be sautéed vegetables with tempeh and tahini sauce, broiled mahimahi, or spinach lasagna. Dinner choices can be grilled chicken or mahimahi baked with mushrooms in lemon and garlic sauce; cream of papaya cashew soup, and a salad bar. Beer, wine, coffee, tea available. Special diet requests (Pritikin, macrobiotic) accommodated. Daily meal plan $24–$27.

Services and Facilities **Exercise Equipment:** Weight-training units, stationary bike, treadmill, free weights. **Services:** Massage (shiatsu, Swedish, Esalen), acupressure, acupuncture, watsu, chiropractic. Counseling on weight loss, diet, nutrition. **Swimming Facilities:** Outdoor pool (Olympic-size), ocean beaches. **Spa Facilities:** 2 Jacuzzi whirlpools, natural pools at nearby springs and steam baths. **Recreation Facilities:** Bicycle rental, tennis court, horseback riding, hiking, volleyball; golf course, ski slopes nearby. **Evening Programs:** Workshops on health and sports conditioning, yoga; cultural performances, traditional Hawaiian feasts.

In the Area Helicopter sightseeing tour of island; scuba trips (fee); Volcanoes National Park, Jaggar Museum (Volcanoes Park history), Kilauea caldera, lava tubes at Wahaula Visitor Center, Hawaii Tropical Botanical Garden, Parker Ranch resort area, Hawaii plantation town, King Kamehameha historic site, Mauna Kea observatory telescope, MacKenzie State Park (hiking, picnics, beach).

Getting Here *From Hilo.* By car, Rte. 11 to Keaau, Rte. 130 to Rte. 137 (45 min). Rental car, limousine, taxi available.

Special Notes No smoking in bathhouse area. Remember to bring sunscreen #15, mosquito repellent, and flashlight.

The Maui Challenge

Sports conditioning

Hawaii
Maui
Exercise and sports help you cross train body and mind during the week-long Maui Challenge program. Each day involves several hours of hiking spectacular and varied terrain. The transitions—from hiking to cycling, from woods to rock and beach—help you develop self-confidence by meeting new challenges.

Arriving on Saturday, you start with a 4-mile beach walk to warm up for the next day's challenge, which is an 8-mile hike to Haleakala's summit. At the top, you board a mountain bike for a 38-mile ride down the paved and winding road to the coast. Tuesday mornings are devoted to water sports, with your choice of windsurfing (instruction available), sea kayaking, or snorkeling. Another day starts with a 5-mile hike up the Oheo Gulch through tall stands of bamboo to the 200-foot Wiamoku Falls; at the base you splash along a rock ridge and plunge into the icy water.

Each day's challenge brings new experiences and a sense of accomplishment; being in relatively good shape helps, but athletic expertise is not emphasized. The group size can range from four to 15 people; the average age of participants is 35 to 55.

Housed at an informal beach hotel, you have optional time to relax, swim, or get a massage. All meals are healthful—low in fat, sugar, and salt, high in complex carbohydrates and fiber.

The Maui Challenge
Box 5489, Glendale, AZ 85312
Tel. 602/878–7071 or 800/448–9816
Fax 602/878–1343

Administration Founder-director, Deborah Sturgess

Season Year-round. Bi-weekly each month, except only 1 week in Jan.

Accommodations 1-bedroom suites at the Maui Coast Resort. All have private bathroom, TV, phone, refrigerator, air-conditioning. Island decor with rattan furniture, lanai, and informal seating.

Rates 1-week program $1,995 single, $3,395 per couple. Deposit: 50%. No credit cards.

Meal Plans All meals included. Breakfast and dinner at the hotel's waterside restaurant. Breakfast includes fresh tropical fruit or juices, whole-wheat pancakes or waffles, egg-white omelet. Lunch box has pita sandwich or croissant, fruit juice, fresh vegetables, low-fat brownie. Dinner choices include vegetarian, fish, and poultry entrées. Juices available throughout the day at the hotel.

Services and Facilities **Exercise Equipment**: Full circuit of cardiovascular and weight-training equipment at nearby World Gym. **Services**: Massage (fee). **Recreation Facilities**: Water sports, including sea kayaking, sailing.

Getting Here *From Kahalui Airport.* Complimentary pickup and return on Saturday. Taxi, rental car available.

Sheraton Hotel Hana-Maui

Nonprogram resort

Hawaii
Hana (Maui)
An aura of the Old West pervades the Hotel Hana-Maui, which is set on an isolated coast in the middle of a cattle ranch. Hawaiian cowboys, called *paniolos*, lead white-face Hereford in from pasture as you hike down the rocky coastal trail to catch the sunset at Red Sand Beach; a session of yoga at the Wellness Center is a nice follow-up, topped off by a shiatsu massage.

Above all, Hana is a place of soothing seclusion. Lodging is in spacious one-story cottages with tropical furnishings and private lanais. During dinner in the Plantation Guest House, talented ensembles offer performances of Hawaiian music and dance in an authentic style not packaged for commercial shows.

The complex has a small wellness center, where you can work out surrounded by panoramic views. The mirrored aerobics studio provides a varied schedule of classes: low-impact aerobics, aquacise, and yoga at $10 per class. A nature walk begins the day at 9:30 AM, complimentary to all guests. The spa director's philosophy takes advantage of the island's natural beauty rather than emphasizing pampering attentions. For serious hikers, there is a four-hour trek into the lush tropical forest, with a stop to swim under the cascades of a waterfall.

Sheraton Hotel Hana-Maui
Box 8, Hana, Maui, HI 967
Tel. 808/248–8211 or 800/782-9488
Fax 808/528-7377

Administration General manager, Charles Bakant

Season Year-round.

Accommodations 97 cottages with wooden floors and walls, tropical furniture. 2 queen-size beds, modern bathroom, private lanai, air-conditioning, ceiling fans.

Rates Daily $305–$535 per suite for 1 or 2 persons; cottages $435. Guest house $1,200 for up to 6 persons. No meals included. Add tax. Credit cards: AE, DC, MC, V.

Meal Plans Menu à la carte.

Services and Facilities **Exercise Equipment:** 2 Precor bikes, 2 Precor stairclimbers, Precor rowing machine, NordicTrack cross-country ski unit, 5-station Paramount gym. **Services:** Swedish and therapeutic massage, facial with coconut, honey, aloe vera; nature walk, hiking, aerobics classes, aquacise. **Swimming Facilities:** Outdoor lap pool, 80′ × 40′; ocean beaches. **Recreation Facilities:** Horseback riding, baseball, hay ride, breakfast cookout. **Evening Programs:** Folklore performances.

In the Area Hana Museum and cultural center, Seven Sacred Pools, lava sand beaches, historic sites; boar hunts, rodeos.

Getting Here *From the U.S. mainland.* Direct flights by United, Delta, American, and Hawaiian Airlines to Kahului Airport. Transfers by van (1½ hr) or Aloha Island Air (15 min). *From Honolulu.* By interisland airlines and American Hawaii cruises. Rental car available.

Strong, Stretched & Centered

Holistic health
Life enhancement
Sports conditioning

Hawaii
Kihei (Maui) Working out with the instructors' instructor is a fitness buff's dream come true. Over 200 graduates of professional sports certification programs come here for six weeks of the body/mind training program originated here by Gloria Keeling.

This is not a quick-fix, so you should be in shape before joining Gloria's beach gang. The techniques used synthesize several cultures, from tai chi chuan to aquacize; in an East-West experience. Weight-reduction methods employ the notion of muscle definition as well as the concept of *ki*, the centered self.

Based at Kihei, the program participants work out at a fully equipped Powerhouse Gym. The staff instructors and advisers from the Maui Holistic Health Center work with you on a one-to-one basis to develop and expand your potential. Training sites include spectacular Haleakala crater (the world's sixth largest dormant volcano) and the numerous white-sand beaches for which Maui is celebrated.

Orchestrated for maximum body movement, you'll learn "gestalt dance" and African jazz rhythms with your aerobics. It's a high-powered experience in interdisciplinary training, with people devoted to nurturing a balance of mind and body fitness. Professional certification is awarded upon completion.

Strong, Stretched & Centered
Box 758, Paia, Maui, HI 96779
Tel. 808/575–2178
Fax 808/575–2275

Administration   Program director, Gloria Keeling

Season   Scheduled sessions year-round.

Accommodations   Lanai-style apartments with 2–3 bedrooms shared by participants. Twin beds, modern bath, ocean-view balcony or terrace. Furnished informally, with white rattan seating, lots of big cotton pillows, tropical fabrics; color TV, completely equipped kitchen. Beach area has shaded Jacuzzi and swimming pool. No maid service; laundry unit in each apartment.

Rates   6-week program $5,300 single, $4,705 per person, double occupancy. $1,000 advance payment. No credit cards.

Meal Plans   3 meals served family-style weekdays. Mostly vegetarian menu includes enchiladas with beans, choice of vegetables or chicken, eggplant Parmesan casserole, baked mahimahi fish, Thai satay noodles with oyster sauce, vegetables, and peanuts. On weekends, guests prepare their own meals.

Services and Facilities   **Exercise Equipment:** Universal Gym, free weights, treadmills, Lifecycles, StairMaster. **Services:** Sports conditioning, weight-lifting training, massage, video analysis, instructor certification. **Swimming Facilities:** Outdoor pool, ocean beach. **Recreation Facilities:** Water sports, hiking; nearby tennis courts, golf course, bike rental, horseback riding, scuba and water sports, all for extra fees. **Evening Programs:** Workshops on health and fitness.

In the Area   Group outings for snorkeling, overnight hike in Hana State Park, sunrise hike on Haleakala crater. Interisland cruises, helicopter sightseeing, shopping and nightlife in Lahaina, sugar-cane train ride, Grand Wailea Resort & Spa.

Getting Here   Direct flights to Maui's airport from Chicago and West Coast on United Airlines. *From Kahului.* About 20 min to Kihei by taxi or rental car. Rental car available for group use.

Special Notes   Program presented during July and Aug. at the Coolfont Resort, West Virginia. (*See* Middle Atlantic States, *above.*)

The Westin Maui

Nonprogram resort

Hawaii
Lahaina (Maui)   Breathtaking waterfalls, meandering streams, and a health club are among the attractions of this mega resort. The Westin Maui is set on 12 oceanfront acres and is bordered by two golf courses and a tennis complex; it has all the pleasures of paradise and none of the pain.

Take the wildlife and garden tour offered by Guest Services and you will learn that more than 650,000 gallons of water sustain the resort's aquatic needs. The pool area alone features five free-form swimming pools, two water slides, and a swim-up Jacuzzi hidden away in a grotto. Swans, flamingos, and other charming characters roam freely, adding their individual personalities to the tropical atmosphere.

The coed health club offers weight-training and an exercise room where aerobics classes are held daily. Step and low-impact sessions are offered for a modest charge per class plus the daily admission fee ($15), which is waived for hotel guests. There is a steam room, sauna, and Jacuzzi for relaxing stiff, sore muscles. Massage therapy is available by appointment.

The Westin Maui
2365 Kaanapali Pkwy., Lahaina, HI 96761
Tel. 808/667–2525 or 800/228–3000
Fax 808/661–5764

Administration General manager, Steve Shalit; spa director, Karl Stolmeier

Season Year-round.

Accommodations 761-room resort has 2 towers, each 11 floors. Luxury rooms and suites, including the exclusive Royal Beach Club. Air-conditioned, private lanais, king-size or double beds, views of ocean or golf course.

Rates $210–$395 single or double occupancy, Royal Beach Club rooms $395, suites from $600. Add taxes, gratuities. Deposit: 2 nights' advance payment or credit-card confirmation. Credit cards: AE, DC, MC, V.

Meal Plans No special dining plan. 3 restaurants, snacks to Continental fare. Best choice: Sound of the Falls.

Services and Facilities **Exercise Facilities:** 10 Sprint weight-training units, 2 StairMasters, 3 Lifecycles, Cybex Smithpress, treadmill, dumbbells (to 40 lb). **Services:** Lomi-Lomi massage, Swedish massage, shiatsu, reflexology, acupressure; beauty salon for facial, hair, and nail care. **Swimming Facilities:** 5 outdoor pools, ocean beach. **Recreation Facilities:** 11 tennis courts (6 lighted), 2 18-hole golf courses, water sports. **Evening Programs:** Resort entertainment, Hawaiiana demonstrations.

In the Area Guided tours of the resort, includes art collection and gardens. Lahaina (old whaling capital) shops, bars, restaurants; Mt. Haleakala; up-country ranches and rodeos; Sugar Cane Train Ride; winery tour; Maui Tropical Plantation (botanic gardens).

Getting Here *From Kapalua-West Airport.* By car, Hwy. 30 (Honoapiilani Hwy.) via Lahaina (10 min). Complimentary transfers at airport. Rental car, taxi, shuttle van available.

Special Notes 10 barrier-free rooms specially appointed for the disabled. Children can enjoy Hawaiian arts and crafts classes and seasonal day camp (Easter, summer, Thanksgiving, Christmas). No smoking in designated areas of the dining room and in health club; 2 nonsmoking floors in Ocean Tower. Spa open daily 7 AM–8 PM. Spa open to nonhotel guests; daily facility fee $15.

Canada

Scenic splendor is an essential part of the fitness vacation in many areas of Canada. Still, Canadian resorts include state-of-the-art health clubs in addition to outdoor hikes, kayaking, and mountain biking.

The Sea Spa Nova Scotia, scheduled to open in 1995, brought seawater and seaweed treatments to Canada's Atlantic Coast. While marine cures are popular in French-speaking Quebec, the high-tech facilities in Nova Scotia mark a breakthrough in transatlantic therapies. Both a destination spa and conference center, this new resort is the perfect base for exploring the Maritime Provinces.

Western Canada is endowed with a number of hot springs where outdoor activity is oriented toward tennis, hiking, skiing, and horseback riding. With the introduction in 1995 of a full-service fitness center at the venerable Banff Springs Hotel, visitors now can combine sports and personal training with a visit to the historic thermal springs, and enjoy the most extensive selection of bodywork in Canada.

Canadian resort spas range from luxurious at the Inn at Manitou in Ontario, to farm-like at the Eastman Health Centre in Quebec. For a demanding yoga regimen, try the Sivananda Ashram near Montreal. On the Pacific Coast, the Ocean Pointe Resort has a full fitness program plus walks in Victoria's historic harbor area and museums. Also in British Columbia is the rustic Hollyhock Farm, where holistic programs and sea kayaking are offered from spring to fall.

The first destination spa opened in 1983 at the Hills Health & Guest Ranch in cariboo country, the heart of British Columbia. Recently expanded and upgraded, the fitness facilities are the core of the sports training and weight management programs, while the trail rides and cross-country skiing provide a balanced, family-oriented activity year-round. The Hills' "Executive Renewal Week" even attracts Japanese businessmen.

Rates in Canada will include a room tax as well as a GST (Goods & Services tax, which is refunded to visitors upon departure). As of summer 1994, $1US was worth $1.36 in Canadian currency. Remember to bring identification papers for Canadian customs: a voter registration card with photo, birth certificate, or passport. Persons from outside the USA wishing to enter the States from Canada should make arrangements before leaving their home country; those planning to re-enter the States should check that they can comply with regulations of the U.S. Customs.

Banff Springs Hotel

Taking the waters

Alberta
Banff
Before the railroad and hotel builders arrived in 1885, the hot springs were sacred, shrouded in clouds of steam. Rebuilt by the Parks Canada, the spring-fed pools at the venerable Banff Springs Hotel are again open, with a high-tech health club

where you can get a shiatsu massage, and then dine on sushi at one of the hotel's restaurants.

The turreted property—the largest in Canada west of Toronto—looks like a castle out of Camelot, and it is equally majestic inside. Most of the rooms are uniquely decorated, and many are historically furnished. But instead of English lords and ladies, the baronial halls may be filled with Japanese tour groups.

The hotel has 14 restaurants plus the new spa café, where healthy breakfasts and lunches are available every day. A grand staircase leads down from the main lobby to the three-level health club, with an aerobics studio and strength-training equipment room whose glass walls overlook the Bow River valley and majestic mountains. The next level down is devoted to skin care and a beauty salon, and access to the pool is via interior stairs from the men's and women's locker rooms. Locker rooms have a lounge with fireplace, glass-walled sauna, inhalation room, steambath, and whirlpool.

Swimmers can use the indoor saltwater pool or outdoor pool or the spa's private lap pool. There are 16 treatment rooms on the pool level, two specially designed for wet bodywork, and also a cascade shower. Designed by Canadian architects and Florida-based spa consultants, this state-of-the-art health club is the best of the Northwest.

Despite all the pampering activities, golf and skiing are still the main attractions here, but other summer oportunities bring cyclists and horseback riders, backpackers and river rafters. With the addition of seasonal packages, Banff Springs has become even more of a fitness buff's dream.

Banff Springs Hotel
Box 960, Banff, Alberta T0L 0C0
Tel. 403/762-2211 or 800/268-9411
Telex 038-21705
Fax 403/762-5755

Administration General manager, Ted Kissane; spa manager, Gordon Tareta

Season Year-round.

Accommodations 867 rooms and suites in original hotel and annex, Banff Springs Manor. Suites in several sizes with nooks and antiques. 3-story VIP suite with private glass elevator, sauna, whirlpool, and lap pool. All rooms have private bath, TV, phone, air-conditioning.

Rates Mid-May–Sept., $135–$184 (C$) daily, single or double. Winter to $232, single or double. Suite with Jacuzzi (2–4 beds) $310–$860; VIP suite $1,500. Week-long spa packages from $302 plus lodging. Confirm room with credit card. Credit cards: AE, MC, V.

Meal Plans Traditional à la carte menu in main dining room. Japanese and Italian restaurants. Spa Cafe open daily for breakfast and lunch.

Services and Facilities **Exercise Equipment:** 10-station Universal Gym Equipment, 2 Lifecycles, 2 stationary bikes, rowing machine, treadmills. **Swimming Facilities:** Large indoor and outdoor pools, 30-ft circular lap pool. **Recreation Facilities:** Bowling alley, tennis courts, 3 ski areas: Mt. Norquay with 17 runs on 123 acres is closest and open till 9 PM Wed.–Sat. Sunshine Village has a

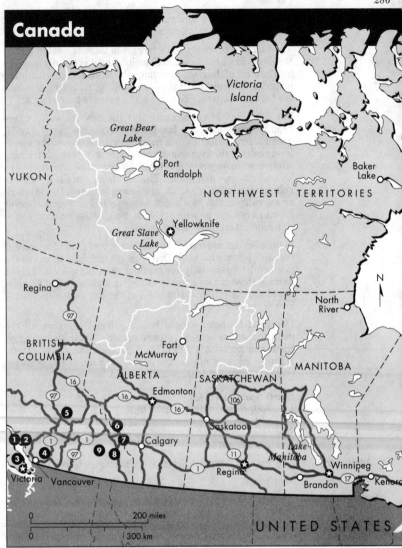

Canada

Alberta
Banff Springs Hotel, **7**
Mountain Escape at
Lake Louise Inn, **6**

British Columbia
Chateau Whistler
Resort, **2**
Fairmont Hot Springs
Resort, **8**
Harrison Hot Springs
Hotel, **4**
The Hills Health and
Guest Ranch, **5**

Hollyhock Farm, **1**
Mountain Trek Fitness
Retreat & Health
Spa, **9**
Ocean Pointe
Resort, **3**

New Brunswick
Manan Island Spa, **17**

Nova Scotia
Sea Spa Nova
Scotia, **18**

Ontario
The Inn at Manitou, **10**
Wheels Country Spa at
Wheels Inn, **11**

Quebec
Aqua-Mer Center, **20**
Auberge du Parc
Inn, **19**
Auberge Villa
Bellevue, **12**
Center d'Sante
d'Eastman, **16**

Gray Rocks Inn, **14**
Sivananda Ashram, **13**
Spa Concept at
Le Château
Bromont, **15**

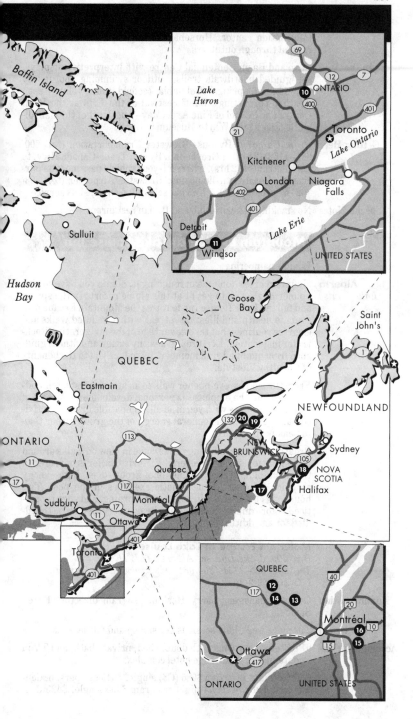

3,514-ft vertical drop and cross-country skiing on 20 mi of groomed trails. Bicycle rentals in Banff. Trail maps at the park information center. Horseback riding and guided treks arranged through outfitters.

In the Area Cave and Basin Centennial Centre with interpretive displays, self-guided boardwalk trails, outdoor swimming pool fed by hot mineral springs. Columbia Icefield tours (May–Sept., weather permitting); Banff Festival of the Arts at the Banff Centre and School of Fine Arts (May–Aug.); art of the Canadian Rockies at the Whyte Museum in Banff.

Getting Here *From Calgary.* By bus, Brewster Transportation (tel. 800/661–1152) (2 hrs) or Greyhound. By car, Trans-Canada Hwy. to park entrances (2 hrs), where a 1-year vehicle pass must be purchased. Local taxi, limousine, Brewster Airporter (tel. 403/762–6700 or 800/661–1152) has scheduled shuttle bus service.

Special Notes No smoking in health club and Italian restaurant.

Mountain Escape at Lake Louise Inn

Luxury pampering

Alberta Mountain hikes don't mean roughing it, nor do you have to give
Lake Louise up morning coffee to get fit at this alpine resort. In the spring and fall the Lake Louise Inn features the Mountain Escape program, a health and lifestyle retreat with scheduled walks and exercise routines that take advantage of the invigorating Rockies for inspiration. Lectures on healthy eating and fitness guidance from qualified staff members introduce you to the benefits of a healthy lifestyle.

From the sunrise eye-opener walk to an afternoon stretch-and-tone session, the emphasis is personal development. A team of instructors works with you in small, compatible groups. Activities are geared to the general energy of the group rather than to peak performance.

Breathtaking surrounding peaks come in view on walks around Lake Louise, and snow-covered Victoria Glacier is mirrored in the aqua-blue water. While one group does high-energy aerobics, another learns aquatic exercises in the pool. Two hour-long classes are scheduled each morning, and yoga is practiced before dinner. Massage and beauty services can be scheduled for an additional charge.

Mountain Escape at Lake Louise Inn
Box 209, Lake Louise, Alberta T0L 1E0
Tel. 403/522–3791 (800/661–9237 in western Canada)
Fax 403/522–2018

Administration General manager, Larry Hoskin; program director, Karen Samuels

Season 2 or more week-long sessions per spring and fall seasons.

Accommodations 91 motel-style rooms with double bed, private bath, and TV in a contemporary ski-lodge hotel complex.

Rates 6-day/6-night program $685 (C$) single, $545 per person, double occupancy. 4-day/4-night program $495 single, $425 dou-

ble. Add 5% provincial tax, 7% service charge, G.S.T. Deposit:
$100 check with reservation. Credit cards: AE, MC, V.

Meal Plans 3 daily meals prepared with spa cuisine recipes provided to
guests on departure. Some vegetarian meals included in the
1,700-calorie diet (per day) plus between-meal refreshments.
Nonalcoholic reception on Sunday evening.

Services and **Exercise Equipment:** Exercycles, Universal Gym Equipment.
Facilities **Services:** Massage (Swedish, sports), facial; beauty salon for
hair, nail, and skin care. **Swimming Facilities:** Heated indoor
pool. **Spa Facilities:** Whirlpool, sauna. **Recreation Facilities:** Bicycle rental, 3 outdoor tennis courts, nearby horseback riding,
downhill and cross-country skiing. **Evening Programs:** Lifestyle lectures.

In the Area Trail hiking, gondola rides at ski area, 2½-mi trail to Lake Ag-
nes teahouse.

Getting Here *From Calgary.* By car, 110 mi on Trans-Canada Hwy. By
bus, Greyhound and Brewster Transportation (tel. 800/661–
1152).

Special Notes Bring hiking boots, warm clothing, gloves. Spa hours: daily
7 AM–10 PM.

Chateau Whistler Resort

Sports conditioning

British Columbia Any season is the right time to visit Whistler/Blackcomb.
Whistler/Blackcomb There's year-round skiing on the greatest vertical rise in North
Mountain America, water sports in summer, and alpine hiking and horseback riding in summer, spring, and fall. And Whistler/
Blackcomb vacation area continues to expand its fitness facilities. The baronial Chateau Whistler Resort, the largest hotel
in Whistler Village, has a complete health club with a pre-ski
stretch class, tennis instruction, and licensed therapists for
sports massage. There are aerobics classes, a 30-foot indoor-
outdoor pool, cardiovascular exercise equipment, coed sauna as
well as separate sets of saunas and steam rooms for men and
women.

Designed around a pedestrian plaza, Whistler Village has doz-
ens of boutiques and restaurants within a short walk from the
hotel. The 12-story Chateau was built on a grand scale in 1990.
The cathedral-ceiling lobby offers unobstructed views of
Blackcomb Mountain's famed slopes, and guest rooms feature
folk art and carpets inspired by Mennonite hooked rugs. Deco-
rating the hotel are Québec armoires, birdhouses, and baskets
of apples. On an outdoor deck, a Jacuzzi beckons. A therapy
center for treatment of sport-related problems with hydrotherapy, massage, and a flotation tank is in the village.

Chateau Whistler Resort
*4599 Chateau Blvd., Box 100, Whistler, British
Columbia V0N 1B0
Tel. 604/938–8000 or 800/268–9411
Fax 604/938–2055*

Administration General manager, David J. G. Roberts; health and tennis manager, Gary Winter

Season Year-round.

Accommodations 343-room high rise with standard rooms and deluxe suites, concierge club floor services. All with full bathroom and amenities, TV, telephone, radio, climate control.

Rates $130–$195 (C$) daily in summer, single or double occupancy; winter rates $260–$295 daily, suites $350–$900. Add 7% GST, 10% tax. Deposit: 1 night's room and tax. Credit cards: AE, MC, V.

Meal Plans Innovative menu in the Wildflower Restaurant with natural, organic ingredients from the area; fresh seafood, wild boar, venison in season. There is also a tapas bar and a lounge for light meals.

Services and Facilities **Exercise Equipment:** 6-unit Keiser pneumatic weight-training circuit, 3 ClimbMax stairclimbers, 2 Universal Aerobicycles, Universal treadmill, Concept 2 rowing ergometer, dumbbells. **Services:** Sports massage, 1-on-1 training, tennis lessons and camps. **Swimming Facilities:** Heated outdoor pool accessible from inside the health club. **Recreation Facilities:** Tennis courts and bike rental at the hotel; golf, canoeing, horseback riding nearby. 25 lifts and a gondola for downhill skiing; cross-country ski trails, glacier skiing (summer). Outdoor croquet court, fishing, paragliding school, ice skating. 2 18-hole golf courses. **Evening Programs:** sleigh rides.

In the Area Whistler Museum, ferry to Vancouver Island.

Getting Here *From Vancouver.* By car, Hwy. 99 past Horseshoe Bay, Squamish, and Howe Sound (70 mi; 90 min). By train, B.C. Rail (tel. 604/932–4003) daily at 7:30 AM (2½ hrs). By bus, Maverick Coach Lines (tel. 604/932–5031) from city terminal, Perimeter Airporter at 2 PM (tel. 604/261–2299). By air, B.C. Air Helijet Airways (tel. 604/938–1878) has scheduled flights on a private plane to Pemberton Airport. Rental car, taxi, limousine available.

Special Notes Specially equipped guest rooms for people with disabilities. No smoking in therapy center and designated dining areas. 1 floor of nonsmoking rooms. Spa hours: daily 6 AM–11 PM.

Fairmont Hot Springs Resort

Nonprogram resort
Taking the waters

British Columbia
Fairmont Hot Springs

Canada's largest hot mineral pools are an attraction of this family-oriented vacation complex in the Rocky Mountains. There's golf, skiing, and a deluxe Sports Center where spa treatments and exercise equipment make it possible to assemble your own spa program. The privately owned Fairmont Hot Springs Resort has large swimming pools for day visitors who come for sports and relaxation. The beautifully landscaped grounds are surrounded by mountain forests.

The recently completed fitness facilities and a private pool are for guests in the lodge and villas. Two full-sized racquetball courts, one squash court, coed saunas and whirlpool, and hydra-fitness exercise equipment are available. An optional spa-cuisine menu has been introduced to accompany fitness programs.

Fairmont Hot Springs Resort
*Box 10, Fairmont Hot Springs, British Columbia V0B
1L0
Tel. 604/345–6311 or 800/663–4979
Telex 041–45108; Fax 604/345–6616*

Administration	General manager, Donald Bilodeau; therapist, Gordon Fraser
Season	Year-round.
Accommodations	139 rooms with private baths in the main lodge. 75 deluxe villas, 5 cottages and 48 suites with cooking facilities. All with air-conditioning, TV, telephone, bath.
Rates	$80–$170 (C$) daily per person, double occupancy. 2-night/2-day spa package, $157–$189 (C$) per person, double occupancy. Add 7% GST, 8% tax. Deposit: 1 night. Credit cards: AE, MC, V.
Meal Plans	Health breakfast daily included in package. Breakfast buffet has fresh juices, bran muffins, yogurt, cottage cheese. Lunch menu is cold cucumber soup, salad of red cabbage and apple, pasta, curried chicken with yogurt dressing, fillet of sole with braised leeks. Dinner entrées include veal cutlet with wild mushrooms, breast of chicken stuffed with lobster, fillet of red snapper with curry sauce.
Services and Facilities	**Exercise Equipment:** 9 Hydra weight-training units, stationary bike. **Services:** Swedish massage, fango, herbal wrap, loofah body scrub, salt-glow scrub; guided hikes, yoga, aerobics, aquacise classes. **Swimming Facilities:** Indoor and outdoor pools open year-round. **Spa Facilities:** Odorless mineral water for hot soaks and swimming pools, outdoor and indoor whirlpools. **Recreation Facilities:** 4 tennis courts, 2 racquetball courts, 1 squash court, 2 18-hole golf courses, water skiing, sailing, fishing, rafting; horseback riding; downhill and cross-country skiing; hiking.
In the Area	Banff Springs National Park, Columbia Ice Field.
Getting Here	*From Calgary.* By car, Hwy. 93, north of Cranbrook (3 hr). By air, private airstrip. By bus, Greyhound (4 hr). Spa open daily 8 AM–10 PM.

Harrison Hot Springs Hotel

Nonprogram resort
Taking the waters

British Columbia *Harrison Hot Springs*	The large, modern hydrotherapy pavilion complements the new fitness facilities and refurbished guest rooms at the Harrison Hot Springs Hotel. The indoor-pool pavilion is constructed of wood and brick and decorated with native carvings, and looks onto the garden where an Olympic-size indoor swimming pool is filled with warm spring water year-round. The sulfurous, 104°F spring water provides effective if temporary relief for aching muscles. Future plans include adding mud baths, Jacuzzis, herbal wraps, and Oriental massage.

The pavilion has separate facilities for men and women, including private Roman baths with sunken seating. There's also an indoor tennis court and exercise room, where aerobics classes are scheduled; aquatic workouts are offered in the thermal pool. Joggers have the choice of running along the lake or on a Dynatrak paved circuit.

From the main road Lake Harrison looks scruffy: The strip of rocky, gray beach is lined with parked cars and RVs, but beyond the tourist bars and souvenir stands are wilderness tracks for hiking and quiet country roads. The hotel, long popular with honeymooners and conventioneers, is in the process of being upgraded and refurbished, but it's business as usual: afternoon tea is still served daily in front of the lobby fireplace.

Harrison Hot Springs Hotel

Harrison Hot Springs, British Columbia V0M 1K0
Tel. 604/796-2244 (800/663-2266 in the western United
States and Canada), Telex 04-361551
Fax 604/796-9374

Administration General manager, Gerald Hadway; spa manager, Sharon Janney

Season Year-round.

Accommodations 300 motel-style rooms in main building, cottages in private garden area. Deluxe rooms in the new tower, some with lake view.

Rates $80–$180 (C$) daily, double or single occupancy; 4 day/3 night midweek package $187–$289 per person, double occupancy, $289–$493 single. Add 7% GST, 8% tax. Credit cards: AE, D, MC, V.

Services and Facilities **Exercise Equipment:** 5 Hydra-Fitness units, 18-station Universal Gym Equipment, 2 Lifecycles, 2 StairMasters. **Services:** Massage, 1-on-1 training. **Swimming Facilities:** Indoor pavilion and outdoor pool open 24 hr, 104°F for soaking, 94°F for swimming; lake. **Recreation Facilities:** Indoor and outdoor tennis courts, volleyball court; horseback riding, golf nearby; cross-country skiing. Bicycle rental. **Evening Programs:** Dinner dancing in the Copper Room.

In the Area Boat trips and fishing on the lake in summer. Minter Gardens showpieces in bloom Mar.–Oct.

Getting Here *From Vancouver.* By car, Trans-Canada Hwy. (Rte. 1) east to exit for Rte. 9 at Minter Gardens; continue to Lake Harrison (2 hrs). By bus, Cascade Lines (tel. 604/662-7953) (3 hrs).

Special Notes Some specially equipped rooms for people with disabilities. Indoor pool open 24 hours, outdoor pool open 10–10.

The Hills Health and Guest Ranch

Luxury pampering
Nutrition and diet
Weight management

British Columbia
100 Mile House
Saddle up for a Western-style ranch workout replete with horse rides and line dancing at the Hills Health Ranch in cariboo country, in the heart of British Columbia. Facials, skin treatments, and massages mix with hayrides and trail rides or, in winter, cross-country skiing. Bringing together fun and fitness, the Hills' wellness program is organized to help you adjust to problems by adopting a physically and emotionally healthy lifestyle.

Woodsy A-frame chalets fan out from the two-story, log-sided main lodge where the spa and indoor swimming pool are located. During winter the ranch is busy with skiiers (several teams train here), but it's an all-season resort that offers special packages for weight management, beauty treatments, and an "Executive Renewal Week." Weekends and 11-day programs are available year-round; alternatively, you can schedule treatments and classes à la carte.

If you join the wellness program you'll participate in exercise, nutrition, and stress management sessions, and receive bodywork treatments. After an initial fitness evaluation you'll begin your scheduled activities: morning power walks, daily guided hikes, aerobics and step classes, line dancing, aquaerobics in the indoor pool, circuit and weight-training, and stretching/relaxation classes. A physician will address medical concerns and a kinesiologist, estheticians, massage therapist, and fitness instructor will work with you throughout the program. Guests have a choice of hearty fare or spa cuisine, as the staff caters to the whole person, providing a high level of personal service.

The Hills Health and Guest Ranch

C-26, 108 Ranch, British Columbia V0K 2Z0
Tel. 604/791–5225
Fax 604/791–6384

Administration President, Patrick Corbett; program director, Juanita Corbett; fitness director, Tim Cooper

Season Year-round.

Accommodations 20 private chalets with up to 3 bedrooms, kitchen, bath, TV, and balcony; alpine cottages for couples and singles. 10 deluxe rooms in the Ranch House have private bathroom, air-conditioning, telephone. 18 larger rooms, each with balcony, in new Manor House.

Rates Weekend $239 (C$) per person, double occupancy, $329 single; 7-day Executive Renewal package $1,299 per person double, $1,575 single. 7-day Inches Off package $895 per person double, $1,175 single. Deposit of $50 or 25% of total cost 2 weeks prior to arrival. Cancellations within 2 weeks of reservation not refundable. Add 10% service charge, 7% G.S. tax. Credit cards: AE, MC, V.

Meal Plans 3 calorie-counted meals a day with health packages. 1,000–1,200 calories a day diet recommended for weight loss.

Services and Facilities **Exercise Equipment:** 8-station Apex circuit, Alpine 2000 stepper, HRT preference stationary bicycles, Quinton treadmill, free weights. **Services:** Massage, facial, herbal wrap, loofah scrub, full-body mud pack, manicure, pedicure. **Swimming Facilities:** Indoor swimming pool. **Spa Facilities:** 2 whirlpools, 2 saunas. **Recreation Facilities:** Stables, horseback riding (1 and 2 hr and overnight rides), cross-country skiing, hiking, curling, ice skating, tobogganing. Nearby tennis courts, golf course, mountain biking, lake fishing and swimming. **Evening Programs:** Western dancing with live local music; workshops on nutrition and wellness.

In the Area Williams Lake (art gallery, July 4th stampede), Gibraltar Gold Mine.

Getting Here By air, Air Canada/B.C. Air (tel. 800/776–3000) daily flights to Williams Lake Airport. Transfers on arrival/departure. *From Vancouver.* By car, use main routes through the Rockies to the village of 100 Mile House, Hwy. 97. By train, BC Rail's (tel. 604/932–4000) Cariboo Dayliner operates 3 times weekly on scenic route to Williams Lake (5 hrs). Complimentary transfers on arrival/departure.

Special Notes Riding and skiing instruction and tepee parties for children. No smoking in dining room and spa. Bring warm clothing and 2 pairs of running shoes. Spa open daily 8 AM–10 PM.

Hollyhock Farm

Holistic health
Life enhancement
Spiritual awareness

British Columbia This secluded holistic island community situated 100 miles
Cortes Island north of Vancouver and reached only by air or ferry, welcomes summer visitors for weekend getaways or for one of the more than 70 seminars and workshops offered here. Subjects range from health and healing to shamanism, a spiritual retreat for couples, and tai chi chuan training. Guests are free to enjoy the island retreat's guided nature walks, organic gardens, and beaches, and bodywork is available for a fee.

Since 1982, specialists in alternative therapies and spiritual health have drawn inspiration from each other in this island setting. The informal "campus," where group discussions are held, is made up of wood dormitories surrounded by the forest and beach. The environment allows for room to jog, swim, or find the solitude to meditate.

Mornings begin with yoga and meditation. Arrangements can be made for bodywork including Swedish massage or skin care. Families camp or share rooms, and kids can enroll in kayaking or other special programs. For relaxation, there are forest trails and beaches, the water, and the hot tub.

Hollyhock Farm
Box 127, Manson's Landing, Cortes Island,
British Columbia V0P 1K0
Tel. 604/935–6465
Fax 604/935–6424

Administration Executive director, Brian Fryer

Season Apr.–Oct.

Accommodations Semiprivate or dormitory rooms (3–6 people per room). A few double and single rooms come with either shared or private bath. Heated buildings with communal showers and toilets. Tent sites without sleeping gear or tent can be reserved.

Rates Weekend Getaway (2 nights) $169–$229 (C$) single, $139–$179 per person, double occupancy, $119–$149 dormitory; tent, $99–$119. 7-night holiday package $579–$799 single, $479–$629 per person double occupancy; tent, $349–$419. Daily rate $89–$119 single, $74–$94 per person, double occupancy, $64–$79 dormitory; tent, $54–$64. $35–$61 per day for children 4–12. Tuition for workshops and seminars is additional. Deposit: $250 for workshop and holiday package, $125 for short stays. Add 8% BC tax, 7% GST. Credit cards: MC, V.

Meal Plans 3 buffet meals daily included with accommodations. Mostly vegetarian, some seafood. Homemade breads and soups, and Friday evening barbecue oysters and salmon are favorites.

Services and Facilities **Services:** Swedish massage, reflexology, acupressure, deep tissue massage, Breema massage (clothed), body wrap, facial. **Swimming Facilities:** Private lake, ocean beaches. **Recreation Facilities:** Kayaks, canoes, rowboat, sailboats, hot tub.

In the Area Vancouver Island: Hot Springs Cove (natural hot spring), Victoria, British Columbia capitol, provincial museum (native arts and history).

Getting Here *From Seattle and Vancouver.* By car and BC ferries (tel. 604/386–3431), via Vancouver Island. By air, scheduled commuter flights on Air Canada/BC Air (tel. 800/663–3721) from Seattle and Vancouver to Campbell River for nearest ferry connection. Direct flights to Cortes Island by scheduled seaplane service: Kenmore Air (tel. 206/486–8400) from Seattle, Coval Airlines (tel. 604/287–8871) from Vancouver. Complimentary transfers on arrival/departure at Manson's Landing for 11-mi trip to Farm.

Special Notes No smoking indoors. Bring warm clothes, flashlight, rainwear, sturdy walking shoes, and footwear that slips on and off easily. Children's programs include sailing and kayak expeditions for 12–15 year olds, and kid's camp.

Mountain Trek Fitness Retreat & Health Spa

Holistic health

British Columbia
Ainsworth Hot Springs

Mountain Trek Fitness Retreat and Health Spa runs integrated wellness weeks spring through autumn, for adventure-minded men and women. Situated on 34 acres of forest overlooking Kootenay Lake and the Purcell Mountains, the rustic cedar lodge is a comfortable base from which to explore high country trails, picnic in pristine meadows, and soak in the hot springs.

Hiking, the core activity of the program (there are six daily treks per package) begins with an orientation on Saturday afternoon. You'll learn some local lore, including information about the Whitewater Glacier Trail, one of the most accessible, that once attracted miners searching for gold and silver in the White Grizzly Wilderness (called Pic-ha-kee-lowna by indigenous people). You may see grizzlies, deer, mountain goats, and marmots as you explore alpine slopes, expansive flower meadows, and a variety of ecological zones with soapstone and serpentine in temperate forests. The lead-and-shepherd guide system allows everyone to go at their own pace.

Workouts in the main lodge are scheduled before and after hikes, and exercise clothing is provided daily. Yoga sessions are held in a wood-floor studio, with views of the mountains and lake. A separate weight-training room has a selection of Cybex equipment and free weights. Located within a five-minute walk are natural thermal spring baths, and there is an outdoor hot tub next to the lodge's sauna.

The all-inclusive week lets you schedule three massages. Each participant or couple has a private bedroom and bathroom, equipped with robes and knapsacks. Optional fasting weeks are structured with daily educational lectures, a colonic, one massage, walks, and a diet of juices.

Mountain Trek Fitness Retreat & Health Spa
Box 1352, Ainsworth Hot Springs, British Columbia
V0G 1A0
Tel. 604/229–5636 or 800/661–5161
Fax 604/229–5636

Administration Founder-director, Wendy Pope

Season Apr.–Oct. scheduled weeks.

Accommodations Cedar 2-story lodge with 6 single bedrooms, 4 double rooms with queen-size bed. All have private toilet with shower. No TV, phone, air-conditioning. Self-service laundry room.

Rates Hiking Week $1,775–$1,875; Gentle Hiking program $1,560–$1,660; 2-week Fit 'n Fast program $2,250–$2,450. Supervised fasting program $700–$800. Add 7% GST, 8% BC tax, and gratuities. Deposit: $500 check. Credit cards: none.

Meal Plans 3 low-fat, high-carbohydrate meals and snacks daily, served buffet style. Breakfast can be cinnamon rice and raisin cereal, fresh fruit and juice, polenta cake with summer fruit sauce, or banana pancakes. Lunch on trail includes spicy tabouli, wholewheat pita sandwich or millet burger, fruit, sweet potato muffin. Dinner entrée is spinach and mushroom lasagna, tofu sukiyaki with rice, angelhair pasta with tomato and artichoke, or cashew/carrot curry with basmati rice. Fresh bread baked daily; steamed vegetables, soup, and salad served with dinner.

Services and Facilities **Exercise Equipment**: 8-unit Cybex weight-training gym, stair stepper, free weights. **Services**: Massage, colonic. **Swimming Facilities**: Nearby pool.

In the Area Nelson (pioneer settlement), hot springs, glacier-fed Kootenay Lake.

Getting Here *From Vancouver and Calgary.* By air, BC Air/Air Canada (tel. 800/776–3000) or Time Air (Canadian International Airlines, tel. 800/426–7000) scheduled flights (1 hr). Tranfers provided from Castlegar Airport for Sat. arrival and Fri. morning departure. By car from Vancouver, Trans-Canada Hwy. to Hope, Hwy. 3 east to Nelson, Hwy. 3A east, Hwy. 31 to Ainsworth (8 hrs). By car from Calgary, Trans-Canada Hwy., Hwy. 93 north to Hwy. 95 past Cranbrook, Hwy. 3 to Creston, Hwy. 3A to Kootenay Bay (ferry), Hwy. 31 (7 hr).

Special Notes Heli-hiking, skiing, and winter fasting programs offered.

Ocean Pointe Resort

Holistic health
Life enhancement
Luxury pampering

British Columbia
Victoria,
Vancouver Island

The Ocean Pointe Resort offers the best of two worlds: the charm and sophistication of Victoria, the capital of British Columbia; and the beauty and solitude of its seaside location. Open to all hotel guests free of charge, the fitness facilities are staffed by trainers with experience in exercise for senior citizens as well as young people. Scheduled classes in aerobics and aquaerobics plus a series of speakers on nutrition and lifestyle round out the holistic program. A wide range of beauty and facial treatments are available à la carte, or with three- or five-day packages, including Thalgo's micronized seaweed products from France, Aveda's line of natural hair-care products, aromatherapy baths and massages, and an anticellulite program.

The goal of the resident owners who opened this spa in 1992 was to offer a facility that would appeal to businesspeople as well as vacationers. Ocean Pointe's fine location and amenities have made this possible. Those on working holiday can take a pre-meeting morning jog along the boardwalk or play a lunchtime game of squash or raquetball in the fitness center. Vacationers who have more free time can luxuriate in the glass-walled ozonated swimming pool (there's no chlorine), taking in panoramic views of the working harbor; or try balneotherapy—underwater massage—in a Somethy tub with air pressure jets; or soak in a tub of mineral salts, essential oils, or marine algae mixed for detoxification.

Ocean Point can also serve as base from which to explore the nearby provincial park on the Pacific side of the Vancouver Island, with facilities for day-trippers. The mild climate enjoyed most of the year makes the island a mecca for golf, sailing, fishing, and scuba, as well. Ocean Pointe Resort's concierge can schedule your tee-off time at the Olympic View golf course or court time on one of the two tennis courts at the hotel grounds. Seacoast expeditions by 12-passenger Zodiac depart from the resort to view marine mammal life, including whales (Apr.–Oct.).

The property is comfortable and finely decorated, with original art and antiques in all the public rooms. Many of the guest rooms are oversized and feature alcoves or dormer windows with a view of the harbor and distant Olympic Mountains.

Ocean Pointe Resort
45 Songhee Rd., Victoria, British Columbia V9A 6T3
Tel. 604/360–2999 or 800/667–4677
Fax 604/360–1041

Administration General manager, Ulrich Stolle; spa director, Kathryn L. Stolle; spa manager, Dawn Woodruff; supervisor, Judith Hill

Season Year-round.

Accommodations 250 rooms, including 34 suites, with king- or queen-size bed, or twins. Choice rooms have Inner Harbour view. All with modern furnishings, private bathroom, TV, telephone, desk, lighted closets. 17 junior suites have compact kitchens.

Rates $99–$270 (C$) single or double occupancy. 3-night Time-Out spa package $825 per person, double occupancy, $995 single; 5-night Rejuvenation package $1,215 per person, double occupancy, $1,507 single; 5-night Anti-Cellulite program $1,420 per person, double occupancy, $1,705 single. Day spa packages (no lodging) $75–$225. Add 7% GST, 7% provincial tax, and gratuities. Credit cards: AE, DC, MC, V.

Meal Plans Lunch and dinner included in spa packages. Menu choices in the Victorian Restaurant include Dungeness crab, fennel and cilantro bisque, medley of organic salad greens, or tea-smoked squab on cellophane noodles for starters; pan-seared arctic char and lobster, or grilled chicken breast with couscous and asparagus as entrées.

Services and Facilities **Exercise Equipment:** 11-station circuit training, 2 StairMasters, 2 Windracer bikes, rowing machine, ergometer. **Services:** Massage (Swedish, reflexology, aromatherapy, relaxation), body wrap, paraffin back treatment, body peeling, facial, anti-age skin treatments. Beauty salon for hair, nails, and makeup. **Swimming Facilities:** Indoor pool. **Recreation Facilities:** 2 tennis courts, squash/racquetball court; 18-hole golf course, marina nearby.

Getting Here *From Seattle and Vancouver.* By air, BC Air/Air Canada (tel. 800/776–3000), Time Air (tel. 800/426–7000), Helijet Airways (tel. 604/938–1878). From Seattle to Inner Harbor, Kenmore Air (tel. 206/486–8400) seaplane (40 min.) or Victoria Clipper (tel. 800/888–2535) ferry (3 hr). By car, B.C. Ferry (tel. 604/386–3431) from Seattle or Tsawwassen to Swartz Bay (3 hr). By bus/ferry, Gray Line (tel. 206/624–5077; 4 hr).

Special Notes 7 rooms specially equipped for people with wheelchairs and people with hearing disabilities. Children's play room. Spa open weekdays 8 AM–10 PM; weekends 9–5.

Manan Island Spa

Luxury pampering

New Brunswick
Grand Manan You won't find an organized spa program at this property, but that's one of Manan Island Spa's primary draws: Guests have the freedom to indulge in hydrotherapy baths and seaweed body wraps (using locally grown dulse, an edible seaweed), or explore the provincial parks, including Fundy National Park with its steep wooded hills, below which the world's highest tides surge upon the cliffs and beaches.

Manan Island, situated in Fundy bay, combines the flavors of New England, Scotland, and France in its heritage, and the design of the eight-bedroom Manon Island Spa reflects the influence: It looks like a New England summer cottage, particularly in the antiques-filled parlor and bedrooms. French thalassotherapy treatments are offered as well as walks in the highlands.

Naturalists have been coming here since James Audubon visited in 1832 and recorded more than 250 different species of birds, including the bald eagle, which still nests here. Whale watching, photography, painting, and rock collecting are popular pastimes. Willa Cather, a frequent visitor during the 1930s, wrote that the island was "tranquilizing to the spirit and seemed to open up great space for it to roam in."

Manan Island Spa

North Head, Grand Manan, New Brunswick E0G 2M0
Tel. 506/662–8624 or 216/562–9171

Administration Director, Joanne Liuzzo

Season June–Sept.

Accommodations 8 bedrooms with private baths. Some king-size brass beds, upstairs views.

Rates Daily B&B $59 (C$), single, $69 for 2 double. 3-day/2-night Island Retreat $225 single, $365 for 2 double; 1-week $490 single, $700 for 2. 3-day/2-night Spa Sampler $135 single, $220 for 2. Deposit: ⅓ advance payment. Cancellation charge for notification less than 48 hr in advance of arrival date. Credit cards: AE, MC, V.

Meal Plans Breakfast cooked to order.

Services and Facilities **Services:** Massage, body wrap, scrub, facial, dulse soak. **Swimming Facilities:** Nearby ocean beaches and lakes. (Water tends to be cool.) **Recreation Facilities:** Bikes available to guests at the inn; canoeing by arrangement. 17 nature trails along the shore to landmarks such as Hole-in-the-Wall cave at Whale Cove, where dulse is harvested.

In the Area Whale-watching expeditions; museum of over 300 island birds,local geological exhibits at Grand Harbour.

Getting Here *From mainland.* By Black Harbor ferry (tel. 506/662–3724), daily (2 hr). Reserve space in advance. Ferry lands at Blacks Harbour on the coastal road (Rte. 1) from St. John and the airport. Short walk from ferry dock on island to inn. *From Maine.* By car, border crossing at Calais/St. Stephen to Rte. 1. Free parking at both ferry terminals.

Special Notes No smoking in the spa or dining room.

Sea Spa Nova Scotia

Luxury pampering
Nutrition and diet
Taking the waters

Nova Scotia
Aspotogan
Peninsula
This beautifully situated $30-million resort opened in 1994, with the intent of taking full advantage of its seaside location as it combines state-of-the-art European thalassotherapy, fitness programs, and tasty Canadian cuisine. Situated on a nature reserve on the Atlantic coast north of Halifax, the Sea Spa Nova Scotia offers stunning views from all the guest rooms, the restaurant, and even the aerobics studio, sending a calming message to guests who have come here for restorative therapy and wellness programs.

Upon arrival you'll be interviewed by a member of the medical staff, then you can choose among numerous activities, including sea-oriented therapies, exercise in the fitness center, or a yoga class in a specially designed meditation room. For more recreation, there are two indoor racquetball courts.

Among the special treatments prescribed by consultants are the therapeutic baths, with a range of equipment that's unprecedented in North America: electro-galvanic tubs, dry carbonic acid gas-bath, and hydrotherapy tubs with underwater massage jets as well as hand-held pressure hose. Stress therapy is another program, which could include biofeedback or a calming walk in the woods.

Seawater is used in a variety of treatments, some using seaweed and marine algae, from body wraps to underwater massage. Drawn directly from the ocean, the salty water is heated to body temperature, and piped into a large indoor swimming pool that's open to all resort guests. Every guest room faces the ocean, and the gentle rhythm of lapping waves acts as a tranquilizer.

Sea Spa Nova Scotia

Box 500, Hubbards, Nova Scotia B0J 1T0
Tel. 902/422–9000 or 800/667–2296
Fax 902/422–0202

Administration Owner-director, Brigitta Hennig

Season Year-round.

Accommodations 116 rooms, including 16 2-level suites. All have private bathroom, TV, clock/radio, phone, air-conditioning; choice of king, queen, or twin beds.

Rates 4-day/3-night package $1,190, single, $980 per person, double occupancy. 8-day/7-night package $2,600 single, $2,240 (US$), double. Additional nights, $345 (US$). Supplement for suite $100 per night. 10% tax and 7% GST and gratuities included. Credit cards: AE, MC, V.

Meal Plans 3 meals daily included in packages. International menu, emphasizing local seafood. Spa cuisine also available at outdoor café in summer. Special diets accommodated.

Services and Facilities **Exercise Equipment:** Nautilus circuit, rowers, cycles, treadmills, StairClimbers, free weights. **Services:** Massage (Swedish, sports, shiatsu), hydrotherapy, herbal wrap, fango, reflexology, aromatherapy, thalassotherapy baths and affusions. Aesthetic salon for facial, lymph drainage, electrolysis, hair and skin care. **Swimming Facilities:** Heated indoor seawater pool. **Spa Facilities:** Separate men's and women's dressing rooms with sauna, steam room, hydrotherapy tubs, Vichy shower, Scotch hose/Swiss shower. **Recreation Facilities:** Racquetball, squash, tennis, 18-hole golf course, sailing, canoeing, fishing.

In the Area Peggy's Cove (fishing village), Annapolis Valley, Halifax historic waterfront.

Getting Here *From Halifax.* By car, Hwy. 103, Rte. 3, Rte. 329 (45 min). Complimentary transfers to and from airport. By car ferry from Portland, Maine, to Yarmouth on Prince of Fundy Cruises (tel. 800/341–7540), or St. John, New Brunswick, to Digby, Nova Scotia.

The Inn at Manitou

Life enhancement
Luxury pampering
Sports conditioning

Ontario
Lake
Manitouwabing

Nestled on the shores of Lake Manitouwabing near Parry Sound, The Inn is a popular retreat for guests seeking peace and seclusion. Tennis clinics have been a staple here since the early 1960s, but in the spring of 1990 The Inn at Manitou opened a full-service spa that provides cross-training as well as luxury pampering. Spa program guests may combine packages for three to seven days with the regular morning or afternoon tennis clinics, and choose from classic French cuisine or gourmet spa dining.

The elegant but tiny spa is in the same building as the indoor tennis court and exercise room, with a maple hardwood "Everflex" floating floor. Among the six private treatment rooms are two designed for wet therapies (mud masks, body wraps, and loofah scrubs) and furnished with a hydrotherapy tub with 47 underwater jets and a hand-operated hose.

The Inn has an extensive menu of massage and mud treatments, including Shiatsu, aromatherapy, and Trager, among others. Premassage facials involve cleansing the skin with a special mud from the Rhine River, and mud is used in several treatments: for body wraps, enabling the minerals and other active ingredients to be absorbed by the body, or for mud baths in the hydrotherapy tub. Known as MoorMud, it was used by monks during the 14th and 15th centuries to cure everything from rheumatism to asthma and depression. The rediscovered, imported mud is said to contain 3,000 organic ingredients.

Natural therapies from leading European spas feature the French line of marine ingredients, Phytomer. A saltwater concentrate used in baths is said to aid slimming and eliminate water retained in tissues. Facials with molecular extracts from amniotic fluid are likewise said to enhance the structure of the skin, while collagen, elastogen, magnesium, and iodine produce similarly beneficial results.

Fitness classes as well as a personal screening and consultation come with all spa packages. The daily schedule includes aerobics, stretching, body sculpting, aquaerobics, and dancercise classes. All guests are invited to join staff-led morning walks and nature hikes.

The Inn at Manitou
McKellar, Ontario P0G 1C0
Winter: 251 Davenport Rd., Toronto, Ontario M5R 1J9
Tel. 705/389–2171 (winter, 416/967–3466)
Fax 705/389–3818 (winter 416/967–6434)

Administration Owners-managers, Sheila and Ben Wise

Season May–Oct.

Accommodations 32 chalet-style rooms, most lakefront, each with log-burning fireplace, modern bathroom; 11 suites with sunken living room, antique marble fireplace, dressing room, bathroom with whirlpool tub, private sauna, sun deck.

Rates $137–$236 per person daily, full American plan, double occupancy. Single supplement $56–$71 per day. 1-day spa sampler $180, 3-day package $449–$609 per person, double occupancy, $902 single. 7-day package $1,212–$1,392 per person double. Add 7% GST, 16% service charge. Deposit: $300 per person. Credit cards: DC, MC, V.

Meal Plans Choice of regular menu or spa cuisine. 3 meals daily, plus mid-morning and afternoon juice and fruit breaks. Spa menu is low in sodium, fat, and cholesterol. Breakfast can be a cold buffet of fresh fruit and juices, cereal, Muesli, granola, yogurt, muffins, brioche, croissants, plus individually cooked egg-white omelet with a ragout of shrimps and coriander tomato. Lunch may be warm white asparagus with blood orange sabayon, pizza with marinated goat cheese, soup of melon and strawberries, or buffet specialties. Dinner entrées include filet of rabbit with sage and pesto sauce, grilled breast of guinea hen with sesame seeds, Georgian Bay trout paper-baked with peaches, Provini veal chop; desserts are poached pears in Beaujolais with vanilla sauce, cream caramel flavored with Grand Marnier, or floating island perfumed with vervan.

Services and Facilities **Exercise Equipment:** 2 Trotter 575 treadmills, 2 Lifecycles, 2 Monark bikes, StairMaster, Legflex, free weights. **Services:** Massage (Swedish, Trager, shiatsu), reflexology, aromatherapy, herbal wraps, mud wraps, Moor therapy (scalp massage, body polish, body mask), facial, seaweed or mineral bath, hand or foot paraffin treatment, waxing, manicure, pedicure; nutrition and fitness consultation. **Swimming Facilities:** Outdoor heated pool 20 × 40 feet. **Recreation Facilities:** 12 outdoor tennis courts, 1 indoor court, horseback riding English style, mountain hiking, water sports, fishing, billiards, mountain bikes, lake cruises.

Getting Here *From Toronto.* By car, Hwy. 400 north to Parry Sound, right on Hwy. 124 to McKellar, right on McKellar Center Rd. for 5 mi (2½ hr). By plane, float-plane charter service ($513 each way); private planes land at Parry Sound District Airport. By limousine from Pearson International Airport ($275 each way). Taxi, rental car available.

Special Notes Men requested to wear jacket at dinner. Tennis camp for teenagers (July–Aug.).

Wheels Country Spa at Wheels Inn

Luxury pampering

Ontario Total fun and fitness is the concept of Wheels Inn, a motel that
Chatham grew into an indoor resort with 7 acres of sports and spa facilities under one roof. Cavort with the kids in the outdoor-indoor swimming pool and water slide, or choose from 42 revitalizing services in the European-style Wheels Country Spa.

Taking a serious approach to shape-ups, staff members have credentials for cardiovascular and muscular testing. They do basic body measurements, a wellness profile, and one-on-one training in a well-equipped fitness center.

Runners and joggers can set courses passing the town's Victorian mansions and modern marina. There are 15 routes mapped out, ranging from 1.8 to 13.5 miles, and an indoor track where 22 laps equal 1 mile.

A wide variety of revitalizing body and skin treatments offered here is unique for Canada. Services are priced on an à la carte basis or on half-day or full-day packages. In this oasis of quiet luxury, stress melts away in the hands of certified masseurs and masseuses. There is also a fully equipped beauty salon. You can schedule a session of reflexology work on nerve centers or be cocooned in a fragrant herbal wrap. Therapeutic Swedish massage and invigorating body scrubs with a loofah sponge working sea salts and avocado oil into your skin are part of package offerings. There is a three-day deluxe spa program and a five-day "Super Tone-Up."

Aerobic classes, with a cushioned floor, are scheduled according to your fitness level, from beginner to high-impact for the super-advanced, and run throughout the day, from 9 AM to 7 PM. People who live nearby can join the club and use the facilities, so you'll never be at a loss for company.

All activities are coed, and you can join a group doing "aquabics" in the fitness pool, or the "renaissance" program for those with arthritis and circulatory problems. Then relax in the whirlpool and steam baths.

Meals are served in the hotel atrium and dining room, or specially prepared lunches can be served in the privacy of the spa lounge for guests who want to avoid temptation. For parents there's a supervised day-care center on the premises.

Wheels Country Spa at Wheels Inn
Best Western Wheels Inn
Box 637, Chatham, Ontario N7M 5K8
Tel. 519/351–1100, 519/436–5500 (spa); 800/265–5265 (in Canada); 800/265–5257 (in U.S.)
Telex 64–7110

Administration President, Steven Bradley; spa director, Jeanette Tielemans

Season Year-round.

Accommodations Spa program limited to 30 participants. The inn has 354 rooms, standard motel amenities, and "club class" rooms.

Rates 3-day package $615 (C$) per person, double occupancy, $705 single. Program includes daily massage, herbal wrap, exercise periods, 3 spa meals, other services. 1-day Pamper Yourself package $160. Add 7% GST; deposit $100. Refundable upon 5-day notice. Rooms-only reservations through Best Western. Credit cards: AE, MC, V.

Meal Plans 3 meals total 1,000 calories per day for spa program participants. Low in salt and fat; choices include meat, fish, salads.

Services and Facilities **Exercise Equipment:** 10 Nautilus weight-training units, 2 Windracer bikes, 2 StairMasters, Universal gym, 6 Schwinn Air Dyne bikes, 3 Concept 2 rowers, free weights (5–200 lb), leg-lift benches. **Services:** Swedish massage, facial, loofah body scrub, herbal wrap, reflexology, relaxation body treatment; beauty salon for hair, nail, and skin care. **Swimming Facilities:** 4-lane lap pool in the Fitness and Racquet Club; Olympic-size pool with indoor and outdoor sections in the atrium. **Spa Facilities:** Saunas, whirlpools. **Recreation Facilities:** Indoor courts:

6 tennis, 9 racquetball, 4 squash; maps of area running and jogging trails; water slides; 24-lane bowling alley.

In the Area Walks through Colasanti's Greenhouses, acres of tropical plants; wine tastings in nearby Blenheim at the Charral Winery. The Guy Lombardo Museum in his hometown, London; Uncle Tom's Cabin, home of Rev. Josiah Henson in Dresden, used on the Underground Railroad.

Getting Here *From border crossing at Detroit/Windsor.* By car, Hwy. 401 to Exit 81 North, then turn right and left at traffic lights (1 hr). *From London, Ontario, and Toronto.* By car, Hwy. 401. By train, VIA Rail (tel. 800/561–3949) serves Chatham from Toronto with 4 trains daily (5 on Thurs.). By air, Windsor/London airport, 1 hr from inn. Local taxi and bus available.

Special Notes Children's programs include day-care center and Kent Kiddie Kollege, with daily activities and special summer outings for children 6–12. No smoking in designated areas. Spa open Mon.–Thurs. 9–9, Fri 9–7, Sat. 9–5, Sun. 9–1.

Aqua-Mer Center

Taking the waters

Québec The complete marine cure at this seaside auberge uses natural
Carleton elements—seawater, algae, mud—and a mild Atlantic climate charged with iodine and negative ions. A combination of European and American therapies revitalizes your body while you relax and enjoy the Gaspé food and scenery at Aqua-Mer Center.

The sequence of treatments prescribed for you after consultation with the professional staff involves bathing and exercising in the indoor swimming pool filled with comfortably heated seawater. There are no cold plunges into the ocean, but brisk walks along the beach and a massage under alternating showers of warm and cold water are encouraged. To stimulate blood circulation and lymph drainage you will be massaged in underwater-jet baths; this will enhance the effect of algae added to seawater that has been heated to a high temperature. Follow this with a toning shower that focuses high-powered jets on every muscle in your body for invigorating results.

Aqua-Mer has a full circuit of treatments with mud, sand, algae, and seawater. Additional complementary treatments include pressotherapy (with pressure cuffs on your legs to enhance circulation), lymphatic drainage massage, shiatsu, and negative ionization. Half of each day is reserved for personal activity, which can be guided mountain tours, excursions to area attractions, or simply relaxing in the quiet room as you enjoy the view.

Aqua-Mer Center
868 Boulevard Perron, Carleton, Québec G0C 1J0
In winter: 145 rue du Pacifique, Laval, Québec H7N 3X9
Tel. spring–fall, 418/364–7055 or 800/463–0867; in
winter, tel. 514/629–5591 or 800/363–2303
Fax spring–fall, 418/364–7351; in winter, 514/629–5591

Administration Director, Yolande Dubois

Season	May 15–Nov. 1.
Accommodations	27 rooms in 3-story auberge and adjoining building. Program participants also stay in the nearby 15-room Thermotel. All have private bath or shower, 2 single beds, bathrobes. No TV, telephone, air-conditioning. Day visitors accommodated on a space-available basis.
Rates	6-day/7-night marine cure $1,045–$1,245 (C$) per person, double occupancy, $1,195–$1,450 single. 5-day marine cure without accommodation includes 5 meals, $575–$625 per person. Add 7% GST; gratuities extra. 25% deposit; balance on arrival. Refunds with notification 30 days prior to reserved dates. Credit cards: AE, MC, V.
Meal Plans	3 meals a day in health café at the Marine Cure Center. Approximately 1,000 calories a day, including fish, chicken, fresh seasonal vegetables. Similar light cuisine at local inns.
Services and Facilities	**Services:** Hydromassage, rain massage, affusion shower, Swiss shower, body wraps, fango, facial, lymphatic massage, pressotherapy, shiatsu, Swedish massage; manicure, pedicure; negative ionization, vertebral board. **Swimming Facilities:** Indoor pool. **Recreation Facilities:** Nearby 9-hole golf course, 3 tennis courts, peddleboats.
In the Area	Mont Saint-Joseph, Miguasha (fossil site), Carleton shops and churches.
Getting Here	*From Montréal.* By bus, Chartered coach departs every Sun. morning, returns Sat. evening (5 hr). By car, Hwy. 20 and 132 east via Mont Joli (4 hr). By air, scheduled Air Canada (tel. 800/776–3000) commuter service to Charlo airport, NB. By train, VIA Rail (tel. 800/561–3949) to Carleton. Complimentary transfers on arrival/departure Sun. at Charlo airport and Carleton train station.
Special Notes	Bring bathing cap, slippers, 2 swim suits, beach towel, workout clothing, walking shoes.

Auberge du Parc Inn

Luxury pampering

Québec
Paspebiac

Settle in for a relaxing week of seawater soaks and gourmet meals at this quiet retreat on the Baie des Chaleurs. Thalassotherapy is the main attraction at this inn, with a touch of Brittany and a style of its own. You are treated with mud, algae, and mineral-rich water pumped directly from the bay. Massage is part of the daily routine for guests on the one-week package.

Group activity is kept to a minimum, but there are stretch-and-tone sessions, and in warm weather groups exercise in the outdoor swimming pool. But a large part of your day is occupied by treatments, a passive program that most of the men and women who come here regularly seem to prefer.

Small and self-contained, the 30-room inn books no more than 40 guests a week for treatments. French is spoken most of the time, though staff members are bilingual. Having some awareness of local customs helps, but with a sense of humor any problem can be solved.

After a walk in the countryside, your appetite sharpened by the salty air, you'll be served low-calorie meals that are a pleasant alternative to typical French-Canadian cooking.

Auberge du Parc Inn

C.P. 40, Paspebiac, Québec G0C 2K0
Tel. 418/752–3355 (800/463–0890 in Québec)

Administration Manager, Madame Le Marquand

Season Year-round.

Accommodations 30 modern bedrooms with private bath in a country manor house. Bathrooms are shared.

Rates 7-day package $1,205–$1,495 (C$) per person double occupancy, $1,325–$1,615 single. 10% advance payment on booking. Add 7% GST, and gratuities. Credit cards: MC, V.

Meal Plans 3 meals a day included in package. Seafood and fresh produce from local farms featured.

Services and Facilities **Services:** Massage, pressotherapy, facial, algae body wrap, hydrotherapy. **Swimming Facilities:** Indoor and outdoor seawater pools; nearby beaches. **Recreation Facilities:** Hiking; golf, tennis, cross-country skiing nearby.

Getting Here *From Québec City.* Located on the main approach to the Gaspé Peninsula. By car, Hwy. 20 to Rivière-du-Loup, then Hwy. 132 east via Mt Jolie through Matapedia (5 hr).

Special Notes No smoking in spa. 2-day marine cure package available.

Auberge Villa Bellevue

Nonprogram resort

Québec
Mont Tremblant Sports training and fitness classes are the specialty of Club Spa Santé at the Auberge Villa Bellevue. Located on a natural lake close to the provincial park, the resort is near one of eastern Canada's most popular vacation playgrounds. The indoor swimming pool, exercise room, whirlpool and sauna are open for year-round use by guests at no extra charge, and are open to others for a daily fee ($7.75 C$). Aerobics classes and aquacise exercise in the pool are scheduled daily during the ski season.

Conditioning prior to skiing can begin with an evaluation of your physical fitness by a credentialed member of the club staff. A personal training program is developed in this hour-long consultation ($65 CAN). Fitness instructors are on hand daily to help you get started on the program. An alpine ski school operates at the resort, and there is free transportation to the slopes of Mt. Tremblant every day. For cross-country skiing, the resort maintains trails and a heated hut where equipment can be rented.

There is tennis instruction with a resident professional, and four courts can be rented by the hour ($10). The resort has mountain bikes which can be rented by the hour ($8 C$) or for a half day ($18 C$). Guests are invited to join a guided bike outing every Tuesday at 2 PM, which includes use of equipment ($20 C$). Summer brings family-oriented programs, and children from age 3 to teens can join activity every afternoon.

The meal plans allow you to select heart-healthy cuisine among five items on the fixed menu. Planned by a local dietitian in consultation with the executive chef, the Menu Santé provides a balance of high-energy and low-calorie food.

Auberge Villa Bellevue
Chemin Principal, Mont Tremblant, Que. J0T 2H0
Tel. 819/425–2734 or 800/567–6763
Fax 819/425–9360

Administration Owner-director, Serge DuBois

Season Year-round.

Accommodations 102 bedrooms including 14 deluxe rooms with king-size or 2 queen-size beds, air conditioning, TV, phone, and screened windows. Also, 8 condominium apartments have fully equipped kitchen, 2–3 bedrooms and baths, furnished in contemporary style, with fireplace, TV, phone, balcony or patio.

Rates 5-night package $255–$365 US in lodge or pavilion room, per person double occupancy, $388–$510 single; apartment $365 per person. Daily rate $54–$79 per person double, $74–$113 single. Children stay free of charge with parents. Add 4%–6% tax, 7% GST. Rates include gratuities. Credit cards: AE, DC, MC, V.

Meal Plans Breakfast and dinner daily included in the 5-night package and daily rate. Menu Santé dinner selections include grilled salmon, roast skinless chicken, pasta, veal, seasonal salads. Special diets accommodated with advance request.

Services and Facilities **Exercise Equipment:** 8 Solaris weight training units, Sprint stepper, 2 Cateye stationary bikes, free weights. **Services:** Swedish massage. **Swimming Facilities:** Private beach on Lake Ouimet; heated indoor lap pool 20 meters (65 ft). **Recreation Facilities:** 4 Har-Tru clay tennis courts ($10 per hour), windsurfing and sailing on the lake, 7 mountain bicycles for rent, kayaks, canoes, paddleboats. Ski instruction, ski equipment and ice skate rental.

In the Area Mont Tremblant Provincial Park, about 15 mi from the villa, with full range of winter and summer activities. Shopping and antiques hunting in St. Jovite. Musee de la Faune (natural history).

Getting Here *From Montreal and Québec.* By bus, Voyageur Lines (tel. 514/842–2281) from Montreal and Quebec City. By car, from Montreal airports and train station, Rte. 130 (90 min). Rental cars, taxi available.

Special Notes No smoking in designated areas. Spa hours: 7 AM–10 PM daily in ski season; summer hours vary.

Centre d' Santé d'Eastman
Eastman Health Center

Life enhancement

Québec
Eastman On a farm, nestled in the rolling countryside of the Eastern Townships (about an hour's drive southeast of Montréal), the Centre de Sante d'Eastman is a low-key retreat for body and mind. The bucolic setting and up-to-date facilities are a unique

and necessary blend for anyone looking for a relaxing, rejuvenating getaway. Hydrotherapy is the specialty, from algae body wraps to thalasso tub.

Seven buildings house the spa facilities and up to 35 guests. A barn is home to the kitchen and dining areas, and the stone farmhouse, complete with flared roof and jutting dormer windows, is the locale for the hospitality lounge. Exercise is optional, and not strenuous. Three guided walks are held daily, and yoga and tai chi chuan sessions are scheduled. A series of treatments designed to rid the skin of impurities is also available. The spa package includes a daily massage, three meals, and a snack.

The oxygen bath is said to produce vitality and a long-lasting sense of well-being. Encased in what looks like an iron lung, you are bathed in 104°F water mixed with carbon dioxide and jets of essential oils, then you receive 10 minutes of oxygen inhalation. Another house specialty is an algae body wrap with seaweed imported from France.

Centre d' Santé d'Eastman
895 Chemin des Diligences, Eastman, Québec J0E 1P0
Tel. 514/297-3009; in Canada, 800/665-5272

Administration Director-owner, Jocelyna Dubuc; spa director, Jocelyne Veillette

Season Year-round.

Accommodations 20 rooms in main house and cottages, all with private bath. No TV, telephone. Comfortably furnished country rooms, some a short walk from spa and dining.

Rates Health Stay package $85–$155 (C$) daily per person, double occupancy. 2-day spa package $170–$230 per person, double occupancy. Add 7% GST and gratuities. Credit cards: AE, MC, V.

Meal Plans 3 meals a day served family style. Vegetarian menu includes eggs, dairy products, decaffeinated tea and coffee. Breakfast can be an omelet with toast, crepes with Québec maple syrup, cereal, yogurt, fruit, or herb power drink. Lunch is soup, plate of raw vegetables. Chinese stir-fry is a dinner specialty. The buffet typically includes vegetable soup, 3 salads (carrot, sprouts, lettuce), eggplant Parmesan, whole wheat fettucine, vegetable rolls, and French apple pie. At 3 PM tisanes (herbal tea) are set out with fruit, cakes, and cookies.

Services and Facilities **Swimming Facilities:** Outdoor pool, lake. **Services:** Massage, polarity, reflexology, body wrap, hydrotherapy tub, body scrub, facial, oxygen bath, aromatherapy, leg waxing. **Recreation Facilities:** horseback riding. **Evening Programs:** Sleigh rides, cooking class, health lecture, tai chi chuan, yoga.

In the Area Québec City, Gaspé Peninsula, Theatre de la Marjolaine.

Getting Here *From Montréal.* By car, Autoroute 10 exit 106 to Eastman, Rte. 245 to Rte. 112, Chemin du Lac d'Argent (1 hr). By bus, Voyageur (tel. 514/842-2281) to Eastman; call for pickup. *From Vermont.* Hwy. 55.

Gray Rocks Inn

Sports conditioning

Québec
St. Jovite

Gray Rocks was built in 1906 as a hunting lodge, and in the late 1930s it opened the area's first Austrian-style ski school. In 1987 the resort continued evolving as a sports resort with the addition of Le Spa, offering a full-service fitness program. Classes and personal services are provided à la carte, although guests aren't charged for using the exercise equipment, coed sauna, or whirlpools. Along with an active social schedule, there are lean cuisine options for dining, making the Gray Rocks vacation package one of the best values in this part of Canada.

If you start with a fitness appraisal to help establish your goals, staff members, including an exercise physiologist, will test your cardiovascular capacity, body composition, and muscle flexibility. A computerized model provides an in-depth analysis of factors that affect your overall wellness. The spa has gained certification for customized exercise programs on their equipment. There are also aerobic dance sessions, stretch classes, and water-supported exercise in the pool.

Gray Rocks Inn
Box 1000, St. Jovite, Québec J0T 2H0
Tel. 819/425–2771 or 800/567–6767
Fax 819/425–3474

Administration General manager, Philip Robinson; spa director, Helene E. Garrity

Season Year-round.

Accommodations 180 bedroom ski-lodge with Spartan furnishings, private bathrooms. 24-room private, upscale "Le Chateau" located a short distance around the lake. 56 apartments (1–3 bedrooms) in cottages.

Rates Summer 6-night package with 3 meals daily, $630–$906 (C$) per person, double occupancy, $828 single. Daily rates: summer from $114 per person double, winter $99–$152 per person double. Add 7% GST and 4.28% local tax. Credit cards: AE, DC, MC, V.

Services and Facilities **Exercise Equipment:** 4 Nautilus weight-training units, 3 Lifecycles, 2 ergometers, 2 Monark bikes, Liferower, free weights (5–50 lb), leg-extension and leg-curl benches, 2 NordicTracks. **Services:** Massage. **Swimming Facilities:** Outdoor pools (not heated); lap pool in the spa. Private beach on Lake Ouimet. **Recreation Facilities:** 22 tennis courts, horseback riding, golf, jogging and hiking trails. Ski school mid-Nov.–Apr. 30. **Evening Programs:** Dancing and theme parties.

In the Area Sleigh rides, shopping in nearby villages. Mont Tremblant Provincial Park (15 mi) for hiking and skiing.

Getting Here *From Montréal.* By train (2 hr). By air, 4,200-ft landing strip for private aircraft. By bus, Voyageur (tel. 514/842–2281) service direct to inn. Local taxi and rental cars.

Special Notes No smoking in spa. Spa open 7 AM–10 PM daily in summer, 8–8 in winter. Daily facility pass ($10) for nonresidents.

Sivananda Ashram

Kid fitness
Spiritual awareness

Québec
Val Morin

Vacationers come here to relax the mind and revitalize the body by practicing yoga from dawn to sunset. Located just an hour from Montréal, the yoga camp is an accessible oasis of peace and harmony. Yet there is time for skiing and family fun within the daily schedule of meditation and vegetarian diet that you are required to follow.

Aside from the bare essentials of lodging, campers revel in the natural beauty of 350 acres of unspoiled woodland. At dawn, you are called to meditation, followed by yogic exercise or *asanas* that stretch and invigorate the body. A first meal comes at mid-morning, peak energy time; supper follows the 4 PM *asana* session. In between, you are free to enjoy the recreational facilities, to hike, or to get a massage. Sunset meditation and a concert of Indian music and dance conclude most days.

Based on five principles for a long and healthy life prescribed by Swami Vishnu Devananda, the program teaches how to breathe and exercise, and how to combine diet with positive thinking and meditation.

Sivananda Ashram
Eighth Ave., Val Morin, Québec J0T 2R0
Tel. 819/322–3226
Fax 819/322–5876

Administration Founder, Swami Vishnu Devananda; director, Mark Ashley

Season Year-round.

Accommodations 2-story wood lodges with private and dormitory rooms. Simply furnished with 60 beds, linens, chest of drawers. Some rooms with private bath. Tent space on grounds.

Rates Single-price all-inclusive policy $40 per person sharing room with private bath, $25–$35 in other rooms, $30–$34 camping. Single room $50; dormitory bed $35–$40. Reservations by mail, with deposit for $50 per person. Credit cards: AE, MC, V.

Meal Plans 2 vegetarian buffets daily. No meat, fish, eggs, alcohol, or coffee. Brunch has fruit, hot grain cereal, baked casserole of seasonal vegetables, rice, salad, herbal tea.

Services and Facilities **Swimming Facilities:** Large outdoor pool; lake. **Spa Facilities:** Sauna, massage. **Recreation Facilities:** Hiking, biking, volleyball; downhill and cross-country skiing. **Evening programs:** Traditional music and dancing of India; bonfires and silent walks.

Getting Here *From Montréal.* By car, Laurentian Autoroute (Rte. 15), Exit 76. By bus, chartered service for special weekends and peak periods from Centre Sivananda (tel. 514/279–3545); Voyageur lines (tel. 514/842–2281) to Val Morin daily. Taxi service available in Val Morin. Airport pickup arranged for $50 (C$).

Special Notes Kids' Yoga Camp, for ages 4–14, is a month-long combination of yogic exercises, swimming, and other activities. No smoking. Remember to bring an exercise mat or blanket, sandals or shoes that can be slipped on and off easily, and warm clothing.

Spa Concept at Le Château Bromont

Luxury pampering
Nutrition and diet

Québec
Bromont

Revitalization and beautification are the basis of the Spa Concept program at Château Bromont, located 60 miles (100 kilometers) from Montréal and 20 minutes from the U.S. border.

Emphasizing serious shape-ups, the Château has a fully equipped gymnasium, indoor and outdoor swimming pools, and an aerobics studio. The daily schedule includes aquafitness Jazzercise, stretch and tone, and low-impact aerobics classes.

European-style treatments are a major attraction for cosmopolitan Montréalers, who make up the majority of the guests. Included in packages for one to seven nights are body peeling, herbal wraps, and an unusually wide choice of massages—from soothing Swedish to shiatsu, Trager, and reflexology. Special therapies include polarity, lymphatic drainage, and baths with mud, sea algae, or essential oils. There are indoor and outdoor whirlpools, and a sauna.

Health programs are based on an evaluation of your lifestyle and on an energy test. The spa directress may advise energy-balancing exercise and specific treatments if you are on a five-night program. Otherwise there is no minimum stay, and services can be booked à la carte.

Spa Concept at Le Château Bromont
90 Stanstead, Bromont, Québec J0E 1L0
Tel. 514/534–2717 or 800/567–7727

Administration Owner-director, Yvette Pratte Marchessalt

Season Year-round.

Accommodations 154 rooms in a country lodge with rustic furnishings. All rooms with air-conditioning, private bath.

Rates 5-night package $1,190 (C$) per person, double occupancy, $1,410 single; 1-night package $275 double, $320 single. Add 11.28% GST and local tax. Deposit: 1 night's accommodation. Credit cards: MC, V.

Meal Plans 3 meals daily included in packages. Meals are nutritionally balanced, low in calories. Herbal teas available.

Services and Facilities **Services:** Massage (Swedish, Esalen, Trager, shiatsu, aromatherapy, reflexology); lymphatic drainage, electro-puncture, polarity therapy, herbal wrap, body peel, facial, fango pack, algotherapy, pressotherapy; beauty salon for hair, nail, and skin care. **Swimming Facilities:** Indoor and outdoor swimming pools. **Recreation Facilities:** Tennis and squash courts, racquetball, shuffleboard, volleyball, horseshoes, mountain biking; nearby downhill and cross-country skiing, horseback riding, water slides.

Getting Here *From Montréal.* By car, Rte. 10E to Exit 78, right turn on Bromont Blvd. to ski-slope area (1 hr).

Mexico

The concept of spas in Mexico can be traced back to the ancient Aztecs, who bathed and worshipped spirits at the country's steaming hot springs. Throughout Mexico today, these *balnearios* (spa resorts) and *baños termales* (hot-spring baths) are a bargain, offering mud baths, thermal waters, and warm hospitality. The largest and most luxurious of them is in Ixtapan de la Sal, two hours' drive southeast of Mexico City.

A very different experience, and a success since it opened more than 50 years ago, is the Rancho La Puerta in Baja California, founded by Deborah Szekely and her late husband. This is the action-oriented counterpart to the Golden Door in California; its holistic health program, vegetarian meals, and the stress-free environment of the Sierra Madres blend into a seamless vacation experience.

The best equipped example of the new resort-based spas is the Avandaro Golf & Spa Resort, a mountain retreat that provides a good opportunity for contemplating nature or improving your golf game between visits to the spa. If the beach is more to your liking, try the Qualton Club and Spa in Puerto Vallarta. On the Caribbean coast, Cancun now has a full-service facility at the Melia Cancun Resort & Spa.

Avandaro Golf & Spa Resort

Luxury pampering

Valle de Bravo Perhaps the last thing you'd expect to find 80 miles west of Mexico City is this miniature alpine village, set in the pines beside a vast lake. The cooler temperatures can be attributed to the area's high altitude, 6,000 feet above sea level. The climate allows for some very unlikely south-of-the-border experiences: crackling fires in guest suites at night to fend off the chill, and invigorating hikes over the hills to witness the annual migration of the monarch butterflies. Programs are customized, as there is no group activity.

The spa is housed in a tile-roof hacienda overlooking the golf course. The latest equipment for facials and anticellulite treatments is available in the salon on the lower level of the spa building, and separate facilities for men and women on the main level include Swiss showers and a set of plunge pools (hot and cold) equipped with a waterfall for an invigorating natural massage. Upstairs is a small aerobics studio used for scheduled classes or individual workouts accompanied by video instructors.

Avandaro Golf & Spa Resort
Vega del Rio S/N-Avandaro
Valle de Bravo 51200
Reservations: 800/525-4800
Tel. 726/6-0370
Fax 726/6-0122

Administration General manager, Alexandra Simon

Season Year-round.

Accommodations 108 rooms within Spanish colonial–style cabins and adobe villas. Most have woodburning fireplace, TV, telephone, tiled modern bathroom. New buildings have 60 junior suites with sitting area, dining table, balcony or terrace.

Rates 5-day/6-night Spa Sampler package $1,710–$1,870 for 2 persons, double occupancy, $1,315 single, $799 per person triple. Daily rate without spa, $122–$210 per person, double or single. Tax and gratuity included in package rate. Deposit: 50% advance payment. Credit cards: AE, MC, V.

Meal Plans $30 credit daily for à la carte menu. Daily specials include grilled mountain trout, pasta, seafood, chicken, and steaks. Vegetarian meals on request.

Services and Facilities **Exercise Equipment:** 5 Paramount weight-training units, 2 Lifecycles, 2 Trotter 540 treadmills, 2 Lifesteps, Precor rower, Tunturi stretch unit, Premier barbell bench, dumbbells (3–50 lb). **Services:** Massage (Swedish, sports, aromatherapy), loofah salt glow, facials, herbal wrap, electronic stimulation of facial and body liftings, anticellulite treatment, antistress biofeedback, nutritional analysis. Salon for hair, nail, and skin care. **Swimming Facilities:** Heated outdoor swimming pool. **Recreation Facilities:** 7 tennis courts, 18-hole golf course, hiking and nature trails, Ping-Pong; nearby horseback riding, water sports, hang gliding.

In the Area Lake Avandaro, Valle de Bravo (colonial pueblo), Toluca (Friday market, botanical garden, Spanish colonial architecture), trout farm, La Gavia (16th-century hacienda), volcano hike.

Getting Here *From Mexico City.* By car, Constituyendes Av. to Autopista (toll road) Rte. 15 via Toluca, Hwy. 134 through national forest, Hwy. 86, Hwy. 8 to Valle de Bravo (3 hr). Hotel provides complimentary round-trip transportation from Mexico City International Airport and hotels in Zona Rosa as part of spa packages, Sunday only. 1-way transfer other days $75.

Special Notes Ground-floor accommodations accessible for people with disabilities. Minimum age in spa is 16. No smoking in spa. Spa open Mon.–Thur. and Sun. 9–2 and 4–7, Fri. and Sat. 9–2 and 4–8.

Balnearios

Nonprogram resort
Taking the waters

A central belt cutting all the way to the Gulf of Mexico as well as the Pacific coast of Mexico comprises a vast volcanic zone. Hundreds of hot springs dot the region, and one entire state— Aguascalientes—has been named for the hot waters.

While most of the springs are not developed, some are popular with Mexican families, and within this volcanic area is Mexico's most beautiful mountain scenery. Here are some of the places where "taking the waters" can be enjoyed year-round.

Mexico

ARIZONA

NEW MEXICO

Tijuana

Ciudad Juárez

45

2

15

Hermosillo

16

Chihuahua

1

Ciudad Obregón

Gulf of California

49

Torreón

40

45

Culiacan

1

40

PACIFIC

54

4

5

15

Guadalajara

80

200

OCEAN

Acapulco

N

0   200 miles

0   300 km

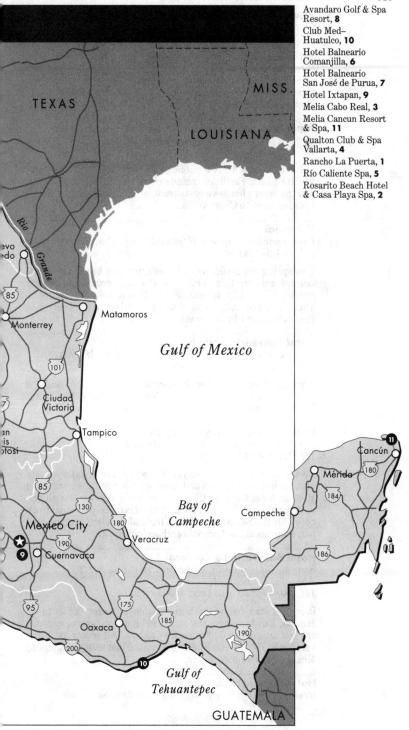

Avandaro Golf & Spa
Resort, **8**

Club Med–
Huatulco, **10**

Hotel Balneario
Comanjilla, **6**

Hotel Balneario
San José de Purua, **7**

Hotel Ixtapan, **9**

Melia Cabo Real, **3**

Melia Cancun Resort
& Spa, **11**

Qualton Club & Spa
Vallarta, **4**

Rancho La Puerta, **1**

Río Caliente Spa, **5**

Rosarito Beach Hotel
& Casa Playa Spa, **2**

Agua Blanca Hotel, Jungapeo, Michoacán
Carretera Zitacuaro, Cd. Hidalgo
Tel. 8 in Jungapeo

Set deep in a canyon, is the 10-room Agua Blanca hotel with three thermal pools fed by radioactive waters. Silence, manicured lawns, and luxuriant flower beds enhance this serene escape. Nearby are San Jose de Purua and the sanctuary of Monarch butterflies.

Aqua Hedionda
Av. Progreso s/n, Cuautla, Morelos
Tel. 735/2–044

Sulfuric waters fill two public pools, wading pools, and eight private pools. Facilities include showers and dressing rooms, and the resort houses a restaurant with dancing on weekends. Located close to Cuernavaca.

El Almeal
Prolongacion Virginia Hernandez s/n. Cuautla, Morelos
Tel. 735/2–1751

Two spring-fed pools, wading pools, playing fields, and a restaurant enhance this public spa. Dressing rooms and lockers provided for daily admission fee. Scenic railroad excursion Thursday, Saturday, and Sunday. Hiking trails nearby to Popacatepti and Ixtaccihuatl.

Hotel Balneario Atzimba
Av. Lazaro Cardenas, 58930 Zinapecuaro, Michoacán
Tel. 455/5–0042 and 455/5–0050

A rustic 12-room hotel with thermal water baths, Atzimba is located about 30 minutes from Morelia, capital of the state. There is a small restaurant and lots of space for unwinding.

Hotel Balneario Chignahuapan
Km. 5 Carretera de Chignahuapan, Puebla
Tel. 777/1–0313

Located at the edge of a canyon into which a cold-water stream plunges hundreds of feet and mixes with hot sulfur springs, the 40-room hotel has huge tiled bathing pools. All rooms with private bath, small balcony. Nearby are Tiaxcala, a colonial town noted for the Sanctuary of the Virgin of Ocotlan, and pre-Hispanic murals at the Cacaxtla archaeological site.

Hotel Balneario La Caldera
Km. 29 Libramiento, Carretera Abosolo, 36970,
Abasolo, Guanajuato
Tel. 460/3–0020 and 460/3–0021

Private baths fed with thermal mineral water, an outdoor Jacuzzi, four tennis courts, soccer field, and extensive gardens are features of the 120-room La Caldera. All rooms have private bath, TV, air-conditioning. Located just west of Irapuato, Mexico's strawberry center.

Hotel Balneario Lourdes
Reservation office: Francisco Zarco 389, San Luis
Potosi, S.L.P.
Tel. 481/2–3232 or 481/3–8065

Located 59 kilometers (37 miles) south of the picturesque colonial city of San Luis Potosi, is this spa, with 36 double rooms, a heated pool fed by mineral waters, horseback riding, squash and tennis courts.

Hotel Tainul

Km. 15 Carretera Cd.
Valles-Tampico, Cd. Valles
Mailing Address: Box 87, Cd. Valles, S.L.P.
Tel. 91–138/2–0000
Fax 91–138/2–4414

Located 15 minutes from Ciudad Valles and 100 kilometers (62 miles) from Tampico, the three-star Hotel Tainul has 142 air-conditioned rooms and 16 suites. The thermal-water swimming pool, fed by sulfur springs, and a freshwater pool, are part of the spa complex; services include facial, massage, manicure, and pedicure. Restaurant and tennis courts for hotel guests.

Oaxtepec Vacation Center, Oaxtepec, Morelos

Reservations: Apdo. 153, Oaxtepec, Morelos 62738
Tel. 52–735/6–0101 or 52–735/6–0202
Fax 52–735/6–0077

This spa, located 56 kilometers (35 miles) east of Cuernavaca, near Cuautla, was a favorite retreat of Moctezuma. The vast swimming pools, athletic fields, and restaurants are run by the Mexican Social Security Institute. Overnight accommodations available in cottages or guest rooms for 6 persons.

Club Med-Huatulco

Sports conditioning

Oaxaca
Santa Cruz
The green hills and emerald waters of Club Med's Huatulco village are located on the Pacific coast 525 kilometers (325 miles) from Acapulco. Sports-oriented activities are available year-round, and the modern fitness center is equipped with state-of-the-art Paramount workout machines.

Choose between exercise and aerobics classes to help work off the éclairs or chocolate mousse from last night's dinner. Sessions of low- and high-impact aerobics, and stretching (45–60 minutes), are offered throughout the day. You have unlimited access to three air-conditioned squash courts, tennis on 12 courts, and a practice golf course. Water-sports activities are popular, too.

Located on twin coves, Huatulco has casita-style lodgings terraced on the hillsides. There are three large freshwater swimming pools (one is Olympic-size) and a choice of five specialty dining rooms. The all-inclusive package, which is a Club Med tradition, takes the stress out of a week devoted to well-being.

Club Med-Huatulco
Bahia de Tangolunda, Santa Cruz, Oaxaca
Tel. 52-958/1-0033
Fax 52-958/1-0101
Reservations: 3 E. 54th St., New York, NY 10019
Tel. 212/977-2100 or 800/258-2633

Administration Rotating Club Med manager

Season Year-round.

Accommodations 500 air-conditioned units furnished with twin beds, optional partition. Rattan furniture, local crafts and bedspreads; private sea-view terrace with hammock. Each casita has a bathroom and shower; electrical voltage is 110.

Rates All-inclusive weekly rate, $650–$1,390 per person, double occupancy; add 10% for single room. Payment of 25% deposit due within a week of reservation, plus club membership fee ($50 annual, $30 initiation). Credit cards: AE, MC, V.

Meal Plans Buffets with unlimited choices for breakfast, lunch, and dinner. Choice of 5 restaurants serving Italian, Argentine, Moroccan, seafood, and Club Med salads, grilled chicken, and tropical fruits. Milk, coffee, tea, and dinner wine included; bottled water available.

Services and Facilities **Exercise Equipment:** 14-unit Paramount weight-training circuit, StairMaster, free weights (3–70 lb), 2 bench presses, incline benches. **Services:** Scheduled classes for aerobics, stretch, and water exercises; massage. **Swimming Facilities:** 3 outdoor pools, 2 ocean beaches. **Recreation Facilities:** sailing, kayaking, windsurfing, snorkeling, 12 tennis courts (7 lighted), 3 indoor squash courts, practice golf course, volleyball, basketball, softball, billiards, Ping-Pong. Golf course (9-hole) nearby (extra charge). **Evening Programs:** Nightly entertainment and dancing.

In the Area Monte Alban (Zapotec archaeological ruins), Oaxaca (16th-century colonial architecture, Indian marketplace), Mitla (Aztec ruins).

Getting Here *From Dallas.* Club Med charter flights on American Airlines every Sunday. Transfers to club provided. Taxi 1-way $25.

Special Notes Registered nurse in residence. Airport fee required with proof of U.S. citizenship. Children 6 and over accommodated with parents.

Hotel Balneario Comanjilla

Taking the waters

Guanajuato Located in the heart of the fertile Bajio region, the pleasantly
León old-fashioned Hotel Balneario Comanjilla is a quiet, secluded resort convenient to beautiful nearby colonial city of Guanajuato and industrial León (the leather capital of Mexico). Gardens surround the two-story guest buildings, one of which houses an aerobics studio and conference facilities.

Exercise programs are organized on request only, and massage ($15) appointments must be made well in advance. Medical and nutritional consultation is available to guests in Spanish only. Nevertheless, two swimming pools filled with warm thermal water, well-appointed guest rooms, tennis courts, and stables make the trip worthwhile for honeymooners, Texas snowbirds, and, perhaps, you, regardless of language barriers.

Hotel Balneario Comajilla

Carretera Panamericana 45, Km. 385
Apt. Postal 111, 37000 León, Gto.
Tel. 52–47/12–0091
Fax 52–47/12–2479

Administration	Manager, Sr. Arturo Sainz
Season	Year-round.
Accommodations	120 rooms in 2-story Spanish-colonial buildings. All with tiled private bathroom, phone, TV, and air-conditioning. 4 suites have step-down Roman bath with thermal water. All with 2 king-size beds, balcony or patio, view of forest or pool.
Rates	Daily rate includes 3 meals. 430 pesos for two persons in standard double room; 580 pesos for two persons in suite.
Meal Plan	3 meals daily included in daily room rate. An à la carte menu is offered in the hotel dining room.
Services and Facilities	**Exercise Facilities:** 2 stationary bikes, free weights. **Services:** Massage, facial; medical evaluation. **Spa Facilities:** 2 outdoor pools. **Recreation Facilities:** 2 tennis courts, bicycles, horseback riding, billiards, Ping-Pong.
In the Area	San Miguel de Allende, Guanajuato (museums, university, fall festival), Leon (leather shopping, particularly for shoes)
Getting Here	*From León.* By car, Hwy. 45 to Silao, Km 385; follow rural road signs to hotel (40 min). Taxi, rental car available at Bajio Regional Airport (20 min).
Special Notes	Ground-floor rooms are accessible for people with disabilities.

Hotel Balneario San José de Purua

Taking the waters

Michoacán
San José Purua

Set on the edge of a small canyon, with spectacular views of the mountains and a nearby waterfall, the Hotel Balneario San José de Purua has been a popular watering place since the times of the Tarascan Empire (AD 1200). Lush gardens and giant trees bearing orchids surround the bathhouse where thermal waters from several springs on the hillside are piped into private bathing pools. Dipping into the fizzy, highly carbonated water is a daily ritual that relaxes travelers' aches and pains. The mineral-radioactive water flows from springs at 89°F (32°C).

Mud packs are a specialty here. Facials using a mixture of the thermal water and highly mineralized mud are said to be beneficial to the complexion. Gently applied, the mud mask dries as you relax, and it is followed by a massage with herbal and fruit-based creams.

Treatments are booked on an à la carte basis. While there is no planned fitness program, the costs for a facial or massage are modest. And the resort offers a full complement of diversions, from golf and tennis to bowling and horseback riding.

Secluded and quiet, the hotel has the atmosphere of a colonial hacienda. Guest rooms with red-tile roofs, private terraces, and garden walks line the canyon to a small lake filled with ducks. The 55-year-old hotel has undergone extensive renovations but maintains a graceful, old-world ambience.

Hotel Balneario San José de Purua

Apdo. Postal 43, Zitacuaro, Michoacán
Paseo de la Reforma, Esq. Colon, 06030, Mexico City,
D.F.
Tel. 905/510–4949 for reservations in Mexico City;
52–725/7–0200 for hotel
Fax 52–725/7–0150 at hotel

Administration Director, Juan Gonzalez Rojas

Season Year-round.

Accommodations 250 rooms in the hacienda-style hotel; heavy wood furniture, handwoven bedspreads, colorful decorations; all rooms with large private baths, modern facilities. Some small private terraces; 1 suite comes with private swimming pool. No air-conditioning. TV lounge with programs by satellite.

Rates Double room with 3 meals 390–432 pesos per day for 2, 230–277 pesos single. Tax included; gratuities optional. Credit cards: AE, MC, V.

Meal Plans Trained under German and Spanish master chefs, the restaurant staff takes a light approach to traditionally spicy Mexican cuisine. Fresh fish grilled over wood, without butter on request. Chicken, lamb, and beef usually well done. Lentil soup with plantain or baked zucchini are dinner choices.

Services and Facilities **Services:** Massage, facials, mud packs. **Bathing Facilities:** Private bath, 5 outdoor pools. **Swimming Facilities:** Outdoor pool. **Recreation Facilities:** Minigolf, tennis, bowling, riding, game rooms for billiards, Ping-Pong, cards. **Evening Programs:** Folkloric groups.

In the Area Michoacán Museum (Museo Michoacano) in an 18th-century palace on Morelia's main plaza houses Indian artifacts, a puppet collection, colonial furniture, and paintings; Museum of Contemporary Art (Museo de Arte Contemporaneo) in Morelia has changing exhibitions, as does the Casa de la Cultura; Church of the Christ of Health (Iglesia del Niño de la Salud) on Rte. 15 near Morelia, has an image of the Christ Child said to have healing powers.

Getting Here *From Mexico City.* By car, Hwy. 15 northwest via Zitacuaro and Cd. Hidalgo, then 7 km to archway, 5 km south of Hwy. 15 (4 hr). By bus, from the Northern Bus Terminal, Transportes Norte de Sonora (tel. 567–9221, 567–9664, 587–5633), 4½ hr. By hotel van, service costs $25 per person, 1 way. Rental car available.

Special Notes Limited access for people with disabilities. Organized games for children. No smoking in the bathhouse.

Hotel Ixtapan

Luxury pampering
Taking the waters

Ixtapan de la Sal Hotel Ixtapan, the largest and most luxurious thermal springs health resort in Mexico, is located in Ixtapan de la Sal, which has been a popular center for cures since the 16th-century Aztec emperor Móctezuma came to bathe. It is 119 kilometers (65 miles) southwest of Mexico City, easily accessible from the capital by car or limousine service.

Its health and beauty programs are designed to revitalize, rejuvenate, and refresh the total person. Family-owned and run, the hotel has been extensively modernized. A water treatment plant and a power plant have been added, as have new, but somewhat limited facilities for aerobics classes and exercise equipment. The centerpiece of the new spa is the marble whirlpool, where you can relax while awaiting a facial or massage in private cubicles.

The thermal waters originate from an extinct volcano about an hour away and are piped into a huge lake in the Parque Acuatico as well as into a swimming pool in the hotel gardens. In a public bathhouse across from the gardens, you can have a private soak in 20 marble-walled Roman baths. The sunken whirlpools are filled with warm mineral water, ideal for a late-afternoon soak or a Sunday indulgence when hotel masseuses have the day off.

Packages include daily massage and treatments in four- and seven-day programs, but you must arrive on a Sunday. The rate includes accommodations, meals, and treatments. Treatments are gentle and relaxing, and exercises are not strenuous. The masseuses work muscles by hand and utilize electric vibrators as well. Optional diet plan and medical supervision, are available with the spa packages.

Among recreational facilities at this 35-acre family resort are a disco, bars, train rides, horse-drawn carriages, water slides, and a bowling alley. Avoid weekend crowds if possible.

Hotel Ixtapan
Ixtapan de la Sal, 51900
Office: Tonala 177, Col. Roma, 06700, Mexico City, D.F.
Tel. 52–5/264–26 for office in Mexico City
Fax 52–5/264–2529
U.S. Reservation Center
Tel. 210/341–8151 or 800/638–7950
Fax 210/342–9789

Administration Director, Roberto San Roman; Spa manager, Juan Martinez

Season Year-round.

Accommodations 200 rooms plus 50 private chalets; pre-Hispanic motifs, colorful native fabrics; rooms comfortable with king-size bed plus sofa bed standard; all suites with private baths and air-conditioning. Superior rooms with balcony face gardens.

Rates 7-day/6-night spa program, (Sun.–Sat.) $784–$825 per person double occupancy, $945–$995 single. 4-day/ 4-night program (Sun.–Thurs. or Wed.–Sun.), $404–$425 double, $565–$650 single. Daily $135–$210 for 2 persons double, full American plan. Add 10% tax plus gratuities. Deposit: 50% at time of booking, plus $95 transfer ($85 return to Mexico City) if requested. No credit cards.

Meal Plans 900-calorie diet menu has fruit or juice with either tea or coffee for breakfast; cream of carrot soup, fresh fruit, and either chicken with mushrooms or plain tuna fish for lunch; dinner choices include fresh rainbow trout, omelet, and cheese plate.

Services and Facilities **Exercise Equipment:** 14-station CalGym, 2 Lifecycles, 2 Precor 9.5 treadmills, Precor X-country skier, free weights, benches. **Services:** Massage, reflexology, mud packs, facial; hair, skin, and nail treatments. **Bathing Facilities:** Indoor and outdoor pools, private whirlpools. **Swimming Facilities:** Outdoor pools. **Recreation Facilities:** Tennis courts, 9-hole golf course, horseback riding, volleyball, badminton. **Evening Programs:** Resort entertainment, movies, folkloric ballet.

In the Area Taxco (artisan center), archaeological sites.

Getting Here *From Mexico City.* By car, Hwy. 15 to toll road (Autopista) via Toluca, then Hwy. 55 to Ixtapan de la Sal toll road (Cuota) (2 hr). By bus from Observatorio terminal. Hotel provides transfers on arrival/departure at airport or downtown hotels $180 round-trip, including tolls and tax. Taxi, rental car available.

Special Notes Elevators and ground-floor rooms are accessible for people with disabilities. Minicamp and play areas for children. No smoking in baths.

Melia Cabo Real

Nonprogram resort

Baja California
San Jose del Cabo Perched on the rugged tip of Baja California, where the Sea of Cortés meets the Pacific Ocean, the spa at the Melia Cabo Real resort is enjoyed by nature lovers and fitness buffs alike. Whale-watching in the Sea of Cortés is a popular pastime, as are desert cycling, mountain jogging, horseback riding, and a full range of water sports. Deep-sea fishing for marlin is also a major attraction.

The hotel is crowned by a unique glass-and-marble pyramid, and bordered by cactus gardens, flowering bougainvillea, and palms. A beachfront restaurant and two swimming pools are reached by cobblestone walkways. The health center's coed gym offers sessions of yoga and tai chi chuan, in addition to personalized exercise supervised by trained fitness instructors. Aquacise and weight-training classes are scheduled in the pool. For relaxation, each locker room has a sauna, steam room, and Jacuzzi. Exercise equipment is minimal, and bodywork is limited to massage and wraps with herbs or mineral salts. Beauty salon services are available as part of the Avanti spa package, or à la carte.

Melia Cabo Real
Carretera Cabo San Lucas, Sector 5, Km 19.5
San Jose del Cabo, 23410
Tel. 52–114/3–0999 or 800/336–3542
Fax 52–114/3–1003

Administration General manager, Cristobal Tortosa; spa director, Lucrecia M. Aguilar

Season Year-round.

Accommodations 292 double rooms and 7 suites, all with oceanfront view, air-conditioning, satellite TV, telephone, marble-floor bathroom with 110-volt (U.S.) electricity outlets. Garden-level rooms have landscaped private terrace: all others have private balcony.

Rates 5-day/4-night Health, Beauty and Pamper Package, including 3 meals daily, spa services, and airport transfers, $897 per person, double occupancy. 1-day spa package (no lodging) $260 per person. Tax included. Daily room rate $119–$205 for 2 persons, $109–$185 single. Suites $287–$400. Add 20% tax, plus gratuities. Deposit: guarantee by credit card. Credit cards: AE, DC, MC, V.

Meal Plans 3 meals daily included in spa package. The weight-loss menu for breakfast is egg-white omelet or granola with low-fat milk, peach melva, juices, coffee, tea, and toast. Lunch can be soup, steamed broccoli and cauliflower, chicken breast, tossed salad, or broiled fish, zucchini and tomato. Dessert is an apple or apricot. Dinner entrées include broiled beef, fish, or chicken; vegetarian plate with cottage cheese; or spinach salad.

Services and Facilities **Exercise Equipment:** 2 Universal weights units, 2 stationary bikes, EZ Stepper, free weights, slant board. **Services:** Massage, herbal wrap, mineral salt wraps, reflexology; 1-on-1 instruction; salon for hair, nail, and skin care. **Swimming Facilities:** 2 outdoor freshwater pools, ocean beach. **Recreation Facilities:** Water sports, scuba, beach volleyball, table tennis, 2 tennis courts (lighted, $9 per hr); 18-hole golf course nearby, horseback riding, boat tours. **Evening Programs:** Live music and dancing nightly.

Getting Here *From Cabo San Lucas International Airport.* By car, Hwy. 1 southwest (25 km), resort entrance at Km 19 (30 min). Complimentary transfers included in 5-day spa package. Taxi, rental car available.

Special Notes Ground-floor rooms available for people with disabilities. Ferry service to Puerto Vallarta scheduled daily.

Melia Cancun Resort & Spa

Nonprogram resort

Quintana Roo
Cancún Amid the strip of high-rise hotels for which Cancún is renowned, is the newly opened (1994) boutique spa at the Melia Cancún Resort, notable because it's the only such beachfront facility in this popular resort town. Perched on a spectacular white sand beach, well-acclaimed Melia Hotel overlooks the turquoise waters of the Caribbean. Enjoying massages poolside is the prescription for relaxation, and outdoor treatment cabanas let you enjoy the sea air without sun. Aerobics classes are held on the pool terrace and in the pool. When you've had enough sun, the spa is a cool retreat, with fully equipped fitness room, and salon for facials and skin and hair treatments.

At day's end try the spa's aloe spritzer—a soothing tonic, involving a body shampoo followed by a cooling aloe body gel.

Other specialties are the Mayan clay mask, sea-salt loofah scrub, and aromatherapy massage.

Melia Cancún Resort & Spa

Blvd. Kukulkan, No. 23 Zona Hotelera
77500 Cancún, Quintana Roo
Tel. 52–988/5–1160 or 800/336–3542
Fax 52–988/5–1085

Administration Managing director, Eberhard Linke

Season Year-round.

Accommodations 413 deluxe rooms, 36 junior suites, 1 presidential suite. All have balcony with ocean or lagoon view, private bathroom, TV, telephone, air-conditioning.

Rates Daily per room (single or double occupancy) from $170 low season, from $285 high season. Spa packages from $175 per day. Add 10% tax and 15% service charge. Credit cards: AE, DC, MC, V.

Meal Plans No meal plan is available, but the Melia has 4 restaurants, all of which feature local seafood and offer spa cuisine. Grilled grouper with fresh lime is a favorite.

Services and Facilities **Exercise Equipment**: Badger strength conditioning units, 3 Quinton treadmills, 2 LifeSteps, 3 Lifecycles, free weights. **Services**: Massage, aromatherapy, hydrating facial, clay mask, loofah body scrub, aloe body wrap; salon for hair, nail, and skin care. **Swimming Facilities**: 3 outdoor pools, ocean beach. **Recreation Facilities**: 3 tennis courts (lighted, hard surface), executive golf course, water sports. **Evening Programs**: music, Ballet Folklorico.

In the Area Mayan ruins, Cozumel (scuba).

Getting Here *From Miami.* By air, United, Mexicana, American Airlines and others have scheduled service. Taxi, rental car available.

Qualton Club & Spa Vallarta

Luxury pampering

Jalisco
Puerto Vallarta The steamy romance of Elizabeth Taylor and Richard Burton put Puerto Vallarta on the international tourist map, and the Qualton Club & Spa Vallarta will keep it there. Located in a seaside complex of high-rise hotels near the international airport, here's a budget-priced property for fitness buffs on a beach holiday. The club has a large fitness center where you can join yoga, step-aerobics, and water-aerobics classes daily, or use a full circuit of weight-training equipment in air-conditioned studios. The club's all-inclusive daily rate includes spa admission, meals, and refreshments. (A daily $10 spa pass is available to nonresidents.)

Supervised by certified aerobics instructors, activities are scheduled from 7AM to 7:30PM. At 7AM a tennis clinic starts the day, followed by low-impact aerobics, cross-training workout sessions, and yoga. There are also bodywork and beauty-salon services available daily at an additional charge. Fitness evaluations are conducted in specially equipped testing rooms. Staff members test your aerobic capacity, strength, flexibility, and blood pressure prior to starting you on a schedule of exercise.

A wide range of relaxing massages, herbal wraps, and facials are available, too, and guests are pampered with body and beauty treatments using natural extracts and herbs. Even the mud in fango treatments has a history: It comes from a volcanic source in Michoacán, where it is purified for exclusive use here.

Qualton Club & Spa Vallarta

Km 2.5 Av. Las Palmas, Puerto Vallarta, Jalisco, 48 300
Reservations: 800/421–2134
Tel. 52–322/4–4446
Fax 52–322/4–4445

Administration	General manager, Roland Bernard; spa manager, Silvia Elena Velasco Santana
Season	Year-round.
Accommodations	248 deluxe rooms with balcony in a 4-star resort with 2 5-story wings connected by a 14-story tower. Top floors have 26 deluxe rooms, 4 master suites, 2 presidential suites with private Jacuzzi and terrace. Club guests get all food and drinks in the room rates. All rooms are air-conditioned, with marble-floored bathroom, color TV, telephone.
Rates	Daily rate $75 per person double, $105 single, $65 per person triple. Add 10% tax, plus gratuities. Deposit: 1 night's lodging. Credit cards: AE, DC, MC, V.
Meal Plans	Breakfast choices include egg-white omelet with steamed vegetables, yogurt, whole-grain cereal, tropical fruit. Lunch can be vegetarian chili, grilled fish, or sautéed vegetables. Dinner choices (available in the Villa Linda restaurant) include skinless chicken fajitas, pasta primavera, baked snapper, broiled chicken breast Florentine with steamed vegetables over spinach, or fish fillet.
Services and Facilities	**Exercise Equipment:** 22-unit Paramount weight-training circuit, 3 Lifecycles, 2 Lifesteps, 2 Lifestride treadmills, Precor step machine, dumbbells, barbells (1¼–45 lb), benches. **Services:** Massage, herbal wrap, loofah body scrub, facial, fango, aromatherapy; computerized health and fitness evaluations; skin, nail care. **Spa Facilities:** Steam room, sauna, whirlpool. **Swimming Facilities:** Outdoor pool, ocean beach. **Recreation Facilities:** Tennis court (concrete surface, lighted) in spa, 8 courts nearby, water sports; Los Flamingos golf course (PGA par-72, designed by Percy Cliff), horseback riding on the beach.
In the Area	Gringo Gulch (celebrity homes), Mismaloya (John Huston's setting for *Night of the Iguana*), Villa Vallarta Mall (shopping), Yelapa (beach restaurants, freshwater lagoon), Playa Las Animas (natural beach), ferry to Baja California.
Getting Here	*From Mexico City.* By air, scheduled flights by Mexicana, Aeromexico, American (45 min). Also direct service from Dallas by Continental. Taxi, rental car available.
Special Notes	Ground-floor accommodations, ramps, elevators for people with disabilities. Spa open Mon.–Sat. 7 AM–8:30 PM. Rubber-sole shoes required in workout rooms.

Rancho La Puerta

Life enhancement
Weight management

Baja California
Tecate

The Rancho La Puerta regimen can be easy or challenging. Hiking on sacred Mount Kuchumaa, a broad range of exercise classes (more than 60 daily), meatless meals spiced with Mexican specialties, and spa pampering are among your options.

The original formula for fitness has expanded since the resort opened 53 years ago, but the basic attractions endure: a nearly perfect year-round climate that's dry (an average of 341 sunny days) and pollen-free, the natural beauty of purple foothills ringed by impressive mountains, and the ovo-lacto vegetarian diet. The ranch has had a high percentage of repeaters, and newcomers quickly get into the swing of things.

Encouraged by instructors who use innovative techniques in workouts, and soothed by a massage or herbal wrap, you focus on recharging body and mind. Some classes are intense, others relaxing; counselors are on hand to help with your schedule.

Designed in the style of a Mexican village, there is a central complex of swimming pools, men's and women's health centers (each with sauna, steam room, Jacuzzi), library, and lounges, linked by brick-paved walkways to casitas and villas that accommodate 150 guests. Gyms dot the landscape: some open-air, others enclosed for cool days. No signup is required for any of the numerous classes, including aerobic circuit training, back-care workshop, better breathing, body awareness, hatha-yoga, self-defense, and a progressive series of fitness and stretching sessions for men.

This flowering oasis, set amid 575 acres of seclusion, also gives you a taste of Mexican resort life. Accommodations vary from studiolike rancheras to luxury haciendas and villas decorated with native handmade furniture and rugs. Many feature tile floors, fireplaces, and kitchenettes. (Large units can be shared by single guests on request.)

After two or three days on a low-fat, high-carbohydrate diet, without distractions from TV, newspapers, or telephone, guests usually discover that their appetite for food has decreased remarkably, while they look and feel healthier. Some do go "over the hill," tempted by Tecate's shops and burrito bars.

Rancho La Puerta
Tecate, Baja California
Tel. 52–6/654–1155
Reservations: Box 463057, Escondido, CA 92046
Tel. 619/744–4222 or 800/443–7565
Fax 619/744–5007

Administration Manager, Jose Manuel Jasso; fitness director, Phyllis Pilgrim

Season Year-round; special weeks for couples only during Mar. and Oct.

Accommodations Single-level ranchera rooms and deluxe studio suites (75) with bath in adobe haciendas and villas. Some large units with 2 bedrooms, 2 baths, southwestern-style beamed ceilings, fireplace, and dining-living area. The maximum number of guests is 150, cared for by a staff of more than 350. No air-conditioning, TV, telephone.

Rates The week-long program, Sat.–Sat., includes use of all fitness facilities, 3 meals a day. Rate varies according to accommodation. Treatments and personal services charged on an individual basis. Single accommodations $1,530–$2,200, double $1,215–$1,750 per person, plus tax. Villa Studios have additional single bed, Villa Suites accommodate up to 4 persons. Gratuities optional. Minimum stay 1 week. Deposit: $250 per person within 14 days of request for accommodations; balance payable 30 days prior to arrival. Credit cards: MC, V.

Meal Plans The ovo-lacto-vegetarian diet includes fish 2 times a week; wine on Fri. optional. Breakfast choices change daily: scrambled eggs and tofu with tortilla, hot and cold cereal, boiled egg, and fresh fruits are typically offered. The lunch buffet may include vegetable soup, tofu sandwiches, a vegetable platter, quesadillas of ricotta cheese and tofu, and garlic herbed pizza. Dinner entrées include lasagna, enchiladas, shrimp casserole, Thai spring roll, grilled swordfish, and steamed vegetables spiced with cilantro-based salsa. Fasting on liquified fruits fortified with fresh vegetables and nuts on Mon.

Services and Facilities **Exercise Equipment:** Supervised weight-training gym with 6 StarTrac treadmills, 15 CamStar weight units, 6 StairMasters (4000 PT), 8 Monark bikes, PTS recumbent bike, 4 Bio-Health computerized bikes, dumbbells, incline benches. **Services:** Massage, herbal wraps, beauty salon for hair, nail, and skin care daily by appointment. Charges will be added to your account. Golden Door hypoallergenic cosmetics used exclusively. **Swimming Facilities:** 3 outdoor pools, 1 heated, used primarily for aquatic exercise classes. **Recreation Facilities:** Tennis on 6 lighted courts, a putting green, volleyball and basketball courts. Hiking ranges from "moderate" to a challenging climb up Mt. Kuchumaa. Outdoor running track. **Evening Programs:** Movie and lecture scheduled nightly. Recreation hall is open for ping-pong and other games.

In the Area Tecate is 3 mi (5 km) from the ranch; Tijuana, 25 mi (40 km) west, bustles with curio shops, a cultural center, and, on summer Sun., bullfights.

Getting Here *From San Diego airport.* Complimentary transfers on arrival/departure. By car, I-5 south to Hwy. 94, Tecate turnoff to Rt. 188, south to border crossing, right at 2nd light, onto Hwy. 2, 3 mi on right (1½ hr). Taxi, rental car available.

Special Notes Most facilities are barrier-free and ground-level. Call for reservations. Families are welcome, though no special activity for young guests is organized; $675 per week for children ages 7–14. No smoking inside buildings. Treatment facilities open daily 7 AM–noon; daily 2–8 PM except Sat.

Río Caliente Spa

Life enhancement
Nutrition and diet
Taking the waters

Jalisco
Guadalajara

For thousands of years, Indians used the meandering river of hot mineral water for curative purposes. Now the fertile valley around the tiny village of La Primavera is a national forest. And the Río Caliente Spa offers nature-oriented holidays, including vegetarian meals and convivial company.

The synthesis of therapies, diet, sun, and bathing is the key to enjoying this unique health resort. As you enter the bathhouse you'll encounter a 20-foot wall of volcanic rock, in front of which are wooden benches where guests relax while enjoying a sweat. A stream of hot thermal water snakes through the room, emitting puffs of steam. Welcome to the Aztec steam room.

Classes in yoga, tai chi chuan, and aquatics are scheduled for all guests who want to participate. Spa services are provided by a well-trained staff.

Río Caliente Spa

Apdo. Postal 5-67 Colonia Chapalita, Guadalajara
43042, Jalisco
No telephone at spa
Reservations: Box 897, Millbrae, CA 94030
Tel. 415/615-9543

Administration   Director, Caroline Durston

Season   Year-round.

Accommodations   48 cabanas and rooms for 80 guests in the main buildings; hand-crafted beds and chairs; colorful fabrics by local artisans; small and simple rooms, all with private baths; no phones, TV, or air-conditioning.

Rates   Daily rate $75–$86 per person, double occupancy, $90–$103 single. Rate includes vegetarian buffet meals, activity program, lodging. Personal services and trips range from $5 to $18. 10% discount for stays of 30 days or longer. Taxes and gratuity additional. $100 deposit. No credit cards.

Meal Plans   Vegetarian meals served buffet style 3 times daily. Tropical foods in season include guavas, jícama, zapote, and guanabana. Organically grown raw greens, raw and cooked vegetables, soups and home-baked grain casseroles supplement vegetarian platters.

Services and
Facilities

Services: Massage, reflexology, facial, manicure, pedicure, fango mudpacks. **Bathing Facilities:** Separate walled plunge pools for men and women, swimming pool; waterfall for nude bathing. **Swimming Facilities:** outdoor pool. **Recreation Facilities:** Hiking.

In the Area   Group trips into Guadalajara (crafts market, Orozco murals), Tlaquepaque (colonial architecture, crafts center), Tequila (brewery). Other attractions include Lake Chapala, Cabanas Institute (center for arts), and Plaza of the Mariachis in Guadalajara.

Getting Here   *From Guadalajara.* By car, Hwy. 80 to La Primavera (60 min). Taxi, rental car available.

Special Notes Limited access for people with disabilities. No smoking indoors. Electrical voltage is 110 A.C. (compatable to U.S.).

Rosarito Beach Hotel & Casa Playa Spa

Luxury pampering

Baja California
Rosarito Beach

Built in the 1930s, when glamorous getaways were for Hollywood celebrities, the Rosarito Beach Hotel has an ornately decorated, Old Mexico ambience, combined with a modern hotel wing. Add to the striking aesthetics the state-of-the-art Casa Playa Spa, housed in a former beach mansion. Programs are personalized by the director, and spa packages are customized.

As you enter the whitewashed, red-tiled archway, you'll discover a romantic garden, and the hotel lobby tiled and decorated with murals by Matias Santoyo. In the spa adjoining the hotel, you are offered an extensive list of bodywork and beauty-salon services. Sandals, a robe, towels, and a personal locker are issued daily. The coed Jacuzzi, sauna, steam room, and fitness gym are open to all hotel guests. A daily membership fee ($10) is charged for use of the facilities, exercise classes cost $5 each. Seaweed and fango treatments are the specialty here.

Rosarito Beach Hotel & Casa Playa Spa
Blvd. Benito Juarez #31, Plaza Rosarito
Baja California Norte 2271
Tel. 52–661/2–0144 or 800/343–8582

Administration General manager, Xavier Hinoko; spa director, Gilda Mayen

Season Year-round.

Accommodations 280 ocean-front rooms and suites, including an 8-story addition built in 1994. All rooms air-conditioned, with balcony or patio, private bathroom, TV, phone.

Rates $49–$89 per room for 2. Day of Beauty $151 including spa lunch. 4-hour thalassotherapy package including spa lunch $136. Packages include tax. Add 10% VAT, plus gratuity to room rates. Credit cards: AE, MC, V.

Meal Plans All meals à la carte. Spa lunch can be steamed halibut, skinless roasted chicken with steamed vegetable and rice, or spinach salad. Dinner entrées include tequilla-sautéed salmon with mushrooms, spinach pasta with tomato sauce, green gazpacho.

Services and Facilities **Exercise Equipment:** 2 multi-station Universal gyms, 4 Nautilus units, 12 Lifecycles, 4 Monark stationary bikes, 2 treadmills, StairMaster, 4 Nautilus units, free weights. **Services:** Swedish massage, reflexology, body wrap, salt-glow scrub, body polish, parafango heat pack, hydrotherapy bath, facial, aromatherapy; hair, nail, and skin care; cholesterol test, fitness profile, personal training. **Swimming Facilities:** 2 outdoor pools, children's pool. **Recreation Facilities:** Tennis, racquetball, volleyball, surfing, miniature golf. Nearby horseback riding. **Evening Programs:** Fri. and Sat. evening fiestas.

In the Area Tijuana (crafts market, Sun. bullfights), Los Cabos (fishing), Puerto Nuevo (lobster feast).

Getting Here *From San Diego.* By car, I-5 or I-805 to the U.S./Mexico border at Tijuana, follow signs to Hwy. 1-D "Rosarito-Ensenada

Cuota" (toll road), south to 3rd Rosarito Beach exit (45 min). By bus, Baja California Tours (tel. 619/454–7166). Rental car available.

Special Notes Spa open Mon.–Sat. 8:30–6:30, Sun., 8–5. Minimum age is 16. No smoking in spa, but other areas are unrestricted.

The Caribbean, the Bahamas, Bermuda

The current trend in the Caribbean is to import European thalassotherapy and American fitness programs. The French touch may be experienced at the new Privilege Resort and Spa on St. Martin, which has sailing and tennis options. Spas on St. Lucia hark back to the time of King Louis XIV, who built baths in the 17th century for his troops at the hot springs, which are still in use. Today you can relax at the tony Jalousie Plantation or LeSport, the fitness buff's counterpart to Club Med.

Jamaica has the widest range of options, among them the luxurious Charlie's Spa at the all-inclusive Sans Souci Lido resort, the rustic mineral water baths at Milk River Spa, and Negril's sports-oriented Swept Away resort, all outstanding opportunities for combining a Caribbean holiday with a healthy regime.

Bermuda vacations may include French facials and bodywork at two resorts, the Sonesta Beach Hotel and Cambridge Beaches, both with well-appointed spas operated by Bersalon group. Cruise ship passengers are welcome to use the spa facilities. A hike along the Railway Trail adds to your fitness regimen on the island.

Holistic island retreats are good healthy alternatives to resorts. At Jamaica's Doral Enchanted Garden, try a soothing aromatherapy massage alongside a mountain stream. St. John in the U.S. Virgin Islands is the winter outpost for the New York-based Omega Institute's programs. And in Puerto Rico the rain forest and the ocean provide a backdrop for bodywork at La Casa de Vida Natural.

Today the Caribbean spa experience is a mixture of fun and fitness. Don't expect a self-contained spa with structured programs; instead look for a resort within your budget that offers many options.

Hyatt Regency Aruba Resort

Nonprogram resort

Aruba
Palm Beach

Set on 12 acres of powdery white sand, 2 miles from the island's pastel-colored capital of Oranjestad, the $52 million Hyatt Regency Aruba Resort & Casino opened in 1990. An 8,000-square-foot three-level swimming pool with cascading waterfalls and tropical lagoons graces this water-sports-oriented resort. Canoe rentals, sailboats, and a 50-foot luxury catamaran for sunset cruises are all available, and two dive boats ferry guests to coral reefs and sunken shipwrecks.

The health and fitness facilities—including exercise room, coed sauna, steam room, outdoor whirlpool, and sun deck for aerobics classes—are open to hotel guests without charge. For those who don't want to get wet or sweat, the gardens feature a 5,000-square-foot saltwater lagoon replete with native fish and

Aruba

Hyatt Regency
Aruba Resort, **24**

The Bahamas

Le Meridien Hotel &
Villas, **3**

Sivananda Ashram
Yoga Retreat, **4**

Bermuda

Cambridge Beaches, **2**

Sonesta Beach Hotel
& Spa, **1**

Dominican Republic

La Mansion Aveda
Spa, **11**

Renaissance Jaragua
Resort, **10**

Grenada

LaSource, **23**

Guadeloupe

Guadeloupe Thermal
Springs, **18**

Hotel PLM
Marissol, **19**

Jamaica

Ciboney, **8**

The Enchanted
Garden, **6**

Jamaican Mineral
Springs, **9**

The San Souci Lido, **7**

Swept Away, **5**

Martinique

Centre de
Thalassothérapie
du Carbet, **20**

Nevis

Four Seasons
Resort, **17**

Puerto Rico

La Casa de
Vida Natural, **12**

Spa Caribe at the
Hyatt Resorts, **13**

St. Lucia

Jalousie Plantation, **21**

Le Sport, **22**

St. Maarten-St. Martin

Port de Plaisance, **16**

Privilege Resort and
Spa, **15**

U.S. Virgin Islands

Omega Journeys at
Maho Bay, **14**

The Caribbean, the Bahamas,

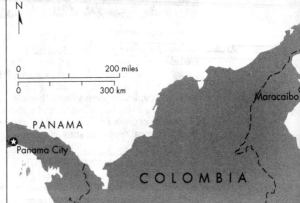

Bermuda

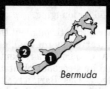

Bermuda

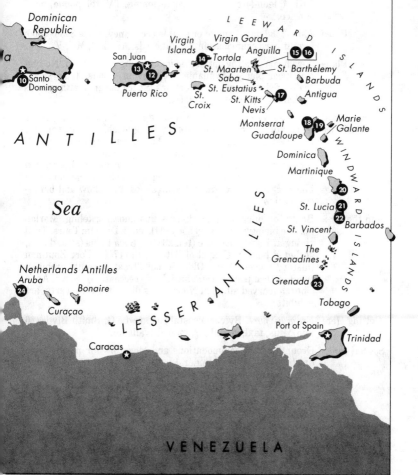

ATLANTIC OCEAN

LEEWARD ISLANDS

Dominican
Republic

Santo
Domingo

San Juan

Virgin
Islands

Puerto Rico

St.
Croix

Virgin Gorda

Tortola

St. Maarten

Saba

St. Eustatius

St. Kitts

Nevis

Montserrat

Guadaloupe

Anguilla

St. Barthélemy

Barbuda

Antigua

Marie
Galante

ANTILLES

Sea

Netherlands Antilles
Aruba

Bonaire

Curaçao

LESSER ANTILLES

Dominica

Martinique

St. Lucia

St. Vincent

The
Grenadines

Grenada

Barbados

Tobago

WINDWARD ISLANDS

Caracas

Port of Spain

Trinidad

VENEZUELA

wildlife; a poolside restaurant fashioned out of native coral stone is good for lounging.

Beaches are public throughout the island. Hike from the natural bridge (carved by the sea), on the rugged coast near Boca Prins, to Andicouri for a romantic picnic on a secluded beach surrounded by a coconut plantation. Aruba's volcanic origins are revealed at Casi Bari, a rock garden of giants, and at tall, unusual rock formations called *Ayo*. Hikers can enjoy panoramic, breezy views from paths cut into the rock.

Hyatt Regency Aruba Resort
L. G. Smith Blvd., Aruba
Tel. 29/783–1234 or 800/233–1234

Administration	General Manager, Carlos Cabrera
Season	Year-round.
Accommodations	360 rooms and suites in 9-story tower and 2 wings of 4 and 5 stories. Regency Club has 27 deluxe rooms, lounge, concierge service. All rooms are spacious, with balcony and full modern bath, queen-size beds. Air-conditioning, TV, telephone, maid service.
Rates	$145–$430 daily, single or double occupancy, suite $450–$600; Credit-card confirmation. Credit cards: AE, DC, MC, V.
Meal Plans	New heart-healthy options on main dining room menu. No special meal plan is available. Vegetarian dishes, fruit salad, grilled fish among daily selections. Snack bar in health spa has herbal teas, protein drinks, fruit.
Services and Facilities	**Exercise Equipment:** Universal gym, StairMaster, Precor treadmill, Lifecycle, Concept 2 rowing machine, free weights. **Services:** Massage (Swedish, shiatsu, acupressure, reflexology). Beauty salon for hairstyling, manicure, pedicure. **Swimming Facilities:** Outdoor pool, ocean beach. **Recreation Facilities:** 2 tennis courts, water sports, cruiser and mountain bikes. **Evening Programs:** Carnival costume show and barbecue; casino.
In the Area	Boats to underwater gardens; scuba and snorkeling. Marlab marine biology tour (3 hr) booked through DePalm Tours. Trail riding at Rancho El Paso (tel. 23310). Boca Prins (sand dunes, secluded beach), Chapel of Alto Vista (1750), Fort Zoutman (history museum) and Olde School Straat (colonial architecture) in Oranjestad, DePalm Island (recreation), Santa Anna Church (carved altar) in Noord, Cas di Cultura (concerts, art exhibits).
Getting Here	*From airport.* By car, coastal road to L. G. Smith Blvd. (20 min). Bus, taxi, rental car, moped available.
Special Notes	Ground-floor accommodations and elevators for people with disabilities. Children under 12 stay with parents free; Camp Hyatt features nature walks. No smoking in spa.

Le Meridien Hotel & Villas

Luxury pampering
Nonprogram resort

The Bahamas
Cable Beach,
Nassau

This grand manor, reeking of Colonial decadence, is stylishly managed by Le Meridien, and has one of the best little spas in the Bahamas. Created as part of a $9 million renovation in 1985, the Royal Bahamian Hotel & Villas facilities include mud baths and a large whirlpool, sauna and steam rooms, and an aerobics studio with exercise equipment.

The resort was originally a private reserve for the rich and titled and is still an oasis for those who seek peace and quiet. A modest strip of powdery sand, manicured gardens abloom with bougainvillea, and a parlor where tea is served with cucumber sandwiches are among the attractions enjoyed by its international clientele.

Tarted up but showing its age, the six-story hotel offers more spacious rooms than any of the fancier neighbors down the road. And for those with a taste for privacy (and the means) there are 10 villas, all pink with sugar-white roofs. Three are individual town houses—each boasting three bedrooms, a private pool, sun room, and a whirlpool in the master suite.

The spa can be reached by elevator in the main building or by a private entrance alongside the swimming pool terrace. Chrome and mirrors add a sleek, modern look to the smallish spaces where you can work out at leisure or book private treatments. Services are offered à la carte, billed to your account, or payable with credit card. Aerobics classes are complimentary to all guests weekdays at 10:30 AM and 6:30 PM.

Try a luxurious mud bath for the ultimate in body-stimulating treatments. The ancient therapy of soaking in herbs and algae has been re-created here with a mixture of peat mud taken from deposits in the Neydharting Valley Basin of northern Austria. The therapeutic effect soothes nerves, eliminates sleeplessness, improves circulation, and rejuvenates the skin.

The physiotherapy specialist Charles Bowleg is both manager and head masseur; a graduate of Dr. Swanson's School of Swedish Massage in Chicago, he returned to the Bahamas more than 30 years ago to work on the muscles of such notables as the Duke of Windsor, the prime minister of the Bahamas, and the screen star Sidney Poitier.

The facilities are designed to pamper and relax rather than give a serious workout. Outside guests can drop in for a day by making advance reservations for treatments. With one of the classiest restaurants on the island, the resort is the kind of place that makes you yearn for an extra day in which to do nothing.

For more active pursuits, try the sports center at the Crystal Palace complex. Just a few minutes' walk from the Royal Bahamian, the indoor, air-conditioned facilities include squash and racquetball/handball courts. Nearby is a championship 18-hole (par 72) golf course. Guests at both hotels get special rates. For a taste of Bahamian cooking, the Casuarinas Round House restaurant just across from the hotel entrance has a "Fit for Life" menu.

Le Meridien Hotel & Villas

Box N 10422, Cable Beach, Nassau, Bahamas
Tel. 809/327–6400 or 800/543–4300
Telex 20317

Administration General manager, Louis Olivier; fitness director, Charles Bowleg

Season Year-round.

Accommodations Beachfront main building has 145 rooms; villas and town houses offer suites with 25 bedrooms. Ocean view, twin queen-size beds, dressing room, twin baths with shower or bathtub, balcony. Cable TV, air-conditioning, bathrobes.

Rates In winter, $165–$306 daily, single or double occupancy; summer $135–$235. Tariffs for suites/town houses depend on length of stay and include butler or maid service. Add 10% tax, $2.85 daily service charge. First-night confirmation by credit card. Credit cards: AE, DC, MC, V.

Meal Plans Buffet breakfast and dinner in Cafe Royale, dinner only (jacket and tie required) in Baccarat pavilion. Dinner offers innovative crossovers of Continental and island fare: Gâteau de Conch et Saint-Jacques au Safron is a mousse of Bahamian conch and scallops baked in delicate saffron sauce. Other specialties include grouper baked in pastry shell with sabayan sauce and rack of lamb dusted with herbs, roasted and broiled.

Services and Facilities **Exercise Equipment:** Universal weight system (6 stations), 2 digital stationary bikes, treadmill. **Services:** Swedish massage, mud bath, facial, manicure, pedicure, waxing. **Swimming Facilities:** Outdoor freshwater pool, ocean beach. **Recreation Facilities:** 2 tennis courts, chess tables. Nearby bicycle rental, golf course, indoor sports center. **Evening Programs:** Casino and theater nearby, with complimentary transportation.

In the Area Island tours, interisland flights, charter boats for fishing and scuba; Seafloor Aquarium (performing dolphins and sea lions), Fort Charlotte, botanic garden, Adastra Gardens (performing flamingos), Junkanoo Art Gallery.

Getting Here *From airport.* By car, coastal road (10 min). Jitney minibus for trips into town. Taxi, rental car available.

Special Notes Elevator to all floors of main building. No smoking in spa or designated dining areas. Spa open daily 9 AM–7:30 PM.

Sivananda Ashram Yoga Retreat

Spiritual awareness

The Bahamas
Paradise Island,
Nassau

A few steps from one of the best-known beaches in the Bahamas, secluded in a grove of pines and palm trees, is a unique combination of spiritual retreat and tropical holiday. Based on the teachings of Swami Vishnu Devananda, the yogic discipline and vegetarian diet at the Sivananda Ashram Yoga Retreat are identical to Sivananda ashrams in Canada, New York, and California, but the sunny climate and beach make this one of the best bargains anywhere. People come here to recuperate from job burnout or to heal after surgery.

The regimen is intensive; attendance at classes and meditations is mandatory for all guests. Mornings begin at 6 with a session of yogic exercises, or *asanas*, to stretch and invigorate the body. Brunch is served at 10, then you are free to enjoy the beach or a relaxing massage until the 4 PM yoga session.

Although there are glitzy hotels and casinos a short walk away, the environment here is totally suffused with a mystical quality—partly due to the quaint appearance of the buildings, some on stilts, some on houseboats. The main house, once the retreat of a wealthy family and leased since 1967 to the Sivananda group in appreciation for healing services, might have sunk into the sand long ago without the volunteer labor of the retreat members. Many guests prefer to bring their own tent and camp among the tropical shrubbery. Arrival can be any day; average stay is two weeks.

To provide the proper nutritional balance, there is an organic garden in which herbs and vegetables are grown. Coconuts come gratis from the palm trees that shelter the 4½-acre compound. For snacks and sweets, a canteen is tucked into a building near the communal laundry and shower facilities. After meals, guests wash their own plates and utensils and dry them on open-air racks. There's no air-conditioning at this retreat, but a new filtration system provides plenty of cool, chemical-free drinking water.

Sivananda Ashram Yoga Retreat
Box N7550, Paradise Island, Nassau, Bahamas
Tel. 809/363–2902
Fax 809/363–3783

Administration Program director, Swami Swaroopanada

Season Year-round.

Accommodations Wooden huts on the beach, dormitory rooms, and cottages provide 103 beds. Furnished with 2–6 beds and table; linens and towels provided. Communal shower and toilet facilities, laundry equipment. Tent space: 50 sites.

Rates $45–$60 daily, rooms shared by 2–6 persons. Single cabin $75. Beachfront meditation huts are preferred location. Tent space $40 per night. $200 advance payment. Credit cards: MC, V.

Meal Plans The lacto-vegetarian diet includes midmorning meal of whole-grain cereal, fresh fruit, homemade yogurt and wheat bread. Dinner dishes include stir-fried tofu and rice, steamed vegetables, green salad. No fish, meat, fowl, eggs, or coffee served.

Services and Facilities **Services:** Massage (shiatsu, reflexology), personal counseling. **Swimming Facilities:** Ocean beach. **Recreation Facilities:** Tennis court, volleyball, walks. **Evening Programs:** Workshops in Hindu culture, philosophy. Concerts.

In the Area Boat trips; botanical gardens, Colonial and Victorian architecture.

Getting Here *From Nassau airport.* Shared taxi van (fixed fee) to Mermaid Marina, Bay and Deveaux streets. Shuttle service by Ashram boat operates on daily schedule.

Special Notes Yoga training for children. No smoking on premises. Remember to bring beach towel, blankets during winter months.

Cambridge Beaches

Luxury pampering

Bermuda
Somerset
New in 1993, the Spa at Cambridge Beaches is set in a 25-acre bayside cottage colony that is more like a club than a resort. A private retreat here can combine classic treatments with the latest in European therapies. Planned as a one-day package or in combination with Bermuda's golf courses, sailing, and heritage-home tours, this is an easy-paced escape.

Several treatments available in the spa salon are considered to be making their debut in North America. Cathiodermie facials by Guinot of Paris incorporate gentle stimulation of skin tissue with electronic rollers which cause a tingling sensation. Using a thermal clay mask, the licensed esthetician dissolves impurities and toxins, leaving the tissue rehydrated and rejuvenated. Ionithermie treatments firm and tone slack skin, and help rid the body of cellulite. Using galvanic current, the Ionithermie machine is attached to your face, body, or bust. Treatments over a period of several days are said to shed inches. This can be combined with bodywraps using seaweed, plant extracts, and other natural ingredients.

A Cambridge Beaches "Day of Fitness" might start with a consultation and computerized body fat analysis, followed by exercise, sauna, and massage. Several spa packages (from four to six days) offer combinations of services for men and women. A personalized spa holiday program can be developed to focus on your special needs and interests, but it requires a minimum stay of five days. All spa holiday packages include deluxe waterview accommodations as well as afternoon tea, full breakfast and dinner daily, with the option of having spa cuisine cooked to order. Evenings are dress-up occasions, with music and often dancing outdoors on a terrace that overlooks Cambridge's private marina.

Somerset's shady lanes are ideal for walks, jogging, and hikes. A moped can be rented at Cambridge Beaches and taken aboard a ferry for a trip to St. George's at the eastern end of the island, via Hamilton where the best shops and pubs are located. A short hike from Cambridge Beaches along the Railway Trail brings you to Scaur Hill Fort, built in the 1870s to protect the Royal Naval Dockyard. Now it's a 22-acre park with breathtaking views of the Great Sound and its armada of sailboats. Spend a day at the restored Dockyard complex, a maritime museum and crafts center, with several pleasant places to dine. Hikers and bikers can use the Railway Trail, a secluded 18-mile track that runs toward Southampton along the route of the old Bermuda Railway, past beautiful estates, the Lantana Cottages (where you can dine on an exchange plan with Cambridge Beaches), and the Somerset Squire pub.

Cambridge Beaches
30 Kings Point Rd., Somerset MA 02 Bermuda
Tel. 809/234–0331 or 800/468–7300 (800/463–5990 in Canada)
Fax 809/234–3352

Administration
General manager, Michael J. Winfield; spa director, Michael Ternant

Season Year-round.

Accommodations 82 individually decorated cottage rooms and suites, recently refurbished or newly built. All have private bathroom, some with whirlpool bath. Furnishings are traditional, with flowered chintz drapery, large closets. Air-conditioning, telephone, and screened windows. No TV but a set can be rented.

Rates Daily $310–$500 for 2 persons, double occupancy, plus 10% tax, and gratuities. 5-day/4-night Personalized Spa Holiday $2,200 single, $3,000 per couple. 5-day/4 night Bermuda Escape $2,075 single, $2,750 per couple. 5-day/4-night Relaxation Package $2,300 single, $3,200 per couple. 6-day/5 night Beauty Holiday $3,000 single, $4,250 per couple. Taxes and gratuities included in package rates. Deposit: 2 nights payment. No credit cards.

Meal Plans Breakfast, dinner, and tea included in daily tariff and spa packages. Breakfast buffet has granola and health cereals, fresh fruit, juices. Eggs can be ordered. Dinner specialties include grilled fish with steamed vegetables, skinless breast of chicken with couscous, and vegetarian plate. Special diets accommodated. Room service in cottage. Exchange dining at six other hotels.

Services and Facilities **Exercise Equipment:** Multi-station Universal gym, computerized FitStep climber, 2 Aerobicycles, Tredex treadmill, free weights. **Services:** Massage (Swedish, shiatsu, sports, reflexology, aromatherapy), paraffin body treatments and wraps, salt-glow polish, G-5 toning, peel, Ionithermie, Cathiodermie; salon for hair, nail, skin care. Fitness consultation, computerized body-fat analysis, nutrition consultation. **Swimming Facilities:** Heated saltwater pool, 5 beaches. **Recreation Facilities:** Marina with power and sail boats, windsurfing, snorkeling equipment, canoes, kayaks. 3 tennis courts (1 lighted), croquet lawn, putting green. Golf courses nearby offer member privileges. Moped and cycle rental. **Evening Programs:** Nightly entertainment, special cruise, dancing.

In the Area Dockyard (maritime museum), Art Centre, Crafts Market, Heydon Trust Chapel, Gibb's Hill Lighthouse, St. George's (colonial capital), Hamilton (City Hall art museum and theater, Parliament buildings, shopping, botanical garden, Bermuda Biological Station (ocean studies).

Getting Here *From East Coast.* By air, USAir and United Airlines have scheduled service daily. By ship, summer sailings include Celebrity Cruise Lines' SS *Meridian* from New York, which docks in Somerset at King's Wharf; Majesty Cruise Lines' *Royal Majesty* on regular service from Boston to Old Town in St. George's; and Cunard. By ferry from Hamilton, complimentary trip 3 times per week, with scheduled service to Watford Bridge (20 min). By bus, frequent service on shore road to Somerset (45 min). Taxi available, no rental car.

Sonesta Beach Hotel & Spa

Nonprogram resort

Bermuda
Southampton

Workouts and relaxation are the program at the Sonesta Beach Hotel & Spa. You can drop in between business meetings or after a round of golf or plan a comprehensive schedule of treatments and exercise classes for three to seven days. Package plans can begin any day of the week.

Aerobics are moderate or vigorous, plotted over 30- or 40-minute periods, alternating active and passive exercise with relaxing stretches. You can select from early morning walks (moderate), circuit training (vigorous), workouts in the water, and yoga; morning yoga sessions are held on the lawn overlooking the sea.

If you simply want to be pampered and left alone to swim or shop, there is a three-day "spa refresher break." For a person who wants to try many different activities and treatments, there are dance exercise routines and easy aerobics, hiking and walking on the beach, and clinics devoted to awareness of proper posture for exercise and running. All can be included in a spa package, or you can simply pay a daily facility charge ($10) and use the whirlpool baths, Finnish sauna, Turkish steam bath, and Universal equipment room.

The larger brother of the spa at Cambridge Beaches, this hotel facility has 12 treatment rooms, an aerobics studio, a large weight-training room, and separate facilities for men and women. Workout clothing is provided daily; a leotard, warm-up suit, gym shorts, shirt, robe, and slippers.

Sonesta Beach Hotel & Spa
South Rd., Horseshoe Bay, Southampton
Tel. 809/238-8122 or 800/766-3782
Fax 809/238-8463

Bersalon Co. Ltd.
Box HM1044, Hamilton HM EX, Bermuda
Tel. 809/292-8570 or 809/238-1226
Fax 809/295-2506

Administration Spa director, Michael J. Ternent; general manager, David Boyd; assistant spa manager, Diane Horbacewiez

Season Year-round.

Accommodations 25-acre peninsula setting. 6-story hotel and Bay Wing suites with 403 guest rooms, ocean or bay view. Spacious split-level units have sitting area and dressing room, full bath, modern rattan furniture, floor-to-ceiling windows, balcony or patio (all rooms). Queen- or king-size beds, full carpeting, air-conditioning, color TV, telephone.

Rates 3-night Spa Sampler package $1,864 per person, double occupancy; $1,280 single. 6-night package, $5,376 for 2, double occupancy, $3,387 single. 4-night Eurospa package also available. Taxes and gratuities included in spa packages. Daily tariff $180–$345 per room, plus 6% tax, $9 daily service charge. Deposit: 2-night payment at booking. Credit cards: AE, DC, MC, V.

Meal Plans 3 meals daily included in 4- and 6-night packages, Breakfast may be a whole-grain cereal with fruit; lunch, a garden salad or cold seafood platter. Dinner entrées include grilled swordfish, vegetarian lasagna, and skewers of vegetables broiled with sea scallops. 2 juice breaks are included in the daily program.

Services and Facilities **Exercise Equipment:** Universal weight-training gym (5 stations), 2 Aerobicycles, Tredex computerized bicycle, recumbent bike, 2 Fitstep stairclimbers, 2 treadmills, hand weights.

Services: Massage (Swedish, aromatherapy, reflexology, G-5 mechanical), facials for men and women, loofah body scrub, herbal wrap, manicure, pedicure, Cathiodermie facial, Ionithermie cellulite control treatments. Hairstyling and beauty-salon services. Paraffin treatments for hands and feet; depilatory treatments. **Swimming Facilities:** Outdoor freshwater pool, indoor pool, 3 ocean beaches. **Recreation Facilities:** 6 lighted tennis courts, volleyball, badminton, croquet, shuffleboard, table tennis. Golf and bicycle rental nearby. Water sports include helmet and scuba diving, windsurfing. Horseback riding available at Spicelands Riding Centre, Warwick. **Evening Programs:** Resort entertainment.

In the Area Island tours; St. George's (replica of colonists' ship *Deliverance*), Blue Grotto (dolphin show), Verdmont House (Georgian antiques), Hamilton (shopping, museums), Maritime Museum at the Dockyard.

Getting Here *From airport.* By taxi, North Shore Rd. to South Rd. (45 min). Public bus for trips to town. Frequent ferry service to points on the island. Moped available.

Special Notes Play area in gardens for children; under 18 not permitted in spa. No smoking in spa or designated sections of the dining room.

La Mansion Aveda Spa

Life enhancement
Luxury pampering
Weight management

Dominican
Republic
Los Pinos
National Park

Set in a pine forest overlooking the Caribbean, La Mansion Aveda Spa has luxury accommodations in private casitas and the main house, as well as the region's first full-service Aveda spa. An organic garden on the property provides fresh produce year-round; the all-natural Aveda products come from Minneapolis. Aerobics done to merengue and salsa music add to the exotic ambience, and you can also join classes in yoga, stretching, or aquarobics.

Trained by Aveda estheticians, the Dominican staffers are experienced in a wide range of rejuvenation therapies. A choice of five services comes with the one-week package, including massage, scalp treatment, and (for men) skin care and shaving consultation. A medical doctor is on staff for consultation and personal health assessment.

The spa visit begins with a fitness evaluation and wellness profile that includes nutritional analysis and iridology. With the help of a staff trainer, you can tailor a program for weight loss, maintenance, or relaxation. Activities open to all guests include cooking classes, a photography workshop, and crafts. The spa also has opportunities outdoors for group hikes, croquet, tennis, horseback riding, mountain biking, swimming, volleyball, and fishing.

Located on the island's central ridge, within driving distance of undeveloped beaches as well as the capital city, Santo Domingo, the 1,800-acre resort is surrounded by Los Pinos National Park. There are organized excursions for an additional fee. Balmy weather prevails throughout the year; the mountain lo-

cation keeps temperatures comfortable in August, and the
rainy season is at the end of April.

La Mansion Aveda Spa
San Jose de las Matas, Dominican Republic
Reservations: 126 E. 56th St., New York, NY 10022
Tel. 212/754–8022 or 800/826–1550
Fax 212/750–0160

Administration Spa director, Jeffrey Stone; medical director, Carolyn Matias,
M.D.; resort owner and operator, Occidental Hoteles

Season Year-round.

Accommodations 20 rooms in the main house each have 2 double beds, private
bathroom, air-conditioning. 100 casita cottages near main
house each have 1 or 2 bedrooms, private bathrooms, air-conditioning. No telephone in rooms; TV lounge in main house.

Rates 7-night package $1,350 per person, 3-night/4-day package $595
per person. Deposit: 50% payment at time of booking. Credit
cards: AE, MC, V.

Meal Plans 3 meals daily included in packages. Mostly vegetarian menu
also has fish or chicken entrées. Tropical fruit and juices available throughout the day. Bottled water in rooms.

Services and **Exercise Equipment**: Weight-training gym. **Services**: Massage,
Facilities body wrap, scalp treatment, reflexology, facials, manicure,
pedicure, hair salon, skin care. **Swimming Facilities**: Outdoor
pool. **Recreation Facilities**: Tennis, volleyball, croquet, badminton, ping-pong, horseback riding, mountain biking.

In the Area Santiago (colonial architecture, university), sulfur springs.

Getting Here *From Santo Domingo.* By car or bus (2 hr). Rental car available. By air, scheduled commuter flights to Santiago (45 min).

Renaissance Jaragua Resort

Luxury pampering

Dominican The Jaragua Resort is an impressive Caribbean casino-cum-
Republic spa in the center of the hemisphere's oldest capital city. A few
Santo Domingo minutes' drive from the flashy ocean boulevard is the colonial
capital founded by Bartholomew Columbus, the brother of the
Discoverer. Vacationers can combine culture and fitness with
casino action.

The new and the old meet on Avenida George Washington, a
lively strip of hotels, restaurants, and shops fronting the
ocean. There is no beach here, but spa goers hardly notice; with
an oversize swimming pool surrounded by tropical gardens,
Scandinavian saunas, Turkish steam bath, Roman whirlpool,
and cold plunge, the resort complex has an ample supply of water sports. Daily beach trips are complimentary.

The freestanding fitness facility is a world unto itself. All marble and glass, it is an oasis of aerobics and bodywork. You work
out on the latest in exercise equipment or join a calisthenics
class. Exercise is scheduled in the Olympic-size swimming
pool, as well as in the air-conditioned cushion-floored aerobics
studio.

Pampering services come in several packages or à la carte. You can get an herbal wrap, a body scrub, a facial, or a massage. Grandly titled the European Spa, the facilities include no thalassotherapy tubs or seawater treatments, but you may bliss out in a private Jacuzzi, then get a surge of energy from the cold plunge.

The daily entrance fee of $10 is waived when you book a massage, or a 7-day/6-night Lifestyle package. With the latter come robe, slippers, and snacks of fresh fruit and juices throughout the day.

Secluded on 14½ palm-fringed acres, the resort has a tennis stadium with four clay courts and spectator seating. During the day this facility can be used by spa guests free of charge. From your room it's a pleasant walk or jog through the garden and alongside the lagoon to the spa. Serious spa buffs may find the program too loose; your best bet is to relax and join the merengue beat.

Renaissance Jaragua Resort
367 George Washington Ave., Santo Domingo,
Dominican Republic
Tel. 809/221–2222 or 800/468–3561
Fax 809/686–0528

Administration	General manager, Alvaro Soto; spa director, Docia Sanchez
Season	Year-round.
Accommodations	10-story Jaragua Tower and an older 2-level wing of garden suites provide 355 luxury rooms. 6 suites with butler, marble baths. All rooms with modern rattan furniture, large bath with magnified makeup mirror, hair dryer. Air-conditioned, carpeted; 3 telephones with direct dial, color cable TV, decorative works by Dominican artists.
Rates	$110–$220 daily for 2 persons; 1- and 2-bedroom suties $300–$820 for 2 persons. Add 13% tax, 10% service charge. 7-day/6-night Lifestyle spa package $1,350 single, $900 per person, double occupancy. Tax and gratuities included in package. Deposit: 1 night's payment at time of booking. Credit cards: AE, DC, MC, V.
Meal Plans	3 daily spa-cuisine meals included in Lifestyle package. Choice of 4 restaurants: Latin American Cafe for meats char-broiled, grilled, or cooked on a spit; Oriental Cafe for stir-fry specialties; fresh homemade pasta in the Italian Cafe; New York deli.
Services and Facilities	**Exercise Equipment:** Nautilus gym (10 stations), stationary bicycles, treadmills, rowing machine, free weights. **Services:** Swedish massage, loofah body scrub, herbal wrap, facial, depilation, personalized nutrition program. Beauty salon for hair, nail, and skin care. **Swimming Facilities:** Olympic-size outdoor pool. **Recreation Facilities:** 4 lighted tennis courts. **Evening Programs:** Casino theater; National Theater for concerts and opera.
In the Area	Daily beach trip (complimentary), walking tour of the colonial area, Columbus lighthouse museum. Cathedral of Santa Maria la Menor (oldest in the Hemisphere, Columbus monument), Museum of the Royal Houses in the colonial quarter; Gallery of Modern Art and Natural History Museum downtown; National

Botanical Gardens (train ride) in northern section of the city; Altos de Chavon (artisans, museum of Taino Indian artifacts) near La Romana. Baseball (Oct.–Feb.), Merengue Festival (July), Polo (Casa de Campo).

Getting Here *From airport.* By taxi (45 min). Public bus, rental car available.

Special Notes Elevators and ramps to all levels for people with disabilities. No smoking in the spa. Spa open weekdays 7 AM–9 PM, Sat. 9 AM–7 PM, Sun. 9 AM–4 PM.

LaSource

Grenada
Pink Gin Beach

The fitness buff's alternative to Club Med, LaSource opened in late 1993 as an all-inclusive resort that offers the benefits of an active beach vacation combined with health and beauty treatments.

The body holiday package introduced at LeSport, its sister resort on St. Lucia, has been updated with a lighter menu, first-class accommodations, and a private nine-hole golf course. Once you arrive you can forget about money matters; even wine and bottled waters are included in the package, and tipping is not permitted.

The Oasis spa provides European-style services such as thalassotherapy in seaweed body wraps, and aromatherapy massage with essential oils of herbs and flowers. After an examination by the resort's nurse, you are programmed for complimentary treatments. (Additional services may be booked based on availability.) Aerobics classes (one hour) include step, stretch and tone, and floor exercise with reggae music. Daily sessions of yoga are scheduled, and a group jog takes place on the beach each morning. Join the optional daily hike at 7 AM to explore the island, then relax in the coed sauna and outdoor whirlpool.

The wooden cottages are designed in the fashion of a Victorian-era West Indian village, sitting amid 40 lush acres between two hills on Grenada's southwestern coast. The elegant colonial architecture features handcrafted wooden trellises and high-ceiling rooms, some of them beamed. Custom-carved four-poster beds, doors, and shutters enhance the rooms. Wood, including mahogany and teak imported from Venezuela, is used extensively in buildings on the grounds.

From a landscaped courtyard, you reach the broad expanse of Pink Gin Beach, where a free-form two-level swimming pool and oversize whirlpool beckon. The pool-terrace bar and restaurant serve buffet breakfast and lunch.

LaSource
Box 852, St. George's, Grenada, West Indies
Tel. 809/444–2556 or 800/544–2883
Fax 809 809/444–2561

Administration General manager, Kurt Vogel; spa director, Hazel Dawson

Season Year-round.

Accommodations 100 rooms, including 9 suites, in pastel-color low-rise buildings on a sloping hill. Guest rooms have marble floors, Bokhara rugs, chenille bedspreads. Slatted shutters and terra-cotta tile balconies frame beach and ocean views. All rooms have walk-in closets, air-conditioning, ceiling fans, clock radio, telephone. Bathrooms are oversize, with marble floor and walls, hair dryer, makeup mirror, and bathrobes. Suites come with bay window area and pullout sofabed. No TV. Top-floor rooms have 18-foot beamed ceilings.

Rates   Daily package $240–$295 per person, double occupancy. Single supplement $40 per night. Taxes and gratuities included. Credit cards: AE, DC, MC, V.

Meal Plans   3 meals and tea included in the daily tariff. Breakfast buffet includes eggs, hot and cold cereals, meats, breads and pastries, yogurt, tropical fruit, and juices. Lunch at the Terrace Restaurant is a buffet of hot and cold items, with salads, pasta, fish, and meat. Dinner entrées can be ordered from light cuisine menu including cabbage roll of risotto and local vegetables in callaloo puree, or from a menu of Great House specialties: callaloo soup, spicy crab cakes, cassoulet of duck and sausage with white haricot beans, Wiener schnitzel, char-grilled marlin with aubergine caviar. Desserts include tropical fruit, Spice Island meringue, and mango ice cream. Wine comes with lunch and dinner.

Services and Facilities   **Exercise Equipment:** Weight-training circuit with Universal 10-station multigym, total hip machine, abdominal crunch, incline and flat benches, dumbbells, hand weights, 2 step machines, rowing machine, 2 stationary bicycles. **Services:** Massage (Swedish, aromatherapy), reflexology, body wrap, loofah salt rub, facial, scalp massage. Class in couples massage, jazz warmup, reggae, stress management. Beauty salon services (extra fee). **Swimming Facilities:** 2 freshwater pools, 2 ocean beaches. **Recreation Facilities:** 2 tennis courts (lighted), 9-hole golf course and putting green, archery, fencing, volleyball, table tennis, water sports, snorkeling equipment. **Evening Programs:** music, barbecue.

In the Area   St. George's (19th-century English colonial capital), Grenada National Museum (island history), Market Square, Fort George, spice-processing station near Gouyave, Grand Etang Forest National Park (hiking trails, lake).

Getting Here   *From Point Salines International Airport.* Transfers provided (5 min). Taxi, rental car available.

Special Notes   Minimum age in spa is 16. Limited facilities for people with disabilities.

Guadeloupe Thermal Springs

Nonprogram resort
Taking the waters

Guadeloupe   Christopher Columbus saw the volcano La Soufrière erupting
Basse-Terre   when he stepped ashore November 4, 1493, at Sainte-Marie, a fishing village along the road to the island's present-day capital, Basse-Terre. The native Caribs were not hospitable to the Discoverer. All that's left of that time are primitive drawings scratched into black rocks at Trois-Rivières, where the road branches toward a nature preserve around La Soufrière.

A more recent discovery is Centre Thermal Harry Hamousin, a therapy center that taps the natural healing power of the mineral springs. French hydrotherapy equipment and therapists trained at leading French spas provide treatments for rheumatism, asthma, and dermatology problems. The classic "cure" has come to the Caribbean.

As an overseas department of France (not a colony or an independent country), Guadeloupe offers its citizens all the benefits of the mother country, including health coverage for the cost of spa therapy. Thus the Centre Thermal Harry Hamousin, a private institution, enjoys a steady stream of visitors from Europe and other islands in the French Antilles. Opened in 1978 with state-of-the-art facilities, the center now welcomes any visitors needing massage or special therapy.

Physical training to aid recovery from injuries includes exercise in shallow pools of mineral water and on special equipment in the gymnasium. Respiratory problems are treated with aerosol-like inhalations of mineral water. There are douches with high-powered jets of water and sulfur baths. The thermal center is open every morning except Sunday and accepts reservations for one-time treatments. Serious problems require consultation with a doctor at the nearby clinic Les Eaux Vives. Arrangements can be made by your hotel or directly with the clinic, and medical records should be brought along for the interview with *le médecin thermal*. Several doctors speak English if your French isn't sufficient.

Newer and oriented less toward medical treatments is *Espace Santè de Ravine Chaude* at the Station Thermale Renè Toribio. Operated as a day spa, the facilities include baths and two swimming pools filled with thermal water, three restaurants (dietetic and gastronomic), and a solarium. A medical doctor is on staff to consult with visitors on treatments. Therapies for rheumatism and anti-stress are structured as a "cure" over several days. Postnatal care also is provided through underwater massage, aromatherapy, and pressotherapy. Open daily from 10 AM to 11 PM, the spa charges an admission fee of 320 francs, and treatments are priced individually.

Hotel arrangements are not provided by the two thermal centers. One of the most interesting places to stay is the Hotel Relais de la Grande Soufrière. Located at the base of the volcano, it reflects the old-world charm of the banana plantations that cover nearby fields. Once a government-owned *relais*, or country inn, the hotel is now under private management. The dining room is popular with local families and businesspeople who escape from the city for lunch.

On market days the stalls are filled with herb sellers hawking natural seasonings and medicines: *matriquin*, Marie-Perrine, *zhèbe-gras*, *fleupapillon*, *bois-de l'homme*, *bonnet-carré*, and the like. All the tastes and stimulations of the old Carib Indian flavorings and remedies are still on sale, alongside modern pharmacies and boutiques laden with Parisian fashions.

Centre Thermal Harry Hamousin
Matouba Papaye, 97120 Saint-Claude, Guadeloupe
Tel. 590/89–53–53
Fax 590/80–06–08

Espace Santè de Ravine Chaude
97129 Le Lamentin, Guadeloupe
Tel. 590/27–75–92
Fax 590/25–76–28

Hotel Relais de la Grande Soufrière
Camp-Jacob, B.P. 17, 97120 Saint-Claude, Guadeloupe
Tel. 590/80–01–27
Fax 590/8001–025

Administration	Centre Thermal Harry Hamousin director, Harry Beaubois; Espace Sante director, Rene Toribio
Season	Year-round.
Accommodations	The Hotel Relais de la Grande Soufrière is a 22-room plantation great house decorated with fine antiques. Spacious and airy rooms have no air-conditioning, telephone, or TV. All have private bath.
Rates	Daily hotel tariff is 250–300 French francs, single, 200–250 francs per person, double occupancy. Clinique Les Eaux Vives 21-day rheumatism therapy 1,330 francs. Breakfast 30 francs; meal plans additional 150–270 francs daily. Deposit: 1 night payment. Credit cards: AE, MC, V.
Meal Plans	No diet plan available. At local restaurants, Creole cooking specialties include spicy fritters, *accras de morue* (salt cod), stuffed land crab, called crabs *farcis;* goat stew; classic *boudin* sausage.
Services and Facilities	**Exercise Equipment:** Weight-training units, treadmills. **Services:** Massage, underwater massage, steam cabinet, loofah body scrub, Scotch douche, skin peeling, acupuncture, physical therapy. **Swimming Facilities:** Outdoor pool. **Spa Facilities:** Therapy pool, hydrotherapy tubs. **Recreation Facilities:** Hiking, nearby beaches.
In the Area	Ferry to Les Saintes (natural bathing), organized hiking with Friends of the Nature Park, scuba at Club Med; Basse-Terre gardens and Prefecture, botanical garden, Fête des Cuisinères (mid-Aug.), Neuf Château (experimental orchard).
Getting Here	*From airport.* By car, coastal road to Trois Rivières, Allée Dumanoir, Route de la Traversée (50 min). Rental car, taxi, public bus available.
Special Notes	No smoking in the center. Remember to bring passport and medical certificate.

Hotel PLM Marissol

Luxury pampering

Guadeloupe *Gosier*	French and American fitness regimens merge at the large and popular Hotel PLM Marissol beach resort. Set in a tropical garden perfumed by blossoms, the facilities include a "hammam" steam room and private rooms for massage and thalassotherapy. Light gymnastics on the beach and stretching exercises in the swimming pool are offered at no extra charge for all guests.
	The Gym Tropique is open daily, except Sunday, 8–8. There is a coed steam room, aerobics studio, and hydrotherapy tubs but no exercise equipment. Workout clothing is provided daily.

European spa treatments are a plus: underwater massage, steam baths, a facial, and whirlpool treatment with seaweed and oils. Classes are scheduled for yoga and aerobics, all optional.

Hotel PLM Marissol

Bas-du-Fort, 97190 Gosier, Guadeloupe
Tel. 590/909398 or 800/221–4542
Fax 590/938332

Administration Manager, Jean Noel Laviale

Season Year-round.

Accommodations 200 air-conditioned rooms (50 bungalows) with terrace or loggia. Modern furniture accented with island fabrics and prints. All rooms have private bath, radio, direct-dial telephone, color TV with satellite programs.

Rates 7-night package $994–$1,199 per person, double occupancy, $1,245–$1,450 single. Daily rate $111–$243 per room for two; Bungalow for two, $128–$243. 25% payment at time of booking. Credit cards: MC, V.

Meal Plans Fitness package includes breakfast and dinner. Breakfast buffet includes yogurt, croissants, granola, fresh fruit. Selections from the dinner menu include steamed vegetables, fresh grilled fish, salads. Grilled specialties: veal scallops, entrecôte steak, seafood brochette.

Services and Facilities **Services:** Massage, body wrap with seaweed, underwater massage, whirlpool bath with seaweed, skin and nail care. **Swimming Facilities:** Outdoor freshwater pool, ocean beach. **Recreation Facilities:** Tennis, hiking, water sports.

In the Area Scuba, mountain hiking; thermal mineral-water treatments at Centre Harry Hamousin, Nature Park, La Soufrière (volcano).

Getting Here *From airport.* Complimentary transfers on arrival and departure. Taxi, rental car available.

Special Notes No smoking in fitness center. Bring passport.

Ciboney

Nonprogram resort

Jamaica
Ocho Rios
Clustered on a hillside near Ocho Rios, the villas of Ciboney opened in 1990, providing a fresh approach to the all-inclusive resort concept. Designed for privacy, the suites are ideal for honeymoons and romantic escapes. Couples can have an entire villa with its own housekeeper, or share a four-apartment villa.

The spa and fitness facilities are tucked into a rambling Great House that serves as a social center and hotel. Recalling plantation days, the lobby staircase leads down to the Orchids restaurant. Among seven dining options at the resort, Orchids takes spa cuisine seriously. The dinner features are displayed as you enter to help you make selections from the menu created by executive chef Jack Shapansky, a graduate of the Culinary Institute of America who believes proper nutrition is intimately related to good health.

The spa's "Fit for Life" schedule starts with reggae aerobics or a power walk. At 5 PM, you can take a step class or low-impact workout in the air-conditioned gym. Instructors are on hand in the exercise equipment room for circuit training, but no other group activity is scheduled. On request, private instruction is available.

Relaxing personal services are offered at the spa by appointment. If you stay a minimum of three nights, the 25-minute sessions of massage, reflexology, and nail care are complimentary. Treatments are provided in curtained cubicles or on a semireclined chair in a garden atrium, by locally trained masseuses who gently knead sore muscles. The spa salon provides a limited selection of facials, paraffin treatments, and hair styling for men and women at an additional charge. There are separate men's and women's saunas and steam rooms, a coed Jacuzzi with cold-water plunge pool, and a Swiss shower.

While a full body massage can be booked for $35, the bodywork here may disappoint serious spa-goers. On the positive side, the spa includes sports and fine dining in the package price. But the real attraction of this Radisson resort are the villas and the attentive staffers who make you feel at home.

Ciboney

Box 728, Main St., Ocho Rios, St. Ann, Jamaica
Tel. 809/974–1027 or 800/777–7800
Fax 809/974–5838

Administration General manager, Lynn W. Mitchell

Season Year-round.

Accommodations 300 luxury units including 36 rooms in the Great House, 236 villa suites with 1–4 bedrooms, 14 single villas, and studios. Bedrooms have air-conditioning, ceiling fan, TV, VCR, radio, phone, private bathroom with hair dryer. Villa suites have kitchenette with stocked bar and snacks, living room, semi-private swimming pool. Modern island furniture, rattan seating.

Rates Daily all-inclusive tariff for Great House room $190–$205 per person, double occupancy, $290–$305 single; 1-bedroom villa suites $230–$285 per person double, $345–$425 single; larger suites from $520 per person. Minimum stay is 3 nights. Taxes and gratuities included. Credit cards: AE, DC, MC, V.

Meal Plans 3 meals and unlimited snacks, selected wines, and bar service included in daily tariff. Breakfast at the Market includes home-baked breads and pastry, eggs cooked to order, cereals, yogurt, tropical fruits, and juices. Lunch on the beach at Casa Nina can be pasta, salad, grilled fish. Orchids restaurant dinner menu has choice of appetizer such as jumbo shrimp in an island curry sauce, seafood terrine or lasagna, smoked chicken. Low-fat entrée selections are seared marlin with papaya salsa, breast of roast chicken marinated in Zinfandel, medallions of pork with warm cabbage salad. Dessert is tropical marinated fruits with sponge cake, breadfruit pudding, or orange bavarian cream.

Services and Facilities **Exercise Equipment**: 7-station Universal weight-training gym, 5 Lifecycles, 2 StairMaster PT4000, barbells (5–45 lb), hand weights (4–10 lb), slant boards. **Services**: Massage, reflexology, facials, paraffin foot/hand treatment, waxing. Salon for hair, nail, and skin care. **Swimming Facilities:** 2 large free-form pools with Jacuzzi, 90 villa pools, small ocean beach. **Recreation Facilities:** 6 tennis courts (lighted, 4 with Har-Tru surface), 2 squash courts, racquetball court (air-conditioned), croquet, table tennis, basketball half-court, water-sports equipment, paddleboats, canoes. Nearby stables and two 18-hole golf courses. **Evening Programs:** Music, barbecue, folkloric show.

In the Area　Dunn's River Falls, Coyoba River Gardens and Museum (island personalities), 18th-century plantation great house museums, Firefly (Noel Coward home).

Getting Here　*From Montego Bay.* Transfers provided on arrival and departure.

Special Notes　Minimum age at resort is 16. Facilities for people with disabilities are limited. Shuttle bus service to beach club.

The Enchanted Garden

Holistic health
Luxury pampering
Nonprogram resort

Jamaica　Set amid 20 acres of rain forest, botanical gardens, waterfalls,
Ocho Rios　and rolling lawns, this leafy retreat was designed as an alternative to the island's other, more active beach resorts. Activities include spa services and holistic health seminars. Guests may float in a natural pool or get massaged under a waterfall or in one of the private garden nooks where a masseuse awaits with aromatherapy. They may also indulge in the new American cuisine created by Doral's spa specialists and the Jamaican cooks.

The spa is a cheerful, air-conditioned hideaway. Ambitious plans for beauty and fitness services were announced when the resort opened in 1991 but until recently only the basics were available. Improvements began in 1993 when the Doral Hospitality Corporation assumed management of the resort. Emphasis now is on all things natural, from facials with fresh-cut aloe plants to aromatherapy with jasmine oils straight from the garden. More than 50 essential oils are available, custom-mixed to suit your mood.

A typical day may begin with a power walk through the exquisite botanical gardens on the hillside, and may also involve a climb to the top of the falls. Among the scheduled classes in the aerobics studio are stretch amd tone, body sculpting, dancercise, and yoga. Couples can try "Loving Hands" massage training together. The limited selection of exercise equipment may be a disappointment for fitness buffs, though the facilities do include a Turkish steam bath, Finnish sauna, outdoor whirlpools, and Swiss showers with multiple heads.

Holistic health workshops are scheduled during week-long seminars held each month. Topics range from a Native American–style vision quest to finding and releasing energy blocks. Training is available in iridology, the joys of relationships, and art therapy.

The Enchanted Garden
Box 284, Ocho Rios, St. Ann, Jamaica
Tel. 809/974-1400 or 800/223-6725
Fax 809/974-5823

Administration	General manager, Frederick March; spa director, Judith Stewart
Season	Year-round.
Accommodations	112 bedrooms and suites with 1–3 bedrooms terraced into hillside gardens. 40 deluxe, modern town houses include sunken living room, private patio with plunge pool, kitchen. TV with satellite channels, telephone, air-conditioning, maid and turndown service.
Rates	Choice of all-inclusive package with meals and taxes covered but no spa services or European Plan (room only) daily rates. All-inclusive package: $170 single, $145 per person, double occupancy, in standard room. 1-bedroom suite with living room $213–$225 per person double, $238–$250 single. European Plan: $90–$130 single or double occupancy; $225–$250 1-bedroom suite. Taxes included. Add 10% service charge. Credit cards: AE, MC, V.
Meal Plans	The all-inclusive daily rate covers 3 meals, snacks, afternoon tea, and open bar. Specialty restaurants feature pasta, Middle Eastern, and Far Eastern cuisine. New American menu choices at L'Eau Mirage are grilled marlin, fillet of mahi mahi with papaya relish, cold poached scallops with tomato vinaigrette, pepper-crusted beef with white beans, warm curried crab and papaya salad. Breakfast can be egg-white omelet, cereal, tropical fruit, and homemade Jamaican bread. Vegetarian meals available on request.
Services and Facilities	**Exercise Equipment:** Precor treadmill, 3 Schwinn Air Dyne stationary bicycles, 2 rowing machines, NordicTrak cross-country ski machine, free weights. **Services:** Aromatherapy massage, Swedish massage, shiatsu, reflexology, sport massage, aromatherapy bath, facial, body scrub, herbal wrap, manicure, pedicure. **Swimming Facilities:** 3 outdoor swimming pools, nearby ocean beach. **Recreation Facilities:** 2 tennis courts (lighted), nearby golf and riding, water volleyball, reggae lessons. **Evening Programs:** Nightclub, Jamaican show and buffet dinner (Fri.).
Getting Here	*From Montego Bay airport.* Complimentary transfers. Taxi, rental car available.
Special Notes	Minimum age 16. Juice bar in Seaquarium café above spa. Shuttle bus to beach.

Jamaican Mineral Springs

Taking the waters

Jamaica *Milk River and Bath*	Getting off the beaten track is easy, but you need a car to explore some of the most scenic areas of the hilly island of Jamaica. In addition to breathtaking vistas there are botanical gardens, a bird sanctuary, and two spas built around mineral springs that have been attracting cure seekers for nearly two centuries.

Legend holds that an African slave, wounded in an uprising, was healed by bathing in pools of water fed by hot springs located high in the lush valleys between Kingston and Port Antonio. English plantation owners seeking respite from the coastal heat spread the word. By the beginning of the 18th century there was a spa hotel, church, and botanical garden for cultivation of medicinal herbs in the town of Bath. What remains today is primitive, nothing like its Georgian namesake in England. The waters, however, still gush forth in a setting of tropical splendor enjoyed by hill people and an occasional visitor.

From the town, a narrow road cuts through fern gullies alongside the Sulphur River to reach Bath Fountain Hotel. Cut into rocks beneath the hotel are private chambers where you can soak in the sulfurous warm water. European spa experts have confirmed high levels of radioactivity.

The hotel's 10 guest rooms are airy and simply furnished. Meals are prepared to order in the public dining room (no credit cards). *Bath Fountain Hotel, Bath, St. Thomas Parish. Rooms cost $350 (Jam.) per night, without private bath; $420–$473 (Jam.) with bathroom, for 2 persons.*

West of Kingston's high-rise government center, past agricultural and industrial developments, is the former capital city, Spanish Town, and from there you can reach the Milk River spa in about two hours. Stop to admire the main square, surrounded by Georgian buildings that date from 1762. One now houses the Jamaican People's Museum of Craft and Technology. A classical statue of Admiral George Rodney commemorates his 1792 naval victory over the French that saved the British colony.

Continuing westward on Route B12 past the market town of May Pen, you reach the Milk River near a crossroads called Toll Gate. Built on a hillside, the spa hotel has private cubicles hewn from stone that are filled directly from the springs. Here, too, an analysis of the water in 1952 confirmed a high degree of radioactivity and minerals, similar to that of the best European spa waters.

Although there are no special treatments or exercise equipment, the hotel has a large outdoor swimming pool filled with the cool mineral water. Ocean beaches and citrus groves are a few miles away. Trout Hall, which produces *ugli* fruit, can be visited on request.

Most of the guests at Milk River come to soak three times a day, reserving cubicles with the receptionist. Bottles of mineral water are on the tables in the dining room. The hotel has seen better days (and may again); the 22 guest rooms are simple, clean, and inexpensive, with two meals included in the daily tariff.

Milk River Spa and Hotel
Milk River Post Office, Clarendon, Jamaica
Tel. 809/924–9544

Administration General manager, Desmond Edwards

Rates Double room with private bath $900 (Jam.) for 2 persons, single room with private bath $600 (Jam.) with 2 meals daily, tax and service included. Credit cards: MC, V.

The Sans Souci Lido

Luxury pampering
Taking the waters

Jamaica
Ocho Rios

Charlie's Spa at the Sans Souci Lido resort takes a fresh approach to island holidays. More hedonistic than health-oriented, the resort atmosphere up on the hill complements vigorous workouts on the beach. It's a pleasant combination if you're interested in toning up or taking off a few pounds.

With the sea on one side and a cascade of mineral water on the other, the spa provides instant stress reduction. The waters, however, are not used for therapy or beauty treatments; you can soak or swim at leisure, and you may join an exercise class in the pool.

Long noted as a luxurious hideaway, Sans Souci came under SuperClubs management a few years ago, which revamped the facilities—and its image. The Sans Souci Lido is now an all-inclusive resort, including spa services, meals, drinks, and water sports in the daily tariff. All guest rooms were upgraded with marble bathrooms, many of them with whirlpool tubs, and amenities such as hair dryers and robes. New suites in the beach wing are smaller and suffer from noise at night from the 24-hour bar. The beach-level exercise equipment room has been air-conditioned; aerobics classes are held in a sea view open-air pavilion. The result is a program that offers more than the sum of its parts.

Begin with a fast-paced walk through the terraced gardens and along the curve of beach where tennis courts and water sports await your pleasure. The sound of a violin or flute draws you to the beach restaurant, where a permanent band of roving musicians entertains.

Bodywork and facials at the spa require appointments. Check in early at the tiny spa office alongside a pool that's home to mascot Charlie, a huge sea turtle who thrives in the mineral water. The Hideaway is a charming gazebo on the rocks, just big enough for a private massage, limited to 30 minutes in the all-inclusive plan. Facials and other treatments are given inside tiny wooden cottages clinging to the rocks. Higher up are rock-walled wet-treatment rooms with an alfresco shower, called "The Ridge," where seaweed and mud wraps are scheduled. At the top is a beauty salon, where a complimentary manicure and pedicure are offered.

A beach level body-scrub grotto conceals a dry sauna next to steps entering the sea. The shallow water here is a mix of saltiness and refreshingly cool mineral water from the springs. It's ideal for washing off oils and salts used for body scrubs (depending on your skin type, it can be aloe, peppermint, or coconut, plus cornmeal).

Sybarites can enjoy a secluded soak in a whirlpool tucked into the garden. A special treat is hidden in a beach grotto where the springwater seeps into a sand-bottom pool. For extra privacy, request an upper-level suite, or the penthouses, where you can sunbathe among the treetops.

Launched in late 1993, the Sans Souci Lido concept has attracted a younger type of guest than previously encountered here. Couples mix at afternoon tea and make plans for the gala beach party or tennis. Hostesses introduce single newcomers.

The Sans Souci Lido

Box 103, Ocho Rios, Jamaica
Tel. 809/974-2353 or 800/203-7456
Fax 809/974-2544

Administration General manager, Joseph Issa; spa director, Margaret Spencer

Season Year-round.

Accommodations 111 suites and rooms in villa-style buildings overlooking gardens and the sea. Newer suites in 3-story beach wing. All have TV, telephone, private balcony, air-conditioning, but no window screens. Traditional furnishings, with sitting area, tea kettle, mini-bar stocked with complimentary wine, waters, beer. Main building nearby houses the Casanova Restaurant and bar/lounge.

Rates 3 nights in deluxe ocean-view room $845–$1,050, beachfront suite $945–$1,386 per person, double occupancy. 7 nights $1,665–$2,120 in deluxe room, $1,875–$2,810 beachfront suite, per person double. Penthouse for 3 days $1,240–$1,620 per person double. Single supplement: $100 per day. Taxes and gratuities included. Credit cards: AE, DC, MC, V.

Meal Plans Breakfast, lunch, and dinner, snacks, and 24-hr room service included in tariff. Breakfast can be sliced pineapple, granola, or egg-white omelet with whole wheat toast. Lunch buffet has salads, grilled tuna sandwich, shrimp ceviche, pasta primavera, spinach and ricotta cannelloni. Dinner in Casanova restaurant includes seafood fettuccine, smoked marlin appetizer, broiled lobster or vegetarian lasagna. Beach restaurant serves Continental menu at dinner.

Services and Facilities **Exercise Equipment:** 2 Schwinn bikes, Lifecycle 9100, Concept 2 rower, dumbbells (15–50 lb), benches, free weights, 8-station Bodymaster multigym, Precor treadmill. **Services:** Massage, aromatherapy, reflexology, fango mud body and face treatment, paraffin wax hand and foot treatment, seaweed wrap, body scrub, facial; beauty salon for hair, nail, and skin care. **Swimming Facilities:** 2 pools and private beaches. **Spa Facilities:** Mineral springwater swimming and soaking pools, whirlpool, sauna. **Recreation Facilities:** Complimentary golf (18 or 9 holes), bike outing, shopping trip. Free use of water-sports equipment, including scuba trip, snorkeling gear. 3 tennis courts (lighted), croquet on beach. Nearby are St. Ann Polo Club; horseback riding at Chukka Cove. **Evening Programs:** Folkloric groups, combo for dancing on terrace.

In the Area Rose Hall and Greenwood Great House museums, Coyaba River Garden and Museum (pre-Columbian to Bob Marley), Ocho Rios craft market, Dunn's River Falls, Prospect Plantation (agricultural training center).

Getting Here *From Montego Bay Airport.* Transfers (about 2 hr) are included in package plans. Air Jamaica has frequent nonstop flights from U.S. cities and Canada. Taxi or limousine available at all times.

Special Notes Elevator connects guest rooms with spa facilities on the beach. (Hillside location of the hotel requires considerable stair climbing.) Minimum stay is 3 nights.

Swept Away

Sports conditioning *Couples only*

Jamaica As a counterpoint to the laid-back pace of life on the beach at
Negril Jamaica's westernmost point, the Swept Away resort stresses a sports and fitness regimen within its 20-acre complex. Included in the rates are unlimited use of the island's first indoor air-conditioned racquetball and squash courts, tennis lessons with resident professionals, and a fully equipped dive shop.

From the open-air reception area, paths lead to 26 two-story villas set rather close together in beachside gardens. The standard villa has four minisuites arranged on two levels around a plant-filled atrium. It is a quiet environment, far removed from the frenetic pace of most vacation villages, but plenty of action vibrates at the tennis complex and around the beach bar and pool. Most guests are young couples, some are honeymooners.

Set apart from the villas by the island's main road is the sports center. At the reception desk you can book courts, massages, and check on scheduled classes in the aerobics pavilion. An Olympic-length lap pool is used for aquacise sessions. Joggers can check out a nine-station parcourse on the half-mile running track.

Tennis buffs get workouts with pros at three daily clinics. There is a ball machine and racquet stringing equipment. If you haven't brought a racquet, there's no problem; equipment can be loaned. Tournaments are held throughout the week.

Massage therapy is close at hand; two rooms are in a thatch-roofed pavilion in the center of the sports complex, complete with outdoor Jacuzzi. (Massage is not part of the all-inclusive package; charges go on your account.)

The weights room here is an open-air pavilion with high-tech German equipment. Instructors are on hand throughout the day to coach you on proper use of the equipment. Certified in aerobics by AFAA, the staff gives classes in Reebok step, abs and gluts, body sculpting, and stretch. A power-lifting competition is scheduled every Wednesday evening.

In the clubhouse are men's and women's locker rooms with steam rooms and saunas. A sports-theme bar with big-screen TV opens at noon, and there is an open-air restaurant. Resort guests can dine here at no extra charge.

With the fitness facilities comes unlimited use of water sports equipment: Windsurfing, kayaking, sunfish sailing, paddleboating, and waterskiing are all featured. Snorkeling gear is also provided, as well as outings in a glass-bottom boat. For certified divers, scuba trips to nearby reefs depart three times daily in the resort's own dive boat. A certification course is available for an extra fee.

With the ambience of a private club, Swept Away allows you to set your own pace. Bicycles are available when you want to explore the area's more lively beaches at leisure. Relax on your veranda and enjoy the sunset. Room service delivers afternoon tea or Continental breakfast at your bidding while you soak up the romantic vista. In the two-level beachside dining pavilion, diversions range from billiards and a piano bar to a games room with a big-screen color TV that brings in stateside programs. Many guests seem content to simply lounge by the seaside freshwater pool; snacks are always available at the juice and veggie bar.

Swept Away
Box 77, Long Bay, Negril, Jamaica
Tel. 809/957-4061 or 212/941-9239; 800/545-7937
Fax 809/957-4060

Administration General manager, Jeremy Jones; spa manager, Nancy Machado

Season Year-round.

Accommodations 134 suites housed in 2-story villas. Jamaican handwork adds to the tropical look of rooms with wooden louvered walls, furnished with rattan rocker and wicker chairs, and plush cushions. King-size beds have cedar headboard; warm colors and earth-tone materials include decorative clay masks, lamps, and floor tiles. Private veranda; air conditioner, ceiling fan, telephone.

Rates Choice of villa: garden, sea view, beachfront. Per-couple packages for 4 days/3 nights $1,320– $1,850; 8 days/7 nights $2,765–$3,780. Rates include all meals, use of sports equipment and fitness facilities with instruction, alcoholic beverages, gratuities, and hotel taxes. Airport transfers provided. Deposit: 1 night's payment. Minimum stay: 3 nights. Credit cards: AE, DC, MC, V.

Meal Plan Buffet breakfast and lunch; dinner served by candlelight. Spa-cuisine options include egg-white omelet cooked to order, hot and cold cereals for breakfast. Lunch can be steamed vegetables, skinless chicken breast, baked fish. Dinner entrées include goat chops in phyllo dough, curried-goat stew, grilled fish in fruit sauce, homemade fish pâté, pasta. Jamaican buffet on Friday evening includes ackee strudel made with native applelike vegetable. Beach bar serves pita sandwich with tuna fish or chicken, fruit, vegetables, juices, beer, and bottled water. Italian restaurant at sports complex open for lunch and dinner has calorie-controlled pizza and pasta.

Services and Facilities **Exercise Equipment:** 22-unit PROFI weight-training gym, free weights and dumbbells (5–100 lb), 2 Lifecycles, 2 recumbent Lifecycles, NordicTrack cross-country skier, rowing ergometer, 2 Stairmasters. **Services:** Swedish massage (extra charge); tennis clinics and private lessons, introduction to scuba. **Swimming Facilities:** 2 outdoor freshwater pools, lap pool, ocean beach, clothing-optional beach. **Recreation Facilities:** 10 tennis courts (lighted, 4 hard-surface, 5 clay), jogging track, basketball court, 2 racquetball courts, 2 squash courts; dive shop with 3 trips daily. **Evening Programs:** Nightly dancing, band and show weekends.

In the Area Paradise Park (18th-century plantation), Great Morass (bird sanctuary), Savanna-la-Mar (19th-century sugar port), Milk River Bath (geothermal springs).

Getting Here *From Montego Bay.* By car, round-trip transfers provided (1½ hr). By air, scheduled Air Jamaica service. Rental car, taxi available.

Special Notes Ground-floor accommodations for people with disabilities. No children.

Centre de Thalassothérapie du Carbet

Life enhancement
Taking the waters

Martinique Seawater and kinesitherapy are the basis of an aquatic workout
Carbet at the indoor pools of the Centre de Thalassothérapie near Fort-de-France, capital city of the island. Considered effective in the treatment of rheumatism, the four-step procedure takes about 2½ hours and costs 300 francs.

Beginning with a plunge into heated seawater (33°C), you may participate in group exercise or simply relax. The pool has built-in underwater jets to massage sore muscles. A more intense underwater massage is next, in a private tub with jets designed to effect lymphatic drainage. The third step is a *douche à affusion*, a full body massage by a therapist working under a continuous shower of seawater.

The massage therapist devotes special attention to relieving tension in the vertebrae of your spine. The water pressure helps relax muscles. The final douche is in a shower stall lined with high-pressure jets aimed at cellulite points, the abdomen, and the vertebrae.

Supplementary services available include electrotherapy to recondition muscles after injury, an algae body mask, and antiarthritis and antiaging treatments for the skin. Inhalation of seawater mist is advised for asthma sufferers, and negative ions are introduced to relieve nervous tension.

While the center is open to the public every day with the exception of Sunday, there is no fitness program in conjunction with a hotel. Located nearby is the beachfront Hotel Marouba (tel. 596/78–00–21; fax 596/78–05–65), which has single rooms at 440F–620F, double rooms 680F–950F for 2 persons daily, including Continental breakfast. Also within a short walk is the 10-room Hotel Christophe Colomb (tel. 596/78–05–38) with single and double rooms 250F–300F daily.

Popular in France, this is spa therapy that sybarites can combine with a Caribbean holiday.

Centre de Thalassothérapie du Carbet
Grand'Anse
97221 Carbet, Martinique
Tel. 596/78–08–78

Administration General manager, Dr. Jacques-Joseph Louisia

Season Year-round. Open weekdays 7–6, Sat. 7–1; closed Sun.

Getting Here *From Fort-de-France.* By car, coastal road toward St. Pierre, 16 mi (25 min). Taxi, rental car available.

Special Notes Bring bathing cap, sandals, swimwear. Robe and towels provided.

Four Seasons Resort

Nonprogram resort

Nevis
Pinney's Beach

Pristine beaches, aquamarine seas, and tropical rain forests set the scene for the Four Seasons Resort on tiny Nevis. Opened in 1991, this luxurious resort seemed at first to clash with the island culture. But today it has become a welcome part of the community. Visitors arrive aboard a private launch at the resort's dock after a VIP greeting in St. Kitts, Nevis's sister island, 2 miles and 30 minutes across the channel. Or private planes can land at the tiny Nevis airstrip. Guests set their own pace, choosing among a number of sports options.

The resort has a sports-vacation package, available June through October, which is an excellent value; it includes unlimited tennis and golf. The tennis complex has 10 courts supervised by professionals who provide clinics and one-on-one training. The golf course is a major attraction at this resort. Joggers and walkers enjoy circuiting the links on a paved path that goes through lush forest and up into the foothills of Mt. Nevis.

Swimmers gained a dedicated two-lane lap pool in 1994 when facilities at the beach pavilion were expanded. Other watersports opportunities incorporate sailboards, kayaks, and snorkeling equipment.

The Health Club, located in the Sports Pavilion, has men's and ladies' saunas, a unisex hair salon, three massage rooms, and an air-conditioned workout room. Aerobics classes, stretch-and-tone sessions, aqua-aerobics, and early morning walks and beach jogs are open to all guests, free of charge. Croquet, volleyball, and shuffleboard are also offered.

Details make the difference: iced facecloths in the weights room, along with pitchers of fresh fruit juices; morning coffee and muffins laid out at the health club; a library of feature films for your VCR viewing; and in-room massage at your convenience. Experienced massage therapists, a rare commodity in the islands, provide some of the best bodywork anywhere. The dining room is reminiscent of a plantation great house, with a plank floor, a high ceiling with rafters, a cut-stone fireplace, ceiling fans, and a small dance floor.

The 12 plantation-style guest lodges have screened porches on the second floor and private patios with screened doors for ground floor rooms. Each building has about a dozen rooms and suites, provided with robes, TV and VCR, and minibar. Bathrooms are extra-large, with separate stall shower and toilet room.

The legacy of 300 years of British rule is still evident on the 68-square-mile island. Thanks to its sulfur bath and health spa, its 82 sugar estates, and the slave trade, the island once was known as the "Queen of the Caribbees." The Bath Hotel (c. 1778), now in disrepair and used as a police building, overlooks a wooden bathhouse where for $2 you can soak in hot mineral water.

Several magnificent plantation homes can be toured by asking the resort concierge. A perfect way to end your day is on Mt. Nevis, where you can enjoy the spectacular sunset, and perhaps catch a glimpse of wild monkeys with 6-foot-long tails.

Four Seasons Resort
Box 565, Charlestown, Nevis, West Indies
Tel. 809/469–1111
Reservations 800/332–3442 in U.S., 800/268–6282 in Canada
Fax 809/469–1112

Administration General manager, John Stauss; fitness/activities director, Juliette Borcher; tennis director, Greg Smith

Season Year-round.

Accommodations 196 rooms and suites in 2-story plantation-style cottages. Choice of king-size or 2 double beds, beach or golf view. Oversize marble-tiled bathroom with full amenities, hair dryer, lighted makeup mirror. All air-conditioned, with ceiling fans, TV and VCR, refrigerator, telephone. Self-service laundry facility in each cottage.

Rates $200–$550 daily per room, single and double; suites $400 for 1-bedroom, $750–$2,750 for 2-bedroom. Rates are European Plan (room only). Add 17% taxes and service charge. 7-night Romance in Paradise package, $3,300–$6,200 for 2 persons, includes massage, Modified American Plan (breakfast and dinner), unlimited golf and tennis. 7-night Island Fantasy package, $7,500–$12,000 for 2, includes massage for 3 days, crewed sailboat, 3 meals daily. Tax and service charge included in packages. Deposit: 3 nights payment. Credit cards: AE, DC, MC, V.

Meal Plans Modified American Plan $75 for breakfast and dinner daily; included in some packages. The breakfast buffet features tropical fruits and juices in season, Grenadian spice muffins, omelets, meats, and grills. Alternative choices are homemade granola, West Indian frittata, and vegetarian burger. Lunch can be herbed smoked chicken with mixed seasonal greens, salad of Nevis tomato, cucumber, and sweet peppers with marinated Spanish onions; or selections from the Mediterranean appetizer buffet. Dinner choices include grilled Caribbean fish, seafood gumbo, Caesar salad, and rotisserie specialties such as local range hen and lamb. Alternative cuisine selections include blackened local red snapper with sautéed spaghetti squash, Asian seared salmon with warm bean-sprout salad, local yellow tomato with Maui onion and roast pepper vinaigrette, spinach salad with jerk chicken, paw paw. Vegetarian menu available.

Services and Facilities **Exercise Equipment**: 3 Trotter treadmills, 4 StairMasters 4000 PT, 3 Lifecycles, 3 Schwinn Air Dyne bikes, 1 Concept 2 rowing machine, free weights (5–25 lb), bench and incline board. **Services**: Massage (Swedish, aromatherapy, sports); salon for hair, nail, and skin care. **Swimming Facilities**: Freshwater swimming pool, 25-m lap pool, ocean beach. **Recreation Facilities**: 18-hole golf course, 10 tennis courts (6 composition courts,

4 red clay; 3 lighted), water sports, volleyball, croquet, scuba, fishing. Horseback riding nearby. **Evening Programs:** Dancing, folklore show, movie features (Mon. and Fri.), pub with 2 pool tables, darts, shuffleboard table.

In the Area Nevis Peak (wild monkeys), Charlestown (shopping, crafts, colonial architecture), St. Kitts (colonial architecture, Brimstone Hill Fortress (c. 1680).

Getting Here *From San Juan.* American Eagle flights to St. Kitts, resort shuttle by car and 40-passenger launch (transfer $45 round-trip). Also, scheduled flights from St. Martin and Antigua directly to Nevis.

Special Notes Ground-floor rooms accommodate people with disabilities. Complimentary day-long program for children ages 3–10. Nurse on duty daily. Passport and departure tax required. Dress code in Great House.

La Casa de Vida Natural

Holistic health
Preventive medicine

Puerto Rico Secluded in the foothills of the Caribbean National Forest,
Luquillo practically in the shadow of towering El Yunque, the highest peak on the island, La Casa de Vida Natural has carved out a 10-acre center for natural health. Vegetarian meals; mud, herbal, and seaweed treatments; and psychological counseling are offered. With one of the island's best ocean beaches just down the hill at Luquillo, and hiking trails leading into the lush rain forest of El Yunque, this low-key, informal getaway has scheduled sessions winter and summer. Accommodations consist of an old farmhouse and guest house, with space for a dozen guests and staff.

The health center offers nonintrusive diagnostic procedures as well as kinesiology and massage. Workshops on physical and mental health are scheduled periodically, and individual counseling is available by appointment. The focus may be on building a psychological immune system, love and hate in health, or organic farming. Specialists on staff include a naturopathic doctor and a certified acupuncturist.

Taking an integrated biological and psychological approach to prevention and cure of disease, the center's services are geared to serve a wide range of interests. Therapies such as cleansing the body with burial in sand and immersion in mud can be combined with colonics and urine analysis. Aerobics classes and Jazzercise are organized in an open-air pavilion.

The program developed by New York–based psychoanalyst Jane G. Goldberg was introduced in 1988. At present, only 16 guests can be accommodated, and plans are to keep the center small, emphasizing personal attention to each guest.

Surrounded by natural beauty, panoramic views of the ocean, and the mountains, the pristine air and water are in natural harmony with the earth. Luquillo Beach, once a thriving coconut plantation, is protected by barrier reefs. The crescent-shape, white-sand beach is perfect for swimming and picnics. El Yunque, protected by the U.S. National Park Service, encompasses 28,000 acres. Reaching an elevation of 3,526 feet, its rain forest includes 240 different tree species, as well as orchids and wildflowers. Brief tropical showers keep things lush, moist, and cool.

Hot sulfur springs, known to the earliest Taino Indians, are an hour's drive from the center. At the Parador Baños de Coamo you can bathe in the same pool where Franklin D. Roosevelt, Thomas Edison, Alexander Graham Bell, and Frank Lloyd Wright took the waters. Now a modern mountain inn, the Parador offers Puerto Rican meals as well as overnight lodging. (Rte. 546; tel. 809/825–2186).

La Casa de Vida Natural
Rio Grande, Luquillo, Puerto Rico 00673
(Reservations) 222 Park Ave. S, New York, NY 10003
Tel. 809/887–4359 or 212/260–5823

Administration Director, Jane Goldberg

Season Year-round.

Accommodations Renovated farmhouse and cottage have 6 guest rooms, simply furnished with 2 beds or queen-size bed; no air-conditioning; shared baths.

Rates 5-day workshop $495. Advance payment $125 for workshops or 2 nights' lodging. Nonprogram lodging $100 per couple, without meals. Credit cards: MC, V.

Meal Plans 3 meals daily included in program fee. Vegetarian diet emphasizes raw fruits and vegetables grown on the property; whole grain home-baked bread, sprouts, juices, salads. Special diets are accommodated.

Services and Facilities **Services:** Massage (full body, $40; reflexology), colonics, mud pack, sand burial, polarity, herbal/seaweed wrap, facial. Holistic medical counseling, nutritional and psychological consultation. **Swimming Facilities:** Outdoor pool; ocean beaches nearby. **Spa Facilities:** Baños de Coamo (60-min drive). **Recreation Facilities:** Hiking, river boating. **Evening Programs:** Informal workshops.

In the Area Fajardo (marina, ferry to Vieques and St. Thomas); National Park Service interpretive program at El Yunque.

Getting Here *From San Juan.* By car, Rte. 3 east to Luquillo Beach, Carr. 186 to El Verde (60 min). Rental car, taxi, public car (*publico*) available. Complimentary airport transfers.

Special Notes No smoking on property.

Spa Caribe at the Hyatt Resorts

Nonprogram resort

Puerto Rico Talking back to the exercise machines might improve your fit-
Dorado ness rating during a workout at the health clubs in Hyatt's sports-oriented resorts. Like a personal coach, the computerized system monitors your progress. Powercise machines converse not only with the users but with each other. Their composite rating is handed to you at the end of the exercise circuit, with suggestions for additional improvement. These high-tech shape-ups are featured at both the Hyatt Regency Cerromar Beach and the Hyatt Dorado Beach, sis-

ter resorts 2 miles apart, on the north shore of the island, 22 miles west of San Juan. In addition to computerized equipment, they offer aerobics classes and aquaerobics, jogging trails, sauna, and a parcourse. Plus, there's professional pampering.

Geared to serve large groups at conferences and conventions in the resort, the spa also caters to the health club regular. A full day of exercise and bodywork, with facial as well as computerized evaluation, is available with a $195 Spa Sampler package. Groups meeting at both resorts are offered corporate games, seminars, workshops, and spouse programs, all supervised by experts. Spa services are available daily on an à la carte basis. In addition to the usual body and skin care, the specialties include neuromuscular therapy, sports massage, herbal wraps, and loofah body scrub. Peter Burwash-trained tennis pros offer a full agenda on 21 courts.

Spa Caribe at the Hyatt Resorts
Hyatt Resorts in Puerto Rico, Dorado, P.R. 00646
Tel. 809/796–1234 or 800/233–1234
Telex 3859758, Fax 809/796–4647

Administration President, Marietta Fridjohn; program manager, Patricia Lach

Season Year-round.

Accommodations Low-rise construction, luxurious landscaping, and vast swimming pools are hallmarks of these resorts. Hyatt Regency Cerromar Beach has 506 rooms on 7 floors, the Dorado Beach has 300 rooms on 2 floors. Both hotels feature sleek new tropical looks: rattan furniture, pastel fabrics, island prints on bedcovers and window drapery; baths have marble-top counters, tile floors, contemporary lighting.

Rates At Cerromar Beach, $160–$415 daily, at Dorado Beach $155–$725 daily, single or double occupancy. Suites and Regency Club rooms higher. Add 9% tax, 15% service charge. Guarantee by credit card. Credit cards: AE, MC, V.

Meal Plans Hyatt Cuisine Naturale menu of light fare, including fish and salads, available. Modified American Plan (breakfast and dinner) $60 per person for adults, $29 for children.

Services and Facilities **Exercise Equipment:** Powercise system (8 machines), Lifestride treadmill, 4 Lifecycles, Liferower, Hydra-Fitness muscular and cardiovascular training units. Outdoor parcourse with Dynacourt equipment. **Services:** Massage (Swedish, reflexology, sports, neck and shoulder), herbal wrap, loofah body scrub, facial cleansing treatments, aromatherapy. Salon for hair, nail, and skin care. **Swimming Facilities:** Outdoor freshwater pools, ocean beaches. **Recreation Facilities:** 21 tennis courts, 6 golf courses, bicycling, volleyball, pool volleyball, water sports. **Evening Programs:** Resort entertainment; casino.

In the Area Scuba, deep-sea fishing, sightseeing tours; Old San Juan (colonial architecture, art galleries, boutiques, museums), El Yunque rain forest, Camuy caves, Aricebo Observatory, San German (architecture, university).

Getting Here *From San Juan.* By car, Hwy. 22 (De Diego Expwy.), Rte. 693 to Dorado (30 min). By air, Dorado Airport. By public car (*publico*) from Old San Juan (60 min). Airport transfers ($45) by Dorado Transport Van. Rental car, taxi available. Shuttle service between hotels.

Special Notes Specially equipped rooms by advance request for people with disabilities. Elevators to all levels. Supervised Camp Hyatt (fee) for children June 1–Labor Day. No smoking in spa and designated dining areas; nonsmoking rooms available. Daily spa admission: $10.

Jalousie Plantation

Luxury pampering
Taking the waters

St. Lucia
Soufrière
Nestled between the Piton Mountains and a 320-acre nature preserve, Jalousie Plantation resort is an intimate hideaway for the rich and famous. The spa program features a daily 25-minute massage, aerobics classes, and use of the health club. The fitness center complex has separate saunas for men and women, a Jacuzzi, hot and cold plunge pools, a squash court, and massage rooms. Optional services include facials, seaweed body wraps, mud wraps, hydrotherapy, and aromatherapy. Try a combination of the Vichy shower in which alternating jets of warm and cold water massage your muscles, a loofah body scrub with algae oil to revitalize your skin, and for a finishing touch, plankton-rich thermal water forced through underwater jets in a hydrotherapy tub.

In a startlingly scenic forest, the resort occupies the site of a 17th-century sugar mill. The spa pools and Jacuzzi look out on to the ocean and the imposing Pitons. The view can be enjoyed as you sip a glass of soursop juice.

Spa cuisine is served at each of the resort's four restaurants, including the bar at the spa, where nonalcoholic drinks are featured. The one-price all-inclusive policy covers meals, sports, and the basic spa package. The guest accommodations range from private cottages, each with a private plunge pool, to suites in the former sugar mill.

Nearby are the thermal baths at Mt. Soufrière and Diamond Falls. A dormant volcano, with pits and open craters of boiling, sulferous mud, Soufrière has spring-fed pools of heated mineral water that have been used since French forces occupied the island during the 17th century. King Louis XVI had the baths built during this time. Cooler, sweeter-smelling water feeds the pools at Diamond Falls.

Jalousie Plantation
Box 251, Soufrière, St. Lucia
Tel. 809/459–7666 or 800/877–3643
Fax 809/459–7667

Administration General manager, William Banmiller

Season Year-round.

Accommodations 115 1- and 2-bedroom cottages and Sugar Mill junior suites. Each cottage has a covered veranda, air-conditioning, TV, coffeemaker, refrigerator; full bathroom with hair dryer, robes; direct-dial phone, FM radio; private plunge pool in garden.

Rates All-inclusive daily rate $480–$700 suite for 2 persons, double occupancy, from $450 single; $500–$750 cottages for 2 persons double, from $475 single. Tax and gratuities included. Deposit: 1 night's payment. Credit cards: AE, DC, MC, V.

Meal Plans 3 meals daily included in tariff. Spa cuisine options on all menus.

Services and Facilities **Exercise Equipment:** Treadmill, Windracer, Liferower, Schwinn Air Dyne stationary bike, Conquest weight-training system, StairMaster. **Services:** Swedish massage, aromatherapy massage, hydrotherapy, seaweed or mud wrap, loofah body scrub, facial; salon for hair, nail, and skin care. **Swimming Facilities:** Outdoor freshwater pool, ocean beach. **Recreation Facilities:** 4 tennis courts (Plexicushion; 3 lighted), squash court, Sunfish and Hobie Cat sailing, windsurfing, watercycles, floats, waterskiing, scuba, snorkeling, kayaking. Charter yachts at Jalousie Cove Marina.

In the Area Pigeon Island National Park (Fort Rodney), Castries (colonial fortifications, Saturday market). Aqua Action festival and boat races (May) at Reduit Beach. Carnival parades in July.

Getting Here *From Hewanorra International Airport.* Complimentary transfers on arrival and departure (1 hr).

Special Notes Ground-floor accommodations for people with disabilities. Passport required. Supervised daily activity for children.

Le Sport

**Luxury pampering
Sports conditioning
Taking the waters**

St. Lucia
Cariblue Beach
Thalassotherapy came to the tiny nation of St. Lucia in a big way when the all-inclusive Le Sport resort opened in 1989. At the elegant Oasis bathhouse, you are massaged with seawater by jets in the hydrotherapy tub and relaxed with a seaweed wrap. Set on a hill overlooking the sea, the Oasis provides sophisticated European equipment for seawater therapy as part of Le Sport's vacation program called the "Body Holiday."

The food segment of the Body Holiday program is called "cuisine légère," which simply means that calories don't count. Emulating the renowned Michel Guerard, the chefs provide meals balanced in complex carbohydrates and low in sodium and sugar. The regular menu, however, also has interesting options (*see* Meal Plans, *below*). Wine is included with lunch and dinner, and an open bar is available, which is stocked with premium brands, fresh fruit juices, and mineral waters.

Before any treatments, a checkup is scheduled with the staff nurse. Stress-linked fatigue and muscle tension, poor circulation, and lymphatic drainage are noted, and measurements are taken for blood pressure, heart rate, and weight. A prescribed course of treatments can include the "hydrator," a bubbling bath with herbs and sea algae, in which underwater jets needle away at the fatty tissue found on the upper arms, thighs, and calves. Another pool fitted with underwater jets is for exercise in seawater, which is denser than fresh water and thus gives greater support for the body. And the therapeutic nutrients of seaweed act as catalysts to create changes in the skin as you are wrapped, cocoonlike, in a coating of algae and sea mud. The scheduled treatments are included in the price of your holiday package; additional services cannot be booked à la carte.

St. Lucia's natural resources also include sulfur baths. Twin volcanic peaks called Petit Piton and Gros Piton rise dramatically above the tiny village of Soufrière on the southwest coast where signs point to the baths. From bubbling, underground springs, the sulfurous water flows into natural pools. Bathing here is said to cure whatever ails you.

A short jaunt up into the hills, across the ridge, brings you into the rain forest. Located between Soufrière and Fond St. Jacques, it's a three-hour trek through a tropical wonderland of dense foliage, flowering plants, and colorful birds.

Le Sport is a laissez-faire spa, not for those who want a regimented program. The eat- and drink-all-you-want policy may particularly suit the less motivated spa-goer.

Le Sport

Box 437, Castries, St. Lucia
Tel. 809/450–8551
Telex LC 6330; Fax 809/450–0368

Administration	Owner-director, Craig Bernard; manager, Michael Mathews; spa director, Anne Hurrell
Season	Year-round.
Accommodations	102 rooms oceanfront or with garden view in pavilions linked to dining room and lounge. Rooms have tropical contemporary look, rattan furniture. Air-conditioning, private balcony or patio, full modern bath with hair dryer, robes; all rooms with telephone, radio.
Rates	$210–$310 daily per person, double occupancy; $40 daily supplement for single occupancy for standard rooms. No minimum stay. Suite $250–$310 per person, double. 3-bedroom Plantation House $410–$450, single supplement $200. Credit-card guarantee for first night. Tax and gratuities included in rates. Credit cards: AE, DC, MC, V.
Meal Plans	3 meals daily included in program price. Breakfast buffet: fresh fruits and juices, bran and Muesli cereals, omelets, smoked salmon, pastries, coffee, milk, tea. Lunch buffet selections include fresh salads, stuffed chicken legs in leek-and-cream sauce, boiled wild rice, julienne of carrots and zucchini. Dinner options may typically include broccoli soufflé, scallop of veal with champagne sabayon, fresh asparagus. Spa cuisine choices may be steamed kingfish with carrot and pimento sauce, or sea scallops with a julienne of carrots and snowpeas in a raspberry vinaigrette sauce.
Services and Facilities	**Exercise Equipment:** Nautilus-type units, bicycles, fencing outfits. **Services:** Massage, hydrotherapy, facial, reflexology, Scotch douche, body wrap, loofah scrub, scalp treatment. **Swimming Facilities:** Outdoor freshwater pool, seawater pool, ocean beach. **Recreation Facilities:** Tennis courts, bicycling, archery, volleyball, scuba diving, windsurfing, waterskiing. **Evening Programs:** Live entertainment nightly, disco.

In the Area	Pigeon Island National Park (museum), Rodney Bay marina, Castries market (built 1894), Government House. Aqua Action Festival in early June.
Getting Here	*From Castries.* By car, coastal road to Gros Ilet (20 min). Complimentary transfers on arrival/departure at Hewanora Airport (90 min). Taxi, rental car available.

Port de Plaisance

Luxury pampering
Sports conditioning

St. Martin/
St. Maarten
Simpson Bay

Dropping anchor at Port de Plaisance doesn't require a yacht, but you can dock at this ITT Sheraton resort and enjoy the facilities of a first-rate tennis and fitness complex, dine at the island's most elegant seafood restaurant, and try your luck in the casino. Guests arriving by plane also get a nautical greeting: complimentary transfers by water taxi from the airport, complete with refreshing beverages. And cruise ship passengers are welcome to spend a day at the aptly named "Port of Pleasure."

The marina separates residential and recreational activities, necessitating a long walk from your room or riding in one of the electric carts that will transport you around the sprawling resort. At the spa registration desk you can sign up for a tennis clinic, salon services, and a wide variety of body treatments. The three full-day spa packages include unlimited use of the fitness room equipment, aerobics classes, and lunch on the pool patio, all for $90–$150, depending on services selected. Services can also be booked individually by guests at any hotel.

The spa has four massage rooms, two facial rooms, a fitness room, aerobics studio, and beauty salon. Both men's and women's locker rooms have saunas, steamrooms, and whirlpool, as well as showers, hair dryers, and basic amenities. Completing the sports complex are an outdoor lap pool, used for aqua aerobics. Aerobics classes, including step, cardio and tone, are scheduled two or three times daily in an air-conditioned studio. Classes are charged to your account at $5 per session, $8 if you use the locker facilities and visit without a spa package.

The range of skin care services and bodywork at the spa has expanded since the resort opened in 1992. Facial treatments using the Cathiodermie galvanic energy system to stimulate skin tissue, marine algae and collagen facials, and aromatherapy are offered by licensed therapists. Nine different massages are available, including a cool mint treatment, antistress relaxer, and sea mud. For a tropical refresher, fruit enzymes are applied to your face in masks with papaya, ginseng or coconut.

Set amid the privacy of 200 lushly landscaped acres on Simpson Bay, the resort lacks an ocean beach. Close by is L'Aqualigne (tel. 42426), a European-style spa on the beach at the Pelican Resort. Or you can cross the border to the French side of the island and join the naturists at Orient Beach, where Club Orient offers a totally nude environment for workouts and water sports. Reservations at the club, call 590/873385, fax 590/873376.

Port de Plaisance

Box 2089, Philipsburg, St. Maarten, N.A.
Tel. 011/5995–45222 or 800/732–9480
Hotel reservations 800/325–3535; fax 011/5995–42315
Spa and Tennis Reservations: Fax 011/5995–42144
Dockmaster Tel. 011/5995–44201, fax 011/5995–44215

Administration General manager, Christian Brüel; spa manager, Irini Vallianatos

Season Year-round.

Accommodations 88 marina apartments (junior, 1-, and 2-bedroom), with contemporary tropical furniture, king-size or twin beds, full kitchen. All rooms air-conditioned, with telephone, TV and VCR, ceiling fans, screen-doored balcony. Marble bathroom has tub/shower, bidet, hairdryer, robes.

Rates $220–$335 daily for junior suite single or double occupancy, $290–$455 for one-bedroom apartment 2 persons, $385–$600 for 2-bedroom apartment up to 6 persons. Daily Spa admission included. Yacht docking fees based on footage, $22.05 (32 ft.)–$149.60 (110 ft.) daily. Add 5% tax, spa gratuities. Deposit: credit card guarantee for 1 night. Credit cards: AE, DC, MC, V.

Meal Plans Lunch included in spa packages. Dinner from a la carte menu featuring grilled red snapper, sea scallops, grouper blackened or creole style. Friday night seafood buffet. Spa lunch can be tuna salad in pita, salad Nicoise, grilled chicken breast with couscous.

Services and Facilities **Exercise Equipment:** Paramount multistation gym, 3 Lifesteps, 3 Lifecycles, 3 Lifestride treadmills, Liferower, 2 PTS reclining bikes, dumbbells (5–25 lb), free weights (3–30 lbs). **Services:** Massage, facial, reflexology, body polish/wrap; personal training, fitness analysis; salon for hair, nail, and skin care. **Swimming Facilities:** Outdoor lap pool (23.5 meter); recreational pool; ocean beaches nearby. **Recreation Facilities:** 7 DecoTurf II tennis courts (lighted), deep-sea fishing, charter boats; golf course nearby at Mullet Bay. **Evening Programs:** Dancing and entertainment at casino's La Belle Vie Club.

Getting Here *From Princess Juliana Airport.* Complimentary transfers by resort boat. By taxi, 10 minutes. Rental car available only at resort.

In the Area Marigot (shopping, Ft. St. Louis), Philipsburg (shopping), St. Bart, Anguilla.

Special Notes Spa Hours: Daily 7 AM–9 PM. Passport or voter card and photo ID required by Dutch Customs, plus $10 depature tax.

Privilege Resort and Spa

Luxury pampering
Sports conditioning
Taking the waters

St. Martin/
St. Maarten
Anse Marcel

Panoramic views come with spa and sports workouts at the new Privilege Resort and Spa, which is perched on hills overlooking the beach and marina at Anse Marcel on the French side of binational St. Martin/St. Maarten. This unique hideaway provides European treatments to rejuvenate sun-damaged skin and aching muscles, as well as six-day "cures"—courses for slimming, anti-stress, or simply relaxing. For a sampler of French balneotherapy, try an underwater massage in the high-tech Doyer tub, or the Swiss shower temple, a multijet cabinet equipped with a control panel for cascades of varying intensity. The sea-oriented treatments available feature purified marine algae and seaweed from Brittany.

Sailing and sports training can be combined with the spa program, or arranged to fit your own schedule. Aerobics classes are held in the late afternoon, or at 8:30 AM. One of the most popular sessions, open to all resort guests without charge, is "aquagym" in the outdoor swimming pool cantilevered between the spa and restaurant. Close by the pool is the sports complex with tennis, squash, and racquetball courts, and an open-air pavilion with exercise equipment. A trainer is available for body-building and a few rounds of boxing-bag technique.

Opened in 1992, both the hotel and spa at Privilege Resort provide privacy and old-world service not found in neighboring resorts. Creole-style houses provide most of the guest rooms; some visitors are housed in ultra-privacy at the residence of the resort owner. Suites have two bathrooms in addition to a large living room. While all lodging is air-conditioned, there is no screening to protect against mosquitoes if you prefer fresh air at night.

Programs for four to seven nights offer a wide variety of sports and spa options, plus a shopping excursion. Sunday, when the spa is closed, guests sail to neighboring islands, with lunch on board, at no extra charge. For an extended cruise, there is a three-day sailing package. Other seasonal packages take advantage of low summer rates. If you want to do it all, the eight-day "Must" package is a VIP adventure, complete with sightseeing and airport transfers by helicopter.

Privilege Resort and Spa
Anse Marcel, 97150 St. Martin, French West Indies
Tel. 590/87–3838; Fax 590/87–4412
Reservations: 800/874–8541

Administration Owner-director, Robert David

Season Year-round.

Accommodations 80 spacious guest rooms, including 2 suites, with private terrace in 2-story hotel units or villa. Furnished in tropical style, bedrooms come with seating area and pull-out sofa bed, king-size bed, mini-bar, room safe, full modern bathroom with hair dryer, separate toilet. All rooms have ceiling fan, air-conditioning with remote control, TV, telephone, terra-cotta tile floor.

Rates 7-night Health & Spa Trek Program $1,795–$2,065 per person, double occupancy, $2,225–$2,695 single; 5-nights $1,385–$1,550 double, $1,692–$1,980 single. Rate includes treatments, breakfast and dinner daily, helicopter transfer to hotel, tax. 7-night Discovery package (Apr. 10–Nov. 30) $790 single or double. 7-night Must package $4,026–$5,630 per person double. Add gratuities. Third person or child in room free. Credit card guarantee for 1 night. Credit cards: AE, MC, V.

Meal Plans Continental breakfast with fresh orange juice, and choice of lunch or dinner included in package rates, except "Discovery" week. No spa menu; dietetic cuisine can be green salad or grilled tuna steak with steamed vegetables. Gourmet dining terrace has Caribbean fish soup, salmon escalope in a Creole sauce, carpaccio of fish Tahitian style, snails in pastry with white wine and mushrooms, shrimp in a basil sauce, scallop ravioli with leek, duck breast with mango compote.

Services and Facilities **Exercise Equipment:** Multigym, French air pressure weight-training units, free weights and benches, 2 stationary bikes, punching bags and gloves (new equipment to be installed 1995). **Services:** Swedish massage, shiatsu, lymphatic drainage, seaweed or mud wraps, manicure, pedicure, hydrotub, underwater massage. Cures (slimming, anti-stress, anti-cellulite). **Swimming Facilities:** 2 outdoor pools, ocean beach. **Recreation Facilities:** 6 tennis courts, 4 squash, 2 racquetball (all lighted), water sports. Nearby golf (18 holes) at Mullet Bay, horseback riding. **Evening Programs:** Disco dancing, 10 casinos on island.

In the Area Marigot (shopping), Orient Beach (clothing-optional beach), St. Bart, Anguilla.

Getting Here *From Princess Julianna Airport.* Taxi (30 min); complimentary transfers included in some packages. Rental car available at resort. Helicopter service.

Special Notes Access to all facilities for people with disabilities, but terrain is hilly. Spa open Mon.–Sat. 8–8. Electrical current 220 V (converter plug in bathrooms). Passport or voter registration and photo ID required for customs clearance, plus $10 departure tax.

Omega Journeys at Maho Bay

Holistic health
Spiritual awareness

U.S. Virgin Islands
Maho Bay, St. John
Workshops in health, music, movement, and personal growth are mixed with fun in the sun during four week-long programs planned by the New York–based Omega Institute. The annual migration to the sunny beaches of St. John is joined by faculty members who lead explorations into the body, mind, and spirit. Living close to nature in a tent village, the workshop participants experience many dimensions of natural healing.

Early birds can start the day with sunrise meditation, tai chi chuan, or yoga. Workshops run two hours each morning and afternoon, allowing a choice of several subjects. Informal and experiential, the group sessions are devoted to bringing health, aliveness, and peace into the many dimensions of contemporary life.

Drawn from a variety of professions, ages, and backgrounds, the participants find common ground in the open-minded, natural atmosphere. Maho Bay Camp Resort is a unique tent-cottage community dedicated to the concept of simple comforts and life in harmony with nature. Perched in thickly wooded hillsides, the canvas-walled cottages are set on plank decks that cantilever over the forest. The 16-by-16-foot units blend in so naturally that they seem to be part of the environment.

Located within the Virgin Islands National Park, the campground has unrestricted access to miles of pristine beaches and well-marked hiking trails, where you may pursue both ecological and historical interests. The National Park Service conducts free tours and lectures on island flora, fauna, and marine biology, as well as on St. John's colorful history and culture.

A must, if time permits, is a drive over Bordeaux Mountain, with its rain forest and spectacular views, to Coral Bay and East End, where descendants of the Danish settlers still farm in the old style.

Omega Journeys at Maho Bay
Maho Bay, St. John
Reservations: Omega Institute, 260 Lake Dr.,
Rhinebeck, NY 12572
Tel. 914/266–4444 or 800/944–1001

Administration President, Stephan Rechtschaffen, M.D.; program director, Jan Deleics

Season Jan.–mid-Feb.

Accommodations 96 tent/cottages tucked into foliage on 14 acres overlooking white-sand beach. Wooden floors, 2 beds, living/dining area (equipped with 2-burner propane stove), lounge chairs, sofa. Linens and bedding supplied, no maid service. Boardwalks connect to toilets, showers, dining pavilion, commissary.

Rates 1 week with workshops, lodging, meals, and round-trip airfare from New York, $1,275 per person, double occupancy. Lodging for single persons and children available. 50% payment at time of booking. Credit cards: MC, V.

Meal Plans Vegetarian meals 3 times daily. Omega's natural-food chefs prepare sumptuous buffets of vegetables and tropical fruits. Some fish and dairy products are available. Lunch includes salads, home-baked whole-wheat bread. Dinner menus offer vegetarian lasagna, baked eggplant Parmesan, tofu casserole.

Services and Facilities Services: Personal consultation on nutrition, body movement, energy training. Yoga instruction. **Swimming Facilities:** Ocean beaches. **Recreation Facilities:** Tennis, hiking, volleyball. **Evening Programs:** Informal workshops, concerts.

In the Area National Park Service interpretive tours, ferry to Tortola, catamaran trips. Annaberg Plantation (Danish-era ruins, special programs), Trunk Bay (underwater trail).

Getting Here   *From Cruz Bay.* By bus, shuttle service from ferry landing or along Northshore Rd. (15 min.). Car rental, taxi, minimoke, bicycle rental available.

Special Notes   No smoking indoors. Remember to bring flashlight, insect repellent, hiking shoes.

3 Health & Fitness Cruises

Staying fit at sea is no longer a matter of jogging 10 laps around the promenade deck. Today's luxury liners feature fitness facilities and programs that are the equal of anything ashore. Seagoing spas were an innovation of the 1970s. Since water is the basic ingredient in many spa cures, it was argued, a spa on the high seas should only make the experience more enjoyable. With abundant fresh air and sunshine, pools filled with filtered sea water, and aerobics classes on deck, the cruise would be an invigorating escape from health club routines at home.

For cruise connoisseurs, however, diet was a dirty word. And the gourmet meals and lavish buffets aboard ship have been the downfall of many calorie counters. Then came the American Heart Association's "Eating Away From Home" program adapted for shipboard dining by Royal Cruise Line, followed by Albert Roux's vegetarian menu for Celebrity Cruises' liners and the new Spa World program on Cunard's *Queen Elizabeth 2*. Your travel agent can provide details on lean and light shipboard cuisines offered by 22 members of the Cruise Lines Industry Association (CLIA).

Advance planning is important for those on a special diet. Specific foods and general preferences should be discussed with a travel agent, who can then secure a confirmation of your meal plan from the cruise line. All the leading lines offer such services at no extra charge.

Smoke-free cruising is a new option with some of the cruise lines. Introduced by the Majesty Cruise Line in cooperation with the Smoke Free Travel Council, cruises from Miami aboard the *Royal Majesty* offer no-smoking cabins as well as a totally smoke-free dining room. Carnival offers similar options.

For the committed fitness buff, cruising can provide the best of both worlds. Norwegian Cruise Line has annual Fitness and Beauty cruises in October. Guest lecturers on nutrition, sports medicine, hairstyling, and makeup make the trip along with football, golf, and tennis stars. Basketball cruises, baseball cruises, and football cruises allow passengers to team up for fun and fitness aboard the *Seaward* and its sister ship the *Norway*, which has the largest seagoing spa and fitness center.

Shore excursions on these cruises offer more than shopping and sightseeing. Several lines, including Norwegian Cruise Line and the *Cunard Countess*, provide entrée to local racquet clubs, golf courses, and fitness centers. Some ships have access to private ports of call, islands where passengers may swim, snorkel, and sunbathe on their own "deserted island." Others have scheduled nature walks and bicycle tours.

While the Caribbean and the Bahamas account for 60% of all cruise destinations, a steadily growing fleet of ships sails from California and Canadian ports. Alaska, the Mexican Riviera, and the Hawaiian islands offer exciting variations on the cruise theme. The rates we quote are published, but may be discounted at certain times of the year. In addition, some cruise lines offer discounts for early bookings and for repeat passengers.

As a new wave of luxury liners comes on line, look for more adventure cruises exploring off-the-beaten track ports and nature preserves. Small, specially designed expedition vessels are sailing to Alaska and along the Pacific coast for Clipper Adventure Cruises, Seaquest Cruises, and Windstar Cruises.

For newcomers to fitness programs, the cruise may be a good way to inaugurate a personal fitness routine that can then be continued effectively at home. Staff instructors offer one-on-one workouts that teach proper exercise routines—perhaps the best bargain in fitness education. And there's a healthy bonus from mother nature: The bracing effect of the fresh air generated by sea water and sun may be just what the doctor ordered for our high-pressure society.

Carnival Cruise Lines

With the debut of 2,600 passenger superliners *Sensation*, *Ecstacy*, *Fantasy*, and *Fascination* in 1994, Carnival Cruise Lines has spas that are bigger than the casinos (another first!). In the Nautica Spa, with a view of the sea, you work out with row upon row of exercise machines reflected in a mirrored ceiling. Behind the gym are six whirlpools (also with a sea view), two saunas, steam rooms, massage rooms, showers, and locker rooms. Also active throughout the day is a large glass-and-mirror-enclosed aerobics studio. Classes include "Cardio-Funk" and "Cardio-Pump." There are organized walks on the ships' upper decks, and a ⅛th-mile jogging track circles the deck. Familiarizations with the equipment and talks by the spa staff are offered regularly throughout each cruise.

A beauty salon completes the enclosed portion of the 12,000-square-foot spa. Operated by London-based Steiner spa professionals, the services offered include a range of facials, massages, and beauty treatments.

Calorie-conscious passengers can take advantage of a Nautica Spa Selection on the menu at each meal. In addition, a circular salad bar in the grill area is open for lunch and dinner.

Carnival Cruise Lines. *3655 NW 87th Ave., Miami, FL 33178. Tel. 305/599–2600 or 800/327–7353 (800/325–1214 in FL).* Commissioned in 1990–1994. 2,600 passengers. Liberian registry, Italian officers, international staff.

Fitness Facilities: 35 weight-training units and computerized exercise machines, ranging from bikes to bench press. **Services:** Massage, loofah scrub, facial, anticathiodermie facial, herbal pack, aromatherapy, pressotherapy (air bags), G5 weight loss massage, eucalyptus steam inhalation. **Sports:** 2 outdoor pools, trapshooting, table tennis, shuffleboard.

Fares include airfare from major cities: $529–$1,1329 for 4-day cruise to the Bahamas; $1,349–$2,429 for 7-day cruise.

Special Notes: No smoking in dining rooms. Children's playroom available on all ships. Some cabins equipped for people with disabilities. A sister ship, *Imagination*, joins the fleet in 1995. The world's largest ship is scheduled to join the fleet in 1996.

Celebrity Cruises

The top-deck Olympic Health Club, operated by Steiner of London, on the 1,354-passenger *Horizon* and 1,374-passenger *Zenith*, has one of the largest and best spas at sea. Each ship has a window-walled weights room, cushion-floored aerobics studio, three outdoor whirlpools, and a coed sauna. Dieters choose between a full vegetarian menu designed by London restaurateur Albert Roux and the regular menu with highlighted items that are low in sodium and cholesterol.

The extensive selection of beauty services is provided by a professional staff, who also provide fitness classes that range from cardio-funk low-impact aerobics to designer body conditioning and a 30-minute session of aqua-aerobics in the outdoor swimming pool. In addition to a dozen pieces of exercise equipment, there are ½-mile outdoor jogging tracks.

Celebrity Cruises. *800 Blue Lagoon Dr., Miami, FL 33126, tel. 305/262–4322 or 800/437–3111.* Deluxe staterooms and outside cabins; most cabins are compact, all have private shower and toilet. Liberian registry, Greek officers and European staff.

Fitness Facilities: 5-station Universal Gym, 2 Trendex treadmills, NordicTrack cross-country ski machine, 3 Aerobicycles, 2 rowing machines, free weights. 2 outdoor swimming pools, whirlpools. **Services:** Massage, Cathiodermie revitalizing facial, Ionithermie slimming treatment, bodybrushing; personal fitness analysis, body fat analysis, personal training; salon for hair, nail, and skin care.

Fares for 7-day cruise including airfare, $1,145–$3,520 per person double occupancy.

Special Notes Wheelchair-equipped state rooms for people with disabilities.

CostaCruises

The ancient Roman rituals for relaxation and revival of the body and mind are updated with modern technology in the Caracalla Spa aboard Costa Cruise Lines' sister ships, the Italian-inspired *CostaClassica* and *CostaRomantica*. The 7,000-square-foot spa glass-walled for views of the sea, has a full line of Nautilus equipment. Treatments offered include thalassotherapy, aromatherapy, and hydrotherapy. The luxuriously appointed top-deck fitness center offers both complimentary group instruction and one-on-one sessions in aerobics, strength training, stress conditioning, and relaxation. A steam bath, saunas, Jacuzzis, and beauty salon are part of spa complex. Treatments with rejuvenating Moor mud, seaweed, and essential oils can be reserved in advance of sailing. Operated by CTI Group, the spa has packages from half-day treatments to the six-day ($625) Bellisima program. Runners, joggers, and power walkers enjoy a dedicated track overlooking the pool deck.

Costa Cruise Lines. *World Trade Center, 80 S.W. 8th St., Miami, FL 33130, tel. 305/358–7325 or 800/462–6782.* Deluxe outside staterooms, inside cabins, with 2 lower beds that convert to a queen-size bed; shower and toilet. Launched 1992, 1993.

1,300 passengers. Italian registry, Italian officers and dining room staff, European stewardesses.

Fitness Facilities: Complete line of weight-training equipment, 3 Lifecycles, free weights. **Services:** Massage, reflexology, body wrap, body scrub, hydrotherapy bath, deep-cleansing facial, rehydrating facial, personal training.

CostaClassica cruises weekly on Saturday from San Juan: Fares, including airfare, are $795–$2,995 per person, double occupancy. *CostaRomantica* sails from Miami every Sunday on week-long cruises.

Crown Odyssey

The largest of the four ships in the Royal Cruise Line, the 34,250-ton *Crown Odyssey* sports a lavish health center complemented by a healthful alternative dining program approved by the American Heart Association. Principal attractions are an indoor swimming pool, whirlpools, gymnasium, saunas, and a health bar. Reminiscent of a sumptuous Roman bath with its tile walls and floors in shades of green, coral, and white, the health center offers the latest in exercise equipment and programs. Choices include classes in yoga, aerobics, dancercise, walk-a-thon, aquacise workouts, Body Shop for strengthening and tightening muscles, and Sit and Be Fit, which incorporates exercises that can be done while sitting in a chair. In addition, two outdoor whirlpools and a parcourse walking track complement the outdoor pool. Programs include lectures and workshops with guest experts on subjects ranging from stress management to nutrition and self-esteem. The *Crown Odyssey* (and her sister ship the *Royal Odyssey*), offers an expanded New Beginnings program that has included a pain clinic and workshops on retirement adjustment.

Royal Cruise Line. *Maritime Plaza, San Francisco, CA 94111, tel. 415/956–7200 or 800/227–4534.* Launched in 1988. 1,052 passengers. Exclusive suites have private Jacuzzis, balconies, butler service. Most have outside staterooms with picture windows. Bahamian registry and crew.

Fitness Facilities: Universal Gym, 4 LifeFitness bikes, Fitstep stair/climber, computerized treadmill, 2 Precor rowers, aquacourse, free weights, ballet bar. **Services:** Massage, herbal wraps, facials; hair, nail, and skin care. **Sports:** Golf driving instruction; tennis and golf ashore.

Cruises to Canada, New England, the Panama Canal, the Mexico Riviera, the Caribbean, Hawaii. Fares for a 7-day Alaskan cruise from Vancouver $1,439–$6,299 per person double occupancy.

Crystal Harmony

This 960-passenger liner has a 3,000-square-foot oceanview spa and fitness center that offers aerobic and Jazzercise instruction and treatments that include thalassotherapy, moortherapy, and aromatherapy. Passengers relax in men's and women's saunas and steam rooms, tee-off at a golf simulator, jog on a full promenade deck, play on paddle tennis or volleyball courts, swim in a lap pool, soak in Jacuzzis, or socialize in an indoor/ outdoor swimming pool with built-in bar. A fitness trainer is aboard, and there are special slimming programs using the DeCleor program. Operated by CTI Group, services include facials, body wrap, and a French hand treatment. The spa also offers a salon for hair, nail, and skin care, and a men's barber-shop.

Personal service is a hallmark of Crystal Cruises. All state-rooms have bathroom with tub and shower, double vanity. Dinner is served at your choice of time in Italian or Chinese restaurants.

Crystal Cruises. *2121 Ave. of the Stars, Los Angeles, CA 90067, tel. 310/785–9300 or 800/446–6645.* Entered service 1990. 8 passenger decks with 480 deluxe staterooms, including 62 penthouse suites. All outside accommodations except 19 inside cabins; many have private verandas; all have king- or queen-size beds. Bahamian registry, Norwegian and Japanese officers, Italian dining staff, international crew.

Fitness Facilities: 3 treadmills, 3 Lifecycles, 2 StairMasters, 2 rowing machines, 4 Lifecircuit weight-training machines, free weights. **Services:** massage, facials, body scrub, herbal wrap; foot, hand and eye treatments; personal trainer; beauty salon.

Cruises from Los Angeles and New York City; fares including airfare for 21-day trans-Canal cruise $15,360–$23,040 per person, double occupancy.

Cunard Countess

Active vacationers aboard the *Cunard Countess* can take advantage of a state-of-the-art fitness center and the shore excursions offered through "SeaSports" TM program. The 2,000-square-foot exercise facility is packed with the latest in LifeFitness equipment. Trainers are on hand daily to assure proper form in your workout. Aerobics class, weight-training seminars, and nutritional lectures are part of the program at no additional charge for all passengers.

When your workout is over, you can relax in one of two adjacent Jacuzzis, a European-style sauna, and an outdoor swimming pool. Country-and-western entertainment is the ship's specialty, and you can join line dancing aerobics classes with the country sound. Ashore, you can enjoy beach facilities at Cunard resorts and sign up for water skiing, golf, tennis, horseback riding, 5K "fun runs" and hikes in remote jungles. (Shore excursions are booked aboard ship for an additional fee.)

Cunard Line. *555 Fifth Ave., New York, NY 10017, tel. 212/880–7304 or 800/221–4770.* Commissioned in 1976, refurbished 1986. 790 passengers. British registry and officers, international staff.

Fitness Facilities: Lido Deck fitness center with 12-station Paramount circuit, 2 LifeRowers, 5 Lifecycles, 2 Lifesteps, computerized weight-training system; outdoor swimming pool, 2 whirlpools. **Services:** Massage, one-on-one training, barbershop/beauty salon. **Sports:** Golf driving range, basketball practice, paddle tennis court, table tennis, shuffleboard.

Cruises from San Juan every Saturday, alternating itineraries. Fares for a 7-day cruise from $1,565 per person double occupancy, including air fare from U.S. Also available, "Sail 'n Stay" packages with an additional week at Barbados or St. Lucia resorts.

Cunard Royal Viking Sun

The *Royal Viking Sun* joined the Cunard fleet in 1994. Among its features are a computerized indoor golf simulator that enables passengers to play some of the world's most challenging courses and—breaking new ground—the first croquet court on a cruise ship. The elaborate Viking Spa overlooks the ship's pool area, where a swim-up bar permits you to combine exercise and socializing. This liner also has a library with fireplace, and penthouse suites.

Cunard Line. *555 Fifth Ave., New York, NY 10017, tel. 212/880–7304 or 800/221–4770.* Launched 1988. 756 passengers. Bahamian registry, British and European officers.

Fitness Facilities: Gym equipped for toning muscles and building endurance; 2 heated outdoor saltwater swimming pools, saunas for men and women; aerobics studio with classes at all levels. **Services:** Massage; facials; moortherapy facial mask; back and leg treatment; thermal or herbal body wrap; throat and decollete treatment; eye, foot, and hand treatment; exfoliation. Salon for hair, nail and skin care. **Sports:** Badminton, tennis practice court, Ping-Pong, quoits, darts.

Fares for 16-night trans–Panama Canal cruise, New York–San Francisco via the Caribbean, $4,395–$12,075 per person double occupancy including air connections (shorter segments available). Wheelchair accommodations in 4 cabins for people with disabilities.

Holland America Line

With a Passport to Fitness program aboard their entire fleet, Holland America Line offers one of the best values in health and fitness cruises year-round. Passengers pick up a passport aboard the ship to earn stamps for fitness classes, team sports, and beauty treatments. Even ordering lunch and dinner from the Perfect Balance menu in the dining room earns a stamp. Prizes are awarded for 20–40 stamps. Aerobics classes and aquatic workouts are available to all passengers. A newly introduced spa menu has such healthful selections as Thai chicken salad and fresh Pacific snapper. Tennis and golf programs and a scuba certification course are offered on shore excursions. The twin luxury liners, immaculately maintained and decoated with an extensive collection of art and antiques, offer services and amenities in the grand tradition of transatlantic travel.

The Ocean Spas aboard the 1,266-passenger sister ships *Maasdam, Statendam,* and *Ryndam* have 4,126 square feet for aerobics studio, weight-training equipment, sets of saunas and steam rooms, and two outdoor whirlpools. Treatments include aromatherapy, body wraps, and massage as well as hair salon services. Among European therapies are products of René Guinot, Thalgo, Ionitherapie, and Remé Laure Moormud.

Holland America Line. *300 Elliott Ave. W, Seattle, WA 98119, tel. 206/281–3535. Nieuw Amsterdam* Netherlands Antilles registry, Dutch officers, Indonesian and Filipino staff.

Fitness Facilities: Gymnasium with Ultra Mac multipurpose 9-way muscular exercise unit, stationary bicycles, rowing machines, free and pully weights, slant boards, treadmills; 2 outdoor swimming pools (1 has pressure jets), 2 saunas. **Services:** Massage, facials, manicure, pedicure, hairstyling, makeup consultation. **Sports:** Tennis courts, shuffleboard, scuba instruction, volleyball.

Fares for 7-day Alasaka cruise from $1,660 to $2,650 per person, double occupancy. Winter cruises from Ft. Lauderdale and Miami.

Special Note: Four staterooms for people with disabilities.

SS Independence and SS Constitution

Refurbished in 1993 by new owners, American Hawaii Cruises' vessels feature two of the most complete fitness centers afloat in the Pacific. Added in 1990 atop the SS *Constitution* was a 2,000-square-foot Health and Fitness Center. A large open area is used for aerobics classes scheduled several times during each day at sea. A sauna and massage room are located near the barbershop/beauty salon.

The Hawaiian way to watch your waistline on these cruises is, of course, the hula. Lessons are offered in hula dancing as well as dancercise and water aerobics. In the mornings you can join the sports director in "walk-a-mile," followed by exercise in one of the two freshwater swimming pools.

Menus have been updated to include lighter fare. The new *Pu'uwai* ("heart") program offers healthy options at breakfast, lunch, and dinner for passengers who wish to limit their intake of fats and cholesterol, but you have to skip the chocolate-macadamia-nut cream pie for dessert if you have the Herculean resolve, and opt for fresh pineapple. This classic liner, owned by Delta Queen Steamboat Co., attracts older passengers.

American Hawaii Cruises. *550 Kearny St., San Francisco, CA 94108, tel. 415/392–9400 or 800/765–7000.* Commissioned in 1951, rebuilt 1974, renovated 1993. 798 passengers. U.S. registry and officers. 7-day cruise from Honolulu every Saturday evening; fare $995–$3,950 per person double occupancy. Also available are cruise-resort combinations via Hilo, with cruise and 3–4 day stay at selected hotels, transfers included, $669–$1,549 per person, double.

SS Norway

The 14-room, 6,000-square-foot Roman Spa, which opened in 1990 aboard the SS *Norway*, launched a new era of spa luxury at sea. Featuring the first hydrotherapy baths on a cruise ship, the spa employs European-trained specialists in thalassotherapy, shiatsu, reflexology, aromatherapy, thermal body wraps, and a wide range of beauty services. Services can be booked à la carte; five package programs are available for a complete spa vacation. Ranging from a half-day introductory workout and herbal massage for $99 to a 6-day customized regime for $689, packages always include a calorie-controlled luncheon served in the spa lounge, which has a juice bar.

Located on Dolphin Deck, the new Roman Spa is a sybaritic enclave of soothing treatment rooms (each equipped with shower), men's and women's saunas and steam rooms, a seawater aquacise pool and Jacuzzi, and an exercise room with computerized cardiovascular equipment. The *Norway's* spa treatments incorporate ancient Roman hydrotherapy philosophy and a sea theme with Phytomer marine algae, moor mud products by Remé Laure. Advance appointments prior to sailing can be made by calling the spa operator (CTI Group: 800/423–5293; in Dade County, 305/358–9002).

For more active passengers there is a "Fit with Fun" program on the ship's Olympic Deck, where state-of-the-art exercise equipment and a 360-degree jogging/walking track have been installed. Team games are organized in the *"Norway* Olympics," and snorkeling is offered at a beach party on NCL's private uninhabited island in the Bahamas. Added features during the Fitness and Beauty Cruise at the end of October include workshops on nutrition, sports medicine, and skin care; running clinics; and workouts with sports personalities. During the rest of the year, golf and tennis Pro-Am cruises have professionals aboard to help improve your game, and opportunities for play abound on shore. Fitness walks are organized in each port.

Norwegian Cruise Line. *95 Merrick Way, Coral Gables, FL 33134, tel. 305/447–9660 or 800/327–7030.* Entered service as the *France,* in 1962, refitted as the *Norway* in 1979, renovated and expanded in 1990. 2,044 passengers. Norwegian registry and officers, international staff.

Fitness Facilities: Universal Gym Equipment, 2 Liferowers, 3 LifeCycles, 2 Lifesteps, free weights; Roman Spa with Bally cardiovascular equipment; 2 outdoor swimming pools; outdoor jogging track. **Services:** Massage, facials, hydrotherapy bath, body wrap, makeup cleansing; hair, nail, and skin care. **Sports:** Racquetball, basketball, volleyball courts, golf putting and driving areas, skeet shooting.

Cruise fares from $1,325 to $5,179, including air fare and transfers. Year-round 7-night cruises departing from Miami on Saturday. Roman Spa open daily 9–7, until 10 PM port days. Spa packages from $99 plus 12% gratuity, includes facility charge, toga. Massage (50 min) $60.

Princess Cruises

A well-equipped gymnasium affords panoramic views of the sea to those working out on the 1,590-passenger *Crown Princess* and *Regal Princess.* With over a dozen pieces of exercise equipment in the 3,250-square foot fitness center, plus an outdoor ⅙-mile cushioned jogging track on the promenade deck, the facilities are part of the "Cruisercise" program developed by Princess Cruises. You can join two to four workout classes per day, relax in four whirlpools, two sets of saunas and steam rooms. Sign up for facials, massage, body wraps, and hair styling at the salon operated by CTI Group.

The dining room menu offers heart-healthy items that are low in sodium and cholesterol, prepared according to American Heart Association guidelines.

Princess's fleetwide Cruisercise® program was designed by Kathy Smith, fitness trainer for the Stars & Stripes U.S. sailing team. On all ships a daily schedule of classes includes walk-a-mile, stretch and tone, high- or low-impact aerobics, and aquacise. Participation earns you prizes.

Princess Cruises. *10100 Santa Monica Blvd., Los Angeles, CA 90067, tel. 310/553–1770 or 800/568–3262. British registry and officers, Italian dining room staff, British stewards.*

Fitness Facilities: Gymnasium with Hydro-fitness 11-station multipurpose weights unit, rowing machines, treadmill, Paramount Uniflex sports trainer, Lifecycles, slant boards, free weights; aerobics studio with classes at all levels scheduled daily; 4 outdoor swimming pools (with a 33-foot pool for laps), 4 whirlpools, sauna. **Services:** Massage, facials, moortherapy facial mask, leg and back treatment, throat and decolette treatment, foot and hand treatment, body wrap, eye treatment. Salon for hair, nail, and skin care.

Cruises include Alaska, Trans-Panama Canal, Caribbean. Fares for 7-night cruise from Ft. Lauderdale, $1,260–$3,360 per person, double occupancy, including round-trip air connections. Wheelchair accommodations in 10 staterooms.

Queen Elizabeth 2

The new Steiner spa aboard Cunard's majestic *Queen Elizabeth 2* enhances body, mind, and spirit in regal fashion. Steiner, after all, holds royal warrants as hairdresser to the queen. But here the accent is on thalassotherapy, a French concept of seawater-based bodywork and exercise in fresh seawater. A fitness center open to all passengers free of charge, includes a swimming pool, a full line of Cybex equipment and computerized exercise bikes, as well as an aerobics studio. The spa is a separate enclave on the ship's lowest of seven decks, with a unique hydrotherapy pool in which you follow a circuit of underwater jets. The London-trained therapists usher you into one of 10 private treatment rooms for a seaweed body mask, followed by a full-hour massage. Other treatments on the spa's list include hydrotub bath with freeze-dried seaweed, or a water blitz massage in which concentrated jets play across your body. The spacious facility can be used for a daily fee or as part of packages offered by Cunard and Spa-Finders. Three packages are offered during transatlantic crossings in the *QE2* SpaWorld program, which includes a newly created spa cusine menu served in the Columbia dining room or on request in the Grill rooms. The benefits of British Airways' new "Well-Being in the Air" program are an added bonus, as your *QE2* ticket includes one-way air transportation with the option of following a scientifically designed fitness and food plan during the flight.

On all sailings, including Caribbean and Bermuda cruises, passengers can participate in the fitness center's scheduled classes. One-on-one training is offered for a fee, as well as a nutritional assessment and fitness evaluation. Open 7–7, the indoor saltwater swimming pool can be reached by elevator. Additional swimming pools are on deck, including the indoor/outdoor Lido Magrodome Center with glass roof that rolls open in warm weather.

Following a major facelift in 1994, the superliner continues to reflect its distinctive heritage as one of the great ocean liners. Entertainment in the Grand Lounge by celebrity artists, and classical concerts in the theater, complement the grandest new spa experience at sea.

Cunard Line. *555 5th Ave., New York, NY 10017, tel. 212/880–7304 or 800/221–4770.* Launched in 1967, re-entered service 1987; major refurbishment 1994. 1,800 passengers. *QE2* SpaWorld transatlantic crossing (May–Oct.) from $2,670 per person, plus $599 spa package, and port taxes (tel. 800/255–7727). Transfer from airports provided for New York sailings. British registry, British and European officers.

Fitness Facilities: Cybex units, LifeFitness equipment. 2 outdoor swimming pools, 2 indoor pools. **Services:** Massage, facials, Ionithermie, seaweed body wrap, aromatherapy, thalassotherapy body scrub, hydrotherapy. Salon for hair, nail, and skin care.

SSC Radisson Diamond

The entire top deck of the SSC *Radisson Diamond* is devoted to a 3,000-foot spa, golf driving range, and jogging track. And there is a marina that descends into the sea. The twin-hull design accommodates 177 staterooms. New technology called SSC (Semi-Submersible Craft) minimizes engine and propeller noise and maximizes deck space. From the 5-story atrium, you are whisked up a glass elevator to three decks of suites (there are 12 decks total) and a glass-walled dining room. All cabins are suite-size with private balcony, queen-size bed, TV, VCR, stereo, and a full bath with shower. The spa and health club, managed by CTI Group, features two massage and facial rooms, hydrotherapy, moormud, and herbal wrap. There are separate saunas and steam rooms for men and women, as well as European treatment rooms and exercise equipment. The open-air swimming pool and Jacuzzi are tiny, but in port you can swim in a floating marina equipped for snorkeling, windsurfing, and water jet boats.

With an open-seating policy in the main dining room, you can order off the menu, request a special diet, or select from the "Simplicity" menu. Evening entertainment is limited to the casino and TV. The ship's rates do not cover personal services in the spa and salon. Packages are offered for half-day or full-day programs, as well as a 3-day program.

Radisson Diamond Cruises. *600 Corporate Dr., Ft. Lauderdale, FL 33334, tel. 305/776–6123 or 800/333–3333.* Debut in 1992. 354 passengers. Finnish registry, international crew.

Fitness Facilities: Exercise room with 4 David cam weight machines, 2 Lifesteps, 2 Liferowers, 4 Lifecycles, free weights. **Services:** Massage, facials, body wraps, hand and foot treatment, aromatherapy. Salon for hair, nail, and skin care.

Cruises from San Juan and Fort Lauderdale on 4-, 5-, and 7-day itineraries. Fares approximately $600 per person, per day, double occupancy. Spa packages $140–$465.

Royal Majesty

The *Royal Majesty* debuted in 1992 as the first ship to ban smoking in the dining room. 132 of the cabins are also smoke-free.

A well-equipped seaview spa is situated high atop the ship, with Body Waver gym and Vanity Fair Salon. The healthful Regal Bodies spa cuisine is available in the dining room. The spa has an aerobics studio with wooden floor where aerobics and tai chi chuan classes are scheduled daily. There are massage rooms, 2 saunas, a smallish outdoor swimming pool, a pair of whirlpools, and a jogging track.

Majesty Cruise Line. *Box 025420, Miami, FL 33102, tel. 305/530–8900 or 800/645–8111.* Commissioned in 1992. 1,056 passengers. Panamanian registry, Greek officers, international crew.

Fitness Facilities: Gymnasium with 2 StairMasters, LifeCycle, recumbent bike, 4 weight-training machines, free weights, NordicTrack cross-country machine, rowing machine. **Services:** Massage, personal training; hair, nail, and skin salon.

Cruises from Miami. Fares for 3-night Bahamas cruise, including airfare, $489–$969 per person, double occupancy; 4-night cruise to Nassau, Key West, and private island, $599–$1,099 per person. Summer cruises to Bermuda from Boston, $1,099–$3,299.

Seabourn Pride and Seabourn Spirit

With almost an entire upper deck devoted to a seagoing spa, the *Seabourn Pride*—the creation of an experienced team of Norwegian and American designers—and sister ship *Seabourn Spirit*, take aim at the upscale cruiser who demands service and spaciousness. The all-suites ships have six passenger decks, open-seating dining rooms where meals are prepared to order, and many attractive features such as marble baths, 5-foot windows, and walk-in closets in every stateroom. The spa program includes a full range of aerobics and activities. Passengers may request a personalized fitness evaluation and dietary guidance. Treatments include body firming and silhouette refining with marine algae body wraps and baths, herbal massages, and facials. Shore excursions include ports rarely visited by large cruise ships, such as Soufrière Bay in St. Lucia, where a visit to the thermal baths can be arranged.

Seabourn Cruises. *55 Francisco St., San Francisco, CA 94133, tel. 415/391–7444.* Debut season 1988–1989. 212 passengers. Norwegian registry and officers, European staff.

Fitness Facilities: Gymnasium with Nautilus exercise units, computerized exercycles, rowing machines, isotonic exercisers, free weights; outdoor swimming pool and twin whirlpool baths, sauna, steam room, aerobics studio. **Services:** Massage, body wraps, moortherapy facial mask, back and leg treatments, hand and eye treatments, throat and decollete treatment. Salon for hair, nail, and skin care, personal fitness consultation. **Sports:** Swimming from the ship's marina deck.

Fares average $460–$989 per day, plus tips. Seasonal destinations include Montréal, New York, and the Caribbean. A 14-day cruise from Fort Lauderdale costs $7,780–$12,400 per person double occupancy. Airfare included from selected cities.

Seaward

The *Seaward*, a Finnish-built addition to the Norwegian Cruise Line fleet in 1988, is a 42,000-ton beauty complete with cascading waterfall, cushioned running track, and basketball court. Although smaller than her big sister the *Norway*, she has a quarter-mile promenade deck that encircles the ship—a detail missing on many new liners. The top-deck spa, all glass and gleaming chrome, affords panoramic views of the sea to those working out. Separate saunas and showers are provided for men and women, and massage is available. The accent is on sports: The ship's two swimming pools and adjacent whirlpools have splash areas surrounded by Astroturf, where a "dive-in" center offers snorkeling equipment and instruction. Excursions in port take in some of the finest golf courses and tennis courts in the islands. Pro-Am cruises team passengers with golf and tennis pros on designated weeks throughout the year. Racquet Club cruises and Tee-Up golf cruises offer clinics and workshops at sea and special games and matches ashore.

Norwegian Cruise Line. *95 Merrick Way, Coral Gables, FL 33134, tel. 305/447–9660 or 800/327–7030.* Inaugurated in 1988. 1,534 passengers. Bahamian registry, Norwegian officers, international crew.

Fitness Facilities: Health spa with Universal equipment, stationary bicycles, aerobics studio with daily scheduled classes, rowing machines, free weights; 2 outdoor swimming pools, whirlpools, sauna, no steam room. **Services:** Massage, facials; moortherapy facial mask; throat and decollete treatment; eye, foot, and hand treatments; exfoliation; herbal or thermal body wrap; salon for hair, nail, and skin care. **Sports:** Volleyball, snorkeling, skeet shooting, golf driving.

Cruises on Sun. from Miami, for 3–4 nights, are $559–$1,649 per person, double occupancy. Airfare included from major gateways.

Seawind Crown

Sailing from Aruba, the classic *Seawind Crown* offers features not found on larger ships, such as squash and volleyball courts, as well as a fitness center. In addition to the coed sauna and cold plunge pool, there are two outdoor swimming pools (one heated) and a jogging track for deck exercise.

Seawind Cruise Line. *1750 Coral Way, Miami, FL 33145; tel. 305/285–9494 or 800/258–8006.* Commissioned as TSS *Vasco da Gama*, rebuilt 1989. Panamanian registry, Portuguese and Greek officers, European dining room staff, Portuguese cabin service. 624 passengers. Cabins have color TV, terry-cloth robes, bathroom with hair dryer.

Fitness Facilities: Fitness Center with stationary bikes, rowing machine, free weights, whirlpool. **Services:** massage, salon for hair, nail, and skin care.

Cruises from Aruba every Sunday. Fares $895–$2,895, including airfare or discount from U.S. cities. Accommodations for people with disabilities in 2 cabins.

Sovereign of the Seas

Sovereign of the Seas sports a central lobby area, the Centrum, that spans five decks. Located one step down from the Sports Deck, the 1,566-square-foot exercise and relaxation facility has a limited choice of weight-training equipment but features a sauna, massage, and whirlpool. Passengers can participate in shipshape activities that range from yoga and aerobics classes to shooting basketball free throws. The program offers 12 activities, beginning with an 8 AM stretch, followed by a group walkathon; other choices include aquacise in the swimming pools and team sports. Sign up early for classes; space is limited. Muscle tension can be soothed away with a cleansing sauna followed by a relaxing massage by qualified therapists. Dining options include a selection of light items that are highlighted on the regular menu as being low in sodium and cholesterol, in line with the American Heart Association guidelines.

Royal Caribbean Cruise Line. *1050 Caribbean Way, Miami, FL 33132, tel. 305/539–6000 or 800/327–6700 (800/245–7225 in Canada).* Commissioned in 1988. 2,280 passengers. Norwegian registry and officers, international staff.

Fitness Facilities: Gymnasium with David pneumatic pressure exercise units, abdominal board, 5 Lifecycles, 6 Liferowers, StairMaster, Boland dumbbells; two outdoor swimming pools. **Services:** Massage, facials; hair, nail, and skin care; personalized exercise program. **Sports:** PGA sanctioned "Golf Ahoy" program aboard and ashore, tennis clinics, basketball, golf putting, shuffleboard, skeet shooting, outside jogging track.

Cruises from Miami on Sat., calling at San Juan, St. Thomas, and a beach resort. Fares $1,245–$2,945 per person double occupancy. Airfare included from selected cities.

Windjammer Figaro

The *Windjammer Figaro* provides an unusual opportunity for vegetarians and yoga devotees to sail among the islands of Maine aboard a 51-foot yawl that offers programs in nutrition, nature studies, and seamanship. With accommodations for just six passengers, this ocean racing ship cruises from the storybook harbor of Camden, Maine, to secluded coves of Acadia National Park. Meals are based on whole grains, fresh garden vegetables, and fruit, in the macrobiotic tradition, with dairy products and coffee as desired. Passengers can participate in sailing the ship. In July, a week for intermediate students of Iyengar yoga style, is taught. Special weeks are devoted to men's and women's issues. Life aboard is informal; smoking is not permitted.

Figaro Cruises. *Box 1336, Camden, ME 04843, tel. 800/473–6169.* Built in 1965, rebuilt in 1987. 6 passengers (2 double-berth cabins, 2 semiprivate berths). U.S. registry, Coast Guard inspected. Crew of 4. Owners/skippers: Jennifer Martin, Barry King.

Cruises on Mon. for 6 days, fares $575–$650 per person double occupancy; Sails Mon. morning, with sleep-aboard privilege the night before sailing. 3-day weekender cruise $365–$385. Yoga cruise in July, $725 per person, double room.

Wind Spirit and Wind Star

A blend of modern technology and the romance of cruising under sail, the yachtlike *Wind Spirit* and *Wind Star* offer a tiny fitness center and a full program of water sports. While under sail, a computerized system raises the six sails automatically in less than two minutes. While anchored in secluded coves, away from the routes of the large cruise ships, the vessel's crew members organize waterskiing and snorkeling expeditions. For certified divers there is scuba equipment aboard. Shore excursions to golf and tennis resorts can be arranged through the ship's purser.

Windstar Cruises. *300 Elliott Ave. W., Seattle, WA 98119. Tel. 206/281–3535 or 800/258–7245 (Canada, 800/263–0844).* Commissioned in 1988. 148 passengers. Bahamian registry, international crew.

Fitness Facilities: Exercise room with 2 rowing machines, stationary bikes; outdoor swimming pool, sauna. **Services:** Massage. **Sports:** Water sports program, shore excursions for golf and tennis.

Cruises the Windward and Leeward Islands in the West Indies. Fares for 7-day cruise $2,795–$3,595 per person, double occupancy.